William L. Newman

The Politics of Aristotle

Vol. II

William L. Newman

The Politics of Aristotle
Vol. II

ISBN/EAN: 9783743376755

Manufactured in Europe, USA, Canada, Australia, Japa

Cover: Foto ©Thomas Meinert / pixelio.de

Manufactured and distributed by brebook publishing software (www.brebook.com)

William L. Newman

The Politics of Aristotle

THE

POLITICS OF ARISTOTLE

NEWMAN

London

HENRY FROWDE

OXFORD UNIVERSITY PRESS WAREHOUSE

AMEN CORNER, E.C.

THE

POLITICS OF ARISTOTLE

WITH AN INTRODUCTION, TWO PREFATORY ESSAYS AND NOTES CRITICAL AND EXPLANATORY

BY

W. L. NEWMAN, M.A.

FELLOW OF BALLIOL COLLEGE, AND FORMERLY READER IN ANCIENT HISTORY IN THE UNIVERSITY OF OXFORD

VOLUME II

PREFATORY ESSAYS

BOOKS I AND II—TEXT AND NOTES

Oxford

AT THE CLARENDON PRESS

1887

CONTENTS.

THE POLITICS OF ARISTOTLE.

The Politics included in all the lists of Aristotle's works.

A TREATISE on Politics in eight books, probably identical with that known to us as 'the Politics,' finds a place in all the three catalogues of Aristotle's works which have been handed down to us—that given by Diogenes Laertius in his life of Aristotle, that of the anonymous writer first published by Menage in his commentary on Diogenes Laertius, and that of 'Ptolemy the philosopher,' which exists only in an Arabic translation [1].

It is described in the first thus (No. 75)—*πολιτικῆς ἀκροάσεως ὡς ἡ Θεοφράστου* ᾱ β̄ γ̄ δ̄ ε̄ ϛ̄ ζ̄ η̄ : in the second (No. 70)—*πολιτικῆς ἀκροάσεως* η̄ : in the third (No. 32)—if we follow Steinschneider's Latin translation (Aristot. Fragm. 1469 sqq.)—liber de regimine civitatum et nominatur bulitikun (s. bolitikun) tractatus viii.

The list of the Anonymus Menagianus is thought by Heitz [2] not to be copied from that of Diogenes, but to be drawn from a common source. Some of its variations from the text of Diogenes, in fact, are too considerable to have arisen in the process of copying. It omits works named by Diogenes, but also names some which we do not find in his list [3]. We see that the words *ὡς ἡ Θεοφράστου* do not appear in its version of the title of the Politics. They may probably not have existed in the document copied. We cannot tell how they came

[1] The three catalogues will be found at the commencement of the fifth volume of the Berlin Aristotle—the third of them in a Latin translation by Steinschneider.

[2] Die verlorenen Schriften des Aristoteles, p. 17.

[3] Heitz, ibid. p. 15.

to appear in the list of Diogenes[1]. Did he find them in the source from which he copied his list, or did he add them himself? Or are they a gloss which has crept from the margin of Diogenes into his text? Their meaning is as doubtful as their origin. They may merely mean that the Political Teaching both of Theophrastus and of Aristotle was arranged in eight books: more probably they mean that the work was identical with one which was ascribed to Theophrastus as its author. Cicero sometimes cites, as from Theophrastus, statements the like of which we find in the Politics; but it does not follow that he may not owe them to Theophrastus, for Theophrastus may well have repeated remarks originally made by Aristotle, and we know that Cicero distinguishes between the works of Aristotle and Theophrastus on the best constitution[2], so that one part of the Politics at all events cannot have been ascribed by him to Theophrastus.

The term *ἀκρόασις* perhaps implies that the work was delivered in the form of oral lectures[3], and to associates[4], not to *οἱ πολλοί*, but Galen speaks of Aristotle 'writing' his *ἀκροάσεις*, and makes no distinction in this respect between them and the rest of his works[5]. In the Rhetoric (1. 8. 1366 a 21)—a reference which may well have been inserted by some later hand—we find the Politics called

[1] See on this subject Zeller, Gr. Ph. 2. 2. 678. 1.

[2] De Fin. 5. 4. 11: cumque uterque eorum docuisset qualem in re publica principem esse conveniret, pluribus praeterea conscripsisset, qui esset optimus rei publicae status, hoc amplius Theophrastus, quae essent in re publica rerum inclinationes et momenta temporum, quibus esset moderandum, utcumque res postularet.

[3] Aristox. Elem. Rhythm. 2. p. 30 Meibom., *καθάπερ Ἀριστοτέλης ἀεὶ διηγεῖτο τοῦτο πλείστους τῶν ἀκουσάντων παρὰ Πλάτωνος τὴν περὶ τἀγαθοῦ ἀκρόασιν παθεῖν· προσιέναι γὰρ ἕκαστον ὑπολαμβάνοντα λήψεσθαί τι τῶν νομιζομένων τούτων ἀνθρωπίνων ἀγαθῶν κ.τ.λ.* (Quoted by Heitz, ibid. p. 210 n.)

[4] Cp. Galen. de Subst. Facult. 4. p. 758 Kühn (quoted by Heitz, ibid. p. 138), *Ἀριστοτέλους καὶ Θεοφράστου τὰ μὲν τοῖς πολλοῖς γεγραφότων, τὰς δὲ ἀκροάσεις τοῖς ἑταίροις.*

[5] See the passage of Galen quoted in the last note. It seems to have been a common practice for the author of a book to read it aloud to an audience: cp. Cic. Brutus c. 51. 191: (Antimachus) cum, convocatis auditoribus, legeret eis magnum illud quod novistis volumen suum, et cum legentem omnes praeter Platonem reliquissent, 'legam,' inquit, 'nihilo minus, Plato enim mihi unus instar est omnium.'

by the name by which we know it (τὰ πολιτικά)[1]. The Politics itself speaks of its inquiries as being περὶ πολιτείας καὶ τίς ἑκάστη καὶ ποία τις (Pol. 3. 1. 1274 b 32: cp. Pol. 6 (4). 8. 1293 b 29, ἡμῖν δὲ τὴν μέθοδον εἶναι περὶ πολιτείας), and refers at the close of the first book to succeeding portions of the work as τὰ περὶ τὰς πολιτείας (1. 13. 1260 b 12). It is also implied to be περὶ τῶν πολιτειῶν in 6 (4). 2. 1289 a 26[2].

Probable date and origin of the lists given by Diogenes Laertius and the Anonymus Menagianus.

References of any kind to the Politics, especially before the time of Cicero, are scarce, and therefore the question of the probable date and origin of the two first of these lists—the oldest, apparently, of the three—is an interesting one, for, as we have seen, they mention the work by name.

Diogenes Laertius himself lived no earlier than the second century of our era and possibly much later, but, as is well-known, he derives much of his information from far more ancient authorities now lost, and his list of Aristotle's works has been thought by many to have come to him through some intermediate compiler or other from Hermippus of Smyrna, the disciple of Callimachus of Alexandria[3], or at all events to precede the rearrangement of Aristotle's works by Andronicus of Rhodes, who lived in the first century before Christ. A short review of the grounds for this opinion will perhaps not be out of place here.

We are told by Plutarch (Sulla c. 26) that when the MSS. of 'most of the works of Aristotle and Theophrastus,' after being rescued from their long seclusion in careless hands at Scepsis[4], had been carried off by Sulla to Rome

[1] So Alexander of Aphrodisias (in Aristot. Metaph. p. 15. 6 Bonitz), ἐν τοῖς Πολιτικοῖς: Julian (Ep. ad Themist. p. 260 D), ἐν τοῖς πολιτικοῖς συγγράμμασιν. I take these references from Sus.[1] p. xlv, note 85. The work of the Platonist Eubulus also was entitled Ἐπίσκεψις τῶν ὑπ' Ἀριστοτέλους ἐν δευτέρῳ τῶν Πολιτικῶν πρὸς τὴν Πλάτωνος Πολιτείαν ἀντειρημένων (Sus.[1] p. xlv: Zeller, Gr. Ph. 2. 2. 678. 1).

[2] Michael Ephesius, quoting from the Politics, uses the expression ἐν ταῖς Πολιτίαις (*lege* Πολιτείαις), and Eustathius, ἐν Πολιτείαις (Sus.[1] p. xlv, note 85).

[3] Hermippus lived till about the close of the third century before Christ.

[4] See the story in Strabo, p. 608–9. Strabo speaks of 'the library of Theophrastus, which included that of Aristotle,' passing to Neleus, and forgets to make it clear whether Apellicon purchased the libraries as a whole, or only

with the rest of the library of Apellicon of Teos, Tyrannion (a contemporary of Lucullus and Cicero) put them in order (ἐνσκευάσασθαι τὰ πολλά), and Andronicus, 'having obtained from him the copies which had been made of them' (cp. Strabo, p. 609), 'published them, and framed the lists now current' (παρ' αὐτοῦ τὸν Ῥόδιον Ἀνδρόνικον εὐπορήσαντα τῶν ἀντιγράφων εἰς μέσον θεῖναι, καὶ ἀναγράψαι τοὺς νῦν φερομένους πίνακας). We learn further from an equally well-known passage of Porphyry's Life of Plotinus, that Andronicus arranged the works of both writers on a new principle. The passage is as follows:—Ἐπεὶ δὲ αὐτὸς (Plotinus) τὴν διάταξιν καὶ τὴν διόρθωσιν τῶν βιβλίων ποιεῖσθαι ἡμῖν ἐπέτρεψεν, ἐγὼ δὲ κἀκείνῳ ζῶντι ὑπεσχόμην καὶ τοῖς ἄλλοις ἐπηγγειλάμην ποιῆσαι τοῦτο, πρῶτον μὲν τὰ βιβλία οὐ κατὰ χρόνους ἐᾶσαι φύρδην ἐκδεδομένα ἐδικαίωσα, μιμησάμενος δ' Ἀπολλόδωρον τὸν Ἀθηναῖον καὶ Ἀνδρόνικον τὸν περιπατητικόν, ὧν ὁ μὲν Ἐπίχαρμον τὸν κωμῳδιογράφον εἰς δέκα τόμους φέρων συνήγαγεν, ὁ δὲ τὰ Ἀριστοτέλους καὶ Θεοφράστου εἰς πραγματείας διεῖλε, τὰς οἰκείας ὑποθέσεις εἰς ταὐτὸν συναγαγών, οὕτω δὴ καὶ ἐγὼ πεντήκοντα τέσσαρα ὄντα ἔχων τὰ τοῦ Πλωτίνου βιβλία διεῖλον μὲν εἰς ἓξ ἐννεάδας, τῇ τελειότητι τοῦ ἓξ ἀριθμοῦ καὶ ταῖς ἐννεάσιν ἀσμένως ἐπιτυχών, ἑκάστῃ δὲ ἐννεάδι τὰ οἰκεῖα φέρων συνεφόρησα, δοὺς καὶ τάξιν πρώτην τοῖς ἐλαφροτέροις προβλήμασιν (c. 24).

It would seem from this passage that before the time of Andronicus the works of Aristotle were arranged in a confused and merely chronological order—the order of publication, apparently—and that he introduced the new plan of grouping them by their subject-matter, following the example of the grammarian Apollodorus of Athens, who

the writings of Aristotle and Theophrastus included in them. He says that Apellicon purchased 'the books of Aristotle and Theophrastus,' and fails to notice the ambiguity of this expression. His mind is, in fact, absorbed in the story which he is telling about the fate of the writings of the two great Peripatetic teachers, and he forgets that Aristotle and Theophrastus must have possessed many books in addition to their own compositions. Athenaeus in his account speaks more distinctly, and tells us that Apellicon purchased 'the Peripatetic writings' (τὰ περιπατητικά) 'and the library of Aristotle and many others' (Deipn. 214 d).

had in the previous century arranged the Comedies of Epicharmus in ten great τόμοι[1]. The writings of Aristotle would include both dialogues and systematic works, and Andronicus would seem to have grouped them together, making, not form or date, but subject-matter the basis of his arrangement. We conclude that in his issue of the works the περὶ δικαιοσύνης, for instance, would be grouped with other ethical writings ascribed to Aristotle. It is possible also that in some cases Andronicus took separate treatises and formed a new whole out of them under some general name. Heitz (p. 36) thinks it probable that he did this for the treatises which together make up the 'Physics' of our editions. He is not stated, however, to have constructed any new treatise out of fragments of Aristotle, any more than Apollodorus constructed a new comedy of Epicharmus. His work would seem to have been one of arrangement, not of manufacture.

As the dialogues and other exoteric writings were apparently comprised in his edition and interspersed among the rest of the works[2], it must have been very different from our own Aristotle. Many spurious works, again, are included in our Aristotle which can hardly have been ascribed to Aristotle in the time of Theophrastus, or have been republished by Andronicus as part of the Scepsis 'find,' though we can well understand that some works of Theophrastus may have been ascribed to Aristotle or *vice versa*, the writings of the two authors having been mixed up together.

Andronicus' issue of Aristotle's works was probably an event of great importance, though not quite as important as a hasty reader of Strabo might imagine. When Strabo asserts, rightly or wrongly, that the Lyceum library at Athens had come, after the withdrawal of Neleus to Scepsis, to possess only 'a few' of the works of Aris-

[1] 'Τόμος here as everywhere else must mean a papyrus-roll' (Birt, Das antike Buchwesen, p. 496).

[2] It is not easy to see where Andronicus can have placed the letters and poems; it is, however, hardly likely that they formed part of the Scepsis find.

totle, he makes this assertion with respect to that one library; he need not be taken to assert the same thing of other great libraries of the Hellenic world, such as those of Alexandria and Pergamon. Strabo's aim is, in fact, to give an explanation of the comparative torpor of the Peripatetic school at Athens during the interval between Neleus and Andronicus, which was in all probability really due to other causes. His assertion is limited to Athens; the libraries of Alexandria and Pergamon were no doubt in far better case. But even for them the publication of Andronicus' texts may well have been an important event. Not a few spurious works may have found a place among the writings of Aristotle preserved in these two great libraries, and perhaps some of the genuine works were wanting. The Scepsis purchase, on the contrary, would include only those works of Aristotle which were ascribed to him by Theophrastus and Neleus, and would probably include all of these. The publication of Andronicus' edition, and especially its publication at Rome, would serve to concentrate attention on the genuine works of these two writers, and to place them before the world in their entirety, at a moment when the really great philosophers, orators, and artists of Greece were being singled out from the crowd with an ardour which was altogether new. Copies of Aristotle's works acquired after this date would probably be copies of the edition of Andronicus.

The question now arises—Is the list of Aristotle's works given by Diogenes ordered after the fashion of Andronicus or not? The answer is not difficult. The list is not quite the chaos which it appears at first sight to be: on the contrary, it is to a certain extent in order; but its order is not the order of Andronicus. First we have the dialogues and other exoteric works, then two or three early abstracts of Platonic lectures or writings, then we come to a part of the list in which logical works seem to predominate: ethical, political, and rhetorical works predominate towards the middle; then come physical and zoological works; last in order we have works designed in all probability for Aristotle's own use ('hypomnematic works'), letters, and poems[1]. The arrangement can hardly be that of Andronicus[2]. Diogenes' list of Theophrastus' works has been shewn by Usener[3] to be derived from the catalogue of a library, and the same thing may probably be true of his list of Aristotle's works[4]. As the former list is for the most part arranged on alphabetical principles, and the latter is not, it is doubtful whether they can have been derived from the same library-catalogue, for if they were, we should hardly expect to find the works of Theophrastus catalogued in one way and those of Aristotle in another. Be this, however, as it may, Diogenes' list of Aristotle's works is probably derived from the catalogue of some library which had purchased its copy of Aristotle's works before Andronicus issued his edition—very possibly an Alexandrian library, but about this we cannot be certain. The mention of the Politics in it may therefore date as far back as the formation of the libraries of Alexandria, or rather perhaps the adoption by their authorities of the practice of dividing large works into 'books,' which is implied throughout the list. Some believe that this change dates only from the time of Callimachus, who was chief librarian of the Museum from about 260 to 240 B.C.[5], but the point is doubtful.

We are on surer ground in referring Diogenes' list of Aristotle's works to pre-Andronican times than in attempting to fix its exact date, or the exact source from which it ultimately came. Diogenes may have copied it himself from some library-catalogue, or on the other hand

[1] The list is said by Heitz (p. 234) to resemble most of those we find in Diogenes in placing the dialogues first, the letters and poems last, and last but one the hypomnematic writings.

[2] For other reasons which make it unlikely that the list of Aristotle's works given by Diogenes is ultimately derived from Andronicus, see Zeller, Gr. Ph. 2. 2. 51 sq.

[3] Analecta Theophrastea, p. 13 sqq.

[4] Heitz' comment on the title ἄτακτα ιβ̄ (No. 127 in Diogenes' list of Aristotle's works) is as follows: 'one would conjecture that the substantive to be supplied is ὑπομνήματα. For the choice of the title the person who catalogued the papyrus-rolls is unquestionably responsible, and we must no doubt set it down to some Alexandrian librarian' (p. 236-7).

[5] See on this subject Birt, Das antike Buchwesen, p. 482 sqq.

it may have come to him through intermediaries. The latter is perhaps the more probable supposition. Usener believes that Diogenes' list of the works of Theophrastus came to him ultimately from Hermippus of Smyrna, who was the author of a work entitled Βίοι, which dealt, among other subjects, with the lives of philosophers and orators[1]. He admits that there are peculiarities in the structure of this list which at first sight make against his view. It is taken, as he has shewn, from the catalogue of a library, which apparently added from time to time, by purchase or otherwise, to the collection of the writings of Theophrastus which it originally possessed, and catalogued both its original stock and (for the most part at all events) its later acquisitions in alphabetical order. Thus the list consists of a long alphabetical list followed by a shorter alphabetical list, which is in its turn succeeded first by a group of books not arranged in any order, and next by a third alphabetical group. We know that Hermippus was an accomplished writer and scholar[2], and it is natural to ask, would he have made his list a mere transcript of an ill-arranged library-catalogue? Usener replies that few of the early πινακογράφοι did their work any better[3]. Ancient authorities speak of Hermippus and Andronicus as having drawn up lists of Theophrastus' works[4], and mention no one else as having done so; and Diogenes' list of his works is clearly not by Andronicus. But if the Βίοι of Hermippus is the ultimate source from which this list came, it does not follow that Diogenes' list of the works of Aristotle was also derived from it. We do not know

[1] See Müller, Fr. Hist. Gr. 3. 35.

[2] We owe to him the vivid sketch of Theophrastus in his lecture-room which Athenaeus has preserved for us (Deipn. 21 a).

[3] 'Meae sententiae' (the view that the list came through Hermippus) 'illa ipsa obicere possis unde ex bibliothecae usu ortam hanc tabulam esse studui ostendere. uerum haud scio an immerito: nam omnibus antiquorum πινάκων reliquiis—si librorum tabulas ab ipsis scriptoribus aut discipulis familiarissimis confectas ut par est excipias—id proprium est, quod ea tantum quae in certis bibliothecis siue Alexandrina siue Pergamena siue aliis conlecta erant respici solent uolumina' (Usener, Analecta Theophrastea, p. 24).

[4] Heitz, p. 47.

for certain that Hermippus drew up a list of Aristotle's works; and if we admit that it is highly probable that he did, we are still met by the difficulty of accounting for the entire contrast between the structure of the one list and that of the other. The list of Theophrastus' works is alphabetical; that of Aristotle's works is not.

Notwithstanding this difficulty, however, it is perhaps more than possible that both lists may have come from the work of Hermippus. They may even have come from a still earlier source. The Βίοι of Hermippus was probably in part an expansion and revision[1] of portions of the vast work of Callimachus (in 120 books), entitled Πίναξ παντοδαπῶν συγγραμμάτων, or πίνακες τῶν ἐν πάσῃ παιδείᾳ διαλαμψάντων καὶ ὧν συνέγραψαν, which gave lists of authors—orators, poets, lawgivers, philosophers—classified in separate groups according to the nature of their writings, and added in each case the full titles of these writings, the number of books, the initial words, and the number of lines. 'In the case of writers who were the authors of more works than one the total number of lines contained in their works was given[2].' We are at once reminded of the remark with which Diogenes concludes his list of Aristotle's writings, that they contain 445,270 lines. His enumeration of the writings of Theophrastus concludes with a similar mention of the number of lines contained in them. The work of Callimachus, who, as has been said, was chief librarian of the Alexandrian Museum, was probably based on the collection of books preserved in the Museum Library and the stores of other Alexandrian libraries, and this would explain some characteristics of the two lists to which reference has already been made.

The Politics, then, is included in a list of Aristotle's works which dates in all probability from an earlier epoch than that of Andronicus. Other indications of its existence

Other indications of the existence of the Politics.

[1] See Müller, Fr. Hist. Gr. 3. 46: Hermipp. Callimach. fr. 46.

[2] See Birt, Das antike Buchwesen, p. 164.

are derivable from works whose date is less doubtful and also probably earlier.

Thus in the Eudemian Ethics the following passages remind us of passages in the Politics and may perhaps be based on its teaching—3. 1. 1229 a 28, cp. Pol. 4 (7). 7. 1328 a 7 : 3. 4. 1231 b 39 sqq., cp. Pol. 1. 9. 1257 a 6 sqq. (where however both uses of the shoe are said to be καθ' αὑτό) : 7. 2. 1238 b 7 sq., cp. Pol. 4 (7). 13. 1332 a 10 sqq.? : 7. 10. 1242 a 6 sqq., cp. Pol. 3. 6. 1278 b 20 sq. : 7. 10. 1242 a 13–31, cp. Pol. 4 (7). 8. 1328 a 28 sqq.[1].

In the Magna Moralia the following—1. 25. 1192 a 16 sqq., cp. Pol. 1. 9. 1258 a 10 sq. and 10. 1258 a 21 sq. : 1. 34. 1194 b 9, cp. Pol. 6 (4). 11. 1295 b 25 : 1. 34. 1194 b 18, cp. Pol. 1. 4. 1254 a 12.

The so-called first book of the Oeconomics (which is ascribed by Philodemus to Theophrastus[2], though Zeller (Gr. Ph. 2. 2. 944) is half inclined to ascribe it to Eudemus) is to a large extent a reproduction of the teaching of the Politics on this subject, though the writer also makes use of the Laws of Plato and the writings of Xenophon. The compiler of the so-called second book of the Oeconomics, which seems to be of a later date, is also apparently acquainted with the Politics (compare Oecon. 2. 1346 a 26 sqq. with Pol. 1. 11. 1259 a 3 sq.).

Indications of an acquaintance with the Politics appear also in the Rhetorica ad Alexandrum, which is wrongly included among the works of Aristotle : e.g. in 3. 1424 a 12 sqq., with which Zeller (Gr. Ph. 2. 2. 78. 2) has compared Pol. 8 (6). 4. 1318 b 27–38 (cp. also Pol. 8 (6). 5. 1320 b 11 sqq.) : also in 3. 1424 b 3 sqq., cp. Pol. 7 (5). 8. 1308 b 34

[1] Since the above was written, I find that Susemihl has drawn attention to one of these passages (Eth. Eud. 7. 2. 1238 b 5 sqq.) in his third edition of the Politics (p. xix, note). He also thinks that in Eth. Eud. 7. 15. 1248 b 26 sqq. the writer had Pol. 4 (7). 13. 1332 a 21 sqq. before him. Zeller (*Hermes* 15. 553 sqq.) holds that in Eth. Eud. 2. 1. 1218 b 32 sqq. the writer had before him, not only Eth. Nic. 1. 8. 1098 b 9 sqq., but also Pol. 4 (7). 1. 1323 a 21 sqq.

[2] Philodemus de Virtutibus et Vitiis lib. ix. col. 7, reprinted in Aristotelis Oeconomica, ed. Göttling, p. 45.

sqq., 1309 a 22 sq., and Pol. 6 (4). 13. 1297 b 6 sq.: also in 3. 1424 b 10 sqq., cp. Pol. 7 (5). 8. 1309 a 14–23.

An acquaintance with Pol. 7 (5). 4. 1303 b 28 sqq. on the part of the writer of the De Animalium Motione may possibly be indicated in c. 7. 701 b 24 sqq.

So again, in the passage from Theophrastus περὶ βασιλείας of which we have the substance and something more in Dionys. Hal. Ant. Rom. 5. 73–4, we seem to detect many reminiscences of the Politics, and especially a clear reminiscence of Pol. 3. 14. 1285 a 30 sqq. If Bernays is right (Theophrastos über Frömmigkeit, p. 61 sqq.) in regarding Porphyr. de Abstin. 2. 12 sqq. as an excerpt from Theophrastus, the disciple perhaps refers in the words εἰ δὲ λέγοι τις κ.τ.λ. to his master's teaching in Pol. 1. 8. 1256 b 15 sqq.

In the Fragments of Aristoxenus, again, we seem to trace occasional echoes of the Politics: compare, for instance, Fragm. 19 from his Πυθαγορικαὶ ἀποφάσεις (Müller, Fr. Hist. Gr. 2. 278) with Pol. 2. 8. 1269 a 14 sq., and Fragm. 20 with Pol. 4 (7). 16. 1335 a 11 sqq.[1]

[1] It is unfortunate that the loss of a few letters in the Herculanean papyri on which what remains of the work of Philodemus de Virtutibus et Vitiis is written makes it uncertain whether Metrodorus, the friend and disciple of Epicurus, had or had not seen the Politics. Philodemus says in the Ninth Book of this work (col. 21: I quote from the text of it appended to Göttling's edition of the Oeconomica ascribed to Aristotle)—κἄπειτα δ' . . . . ας ἔχειν ὡς τούς τε πολλοὺς ἐξελέγχο[ντε]ς ἔνθ' ἂν ἐναντίως [τι αὐτοῖς] κατηγο[ρῶ]σιν ὑπὲρ τῶν αὐτῶν, καὶ τῶν ἀγ[νο]ουμένων τι διδά[σ]κοντες, ὅ[π]ερ Ἀριστοτέλ[ης] ἔπαθεν [κατὰ] τὸν ἐν τῷ πε[ρ]ὶ π[ολειτικῆς] λόγον ὑπὲρ τοῦ τὸν [μ]ὲν [ἀγα]θὸν ἄνδρα καὶ χρημ[ατιστὴ]ν ἀγαθὸν εἶναι, τὸν δ[ὲ] φ[αῦλ]ον καὶ χρηματιστὴν [φαῦ]λον, ὡς ὁ Μητρόδωρος [ἀ]πέ[δ]ειξεν. Göttling (p. 206) supposes that the reference is to Eth. Nic. 4. 1, but the context (col. 17 sqq.) might equally well be taken to refer to the passage about Thales in Pol. 1. 11. 1259 a 6–18. It is, in fact, just possible that the word which Göttling supplies as πολιτικῆς, or πολειτικῆς, was πολιτείας—Rose supplies πολιτείας and takes the reference to be to Pol. 1. 8–10—but it seems more probable that the reference is to a dialogue, in which case we may supply either πλούτου (with Spengel, followed by Heitz, p. 195, and Zeller, Gr. Ph. 2. 2. 61. 1), or possibly πολιτικοῦ. When Metrodorus is related (Plutarch adv. Colot. c. 33) to have found fault with philosophers, who

Hieronymus of Rhodes, who lived at the close of the fourth and in the first half of the third century B.C., seems from Diog. Laert. 1. 26 to have told in his Σποράδην ὑπομνήματα the story about Thales which we read in Pol. 1. 11, and in a form which, though shortened, is very similar to that of the Aristotelian narrative[1]. It is, however, possible that the two writers derived it from a common source.

In the dialogue entitled Erastae, which is included among Plato's works, though it can hardly be his, there are things which remind us of Aristotle's teaching: the distinction drawn (135 C sqq.) between ὁ τὴν τέχνην ἔχων and ὁ πεπαιδευμένος is perhaps more emphasized than we expect to find it in a pre-Aristotelian work and recalls, among other passages of Aristotle, Pol. 3. 11. 1282 a 3 sqq.; we note also that the teaching of the first book of the Politics is contradicted, intentionally or otherwise, in 138 C. But we cannot say positively that the writer is acquainted with the Politics.

Polybius. Polybius has often been said to show no acquaintance with the Politics, and it must be confessed that though there are passages in his Sixth Book which remind us at once of the Politics[2], it is not clear that he had a first-hand knowledge of it. His account of the origin of society and his constitutional teaching seem rather to be based on the

in their pride misinterpreted the function of philosophy, and made themselves ridiculous by seeking to rival Lycurgus and Solon, he may be referring to the Republic and Laws of Plato, not to Aristotle.

[1] Since the above was written, I find that Prinz (De Solonis Plutarchei fontibus, p. 24) and Susemihl (Sus.[3] p. xix) have already drawn attention to this.

[2] Compare Polyb. 6. 57. 2, δυοῖν δὲ τρόπων ὄντων καθ' οὓς φθείρεσθαι πέφυκε πᾶν γένος πολιτείας, τοῦ μὲν ἔξωθεν, τοῦ δ' ἐν αὐτοῖς φυομένου with Aristot. Pol. 7 (5). 10. 1312 b 38 sq. and other passages: Polyb. 6. 18. 5 with Aristot. Pol. 4 (7). 15. 1334 a 25 sqq.: Polyb. 6. 3. 7 with Aristot. Pol. 2. 6. 1265 b 33 sqq. The account of βασιλεία in Polyb. 6. 6. 10 sqq. reminds us of that of Aristotle: Polybius' fear of αὔξησις ὑπὲρ τὸ δέον (6. 10. 7) reminds us of Aristotle's warnings against αὔξησις παρὰ τὸ ἀνάλογον (7 (5). 3. 1302 b 33 sqq., cp. 7 (5). 8. 1308 b 10 sqq.); and the language of Polybius as to the Roman Constitution (6. 11. 11 sqq.) resembles that of Aristotle about the Lacedaemonian constitution (Pol. 6 (4). 9. 1294 b 13 sqq.), no less than that of Plato (Laws 712 C sqq.).

views which were fashionable in the third century before Christ than on the teaching of the Politics.

Society originates, according to him, in the gregarious tendencies common to man and many other animals, not in the household relation, and just as a herd of bulls is led by the strongest, so the primitive form of Monarchy among men is the rule of the strongest and boldest. It is only after a time, in the view of Polybius, that the experience of social life developes in man an ἔννοια τοῦ δικαίου καὶ τοῦ ἀδίκου, τοῦ καλοῦ καὶ τοῦ αἰσχροῦ (Polyb. 6. 5. 10: 6. 6. 7, 9)[1] —Aristotle, on the contrary, had held perceptions of this kind to be presupposed by human society (Pol. 1. 2. 1253 a 15 sqq.)—and that the Monarchy of the strongest gives place to Kingship, which Aristotle had said to be the primitive constitution. All unmixed constitutions, however, have, according to Polybius, a tendency to degenerate, and so Kingship passes into Tyranny. Aristocracy, the rule of the few good, succeeds, and in its turn passes into Oligarchy, the rule of a bad few. Then comes Democracy, the rule of a virtuous Many, followed by Ochlocracy, the rule of a vicious Many. Combine Kingship, Aristocracy, and Democracy in one constitution, and much will have been done to prevent constitutional decline and change. Thus Polybius recommends a mixture of these three constitutions; this is what mixed government means to him, something quite different from what it means to Aristotle.

We know that even in Aristotle's time there were those who commended the kind of mixed government which Polybius commends[2]. The Lacedaemonian constitution gave the hint of it. But in the century after Aristotle's death the union of kingship, aristocracy, and democracy rose more than ever into credit, vigorously preached by the Stoics, and also probably by the Peripatetic Dicaearchus. Polybius inherited this theory, and handed it on to Cicero and the eulogists of the English constitution in the last century.

[1] Compare the similar view of the Epicureans (Porphyr. de Abstin. 1. 10).

[2] See Aristot. Pol. 2. 6. 1265 b 33 sqq.

A connexion has been ingeniously suggested[1] between the constitutional views of Polybius and those of the Eighth Book of the Nicomachean Ethics of Aristotle (c. 12. 1160 a 31 sqq.). Polybius may perhaps have been acquainted with this treatise[2], but it is more probable that the source from which he drew was the Τριπολιτικός of Dicaearchus[3] or some other intermediate authority[4]. His theory of constitutional change would be suggested or confirmed by the history of Rome, in which the μοναρχία of Romulus was succeeded by the kingship of Numa, and the tyranny of Tarquin by the aristocracy of the early Republic and the mixed constitution which Polybius commends.

Cicero.

Cicero inherited far more from the Politics than Polybius. He lived like Aristotle at a time which greatly needed moral reinvigoration, and, like Aristotle, he sought this at the hands of the State. He accepts Aristotle's account of the end of the State (de Rep. 4. 3. 3 : 5. 6. 8), as he accepts his account of its origin (de Rep. 1. 25. 39), rejecting that of Epicurus (1. 25. 40). It exists to promote 'good and happy life.' But if we ask what kind of State best fulfils this end, the answer is that a combination of kingship, aristocracy, and democracy does so. Here he returns to the views of Polybius. As to unmixed constitutions, kingship is the best of them, but they are all very liable to decline into forms not based on 'iuris consensus et utilitatis communio'—into tyranny, the rule of a faction, and anarchy (de Rep. 1. 45. 69). Cicero goes far beyond Aristotle in his condemnation of the perverted forms and denies to the

[1] By the late Mr. R. Shute in an unpublished essay.

[2] Polyb. 3. 4. 11 at any rate appears to echo Eth. Nic. 2. 2. 1104 b 30 sq.

[3] See Müller, Fr. Hist. Gr. 2. 242.

[4] It is worthy of notice that when Carneades wished to attack Aristotle's notion of justice, he would seem to have sought it in the Περὶ Δικαιοσύνης, not in the Nicomachean Ethics. See Cic. de Rep. 3. 6. 4 : 3. 7. 10 : 3. 8. 12. This, however, does not necessarily prove that the Nicomachean Ethics was not well-known at that time; the other work may have been still better known, or it may have contained in its four large books a fuller treatment of the subject.

communities in which they exist the name of 'res publicae' (de Rep. 1. 25. 39: Augustini argumentum libr. iii: de Rep. 3. 31. 43).

To devise a best State is, in Cicero's view, beyond the power of any single inquirer. The only way to arrive at a true conception of the best State is to study the Roman constitution, which is the work of many generations and centuries, and hence of unsurpassed excellence (de Rep. 1. 46. 70: 2. 1. 2). It is to the experience of Rome, therefore, that Cicero has recourse, when he seeks to discover what institutions best promote a good and happy life. The institutions which do so are Roman institutions—the censorship, the *patria potestas*, and others. Cicero has too much national feeling to follow Greek guidance in politics implicitly, and there is a certain originality in the way in which he accepts the central principle of the Politics without accepting its application in detail. His main aim is a conservative aim—to recall his countrymen to a sense of the value of the triple constitution under which Rome had achieved greatness, and which was increasingly imperilled every day by the rising tendency to autocracy.

Cicero inherited much from the Politics, but it does not necessarily follow that he had a first-hand acquaintance with the book itself. There are passages in the De Republica which seem to indicate such an acquaintance. Thus it is possible that the procedure of Aristotle in the first and third books of the Politics is present to Cicero's mind, when he announces his intention of departing from the practice of those learned inquirers on politics who begin with the union of male and female, the birth of offspring, and the formation of a body of kinsfolk, and frequently distinguish the various meanings in which this or that word is used (de Rep. 1. 24. 38: see vol. i. p. 34). His criticisms on Plato's Communism (de Rep. 4. 4. 4) seem still more clearly to imply an acquaintance with the Politics. The following passages may also be compared: de Rep. 1. 34. 51 with Pol. 1. 2. 1252 a 30 sq. and with 6 (4). 8. 1293 b 38 sqq., 1294 b 17 sq.—de Rep. 1. 35. 55 with Pol. 3. 16. 1287 b

11 sqq.—de Rep. 2. 12. 24 with Pol. 2. 9. 1271 a 20 sq. and 2. 11. 1272 b 38 sqq.—de Rep. 3. 25. 37 *sub fin.* with Pol. 1. 4. 1254 a 14 sq.[1].

One would suppose from the De Finibus[2] that Cicero was at all events acquainted with the part of the Politics which treats of the 'optimus rei publicae status,' were it not that in the De Republica[3] he makes Laelius contrast the method of Plato, who constructed a model State, with that of all other inquirers. All save Plato 'disseruerunt sine ullo certo exemplari formaque rei publicae de generibus et de rationibus civitatum.' Cicero himself will in the De Republica so far follow Plato's example as to investigate 'non vaganti oratione, sed defixa in una re publica.' It certainly looks as if Cicero was not aware, when he wrote the De Republica, that both Aristotle and Theophrastus had sketched the best form of the State.

Philodemus de Musica.

In reading the fragmentary remains of Philodemus de Musica (ed. Kemke), we often notice that Philodemus combats, or refers to, arguments which remind us of those used in the Fifth Book of the Politics. Thus Kemke (pp. xiii–xiv) compares lib. 3. fragm. 52 (in his edition) with Pol. 5 (8). 5. 1340 a 18 sqq.: fragm. 53 with 1340 a 14 sq.: fragm. 65, 66 with 5 (8). 7. 1342 a 8 sqq. One or two other passages of which the same thing may be said are noted by Gomperz, Zu Philodem's Büchern von der Musik, p. 18 sq. (lib. 3. fr. 24: cp. 5 (8). 5. 1340 b 2) and p. 31 (lib. 3. fr. 54: cp. 1340 a 22). Perhaps the following passages may also be added to the list—lib. 1. fr. 16, cp. 5 (8). 3. 1338 b 1: fr. 17, cp. 5 (8). 5. 1340 a 2–5: lib. 3. fr. 45 (where ἀ[π]οφα[ίν]εται[ι] should probably be read in place of ἀ[λλ'] ὁ φά[σκ]εται[ι], Kemke), cp. 5 (8). 5. 1339 b 8–10: fr. 55 and lib. 4. col. 3. 23 sqq., cp. 5 (8). 5. 1340 a 12 sqq.: lib. 4. col. 15. 5 sq., cp. 5 (8). 5. 1339 a 16 sq.: col. 16. 17 sqq., cp. 5 (8). 3. 1338 a 24 sqq. On these similarities the observations of Gomperz, pp. 28–29, are well worth reading. The language

[1] See also Zeller, Gr. Ph. 2. 2. 151. 6.
[2] 5. 4. 11.
[3] 2. 11. 22.

of these passages, as he remarks, differs sufficiently from that of the Politics to make it probable that Philodemus had not the Politics before him, but either some work of Aristotle's (a dialogue, Gomperz thinks) used by him in the composition of the Politics, or some work which reproduced the Politics. It is evident, however, that the subjects discussed in the Fifth Book had been much discussed before Aristotle dealt with them, and possibly some at any rate of the expressions which strike us as similar in the Politics and the De Musica may have been originally used by inquirers of an earlier date than Aristotle, and have come both to him and to Philodemus by inheritance.

If Meineke is right, and the short sketch of the political teaching of the Peripatetics contained in the Eclogae of Stobaeus (2. 6. 17) is taken from the work of Areius Didymus, the instructor of the Emperor Augustus, then we have clear evidence that the Politics was well known to this writer, for nearly everything in the sketch is derived from the Politics [1].

The writer whom Plutarch follows in the latter part of the second chapter of his Life of Crassus was probably acquainted with the Politics, for the following passage contains several expressions familiar to readers of its first book. Plutarch here says of Crassus as an owner of slaves—*τοσούτους ἐκέκτητο καὶ τοιούτους . . . αὐτὸς ἐπιστατῶν μανθάνουσι καὶ προσέχων καὶ διδάσκων καὶ ὅλως νομίζων τῷ δεσπότῃ προσήκειν μάλιστα τὴν περὶ τοὺς οἰκέτας ἐπιμέλειαν ὡς ὄργανα ἔμψυχα τῆς οἰκονομικῆς. Καὶ τοῦτο μὲν ὀρθῶς ὁ Κράσσος, εἴπερ, ὡς ἔλεγεν, ἡγεῖτο τὰ μὲν ἄλλα διὰ τῶν οἰκετῶν χρῆναι, τοὺς δὲ οἰκέτας δι' αὐτοῦ κυβερνᾶν· τὴν γὰρ οἰκονομικὴν ἐν ἀψύχοις χρηματιστικὴν οὖσαν ἐν ἀνθρώποις πολιτικὴν γιγνομένην ὁρῶμεν* [2]*· ἐκεῖνο δὲ οὐκ εὖ, τὸ μηδένα νομίζειν μηδὲ φάσκειν*

[1] See Stobaeus, Eclogae (ed. Meineke), tom. 2. pp. clii., cliv–v., and R. Volkmann, Leben Schriften und Philosophie des Plutarch von Chaeroneia, 1. 154 sqq.

[2] This is of course nowhere said by Aristotle, who would not allow the identity of any section of *οἰκονομική* either with *χρηματιστική* or *πολιτική*, yet his teaching in the Politics perhaps underlies this modification of it.

εἶναι πλούσιον ὃς οὐ δύναται τρέφειν ἀπὸ τῆς οὐσίας στρατόπεδον (ὁ γὰρ πόλεμος οὐ τεταγμένα σιτεῖται κατὰ τὸν Ἀρχίδαμον, ὥσθ' ὁ πρὸς πόλεμον πλοῦτος ἀόριστος). Crassus (c. 3) was interested in the teaching of Aristotle, and was instructed in his doctrines by a Peripatetic named Alexander[1], from whom these facts about him may ultimately be derived.

The writer, again, whom Plutarch followed in Agis c. 5 may possibly have sought to meet the criticisms which Aristotle passes in Pol. 2. 9. 1270 a 18 sqq. on the laws of the Lacedaemonian State, and to show that Lycurgus was not in fault. See my notes on 1270 a 4 and 19.

Those who are well versed in the Greek and Latin writers of the earlier Roman Empire will probably be able to add to the following scanty list of passages from writers of that epoch, which seem to indicate an acquaintance, direct or indirect, with the Politics or with some points of its teaching:—

Plin. Epist. 7. 17 (cp. Pol. 3. 11. 1281 a 42 sqq.)[2]:

Dio Chrysostom, Or. 3. 115 R sqq. (?): the reference in Or. 36. 83 R to the ἀγαθὴν ἐξ ἁπάντων ἀγαθῶν πόλιν: Or. 7. 267 R, cp. Pol. 2. 6. 1264 b 39: Or. 14. 439 R, cp. Pol. 3. 6. 1278 b 36:

Plutarch, De Monarchia Democratia et Oligarchia (if the work be his), c. 1, καθάπερ γὰρ ἀνθρώπου βίοι πλέονες, ἔστι καὶ δήμου πολιτεία βίος (cp. Pol. 6 (4). 11. 1295 a 40): several passages in the Reipublicae Gerendae Praecepta—c. 15. 812 B, where the πρῳρεύς is spoken of as the ὄργανον of the κυβερνήτης (cp. Pol. 1. 4. 1253 b 29): c. 15. 812 D, οὐ γὰρ μόνον τῆς δυνάμεως κ.τ.λ. (cp. Pol. 2. 11. 1273 b 12 sqq.): c. 17 *init.* (cp. Pol. 2. 2. 1261 a 37 sqq.): c. 24 *init.* (cp. Pol. 4 (7). 2. 1324 b 26 sq. and 4 (7). 3. 1325 a 34 sqq. ?): c. 32. 825 A, ἀλλὰ πολλάκις κ.τ.λ. (cp. Pol. 7 (5). 8. 1308 a 31 sqq.). In passages like these, however, Plutarch may well be

[1] Some particulars respecting him will be found in Stahr, Aristoteles bei den Roemern, p. 18.

[2] Plin. Epist. 1. 20 seems to contain a reminiscence of Poet. 7. 1450 b 34 sqq., rather than of Pol. 4 (7). 4. 1326 a 33 sq.

reproducing, not the Politics, but some work which the Politics reproduces—very possibly the Polities of Aristotle—for we find Plutarch in the last-named passage (c. 32. 825 A–C) relating stories similar to those told in Pol. 7 (5). 4. 1303 b 20 sqq., and 37 sqq., but with more fulness of detail, and these are stories which may well have found a place in the Polities. In Plutarch's An Seni sit gerenda Respublica, c. 7. 787 C–D, we are reminded of Pol. 4 (7). 14. 1332 b 38 sqq., but it would be quite unsafe to infer an acquaintance with the Politics from this passage. So again, in the De Cupiditate Divitiarum (c. 8. 527 A) the lovers of wealth are divided into two classes, just as they are in Pol. 1. 9—those who make no use of their wealth and those who squander it on pleasures—but Plutarch here quotes from Aristotle an expression which does not occur in the Politics, and he may well be making use of a dialogue of Aristotle in which similar views were put forth. In [Plutarch] de Liberis Educandis c. 13. 9 C, the saying *πᾶς ὁ βίος ἡμῶν εἰς ἄνεσιν καὶ σπουδὴν διῄρηται* reminds us of Pol. 4 (7). 14. 1333 a 30, but there is so little in the rest of the treatise to point to an acquaintance with the Politics that it is doubtful whether the writer had the Politics before him.

We are reminded of the Politics, again, when we read in Arrian, Epictetus 2. 10, that 'the whole is superior to the part and the State to the citizen,' but doctrines such as this were the common property of the Peripatetic school, and a reference to them in no way implies a first-hand acquaintance with the Politics[1].

Alexander of Aphrodisias.

It is far otherwise when we find Alexander of Aphrodisias distinctly quoting the Politics (in Aristot. Metaph. p. 15. 6 Bonitz, *τὸν γὰρ δοῦλον ἐν τοῖς Πολιτικοῖς εἶναι εἶπεν ὃς ἄνθρωπος ὢν ἄλλου ἐστίν*)[2]. Here we have a direct reference

[1] It is uncertain when the spurious fragments of Hippodamus and other Pythagoreans (see as to these, Zeller, Gr. Ph. 3. 2. 85. 2, ed. 2) came into existence, but we often find in them what seem to be indications of an acquaintance with the Politics.

[2] It should be added, however, that the Laurentian MS. of Alexander (L) has the reading—*τὸν γὰρ δοῦλον ἐν τοῖς Πολιτικοῖς εἶπεν εἶναι τὸν ἄνθρωπον τὸν ἄλλου ὄντα καὶ μὴ ἑαυτοῦ.*

of an indubitable kind. Susemihl's first edition of the Politics (p. xlv. note 85: cp. Sus.[3] p. xviii. sq.) supplies a list of references and quotations subsequent to this date which need not be repeated here.

The passages which have been adduced will suffice to show that we are perhaps in possession of as many indications of the existence of the Politics between the time of Aristotle and that of Alexander of Aphrodisias as could well be expected, considering the extent of our literary losses and the entire change in matters political which resulted from the establishment of the Roman Empire.

The Politics divided into πρῶτοι and other λόγοι.

It is not impossible that one or two large works had already appeared broken up by their authors into 'books'—i.e. volumes, or rather papyrus-rolls, of a portable and handy size[1]—before the Politics came into existence. It would certainly seem that the historical work of Ephorus was published in this form, for it was divided into thirty books, each dealing with a separate subject[2]. Aristotle himself had apparently divided his dialogues—if we may thus interpret the phrase ἐξωτερικοὶ λόγοι in Cic. ad Att. 4. 16. 2—into books, prefixing to each book a separate *prooemium*[3]. But the Politics was not composed after this fashion, which was quite a new one in those days. It was divided by Aristotle into πρῶτοι λόγοι and other λόγοι, the first book having as its subject οἰκονομία καὶ δεσποτεία (3. 6. 1278 b 17) and being thus distinguished from τὰ περὶ τὰς πολιτείας (1. 13. 1260 b 12), but falling nevertheless within

[1] As Blass points out (Handbuch der klassischen Alterthumswissenschaft, i. 313), large works were probably from the first often published in more rolls than one for convenience in perusal, but each scribe who copied them would divide them after a fashion of his own, according to the size of his rolls, without paying much attention to the nature of the contents, and it was a decided step in advance when the sections into which a work was to be divided came to be authoritatively determined at the outset.

[2] See Diod. 5. 1 : 16. 1. Birt (Das antike Buchwesen, p. 471) does not feel absolutely certain (see his remarks on the subject, p. 466 sqq.), but the fact is highly probable, to say the least. See Blass *ubi supra*.

[3] See Cic. ad Att. 4. 16. 2, and Blass *ubi supra*.

the πρῶτοι λόγοι (3. 6. 1278 b 17). Where these πρῶτοι λόγοι end, it is not easy to say, for we cannot infer from the use of the past tense in 3. 18. 1288 a 37, ἐν δὲ τοῖς πρώτοις ἐδείχθη λόγοις, that the πρῶτοι λόγοι are over before the beginning of this chapter, since we have εἴρηται δὴ καὶ κατὰ τοὺς πρώτους λόγους in 3. 6. 1278 b 17—a chapter which certainly seems to form part of the πρῶτοι λόγοι, for in 6 (4). 2. 1289 a 26 sqq. the distinction of the ὀρθαὶ πολιτεῖαι and the παρεκβάσεις (3. 7) is said to fall within the πρώτη μέθοδος. On the other hand, there is nothing to show that the Fourth and Fifth Books belong to the πρῶτοι λόγοι. But if the point at which the πρῶτοι λόγοι close is uncertain, there seems to be no doubt that the distinction between πρῶτοι and other λόγοι is due to Aristotle, while the division into books is probably not so. Still the eight books of the Politics are marked off from each other by clear differences of subject-matter, so that no great violence was done to the composition when it was broken up into books.

Question of the unity of the Politics. (1) How far do the first three books hang together?

If we take the first three books first, and ask how far they hang together, we shall find on examination that there is some want of unity even here. The First Book, as has been already noticed, proves that the household exists by nature, yet the Second treats the question whether it should exist or not as one still open for discussion, and makes no reference to the arguments of the First Book. Perhaps, however, we should not attach too much importance to this, for in the First Book itself the slave is assumed as an element of the household, long before the naturalness of slavery is investigated and established. Then again, the closing sentence of the First Book, as has been noticed elsewhere [1], is not quite in accord with the opening paragraph of the Second, nor is there anything in the conclusion of the First (apart from this closing sentence) to lead us to expect that immediate transition to the subject of the best constitution which we note at the commencement of the Second. There is no clear indication, again, in the Second Book that the First has preceded it. The passage

[1] See notes on 1260 b 20, 27.

2. 2. 1261 b 12 sqq., no doubt, reminds us of 1. 2. 1252 b 28 sq., as do 2. 5. 1263 b 37 sqq. and 2. 9. 1269 b 14 sqq. of 1. 13. 1260 b 13 sqq.; but we are not referred back in these passages to the First Book. The Second Book has one or two links with the Third (compare, for example, 2. 9. 1271 a 18 sq. with 3. 14. 1284 b 37 sqq.), and it stands in a close relation to the Fourth, for in constructing the best State in the Fourth, Aristotle avoids many of the rocks of which we are warned in the Second, and we find one or two subjects discussed in this Book which have been marked out for discussion in the Second (compare 2. 6. 1265 b 16 with 4 (7). 16). The Second Book, in fact, seems to be more closely related to the Third and Fourth Books than to the First. Yet we note that while at the beginning of the Second Book the best constitution is announced as the subject of inquiry, the Third Book, on the contrary, addresses itself (3. 1. 1274 b 32) to an inquiry respecting all constitutions (*περὶ πολιτείας καὶ τίς ἑκάστη καὶ ποία τις*). On the other hand, the Third Book, unlike the Second, distinctly refers to the First (3. 6. 1278 b 17 sqq.: cp. 1. 2. 1253 a 1 sqq.), and its discussion of the virtue of the citizen reminds us of the discussion of the virtue of the woman, child, and slave in the First.

(2) How far do the Fourth and Fifth Books form a satisfactory sequel to the first three?

If we pass on to the Fourth and Fifth Books, and ask how far they form a satisfactory sequel to the first three, we raise a question which has given rise to much debate. Something has already been said on this subject[1]. We have just seen that the Second Book prepares the way for the Fourth[2], and we observe also that the conclusions of the First and Third Books are made use of in more passages than one of the Fourth (compare, for example, 1. 3. 1253 b 18–1. 7. 1255 b 39, 1. 12. 1259 a 37–b 17, and 3. 6.

[1] See vol. i. p. 292 sqq.

[2] I incline on the whole to agree with those who take 4 (7). 4. 1325 b 34, *καὶ περὶ τὰς ἄλλας πολιτείας ἡμῖν τεθεώρηται πρότερον*, as referring to the contents of the Second Book (cp. 2. 1. 1260 b 29, *δεῖ καὶ τὰς ἄλλας ἐπισκέψασθαι πολιτείας*, and 2. 12. 1274 b 26, *τὰ μὲν οὖν περὶ τὰς πολιτείας, τάς τε κυρίας καὶ τὰς ὑπό τινων εἰρημένας, ἔστω τεθεωρημένα τὸν τρόπον τοῦτον*). But the sentence is one which it would be easy to interpolate.

1278 b 30–1279 a 21, with 4 (7). 3. 1325 a 27–31, and 4 (7). 14. 1333 a 3 sqq.: compare also 3. 5. 1278 a 40 sqq. with 4 (7). 14. 1333 a 11 sqq.)[1]. The discrepancies, however, which have already been noted[2] between the Fourth and Fifth Books on the one hand and the first three on the other must not be lost sight of. It is possible that these two books, like the Seventh, were not originally written for insertion in the work of which they now form a part, at all events in its present form, and were incorporated with it by an afterthought[3]. The close relation, however, in which they stand to the Second, must be admitted to make against this view, and the only safe course is to confess that we cannot penetrate the secrets of the workshop, or perhaps we should rather say, the Peripatetic school.

(3) Transition to the remaining three books.

We are far more conscious of a break when we pass from the five books to the remaining three. There are indeed many links between the two groups of books. Not only are anticipations to be found in the earlier group of the teaching of the later (compare, for instance, 2. 6. 1265 b 26–30 with 6 (4). 11. 1295 a 25 sqq.), but we trace in both the same twofold aim—the aim of scientific truth and the aim of utility (1. 11. 1258 b 9: 2. 1. 1260 b 32: 3. 2. 1275 b 21: compare 6 (4). 1. 1288 b 35).

But the emphatic announcement at the outset of the Sixth Book of the multiplicity of the problems of Political Science strikes us as something altogether new. We expect that Aristotle will pass quietly on from the best constitution (or in other words Kingship and Aristocracy) to Polity, the only ὀρθὴ πολιτεία still undiscussed, and if it is true that he gives good reasons (6 (4). 8. 1293 b 22 sqq.) for departing from this course and for studying oligarchy and democracy before he studies the polity, still we are conscious of a considerable change of tone

[1] It should be noted, however, that the references to the πρῶτοι λόγοι in 4 (7). 3. 1325 a 30 and 4 (7). 14. 1333 a 3 can easily be detached from the context in which they stand, and may well have been added by a later hand.

[2] Vol. i. p. 295 sqq.

[3] A further question might be raised, whether they were incorporated with the Politics by the hand of Aristotle.

when we pass to the Sixth Book. Aristotle here becomes suddenly aware that Political Science has a technical as well as an ethical side; he insists that the statesman, like the physician (Eth. Nic. 10. 10. 1180 b 25 sqq.) or the general (Eth. Nic. 1. 11. 1101 a 3 sqq.), must be able to make the best of the material which happens to be at his disposal—nay, that he must understand how to construct any constitution that may be demanded of him, even if it is not the best that the circumstances permit. In the earlier books (1–5) πολιτική and the πόλις seem to be regarded on the whole from a more ideal point of view, as the sources of good life: the keynote of these books is the exaltation of πολιτικὴ ἀρχή over δεσποτική and οἰκονομικὴ ἀρχή, of which we hear so much in the first book. The παρεκβάσεις are viewed throughout them as originating in an erroneous view of justice (as indeed they still are in 7 (5). 1. 1301 a 25 sqq.); in the Sixth Book, on the contrary, we discover for the first time that they are in some cases the only possible constitutions, the social conditions of the community permitting no other forms (6 (4). 12. 1296 b 24 sqq.). The Seventh Book goes so far as to advise a tyranny how to maintain itself in power. Another obvious difference between the two groups of books is that the one is far fuller of historical detail than the other.

A further peculiarity of the later group (6–8) is the emphasis with which these books dwell on a fact which finds no mention elsewhere—that of the existence of many forms of democracy and oligarchy. The Third Book, it is true, had distinguished various kinds of Kingship, so that there is nothing new in the recognition of sub-forms of this or that constitution; but still we nowhere learn outside these three books that democracy and oligarchy have many forms. No truth, however, is more insisted on in the three books, or rather in the Sixth and Eighth, for in the Seventh it is referred to only in the closing chapter[1], a

[1] The only subdivision of oligarchies and democracies recognized in the remainder of the book is that into ἔννομοι and κύριοι (7 (5). 6. 1306 b 20).

chapter which, though quite Aristotelian, may well be of later date than the rest of the book.

Question whether the Fourth and Fifth Books or the Sixth and Eighth were the earlier written.

We might be tempted by the entire silence of the Fourth and Fifth Books with regard to much that comes before us in the Sixth and Eighth to regard the former pair of books as written before the latter. But then it is not by any means certain that the Fourth and Fifth Books were in existence when the Sixth and Eighth were penned. The Sixth Book no doubt refers to the inquiry respecting the best constitution as concluded, but it is not clear that the inquiry referred to is that contained in the Fourth and Fifth Books. It alludes to an inquiry respecting *ἀριστοκρατία* contained in the *πρῶτοι λόγοι*, but we cannot be sure that the Fourth and Fifth Books are intended to be referred to. The passage is as follows (6 (4). 7. 1293 b 1 sqq.):—

ἀριστοκρατίαν μὲν οὖν καλῶς ἔχει καλεῖν περὶ ἧς διήλθομεν ἐν τοῖς πρώτοις λόγοις· τὴν γὰρ ἐκ τῶν ἀρίστων ἁπλῶς κατ' ἀρετὴν πολιτείαν, καὶ μὴ πρὸς ὑπόθεσίν τινα ἀγαθῶν ἀνδρῶν, μόνην δίκαιον προσαγορεύειν ἀριστοκρατίαν· ἐν μόνῃ γὰρ ἁπλῶς ὁ αὐτὸς ἀνὴρ καὶ πολίτης ἀγαθός ἐστιν· οἱ δ' ἐν ταῖς ἄλλαις ἀγαθοὶ πρὸς τὴν πολιτείαν εἰσὶ τὴν αὐτῶν.

The reference here may well be to the Third Book, in which we find all the characteristics of the best constitution here dwelt upon mentioned (cp. 3. 18); and the same thing perhaps holds of the reference in 6 (4). 3. 1290 a 2 to *τὰ περὶ τὴν ἀριστοκρατίαν*, where 3. 12. 1283 a 14 sqq. may possibly be the passage alluded to. It is true that there are two passages in the Sixth Book which remind us of the teaching of the Fourth and Fifth Books—c. 2. 1289 a 32, where both *ἀριστοκρατία* and *βασιλεία* are said to rest on *ἀρετὴ κεχορηγημένη*, and c. 11. 1295 a 25 sqq., where a *πολιτεία κατ' εὐχήν* is spoken of, requiring a type of virtue above the ordinary type and an education presupposing not only high natural gifts, but also a *χορηγία* which only Fortune can give. These passages are quite in harmony with the teaching of the Fourth and Fifth Books, but they might have been written before these books were written. It is far more clear that both the Fourth and Fifth Books, and the Sixth and Eighth, were written after the Third, than that either pair of books was written after the other. These two pairs of books seem to be to a considerable extent independent of each other. Both, we notice, are incomplete; there is no clear evidence that either group was ever finished, though the opening of the Sixth Book (6 (4). 2. 1289 a 30) speaks of the inquiry respecting the best constitution as complete, and the Eighth Book, as we possess it, appears to close in the middle of a sentence[1]. It is possible that Aristotle went on with the Sixth Book after completing the Third, instead of proceeding with the sketch of the best State. If he did so, however, it is strange that we find in the Fourth and Fifth Books so few traces of the teaching of the Sixth and Eighth.

The Sixth Book.

A noteworthy feature of the Sixth Book is the state in which we find its earlier portion. The programme given in its second chapter (1289 b 12–26), as has been pointed out elsewhere (vol. i. p. 492 sqq.), does not altogether correspond with the list of questions marked out for treatment in the first chapter. The repetitions of prior discussions which we remark in c. 4 are still more surprising; c. 4. 1290 a 30–b 20 goes over much the same ground as the eighth chapter of the Third Book, and c. 4. 1290 b 21–1291 b 13 not only repeats (with considerable variations of method and result) the investigations of the preceding chapter, but contains much that is similar to the contents of the eighth chapter of the Fourth Book. The first four chapters of the Sixth Book may perhaps not have received a final revision, or may have been tampered with by some later hand.

The Seventh Book.

The Seventh Book was probably originally written as a separate treatise, and only inserted by an afterthought between the Sixth and Eighth Books. Not many references to other books of the Politics occur in its pages[2], and

[1] 8 (6). 8. 1323 a 9, *περὶ μὲν οὖν τῶν ἀρχῶν, ὡς ἐν τύπῳ, σχεδὸν εἴρηται περὶ πασῶν*, where we have *μὲν οὖν* without any *δέ* to follow.

[2] Such references as those in 7 (5). 1. 1301 a 28 (*ὥσπερ εἴρηται καὶ πρότερον*) and 7 (5). 8. 1308 a 2 (*ποῖα δὲ λέγομεν τῶν πολιτειῶν σοφίσματα, πρότερον εἴρηται*) may easily have been added by a

it has some marked peculiarities. As has been already remarked[1], it systematically distinguishes between μοναρχίαι (including Kingships) and πολιτεῖαι[2], and it takes no notice (till its last chapter) of the many sub-forms of oligarchy and democracy dwelt on in the Sixth and Eighth Books; it also advises in one passage (c. 1. 1302 a 2–8) the blending in constitutions of ἰσότης ἀριθμητική with ἰσότης κατ' ἀξίαν, as the best security for durability[3]. It is perhaps by supposing that the Seventh Book has been inserted between two closely related books composed consecutively, that we shall best explain some difficulties occasioned by the references in the Eighth Book to the Sixth and Seventh Books. On the one hand, the Eighth Book refers more than once to the Seventh as preceding it, and one of these references at all events is too much interwoven with the context to be easily explained away as an addition by a later hand (c. 5. 1319 b 37 sqq.). On the other hand, the Sixth Book is referred to in 8 (6). 2. 1317 b 34 as ἡ μέθοδος ἡ πρὸ ταύτης, and in c. 4. 1318 b 7 as οἱ πρὸ τούτων λόγοι. If these references are from the hand of Aristotle—which is by no means certain, for they can readily be detached from the context—it may well be that they were inserted before the Seventh Book was intruded between the Sixth and the Eighth, and through an oversight escaped excision afterwards.

Promises of future investigations which are not fulfilled in the Politics.

Some further light will be thrown on the subject which we have been considering, if we note down from the pages of the Politics some promises of future investigations which are not fulfilled in the work as we have it.

The earliest of these (1. 13. 1260 b 8 sqq.) prepares us to

later hand, or by Aristotle himself, if he incorporated the Seventh Book with the Politics.

[1] Vol. i. p. 521.

[2] A similar distinction is implied in 3. 15. 1286 b 8–13. Μοναρχία and πολιτεία are often distinguished in the ordinary use of the Greek language (see Liddell and Scott s. v. πολιτεία), and the Seventh Book conforms to the common way of speaking. The Seventh Book also agrees with the Third in tracing the plurality of forms of constitution to varying views of what is just (7 (5). 1. 1301 a 25 sqq.: cp. 3. 9).

[3] This recommendation, it may be noticed, is borrowed from Plato, Laws 757 E.

expect a full investigation of the virtue of husband and wife, father and child, and of the conduct they should observe to each other, and also of the various forms which each of these relations should assume under each constitution; we are to be told how every constitution will educate the women and children who fall under its authority. Perhaps these inquiries were to find a place in the discussions περὶ παιδονομίας to which the Fourth Book (4 (7). 16. 1335 b 2) bids us look forward; but at any rate the intimation of the First Book leads us to expect an interesting ethical investigation which we do not find in the Politics, though the necessity of adapting education to the constitution is often insisted on (e.g. in 5 (8). 1. 1337 a 11 sqq.: 7 (5). 9. 1310 a 12 sqq.: 8 (6). 4. 1319 b 1 sqq.). The Sixth, Seventh, and Eighth Books, as we have them, seem in fact too much preoccupied with purely political problems to find room for the delicate ethical inquiry promised in the First Book. Yet we are told at the beginning of the Eighth Book that only a few subjects remain for discussion, and the subject dwelt upon in this passage of the First Book is not included in its enumeration of them. The announcement there made appears, in fact, to be completely forgotten.

Then again, the intimation in the first chapter of the Sixth Book that the making of laws, as distinguished from constitutions, is a part of the province of πολιτική, and that the whole province of πολιτική must be fully dealt with, leads us to look for an inquiry on the subject of laws in the Politics (cp. 3. 15. 1286 a 5, ἀφείσθω τὴν πρώτην). But, as has been noticed already, the programme given in the very next chapter (the second) omits all mention of this topic, and the opening paragraphs of the Eighth Book fail to include it among the subjects which still demand treatment, though it certainly is not dealt with in any part of the Politics which has come down to us.

Other intimations of future discussions which never actually occur will be found in 4 (7). 5. 1326 b 32 sqq.: 4 (7). 10. 1330 a 4 and 1330 a 31 sqq.: 4 (7). 16. 1335 b 2 sqq.:

4 (7). 17. 1336 b 24: 5 (8). 3. 1338 a 32 sqq.: 5 (8). 7. 1341 b 19 sqq.: 8 (6). 1. 1316 b 39 sqq. These passages, however, only prove what we knew without them, that the inquiry as to the best State and its arrangements is incomplete, and also that the Eighth Book is incomplete. The fact that there are no references in the Politics to past discussions which cannot be explained as relating to existing passages in the treatise as we have it, seems to make it probable that no considerable part of the work has been lost, and that it was never finished.

We see then that though there is a certain amount of unity about the Politics, it is not a well-planned whole. Its component parts fit together more or less, but the fit is not perfect.

The Politics a whole whose parts fit together imperfectly. Question as to the probable causes of this.

How is it that this is so? How is it that the Politics, though indisputably a whole, is yet a whole in which we trace these discrepancies of plan?

Beyond all doubt, we must not expect a Greek philosophical treatise to be arranged precisely in the order in which we expect a modern work of the same kind to be arranged. A modern work would not first prove that the household exists by nature, and then inquire whether it ought to exist. Yet this is what Aristotle does in the First and Second Books of the Politics. Cicero has already noticed in the Tusculan Disputations some peculiarities in the methods of investigation practised by Greek philosophers, as distinguished from Greek geometricians. 'Veruntamen mathematicorum iste mos est, non est philosophorum. Nam geometrae cum aliquid docere volunt, si quid ad eam rem pertinet eorum quae ante docuerunt, id sumunt pro concesso et probato: illud modo explicant, de quo ante nihil scriptum est. Philosophi, quamcunque rem habent in manibus, in eam quae conveniunt congerunt omnia, etsi alio loco disputata sunt. Quod ni ita esset, cur Stoicus, si esset quaesitum, satisne ad beate vivendum virtus posset, multa diceret? cui satis esset respondere se ante docuisse nihil bonum esse, nisi quod honestum esset; hoc probato, consequens esse beatam vitam virtute esse contentam, et quo modo hoc sit consequens illi, sic illud huic, ut si beata vita virtute contenta sit, nisi honestum quod sit, nihil aliud sit bonum. Sed tamen non agunt sic. Nam et de honesto et de summo bono separatim libri sunt, et cum ex eo efficiatur satis magnam in virtute ad beate vivendum esse vim, nihilo minus hoc agunt separatim. Propriis enim et suis argumentis et admonitionibus tractanda quaeque res est, tanta praesertim[1].'

Seneca, again, in an interesting passage of his Fortieth Epistle, contrasts Greek and Roman oratory, and finds more deliberation, reflection, and system in the latter. 'In Graecis hanc licentiam tuleris: nos, etiam cum scribimus, interpungere assuevimus. Cicero quoque noster, a quo Romana eloquentia exsilivit, gradarius fuit. Romanus sermo magis se circumspicit et aestimat praebetque aestimandum.'

But differences of this kind do not suffice to explain the phenomena which need explanation in the Politics. What we remark is that, of the three or four parts of which the work is made up, those which precede and those which follow very nearly correspond to each other, but do not quite do so. In passing from one part to another, we are conscious that the two parts do not completely match: the part which we must place second in order is not quite what the part which precedes it leads us to expect it to be, though it is very nearly so. Some of the discrepancies which we notice in the Politics may be accounted for on the supposition that the work was never finished and never received a final revision at its author's hands, but then it must be remembered that a similar, or even greater, want of unity has been traced in the Nicomachean Ethics, which can hardly have suffered from the same cause.

Whatever may be the case as to the Nicomachean Ethics, perhaps the state of the Politics becomes in general intelligible if we suppose that Aristotle, notwithstanding his turn for systematization, allowed himself some freedom in work-

[1] Cic. Tusc. Disp. 5. 7. 18–19.

ing successively at different parts of the treatise, permitted each part to forget to some extent its membership of a whole, and failed to force on his investigations that complete harmony, of form as well as of substance, which rigorous criticism would require[1]. Very probably his views developed as he passed from one portion of the work to another; he seems throughout it to be feeling his way as a pioneer would, and we need not be surprised to find in the Sixth and Eighth Books ideas of which there is no trace in the earlier ones. Possibly some interval of time elapsed between the composition of the different parts[2]. The Third Book is the centre round which the whole treatise is grouped; it is presupposed both in the inquiries of the Fourth Book and in those of the Sixth.

We notice that we have no such programme of future inquiries at the outset of the Politics as that which the first and second chapters of the Sixth Book set forth for the remainder of the work, and it may well be the case that Aristotle began the Politics without any definite scheme of it before him. He had evidently cast aside the programme which we find at the close of the Nicomachean Ethics, and yet he framed no fresh one to take its place. If he had done so, perhaps he would have prepared us by some intimation early in the work for the break of which we are sensible in passing from the first five books to the remaining three. Something might have been lost in freshness and freedom, if the structure of the Politics had been more rigorously systematic—if a definite programme had been announced at the outset and adhered to throughout, but the bisected aspect which the work wears at present would have been removed, and the gulf would have been

[1] This will not, however, explain everything; it will not explain, for instance, the state in which we find the first four chapters of the Sixth Book.

[2] It is also possible that some of the books were rewritten, and that the Politics, as we have it, is a mixture of two or more editions. For instance, a Second Book may once have existed with a commencement in fuller harmony with the conclusion of the First than that of the present Second Book, and a Fourth Book in fuller harmony with the Third than the present Fourth.

bridged between the ethical πολιτική of the earlier group of books and the largely technical πολιτική of the later.

Apart from possible interpolations, the Politics would seem to be the work of one author, and that author Aristotle, not Theophrastus.

Some may be inclined to suspect that the Politics is the work of more authors than one. It is very possible that it is not free from interpolation, but there seems to be no reason to doubt that the bulk of the treatise is to be referred to one and the same author. The same peculiarities of style appear throughout it—peculiarities which are traceable more or less in other works ascribed to Aristotle, and which afford marked indications of character. We are sensible of a certain combativeness—of a fondness for tacitly contradicting other writers, especially Plato; we feel that we have to do with a writer who is at once eager in utterance and circumspect in drawing conclusions.

If we refuse to trust to the evidence of style, we may note that a work composed by more authors than one, and especially a work on Politics, would probably betray its origin by anachronisms, unless these authors were contemporaries. The works of Theophrastus on Plants, though far removed in subject from current events, mark their own date by referring to events long subsequent to the death of Aristotle[1].

Then again, each of the three or four parts into which the Politics falls seems to be the work of a writer who is thinking out the subject for himself—a pioneer, not a deft expositor and elaborator of another man's system. Perhaps the very discrepancies and variations of view which we note in the Politics indicate this. The system is in making, not made. The earlier books of the treatise appear to be unfamiliar with doctrines which are insisted on with emphasis in the later ones. The writer is evidently one who has known Greece in the days of its freedom and greatness before the defeat of Chaeroneia—one who belongs perhaps rather to the age of Philip than to that of Alexander: the opinions he combats and corrects are those of that day; they are the opinions of Plato or Isocrates or the Socratic Schools, not those of a

[1] See Zeller, Gr. Ph. 2. 2. 98 n.: 811 n.

later time. If the Politics, or any part of it, had been written even twenty years after Alexander's death, would not the fact be readily discoverable? Would a writer of that date have committed himself to the sanguine view that the Greek race, if united, would be able to rule the world? Would the passages recommending the constitution resting on the *μέσοι* have been expressed as they are, if they had been written after Antipater's introduction of a property-qualification for citizenship at Athens? The writer at any rate would not have needed to go back to *οἱ πρότερον ἐφ' ἡγεμονίᾳ γεγονότες* to find a statesman of far-reaching authority who favoured a constitution resembling the polity.

Nothing surprises us more in the Politics than the fact that, though it was apparently written after Chaeroneia, it is almost entirely preoccupied with the petty States of Greece, and the constitutions prevailing in them. Macedon, it is true, might profit by the pages devoted to Kingship, but throughout the greater part of the work the writer evidently has the Greek City-State and its difficulties in view. He seems wholly unconscious that the sceptre had passed irrevocably from Greece to Macedon; he has not fully deciphered the meaning of Chaeroneia. We need not blame him for this: if Greece had been less exhausted and wiser, Chaeroneia might not have been 'finis Graeciae.' But his view of the situation probably shows that he wrote not long after the battle, and before the magnitude of the catastrophe had been fully realized.

The *ὡς ἡ Θεοφράστου* in the list of Diogenes may suggest the question whether Theophrastus was not the writer of the Politics, or of a part of it. Theophrastus was only 12 or 15 years younger than Aristotle, though he survived him apparently 34 years or more. It is very possible that he wrote some of his books before the death of Aristotle; the Politics might belong to that epoch and yet be his. If this were so, we should still feel pretty sure that we possessed the gist of Aristotle's political teaching, for the work of Theophrastus would certainly be based on the views of his master. But we feel in reading the Politics that we are in presence of the master, not of the disciple—of the originator of the system, not of its expositor. There is a difference, again, between the style of Aristotle and that of Theophrastus; the writings of the latter were probably far easier reading than those of the former—sweeter, more flowing, and less sinewy[1]. Opinions also find expression in the Politics which Theophrastus seems not to have held. He would hardly have been willing to assert, as the First Book of the Politics asserts (c. 8. 1256 b 15 sqq.), the naturalness of animal food[2]. He may perhaps also have rated the importance of external and bodily goods to happiness rather higher than we find it rated in the Fourth Book of the Politics[3].

Theophrastus was famed for the freshness with which he could treat a subject already treated by Aristotle[4], and it is probable that the treatise in six books entitled Πολιτικά, which Diogenes Laertius ascribes to him, was different in many respects from the work which we know as Aristotle's Politics. Cicero distinctly implies that the work of Theo-

[1] Cic. Brutus 31. 121: quis Aristotele nervosior, Theophrasto dulcior? Heylbut (de Theophrasti libris περὶ φιλίας, p. 9) remarks: 'taceri quidem nequit nonnulla minus severe et magis ad communem sensum a Theophrasto tractata esse, qui longe suaviore et faciliore quam Aristoteles scribendi genere utebatur.'

[2] See Bernays, Theophrastos' Schrift über Frömmigkeit, *passim*. It is not quite clear that the so-called first book of the Oeconomics (c. 2), which Philodemus ascribes to Theophrastus, contemplates the use of animal food. If, again, as Bernays appears to think (Theophrastos über Frömmigkeit, p. 96 sq.), it is to Theophrastus, and not to Porphyry, that we are to ascribe the strong assertion of the identity of men and animals 'in desires and anger, and also in reasoning (λογισμοῖς), and above all in perceptions,' which we find in Porphyr. de Abstin. 3. 25, Theophrastus can hardly be the writer of such a passage as Pol. 1. 2. 1253 a 15 sqq.

[3] Cicero at all events seems to have thought that he rated these goods higher than Aristotle (see Acad. Post. 1. 9. 33: 10. 35). Theophrastus appears in his Ethics to have thought the question worthy of discussion, whether πρὸς τὰς τύχας τρέπεται τὰ ἤθη καὶ κινούμενα τοῖς τῶν σωμάτων πάθεσιν ἐξίσταται τῆς ἀρετῆς (Plutarch, Pericl. c. 38: Sertor. c. 10). He appears to have speculated whether great calamities might not spoil even a good man's character.

[4] Cic. de Fin. 1. 2. 6: quid? Theophrastus mediocriterne delectat, cum tractat locos ab Aristotele ante tractatos?

phrastus 'De optimo statu reipublicae' was not identical with the work of Aristotle on the same subject, and if it should be suggested that the Fourth and Fifth Books of our 'Aristotle's Politics' are the treatise of Theophrastus or its remains, it may be replied that internal evidence points rather to Aristotle as their author.

The Politics is probably not a pupil's record of Aristotle's lectures, but a composition committed to writing by Aristotle and designed for use in his school.

Thus far we have assumed that the Politics is a composition committed to writing by its author or authors, but this is precisely what has been questioned by some. One or two critics have drawn attention to the accounts given of Aristotle's style by Cicero and others[1] who were familiar with his dialogues—accounts which are borne out by some of the still existing fragments of those dialogues—and have asked whether the extant works of Aristotle, marked as they are by many roughnesses and peculiarities of style, can really have been composed by him—whether they are not, or most of them are not, mere notes of Aristotle's lectures taken down by his hearers and perhaps put in shape by some one disciple. To some of them, indeed, this theory would not apply. The History of Animals can hardly have had this origin, and the hypomnematic works of Aristotle—if they were intended for his own use—must also have been committed to writing by him. But setting these on one side, and setting on one side also works incorrectly connected with his name, it has been asked whether many, if not all, of the remaining works are anything more than reports of his lectures.

There is undoubtedly a colloquial air about them; some have more of it than others, and none more than the Politics. The Politics reads, even more than the Nicomachean Ethics, like the talk of an experienced inquirer engaged with others in a difficult investigation, and feeling his way through it. We know that notes were taken by

[1] See Zeller's note, Gr. Ph. 2. 2. 111. 1, where some of them are collected. Among these is the well-known passage, Cic. Acad. 2. 38. 119: veniet flumen orationis aureum fundens Aristoteles.

pupils in the lecture-rooms of the great Greek teachers. Aristotle himself took notes of Plato's lectures *περὶ τἀγαθοῦ*, and other disciples of Plato did the same[1]. We are told that the Cynic Metrocles 'burnt the lectures of Theophrastus,' an expression which some have taken to mean notes taken by him of Theophrastus' lectures[2]. But then we observe that the works which we associate with the name of Aristotle resemble each other in style more than we should expect, if they had come into existence in this way, unless indeed the report were *verbatim* or nearly so, or the whole of the lectures were reported by a single individual. If the reports were, as they probably would be, by different hands and not very close, it is natural to expect that the rendering of one reporter would differ a good deal from the rendering of another, and that in the result the works ascribed to Aristotle would differ from each other in style more than they actually do. It seems hardly likely that any mere 'redaction' by a single disciple would suffice to restore to them the degree of uniformity which they exhibit. The question then arises—is it likely that the reports would be *verbatim* or nearly so?

Aristotle's report of Plato's lectures *περὶ τἀγαθοῦ* was, it would seem, pretty close[3], so far at all events as certain expressions of Plato were concerned, but it is perhaps hardly likely that a long course of lectures would be taken down in the close way in which we must suppose Aristotle's language to have been taken down, if most of what we call his works are in fact reports of his lectures[4]. If his

[1] Heitz, Verlorenen Schriften des Aristoteles, p. 217 sq.

[2] Diog. Laert. 6. 95, οὗτος τὰ ἑαυτοῦ συγγράμματα κατακαών, ὥς φησιν Ἑκάτων ἐν πρώτῳ Χρειῶν, ἐπέλεγε,

Τάδ' ἔστ' ὀνείρων νερτέρων φαντάσματα,
οἷον λῆρος· οἱ δ', ὅτι τὰς Θεοφράστου ἀκροάσεις καταφλέγων ἐπέλεγε,
Ἥφαιστε, πρόμολ' ὧδε, Θέτις νύ τι σεῖο χατίζει.

[3] Cp. Simplic. in Aristot. Phys. 362 a 12 (quoted by Heitz, p. 217), ἐν τοῖς περὶ τἀγαθοῦ λόγοις, οἷς ὁ Ἀριστοτέλης καὶ Ἡρακλείδης καὶ Ἑστιαῖος καὶ ἄλλοι τοῦ Πλάτωνος ἑταῖροι παραγενόμενοι ἀνεγράψαντο τὰ ῥηθέντα αἰνιγματωδῶς, ὡς ἐρρήθη.

[4] It would seem from Plutarch's treatise De recta ratione audiendi (c. 18) that the lecturers of his day were liable to be interrupted by questions put by some member of their audience, to which they were expected to reply. If this was so in Aristotle's time, a faithful report of a lecture would give

lectures, however, were thus taken down, the reports would differ but little from compositions strictly so called, for ancient authors, like modern, may often have dictated their writings to an amanuensis.

But no ancient authority conceives the works of Aristotle to have come into being in this way. Galen, as we have seen, speaks of Aristotle as 'writing' the ἀκροάσεις for his pupils[1]. Theophrastus, in a letter to the Peripatetic Phanias cited by Diogenes Laertius[2], seems to use the term ἀναγνώσεις of his own lectures. The περὶ τἀγαθοῦ of Aristotle, which consisted of notes of Plato's lectures, was never included among the works of Plato, and it would be equally easy to distinguish between reports of Aristotle's lectures and works written by Aristotle. It seems, besides, only natural that Aristotle should write down a course of lectures which he probably intended to re-deliver. He was not, like Socrates or Carneades, one who systematically abstained from writing; he had been a writer from his youth; and is it likely that after composing his Dialogues and his History of Animals and his work on Constitutions, and even noting down the Problems which suggested themselves to him, and accumulating a mass of memoranda, he trusted his political and other teaching to the chapter of accidents? Even if, on the first occasion on which each course was delivered, he used no notes, and a pupil took down a report of the lectures, is it not likely that he would adopt this report, and use it, possibly in an amplified and revised form, on subsequent occasions?

The remark may be added that if the Politics is a pupil's record of Aristotle's lectures, it is the record of a course of lectures singularly broken up into parts. We ask with some curiosity, why a continuous course of lectures should form so imperfect an unity. One would have expected that a single course delivered without notes would have been far

these replies, and probably record the interruption which elicited them.

[1] Above, p. ii.

[2] 5. 37. It would of course be unsafe to build too much on the testimony of an alleged letter, which may have been, like much of Greek epistolary literature, falsified or spurious.

more of an unity than the Politics seems to be. It is no doubt possible that the work is a pupil's record of three or four courses put together; but, on the whole, the supposition which involves fewest difficulties seems to be that the Politics was written by Aristotle for use in his lecture-room, or at all events for the use of his pupils. It is evident that Greek teachers had to study with some care how best to carry their pupils with them. Some hearers, we are told in the Metaphysics[1], would accept nothing but strict mathematical demonstration; others demanded a frequent use of examples, while others again expected the lecturer to adduce passages from the poets in confirmation of his teaching. Aristotle is careful to explain at the very outset of the Nicomachean Ethics, for the benefit of the first-named class of critics, that ethical and political problems do not lend themselves to mathematical demonstration, but he often illustrates his teaching by familiar examples and often also refers to the poets. These methods would be especially in place in an educational, or acroamatic, treatise. Unlike Plato, who seems for the most part to have written in one and the same way for the outside world and for his pupils, Aristotle made a distinction between the style of his published works and the style of those which he intended for use within his school. With his pupils he seems to have been less attentive to form, less rhetorical, and more colloquial.

His lecturing is not of an *ex cathedra* or formal type; on the contrary, he seems to regard himself rather as the pioneer of a body of investigators, and takes pains to select that path through the thicket along which they will find it most easy to follow him. He never forgets the traditional impressions, prepossessions, and prejudices of the better sort of Greek; he himself has inherited these traditions, which need only a certain amount of sifting and correction to become the basis of his own philosophical system. His tone is thus rather that of a comrade than a teacher. We can imagine how great would be the im-

[1] Metaph. α. 3. 995 a 6 sqq.

pression produced on thoughtful Greeks by the Politics; its teaching would be the more effective, because it was so little *ex cathedra* and was conveyed in an unlaboured and conversational style.

It is not impossible that many of Aristotle's works are records of his teaching drawn up by him after the lectures had been delivered. Several of the treatises comprised in the 'Moralia' of Plutarch are thought to be based on lectures previously given; the treatise De Audiendis Poetis is expressly said by Plutarch to be so (c. 1)[1]. The orators had set the example of writing down their speeches before or after delivery. We need not suppose that all the works of Aristotle were designed for one and the same purpose, or that they all originated in exactly the same way. The extreme brevity and compression of his style in some of them (for instance, in parts of the Metaphysics and in the third book of the De Anima) would seem to render these writings more suitable for private perusal than for reading aloud. We do not often observe a similar degree of compression in the Politics.

How is the displacement of the Fourth and Fifth Books to be accounted for?

The displacement of the Fourth and Fifth Books may be accounted for in many ways. It may be due to the unfinished state of the work: Aristotle may have left his manuscript in pieces, and the 'disiecta membra' may not have been put together aright. Or the particular MS. or MSS. of which the MSS. we possess are reproductions may have had this defect. Several MSS. of the Metaphysics of Aristotle (S, A^b, B^b, C^b, E^b)—among them one of the best (A^b)—place Books M and N before K and Λ[2]. Bekker remarks at the close of the Sixth Book of the History of Animals (581 a 5), that several MSS. place the Eighth Book immediately after the Sixth: 'octavum et A^a subiungit et P Q C^a D^a E^a F^a G^a m n, septimo in noni locum depresso.' So again, according to Bekker's note at the close of the Seventh Book of the same treatise, P A^a C^a

[1] See Volkmann, Leben Schriften und Philosophie des Plutarch, 1. 65.

[2] Bonitz, Aristotelis Metaphysica, p. v sqq.

add after ἄρχονται, the last word of this book, the words προιούσης δὴ τῆς ἡλικίας, 'quod est initium libri decimi': here apparently we have a trace of an arrangement of the books by which the spurious Tenth Book was inserted at the close of the Seventh[1].

Displacements of this kind are said to have frequently occurred, when *codices* of parchment took the place of papyrus-rolls and works were transcribed from papyrus to parchment[2].

Or again, the same thing may have happened to the Politics which some think has happened to the Facta et Dicta Memorabilia of Valerius Maximus[3]. The Fourth and Fifth Books (i. e. the fourth and fifth volumes or papyrus-rolls) may have circulated as a separate work, and may have been wrongly placed, when restored to the work of which they originally formed a part. If, as may well be the case, the displacement of the two books occurred at a very early date, or at all events prior to the general disuse of papyrus-rolls, this may have been the way in which it came about. But indeed a mere mistake in numbering the eight papyrus-rolls of the archetype would suffice to account for it. It is, no doubt, possible that these two books belong to a different edition of the treatise from the Third Book, and that this circumstance has in some way or other led to their being placed at the end of it. It is not easy, however, to see how it can have done so; nor is the position in which we find them accounted for, if we take the view that they were not originally designed to form part of the work, for this may very probably be true of the Seventh Book, which nevertheless stands fifth in order in the MSS.

[1] Some MSS. of William of Moerbeke's Latin Translation of the Politics in the Bibliothèque Nationale at Paris (Fonds de Sorbonne, 928: Fonds de Saint-Victor, 336) are said by Jourdain (Recherches critiques sur l'âge et l'origine des traductions latines d'Aristote, p. 181) 'n'annoncer que sept livres; et le dernier se termine cependant par ces mots: *Palam quia tres hos faciendum ad disciplinam: quod medium, quod possibile, quod decens.* La division des livres varie donc sans que l'ouvrage soit moins complet.'

[2] See Birt, Antike Buchwesen, p. 374. The change came to be of common occurrence, according to this writer, in the fourth and fifth centuries of our era.

[3] See Dict. of Greek and Roman Biography, art. Valerius Maximus.

ON THE MANUSCRIPTS OF THE POLITICS AND THE LATIN TRANSLATION OF WILLIAM OF MOERBEKE.

THE publication in 1872 of Susemihl's critical edition of the Politics will always be regarded as marking an epoch in the study of the work. It comprises a complete collation of all the more important MSS. then known to scholars and a partial collation of the inferior ones; it also contains a revised text of William of Moerbeke's Latin translation of the Politics, based on a collation of a number of MSS. I have not attempted to revise Susemihl's collations. I have, however, collated the first two books of the Politics in MS. 112 belonging to Corpus Christi College, Oxford (referred to by Susemihl in his edition of the Nicomachean Ethics as O^1, but not, I believe, previously collated for the Politics)[1], and I have collated the first two books of William of Moerbeke's Latin translation in MS. 891 of the Phillipps Library, Cheltenham (referred to by me as z), and in MS. 112 belonging to Balliol College, Oxford, named o by Susemihl (Sus.[1] p. xxxviii), whose collation of this MS., made by Dr. M. Schanz, extends, however, only to the First Book. I have also collated a number of passages in the first two books of the same Latin Translation in a Bodleian MS. (Canon. Class. Lat. 174), which I refer to as y. This MS. and the Phillipps MS. have not, so far as I am aware, been collated before. The latter MS. is of some importance, for though it is neither copied from the a of Susemihl (MS. 19, *sciences et arts*, *latin*, of the Bibliothèque de l'Arsenal at Paris) nor a from it, these two MSS. evidently belong to the same family, a family of which a has

[1] See as to this MS., so far as its text of the Politics is concerned, the remarks prefixed to the Critical Notes (below, p. 58 sqq.).

hitherto been the sole representative, and Susemihl (with whom Busse concurs, de praesidiis Aristotelis Politica emendandi, p. 11) says of a (Sus.[1] p. xxxv)—'omnium librorum mihi adhibitorum longe est optimus, quoniam, etsi ceteris non rarius peccat, tamen longe saepius quam alius quis verum retinuit solus.' The words prefixed in a to the Translation of the Politics—*incipit liber politicorum Aristotilis a fratre Guilielmo ordinis praedicatorum de greco in latinum translatus*—which enabled M. Barthélemy St. Hilaire in 1837 (Politique d'Aristote, tome 1, p. lxxix) to establish the truth of Schneider's conjecture and to designate William of Moerbeke as its author, and which have not hitherto been found in any other MS., are prefixed to this translation in z also, though z does not add at the end of it the words which are found at the end of it in a (St. Hilaire, *ubi supra*: Sus.[1] p. xxxiv); the closing words in z are, in fact, *explicit liber polliticorum Aristotilis*[1].

Still it is on Susemihl's *apparatus criticus* that the following remarks are mainly based, so far at least as the more important MSS. of the Politics are concerned, and my aim in them will be to derive as much instruction as possible from the copious data with which he has furnished the student of the Politics, and especially to throw light on the characteristics and comparative value of the two families into which his MSS. fall, and of the more important MSS. individually. I am all the more desirous to acknowledge my debt to Susemihl, because on questions relating to the text I have often been led to conclusions at variance with his. On these questions I shall be able to speak more definitively, when I have completed my commentary, but something must be said at once as to the principles on which I have framed my text.

Some Palimpsest Fragments of the Third and Sixth (Fourth) Books of the Politics ascribed to the tenth century

[1] See below (p. 60 sqq.) as to these MSS. of William of Moerbeke's Latin Translation of the Politics. I will only add here as to z, that though its text often agrees with that of a, it does not by any means always do so; in fact, it occasionally offers readings peculiar to itself, some of them excellent.

have recently been discovered, or rediscovered, in the Vatican Library[1], but no complete MS. of the work is older than the fourteenth. Nor have we any Greek commentaries on the Politics, such as we possess in the case of some other works of Aristotle, which might aid us in the correction of the text. The extant complete MSS. fall, as has been said, into two families, the second of them including a superior and inferior variety. The chief[2] representatives of the first family are the two manuscripts, M^s (B 105, 'ordinis superioris,' of the Ambrosian Library at Milan), belonging to the second half of the fifteenth century, and P^1 (MS. 2023 of the Bibliothèque Nationale at Paris), transcribed by Demetrius Chalcondylas[3], possibly at Milan (see Sus.[1] p. vii), at the close of the fifteenth or the beginning of the sixteenth century[4]. A full account of these manuscripts will be found in Susemihl's large critical edition of the Politics

[1] See the Preface.

[2] They are not its only representatives, for we are furnished with many readings characteristic of this recension by the corrections and various readings found in P^2 and in larger numbers in P^4, two MSS. of the second family. P^5, a manuscript of mixed type, being related to both families, would also be of much use, if it were not very late (it belongs to the sixteenth century), and both for this reason and for others, of very doubtful authority. It is also imperfect, for its earlier portion is lost, and it commences only at 1306 a 6. See on these sources Sus.[3] praef. p. vi sqq.

[3] Or rather Chalcocondylas—'of the bronze pen' (Gardthausen, Gr. Paläographie, p. 72). In studying the readings offered by P^1 it is necessary to bear in mind that Demetrius Chalcondylas was no mere ordinary copyist; he was a learned scholar, and superintended editions of Homer (Florence, 1488), of Isocrates (Milan, 1493), and of Suidas (1499). Susemihl (Sus.[3] p. xiv) is no doubt right in regarding as emendations of his several of the good readings which are found only in P^1. Here and there, however, as Busse has pointed out (de praesidiis, etc., p. 45), P^1 appears to preserve the reading of the archetype more faithfully than any other MS. of the first family (e.g. in 3. 9. 1280 b 5).

[4] P^1 must be classed with the first family, though many of the corrections introduced into it by Demetrius belong to the second, just as P^2 and P^4 must be classed with the second family, though many of the corrections introduced into them by their writers belong to the first. It is singular that each of the writers of these three MSS., and perhaps also the writer of the MS. used by Leonardus Aretinus, should have corrected his MS. from the recension to which it does not belong. This may indicate that some doubt was even then felt as to the comparative value of the two recensions. Some of the corrections of this kind in P^1 are in the same ink as the MS., and were therefore probably made either at the time of writing or not long after.

(1872), pp. vii–xii. Bekker omitted to collate these two MSS. for his edition of Aristotle (1831). Some readings from them, however, had been communicated by Haase to Göttling and had been published by the latter in his edition of the Politics (1824), and M. Barthélemy St. Hilaire (1837) carried the study of the Paris MSS. of the Politics much farther; but any one who compares the full collation of M^s P^1 made on behalf of Susemihl with previous accounts of the text of these MSS. will see that our knowledge of the readings they offer was greatly enlarged by the publication of his edition of 1872. So far then as extant manuscripts are concerned, the text of the first family has only recently come to be thoroughly known, but it must not be forgotten that students of the Politics have had at their disposal from the first an extremely literal Latin translation published probably about 1260 (*Rhein. Mus.* 39. p. 457) and based on a Greek text of the first family. This translation is the work of one of the earliest students of Greek in Western Europe—William of Moerbeke, a Flemish[1] Dominican, who was Archbishop of Corinth at the close of his life (1280–1)[2]—and if we may judge by the number of copies of it which exist, was largely used in the middle ages, notwithstanding the censure passed by Roger Bacon on the class of translations to which it belongs[3] and its occasional almost complete

[1] Moerbeke, or Meerbecke, is a small town of Eastern Flanders, some miles from Ghent. It is not perhaps quite certain in what sense this translation was the work of William of Moerbeke. More hands than one may have been employed upon it: some parts of it (e.g. the last chapter of the Second Book) show much more ignorance of Greek than others. We cannot feel sure that William of Moerbeke translated the whole; indeed, his functions may have been confined to supervising the work of others and editing the book. The MSS. which mention his name are not the earliest. Some scribe or other, perhaps a Dominican, would appear to have added the name, when the work had become famous. We must not, however, lose sight of the fact that a great similarity of method is noticeable throughout the translation; this makes in favour of its being the work of a single author.

[2] Oncken, Die Staatslehre des Aristoteles, p. 70.

[3] Speaking of William of Moerbeke, Roger Bacon says—'Willielmus iste Flemingus, ut notum est omnibus Parisiis literatis, nullam novit scientiam in lingua graeca, de qua praesumit, et ideo

unintelligibility, which is mostly due to its extreme literalness, though not unfrequently it is the result of the translator's imperfect knowledge of Greek[1]. As no known MS. of the Politics except the Vatican Fragments is older than the fourteenth century, this translation is based on a Greek text earlier than any complete text we possess. Not much earlier, however, it would seem, if Susemihl is right, for he says (Politica, ed. 1872, p. xii)—'Rudolphus Schoellius ex compendiorum natura libri M^{s} archetypum saeculo xiii° aut xiv° antiquius non fuisse collegit, unde vel ipsum illum codicem quem vertendo expressit Guilelmus saeculum xii^{um} exiens aut xiii^{um} iniens aetate non superasse ex magno vitiorum numero mirum in modum Guilelmo et Ambrosiano communium concludendum esse videtur.' Still the importance of the Latin translation is great, and here again Susemihl has done excellent service, for he has collated several manuscripts of it for his critical edition of the Politics (Sus.[1] p. xxxiv). The value of this translation as an authority for the text of the Politics only gradually came to be perceived. The Aldine edition (1498) was based on a manuscript of the second family, and it was

omnia transfert falsa et corrumpit sapientiam Latinorum' (quoted by Jourdain, Recherches critiques sur l'âge et l'origine des traductions latines d'Aristote, p. 67), and Sepulveda remarks in the preface to his translation of the Politics: 'vix enim eos in numero interpretum habendos puto, qui verbum verbo inepta quadam fidelitate reddunt.' Yet it is impossible not to respect the feeling which led William of Moerbeke to adopt this mode of translating Aristotle. He followed the example of most of the translators of the Bible in antiquity (Blass, Handbuch der klassischen Alterthums-Wissenschaft 1. 223).

[1] Thus προβούλους is rendered by *praemissos*, 6 (4). 14. 1298 b 29: ἄποικοι by *domestici*, 2. 10. 1271 b 27, and ἀποίκους by *expulsos*, 7 (5). 3. 1303 b 3, while ἀποικία is *vicinia* in 1. 2. 1252 b 17, 21 and 6 (4). 4. 1290 b 14, but *familiaritas* in 2. 10. 1271 b 29. In 2. 5. 1264 a 35, τὰς παρ' ἐνίοις εἱλωτείας τε καὶ πενεστείας καὶ δουλείας is rendered *a quibusdam obsequia et humiliationes et servitutes*, and blunders equally portentous swarm in the translation of the last chapter of the Second Book. In 1. 6. 1255 a 6 the translation has *promulgatio* for ὁμολογία: and in 14 *violentiam pati* for βιάζεσθαι, with ruinous results to the sense of the passage. In 1. 11. 1259 a 15, ἐκμισθοῦντα is rendered by *pretium taxans*. The translator's rendering of ἢ by *quam* in 2. 3. 1261 b 35 seems to show an entire misapprehension of the meaning of the Greek. Ἐκ τῶν ἐν ποσὶ in 2. 5. 1263 a 18 is *ex his quae in potibus*.

not till 1550, when the third Basle edition of Aristotle appeared, that any use was made of the Latin translation in correcting the text (see Sus.[1] p. xxxii: Sus.[2] p. xvii). Two years later, Victorius published his first edition of the Politics, and in 1576 a second edition with a commentary (Sus.[2] p. xviii). He seems to have used the Latin translation for the emendation of the text in both his editions (Schneider, Aristot. Pol. Praefat. p. xx), and he speaks of it thus in his preface to the second:—'quoscunque calamo exaratos codices indagare potui, cunctos deteriores mendosioresque inveni quam fuerit exemplar, quo illa usa est' (see also his commentary on 4 (7). 12. 1331 b 13 sqq. *Distribui autem*, and on 2. 5. 1264 a 17 sqq. *Si namque eodem pacto*). Schneider bears equally strong testimony to its value for critical purposes in the preface to his edition of the Politics, published in 1809 (p. xxv). Susemihl, with manuscripts of the first family before him, takes a somewhat more measured view on the subject. He sees[1] that it is in some cases impossible[2] and in others difficult to say what the translator found in his text. The translator's rendering is not always equally literal[3]. He sometimes, as Susemihl points out, omits or adds small words, and where he finds that the meaning of

[1] Sus.[1], p. xxxiii.

[2] E.g. where questions arise as to the insertion or omission of the article, or as to the spelling of Greek words (if the Greek word is not reproduced). Occasionally indeed, the article is expressed by the translator, as for instance in the important passage 1. 13. 1260 a 8, *quare natura quae plura principantia et subiecta*.

[3] This will be evident from the following examples. In 1. 6. 1255 a 8, γράφονται παρανόμων is rendered, literally enough, *scribunt iniquorum*: in 1. 8. 1256 b 10, συνεκτίκτει is *coepariunt*: in 1. 9. 1257 a 32, τῷ εἰσάγεσθαι is *per adduci*. In 3. 15. 1286 a 9–10, again, the translator finds in his Greek a masculine plural nominative conjoined with a verb in the third person singular. His Latin reproduces this false concord. Literalness could certainly be carried no further. But in other passages the version is not equally exact: thus for instance in 1256 b 9, τελειωθεῖσιν is rendered *secundum perfectionem* (or *perfectam* — sc. *generationem*): in 1259 a 13, ὀλίγου μισθωσάμενον *modico pro pretio dato*: in 1259 a 22, τοῦτον ποιοῦνται τὸν πόρον *hoc modo faciunt divitias* (see also 1255 b 35, 1268 b 5). An exact 'ad verbum' rendering is, in fact, impracticable in Latin, and one or two of these passages seem to show that the translator does not always make his version as literal as he might.

a sentence will thus be made clearer, he does not scruple to add a Latin word or two, for which no equivalent existed in his Greek text (Sus.[1] pp. xxxiii–xxxiv). That Greek text, again, Susemihl allows to have been here and there deformed by chance corruptions, by arbitrary changes, and by the intrusion of glosses (Sus.[1] p. xxxi). Notwithstanding all this, however, Susemihl claimed, in his edition of 1872 at all events, that the Latin translation is 'instar optimi codicis, qui quamvis non eandem auctoritatem quam E in Physicis, Meteorologicis, Psychologicis, et A^c in Poeticis et Rhetoricis, tamen eandem quam K^b in Ethicis et fortasse paulo maiorem habeat' (p. xxxii). Dittenberger in his valuable review of Susemihl's edition of 1872 (published in the *Gött. gelehrt. Anz.* for Oct. 28, 1874, p. 1349 sqq.) expressed a doubt (p. 1363), whether Susemihl had in that edition 'kept himself entirely free from the tendency, which he had noticed in Victorius and Schneider, to over-value the Vetus Interpres,' and though in his two subsequent editions of 1879 and 1882, and especially in the latter, where he abandons (p. xii. n.) the comparison with K^b, Susemihl shows less confidence in the unsupported testimony of the Vetus Interpres, he perhaps still rates it somewhat too high. It is not, to begin with, absolutely clear that we have a right (with Susemihl) to take this translation as a reproduction of a single Greek manuscript. Obviously it renders with great literalness the Greek text which it adopts, but we must bear in mind that a translator, even if he does his work as literally as the author of this ancient translation, is not quite as mechanical a being as a copyist. He may not be invariably faithful to one manuscript[1], and if he is, he may now and then prefer to render some gloss or conjectural reading which he finds in its margin, rather than the reading which stands in its text[2]. He may adopt con-

[1] Susemihl himself points out (Sus.[1], p. xxxv), relying on a marginal annotation in one MS. of the Vet. Int. on 3. 17. 1288 a 15, that 'aut in Γ' (the manuscript which the Vet. Int. is supposed to have used) 'hic illic adscriptae erant variae lectiones, aut praeter Γ hic illic etiam alium codicem vel plures alios (Guilelmus) inspexerat.'

[2] Roemer in the preface to his

jectural emendations of his own or of others. We must, I think, allow for these possibilities in the case of this Latin translation of the Politics, and not rate its testimony quite so high as we should rate that of a Greek manuscript of the same date[1]. We must also remember that William of Moerbeke, its probable author, was not a Greek by birth, and that he may have been as little infallible in deciphering Greek manuscripts as he certainly was in interpreting Greek words.

Nevertheless the readings offered by the thirteenth-century translator commonly deserve attention, and Bekker, who has here and there (for the most part in the wake of earlier editors), with manifest advantage to the text, adopted a reading based on his unsupported authority[2], might well have done something more than he did in his critical edition of the Politics (1831) to call attention to them. He also omitted, as we have already seen, to collate the manuscripts M^s and P^1, though he must have learnt their importance from the imperfect notes of their readings given in Göttling's edition (1824) on the authority of Haase. This omission has now been fully repaired by Susemihl, who has been in his turn, perhaps, in his first two editions at all events, a little inclined to overrate the value of the authorities which he was the first fully to turn to account. In his third and last edition, however, besides being generally more conservative in his

edition of Aristotle's Rhetoric (Teubner, 1885, p. xiii) says of William of Moerbeke's Latin Translation of this treatise—'varietates et glossas, quas pro correctionibus habuisse videtur' (cp. Sus.[1] Praef. p. vi), 'ubique cupide arripientem videmus hominem omni sano iudicio destitutum.'

[1] I have followed Susemihl in designating the Greek text which the Vetus Interpres appears to render by the symbol Γ, but I must not be understood to imply by this that I feel sure that it invariably represents the text of a single manuscript.

[2] E. g. in 2. 1. 1260 b 41 he accepts *εἰς ὁ τῆς* on the authority of the Vet. Int. in place of *ἰσότης*, the reading of all known MSS.: in 2. 7. 1266 b 2 he accepts *δ' ἤδη* on the same authority: in 3. 12. 1283 a 7 he gets *ὑπερέχει* in place of *ὑπερέχειν* from the same source: in 4 (7). 17. 1336 a 6 he is probably right in reading *εἰσάγειν* (Vet. Int. *inducere*): in 6 (4). 4. 1292 a 22 he adds *παρ'* before *ἑκατέροις*, which seems quite indispensable, but which only Vet. Int. gives (*apud*).

dealings with the text, Susemihl is, as we shall see, more cautious in his acceptance of the readings of the first family of manuscripts, and also in his acceptance of the unsupported testimony of the Vetus Interpres. He says himself of his third edition (praef. p. xii), that it is 'Bekkerianis multo similior quam duae priores.'

Besides, however, being the first to give a full record of the readings of the first family of manuscripts, Susemihl has done much to add to our knowledge of the second family also. This is considerably more numerous than the first; it includes, according to Susemihl, nearly a score of manuscripts. The most important of them are P^2, the I^b of Bekker (MS. Coislin 161 in the Bibliothèque Nationale at Paris), a manuscript of the fourteenth century from one of the monasteries on Mount Athos, of which a full account will be found in the preface to Susemihl's edition of 1872 (pp. xvi–xx); and P^3 (MS. 2026 of the Bibliothèque Nationale at Paris), the earliest complete MS. of the Politics known to scholars, for it belongs to the beginning of the fourteenth century (see pp. xx–xxi of the same preface). These two manuscripts have been collated throughout by Susemihl. Of the less good variety of this family[1], only P^4 (MS. 2025 of the Paris Bibliothèque Nationale) appears to have been collated from beginning to end, but Bekker used some of the manuscripts falling under this head for particular books, and Susemihl has had them collated for the passages indicated by him in his critical edition (1872), pp. xxviii–xxix, and in his explanatory edition (1879), pp. xvi–xvii[2]. O^1 belongs to this variety.

[1] See on the MSS. composing it $Sus.^1$ p. xxi sq. Their text has often suffered from the intrusion of glosses (see critical note on 1253 a 12) and supplementary additions (see critical note on 1255 b 12). They also frequently omit words, especially the article. Yet here and there they have alone preserved the true reading (e.g. in 1320 a 16, *μή τοί γε*).

[2] I add an explanation of the chief symbols which I have adopted from Susemihl. Π stands for the consent of the Aldine edition and all extant MSS., so far as these sources have been consulted for Susemihl's editions: $Π^1$ for the consent of the extant MSS. of the first family (in the first two books M^s P^1 only) and the text followed by the Vetus Interpres: $Π^2$ for the consent of the Aldine edition and the MSS. of the second

If we except the Vatican Fragments[1], the manuscripts of the Politics are of a late date, later than the text translated by the Vetus Interpres, which was itself apparently not very early. They are evidently full of the faults which are commonly found in manuscripts. The scribes did their work mechanically for the most part—often without a thought of the meaning of what they were writing—though here and there we seem to detect efforts to emend the text, especially in the case of puzzling words or passages. The manuscripts often incorporate glosses with the text; they often omit whole clauses, especially clauses intervening between repetitions of the same word; still oftener they omit one or more words; they are often led astray by homoeoteleuton; their errors are particularly frequent in relation to certain words; they repeat words from the preceding line; they are apt to place contiguous words in the same case; sometimes they seem to admit two alternative readings together into the text—sometimes we notice that clauses are transposed. To say that they have these defects is, however, only to say that they share the common lot of manuscripts. Their lateness has probably added to their imperfections. We note, for instance, that many of the variations which we observe in them are variations in the termination of words[2], and these may often have arisen from the misreading or miswriting of contractions, which were used with increasing frequency after the eleventh century. How easily they might thus arise will be seen from Gardthausen's work on Greek Palaeography

family, so far as these sources have been examined for Susemihl's editions: Π^3 for the consent of the Aldine edition and the MSS. of the less good variety of the second family, subject to the same limitation. I need hardly explain that the abbreviation 'pr.' prefixed to the name of a MS. refers to its original state and is intended to distinguish an original reading from a correction.

[1] See the Preface.

[2] See, for instance, the various readings in 1271 a 37 (*αὐτῆς* Π^1, *αὐτῶν* P^2, *αὐτοῦ* pr. P^3, *αὐτοῖς* Π^3), 1280 a 24 (*ἐλευθερίη* M^8, *ἐλευθέριοι* Π^2, *ἐλεύθεροι* P^1—the true reading being doubtless *ἐλευθερίᾳ*), 1282 a 27, 1284 b 41, 1286 a 25, 1286 b 24, 33, 1287 b 30, 1288 a 23, 1292 b 36, 1297 a 1: and see Sus.[1], p. xii, note 21. Not many pages, however, of Susemihl's *apparatus criticus* are free from instances of error in terminations.

(p. 246), where we find the remark that the same contraction may be used to represent θεότητος, θεότητι, θεότητα, while another represents πόλις, πολύς, πόλεμος, πολέμιος, πολίτης, and even πολιτεία (though the last word is more usually represented by a different contraction), and that a single contraction may be employed to express βάλλοντος, βάλλοντι, βάλλοντα, βάλλοντες, βάλλοντας.

Occasionally all the manuscripts, in addition to the text used by the Vetus Interpres, offer a reading almost or quite certainly wrong[1], but they seem on the whole to preserve with considerable fidelity the idiosyncrasies of Aristotle's peculiar and highly characteristic style. In a large number of passages earlier critics have condemned readings which a closer and more sympathetic study of Aristotle's use of language has proved to be undoubtedly correct[2]. Often and often the manuscripts have retained little idiosyncrasies of style, which less mechanical copyists, or copyists more ready to insist on the ordinary rules of Greek writing, might well have smoothed away. Peculiarities in the order of words[3], occasional omissions of a word or words[4], *constructiones ad sensum*[5], carelessnesses[6]

[1] E.g. in 2. 12. 1274 b 7, Γ Π (except perhaps pr. P^3) have ἐπίσκεψιν (instead of ἐπίσκηψιν): in 3. 3. 1276 b 9, Γ Π have λέγοιμεν for λέγομεν: in 3. 8. 1279 b 28, προσαγορεύοι or προσαγορεύει, one or other of which appears in Γ Π, must be wrong: in 3. 15. 1286 a 9–10, δοκεῖ . . . οἱ νόμοι Γ Π: in 3. 16. 1287 a 29, Γ Π seem to be wrong, and the Vossian *codex* of Julian alone right. Cases in which all the MSS. are wrong and Γ alone is right also occur: see for example the passages referred to above, p. xlviii, note 2.

[2] Those who do not happen to be acquainted with the second of Vahlen's Aristotelische Aufsätze will thank me for referring to it in illustration of this remark.

[3] E.g. 1. 6. 1255 b 2, ἡ δὲ φύσις βούλεται μὲν τοῦτο ποιεῖν πολλάκις, οὐ μέντοι δύναται (so Γ Π, except that M^s P^1 place τοῦτο after ποιεῖν): 7 (5). 9. 1309 b 27, τέλος δ' οὕτως ὥστε μηδὲ ῥῖνα ποιήσει φαίνεσθαι: 7 (5). 10. 1311 a 23, τὰς αὐτὰς ἀρχὰς δεῖ νομίζειν περί τε τὰς πολιτείας εἶναι τῶν μεταβολῶν καὶ περὶ τὰς μοναρχίας (except that Γ M^s erroneously place τῶν μεταβολῶν before αὐτὰς): 8 (6). 6. 1320 b 33, τὰ μὲν εὖ σώματα διακείμενα πρὸς ὑγίειαν: 4 (7). 1. 1323 b 4, περὶ δὲ τὴν ἔξω κτῆσιν τῶν ἀγαθῶν μετριάζουσιν.

[4] E.g. of πόλις and its parts (see explanatory note on 1266 b 1): of ἀρετήν, 5 (8). 4. 1338 b 15 and 1. 13. 1260 a 24: of ἔχουσιν, 6 (4). 9. 1294 b 27: of πρὸς τὴν ψυχήν, 5 (8). 5. 1340 b 17: of μετέχειν, 6 (4). 6. 1292 b 36.

[5] E.g. 7 (5). 10. 1311 a 33, τῆς δ' ὕβρεως οὔσης πολυμεροῦς, ἕκαστον αὐτῶν αἴτιον γίνεται τῆς ὀργῆς.

[6] E.g. 3. 13. 1283 b 16, δῆλον

or roughnesses[1] of style, and even positively bad writing[2] are faithfully reproduced[3].

We have seen, however, that the complete MSS. fall into two families, and here the question arises—what is the origin and the extent of the distinction between them? We know that in parts of the de Anima and of some other writings of Aristotle two texts exist, which have been thought by some to represent two separate issues or editions, both from the hand of Aristotle, while others have held one of the texts to be a *réchauffé* due, not to Aristotle, but to some expositor who has rewritten the original with slight alterations in the language, not often affecting the meaning. Has the distinction between the two families of manuscripts in the case of the Politics originated in either of these ways? The question is an important one, for if the distinction between them had this origin, it would obviously be altogether improper to blend the readings of the two families together and to form a composite text out of them, as all editors have hitherto sought to do. There is no doubt that the differences existing between the two families are in part of a similar nature to those which exist between the two texts of the second book of the de Anima. As in the de Anima, so in the Politics, we note variations in the order of words, variations in the use of the article, variations in particles and the like. But these variations are far less frequent in the Politics than in the portions of the second book of the de Anima in which a second text exists. In one or two places of the de Anima, again, we trace some slight divergence of

γὰρ ὡς εἴ τις πάλιν εἷς πλουσιώτερος ἁπάντων ἐστί, δῆλον ὅτι κ.τ.λ.: 8 (6). 5. 1319 b 33, ἔστι δ' ἔργον τοῦ νομοθέτου καὶ τῶν βουλομένων συνιστάναι τινὰ τοιαύτην πολιτείαν οὐ τὸ καταστῆσαι μέγιστον ἔργον οὐδὲ μόνον, ἀλλ' ὅπως σώζηται μᾶλλον.

[1] E. g. 2. 6. 1264 b 39–40 (cp. de Gen. An. 2. 7. 746 b 7–9): 1. 10. 1258 a 24.

[2] E. g. 6 (4). 8. 1293 b 26–7.

[3] Some of their mistakes seem to be due to their ultimate derivation from an archetype in which words were neither separated nor accentuated: thus we have ἡ δὴ instead of ἤδη in 1252 b 28, ἀριστάρχεῖν instead of ἄριστ' ἄρχειν in 1273 b 5, ἀλλ' οὐδ' ἔστιν instead of ἄλλου δ' ἐστὶν in 1254 a 15, Χάρητι δὴ instead of Χαρητίδῃ in 1258 b 40.

meaning[1], and this we hardly find in the Politics. And then again, we note that variations in the order of words occur even within the first family, the order followed by M^s P^1 being often different from that followed by Γ, which is in these cases commonly the same as that of the second family. It seems, therefore, hardly necessary to have recourse to the supposition of a double text to account for variations of order[2]. The same thing may be said as to variations in the use of the article and others of the same kind. Besides, many of the differences between the readings of the two families are of a sort which is not equally conspicuous in the two texts of the de Anima. One family uses one form of a word, the other another: the first has ὀψοποιητική, the second ὀψοποιϊκή: the first commonly uses the form μονάρχης, the second μόναρχος[3], and so forth. The second family occasionally avoids *hiatus* where the first does not. Differences of this kind are probably due to grammarian revisers of the text; and if this is so, it seems probable that the differences which might be ascribed to a duality of text have also originated in the same way. Many of the differences, again, between the text of Π^1 and Π^2 appear to be due to a misreading of contractions, or to omissions on the part of one set of manuscripts or the other (most often of Π^1), or to other accidental causes. It does not seem likely that the contrast of the two families runs back (at all events in its present proportions) to anything like so early a date as do the two

[1] E.g. in de An. 2. 9. 421 a 9, where the received text has—*αἴτιον δ' ὅτι τὴν αἴσθησιν ταύτην οὐκ ἔχομεν ἀκριβῆ, ἀλλὰ χείρω πολλῶν ζῴων*, and the second text—*αἴτιον δ' ὅτι οὐκ ἔχομεν ἀκριβῆ ταύτην τὴν αἴσθησιν, ἀλλὰ χείριστα ὀσμᾶται ἄνθρωπος τῶν ζῴων.*

[2] M^s here and there has an order of its own (e.g. in 1267 b 40). It is easy to see from Susemihl's *apparatus criticus* on 1271 a 25, 36 (Sus.[1], pp. 127, 128), how easily these changes of order might arise, and, if they arose in an archetype, how widely they might be diffused.

[3] 'The dependent compounds of the stem ἄρχω end in Attic not in -αρχης, but throughout in -αρχος (γυμνασίαρχος, δήμαρχος, ἵππαρχος, τριήραρχος, etc.): still in an Attic inscription of B. C. 324 we find certain finance officials of the deme Athmone named μεράρχαι' (Meisterhans, Grammatik der attischen Inschriften, pp. 53–54).

texts of portions of the de Anima. Both families agree in the order in which they arrange the books. In both, the first four chapters of the Sixth Book are little better than a chaos. This last defect, it is true, may have existed in the work as Aristotle left it. All the manuscripts, and the *vetus versio* also, have the obvious blunder ἐπίσκεψιν in 2. 12. 1274 b 7: all read ἐκ δὲ τοῦ τετάρτου τῶν τετάρτων in 2. 6. 1266 a 18. The text of the Vatican Fragments is a mixed text, and may possibly belong to a time prior to the rise of a marked contrast between the two families.

It would seem, then, that both families of manuscripts may safely be used in the construction of a text of the Politics. No editor, in fact, has attempted to base his text on one family only and dispensed altogether with the aid of the other. Bekker mainly relies on the second family, but he has adopted several readings from the Vetus Interpres: Susemihl bases his text in the main on the first family, and especially on Γ, but he frequently adopts readings from the second[1]. Editors of the Politics seem to have no option but to make their text more or less a composite text. Ours must be based partly on the first family of manuscripts, partly on the better variety of the second: occasionally perhaps it may be necessary to take a reading from the less good variety of the second. The question whether in a given passage we are to follow the reading given by the first family or the second, which is often a difficult one, must be decided partly by the proba-

[1] E. g. in the following passages of the First and Second Books: 1255 a 5, 1259 b 2, 1260 a 39, 1262 a 30, 1264 a 1, 1264 b 3, 1265 a 30, 35 (χρῆσιν), 1265 b 4, 21, 1266 a 20, 23, 1267 b 40, 1270 a 20, 21, 1271 a 27, 1273 a 10, 1273 b 3. It may be added that Susemihl recognizes in his third edition (praef. p. xvi), how prone the MSS. of the first family are to omit words, and how little they are to be depended on in cases of omission; hence we find him in this edition accepting from the second family not a few words which he had previously eliminated in reliance on the authority of the first family, and generally showing an increased confidence in the second family, though he still prefers the first. Instances of this will be found in the following passages of the first two books, as they stand in Susemihl's third edition—1253 a 25, 1257 b 24, 1260 b 17, 1261 a 22, 1263 b 1, 6, 1264 a 16, 1268 a 26, 1270 a 25, 34, 1273 a 9, b 2, 27, 1274 b 8.

bilities of the particular case, partly in reference to the known tendencies of either family.

The manuscripts of the second family, for instance, as has been said, avoid *hiatus* more frequently than those of the first [1]: here in all probability the less polished version is the more genuine. In matters of spelling, again, the first family has perhaps occasionally preserved peculiarities which the second has smoothed away (e. g. the form συμφυῆναι in 1262 b 13, which is all the more likely to be correct because it is found in K^b in Eth. Nic. 7. 5. 1147 a 22)[2]. When the first family unanimously places words in one order which the second places in another, the order given by the first family is sometimes to my mind more unstudied and more Aristotelian than that given by the second [3]. But in graver matters at any rate the advantage seems to me to rest with the second family [4]. In some cases falling under this head, no doubt, the readings of the first family may well deserve our preference. Thus in 2. 11. 1273 a 41, Π^1 give us *ταύτην οὐχ οἷόν τε βεβαίως ἀριστοκρατεῖσθαι τὴν πολιτείαν*, and Π^2 the softened and probably less genuine reading *ταύτην οὐχ οἷόν τ' εἶναι βεβαίως ἀριστοκρατικὴν πολιτείαν*: and in 2. 1. 1260 b 28 *τίς* Π^1 seems preferable on similar grounds to *ἤ*, which is the reading of the manuscripts of the second family. So again in 4 (7). 12. 1331 b 13 Π^1 have preserved

[1] E. g. in 1254 b 14: 1255 a 11, b 5, 21: 1256 a 33, b 18: 1258 a 31: 1259 b 7: 1261 b 17, 32: 1263 a 28: 1264 a 37, 38, etc. In these passages, however, the elisions by which *hiatus* is avoided are of a trivial and obvious kind: serious cases of *hiatus* are commonly left untouched in both families alike.

[2] It is not, however, always the case that the spelling of Π^1 is to be preferred. For instance, the form φιδίτια (Π^2) seems preferable to φιλίτια (Π^1)—see critical note on 1271 a 27. It is hardly likely that in matters of spelling complete reliance can safely be placed on either family. It should be noted that in questions as to *hiatus* and commonly also in questions of spelling we get no assistance from the Vetus Interpres, and are dependent on M^s P^1, so far as the first family is concerned.

[3] E. g. in 5 (8). 2. 1337 b 20 Π^1 have ὁ δὲ αὐτὸ τοῦτο πράττων πολλάκις δι' ἄλλους θητικὸν καὶ δουλικὸν ἂν δόξειε πράττειν (where πολλάκις is to be taken with ἂν δόξειε—compare the similar displacement of πολλάκις in 1. 6. 1255 b 3), while Π^2 place πολλάκις after δι' ἄλλους (and also ἂν after δόξειεν), thus arranging the words in a more regular and logical, but probably less genuine, order.

[4] The Vatican Fragments agree far more often with the second family than with the first. See the Preface.

the true reading νενεμῆσθαι (Π^2 almost without exception have μεμιμῆσθαι), and in 4 (7). 17. 1336 b 2 ἀπελαύνειν Π^2 seems to be undoubtedly wrong. But on the whole it appears to me that Π^2 less often transmute a puzzling reading into an easier one than Π^1. Thus, for example, in

1. 2. 1252 b 15, ὁμοκάπους, the reading of most MSS. of the second family, is better than ὁμοκάπνους, Π^1 P^4 L^s.

1. 4. 1253 b 27, τῶν οἰκονομικῶν, the reading of almost all the MSS. of the second family, is better than τῷ οἰκονομικῷ, the reading of the first.

1. 9. 1257 b 24, Π^1 seem to be wrong in omitting οὗτος.

1. 11. 1258 b 27, Π^1 have corrected τρίτον into τέταρτον wrongly, though not unnaturally.

2. 2. 1261 b 7, οὔτε Π^2 is probably more genuine than οὐ Π^1.

2. 7. 1267 a 40, Π^1 omit the second ἂν, though the repetition of ἂν is probably right.

2. 8. 1268 b 12, Π^2 retain the singular but quite Aristotelian (Bon. Ind. 454 a 20 sq.) displacement of μὲν, of which indeed there are many traces in the MSS. of the Latin Translation.

21, Π^2 add ἤδη probably rightly.

1269 a 18, Vet. Int. has *qui mutaverit*, and may perhaps have found ὁ added in his text before κινήσας, where M^s P^1 add τις: Π^2 are probably right in reading simply κινήσας.

2. 9. 1270 a 34, Π^1 omit an awkward but idiomatic μὲν.

3. 12. 1282 b 15, δὲ Π^2 is more probably Aristotelian than δὴ Π^1.

3. 14. 1285 b 12, P^2 and (on second thoughts) P^3 give ἐπανάτασις: M^s P^1 and possibly Γ (Vet. Int. *elevatio*) wrongly ἐπανάστασις.

6 (4). 5. 1292 b 5, the difficult word εἰσίῃ ('takes office') becomes εἰς εἴη in Γ M^s pr. P^1.

6 (4). 6. 1293 a 3, Π^2 rightly omit καὶ before εὐπορίας.

6 (4). 12. 1296 b 33, an idiomatic δὲ is omitted by Π^1, but preserved by Π^2.

6 (4). 16. 1300 b 30, παντὶ Π^2 seems to me to be right, not παρόντι Π^1.

8 (6). 8. 1322 b 14, εἰσφοράν Π^2 is undoubtedly correct, though Γ M^s P^1 substitute the commoner word ἐφορείαν.

4 (7). 1. 1323 b 9, the idiomatic use of αὐτῶν is probably correct, but Γ M^s P^1 omit the word.

4 (7). 12. 1331 b 5, τὴν Π^2 is probably right, though its omission by Γ M^s pr. P^1 makes the passage easier. This omission, however, may well be accidental, as τὴν is followed by τῶν.

5 (8). 5. 1339 a 29, τε παισὶν Π², where the place of τε, though not that which we should expect, is justified by many parallel instances (see Bon. Ind. 749 b 44 sqq.), whereas P¹ reads γε and Mˢ omits τε, and possibly Γ also, but of this we cannot be certain, for the Vet. Int. seldom renders τε.

5 (8). 6. 1341 a 13, καὶ, which Π² add, is probably right, though not easy to interpret.

5 (8). 6. 1341 b 1, Π¹ wrongly substitute ἴαμβοι for σαμβῦκαι.

The manuscripts of the first family seem also, I think, to admit glosses into the text more frequently than the better ones of the second (see, for instance, Susemihl's *apparatus criticus* on 1. 8. 1256 b 26: 2. 6. 1265 a 21, 22: 2. 7. 1266 a 37: 2. 10. 1271 b 28: 3. 4. 1277 a 23: 3. 10. 1281 a 28, where σπουδαῖα, which is probably a gloss, takes in Π¹ the place of δίκαια). Clearly, again, as Dittenberger has remarked[1], and Susemihl has now fully recognized (Sus.³ p. xvi), these manuscripts are apt to omit words, probably because their archetype was somewhat carelessly written[2]. Take the following instances from the Third Book:—

1275 a 11, Π¹ om. καὶ γὰρ ταῦτα τούτοις ὑπάρχει: 28, Γ Mˢ pr. P¹ om. καίτοι—ἀρχῆς: 1276 a 4, Mˢ P¹, and possibly Γ, om. τῆς: b 3, Mˢ P¹, and possibly Γ, om. ἂν: 36, Γ Mˢ pr. P¹ om. ἀλλὰ: 1277 a 20, Π¹ om. ἀρετὴ after ἡ αὐτὴ: 24, Γ Mˢ pr. P¹ om. ἴσως: 1278 b 2, om. ἐκ τῶν εἰρημένων: 20, om. οὐκ ἔλαττον: 1279 a 2, Π¹ om. ἕνα, though Mˢ P¹ move εἶναι to its place: 34, Mˢ P¹, and possibly Γ, om. τῶν in τὴν δὲ τῶν ὀλίγων: b 15, Π¹ om. τι: 1280 b 1, Mˢ P¹, and possibly Γ, om. τοῦ: 5, Γ Mˢ pr. P¹ om. πολιτικῆς: 1282 a 7, Π¹ om. καὶ: 17, om. ἢ before βελτίους: 40, Mˢ P¹, and probably Γ, om. τὸ before τούτων: 1283 a 10, Π¹ om. καὶ, and in the next line in πᾶσαν ἀνισότητ' Γ Mˢ pr. P¹ omit the second of the two syllables αν, making ἀνισότητ' into ἰσότητ' or ἰσότητα: 17, Mˢ P¹, and possibly Γ, om. τ': 32,

[1] *Gött. gel. Anz.*, Oct. 28, 1874, p. 1359. If we examine the discrepancies between Π¹ and Π² in the first two books of the Politics, we shall find that in a large proportion of cases they arise from the omission of words in Π¹.

[2] Omissions also occur in Π², and some of them are on a more extensive scale than those of Π¹ (see, for example, 1307 b 32–34, 1334 a 37–38, 1336 b 18, 1337 b 16–19, 34–35), but they fortunately occur less frequently, and they give rise to no critical doubts. They are often obviously due to homoeoteleuton.

Ms P¹, and possibly Γ, om. τὰ: b 2, Π¹ om. τι: 1284 b 11, om. τι (perhaps rightly): 1285 a 6, Ms P¹, and possibly Γ, om. τοὺς: 1286 b 31, Π¹ om. καὶ before κατὰ: 1287 a 16, om. τοίνυν: 25, Γ om. ἐπίτηδες παιδεύσας, Ms P¹ om. παιδεύσας: b 38, Γ Ms pr. P¹ om. καὶ ἄλλο βασιλικὸν: 1288 a 6, Π¹ om. ἤδη: 16, om. τινὰ: 29, om. τοῦτον (as they omit οὗτος in 1257 b 24 and οὗτοι in 1273 a 9).

In his third edition, Susemihl adopts the reading of the first family in only four of the passages which I have just cited. A similar array of passages might be adduced from the Sixth Book, and a somewhat shorter one from the First and Second. I am far from saying that in every one of these passages the sin of omission can be positively brought home to Π¹—on the contrary, in more than one of them it is not clear whether Π¹ omit or Π² add—but I am inclined to think, as Susemihl now thinks (Sus.³ p. xvi), that Π² add a good deal less often than Π¹ omit. At all events, it is evident that omissions in Π¹ must be carefully scrutinized before we can safely accept them.

It has already been said that most of the discrepancies between Π¹ and Π² seem to be due to errors of transcription or to have originated in some other easily intelligible way; but there is a certain percentage of which this cannot be said. In the First and Second Books the following variations may be cited under this head :—

A. 1. 7. 1255 b 26, τούτων Π¹ is replaced by τῶν τοιούτων in Π².

B. 2. 1. 1260 b 28, τίς Π¹, ᾗ Π².

C. 2. 8. 1267 b 26, κόμης Γ Ms pr. P¹, κόσμῳ πολυτελεῖ Π².

D. 2. 9. 1269 b 21, τοιοῦτος ἐστιν Π¹ (so accentuated in Ms P¹), φανερός ἐστι τοιοῦτος ὢν Π².
(Cp. 1269 b 26, where Γ Ms pr. P¹ om. φανερῶς.)

E. 2. 10. 1271 b 28, κρῆτες Γ Ms pr. P¹ (all other MSS. Λύκτιοι).

F. 2. 11. 1273 a 41, ταύτην οὐχ οἷόν τε βεβαίως ἀριστοκρατεῖσθαι τὴν πολιτείαν Π¹: ταύτην οὐχ οἷόν τ' εἶναι βεβαίως ἀριστοκρατικὴν πολιτείαν Π².

In E there can be little doubt that a gloss explanatory of Λύκτιοι has taken the place of this word in Γ Ms pr. P¹. Of B and F something has already been said. A, C, D remain, and these are less easy to classify or account for, but it is noticeable that in all these three passages Π^1 abbreviate, just as elsewhere they omit.

So far we have been considering cases in which Π^1 and Π^2 are at issue[1], and these are the most difficult and perplexing with which we have to deal. It often happens, however, that the three texts of the first family—three, if we include the original of the *vetus versio*—do not agree. M^s and P^1, and also Γ and M^s, often stand apart by themselves, and Γ and P^1 occasionally do so[2]. When M^s P^1 stand alone, we usually find that Γ agrees with the second family, and the same thing may be said of P^1 when Γ M^s stand alone. Against the union of Γ Π^2 not much weight commonly attaches, as it seems to me, to that of M^s P^1, and Γ M^s have also, I think, little weight when matched against P^1 Π^2.

The following passages from the Second Book will illustrate this in reference to M^s P^1, though some of the readings referred to are far better than others, and I would not pronounce positively against all:—

1260 b 32, M^s P^1 om. τ': 1261 a 6, M^s P^1 ἐν τῇ Πλάτωνος πολιτείᾳ: the other MSS. have ἐν τῇ πολιτείᾳ τῇ (some τοῦ) Πλάτωνος: 17, M^s P^1 οὐ for οὐδὲ wrongly: 1261 b 25, M^s P^1 om. τοῖς in ταῖς γυναιξὶ καὶ τοῖς τέκνοις: 28, M^s P^1 om. τίς: 1262 a 35, M^s pr. P^1 om. εἶναι: 1262 b 6, M^s P^1 om. οὕτως wrongly: 7, M^s P^1 om. τε: 1263 b 32, M^s pr. P^1 ἔσται wrongly: 1264 a 1, M^s pr. P^1 ἐκοινώνησε wrongly: 1264 b 20, M^s pr. P^1 ὥσπερ wrongly: 39, M^s P^1 om. λόγοις: 1265 a 18, M^s P^1 μὴ for μηδὲν wrongly: 36, M^s P^1 add μὲν after πράως: 1265 b 27, M^s P^1 place μὲν not after βούλεται like the rest, but after ὅλη, not probably rightly: 1266 b 28, M^s P^1 τάξει instead of τάξειεν: 1268 a 14,

[1] It is possible that the contrast of the two families of MSS. would be less strongly marked, if we possessed a larger number of good MSS. of the Politics. We might probably in that case possess MSS. occupying an intermediate position between the two. This hardly any of our MSS. can be said to do. [My surmise has been verified by the discovery of the Vatican Fragments.]

[2] We find Γ and P^1 standing together alone far less often than Γ and M^s, or M^s and P^1. The remarks in the text were written before I became acquainted with Susemihl's third edition, in which I find that they are to some extent anticipated.

Ms pr. P[1] om. καὶ ξενικῶν: 37, Ms P[1] γεωργεῖν wrongly: 1268 b 23, Ms P[1] γενέσθαι for γίνεσθαι: 1269 a 18, Ms P[1] add τις before κινήσας (wrongly, I think): 1269 b 28, Ms P[1] πρώτως in place of πρῶτος: 32, Ms P[1] διώκητο wrongly for διωκεῖτο: 1270 a 1, Ms pr. P[1] om. τῆς οἰκείας wrongly: 8, Ms P[1] γινομένων wrongly for γενομένων: 17, Ms P[1] om. λίαν before οὐσίαν: τὸν Ms, τῶν P[1] wrongly for τοῖς: 26, Ms P[1] om. ἢ before καὶ wrongly: 1270 b 2, Ms P[1] om. τοὺς πολίτας wrongly: 8, Ms P[1] om. ἐστίν: 26, Ms P[1] ἤδη wrongly for ἔδει: 1271 a 16, Ms P[1] om. ἂν wrongly: 1271 b 22, Ms P[1] τε wrongly for δέ: 1272 b 31, Ms P[1] om. ἔχουσαν (wrongly, as I think), and om. ἐν wrongly: 1273 b 25, Ms P[1] κρήτης wrongly for κρητικῆς: 37, Ms P[1] om. γὰρ wrongly[1].

Changes in the order of words peculiar to Ms P[1] occur not unfrequently; the following instances may be adduced from the Second Book:—

1260 b 41, 1261 b 7, 1263 a 22, b 16, 17, 1264 a 9, 1265 b 15, 1267 a 38, 1268 a 39, 1271 a 36, b 7, 1272 b 24.

It would be rash to alter the order of words on the authority of these two manuscripts unsupported by others.

As to the readings peculiar to Γ Ms, not many of them, I think, possess merit. Take the following list from the Second Book:—

1261 a 21, Γ Ms om. καὶ before δυνατός (wrongly, I think): 33, Γ Ms read δὲ for γὰρ wrongly: 1264 a 19, Γ Ms παθόντες (P[1] Π[2] μαθόντες): b 9, Γ Ms εἴπουθεν δὴ wrongly for ἤπουθεν δή: 1267 a 2, Γ pr. Ms om. καὶ wrongly: 1268 b 9, Γ Ms om. καὶ wrongly: 1269 a 25, Γ Ms om. καὶ before κινητέοι: 1270 a 12, Γ Ms om. ἔοικεν wrongly: b 8, Γ Ms om. αὐτὴ wrongly: 1271 a 18, Γ Ms om. διὰ: b 7, Γ Ms om. μέν: 1272 b 1, Γ Ms have διαφερόντων wrongly for διαφθερούντων: 1273 a 40, Γ Ms have πολιτειῶν wrongly for πολιτῶν: b 4, Γ Ms have ἂν wrongly for ὧν: 1274 a 8, Γ Ms om. τὰ—Περικλῆς (homoeoteleuton): 28, Γ Ms om. μαντικήν: b 20, Γ Ms om. γὰρ wrongly[2].

[1] Ms P[1] perhaps diverge rather more frequently from the other texts in the Second Book than in the First and Third, but the readings peculiar to these two MSS. in the First, Third, and Sixth Books seem to me to be of even less value than in the Second.

[2] The record of these two MSS. is no better in the First, Third, and Sixth Books.

Readings resting on the authority of only one of the manuscripts of the Politics possess, as a rule, but little weight. 'Such readings,' remarks Dittenberger (*Gött. gel. Anz.*, Oct. 28, 1874, p. 1362), 'should only be adopted after convincing proof, (1) that the reading unanimously given by the other MSS. and probably inherited from the archetype is on internal grounds untenable, and (2) that the emendation offered by the single MS. in question is the easiest, simplest, and most satisfactory that can be offered.' M^s is a carelessly written manuscript, and very little importance can be attached to its unsupported testimony. We have already seen that not a few tempting readings peculiar to P^1 are probably conjectural emendations of its learned transcriber, and we must beware of attaching too much importance to its unsupported testimony[1]. The same thing may be said of P^2, and also of P^3.

When, however, we ask what value is to be attached to the unsupported testimony of the text followed by the Vetus Interpres, we are on more debatable ground. Susemihl still attaches much importance to it, though, as has been said, considerably less in his third edition than in his previous ones. But even he accepts only a moderate proportion of the many readings which rest on its unsupported testimony. Dittenberger unhesitatingly applies to Γ the rule which we have just cited from him. 'From this rule,' he says (*Gött. gel. Anz.* p. 1363), 'no exception should be made even in favour of the translation of William of Moerbeke. No doubt it is quite true that it represents the best of all the manuscripts of the Politics, but even the testimony of the best single manuscript, as it is not the sole representative of a family, has from a diplomatic point of view no weight whatever in opposition to the concurrence of all other manuscripts of both families.'

The question, however, arises, as we have seen, how far the translation faithfully reproduces the Greek text (or texts)

[1] Its value may be studied in the following passages from the Sixth Book :—1289 a 10, 15, b 1 : 1290 a 1 : 1291 b 31 : 1292 a 1, b 13 : 1293 a 30 : 1294 a 3, 12, b 8, 23, 24 : 1296 a 16, b 7, 10 : 1297 b 16 : 1298 a 7, 18 : 1299 a 30 : 1300 a 3, 5, b 13, 18.

used by the translator[1]. Susemihl recognizes even in his first edition that in some matters it is not rigidly faithful to its original. 'Denique, quamvis omnia ad verbum vertere soleat Guilelmus, cavendum tamen est, ne, ubicunque paulo liberiore ratione utatur, semper aliud quid in eius exemplo scriptum fuisse credamus atque in nostris hodie legitur. Nam non solum idem vocabulum Graecum non eodem semper reddit Latino, verum sunt etiam parvulae voces, quas contra codicis sui auctoritatem aut addiderit aut omiserit, velut copulam saepissime adiecit, ubi deest in exemplaribus Graecis[2], praepositionem cum plurium nominum casibus copulatam ante unumquodque eorum repetere solet[3], τε et γε particulas plerumque non vertit, in διόπερ et aliis vocabulis cum περ compositis modo hoc περ *quidem* voce exprimit, modo silentio transit. Quae cum ita sint, etiam verba quaedam in omnibus aut paene omnibus codicibus omissa, quae Guilelmi auctoritate fretus Aristoteli reddidi, velut 2. 3. 1262 a 12 ἥ, 2. 5. 1263 a 35 ὡς, b 34 ἔσται, 2. 6. 1265 a 34 ζῆν, 3. 3. 1276 a 25 τόπον, 4 (7). 17. 1337 a 7 εἶναι (cf. 2. 7. 1267 b 18 ὡς, 4 (7). 16. 1335 a 30 χρόνῳ), in dubium posse vocari, utrum revera in exemplo suo invenerit an Latine tantum reddiderit sententia et sermonis Latini ratione permotus, eo libentius concedo, quo minus aliis locis tale quid factum esse potest negari, velut vix 1. 9. 1257 b 38 τέλος post αὔξησις legisse censendus est, quamquam vertit *huius autem augmentatio finis*' (Sus.[1], pp. xxxiii–xxxiv).

This list, however, is far from exhausting the laxities

[1] I regret that Busse's excellent dissertation 'de praesidiis Aristotelis Politica emendandi' (Berlin, 1881) did not come to my knowledge till some months after my remarks on the Vetus Interpres and my critical notes had been written. I find that he has anticipated several of the criticisms which I have ventured to make on the thirteenth-century translation as an authority for the text of the Politics. Perhaps however the fact that we have independently arrived at many similar results on this subject may lend some additional weight to our common conclusions.

[2] He adds *est* in the following passages of the first two books —1253 a 16, 1255 b 7, 31, 1256 a 21, 1261 a 2, 1264 a 34, 1271 a 5, 1274 b 9: *esse* in 1260 b 37, 1264 a 9: *erit* in 1263 b 34, 1266 b 27.

[3] See 1258 a 1, 1262 b 3, 1269 a 10, 1271 b 8. So too *ut*, 1253 b 16 (in most MSS.).

which the worthy translator permits himself. He omits μὲν without support from any extant manuscript (so far as they have been examined) in twelve passages of the first two books [1], καὶ in sixteen [2], δὲ in eight [3], γὰρ in three [4], ἂν in four [5]. He fails to render οὔτε in 1253 b 38, τι in 1253 b 32. He often reads γε (1254 a 9, 1266 b 34, 1269 b 9) or δὲ (1268 b 41, 1271 b 15) for τε, though sometimes τε for γε (1254 b 34, 1273 b 7, 1274 a 15) or for δὲ (1258 a 26), and γε for δὲ (1252 b 8, 1268 b 16). He renders ἢ by *et* in 1252 a 13, 1253 b 34, 1256 a 37, 1258 b 19, and καὶ by *aut* in 1262 a 8. He occasionally adds words—*civitates* in 1266 b 1, *scilicet* in 1274 a 1, *eorum* in 1258 a 5. His voices, moods, and tenses often fail to reproduce the voices, moods, and tenses of the original. Thus we find him substituting the passive for the active [6], the active for the passive [7], the indicative for the subjunctive [8], the subjunctive for the indicative [9], the present for the past [10], the past for the present [11]. He sometimes, though not very often, omits words of some length, or even two or three words together [12]. This is probably the result of accident. He usually adheres to the order of the words

[1] 1252 a 27, 1257 a 7, 1258 b 11, 1259 a 28, 1265 a 9, 1266 b 3, 1270 a 4, b 11, 37, 1273 a 26, 1274 a 26, b 15. The omissions noted in the text may be due in part to errors committed by copyists of the translation, but they appear in all Susemihl's MSS. of it.

[2] 1252 a 29, 1253 a 31, 1258 a 2 (z adds *et* here), 1259 a 33, b 8, 29, 1260 a 31, 1262 a 18, 1263 b 34, 1264 a 15, 1266 b 28, 1267 b 24, 1269 a 38, 1270 a 26, 1274 a 25, b 17.

[3] 1252 a 13, b 23, 1254 b 24, 1256 b 33, 1262 a 38, 1266 a 11, b 2, 1269 a 19.

[4] 1264 a 36, 1268 b 13, 1274 b 21.

[5] 1254 b 1, 1256 a 4, 1265 a 30, 1269 b 26. I am far from saying that the Vet. Int. always makes these omissions without MS. authority, but their frequency makes it probable that they are largely his own.

[6] E.g. in 1256 b 41, 1259 a 3, 1262 b 25, 1264 b 14, 1265 b 7, 1266 b 20, 1267 a 38, b 5, 1268 b 21, 1271 b 5, 1274 a 7. Busse makes the same remark (p. 25).

[7] E.g. in 1262 a 5, 1265 b 10, 1266 a 11, 1269 a 18, 1271 a 22.

[8] E.g. in 1270 a 27.

[9] E.g. in 1253 a 22, 1265 b 15, 1288 b 36.

[10] E.g. in 1265 a 27, 1266 a 37, b 3, 7, 27, 1268 b 38, 1269 b 16, 1271 b 4, 22, 1272 b 32, 1273 b 17, 1274 a 3.

[11] E.g. in 1262 b 6, 1273 b 39.

[12] Πάντων, 1254 b 15, 1261 a 2: τῇ φύσει, 1253 a 19: γινομένων, 1257 b 17: καὶ τῆς Κρητικῆς, 1269 a 29: ἔξω Κελτῶν, 1269 b 26: ἕκαστον, 1271 a 29: καθέστηκεν, 1271 a 41: αὐτὸν, 1274 a 27.

in the Greek, but not unfrequently he makes slight changes in it, which do not probably for the most part correspond to anything in the text before him[1]. Here and there (e.g. in 1257 a 30–31) these changes are forced on him by the difference between Latin and Greek. We must remember that, however useful this translation may be to us for textual purposes, its author never dreamed of its being thus used. He never designed it to serve as a substitute for a manuscript.

In addition to the minute inaccuracies we have been noting, blunders in translation often occur, and also apparently blunders in the decipherment of the Greek text. Of the former class of blunders a few specimens have already been given; it would be easy to add to their number indefinitely. The last chapter of the Second Book offers some remarkable examples. It is hardly likely that so poor a Greek scholar can have been perfect as a decipherer of Greek writing; it is perhaps owing to this, that he renders ἀνέστιος as ἀνόσιος in 1253 a 5, τοῦ δεῖνος as τοῦδε υἱός in 1262 a 3, ἐθέλειν as μέλλειν or ὀφείλειν in 1267 a 34, ἀρίστην as ἀρετῆς in 1269 a 32, ἐπίκειται as ὑπόκειται in 1271 b 34, and γέρας as γῆρας in 1272 a 37, unless indeed we suppose his Greek text to have been exceptionally defective in these passages. We can sometimes account for errors in the *vetus versio* by the supposition that the translator used a manuscript in which ambiguous contractions similar to those found in M^s occasionally occurred, for in one or two places where M^s has a contraction of this kind we find the translator going astray: thus in 1335 a 27, where instead of πληθύον M^s has a contraction which might be taken to stand for πλῆθος, the rendering of the Vet. Int. is *multum*, and in 1337 a 28 under similar circumstances Vet. Int. has *ipsorum* where we expect *ipsum*. Here and there, again, as Busse has pointed out (pp. 14–28), the translator would seem to have sought to mend defects in his Greek text by conjectures of his own: one of the clearest cases of this is to

[1] His plan is, according to Busse (p. 13), 'ea quae forma ac sensu cohaereant etiam collocatione arctius coniungere.'

be found in 4 (7). 14. 1334 a 2 sqq., where the omission of some words in the translator's Greek text (and in M[s]) makes nonsense of the sentence, and he has sought to remedy this by rendering τάξῃ *ordinis*, as if it were τάξεως. So too in 8 (6). 7. 1321 a 6, finding probably in his text the same meaningless fragment of βαναυσικὸν (ναυσικὸν) which appears in M[s], the translator renders it *nautica* to make sense, and in 1. 8. 1256 a 30 he has *multis* for the same reason, though the reading he found in his text was in all probability the blunder πολλοὶ.

It is evident that, however good the manuscript or manuscripts used by the Vetus Interpres may have been[1], we have only an imperfect reproduction of them in his translation. Before, therefore, we can accept a reading which rests on its unsupported authority, we must in the first place make sure that he has manuscript authority for it, and that it has not originated in some error or inaccuracy or conjecture of his own. It is only of a certain number of the readings peculiar to the Vetus Interpres that we can assert this with confidence. The following are instances of readings too remarkable to have originated with the translator :—

2. 1. 1260 b 41, εἶς ὁ τῆς in place of ἰσότης Π.
2. 7. 1266 b 2, δ' ἤδη.
3. 12. 1283 a 7, ὑπερέχει.
4 (7). 17. 1336 a 6, εἰσάγειν.
1. 2. 1253 a 7, πετεινοῖς for πεττοῖς.

In the first four of these passages I am inclined to think that the translator's Greek text preserved the true reading. In the fifth he may probably have translated a marginal

[1] They seem to have suffered from the incorporation of glosses with the text (e.g. in 1254 b 1, φαύλως appears to be a gloss, μοχθηρῶς the true reading: glosses have found their way into the Greek text followed by the Vet. Int. in 1259 b 14 and 1287 a 10; and in 1291 b 29, ὅμοια, which is probably a gloss intended to explain τὰ τούτοις λεγόμενα κατὰ τὴν αὐτὴν διαφοράν, has been added to these words). We must also credit the text followed by the Vet. Int. with the many erroneous readings common to it with M[s].

correction, for the correction πετεινοῖς appears in the margin of more than one extant manuscript.

So far as to varieties of reading; but manuscripts are liable to still graver defects—to interpolation, chasms in the text, displacement of words, clauses, and paragraphs, and the like. In the text of Aristotle's treatise de Generatione Animalium, for instance, a chasm is thought to be traceable in 2. 1. 735 a 11 (after θεωροῦντος)[1], and whole paragraphs in more cases than one seem to be out of their true place[2]. How has it fared with the Politics in respect of these matters?

As to interpolation, I have elsewhere pointed to more than one passage in which it may reasonably be suspected. Susemihl, as is well known, holds that chasms in the text of the Politics occur not unfrequently, and that in many cases the transposition of clauses and paragraphs is called for. There would be nothing surprising in this. We occasionally find sentences obviously displaced in manuscripts of the Politics[3], and here and there we seem to trace a minute but indubitable chasm (there is a chasm of this kind in the better manuscripts in 1285 a 19). The question is one on which I would rather not express a definitive opinion, till I have completed my commentary, but so far as I can judge at present, I doubt whether Susemihl has made out his case. Problems of this kind, however, are best discussed in notes on the particular passages in reference to which they arise.

The question whether double versions occur is also an interesting one. This, again, is one for discussion in detail. I will only say that they need to be very clearly established, and that I am inclined to doubt whether they are really traceable in many of the cases in which they have been supposed to be so. The double inquiry into the cause

[1] So think Aubert and Wimmer: see their edition of the de Gen. An., p. 140.

[2] De Gen. An. 1. 19. 726 b 24–30: 2. 3. 737 a 34–737 b 7 (Aubert and Wimmer, pp. 98, 152).

[3] E.g. in 1264 b 3, 1287 b 18, 1290 a 32.

of the existence of a multiplicity of constitutions contained in the first four chapters of the Sixth Book is, however, certainly suspicious[1], and, as I have said elsewhere, these four chapters are in a condition the origin of which it is difficult to penetrate.

But here we find ourselves in face of those broader problems in relation to the state of the text of the Politics, as to which something has already been said.

[1] Attention has been called to this both by Susemihl and by Mr. J. C. Wilson.

ΠΟΛΙΤΙΚΩΝ Α'.

Ἐπειδὴ πᾶσαν πόλιν ὁρῶμεν κοινωνίαν τινὰ οὖσαν καὶ 1252 a
πᾶσαν κοινωνίαν ἀγαθοῦ τινὸς ἕνεκεν συνεστηκυῖαν (τοῦ γὰρ εἶναι δοκοῦντος ἀγαθοῦ χάριν πάντα πράττουσι πάντες), δῆλον ὡς πᾶσαι μὲν ἀγαθοῦ τινὸς στοχάζονται, μάλιστα δὲ καὶ τοῦ κυριωτάτου πάντων ἡ πασῶν κυριωτάτη καὶ πάσας περιέχουσα τὰς ἄλλας· αὕτη δέ ἐστιν ἡ καλουμένη πόλις
2 καὶ ἡ κοινωνία ἡ πολιτική. ὅσοι μὲν οὖν οἴονται πολιτικὸν καὶ βασιλικὸν καὶ οἰκονομικὸν καὶ δεσποτικὸν εἶναι τὸν αὐτόν, οὐ καλῶς λέγουσιν· πλήθει γὰρ καὶ ὀλιγότητι νομίζουσι διαφέρειν, ἀλλ' οὐκ εἴδει τούτων ἕκαστον, οἷον ἂν μὲν ὀλίγων, δεσπότην, ἂν δὲ πλειόνων, οἰκονόμον, ἂν δ' ἔτι πλειόνων, πολιτικὸν ἢ βασιλικόν, ὡς οὐδὲν διαφέρουσαν μεγάλην οἰκίαν ἢ μικρὰν πόλιν, καὶ πολιτικὸν δὲ καὶ βασιλικόν, ὅταν μὲν αὐτὸς ἐφεστήκῃ, βασιλικόν, ὅταν δὲ κατὰ τοὺς λόγους τῆς ἐπιστήμης τῆς τοιαύτης κατὰ μέρος ἄρχων καὶ ἀρχόμενος, πολιτικόν· ταῦτα δ' οὐκ ἔστιν ἀληθῆ·
3 δῆλον δ' ἔσται τὸ λεγόμενον ἐπισκοποῦσι κατὰ τὴν ὑφηγημένην μέθοδον. ὥσπερ γὰρ ἐν τοῖς ἄλλοις τὸ σύνθετον μέχρι τῶν ἀσυνθέτων ἀνάγκη διαιρεῖν (ταῦτα γὰρ ἐλάχιστα μόρια τοῦ παντός), οὕτω καὶ πόλιν ἐξ ὧν σύγκειται σκοποῦντες ὀψόμεθα καὶ περὶ τούτων μᾶλλον, τί τε διαφέρουσιν ἀλλήλων, καὶ εἴ τι τεχνικὸν ἐνδέχεται λαβεῖν περὶ ἕκαστον τῶν ῥηθέντων.

Εἰ δή τις ἐξ ἀρχῆς τὰ πράγματα φυόμενα βλέψειεν, 2
ὥσπερ ἐν τοῖς ἄλλοις, καὶ ἐν τούτοις κάλλιστ' ἂν

οὕτω θεωρήσειεν. ἀνάγκη δὴ πρῶτον συνδυάζεσθαι τοὺς ἄνευ 2
ἀλλήλων μὴ δυναμένους εἶναι, οἷον θῆλυ μὲν καὶ ἄρρεν τῆς
γενέσεως ἕνεκεν (καὶ τοῦτο οὐκ ἐκ προαιρέσεως, ἀλλ' ὥσπερ
καὶ ἐν τοῖς ἄλλοις ζῴοις καὶ φυτοῖς φυσικὸν τὸ ἐφίεσθαι,
οἷον αὐτό, τοιοῦτον καταλιπεῖν ἕτερον), ἄρχον δὲ φύσει καὶ
ἀρχόμενον διὰ τὴν σωτηρίαν· τὸ μὲν γὰρ δυνάμενον τῇ
διανοίᾳ προορᾶν ἄρχον φύσει καὶ δεσπόζον φύσει, τὸ δὲ
δυνάμενον τῷ σώματι ταῦτα ποιεῖν ἀρχόμενον καὶ φύσει
δοῦλον· διὸ δεσπότῃ καὶ δούλῳ ταὐτὸ συμφέρει. φύσει μὲν 3
1252 b οὖν διώρισται τὸ θῆλυ καὶ τὸ δοῦλον (οὐθὲν γὰρ ἡ φύσις
ποιεῖ τοιοῦτον οἷον χαλκοτύποι τὴν Δελφικὴν μάχαιραν
πενιχρῶς, ἀλλ' ἓν πρὸς ἕν· οὕτω γὰρ ἂν ἀποτελοῖτο κάλλιστα τῶν ὀργάνων ἕκαστον, μὴ πολλοῖς ἔργοις ἀλλ' ἑνὶ
δουλεῦον)· ἐν δὲ τοῖς βαρβάροις τὸ θῆλυ καὶ δοῦλον τὴν 4
αὐτὴν ἔχει τάξιν. αἴτιον δὲ ὅτι τὸ φύσει ἄρχον οὐκ ἔχουσιν, ἀλλὰ γίνεται ἡ κοινωνία αὐτῶν δούλης καὶ δούλου. διό
φασιν οἱ ποιηταὶ "βαρβάρων δ' Ἕλληνας ἄρχειν εἰκός,"
ὡς ταὐτὸ φύσει βάρβαρον καὶ δοῦλον ὄν. ἐκ μὲν οὖν τού- 5
των τῶν δύο κοινωνιῶν οἰκία πρώτη, καὶ ὀρθῶς Ἡσίοδος
εἶπε ποιήσας "οἶκον μὲν πρώτιστα γυναῖκά τε βοῦν τ' ἀρο-
τῆρα"· ὁ γὰρ βοῦς ἀντ' οἰκέτου τοῖς πένησίν ἐστιν. ἡ μὲν
οὖν εἰς πᾶσαν ἡμέραν συνεστηκυῖα κοινωνία κατὰ φύσιν
οἶκός ἐστιν, οὓς Χαρώνδας μὲν καλεῖ ὁμοσιπύους, Ἐπιμενίδης
δὲ ὁ Κρὴς ὁμοκάπους· ἡ δ' ἐκ πλειόνων οἰκιῶν κοινωνία
πρώτη χρήσεως ἕνεκεν μὴ ἐφημέρου κώμη. μάλιστα δὲ 6
κατὰ φύσιν ἔοικεν ἡ κώμη ἀποικία οἰκίας εἶναι· οὓς κα-
λοῦσί τινες ὁμογάλακτας παῖδάς τε καὶ παίδων παῖδας.
διὸ καὶ τὸ πρῶτον ἐβασιλεύοντο αἱ πόλεις, καὶ νῦν ἔτι τὰ
ἔθνη· ἐκ βασιλευομένων γὰρ συνῆλθον· πᾶσα γὰρ οἰκία
βασιλεύεται ὑπὸ τοῦ πρεσβυτάτου, ὥστε καὶ αἱ ἀποικίαι διὰ
τὴν συγγένειαν. καὶ τοῦτ' ἐστὶν ὃ λέγει Ὅμηρος, "θεμιστεύει 7
δὲ ἕκαστος παίδων ἠδ' ἀλόχων"· σποράδες γάρ· καὶ οὕτω
τὸ ἀρχαῖον ᾤκουν. καὶ τοὺς θεοὺς δὲ διὰ τοῦτο πάντες φασὶ

βασιλεύεσθαι, ὅτι καὶ αὐτοὶ οἱ μὲν ἔτι καὶ νῦν, οἱ δὲ τὸ
ἀρχαῖον ἐβασιλεύοντο, ὥσπερ δὲ καὶ τὰ εἴδη ἑαυτοῖς ἀφο-
8 μοιοῦσιν οἱ ἄνθρωποι, οὕτω καὶ τοὺς βίους τῶν θεῶν. ἡ δ' ἐκ
πλειόνων κωμῶν κοινωνία τέλειος πόλις ἤδη, πάσης ἔχουσα
πέρας τῆς αὐταρκείας ὡς ἔπος εἰπεῖν, γινομένη μὲν οὖν τοῦ
ζῆν ἕνεκεν, οὖσα δὲ τοῦ εὖ ζῆν. διὸ πᾶσα πόλις φύσει ἐστίν,
εἴπερ καὶ αἱ πρῶται κοινωνίαι· τέλος γὰρ αὕτη ἐκείνων,
ἡ δὲ φύσις τέλος ἐστίν· οἷον γὰρ ἕκαστόν ἐστι τῆς γενέσεως
τελεσθείσης, ταύτην φαμὲν τὴν φύσιν εἶναι ἑκάστου, ὥσπερ
9 ἀνθρώπου ἵππου οἰκίας. ἔτι τὸ οὗ ἕνεκα καὶ τὸ τέλος βέλ-
τιστον· ἡ δ' αὐτάρκεια καὶ τέλος καὶ βέλτιστον. ἐκ τούτων
οὖν φανερὸν ὅτι τῶν φύσει ἡ πόλις ἐστί, καὶ ὅτι ἄνθρωπος
φύσει πολιτικὸν ζῷον, καὶ ὁ ἄπολις διὰ φύσιν καὶ οὐ διὰ
τύχην ἤτοι φαῦλός ἐστιν ἢ κρείττων ἢ ἄνθρωπος, ὥσπερ
καὶ ὁ ὑφ' Ὁμήρου λοιδορηθεὶς "ἀφρήτωρ ἀθέμιστος ἀνέστιος"·
10 ἅμα γὰρ φύσει τοιοῦτος καὶ πολέμου ἐπιθυμητής, ἅτε περ
ἄζυξ ὢν ὥσπερ ἐν πεττοῖς. διότι δὲ πολιτικὸν ὁ ἄνθρωπος
ζῷον πάσης μελίττης καὶ παντὸς ἀγελαίου ζῴου μᾶλλον,
δῆλον. οὐδὲν γάρ, ὡς φαμέν, μάτην ἡ φύσις ποιεῖ, λόγον
11 δὲ μόνον ἄνθρωπος ἔχει τῶν ζῴων· ἡ μὲν οὖν φωνὴ τοῦ
λυπηροῦ καὶ ἡδέος ἐστὶ σημεῖον, διὸ καὶ τοῖς ἄλλοις ὑπάρχει ζῴοις· μέχρι γὰρ τούτου ἡ φύσις αὐτῶν ἐλήλυθε τοῦ
ἔχειν αἴσθησιν λυπηροῦ καὶ ἡδέος καὶ ταῦτα σημαίνειν
ἀλλήλοις· ὁ δὲ λόγος ἐπὶ τῷ δηλοῦν ἐστὶ τὸ συμφέρον καὶ
12 τὸ βλαβερόν, ὥστε καὶ τὸ δίκαιον καὶ τὸ ἄδικον· τοῦτο γὰρ
πρὸς τὰ ἄλλα ζῷα τοῖς ἀνθρώποις ἴδιον, τὸ μόνον ἀγαθοῦ
καὶ κακοῦ καὶ δικαίου καὶ ἀδίκου καὶ τῶν ἄλλων αἴσθησιν
ἔχειν· ἡ δὲ τούτων κοινωνία ποιεῖ οἰκίαν καὶ πόλιν. καὶ
πρότερον δὴ τῇ φύσει πόλις ἢ οἰκία καὶ ἕκαστος ἡμῶν ἐστίν.
13 τὸ γὰρ ὅλον πρότερον ἀναγκαῖον εἶναι τοῦ μέρους· ἀναιρου-
μένου γὰρ τοῦ ὅλου οὐκ ἔσται ποὺς οὐδὲ χείρ, εἰ μὴ ὁμωνύμως,
ὥσπερ εἴ τις λέγει τὴν λιθίνην· διαφθαρεῖσα γὰρ ἔσται
τοιαύτη, πάντα δὲ τῷ ἔργῳ ὥρισται καὶ τῇ δυνάμει, ὥστε

μηκέτι τοιαῦτα ὄντα οὐ λεκτέον τὰ αὐτὰ εἶναι, ἀλλ' ὁμώ-
νυμα. ὅτι μὲν οὖν ἡ πόλις καὶ φύσει καὶ πρότερον ἢ ἕκα- 14
στος, δῆλον· εἰ γὰρ μὴ αὐτάρκης ἕκαστος χωρισθείς, ὁμοίως
τοῖς ἄλλοις μέρεσιν ἕξει πρὸς τὸ ὅλον· ὁ δὲ μὴ δυνάμενος κοινωνεῖν, ἢ μηδὲν δεόμενος δι' αὐτάρκειαν, οὐδὲν μέρος
πόλεως, ὥστε ἢ θηρίον ἢ θεός. φύσει μὲν οὖν ἡ ὁρμὴ ἐν 15
πᾶσιν ἐπὶ τὴν τοιαύτην κοινωνίαν· ὁ δὲ πρῶτος συστήσας
μεγίστων ἀγαθῶν αἴτιος. ὥσπερ γὰρ καὶ τελεωθὲν βέλτιστον τῶν ζῴων ἄνθρωπός ἐστιν, οὕτω καὶ χωρισθὲν νόμου καὶ
δίκης χείριστον πάντων. χαλεπωτάτη γὰρ ἀδικία ἔχουσα 16
ὅπλα· ὁ δὲ ἄνθρωπος ὅπλα ἔχων φύεται φρονήσει καὶ
ἀρετῇ, οἷς ἐπὶ τἀναντία ἔστι χρῆσθαι μάλιστα. διὸ ἀνοσιώτατον καὶ ἀγριώτατον ἄνευ ἀρετῆς, καὶ πρὸς ἀφροδίσια
καὶ ἐδωδὴν χείριστον. ἡ δὲ δικαιοσύνη πολιτικόν· ἡ γὰρ δίκη
πολιτικῆς κοινωνίας τάξις ἐστίν· ἡ δὲ δίκη τοῦ δικαίου κρίσις.

1253 b. 3 Ἐπεὶ δὲ φανερὸν ἐξ ὧν μορίων ἡ πόλις συνέστηκεν,
ἀναγκαῖον πρῶτον περὶ οἰκονομίας εἰπεῖν· πᾶσα γὰρ σύγκειται
πόλις ἐξ οἰκιῶν. οἰκονομίας δὲ μέρη, ἐξ ὧν πάλιν οἰκία
συνέστηκεν· οἰκία δὲ τέλειος ἐκ δούλων καὶ ἐλευθέρων. ἐπεὶ
δ' ἐν τοῖς ἐλαχίστοις πρῶτον ἕκαστον ζητητέον, πρῶτα δὲ
καὶ ἐλάχιστα μέρη οἰκίας δεσπότης καὶ δοῦλος καὶ πόσις
καὶ ἄλοχος καὶ πατὴρ καὶ τέκνα, περὶ τριῶν ἂν τούτων
σκεπτέον εἴη τί ἕκαστον καὶ ποῖον δεῖ εἶναι. ταῦτα δ' 2
ἐστὶ δεσποτικὴ καὶ γαμική (ἀνώνυμον γὰρ ἡ γυναικὸς καὶ ἀνδρὸς σύζευξις) καὶ τρίτον τεκνοποιητική· καὶ γὰρ αὕτη οὐκ
ὠνόμασται ἰδίῳ ὀνόματι. ἔστωσαν δ' αὗται τρεῖς ἃς εἴπομεν. ἔστι δέ τι μέρος ὃ δοκεῖ τοῖς μὲν εἶναι οἰκονομία, 3
τοῖς δὲ μέγιστον μέρος αὐτῆς· ὅπως δ' ἔχει, θεωρητέον.
λέγω δὲ περὶ τῆς καλουμένης χρηματιστικῆς. πρῶτον δὲ
περὶ δεσπότου καὶ δούλου εἴπωμεν, ἵνα τά τε πρὸς τὴν
ἀναγκαίαν χρείαν ἴδωμεν, κἂν εἴ τι πρὸς τὸ εἰδέναι περὶ
αὐτῶν δυναίμεθα λαβεῖν βέλτιον τῶν νῦν ὑπολαμβανομέ-
νων. τοῖς μὲν γὰρ δοκεῖ ἐπιστήμη τέ τις εἶναι ἡ δεσποτεία, 4

καὶ ἡ αὐτὴ οἰκονομία καὶ δεσποτεία καὶ πολιτικὴ καὶ βασιλική, καθάπερ εἴπομεν ἀρχόμενοι· τοῖς δὲ παρὰ φύσιν τὸ δεσπόζειν. νόμῳ γὰρ τὸν μὲν δοῦλον εἶναι τὸν δ' ἐλεύθερον, φύσει δ' οὐδὲν διαφέρειν. διόπερ οὐδὲ δίκαιον· βίαιον γάρ. ἐπεὶ οὖν ἡ κτῆσις μέρος τῆς οἰκίας ἐστὶ καὶ ἡ κτητικὴ **4**
μέρος τῆς οἰκονομίας (ἄνευ γὰρ τῶν ἀναγκαίων ἀδύνατον καὶ ζῆν καὶ εὖ ζῆν), ὥσπερ δὲ ταῖς ὡρισμέναις τέχναις ἀναγκαῖον ἂν εἴη ὑπάρχειν τὰ οἰκεῖα ὄργανα, εἰ μέλλει
2 ἀποτελεσθήσεσθαι τὸ ἔργον, οὕτω καὶ τῶν οἰκονομικῶν· τῶν δ' ὀργάνων τὰ μὲν ἄψυχα τὰ δ' ἔμψυχα, οἷον τῷ κυβερνήτῃ ὁ μὲν οἴαξ ἄψυχον, ὁ δὲ πρωρεὺς ἔμψυχον (ὁ γὰρ ὑπηρέτης ἐν ὀργάνου εἴδει ταῖς τέχναις ἐστίν), οὕτω καὶ τὸ κτῆμα ὄργανον πρὸς ζωήν ἐστι, καὶ ἡ κτῆσις πλῆθος ὀργάνων ἐστί, καὶ ὁ δοῦλος κτῆμά τι ἔμψυχον, καὶ ὥσπερ
3 ὄργανον πρὸ ὀργάνων πᾶς ὁ ὑπηρέτης· εἰ γὰρ ἠδύνατο ἕκαστον τῶν ὀργάνων κελευσθὲν ἢ προαισθανόμενον ἀποτελεῖν τὸ αὑτοῦ ἔργον, ὥσπερ τὰ Δαιδάλου φασὶν ἢ τοὺς τοῦ Ἡφαίστου τρίποδας, οὕς φησιν ὁ ποιητὴς αὐτομάτους θεῖον δύεσθαι ἀγῶνα, οὕτως αἱ κερκίδες ἐκέρκιζον αὐταὶ καὶ τὰ πλῆκτρα ἐκιθάριζεν, οὐδὲν ἂν ἔδει οὔτε τοῖς ἀρχιτέκτοσιν
4 ὑπηρετῶν οὔτε τοῖς δεσπόταις δούλων. τὰ μὲν οὖν λεγόμενα 1254 a
ὄργανα ποιητικὰ ὄργανά ἐστι, τὸ δὲ κτῆμα πρακτικόν· ἀπὸ μὲν γὰρ τῆς κερκίδος ἕτερόν τι γίνεται παρὰ τὴν χρῆσιν αὐτῆς, ἀπὸ δὲ τῆς ἐσθῆτος καὶ τῆς κλίνης ἡ χρῆσις μόνον. ἔτι δ' ἐπεὶ διαφέρει ἡ ποίησις εἴδει καὶ ἡ πρᾶξις, καὶ δέονται ἀμφότεραι ὀργάνων, ἀνάγκη καὶ ταῦτα τὴν
5 αὐτὴν ἔχειν διαφοράν· ὁ δὲ βίος πρᾶξις, οὐ ποίησίς ἐστιν· διὸ καὶ ὁ δοῦλος ὑπηρέτης τῶν πρὸς τὴν πρᾶξιν. τὸ δὲ κτῆμα λέγεται ὥσπερ καὶ τὸ μόριον· τό τε γὰρ μόριον οὐ μόνον ἄλλου ἐστὶ μόριον, ἀλλὰ καὶ ὅλως ἄλλου· ὁμοίως δὲ καὶ τὸ κτῆμα. διὸ ὁ μὲν δεσπότης τοῦ δούλου δεσπότης μόνον, ἐκείνου δ' οὐκ ἔστιν· ὁ δὲ δοῦλος οὐ μόνον δεσπότου δοῦλός
6 ἐστιν, ἀλλὰ καὶ ὅλως ἐκείνου. τίς μὲν οὖν ἡ φύσις τοῦ δούλου

καὶ τίς ἡ δύναμις, ἐκ τούτων δῆλον· ὁ γὰρ μὴ αὑτοῦ φύσει ἀλλ᾽ ἄλλου, ἄνθρωπος ὤν, οὗτος φύσει δοῦλός ἐστιν, ἄλλου
δ᾽ ἐστὶν ἄνθρωπος, ὃς ἂν κτῆμα ᾖ ἄνθρωπος ὤν, κτῆμα δὲ
5 ὄργανον πρακτικὸν καὶ χωριστόν. πότερον δ᾽ ἐστί τις φύσει
τοιοῦτος ἢ οὔ, καὶ πότερον βέλτιον καὶ δίκαιόν τινι δουλεύειν
ἢ οὔ, ἀλλὰ πᾶσα δουλεία παρὰ φύσιν ἐστί, μετὰ ταῦτα
σκεπτέον. οὐ χαλεπὸν δὲ καὶ τῷ λόγῳ θεωρῆσαι καὶ ἐκ
τῶν γινομένων καταμαθεῖν. τὸ γὰρ ἄρχειν καὶ ἄρχεσθαι 2
οὐ μόνον τῶν ἀναγκαίων ἀλλὰ καὶ τῶν συμφερόντων ἐστί,
καὶ εὐθὺς ἐκ γενετῆς ἔνια διέστηκε τὰ μὲν ἐπὶ τὸ ἄρχεσθαι
τὰ δ᾽ ἐπὶ τὸ ἄρχειν. καὶ εἴδη πολλὰ καὶ ἀρχόντων καὶ
ἀρχομένων ἐστίν, καὶ ἀεὶ βελτίων ἡ ἀρχὴ ἡ τῶν βελτιόνων
ἀρχομένων, οἷον ἀνθρώπου ἢ θηρίου· τὸ γὰρ ἀποτελούμενον 3
ἀπὸ τῶν βελτιόνων βέλτιον ἔργον, ὅπου δὲ τὸ μὲν ἄρχει
τὸ δ᾽ ἄρχεται, ἐστί τι τούτων ἔργον. ὅσα γὰρ ἐκ πλειόνων
συνέστηκε καὶ γίνεται ἕν τι κοινόν, εἴτε ἐκ συνεχῶν εἴτε ἐκ
διῃρημένων, ἐν ἅπασιν ἐμφαίνεται τὸ ἄρχον καὶ τὸ ἀρχόμενον. καὶ τοῦτ᾽ ἐκ τῆς ἁπάσης φύσεως ἐνυπάρχει τοῖς 4
ἐμψύχοις· καὶ γὰρ ἐν τοῖς μὴ μετέχουσι ζωῆς ἐστί τις
ἀρχή, οἷον ἁρμονίας. ἀλλὰ ταῦτα μὲν ἴσως ἐξωτερικωτέρας ἐστὶ σκέψεως, τὸ δὲ ζῷον πρῶτον συνέστηκεν ἐκ ψυχῆς
καὶ σώματος, ὧν τὸ μὲν ἄρχον ἐστὶ φύσει τὸ δ᾽ ἀρχόμενον. δεῖ δὲ σκοπεῖν ἐν τοῖς κατὰ φύσιν ἔχουσι μᾶλλον 5
τὸ φύσει, καὶ μὴ ἐν τοῖς διεφθαρμένοις. διὸ καὶ τὸν βέλτιστα διακείμενον καὶ κατὰ σῶμα καὶ κατὰ ψυχὴν ἄνθρωπον θεωρητέον, ἐν ᾧ τοῦτο δῆλον· τῶν γὰρ μοχθηρῶν ἢ
1254 b μοχθηρῶς ἐχόντων δόξειεν ἂν ἄρχειν πολλάκις τὸ σῶμα
τῆς ψυχῆς διὰ τὸ φαύλως καὶ παρὰ φύσιν ἔχειν. ἔστι 6
δ᾽ οὖν, ὥσπερ λέγομεν, πρῶτον ἐν ζῴῳ θεωρῆσαι καὶ δεσποτικὴν ἀρχὴν καὶ πολιτικήν· ἡ μὲν γὰρ ψυχὴ τοῦ σώματος ἄρχει δεσποτικὴν ἀρχήν, ὁ δὲ νοῦς τῆς ὀρέξεως πολιτικὴν καὶ βασιλικήν· ἐν οἷς φανερόν ἐστιν ὅτι κατὰ φύσιν καὶ συμφέρον τὸ ἄρχεσθαι τῷ σώματι ὑπὸ τῆς ψυ-

χῆς καὶ τῷ παθητικῷ μορίῳ ὑπὸ τοῦ νοῦ καὶ τοῦ μορίου τοῦ
λόγον ἔχοντος, τὸ δ' ἐξ ἴσου ἢ ἀνάπαλιν βλαβερὸν πᾶσιν.
7 πάλιν ἐν ἀνθρώπῳ καὶ τοῖς ἄλλοις ζῴοις ὡσαύτως· τὰ
μὲν γὰρ ἥμερα τῶν ἀγρίων βελτίω τὴν φύσιν, τούτοις δὲ
πᾶσι βέλτιον ἄρχεσθαι ὑπ' ἀνθρώπου· τυγχάνει γὰρ σω-
τηρίας οὕτως. ἔτι δὲ τὸ ἄρρεν πρὸς τὸ θῆλυ φύσει τὸ μὲν
κρεῖττον τὸ δὲ χεῖρον, τὸ μὲν ἄρχον τὸ δὲ ἀρχόμενον. τὸν
αὐτὸν δὲ τρόπον ἀναγκαῖον εἶναι καὶ ἐπὶ πάντων ἀνθρώ-
8 πων. ὅσοι μὲν οὖν τοσοῦτον διεστᾶσιν ὅσον ψυχὴ σώματος
καὶ ἄνθρωπος θηρίου (διάκεινται δὲ τοῦτον τὸν τρόπον, ὅσων
ἐστὶν ἔργον ἡ τοῦ σώματος χρῆσις, καὶ τοῦτ' ἔστ' ἀπ' αὐτῶν
βέλτιστον), οὗτοι μέν εἰσι φύσει δοῦλοι, οἷς βέλτιόν ἐστιν
9 ἄρχεσθαι ταύτην τὴν ἀρχήν, εἴπερ καὶ τοῖς εἰρημένοις. ἔστι
γὰρ φύσει δοῦλος ὁ δυνάμενος ἄλλου εἶναι (διὸ καὶ ἄλλου
ἐστίν) καὶ ὁ κοινωνῶν λόγου τοσοῦτον ὅσον αἰσθάνεσθαι ἀλλὰ
μὴ ἔχειν· τὰ γὰρ ἄλλα ζῷα οὐ λόγου αἰσθανόμενα, ἀλλὰ
παθήμασιν ὑπηρετεῖ. καὶ ἡ χρεία δὲ παραλλάττει μικρόν·
ἡ γὰρ πρὸς τἀναγκαῖα τῷ σώματι βοήθεια γίνεται παρ'
ἀμφοῖν, παρά τε τῶν δούλων καὶ παρὰ τῶν ἡμέρων ζῴων.
10 βούλεται μὲν οὖν ἡ φύσις καὶ τὰ σώματα διαφέροντα
ποιεῖν τὰ τῶν ἐλευθέρων καὶ τῶν δούλων, τὰ μὲν ἰσχυρὰ
πρὸς τὴν ἀναγκαίαν χρῆσιν, τὰ δ' ὀρθὰ καὶ ἄχρηστα πρὸς
τὰς τοιαύτας ἐργασίας, ἀλλὰ χρήσιμα πρὸς πολιτικὸν
βίον (οὗτος δὲ καὶ γίνεται διῃρημένος εἴς τε τὴν πολεμικὴν
χρείαν καὶ τὴν εἰρηνικήν), συμβαίνει δὲ πολλάκις καὶ τοὐναντίον, τοὺς μὲν τὰ σώματα ἔχειν ἐλευθέρων τοὺς δὲ τὰς
ψυχάς· ἐπεὶ τοῦτό γε φανερόν, ὡς εἰ τοσοῦτον γένοιντο διά-
φοροι τὸ σῶμα μόνον ὅσον αἱ τῶν θεῶν εἰκόνες, τοὺς ὑπολειπομένους πάντες φαῖεν ἂν ἀξίους εἶναι τούτοις δουλεύειν.
11 εἰ δ' ἐπὶ τοῦ σώματος τοῦτ' ἀληθές, πολὺ δικαιότερον ἐπὶ
τῆς ψυχῆς τοῦτο διωρίσθαι· ἀλλ' οὐχ ὁμοίως ῥᾴδιον ἰδεῖν
τό τε τῆς ψυχῆς κάλλος καὶ τὸ τοῦ σώματος. ὅτι μὲν
τοίνυν εἰσὶ φύσει τινὲς οἱ μὲν ἐλεύθεροι οἱ δὲ δοῦλοι, φα- 1255 a

νερόν, οἷς καὶ συμφέρει τὸ δουλεύειν καὶ δίκαιόν ἐστιν·
6 ὅτι δὲ καὶ οἱ τἀναντία φάσκοντες τρόπον τινὰ λέγουσιν
ὀρθῶς, οὐ χαλεπὸν ἰδεῖν· διχῶς γὰρ λέγεται τὸ δουλεύειν
καὶ ὁ δοῦλος· ἔστι γάρ τις καὶ κατὰ νόμον δοῦλος καὶ
δουλεύων· ὁ γὰρ νόμος ὁμολογία τίς ἐστιν, ἐν ᾧ τὰ κατὰ
πόλεμον κρατούμενα τῶν κρατούντων εἶναί φασιν. τοῦτο δὴ 2
τὸ δίκαιον πολλοὶ τῶν ἐν τοῖς νόμοις ὥσπερ ῥήτορα γράφονται παρανόμων, ὡς δεινὸν εἰ τοῦ βιάσασθαι δυναμένου
καὶ κατὰ δύναμιν κρείττονος ἔσται δοῦλον καὶ ἀρχόμενον
τὸ βιασθέν· καὶ τοῖς μὲν οὕτω δοκεῖ τοῖς δὲ ἐκείνως, καὶ
τῶν σοφῶν. αἴτιον δὲ ταύτης τῆς ἀμφισβητήσεως, καὶ ὃ 3
ποιεῖ τοὺς λόγους ἐπαλλάττειν, ὅτι τρόπον τινὰ ἀρετὴ τυγ-
χάνουσα χορηγίας καὶ βιάζεσθαι δύναται μάλιστα, καὶ
ἔστιν ἀεὶ τὸ κρατοῦν ἐν ὑπεροχῇ ἀγαθοῦ τινός, ὥστε δοκεῖν
μὴ ἄνευ ἀρετῆς εἶναι τὴν βίαν, ἀλλὰ περὶ τοῦ δικαίου μόνον εἶναι τὴν ἀμφισβήτησιν· διὰ γὰρ τοῦτο τοῖς μὲν εὔνοια 4
δοκεῖ τὸ δίκαιον εἶναι, τοῖς δ' αὐτὸ τοῦτο δίκαιον, τὸ τὸν
κρείττονα ἄρχειν, ἐπεὶ διαστάντων γε χωρὶς τούτων τῶν λόγων οὔτε ἰσχυρὸν οὐδὲν ἔχουσιν οὔτε πιθανὸν ἅτεροι λόγοι, ὡς
οὐ δεῖ τὸ βέλτιον κατ' ἀρετὴν ἄρχειν καὶ δεσπόζειν. ὅλως 5
δ' ἀντεχόμενοί τινες, ὡς οἴονται, δικαίου τινός (ὁ γὰρ νόμος
δίκαιόν τι) τὴν κατὰ πόλεμον δουλείαν τιθέασι δικαίαν,
ἅμα δὲ οὔ φασιν· τήν τε γὰρ ἀρχὴν ἐνδέχεται μὴ δικαίαν εἶναι τῶν πολέμων, καὶ τὸν ἀνάξιον δουλεύειν οὐδαμῶς ἂν φαίη τις δοῦλον εἶναι· εἰ δὲ μή, συμβήσεται τοὺς
εὐγενεστάτους εἶναι δοκοῦντας δούλους εἶναι καὶ ἐκ δούλων,
ἐὰν συμβῇ πραθῆναι ληφθέντας. διόπερ αὐτοὺς οὐ βούλονται 6
λέγειν δούλους, ἀλλὰ τοὺς βαρβάρους. καίτοι ὅταν τοῦτο λέγωσιν, οὐδὲν ἄλλο ζητοῦσιν ἢ τὸ φύσει δοῦλον, ὅπερ ἐξ
ἀρχῆς εἴπομεν· ἀνάγκη γὰρ εἶναί τινας φάναι τοὺς μὲν
πανταχοῦ δούλους τοὺς δὲ οὐδαμοῦ. τὸν αὐτὸν δὲ τρόπον καὶ 7
περὶ εὐγενείας· αὐτοὺς μὲν γὰρ οὐ μόνον παρ' αὑτοῖς εὐγενεῖς ἀλλὰ πανταχοῦ νομίζουσιν, τοὺς δὲ βαρβάρους οἴκοι μό-

νον, ὡς ὄν τι τὸ μὲν ἁπλῶς εὐγενὲς ἐλεύθερον, τὸ δ' οὐχ
ἁπλῶς, ὥσπερ καὶ ἡ Θεοδέκτου Ἑλένη φησὶν

> θείων δ' ἀπ' ἀμφοῖν ἔκγονον ῥιζωμάτων
> τίς ἂν προσειπεῖν ἀξιώσειεν λάτριν;

8 ὅταν δὲ τοῦτο λέγωσιν, οὐδενὶ ἀλλ' ἢ ἀρετῇ καὶ κακίᾳ διο-
ρίζουσι τὸ δοῦλον καὶ ἐλεύθερον καὶ τοὺς εὐγενεῖς καὶ τοὺς
δυσγενεῖς. ἀξιοῦσι γάρ, ὥσπερ ἐξ ἀνθρώπου ἄνθρωπον καὶ 1255 b
ἐκ θηρίων γίνεσθαι θηρίον, οὕτω καὶ ἐξ ἀγαθῶν ἀγαθόν· ἡ
δὲ φύσις βούλεται μὲν τοῦτο ποιεῖν πολλάκις, οὐ μέντοι
9 δύναται. ὅτι μὲν οὖν ἔχει τινὰ λόγον ἡ ἀμφισβήτησις,
καὶ οὐκ εἰσὶν οἱ μὲν φύσει δοῦλοι οἱ δὲ ἐλεύθεροι, δῆλον·
καὶ ὅτι ἔν τισι διώρισται τὸ τοιοῦτον, ὧν συμφέρει τῷ μὲν τὸ
δουλεύειν τῷ δὲ τὸ δεσπόζειν καὶ δίκαιον, καὶ δεῖ τὸ μὲν
ἄρχεσθαι τὸ δ' ἄρχειν, ἣν πεφύκασιν ἀρχὴν ἄρχειν, ὥστε
10 καὶ δεσπόζειν. τὸ δὲ κακῶς ἀσυμφόρως ἐστὶν ἀμφοῖν· τὸ
γὰρ αὐτὸ συμφέρει τῷ μέρει καὶ τῷ ὅλῳ καὶ σώματι καὶ
ψυχῇ, ὁ δὲ δοῦλος μέρος τι τοῦ δεσπότου, οἷον ἔμψυχόν τι
τοῦ σώματος κεχωρισμένον δὲ μέρος. διὸ καὶ συμφέρον
ἐστί τι καὶ φιλία δούλῳ καὶ δεσπότῃ πρὸς ἀλλήλους τοῖς
φύσει τούτων ἠξιωμένοις· τοῖς δὲ μὴ τοῦτον τὸν τρόπον,
ἀλλὰ κατὰ νόμον καὶ βιασθεῖσι, τοὐναντίον.

Φανερὸν δὲ καὶ ἐκ τούτων ὅτι οὐ ταὐτόν ἐστι δεσποτεία **7**
καὶ πολιτική, οὐδὲ πᾶσαι ἀλλήλαις αἱ ἀρχαί, ὥσπερ τινές
φασιν· ἡ μὲν γὰρ ἐλευθέρων φύσει ἡ δὲ δούλων ἐστίν, καὶ
ἡ μὲν οἰκονομικὴ μοναρχία (μοναρχεῖται γὰρ πᾶς οἶκος),
2 ἡ δὲ πολιτικὴ ἐλευθέρων καὶ ἴσων ἀρχή. ὁ μὲν οὖν δεσπότης οὐ λέγεται κατὰ ἐπιστήμην, ἀλλὰ τῷ τοιόσδε εἶναι,
ὁμοίως δὲ καὶ ὁ δοῦλος καὶ ὁ ἐλεύθερος· ἐπιστήμη δ' ἂν
εἴη καὶ δεσποτικὴ καὶ δουλική, δουλικὴ μὲν οἵαν περ ὁ ἐν
Συρακούσαις ἐπαίδευεν· ἐκεῖ γὰρ λαμβάνων τις μισθὸν
3 ἐδίδασκε τὰ ἐγκύκλια διακονήματα τοὺς παῖδας. εἴη δ'
ἂν καὶ ἐπὶ πλεῖον τῶν τοιούτων μάθησις, οἷον ὀψοποιικὴ
καὶ τἆλλα τὰ τοιαῦτα γένη τῆς διακονίας· ἔστι γὰρ ἕτερα

ἑτέρων τὰ μὲν ἐντιμότερα ἔργα τὰ δ' ἀναγκαιότερα, καὶ
κατὰ τὴν παροιμίαν δοῦλος πρὸ δούλου, δεσπότης πρὸ δεσπότου. αἱ μὲν οὖν τοιαῦται πᾶσαι δουλικαὶ ἐπιστῆμαί εἰσι, 4
δεσποτικὴ δ' ἐπιστήμη ἐστὶν ἡ χρηστικὴ δούλων· ὁ γὰρ δεσπότης οὐκ ἐν τῷ κτᾶσθαι τοὺς δούλους, ἀλλ' ἐν τῷ χρῆσθαι
δούλοις. ἔστι δ' αὕτη ἡ ἐπιστήμη οὐδὲν μέγα ἔχουσα οὐδὲ
σεμνόν· ἃ γὰρ τὸν δοῦλον ἐπίστασθαι δεῖ ποιεῖν, ἐκεῖνον δεῖ
ταῦτα ἐπίστασθαι ἐπιτάττειν. διὸ ὅσοις ἐξουσία μὴ αὐτοὺς 5
κακοπαθεῖν, ἐπίτροπος λαμβάνει ταύτην τὴν τιμήν, αὐτοὶ
δὲ πολιτεύονται ἢ φιλοσοφοῦσιν. ἡ δὲ κτητικὴ ἑτέρα ἀμφοτέρων τούτων, οἷον ἡ δικαία, πολεμική τις οὖσα ἢ θηρευτική. περὶ μὲν οὖν δούλου καὶ δεσπότου τοῦτον διωρίσθω
τὸν τρόπον·

1256 a. **8** Ὅλως δὲ περὶ πάσης κτήσεως καὶ χρηματιστικῆς θεω-
ρήσωμεν κατὰ τὸν ὑφηγημένον τρόπον, ἐπείπερ καὶ ὁ δοῦλος τῆς κτήσεως μέρος τι ἦν. πρῶτον μὲν οὖν ἀπορήσειεν
ἄν τις πότερον ἡ χρηματιστικὴ ἡ αὐτὴ τῇ οἰκονομικῇ ἐστὶν
ἢ μέρος τι ἢ ὑπηρετική, καὶ εἰ ὑπηρετική, πότερον ὡς ἡ
κερκιδοποιικὴ τῇ ὑφαντικῇ ἢ ὡς ἡ χαλκουργικὴ τῇ ἀν-
δριαντοποιίᾳ· οὐ γὰρ ὡσαύτως ὑπηρετοῦσιν, ἀλλ' ἡ μὲν ὄργανα παρέχει, ἡ δὲ τὴν ὕλην· λέγω δὲ ὕλην τὸ ὑποκεί- 2
μενον, ἐξ οὗ τι ἀποτελεῖται ἔργον, οἷον ὑφάντῃ μὲν ἔρια,
ἀνδριαντοποιῷ δὲ χαλκόν. ὅτι μὲν οὖν οὐχ ἡ αὐτὴ οἰκονομικὴ τῇ χρηματιστικῇ, δῆλον· τῆς μὲν γὰρ τὸ πορίσασθαι, τῆς δὲ τὸ χρήσασθαι· τίς γὰρ ἔσται ἡ χρησομένη
τοῖς κατὰ τὴν οἰκίαν παρὰ τὴν οἰκονομικήν; πότερον δὲ
μέρος αὐτῆς ἐστί τι ἢ ἕτερον εἶδος, ἔχει διαμφισβήτησιν.
εἰ γάρ ἐστι τοῦ χρηματιστικοῦ θεωρῆσαι πόθεν χρήματα καὶ 3
κτῆσις ἔσται, ἡ δὲ κτῆσις πολλὰ περιείληφε μέρη καὶ ὁ
πλοῦτος, ὥστε πρῶτον ἡ γεωργικὴ πότερον μέρος τι τῆς χρηματιστικῆς ἢ ἕτερόν τι γένος, καὶ καθόλου ἡ περὶ τὴν τροφὴν ἐπιμέλεια καὶ κτῆσις; ἀλλὰ μὴν εἴδη γε πολλὰ τρο- 4
φῆς, διὸ καὶ βίοι πολλοὶ καὶ τῶν ζῴων καὶ τῶν ἀνθρώπων

εἰσίν· οὐ γὰρ οἷόν τε ζῆν ἄνευ τροφῆς, ὥστε αἱ διαφοραὶ τῆς τροφῆς τοὺς βίους πεποιήκασι διαφέροντας τῶν ζῴων.
5 τῶν τε γὰρ θηρίων τὰ μὲν ἀγελαῖα τὰ δὲ σποραδικά ἐστιν, ὁποτέρως συμφέρει πρὸς τὴν τροφὴν αὐτοῖς, διὰ τὸ τὰ μὲν ζῳοφάγα τὰ δὲ καρποφάγα τὰ δὲ παμφάγα αὐτῶν εἶναι, ὥστε πρὸς τὰς ῥᾳστώνας καὶ τὴν αἵρεσιν τὴν τούτων ἡ φύσις τοὺς βίους αὐτῶν διώρισεν, ἐπεὶ δ' οὐ ταὐτὸ ἑκάστῳ ἡδὺ κατὰ φύσιν ἀλλὰ ἕτερα ἑτέροις, καὶ αὐτῶν τῶν ζῳοφάγων καὶ τῶν
6 καρποφάγων οἱ βίοι πρὸς ἄλληλα διεστᾶσιν· ὁμοίως δὲ καὶ τῶν ἀνθρώπων· πολὺ γὰρ διαφέρουσιν οἱ τούτων βίοι. οἱ μὲν οὖν ἀργότατοι νομάδες εἰσίν· ἡ γὰρ ἀπὸ τῶν ἡμέρων τροφὴ ζῴων ἄνευ πόνου γίνεται σχολάζουσιν, ἀναγκαίου δὲ ὄντος μεταβάλλειν τοῖς κτήνεσι διὰ τὰς νομὰς καὶ αὐτοὶ ἀναγκάζονται συνακολουθεῖν, ὥσπερ γεωργίαν ζῶσαν
7 γεωργοῦντες· οἱ δ' ἀπὸ θήρας ζῶσι, καὶ θήρας ἕτεροι ἑτέρας, οἷον οἱ μὲν ἀπὸ λῃστείας, οἱ δ' ἀφ' ἁλιείας, ὅσοι λίμνας καὶ ἕλη καὶ ποταμοὺς ἢ θάλατταν τοιαύτην προσοικοῦσιν, οἱ δ' ἀπ' ὀρνίθων ἢ θηρίων ἀγρίων· τὸ δὲ πλεῖστον γένος τῶν ἀνθρώπων ἀπὸ τῆς γῆς ζῇ καὶ τῶν ἡμέρων καρ-
8 πῶν. οἱ μὲν οὖν βίοι τοσοῦτοι σχεδόν εἰσιν, ὅσοι γε αὐτόφυτον ἔχουσι τὴν ἐργασίαν καὶ μὴ δι' ἀλλαγῆς καὶ καπηλείας πορίζονται τὴν τροφήν, νομαδικὸς γεωργικὸς λῃστρικὸς ἁλιευτικὸς θηρευτικός· οἱ δὲ καὶ μιγνύντες ἐκ τούτων ἡδέως ζῶσι, προσαναπληροῦντες τὸν ἐνδεέστατον βίον, ᾗ τυγχάνει ἐλλείπων πρὸς τὸ αὐτάρκης εἶναι, οἷον οἱ μὲν νομαδικὸν ἅμα καὶ λῃστρικόν, οἱ δὲ γεωργικὸν καὶ θηρευ-
9 τικόν· ὁμοίως δὲ καὶ περὶ τοὺς ἄλλους, ὡς ἂν ἡ χρεία συναναγκάζῃ, τοῦτον τὸν τρόπον διάγουσιν. ἡ μὲν οὖν τοιαύτη κτῆσις ὑπ' αὐτῆς φαίνεται τῆς φύσεως διδομένη πᾶσιν, ὥσπερ κατὰ τὴν πρώτην γένεσιν εὐθύς, οὕτω καὶ τελειω-
10 θεῖσιν. καὶ γὰρ κατὰ τὴν ἐξ ἀρχῆς γένεσιν τὰ μὲν συνεκτίκτει τῶν ζῴων τοσαύτην τροφὴν ὡς ἱκανὴν εἶναι μέχρις οὗ ἂν δύνηται αὐτὸ αὑτῷ πορίζειν τὸ γεννηθέν, οἷον ὅσα

σκωληκοτοκεῖ ἢ ᾠοτοκεῖ· ὅσα δὲ ζῳοτοκεῖ, τοῖς γεννωμένοις
ἔχει τροφὴν ἐν αὑτοῖς μέχρι τινός, τὴν τοῦ καλουμένου γάλακτος φύσιν. ὥστε ὁμοίως δῆλον ὅτι καὶ γενομένοις οἰη- 11
τέον τά τε φυτὰ τῶν ζῴων ἕνεκεν εἶναι καὶ τὰ ἄλλα ζῷα
τῶν ἀνθρώπων χάριν, τὰ μὲν ἥμερα καὶ διὰ τὴν χρῆσιν
καὶ διὰ τὴν τροφήν, τῶν δὲ ἀγρίων, εἰ μὴ πάντα, ἀλλὰ
τά γε πλεῖστα τῆς τροφῆς καὶ ἄλλης βοηθείας ἕνεκεν, ἵνα
καὶ ἐσθὴς καὶ ἄλλα ὄργανα γίνηται ἐξ αὐτῶν. εἰ οὖν ἡ 12
φύσις μηδὲν μήτε ἀτελὲς ποιεῖ μήτε μάτην, ἀναγκαῖον
τῶν ἀνθρώπων ἕνεκεν αὐτὰ πάντα πεποιηκέναι τὴν φύσιν.
διὸ καὶ ἡ πολεμικὴ φύσει κτητική πως ἔσται, ἡ γὰρ θηρευτικὴ μέρος αὐτῆς, ᾗ δεῖ χρῆσθαι πρός τε τὰ θηρία καὶ
τῶν ἀνθρώπων ὅσοι πεφυκότες ἄρχεσθαι μὴ θέλουσιν, ὡς
φύσει δίκαιον τοῦτον ὄντα τὸν πόλεμον. ἓν μὲν οὖν εἶδος 13
κτητικῆς κατὰ φύσιν τῆς οἰκονομικῆς μέρος ἐστίν· ὃ δεῖ
ἤτοι ὑπάρχειν ἢ πορίζειν αὐτὴν ὅπως ὑπάρχῃ, ὧν ἐστὶ θησαυρισμὸς χρημάτων πρὸς ζωὴν ἀναγκαίων καὶ χρησίμων
εἰς κοινωνίαν πόλεως ἢ οἰκίας. καὶ ἔοικεν ὅ γ᾽ ἀληθινὸς 14
πλοῦτος ἐκ τούτων εἶναι. ἡ γὰρ τῆς τοιαύτης κτήσεως
αὐτάρκεια πρὸς ἀγαθὴν ζωὴν οὐκ ἄπειρός ἐστιν, ὥσπερ Σόλων φησὶ ποιήσας "πλούτου δ᾽ οὐδὲν τέρμα πεφασμένον ἀνδράσι κεῖται." κεῖται γὰρ ὥσπερ καὶ ταῖς ἄλλαις τέχναις· 15
οὐδὲν γὰρ ὄργανον ἄπειρον οὐδεμιᾶς ἐστὶ τέχνης οὔτε πλήθει
οὔτε μεγέθει, ὁ δὲ πλοῦτος ὀργάνων πλῆθός ἐστιν οἰκονομικῶν καὶ πολιτικῶν. ὅτι μὲν τοίνυν ἔστι τις κτητικὴ
κατὰ φύσιν τοῖς οἰκονόμοις καὶ τοῖς πολιτικοῖς, καὶ δι᾽ ἣν
αἰτίαν, δῆλον·

9 Ἔστι δὲ γένος ἄλλο κτητικῆς, ἣν μάλιστα καλοῦσι, καὶ
δίκαιον αὐτὸ καλεῖν, χρηματιστικήν, δι᾽ ἣν οὐδὲν δοκεῖ
1257 a πέρας εἶναι πλούτου καὶ κτήσεως· ἣν ὡς μίαν καὶ τὴν
αὐτὴν τῇ λεχθείσῃ πολλοὶ νομίζουσι διὰ τὴν γειτνίασιν·
ἔστι δ᾽ οὔτε ἡ αὐτὴ τῇ εἰρημένῃ οὔτε πόρρω ἐκείνης. ἔστι δ᾽
ἡ μὲν φύσει ἡ δ᾽ οὐ φύσει αὐτῶν, ἀλλὰ δι᾽ ἐμπειρίας

2 τινὸς καὶ τέχνης γίνεται μᾶλλον. λάβωμεν δὲ περὶ αὐτῆς
τὴν ἀρχὴν ἐντεῦθεν. ἑκάστου γὰρ κτήματος διττὴ ἡ χρῆσίς
ἐστιν, ἀμφότεραι δὲ καθ' αὑτὸ μὲν ἀλλ' οὐχ ὁμοίως καθ'
αὑτό, ἀλλ' ἡ μὲν οἰκεία ἡ δ' οὐκ οἰκεία τοῦ πράγματος,
οἷον ὑποδήματος ἥ τε ὑπόδεσις καὶ ἡ μεταβλητική. ἀμ-
3 φότεραι γὰρ ὑποδήματος χρήσεις· καὶ γὰρ ὁ ἀλλαττό-
μενος τῷ δεομένῳ ὑποδήματος ἀντὶ νομίσματος ἢ τροφῆς
χρῆται τῷ ὑποδήματι ᾗ ὑπόδημα, ἀλλ' οὐ τὴν οἰκείαν
χρῆσιν· οὐ γὰρ ἀλλαγῆς ἕνεκεν γέγονεν. τὸν αὐτὸν δὲ
4 τρόπον ἔχει καὶ περὶ τῶν ἄλλων κτημάτων. ἔστι γὰρ ἡ
μεταβλητικὴ πάντων, ἀρξαμένη τὸ μὲν πρῶτον ἐκ τοῦ
κατὰ φύσιν, τῷ τὰ μὲν πλείω τὰ δ' ἐλάττω τῶν ἱκανῶν
ἔχειν τοὺς ἀνθρώπους. ᾗ καὶ δῆλον ὅτι οὐκ ἔστι φύσει τῆς
χρηματιστικῆς ἡ καπηλική· ὅσον γὰρ ἱκανὸν αὐτοῖς, ἀναγ-
5 καῖον ἦν ποιεῖσθαι τὴν ἀλλαγήν. ἐν μὲν οὖν τῇ πρώτῃ
κοινωνίᾳ (τοῦτο δ' ἐστὶν οἰκία) φανερὸν ὅτι οὐδέν ἐστιν ἔργον
αὐτῆς, ἀλλ' ἤδη πλείονος τῆς κοινωνίας οὔσης. οἱ μὲν γὰρ
τῶν αὐτῶν ἐκοινώνουν πάντων, οἱ δὲ κεχωρισμένοι πολλῶν
πάλιν καὶ ἑτέρων· ὧν κατὰ τὰς δεήσεις ἀναγκαῖον ποιεῖσθαι τὰς μεταδόσεις, καθάπερ ἔτι πολλὰ ποιεῖ καὶ τῶν
6 βαρβαρικῶν ἐθνῶν, κατὰ τὴν ἀλλαγήν. αὐτὰ γὰρ τὰ
χρήσιμα πρὸς αὐτὰ καταλλάττονται, ἐπὶ πλέον δ' οὐδέν,
οἷον οἶνον πρὸς σῖτον διδόντες καὶ λαμβάνοντες, καὶ τῶν
ἄλλων τῶν τοιούτων ἕκαστον. ἡ μὲν οὖν τοιαύτη μεταβλητικὴ οὔτε παρὰ φύσιν οὔτε χρηματιστικῆς ἐστὶν εἶδος οὐδέν,
7 εἰς ἀναπλήρωσιν γὰρ τῆς κατὰ φύσιν αὐταρκείας ἦν· ἐκ
μέντοι ταύτης ἐγένετ' ἐκείνη κατὰ λόγον. ξενικωτέρας γὰρ
γινομένης τῆς βοηθείας τῷ εἰσάγεσθαι ὧν ἐνδεεῖς καὶ ἐκπέμπειν ὧν ἐπλεόναζον, ἐξ ἀνάγκης ἡ τοῦ νομίσματος ἐπο-
8 ρίσθη χρῆσις. οὐ γὰρ εὐβάστακτον ἕκαστον τῶν κατὰ φύσιν
ἀναγκαίων· διὸ πρὸς τὰς ἀλλαγὰς τοιοῦτόν τι συνέθεντο
πρὸς σφᾶς αὐτοὺς διδόναι καὶ λαμβάνειν, ὃ τῶν χρησίμων
αὐτὸ ὂν εἶχε τὴν χρείαν εὐμεταχείριστον πρὸς τὸ ζῆν, οἷον

σίδηρος καὶ ἄργυρος κἂν εἴ τι τοιοῦτον ἕτερον, τὸ μὲν πρῶτον ἁπλῶς ὁρισθὲν μεγέθει καὶ σταθμῷ, τὸ δὲ τελευταῖον
καὶ χαρακτῆρα ἐπιβαλλόντων, ἵν᾽ ἀπολύσῃ τῆς μετρή-
σεως αὐτούς· ὁ γὰρ χαρακτὴρ ἐτέθη τοῦ ποσοῦ σημεῖον. πο- 9
1257 b ρισθέντος οὖν ἤδη νομίσματος ἐκ τῆς ἀναγκαίας ἀλλαγῆς
θάτερον εἶδος τῆς χρηματιστικῆς ἐγένετο, τὸ καπηλικόν, τὸ
μὲν οὖν πρῶτον ἁπλῶς ἴσως γινόμενον, εἶτα δι᾽ ἐμπειρίας ἤδη
τεχνικώτερον, πόθεν καὶ πῶς μεταβαλλόμενον πλεῖστον
ποιήσει κέρδος. διὸ δοκεῖ ἡ χρηματιστικὴ μάλιστα περὶ τὸ 10
νόμισμα εἶναι, καὶ ἔργον αὐτῆς τὸ δύνασθαι θεωρῆσαι πόθεν ἔσται πλῆθος χρημάτων· ποιητικὴ γὰρ εἶναι τοῦ πλούτου
καὶ χρημάτων. καὶ γὰρ τὸν πλοῦτον πολλάκις τιθέασι νομίσματος πλῆθος, διὰ τὸ περὶ τοῦτ᾽ εἶναι τὴν χρηματιστικὴν
καὶ τὴν καπηλικήν. ὁτὲ δὲ πάλιν λῆρος εἶναι δοκεῖ τὸ 11
νόμισμα καὶ νόμος παντάπασι, φύσει δ᾽ οὐδέν, ὅτι μεταθεμένων τε τῶν χρωμένων οὐδενὸς ἄξιον οὔτε χρήσιμον πρὸς
οὐδὲν τῶν ἀναγκαίων ἐστί, καὶ νομίσματος πλουτῶν πολλάκις ἀπορήσει τῆς ἀναγκαίας τροφῆς· καίτοι ἄτοπον τοιοῦτον
εἶναι πλοῦτον οὗ εὐπορῶν λιμῷ ἀπολεῖται, καθάπερ καὶ τὸν
Μίδαν ἐκεῖνον μυθολογοῦσι διὰ τὴν ἀπληστίαν τῆς εὐχῆς
πάντων αὐτῷ γιγνομένων τῶν παρατιθεμένων χρυσῶν. διὸ 12
ζητοῦσιν ἕτερόν τι τὸν πλοῦτον καὶ τὴν χρηματιστικήν, ὀρθῶς
ζητοῦντες. ἔστι γὰρ ἑτέρα ἡ χρηματιστικὴ καὶ ὁ πλοῦτος ὁ
κατὰ φύσιν, καὶ αὕτη μὲν οἰκονομική, ἡ δὲ καπηλική,
ποιητικὴ χρημάτων οὐ πάντως, ἀλλ᾽ ἢ διὰ χρημάτων μεταβολῆς. καὶ δοκεῖ περὶ τὸ νόμισμα αὕτη εἶναι· τὸ γὰρ
νόμισμα στοιχεῖον καὶ πέρας τῆς ἀλλαγῆς ἐστίν. καὶ ἄπει- 13
ρος δὴ οὗτος ὁ πλοῦτος ὁ ἀπὸ ταύτης τῆς χρηματιστικῆς·
ὥσπερ γὰρ ἡ ἰατρικὴ τοῦ ὑγιαίνειν εἰς ἄπειρόν ἐστι καὶ
ἑκάστη τῶν τεχνῶν τοῦ τέλους εἰς ἄπειρον (ὅτι μάλιστα γὰρ
ἐκεῖνο βούλονται ποιεῖν), τῶν δὲ πρὸς τὸ τέλος οὐκ εἰς ἄπειρον (πέρας γὰρ τὸ τέλος πάσαις), οὕτω καὶ ταύτης τῆς
χρηματιστικῆς οὐκ ἔστι τοῦ τέλους πέρας, τέλος δὲ ὁ τοιοῦτος

14 πλοῦτος καὶ χρημάτων κτῆσις· τῆς δ' οἰκονομικῆς, οὐ χρηματιστικῆς, ἔστι πέρας· οὐ γὰρ τοῦτο τῆς οἰκονομικῆς ἔργον.
διὸ τῇ μὲν φαίνεται ἀναγκαῖον εἶναι παντὸς πλούτου πέρας,
ἐπὶ δὲ τῶν γινομένων ὁρῶ(μεν) συμβαῖνον τοὐναντίον· πάντες
γὰρ εἰς ἄπειρον αὔξουσιν οἱ χρηματιζόμενοι τὸ νόμισμα.
15 αἴτιον δὲ τὸ σύνεγγυς αὐτῶν· ἐπαλλάττει γὰρ ἡ χρῆσις
τοῦ αὐτοῦ οὖσα ἑκατέρα τῆς χρηματιστικῆς, τῆς γὰρ αὐτῆς
ἐστὶ χρήσεως κτῆσις, ἀλλ' οὐ κατὰ ταὐτόν, ἀλλὰ τῆς μὲν
ἕτερον τέλος, τῆς δ' ἡ αὔξησις. ὥστε δοκεῖ τισὶ τοῦτ' εἶναι
τῆς οἰκονομικῆς ἔργον, καὶ διατελοῦσιν ἢ σώζειν οἰόμενοι
16 δεῖν ἢ αὔξειν τὴν τοῦ νομίσματος οὐσίαν εἰς ἄπειρον. αἴτιον
δὲ ταύτης τῆς διαθέσεως τὸ σπουδάζειν περὶ τὸ ζῆν, ἀλλὰ
μὴ τὸ εὖ ζῆν· εἰς ἄπειρον οὖν ἐκείνης τῆς ἐπιθυμίας οὔσης, 1258 a
καὶ τῶν ποιητικῶν ἀπείρων ἐπιθυμοῦσιν. ὅσοι δὲ καὶ τοῦ εὖ
ζῆν ἐπιβάλλονται, τὸ πρὸς τὰς ἀπολαύσεις τὰς σωματικὰς
ζητοῦσιν, ὥστ' ἐπεὶ καὶ τοῦτ' ἐν τῇ κτήσει φαίνεται ὑπάρχειν, πᾶσα ἡ διατριβὴ περὶ τὸν χρηματισμόν ἐστι, καὶ τὸ
17 ἕτερον εἶδος τῆς χρηματιστικῆς διὰ τοῦτ' ἐλήλυθεν. ἐν ὑπερ-
βολῇ γὰρ οὔσης τῆς ἀπολαύσεως, τὴν τῆς ἀπολαυστικῆς
ὑπερβολῆς ποιητικὴν ζητοῦσιν· κἂν μὴ διὰ τῆς χρηματιστικῆς δύνωνται πορίζειν, δι' ἄλλης αἰτίας τοῦτο πειρῶνται,
ἑκάστῃ χρώμενοι τῶν δυνάμεων οὐ κατὰ φύσιν· ἀνδρίας
γὰρ οὐ χρήματα ποιεῖν ἐστὶν ἀλλὰ θάρσος, οὐδὲ στρατηγικῆς
18 καὶ ἰατρικῆς, ἀλλὰ τῆς μὲν νίκην τῆς δ' ὑγίειαν· οἱ δὲ
πάσας ποιοῦσι χρηματιστικάς, ὡς τοῦτο τέλος ὄν, πρὸς δὲ
τὸ τέλος ἅπαντα δέον ἀπαντᾶν. περὶ μὲν οὖν τῆς τε μὴ
ἀναγκαίας χρηματιστικῆς, καὶ τίς, καὶ δι' αἰτίαν τίνα ἐν
χρείᾳ ἐσμὲν αὐτῆς, εἴρηται· καὶ περὶ τῆς ἀναγκαίας, ὅτι
ἑτέρα μὲν αὐτῆς οἰκονομικὴ δὲ κατὰ φύσιν ἡ περὶ τὴν
τροφήν, οὐχ ὥσπερ αὐτὴ ἄπειρος, ἀλλὰ ἔχουσα ὅρον·
δῆλον δὲ καὶ τὸ ἀπορούμενον ἐξ ἀρχῆς, πότερον τοῦ 10
οἰκονομικοῦ καὶ πολιτικοῦ ἐστὶν ἡ χρηματιστικὴ ἢ οὔ, ἀλλὰ
δεῖ τοῦτο μὲν ὑπάρχειν· ὥσπερ γὰρ καὶ ἀνθρώπους οὐ ποιεῖ

ἡ πολιτική, ἀλλὰ λαβοῦσα παρὰ τῆς φύσεως χρῆται
αὐτοῖς, οὕτω καὶ τροφὴν τὴν φύσιν δεῖ παραδοῦναι γῆν ἢ
θάλατταν ἢ ἄλλο τι· ἐκ δὲ τούτων ὡς δεῖ ταῦτα διαθεῖναι προσήκει τὸν οἰκονόμον. οὐ γὰρ τῆς ὑφαντικῆς ἔρια 2
ποιῆσαι, ἀλλὰ χρήσασθαι αὐτοῖς, καὶ γνῶναι δὲ τὸ ποῖον
χρηστὸν καὶ ἐπιτήδειον ἢ φαῦλον καὶ ἀνεπιτήδειον. καὶ γὰρ
ἀπορήσειεν ἄν τις διὰ τί ἡ μὲν χρηματιστικὴ μόριον τῆς
οἰκονομίας, ἡ δ' ἰατρικὴ οὐ μόριον· καίτοι δεῖ ὑγιαίνειν τοὺς
κατὰ τὴν οἰκίαν, ὥσπερ ζῆν ἢ ἄλλο τι τῶν ἀναγκαίων.
ἐπεὶ δὲ ἔστι μὲν ὡς τοῦ οἰκονόμου καὶ τοῦ ἄρχοντος καὶ περὶ 3
ὑγιείας ἰδεῖν, ἔστι δὲ ὡς οὔ, ἀλλὰ τοῦ ἰατροῦ, οὕτω καὶ περὶ
τῶν χρημάτων ἔστι μὲν ὡς τοῦ οἰκονόμου, ἔστι δὲ ὡς οὔ, ἀλλὰ
τῆς ὑπηρετικῆς· μάλιστα δέ, καθάπερ εἴρηται πρότερον, δεῖ
φύσει τοῦτο ὑπάρχειν· φύσεως γάρ ἐστιν ἔργον τροφὴν τῷ
γεννηθέντι παρέχειν· παντὶ γάρ, ἐξ οὗ γίνεται, τροφὴ τὸ
λειπόμενόν ἐστιν. διὸ κατὰ φύσιν ἐστὶν ἡ χρηματιστικὴ 4
πᾶσιν ἀπὸ τῶν καρπῶν καὶ τῶν ζῴων. διπλῆς δ' οὔσης
αὐτῆς, ὥσπερ εἴπομεν, καὶ τῆς μὲν καπηλικῆς τῆς δ' οἰκονομικῆς, καὶ ταύτης μὲν ἀναγκαίας καὶ ἐπαινουμένης, τῆς
1258 b δὲ μεταβλητικῆς ψεγομένης δικαίως (οὐ γὰρ κατὰ φύσιν
ἀλλ' ἀπ' ἀλλήλων ἐστίν), εὐλογώτατα μισεῖται ἡ ὀβολο-
στατικὴ διὰ τὸ ἀπ' αὐτοῦ τοῦ νομίσματος εἶναι τὴν κτῆσιν
καὶ οὐκ ἐφ' ὅπερ ἐπορίσθη· μεταβολῆς γὰρ ἐγένετο χάριν, 5
ὁ δὲ τόκος αὐτὸ ποιεῖ πλέον. ὅθεν καὶ τοὔνομα τοῦτ' εἴληφεν·
ὅμοια γὰρ τὰ τικτόμενα τοῖς γεννῶσιν αὐτά ἐστιν, ὁ δὲ
τόκος γίνεται νόμισμα νομίσματος· ὥστε καὶ μάλιστα παρὰ
φύσιν οὗτος τῶν χρηματισμῶν ἐστίν.

11 Ἐπεὶ δὲ τὰ πρὸς τὴν γνῶσιν διωρίκαμεν ἱκανῶς, τὰ
πρὸς τὴν χρῆσιν δεῖ διελθεῖν. πάντα δὲ τὰ τοιαῦτα τὴν
μὲν θεωρίαν ἐλεύθερον ἔχει, τὴν δ' ἐμπειρίαν ἀναγκαίαν.
ἔστι δὲ χρηματιστικῆς μέρη χρήσιμα τὸ περὶ τὰ κτήματα
ἔμπειρον εἶναι, ποῖα λυσιτελέστατα καὶ ποῦ καὶ πῶς, οἷον
ἵππων κτῆσις ποία τις ἢ βοῶν ἢ προβάτων, ὁμοίως δὲ καὶ

2 τῶν λοιπῶν ζῴων (δεῖ γὰρ ἔμπειρον εἶναι πρὸς ἄλληλά
τε τούτων τίνα λυσιτελέστατα, καὶ ποῖα ἐν ποίοις τόποις·
ἄλλα γὰρ ἐν ἄλλαις εὐθηνεῖ χώραις), εἶτα περὶ γεωργίας,
καὶ ταύτης ἤδη ψιλῆς τε καὶ πεφυτευμένης, καὶ μελιττουργίας, καὶ τῶν ἄλλων ζῴων τῶν πλωτῶν ἢ πτηνῶν, ἀφ'
3 ὅσων ἔστι τυγχάνειν βοηθείας. τῆς μὲν οὖν οἰκειοτάτης χρηματιστικῆς ταῦτα μόρια καὶ πρῶτα, τῆς δὲ μεταβλητικῆς
μέγιστον μὲν ἐμπορία (καὶ ταύτης μέρη τρία, ναυκληρία
φορτηγία παράστασις· διαφέρει δὲ τούτων ἕτερα ἑτέρων τῷ
τὰ μὲν ἀσφαλέστερα εἶναι, τὰ δὲ πλείω πορίζειν τὴν ἐπι-
4 καρπίαν), δεύτερον δὲ τοκισμός, τρίτον δὲ μισθαρνία· ταύτης δ' ἡ μὲν τῶν βαναύσων τεχνῶν, ἡ δὲ τῶν ἀτέχνων
καὶ τῷ σώματι μόνῳ χρησίμων· τρίτον δὲ εἶδος χρηματιστικῆς μεταξὺ ταύτης καὶ τῆς πρώτης (ἔχει γὰρ καὶ τῆς
κατὰ φύσιν τι μέρος καὶ τῆς μεταβλητικῆς), ὅσα ἀπὸ γῆς
καὶ τῶν ἀπὸ γῆς γινομένων ἀκάρπων μὲν χρησίμων δέ,
5 οἷον ὑλοτομία τε καὶ πᾶσα μεταλλευτική. αὕτη δὲ πολλὰ
ἤδη περιείληφε γένη· πολλὰ γὰρ εἴδη τῶν ἐκ γῆς μεταλ-
λευομένων ἐστίν. περὶ ἑκάστου δὲ τούτων καθόλου μὲν εἴρηται
καὶ νῦν, τὸ δὲ κατὰ μέρος ἀκριβολογεῖσθαι χρήσιμον μὲν
6 πρὸς τὰς ἐργασίας, φορτικὸν δὲ τὸ ἐνδιατρίβειν. εἰσὶ δὲ
τεχνικώταται μὲν τῶν ἐργασιῶν ὅπου ἐλάχιστον τύχης,
βαναυσόταται δ' ἐν αἷς τὰ σώματα λωβῶνται μάλιστα,
δουλικώταται δὲ ὅπου τοῦ σώματος πλεῖσται χρήσεις, ἀγεννέ-
7 σταται δὲ ὅπου ἐλάχιστον προσδεῖ ἀρετῆς. ἐπεὶ δ' ἐστὶν ἐνίοις
γεγραμμένα περὶ τούτων, οἷον Χαρητίδῃ τῷ Παρίῳ καὶ
Ἀπολλοδώρῳ τῷ Λημνίῳ περὶ γεωργίας καὶ ψιλῆς καὶ
πεφυτευμένης, ὁμοίως δὲ καὶ ἄλλοις περὶ ἄλλων, ταῦτα
μὲν ἐκ τούτων θεωρείτω ὅτῳ ἐπιμελές· ἔτι δὲ καὶ τὰ λεγόμενα σποράδην, δι' ὧν ἐπιτετυχήκασιν ἔνιοι χρηματιζό-
8 μενοι, δεῖ συλλέγειν· πάντα γὰρ ὠφέλιμα ταῦτ' ἐστὶ τοῖς
τιμῶσι τὴν χρηματιστικήν, οἷον καὶ τὸ Θάλεω τοῦ Μιλησίου·
τοῦτο γάρ ἐστι κατανόημά τι χρηματιστικόν, ἀλλ' ἐκείνῳ

μὲν διὰ τὴν σοφίαν προσάπτουσι, τυγχάνει δὲ καθόλου τι
ὄν. ὀνειδιζόντων γὰρ αὐτῷ διὰ τὴν πενίαν ὡς ἀνωφελοῦς 9
τῆς φιλοσοφίας οὔσης, κατανοήσαντά φασιν αὐτὸν ἐλαιῶν
φορὰν ἐσομένην ἐκ τῆς ἀστρολογίας, ἔτι χειμῶνος ὄντος
εὐπορήσαντα χρημάτων ὀλίγων ἀρραβῶνας διαδοῦναι τῶν
ἐλαιουργείων τῶν τ' ἐν Μιλήτῳ καὶ Χίῳ πάντων, ὀλίγου μισθωσάμενον ἅτ' οὐδενὸς ἐπιβάλλοντος· ἐπειδὴ δ' ὁ καιρὸς ἧκε,
πολλῶν ζητουμένων ἅμα καὶ ἐξαίφνης, ἐκμισθοῦντα ὃν τρόπον
ἠβούλετο, πολλὰ χρήματα συλλέξαντα ἐπιδεῖξαι ὅτι ῥᾴδιόν
ἐστι πλουτεῖν τοῖς φιλοσόφοις, ἂν βούλωνται, ἀλλ' οὐ τοῦτ'
ἐστὶ περὶ ὃ σπουδάζουσιν. Θαλῆς μὲν οὖν λέγεται τοῦτον 10
τὸν τρόπον ἐπίδειξιν ποιήσασθαι τῆς σοφίας· ἔστι δ', ὥσπερ
εἴπομεν, καθόλου τὸ τοιοῦτον χρηματιστικόν, ἐάν τις δύνηται
μονοπωλίαν αὑτῷ κατασκευάζειν. διὸ καὶ τῶν πόλεων ἔνιαι
τοῦτον ποιοῦνται τὸν πόρον, ὅταν ἀπορῶσι χρημάτων· μονοπωλίαν γὰρ τῶν ὠνίων ποιοῦσιν. ἐν Σικελίᾳ δέ τις τεθέντος 11
παρ' αὐτῷ νομίσματος συνεπρίατο πάντα τὸν σίδηρον ἐκ
τῶν σιδηρείων, μετὰ δὲ ταῦτα ὡς ἀφίκοντο ἐκ τῶν ἐμπορίων οἱ ἔμποροι, ἐπώλει μόνος, οὐ πολλὴν ποιήσας ὑπερβολὴν τῆς τιμῆς· ἀλλ' ὅμως ἐπὶ τοῖς πεντήκοντα ταλάντοις
ἐπέλαβεν ἑκατόν. τοῦτον μὲν οὖν ὁ Διονύσιος αἰσθόμενος τὰ 12
μὲν χρήματα ἐκέλευσεν ἐκκομίσασθαι, μὴ μέντοι γε ἔτι
μένειν ἐν Συρακούσαις, ὡς πόρους εὑρίσκοντα τοῖς αὑτοῦ
πράγμασιν ἀσυμφόρους· τὸ μέντοι ὅραμα Θάλεω καὶ τοῦτο
ταὐτόν ἐστιν· ἀμφότεροι γὰρ ἑαυτοῖς ἐτέχνασαν γενέσθαι
μονοπωλίαν. χρήσιμον δὲ γνωρίζειν ταῦτα καὶ τοῖς πολι- 13
τικοῖς· πολλαῖς γὰρ πόλεσι δεῖ χρηματισμοῦ καὶ τοιούτων
πόρων, ὥσπερ οἰκίᾳ, μᾶλλον δέ. διόπερ τινὲς καὶ πολιτεύονται τῶν πολιτευομένων ταῦτα μόνον.

12 Ἐπεὶ δὲ τρία μέρη τῆς οἰκονομικῆς ἦν, ἓν μὲν δεσποτική, περὶ ἧς εἴρηται πρότερον, ἓν δὲ πατρική, τρίτον δὲ
γαμική· καὶ γὰρ γυναικὸς ἄρχειν καὶ τέκνων, ὡς ἐλευθέρων μὲν ἀμφοῖν, οὐ τὸν αὐτὸν δὲ τρόπον τῆς ἀρχῆς, ἀλλὰ

γυναικὸς μὲν πολιτικῶς, τέκνων δὲ βασιλικῶς· τό τε γὰρ 1259 b
ἄρρεν φύσει τοῦ θήλεος ἡγεμονικώτερον, εἰ μή που συνέστηκε παρὰ φύσιν, καὶ τὸ πρεσβύτερον καὶ τέλειον τοῦ νεω-
2 τέρου καὶ ἀτελοῦς. ἐν μὲν οὖν ταῖς πολιτικαῖς ἀρχαῖς ταῖς
πλείσταις μεταβάλλει τὸ ἄρχον καὶ τὸ ἀρχόμενον (ἐξ ἴσου
γὰρ εἶναι βούλεται τὴν φύσιν καὶ διαφέρειν μηδέν), ὅμως
δέ, ὅταν τὸ μὲν ἄρχῃ τὸ δὲ ἄρχηται, ζητεῖ διαφορὰν εἶναι
καὶ σχήμασι καὶ λόγοις καὶ τιμαῖς, ὥσπερ καὶ Ἄμασις
3 εἶπε τὸν περὶ τοῦ ποδανιπτῆρος λόγον· τὸ δ' ἄρρεν ἀεὶ πρὸς
τὸ θῆλυ τοῦτον ἔχει τὸν τρόπον. ἡ δὲ τῶν τέκνων ἀρχὴ
βασιλική· τὸ γὰρ γεννῆσαν καὶ κατὰ φιλίαν ἄρχον καὶ
κατὰ πρεσβείαν ἐστίν, ὅπερ ἐστὶ βασιλικῆς εἶδος ἀρχῆς. διὸ
καλῶς Ὅμηρος τὸν Δία προσηγόρευσεν εἰπὼν "πατὴρ ἀνδρῶν τε θεῶν τε," τὸν βασιλέα τούτων ἁπάντων. φύσει γὰρ
τὸν βασιλέα διαφέρειν μὲν δεῖ, τῷ γένει δ' εἶναι τὸν αὐτόν·
ὅπερ πέπονθε τὸ πρεσβύτερον πρὸς τὸ νεώτερον καὶ ὁ γεν-
νήσας πρὸς τὸ τέκνον.

Φανερὸν τοίνυν ὅτι πλείων ἡ σπουδὴ τῆς οἰκονομίας **13**
περὶ τοὺς ἀνθρώπους ἢ περὶ τὴν τῶν ἀψύχων κτῆσιν, καὶ
περὶ τὴν ἀρετὴν τούτων ἢ περὶ τὴν τῆς κτήσεως, ὃν καλοῦμεν
2 πλοῦτον, καὶ τῶν ἐλευθέρων μᾶλλον ἢ δούλων. πρῶτον μὲν
οὖν περὶ δούλων ἀπορήσειεν ἄν τις, πότερόν ἐστιν ἀρετή τις
δούλου παρὰ τὰς ὀργανικὰς καὶ διακονικὰς ἄλλη τιμιωτέρα
τούτων, οἷον σωφροσύνη καὶ ἀνδρία καὶ δικαιοσύνη καὶ τῶν
ἄλλων τῶν τοιούτων ἕξεων, ἢ οὐκ ἔστιν οὐδεμία παρὰ τὰς
3 σωματικὰς ὑπηρεσίας. ἔχει γὰρ ἀπορίαν ἀμφοτέρως· εἴτε
γὰρ ἔστι, τί διοίσουσι τῶν ἐλευθέρων; εἴτε μή ἐστιν, ὄντων
ἀνθρώπων καὶ λόγου κοινωνούντων ἄτοπον. σχεδὸν δὲ
ταὐτόν ἐστι τὸ ζητούμενον καὶ περὶ γυναικὸς καὶ παιδός,
πότερα καὶ τούτων εἰσὶν ἀρεταί, καὶ δεῖ τὴν γυναῖκα εἶναι
σώφρονα καὶ ἀνδρείαν καὶ δικαίαν, καὶ παῖς ἐστι καὶ ἀκό-
4 λαστος καὶ σώφρων, ἢ οὔ; καὶ καθόλου δὴ τοῦτ' ἐστὶν ἐπισκεπτέον περὶ ἀρχομένου φύσει καὶ ἄρχοντος, πότερον ἡ αὐτὴ

ἀρετὴ ἢ ἑτέρα. εἰ μὲν γὰρ δεῖ ἀμφοτέρους μετέχειν καλοκἀγαθίας, διὰ τί τὸν μὲν ἄρχειν δέοι ἂν τὸν δὲ ἄρχεσθαι
καθάπαξ; οὐδὲ γὰρ τῷ μᾶλλον καὶ ἧττον οἷόν τε διαφέ-
ρειν· τὸ μὲν γὰρ ἄρχεσθαι καὶ ἄρχειν εἴδει διαφέρει, τὸ
δὲ μᾶλλον καὶ ἧττον οὐδέν· εἰ δὲ τὸν μὲν δεῖ τὸν δὲ μή, 5
θαυμαστόν. εἴτε γὰρ ὁ ἄρχων μὴ ἔσται σώφρων καὶ δίκαιος, πῶς ἄρξει καλῶς; εἴθ' ὁ ἀρχόμενος, πῶς ἀρχθή-
1260 a σεται καλῶς; ἀκόλαστος γὰρ ὢν καὶ δειλὸς οὐδὲν ποιήσει
τῶν προσηκόντων. φανερὸν τοίνυν ὅτι ἀνάγκη μὲν μετέχειν
ἀμφοτέρους ἀρετῆς, ταύτης δ' εἶναι διαφοράς, ὥσπερ καὶ
τῶν φύσει ἀρχομένων. καὶ τοῦτο εὐθὺς ὑφήγηται περὶ τὴν 6
ψυχήν· ἐν ταύτῃ γάρ ἐστι φύσει τὸ μὲν ἄρχον τὸ δ'
ἀρχόμενον, ὧν ἑτέραν φαμὲν εἶναι ἀρετήν, οἷον τοῦ λόγον
ἔχοντος καὶ τοῦ ἀλόγου. δῆλον τοίνυν ὅτι τὸν αὐτὸν τρόπον
ἔχει καὶ ἐπὶ τῶν ἄλλων, ὥστε φύσει τὰ πλείω ἄρχοντα
καὶ ἀρχόμενα· ἄλλον γὰρ τρόπον τὸ ἐλεύθερον τοῦ δούλου 7
ἄρχει καὶ τὸ ἄρρεν τοῦ θήλεος καὶ ἀνὴρ παιδός· καὶ πᾶσιν
ἐνυπάρχει μὲν τὰ μόρια τῆς ψυχῆς, ἀλλ' ἐνυπάρχει δια-
φερόντως· ὁ μὲν γὰρ δοῦλος ὅλως οὐκ ἔχει τὸ βουλευτικόν,
τὸ δὲ θῆλυ ἔχει μέν, ἀλλ' ἄκυρον, ὁ δὲ παῖς ἔχει μέν,
ἀλλ' ἀτελές. ὁμοίως τοίνυν ἀναγκαῖον ἔχειν καὶ περὶ τὰς 8
ἠθικὰς ἀρετὰς ὑποληπτέον, δεῖν μὲν μετέχειν πάντας, ἀλλ'
οὐ τὸν αὐτὸν τρόπον, ἀλλ' ὅσον ἑκάστῳ πρὸς τὸ αὑτοῦ
ἔργον. διὸ τὸν μὲν ἄρχοντα τελέαν ἔχειν δεῖ τὴν ἠθικὴν
ἀρετήν (τὸ γὰρ ἔργον ἐστὶν ἁπλῶς τοῦ ἀρχιτέκτονος, ὁ δὲ
λόγος ἀρχιτέκτων), τῶν δ' ἄλλων ἕκαστον, ὅσον ἐπιβάλλει
αὐτοῖς. ὥστε φανερὸν ὅτι ἐστὶν ἠθικὴ ἀρετὴ τῶν εἰρημένων 9
πάντων, καὶ οὐχ ἡ αὐτὴ σωφροσύνη γυναικὸς καὶ ἀνδρός,
οὐδ' ἀνδρία καὶ δικαιοσύνη, καθάπερ ᾤετο Σωκράτης, ἀλλ'
ἡ μὲν ἀρχικὴ ἀνδρία, ἡ δ' ὑπηρετική. ὁμοίως δ' ἔχει καὶ
περὶ τὰς ἄλλας. δῆλον δὲ τοῦτο καὶ κατὰ μέρος μᾶλλον 10
ἐπισκοποῦσιν· καθόλου γὰρ οἱ λέγοντες ἐξαπατῶσιν ἑαυτούς,
ὅτι τὸ εὖ ἔχειν τὴν ψυχὴν ἀρετή, τὸ ὀρθοπραγεῖν, ἤ τι

τῶν τοιούτων· πολὺ γὰρ ἄμεινον λέγουσιν οἱ ἐξαριθμοῦντες
11 τὰς ἀρετάς, ὥσπερ Γοργίας, τῶν οὕτως ὁριζομένων. διὸ δεῖ,
ὥσπερ ὁ ποιητὴς εἴρηκε περὶ γυναικός, οὕτω νομίζειν ἔχειν
περὶ πάντων, "γυναικὶ κόσμον ἡ σιγὴ φέρει," ἀλλ' ἀνδρὶ
οὐκέτι τοῦτο. ἐπεὶ δ' ὁ παῖς ἀτελής, δῆλον ὅτι τούτου μὲν καὶ
ἡ ἀρετὴ οὐκ αὐτοῦ πρὸς αὐτόν ἐστιν, ἀλλὰ πρὸς τὸ τέλος
12 καὶ τὸν ἡγούμενον. ὁμοίως δὲ καὶ δούλου πρὸς δεσπότην. ἔθεμεν δὲ πρὸς τἀναγκαῖα χρήσιμον εἶναι τὸν δοῦλον, ὥστε δῆλον ὅτι καὶ ἀρετῆς δεῖται μικρᾶς, καὶ τοσαύτης ὅπως μήτε
δι' ἀκολασίαν μήτε διὰ δειλίαν ἐλλείψῃ τῶν ἔργων. ἀπορήσειε δ' ἄν τις, τὸ νῦν εἰρημένον εἰ ἀληθές, ἆρα καὶ τοὺς
τεχνίτας δεήσει ἔχειν ἀρετήν· πολλάκις γὰρ δι' ἀκολασίαν
13 ἐλλείπουσι τῶν ἔργων. ἢ διαφέρει τοῦτο πλεῖστον; ὁ μὲν γὰρ
δοῦλος κοινωνὸς ζωῆς, ὁ δὲ πορρώτερον, καὶ τοσοῦτον ἐπιβάλλει ἀρετῆς ὅσον περ καὶ δουλείας· ὁ γὰρ βάναυσος τεχνίτης ἀφωρισμένην τινὰ ἔχει δουλείαν· καὶ ὁ μὲν δοῦλος 1260 b
τῶν φύσει, σκυτοτόμος δ' οὐδείς, οὐδὲ τῶν ἄλλων τεχνιτῶν.
14 φανερὸν τοίνυν ὅτι τῆς τοιαύτης ἀρετῆς αἴτιον εἶναι δεῖ τῷ
δούλῳ τὸν δεσπότην, ἀλλ' οὐ τὴν διδασκαλικὴν ἔχοντα τῶν
ἔργων δεσποτικήν. διὸ λέγουσιν οὐ καλῶς οἱ λόγου τοὺς δούλους ἀποστεροῦντες καὶ φάσκοντες ἐπιτάξει χρῆσθαι μόνον·
νουθετητέον γὰρ μᾶλλον τοὺς δούλους ἢ τοὺς παῖδας.

15 Ἀλλὰ περὶ μὲν τούτων διωρίσθω τὸν τρόπον τοῦτον· περὶ
δ' ἀνδρὸς καὶ γυναικὸς καὶ τέκνων καὶ πατρός, τῆς τε περὶ
ἕκαστον αὐτῶν ἀρετῆς καὶ τῆς πρὸς σφᾶς αὐτοὺς ὁμιλίας,
τί τὸ καλῶς καὶ μὴ καλῶς ἐστί, καὶ πῶς δεῖ τὸ μὲν εὖ διώκειν τὸ δὲ κακῶς φεύγειν, ἐν τοῖς περὶ τὰς πολιτείας ἀναγκαῖον ἐπελθεῖν· ἐπεὶ γὰρ οἰκία μὲν πᾶσα μέρος πόλεως,
ταῦτα δ' οἰκίας, τὴν δὲ τοῦ μέρους πρὸς τὴν τοῦ ὅλου δεῖ βλέπειν ἀρετήν, ἀναγκαῖον πρὸς τὴν πολιτείαν βλέποντας παι-
δεύειν καὶ τοὺς παῖδας καὶ τὰς γυναῖκας, εἴπερ τι διαφέρει πρὸς
τὸ τὴν πόλιν εἶναι σπουδαίαν καὶ τοὺς παῖδας εἶναι σπουδαίους
16 καὶ τὰς γυναῖκας σπουδαίας. ἀναγκαῖον δὲ διαφέρειν· αἱ μὲν

γὰρ γυναῖκες ἥμισυ μέρος τῶν ἐλευθέρων, ἐκ δὲ τῶν παίδων οἱ κοινωνοὶ γίνονται τῆς πολιτείας. ὥστ' ἐπεὶ περὶ μὲν τούτων διώρισται, περὶ δὲ τῶν λοιπῶν ἐν ἄλλοις λεκτέον, ἀφέντες ὡς τέλος ἔχοντας τοὺς νῦν λόγους, ἄλλην ἀρχὴν ποιησάμενοι λέγωμεν, καὶ πρῶτον ἐπισκεψώμεθα περὶ τῶν ἀποφηναμένων περὶ τῆς πολιτείας τῆς ἀρίστης.

Β'.

Ἐπεὶ δὲ προαιρούμεθα θεωρῆσαι περὶ τῆς κοινωνίας τῆς πολιτικῆς, τίς κρατίστη πασῶν τοῖς δυναμένοις ζῆν ὅτι μάλιστα κατ' εὐχήν, δεῖ καὶ τὰς ἄλλας ἐπισκέψασθαι πολιτείας, αἷς τε χρῶνταί τινες τῶν πόλεων τῶν εὐνομεῖσθαι λεγομένων, κἂν εἴ τινες ἕτεραι † τυγχάνωσιν † ὑπό τινων εἰρημέναι καὶ δοκοῦσαι καλῶς ἔχειν, ἵνα τό τ' ὀρθῶς ἔχον ὀφθῇ καὶ τὸ χρήσιμον, ἔτι δὲ τὸ ζητεῖν τι παρ' αὐτὰς ἕτερον μὴ δοκῇ πάντως εἶναι σοφίζεσθαι βουλομένων, ἀλλὰ διὰ τὸ μὴ καλῶς ἔχειν ταύτας τὰς νῦν ὑπαρχούσας, διὰ τοῦτο ταύτην δοκῶμεν ἐπιβαλέσθαι τὴν μέθοδον. ἀρχὴν δὲ πρῶτον ποιη- 2
τέον ἥπερ πέφυκεν ἀρχὴ ταύτης τῆς σκέψεως. ἀνάγκη γὰρ ἤτοι πάντας πάντων κοινωνεῖν τοὺς πολίτας, ἢ μηδενός, ἢ τινῶν μὲν τινῶν δὲ μή. τὸ μὲν οὖν μηδενὸς κοινωνεῖν φανερὸν ὡς ἀδύνατον· ἡ γὰρ πολιτεία κοινωνία τίς ἐστι, καὶ πρῶτον ἀνάγκη τοῦ τόπου κοινωνεῖν· ὁ μὲν γὰρ τόπος εἷς ὁ τῆς
1261 a μιᾶς πόλεως, οἱ δὲ πολῖται κοινωνοὶ τῆς μιᾶς πόλεως·
ἀλλὰ πότερον ὅσων ἐνδέχεται κοινωνῆσαι, πάντων βέλτιον 3
κοινωνεῖν τὴν μέλλουσαν οἰκήσεσθαι πόλιν καλῶς, ἢ τινῶν μὲν τινῶν δὲ οὐ βέλτιον; ἐνδέχεται γὰρ καὶ τέκνων καὶ γυναικῶν καὶ κτημάτων κοινωνεῖν τοὺς πολίτας ἀλλήλοις, ὥσπερ ἐν τῇ πολιτείᾳ τῇ Πλάτωνος· ἐκεῖ γὰρ ὁ Σωκράτης φησὶ δεῖν κοινὰ τὰ τέκνα καὶ τὰς γυναῖκας εἶναι καὶ τὰς κτήσεις. τοῦτο δὴ πότερον ὡς νῦν οὕτω βέλτιον ἔχειν, ἢ κατὰ
2 τὸν ἐν τῇ πολιτείᾳ γεγραμμένον νόμον; ἔχει δὴ δυσχερείας

ἄλλας τε πολλὰς τὸ πάντων εἶναι τὰς γυναῖκας κοινάς, καὶ δι' ἣν αἰτίαν φησὶ δεῖν νενομοθετῆσθαι τὸν τρόπον τοῦτον ὁ Σωκράτης, οὐ φαίνεται συμβαῖνον ἐκ τῶν λόγων· ἔτι δὲ πρὸς τὸ τέλος ὅ φησι τῇ πόλει δεῖν ὑπάρχειν, ὡς μὲν εἴρη-
2 ται νῦν, ἀδύνατον, πῶς δὲ δεῖ διελεῖν, οὐδὲν διώρισται. λέγω δὲ τὸ μίαν εἶναι τὴν πόλιν ὡς ἄριστον ὃν ὅτι μάλιστα πᾶσαν· λαμβάνει γὰρ ταύτην ὑπόθεσιν ὁ Σωκράτης. καίτοι φανερόν ἐστιν ὡς προϊοῦσα καὶ γινομένη μία μᾶλλον οὐδὲ πόλις ἔσται· πλῆθος γάρ τι τὴν φύσιν ἐστὶν ἡ πόλις, γινομένη τε μία μᾶλλον οἰκία μὲν ἐκ πόλεως, ἄνθρωπος δ' ἐξ οἰκίας ἔσται· μᾶλλον γὰρ μίαν τὴν οἰκίαν τῆς πόλεως φαίημεν ἄν, καὶ τὸν ἕνα τῆς οἰκίας· ὥστ' εἰ καὶ δυνατός τις εἴη τοῦτο
3 δρᾶν, οὐ ποιητέον· ἀναιρήσει γὰρ τὴν πόλιν. οὐ μόνον δ' ἐκ πλειόνων ἀνθρώπων ἐστὶν ἡ πόλις, ἀλλὰ καὶ ἐξ εἴδει διαφερόντων· οὐ γὰρ γίνεται πόλις ἐξ ὁμοίων. ἕτερον γὰρ συμμαχία καὶ πόλις· τὸ μὲν γὰρ τῷ ποσῷ χρήσιμον, κἂν ᾖ τὸ αὐτὸ τῷ εἴδει (βοηθείας γὰρ χάριν ἡ συμμαχία πέφυκεν), ὥσπερ ἂν εἰ σταθμὸς πλεῖον † ἑλκύσῃ †· διοίσει δὲ τῷ τοιούτῳ καὶ πόλις ἔθνους, ὅταν μὴ κατὰ κώμας ὦσι κεχωρισμένοι τὸ πλῆθος, ἀλλ' οἷον Ἀρκάδες· ἐξ ὧν δὲ δεῖ ἓν
4 γενέσθαι, εἴδει διαφέρει. διόπερ τὸ ἴσον τὸ ἀντιπεπονθὸς σῴζει τὰς πόλεις, ὥσπερ ἐν τοῖς ἠθικοῖς εἴρηται πρότερον· ἐπεὶ καὶ ἐν τοῖς ἐλευθέροις καὶ ἴσοις ἀνάγκη τοῦτ' εἶναι· ἅμα γὰρ οὐχ οἷόν τε πάντας ἄρχειν, ἀλλ' ἢ κατ' ἐνιαυτὸν ἢ
5 κατά τινα ἄλλην τάξιν ἢ χρόνον. καὶ συμβαίνει δὴ τὸν τρόπον τοῦτον ὥστε πάντας ἄρχειν, ὥσπερ ἂν εἰ μετέβαλλον οἱ σκυτεῖς καὶ οἱ τέκτονες καὶ μὴ οἱ αὐτοὶ ἀεὶ σκυτοτόμοι
6 καὶ τέκτονες ἦσαν. ἐπεὶ δὲ βέλτιον οὕτως ἔχειν καὶ τὰ περὶ τὴν κοινωνίαν τὴν πολιτικήν, δῆλον ὡς τοὺς αὐτοὺς ἀεὶ βέλτιον ἄρχειν, εἰ δυνατόν· ἐν οἷς δὲ μὴ δυνατὸν διὰ τὸ τὴν φύσιν ἴσους εἶναι πάντας, ἅμα δὲ καὶ δίκαιον, εἴτ' ἀγαθὸν 1261 b
εἴτε φαῦλον τὸ ἄρχειν, πάντας αὐτοῦ μετέχειν, † τοῦτο δὲ μιμεῖται τὸ ἐν μέρει τοὺς ἴσους εἴκειν τὸ δ' ὡς ὁμοίους εἶναι ἐξ

ἀρχῆς †· οἱ μὲν γὰρ ἄρχουσιν οἱ δ' ἄρχονται κατὰ μέρος, 7
ὥσπερ ἂν ἄλλοι γενόμενοι. καὶ τὸν αὐτὸν δὴ τρόπον ἀρχόντων
ἕτεροι ἑτέρας ἄρχουσιν ἀρχάς. φανερὸν τοίνυν ἐκ τούτων ὡς
οὔτε πέφυκε μίαν οὕτως εἶναι τὴν πόλιν ὥσπερ λέγουσί τινες,
καὶ τὸ λεχθὲν ὡς μέγιστον ἀγαθὸν ἐν ταῖς πόλεσιν ὅτι τὰς
πόλεις ἀναιρεῖ· καίτοι τό γε ἑκάστου ἀγαθὸν σώζει ἕκαστον.
ἔστι δὲ καὶ κατ' ἄλλον τρόπον φανερὸν ὅτι τὸ λίαν ἑνοῦν ζη- 8
τεῖν τὴν πόλιν οὐκ ἔστιν ἄμεινον. οἰκία μὲν γὰρ αὐταρκέστερον ἑνός, πόλις δ' οἰκίας· καὶ βούλεταί γ' ἤδη τότ' εἶναι πόλις, ὅταν αὐτάρκη συμβαίνῃ τὴν κοινωνίαν εἶναι τοῦ πλήθους.
εἴπερ οὖν αἱρετώτερον τὸ αὐταρκέστερον, καὶ τὸ ἧττον ἓν τοῦ
μᾶλλον αἱρετώτερον.

3 Ἀλλὰ μὴν οὐδ' εἰ τοῦτο ἄριστόν ἐστι, τὸ μίαν ὅτι μάλιστ' εἶναι τὴν κοινωνίαν, οὐδὲ τοῦτο ἀποδείκνυσθαι φαίνεται
κατὰ τὸν λόγον, ἐὰν πάντες ἅμα λέγωσι τὸ ἐμὸν καὶ τὸ μὴ
ἐμόν· τοῦτο γὰρ οἴεται ὁ Σωκράτης σημεῖον εἶναι τοῦ τὴν
πόλιν τελέως εἶναι μίαν. τὸ γὰρ πάντες διττόν. εἰ μὲν οὖν 2
ὡς ἕκαστος, τάχ' ἂν εἴη μᾶλλον ὃ βούλεται ποιεῖν ὁ Σωκράτης, ἕκαστος γὰρ υἱὸν ἑαυτοῦ φήσει τὸν αὐτὸν καὶ γυναῖκα δὴ τὴν αὐτήν, καὶ περὶ τῆς οὐσίας καὶ περὶ ἑκάστου
δὴ τῶν συμβαινόντων ὡσαύτως· νῦν δ' οὐχ οὕτω φήσουσιν οἱ
κοιναῖς χρώμενοι ταῖς γυναιξὶ καὶ τοῖς τέκνοις, ἀλλὰ πάντες μέν, οὐχ ὡς ἕκαστος δ' αὐτῶν. ὁμοίως δὲ καὶ τὴν οὐσίαν 3
πάντες μέν, οὐχ ὡς ἕκαστος δ' αὐτῶν. ὅτι μὲν τοίνυν παραλογισμός τίς ἐστι τὸ λέγειν πάντας, φανερόν· τὸ γὰρ πάντες καὶ ἀμφότερα καὶ περιττὰ καὶ ἄρτια διὰ τὸ διττὸν καὶ
ἐν τοῖς λόγοις ἐριστικοὺς ποιεῖ συλλογισμούς· διὸ ἐστὶ τὸ πάντας τὸ αὐτὸ λέγειν ὡδὶ μὲν καλόν, ἀλλ' οὐ δυνατόν, ὡδὶ δ'
οὐδὲν ὁμονοητικόν· πρὸς δὲ τούτοις ἑτέραν ἔχει βλάβην τὸ 4
λεγόμενον. ἥκιστα γὰρ ἐπιμελείας τυγχάνει τὸ πλείστων
κοινόν· τῶν γὰρ ἰδίων μάλιστα φροντίζουσιν, τῶν δὲ κοινῶν
ἧττον, ἢ ὅσον ἑκάστῳ ἐπιβάλλει· πρὸς γὰρ τοῖς ἄλλοις ὡς
ἑτέρου φροντίζοντος ὀλιγωροῦσι μᾶλλον, ὥσπερ ἐν ταῖς οἰκε-

τικαῖς διακονίαις οἱ πολλοὶ θεράποντες ἐνίοτε χεῖρον ὑπηρε-
5 τοῦσι τῶν ἐλαττόνων. γίνονται δ' ἑκάστῳ χίλιοι τῶν πολιτῶν
υἱοί, καὶ οὗτοι οὐχ ὡς ἑκάστου, ἀλλὰ τοῦ τυχόντος ὁ τυχὼν
ὁμοίως ἐστὶν υἱός· ὥστε πάντες ὁμοίως ὀλιγωρήσουσιν. ἔτι 1262 a
οὕτως ἕκαστος ἐμὸς λέγει τὸν εὖ πράττοντα τῶν πολιτῶν ἢ
κακῶς, ὁπόστος τυγχάνει τὸν ἀριθμόν, οἷον ἐμὸς ἢ τοῦ δεῖνος,
τοῦτον τὸν τρόπον λέγων καθ' ἕκαστον τῶν χιλίων, ἢ ὅσων
ἡ πόλις ἐστί, καὶ τοῦτο διστάζων· ἄδηλον γὰρ ᾧ συνέβη γενέ-
6 σθαι τέκνον καὶ σωθῆναι γενόμενον. καίτοι πότερον οὕτω
κρεῖττον τὸ ἐμὸν λέγειν ἕκαστον τὸ αὐτὸ μὲν προσαγορεύοντας δισχιλίων καὶ μυρίων, ἢ μᾶλλον ὡς νῦν ἐν ταῖς πόλεσι
7 τὸ ἐμὸν λέγουσιν; ὁ μὲν γὰρ υἱὸν αὑτοῦ ὁ δ' ἀδελφὸν αὑτοῦ
προσαγορεύει τὸν αὐτόν, ὁ δ' ἀνεψιόν, ἢ κατ' ἄλλην τινὰ
συγγένειαν, ἢ πρὸς αἵματος, ἢ κατ' οἰκειότητα καὶ κηδείαν
αὑτοῦ πρῶτον ἢ τῶν αὑτοῦ, πρὸς δὲ τούτοις ἕτερον φράτορα
φυλέτην· κρεῖττον γὰρ ἴδιον ἀνεψιὸν εἶναι ἢ τὸν τρόπον τοῦ-
8 τον υἱόν. οὐ μὴν ἀλλ' οὐδὲ διαφυγεῖν δυνατὸν τὸ μή τινας
ὑπολαμβάνειν ἑαυτῶν ἀδελφούς τε καὶ παῖδας καὶ πατέρας
καὶ μητέρας· κατὰ γὰρ τὰς ὁμοιότητας αἳ γίνονται τοῖς
τέκνοις πρὸς τοὺς γεννήσαντας, ἀναγκαῖον λαμβάνειν περὶ
9 ἀλλήλων τὰς πίστεις. ὅπερ φασὶ καὶ συμβαίνειν τινὲς τῶν
τὰς τῆς γῆς περιόδους πραγματευομένων· εἶναι γάρ τισι
τῶν ἄνω Λιβύων κοινὰς τὰς γυναῖκας, τὰ μέντοι γενόμενα
τέκνα διαιρεῖσθαι κατὰ τὰς ὁμοιότητας. εἰσὶ δέ τινες καὶ
γυναῖκες καὶ τῶν ἄλλων ζῴων, οἷον ἵπποι καὶ βόες, αἳ
σφόδρα πεφύκασιν ὅμοια ἀποδιδόναι τὰ τέκνα τοῖς γονεῦσιν, ὥσπερ ἡ ἐν Φαρσάλῳ κληθεῖσα Δικαία ἵππος. ἔτι δὲ **4**
καὶ τὰς τοιαύτας δυσχερείας οὐ ῥᾴδιον εὐλαβηθῆναι τοῖς
ταύτην κατασκευάζουσι τὴν κοινωνίαν, οἷον αἰκίας καὶ φόνους
ἀκουσίους, τοὺς δὲ ἑκουσίους, καὶ μάχας καὶ λοιδορίας· ὧν
οὐδὲν ὅσιόν ἐστι γίνεσθαι πρὸς πατέρας καὶ μητέρας καὶ τοὺς
μὴ πόρρω τῆς συγγενείας ὄντας, ὥσπερ πρὸς τοὺς ἄποθεν·
ἀλλὰ καὶ πλεῖον συμβαίνειν ἀναγκαῖον ἀγνοούντων ἢ γνω-

ριζόντων, καὶ γενομένων τῶν μὲν γνωριζόντων ἐνδέχεται τὰς
νομιζομένας γίνεσθαι λύσεις, τῶν δὲ μηδεμίαν. ἄτοπον δὲ 2
καὶ τὸ κοινοὺς ποιήσαντα τοὺς υἱοὺς τὸ συνεῖναι μόνον ἀφελεῖν τῶν ἐρώντων, τὸ δ' ἐρᾶν μὴ κωλῦσαι, μηδὲ τὰς χρήσεις τὰς ἄλλας, ἃς πατρὶ πρὸς υἱὸν εἶναι πάντων ἐστὶν
ἀπρεπέστατον καὶ ἀδελφῷ πρὸς ἀδελφόν, ἐπεὶ καὶ τὸ ἐρᾶν
μόνον. ἄτοπον δὲ καὶ τὸ τὴν συνουσίαν ἀφελεῖν δι' ἄλλην 3
μὲν αἰτίαν μηδεμίαν, ὡς λίαν δὲ ἰσχυρᾶς τῆς ἡδονῆς γινο-
μένης· ὅτι δ' ὁ μὲν πατὴρ ἢ υἱός, οἱ δ' ἀδελφοὶ ἀλλήλων,
μηδὲν οἴεσθαι διαφέρειν. ἔοικε δὲ μᾶλλον τοῖς γεωργοῖς 4
εἶναι χρήσιμον τὸ κοινὰς εἶναι τὰς γυναῖκας καὶ τοὺς παῖ-
1262 b δας ἢ τοῖς φύλαξιν· ἧττον γὰρ ἔσται φιλία κοινῶν ὄντων
τῶν τέκνων καὶ τῶν γυναικῶν, δεῖ δὲ τοιούτους εἶναι τοὺς ἀρχομένους πρὸς τὸ πειθαρχεῖν καὶ μὴ νεωτερίζειν. ὅλως δὲ 5
συμβαίνειν ἀνάγκη τοὐναντίον διὰ τὸν τοιοῦτον νόμον ὧν
προσήκει τοὺς ὀρθῶς κειμένους νόμους αἰτίους γίνεσθαι, καὶ
δι' ἣν αἰτίαν ὁ Σωκράτης οὕτως οἴεται δεῖν τάττειν τὰ περὶ
τὰ τέκνα καὶ τὰς γυναῖκας· φιλίαν τε γὰρ οἰόμεθα μέγιστον 6
εἶναι τῶν ἀγαθῶν ταῖς πόλεσιν (οὕτω γὰρ ἂν ἥκιστα στασιά-
ζοιεν), καὶ τὸ μίαν εἶναι τὴν πόλιν ἐπαινεῖ μάλισθ' ὁ Σω-
κράτης· ὃ καὶ δοκεῖ κἀκεῖνος εἶναί φησι τῆς φιλίας ἔργον,
καθάπερ ἐν τοῖς ἐρωτικοῖς λόγοις ἴσμεν λέγοντα τὸν Ἀρι-
στοφάνην ὡς τῶν ἐρώντων διὰ τὸ σφόδρα φιλεῖν ἐπιθυμούν-
των συμφυῆναι καὶ γενέσθαι ἐκ δύο ὄντων ἀμφοτέρους ἕνα.
ἐνταῦθα μὲν οὖν ἀνάγκη ἀμφοτέρους ἐφθάρθαι ἢ τὸν ἕνα· ἐν 7
δὲ τῇ πόλει τὴν φιλίαν ἀναγκαῖον ὑδαρῆ γίνεσθαι διὰ τὴν
κοινωνίαν τὴν τοιαύτην, καὶ ἥκιστα λέγειν τὸν ἐμὸν ἢ υἱὸν
πατέρα ἢ πατέρα υἱόν. ὥσπερ γὰρ μικρὸν γλυκὺ εἰς πολὺ 8
ὕδωρ μιχθὲν ἀναίσθητον ποιεῖ τὴν κρᾶσιν, οὕτω συμβαίνει
καὶ τὴν οἰκειότητα τὴν πρὸς ἀλλήλους τὴν ἀπὸ τῶν ὀνομά-
των τούτων, διαφροντίζειν ἥκιστα ἀναγκαῖον ὂν ἐν τῇ πολιτείᾳ τῇ τοιαύτῃ, ἢ πατέρα ὡς υἱῶν ἢ υἱὸν ὡς πατρός, ἢ ὡς
ἀδελφοὺς ἀλλήλων. δύο γάρ ἐστιν ἃ μάλιστα ποιεῖ κήδεσθαι 9

τοὺς ἀνθρώπους καὶ φιλεῖν, τό τε ἴδιον καὶ τὸ ἀγαπητόν· ὧν
οὐδέτερον οἷόν τε ὑπάρχειν τοῖς οὕτω πολιτευομένοις. ἀλλὰ
μὴν καὶ περὶ τοῦ μεταφέρειν τὰ γινόμενα τέκνα, τὰ μὲν ἐκ
τῶν γεωργῶν καὶ τεχνιτῶν εἰς τοὺς φύλακας, τὰ δ' ἐκ τούτων εἰς ἐκείνους, πολλὴν ἔχει ταραχήν, τίνα ἔσται τρόπον·
καὶ γινώσκειν ἀναγκαῖον τοὺς διδόντας καὶ μεταφέροντας
10 τίσι τίνας διδόασιν. ἔτι δὲ καὶ τὰ πάλαι λεχθέντα μᾶλλον
ἐπὶ τούτων ἀναγκαῖον συμβαίνειν, οἷον αἰκίας ἔρωτας φόνους·
οὐ γὰρ ἔτι προσαγορεύουσιν ἀδελφοὺς καὶ τέκνα καὶ πατέρας
καὶ μητέρας τοὺς φύλακας οἵ τε εἰς τοὺς ἄλλους πολίτας δοθέντες καὶ πάλιν οἱ παρὰ τοῖς φύλαξι τοὺς ἄλλους πολίτας, ὥστε εὐλαβεῖσθαι τῶν τοιούτων τι πράττειν διὰ τὴν
συγγένειαν. περὶ μὲν οὖν τῆς περὶ τὰ τέκνα καὶ τὰς
γυναῖκας κοινωνίας διωρίσθω τὸν τρόπον τοῦτον·

Ἐχόμενον δὲ τούτων ἐστὶν ἐπισκέψασθαι περὶ τῆς κτή- **5**
σεως, τίνα τρόπον δεῖ κατασκευάζεσθαι τοῖς μέλλουσι πολιτεύεσθαι τὴν ἀρίστην πολιτείαν, πότερον κοινὴν ἢ μὴ κοινὴν
2 εἶναι τὴν κτῆσιν. τοῦτο δ' ἄν τις καὶ χωρὶς σκέψαιτο ἀπὸ
τῶν περὶ τὰ τέκνα καὶ τὰς γυναῖκας νενομοθετημένων, λέγω
δὲ τὰ περὶ τὴν κτῆσιν πότερον κἂν ᾖ ἐκεῖνα χωρίς, καθ' 1263 a
ὃν νῦν τρόπον ἔχει πᾶσι, τάς τε κτήσεις κοινὰς εἶναι βέλτιον καὶ τὰς χρήσεις, οἷον τὰ μὲν γήπεδα χωρίς, τοὺς δὲ
καρποὺς εἰς τὸ κοινὸν φέροντας ἀναλίσκειν (ὅπερ ἔνια ποιεῖ
τῶν ἐθνῶν), ἢ τοὐναντίον τὴν μὲν γῆν κοινὴν εἶναι καὶ γεωργεῖν κοινῇ, τοὺς δὲ καρποὺς διαιρεῖσθαι πρὸς τὰς ἰδίας χρήσεις (λέγονται δέ τινες καὶ τοῦτον τὸν τρόπον κοινωνεῖν τῶν
3 βαρβάρων), ἢ καὶ τὰ γήπεδα καὶ τοὺς καρποὺς κοινούς. ἑτέρων μὲν οὖν ὄντων τῶν γεωργούντων ἄλλος ἂν εἴη τρόπος καὶ
ῥᾴων, αὐτῶν δ' αὑτοῖς διαπονούντων τὰ περὶ τὰς κτήσεις
πλείους ἂν παρέχοι δυσκολίας· καὶ γὰρ ἐν ταῖς ἀπολαύσεσι
καὶ ἐν τοῖς ἔργοις μὴ γινομένων ἴσων ἀναγκαῖον ἐγκλήματα γίνεσθαι πρὸς τοὺς ἀπολαύοντας μὲν [ἢ λαμβάνοντας]
πολλά, ὀλίγα δὲ πονοῦντας, τοῖς ἐλάττω μὲν λαμβάνουσι,

πλείω δὲ πονοῦσιν. ὅλως δὲ τὸ συζῆν καὶ κοινωνεῖν τῶν ἀν- 4 θρωπικῶν πάντων χαλεπόν, καὶ μάλιστα τῶν τοιούτων. δηλοῦσι δ' αἱ τῶν συναποδήμων κοινωνίαι· σχεδὸν γὰρ οἱ πλεῖστοι διαφερόμενοι ἐκ τῶν ἐν ποσὶ καὶ ἐκ μικρῶν προσκρούοντες ἀλλήλοις. ἔτι δὲ τῶν θεραπόντων τούτοις μάλιστα προσκρούομεν, οἷς πλεῖστα προσχρώμεθα πρὸς τὰς διακονίας τὰς ἐγκυκλίους. τὸ μὲν οὖν κοινὰς εἶναι τὰς κτήσεις ταύτας 5 τε καὶ ἄλλας τοιαύτας ἔχει δυσχερείας, ὃν δὲ νῦν τρόπον ἔχει καὶ ἐπικοσμηθὲν ἤθεσι καὶ τάξει νόμων ὀρθῶν, οὐ μικρὸν ἂν διενέγκαι· ἕξει γὰρ τὸ ἐξ ἀμφοτέρων ἀγαθόν· λέγω δὲ τὸ ἐξ ἀμφοτέρων τὸ ἐκ τοῦ κοινὰς εἶναι τὰς κτήσεις καὶ τὸ ἐκ τοῦ ἰδίας. δεῖ γὰρ πῶς μὲν εἶναι κοινάς, ὅλως δ' ἰδίας· αἱ μὲν γὰρ ἐπιμέλειαι διῃρημέναι τὰ ἐγκλήματα 6 πρὸς ἀλλήλους οὐ ποιήσουσιν, μᾶλλον δὲ ἐπιδώσουσιν ὡς πρὸς ἴδιον ἑκάστου προσεδρεύοντος· δι' ἀρετὴν δ' ἔσται πρὸς τὸ χρῆσθαι κατὰ τὴν παροιμίαν κοινὰ τὰ φίλων. ἔστι δὲ καὶ νῦν τὸν τρόπον τοῦτον ἐν ἐνίαις πόλεσιν οὕτως ὑπογεγραμμένον ὡς οὐκ ὂν ἀδύνατον, καὶ μάλιστα ἐν ταῖς καλῶς οἰκουμέναις τὰ μὲν ἔστι τὰ δὲ γένοιτ' ἄν· ἰδίαν γὰρ ἕκαστος τὴν κτῆσιν 7 ἔχων τὰ μὲν χρήσιμα ποιεῖ τοῖς φίλοις, τοῖς δὲ χρῆται κοινοῖς, οἷον καὶ ἐν Λακεδαίμονι τοῖς τε δούλοις χρῶνται τοῖς ἀλλήλων ὡς εἰπεῖν ἰδίοις, ἔτι δ' ἵπποις καὶ κυσίν, κἂν δεηθῶσιν ἐφοδίων ἐν τοῖς ἀγροῖς κατὰ τὴν χώραν. φανερὸν 8 τοίνυν ὅτι βέλτιον εἶναι μὲν ἰδίας τὰς κτήσεις, τῇ δὲ χρήσει ποιεῖν κοινάς· ὅπως δὲ γίνωνται τοιοῦτοι, τοῦ νομοθέτου τοῦτ' ἔργον ἴδιόν ἐστιν. ἔτι δὲ καὶ πρὸς ἡδονὴν ἀμύθητον ὅσον διαφέρει τὸ νομίζειν ἴδιόν τι· μὴ γὰρ οὐ μάτην τὴν πρὸς
1263 b αὑτὸν αὐτὸς ἔχει φιλίαν ἕκαστος, ἀλλ' ἔστι τοῦτο φυσικόν. τὸ δὲ φίλαυτον εἶναι ψέγεται δικαίως· οὐκ ἔστι δὲ τοῦτο τὸ 9 φιλεῖν ἑαυτόν, ἀλλὰ τὸ μᾶλλον ἢ δεῖ φιλεῖν, καθάπερ καὶ τὸν φιλοχρήματον, ἐπεὶ φιλοῦσί γε πάντες ὡς εἰπεῖν ἕκαστον τῶν τοιούτων. ἀλλὰ μὴν καὶ τὸ χαρίσασθαι καὶ βοηθῆσαι φίλοις ἢ ξένοις ἢ ἑταίροις ἥδιστον· ὃ γίνεται τῆς

10 κτήσεως ἰδίας οὔσης. ταῦτά τε δὴ οὐ συμβαίνει τοῖς λίαν ἓν
ποιοῦσι τὴν πόλιν, καὶ πρὸς τούτοις ἀναιροῦσιν ἔργα δυοῖν
ἀρεταῖν φανερῶς, σωφροσύνης μὲν τὸ περὶ τὰς γυναῖκας
(ἔργον γὰρ καλὸν ἀλλοτρίας οὔσης ἀπέχεσθαι διὰ σωφροσύνην), ἐλευθεριότητος δὲ τὸ περὶ τὰς κτήσεις· οὔτε γὰρ ἔσται
φανερὸς ἐλευθέριος ὤν, οὔτε πράξει πρᾶξιν ἐλευθέριον οὐδε-
μίαν· ἐν τῇ γὰρ χρήσει τῶν κτημάτων τὸ τῆς ἐλευθεριότητος ἔργον ἐστίν.
11 Εὐπρόσωπος μὲν οὖν ἡ τοιαύτη νομοθεσία καὶ φιλάνθρωπος ἂν εἶναι δόξειεν· ὁ γὰρ ἀκροώμενος ἄσμενος ἀποδέχεται, νομίζων ἔσεσθαι φιλίαν τινὰ θαυμαστὴν πᾶσι πρὸς
ἅπαντας, ἄλλως τε καὶ ὅταν κατηγορῇ τις τῶν νῦν ὑπαρχόντων ἐν ταῖς πολιτείαις κακῶν ὡς γινομένων διὰ τὸ μὴ
κοινὴν εἶναι τὴν οὐσίαν, λέγω δὲ δίκας τε πρὸς ἀλλήλους
περὶ συμβολαίων καὶ ψευδομαρτυριῶν κρίσεις καὶ πλουσίων
12 κολακείας· ὧν οὐδὲν γίνεται διὰ τὴν ἀκοινωνησίαν ἀλλὰ
διὰ τὴν μοχθηρίαν, ἐπεὶ καὶ τοὺς κοινὰ κεκτημένους καὶ κοινωνοῦντας πολλῷ διαφερομένους μᾶλλον ὁρῶμεν ἢ τοὺς χωρὶς
τὰς οὐσίας ἔχοντας· ἀλλὰ θεωροῦμεν ὀλίγους τοὺς ἐκ τῶν κοινωνιῶν διαφερομένους πρὸς πολλοὺς συμβάλλοντες τοὺς κεκτη-
13 μένους ἰδίᾳ τὰς κτήσεις. ἔτι δὲ δίκαιον μὴ μόνον λέγειν
ὅσων στερήσονται κακῶν κοινωνήσαντες, ἀλλὰ καὶ ὅσων
ἀγαθῶν· φαίνεται δ' εἶναι πάμπαν ἀδύνατος ὁ βίος. αἴτιον
δὲ τῷ Σωκράτει τῆς παρακρούσεως χρὴ νομίζειν τὴν ὑπόθε-
14 σιν οὐκ οὖσαν ὀρθήν. δεῖ μὲν γὰρ εἶναί πως μίαν καὶ τὴν
οἰκίαν καὶ τὴν πόλιν, ἀλλ' οὐ πάντως. ἔστι μὲν γὰρ ὡς οὐκ
ἔσται προϊοῦσα πόλις, ἔστι δ' ὡς ἔσται μέν, ἐγγὺς δ' οὖσα
τοῦ μὴ πόλις εἶναι χείρων πόλις, ὥσπερ κἂν εἴ τις τὴν
συμφωνίαν ποιήσειεν ὁμοφωνίαν ἢ τὸν ῥυθμὸν βάσιν μίαν.
15 ἀλλὰ δεῖ πλῆθος ὄν, ὥσπερ εἴρηται πρότερον, διὰ τὴν παιδείαν κοινὴν καὶ μίαν ποιεῖν· καὶ τόν γε μέλλοντα παιδείαν
εἰσάγειν, καὶ νομίζοντα διὰ ταύτης ἔσεσθαι τὴν πόλιν σπουδαίαν, ἄτοπον τοῖς τοιούτοις οἴεσθαι διορθοῦν, ἀλλὰ μὴ τοῖς

ἔθεσι καὶ τῇ φιλοσοφίᾳ καὶ τοῖς νόμοις, ὥσπερ τὰ περὶ
τὰς κτήσεις ἐν Λακεδαίμονι καὶ Κρήτῃ τοῖς συσσιτίοις ὁ
1264 a νομοθέτης ἐκοίνωσεν. δεῖ δὲ μηδὲ τοῦτο αὐτὸ ἀγνοεῖν, ὅτι χρὴ 16
προσέχειν τῷ πολλῷ χρόνῳ καὶ τοῖς πολλοῖς ἔτεσιν, ἐν οἷς
οὐκ ἂν ἔλαθεν εἰ ταῦτα καλῶς εἶχεν· πάντα γὰρ σχεδὸν
εὕρηται μέν, ἀλλὰ τὰ μὲν οὐ συνῆκται, τοῖς δ' οὐ χρῶνται
γινώσκοντες. μάλιστα δ' ἂν γένοιτο φανερόν, εἴ τις τοῖς ἔρ- 17
γοις ἴδοι τὴν τοιαύτην πολιτείαν κατασκευαζομένην· οὐ γὰρ
δυνήσεται μὴ μερίζων αὐτὰ καὶ χωρίζων ποιῆσαι τὴν πόλιν, τὰ μὲν εἰς συσσίτια, τὰ δὲ εἰς φρατρίας καὶ φυλάς.
ὥστε οὐδὲν ἄλλο συμβήσεται νενομοθετημένον πλὴν μὴ γεωργεῖν τοὺς φύλακας· ὅπερ καὶ νῦν Λακεδαιμόνιοι ποιεῖν ἐπιχειροῦσιν. οὐ μὴν ἀλλ' οὐδὲ ὁ τρόπος τῆς ὅλης πολιτείας τίς 18
ἔσται τοῖς κοινωνοῦσιν, οὔτ' εἴρηκεν ὁ Σωκράτης οὔτε ῥᾴδιον
εἰπεῖν. καίτοι σχεδὸν τό γε πλῆθος τῆς πόλεως τὸ τῶν ἄλλων πολιτῶν γίνεται πλῆθος, περὶ ὧν οὐδὲν διώρισται, πότερον καὶ τοῖς γεωργοῖς κοινὰς εἶναι δεῖ τὰς κτήσεις ἢ καὶ
καθ' ἕκαστον ἰδίας, ἔτι δὲ καὶ γυναῖκας καὶ παῖδας ἰδίους
ἢ κοινούς. εἰ μὲν γὰρ τὸν αὐτὸν τρόπον κοινὰ πάντα πάν- 19
των, τί διοίσουσιν οὗτοι ἐκείνων τῶν φυλάκων; ἢ τί πλεῖον
τοῖς ὑπομένουσι τὴν ἀρχὴν αὐτῶν; ἢ τί μαθόντες ὑπομενοῦσι
τὴν ἀρχήν, ἐὰν μή τι σοφίζωνται τοιοῦτον οἷον Κρῆτες;
ἐκεῖνοι γὰρ τἆλλα ταὐτὰ τοῖς δούλοις ἐφέντες μόνον ἀπειρήκασι τὰ γυμνάσια καὶ τὴν τῶν ὅπλων κτῆσιν. εἰ δέ, κα- 20
θάπερ ἐν ταῖς ἄλλαις πόλεσι, καὶ παρ' ἐκείνοις ἔσται τὰ
τοιαῦτα, τίς ὁ τρόπος ἔσται τῆς κοινωνίας; ἐν μιᾷ γὰρ πόλει δύο πόλεις ἀναγκαῖον εἶναι, καὶ ταύτας ὑπεναντίας
ἀλλήλαις· ποιεῖ γὰρ τοὺς μὲν φύλακας οἷον φρουρούς, τοὺς δὲ
γεωργοὺς καὶ τοὺς τεχνίτας καὶ τοὺς ἄλλους πολίτας. ἐγκλή- 21
ματα δὲ καὶ δίκαι, καὶ ὅσα ἄλλα ταῖς πόλεσιν ὑπάρχειν
φησὶ κακά, πάνθ' ὑπάρξει καὶ τούτοις. καίτοι λέγει ὁ Σωκράτης ὡς οὐ πολλῶν δεήσονται νομίμων διὰ τὴν παιδείαν,
οἷον ἀστυνομικῶν καὶ ἀγορανομικῶν καὶ τῶν ἄλλων τῶν

22 τοιούτων, ἀποδιδοὺς μόνον τὴν παιδείαν τοῖς φύλαξιν. ἔτι δὲ
κυρίους ποιεῖ τῶν κτημάτων τοὺς γεωργοὺς ἀποφορὰν φέρον-
τας· ἀλλὰ πολὺ μᾶλλον εἰκὸς εἶναι χαλεποὺς καὶ φρονη-
μάτων πλήρεις ἢ τὰς παρ' ἐνίοις εἱλωτείας τε καὶ πενεστείας
23 καὶ δουλείας. ἀλλὰ γὰρ εἴτ' ἀναγκαῖα ταῦθ' ὁμοίως εἴτε
μή, νῦν γε οὐδὲν διώρισται, καὶ περὶ τῶν ἐχομένων, τίς ἥ
τούτων τε πολιτεία καὶ παιδεία καὶ νόμοι τίνες. ἔστι δ' οὔτε
εὑρεῖν ῥᾴδιον, οὔτε τὸ διαφέρον μικρόν, τὸ ποιούς τινας εἶναι
24 τούτους πρὸς τὸ σώζεσθαι τὴν τῶν φυλάκων κοινωνίαν. ἀλλὰ
μὴν εἴ γε τὰς μὲν γυναῖκας ποιήσει κοινὰς τὰς δὲ κτήσεις 1264 b
ἰδίας, τίς οἰκονομήσει ὥσπερ τὰ ἐπὶ τῶν ἀγρῶν οἱ ἄνδρες
αὐτῶν, κἂν εἰ κοιναὶ αἱ κτήσεις καὶ αἱ τῶν γεωργῶν γυναῖκες; ἄτοπον δὲ καὶ τὸ ἐκ τῶν θηρίων ποιεῖσθαι τὴν πα-
ραβολήν, ὅτι δεῖ τὰ αὐτὰ ἐπιτηδεύειν τὰς γυναῖκας τοῖς
25 ἀνδράσιν, οἷς οἰκονομίας οὐδὲν μέτεστιν. ἐπισφαλὲς δὲ καὶ
τοὺς ἄρχοντας ὡς καθίστησιν ὁ Σωκράτης· ἀεὶ γὰρ ποιεῖ τοὺς
αὐτοὺς ἄρχοντας, τοῦτο δὲ στάσεως αἴτιον γίνεται καὶ παρὰ
τοῖς μηδὲν ἀξίωμα κεκτημένοις, ἤπουθεν δὴ παρά γε θυ-
26 μοειδέσι καὶ πολεμικοῖς ἀνδράσιν. ὅτι δ' ἀναγκαῖον αὐτῷ
ποιεῖν τοὺς αὐτοὺς ἄρχοντας, φανερόν· οὐ γὰρ ὁτὲ μὲν ἄλλοις
ὁτὲ δὲ ἄλλοις μέμικται ταῖς ψυχαῖς ὁ παρὰ τοῦ θεοῦ χρυ-
σός, ἀλλ' ἀεὶ τοῖς αὐτοῖς. φησὶ δὲ τοῖς μὲν εὐθὺς γινομένοις μῖξαι χρυσόν, τοῖς δ' ἄργυρον, χαλκὸν δὲ καὶ σίδηρον
27 τοῖς τεχνίταις μέλλουσιν ἔσεσθαι καὶ γεωργοῖς. ἔτι δὲ καὶ
τὴν εὐδαιμονίαν ἀφαιρούμενος τῶν φυλάκων, ὅλην φησὶ δεῖν
εὐδαίμονα ποιεῖν τὴν πόλιν τὸν νομοθέτην. ἀδύνατον δὲ
εὐδαιμονεῖν ὅλην, μὴ τῶν πλείστων ἢ μὴ πάντων μερῶν ἤ
τινῶν ἐχόντων τὴν εὐδαιμονίαν. οὐ γὰρ τῶν αὐτῶν τὸ εὐδαιμονεῖν ὧνπερ τὸ ἄρτιον· τοῦτο μὲν γὰρ ἐνδέχεται τῷ ὅλῳ
ὑπάρχειν, τῶν δὲ μερῶν μηδετέρῳ, τὸ δὲ εὐδαιμονεῖν ἀδύ-
28 νατον. ἀλλὰ μὴν εἰ οἱ φύλακες μὴ εὐδαίμονες, τίνες ἕτεροι; οὐ γὰρ δὴ οἵ γε τεχνῖται καὶ τὸ πλῆθος τὸ τῶν βαναύσων. ἡ μὲν οὖν πολιτεία περὶ ἧς ὁ Σωκράτης εἴρηκεν,

ταύτας τε τὰς ἀπορίας ἔχει καὶ τούτων οὐκ ἐλάττους
ἑτέρας·

6 Σχεδὸν δὲ παραπλησίως καὶ περὶ τοὺς νόμους ἔχει τοὺς
ὕστερον γραφέντας· διὸ καὶ περὶ τῆς ἐνταῦθα πολιτείας ἐπισκέψασθαι μικρὰ βέλτιον. καὶ γὰρ ἐν τῇ πολιτείᾳ περὶ
ὀλίγων πάμπαν διώρικεν ὁ Σωκράτης, περί τε γυναικῶν
καὶ τέκνων κοινωνίας, πῶς ἔχειν δεῖ, καὶ περὶ κτήσεως, καὶ
τῆς πολιτείας τὴν τάξιν· διαιρεῖται γὰρ εἰς δύο μέρη τὸ 2
πλῆθος τῶν οἰκούντων, τὸ μὲν εἰς τοὺς γεωργούς, τὸ δὲ εἰς τὸ
προπολεμοῦν μέρος, τρίτον δ' ἐκ τούτων τὸ βουλευόμενον καὶ
κύριον τῆς πόλεως· περὶ δὲ τῶν γεωργῶν καὶ τῶν τεχνιτῶν, 3
πότερον οὐδεμιᾶς ἢ μετέχουσί τινος ἀρχῆς, καὶ πότερον ὅπλα
δεῖ κεκτῆσθαι καὶ τούτους καὶ συμπολεμεῖν ἢ μή, περὶ τούτων οὐδὲν διώρικεν ὁ Σωκράτης, ἀλλὰ τὰς μὲν γυναῖκας
οἴεται δεῖν συμπολεμεῖν καὶ παιδείας μετέχειν τῆς αὐτῆς
τοῖς φύλαξιν, τὰ δ' ἄλλα τοῖς ἔξωθεν λόγοις πεπλήρωκε
τὸν λόγον καὶ περὶ τῆς παιδείας, ποίαν τινὰ δεῖ γίνεσθαι
1265 a τῶν φυλάκων. τῶν δὲ νόμων τὸ μὲν πλεῖστον μέρος νόμοι 4
τυγχάνουσιν ὄντες, ὀλίγα δὲ περὶ τῆς πολιτείας εἴρηκεν, καὶ
ταύτην βουλόμενος κοινοτέραν ποιεῖν ταῖς πόλεσι, κατὰ μικρὸν περιάγει πάλιν εἰς τὴν ἑτέραν πολιτείαν· ἔξω γὰρ 5
τῆς τῶν γυναικῶν κοινωνίας καὶ τῆς κτήσεως, τὰ ἄλλα
ταὐτὰ ἀποδίδωσιν ἀμφοτέραις ταῖς πολιτείαις· καὶ γὰρ
παιδείαν τὴν αὐτήν, καὶ τὸ τῶν ἔργων τῶν ἀναγκαίων ἀπε-
χομένους ζῆν, καὶ περὶ συσσιτίων ὡσαύτως· πλὴν ἐν ταύτῃ
φησὶ δεῖν εἶναι συσσίτια καὶ γυναικῶν, καὶ τὴν μὲν χιλίων
τῶν ὅπλα κεκτημένων, ταύτην δὲ πεντακισχιλίων. τὸ μὲν 6
οὖν περιττὸν ἔχουσι πάντες οἱ τοῦ Σωκράτους λόγοι καὶ τὸ
κομψὸν καὶ τὸ καινοτόμον καὶ τὸ ζητητικόν, καλῶς δὲ
πάντα ἴσως χαλεπόν, ἐπεὶ καὶ τὸ νῦν εἰρημένον πλῆθος δεῖ
μὴ λανθάνειν ὅτι χώρας δεήσει τοῖς τοσούτοις Βαβυλωνίας
ἤ τινος ἄλλης ἀπεράντου τὸ πλῆθος, ἐξ ἧς ἀργοὶ πεντακισ-
χίλιοι θρέψονται, καὶ περὶ τούτους γυναικῶν καὶ θεραπόν-

7 των ἕτερος ὄχλος πολλαπλάσιος. δεῖ μὲν οὖν ὑποτίθεσθαι
κατ' εὐχήν, μηδὲν μέντοι ἀδύνατον. λέγεται δ' ὡς δεῖ τὸν
νομοθέτην πρὸς δύο βλέποντα τιθέναι τοὺς νόμους, πρός τε
τὴν χώραν καὶ τοὺς ἀνθρώπους. ἔτι δὲ καλῶς ἔχει προσθεῖ-
ναι καὶ πρὸς τοὺς γειτνιῶντας τόπους, εἰ δεῖ τὴν πόλιν ζῆν
βίον πολιτικόν· οὐ γὰρ μόνον ἀναγκαῖόν ἐστιν αὐτὴν τοιούτοις
χρῆσθαι πρὸς τὸν πόλεμον ὅπλοις ἃ χρήσιμα κατὰ τὴν
8 οἰκείαν χώραν ἐστίν, ἀλλὰ καὶ πρὸς τοὺς ἔξω τόπους. εἰ δέ
τις μὴ τοιοῦτον ἀποδέχεται βίον, μήτε τὸν ἴδιον μήτε τὸν
κοινὸν τῆς πόλεως, ὅμως οὐδὲν ἧττον δεῖ φοβεροὺς εἶναι τοῖς
πολεμίοις, μὴ μόνον ἐλθοῦσιν εἰς τὴν χώραν ἀλλὰ καὶ
ἀπελθοῦσιν. καὶ τὸ πλῆθος δὲ τῆς κτήσεως ὁρᾶν δεῖ, μήποτε
βέλτιον ἑτέρως διορίσαι τῷ σαφῶς μᾶλλον, τοσαύτην γὰρ
εἶναί φησι δεῖν ὥστε ζῆν σωφρόνως, ὥσπερ ἂν εἴ τις εἶπεν
9 ὥστε ζῆν εὖ (τοῦτο γάρ ἐστι καθόλου μᾶλλον· ἔτι δ' ἔστι σωφρόνως μὲν ταλαιπώρως δὲ ζῆν). ἀλλὰ βελτίων ὅρος τὸ
σωφρόνως καὶ ἐλευθερίως (χωρὶς γὰρ ἑκάτερον τὸ μὲν τῷ
τρυφᾶν ἀκολουθήσει, τὸ δὲ τῷ ἐπιπόνως), ἐπεὶ μόναι γ'
εἰσὶν ἕξεις αἱρεταὶ περὶ τὴν τῆς οὐσίας χρῆσιν αὗται, οἷον
οὐσίᾳ πράως ἢ ἀνδρείως χρῆσθαι οὐκ ἔστιν, σωφρόνως δὲ καὶ
ἐλευθερίως ἔστιν, ὥστε καὶ τὰς χρήσεις ἀναγκαῖον περὶ αὐτὴν
10 εἶναι ταύτας. ἄτοπον δὲ καὶ τὸ τὰς κτήσεις ἰσάζοντα τὸ
περὶ τὸ πλῆθος τῶν πολιτῶν μὴ κατασκευάζειν, ἀλλ' ἀφεῖναι τὴν τεκνοποιίαν ἀόριστον ὡς ἱκανῶς ἂν ὁμαλισθησομένην
εἰς τὸ αὐτὸ πλῆθος διὰ τὰς ἀτεκνίας ὁσωνοῦν γεννωμένων,
11 ὅτι δοκεῖ τοῦτο καὶ νῦν συμβαίνειν περὶ τὰς πόλεις. δεῖ δὲ
τοῦτ' οὐχ ὁμοίως ἀκριβῶς ἔχειν περὶ τὰς πόλεις τότε καὶ νῦν·
νῦν μὲν γὰρ οὐδεὶς ἀπορεῖ διὰ τὸ μερίζεσθαι τὰς οὐσίας εἰς
ὁποσονοῦν πλῆθος, τότε δὲ ἀδιαιρέτων οὐσῶν ἀνάγκη τοὺς παράζυγας μηδὲν ἔχειν, ἐάν τε ἐλάττους ὦσι τὸ πλῆθος ἐάν τε
12 πλείους. μᾶλλον δὲ δεῖν ὑπολάβοι τις ἂν ὡρίσθαι τῆς οὐσίας
τὴν τεκνοποιίαν, ὥστε ἀριθμοῦ τινὸς μὴ πλείονα γεννᾶν· τοῦτο
δὲ τιθέναι τὸ πλῆθος ἀποβλέποντα πρὸς τὰς τύχας, ἂν

συμβαίνῃ τελευτᾶν τινὰς τῶν γεννηθέντων, καὶ πρὸς τὴν
τῶν ἄλλων ἀτεκνίαν. τὸ δ' ἀφεῖσθαι, καθάπερ ἐν ταῖς 13
πλείσταις πόλεσι, πενίας ἀναγκαῖον αἴτιον γίνεσθαι τοῖς πολίταις, ἡ δὲ πενία στάσιν ἐμποιεῖ καὶ κακουργίαν. Φείδων
μὲν οὖν ὁ Κορίνθιος, ὢν νομοθέτης τῶν ἀρχαιοτάτων, τοὺς
οἴκους ἴσους ᾠήθη δεῖν διαμένειν καὶ τὸ πλῆθος τῶν πολιτῶν,
καὶ εἰ τὸ πρῶτον τοὺς κλήρους ἀνίσους εἶχον πάντες κατὰ μέ-
γεθος· ἐν δὲ τοῖς νόμοις τούτοις τοὐναντίον ἐστίν. ἀλλὰ περὶ 14
μὲν τούτων πῶς οἰόμεθα βέλτιον ἂν ἔχειν, λεκτέον ὕστερον·
ἐλλέλειπται δὲ τοῖς νόμοις τούτοις καὶ τὰ περὶ τοὺς ἄρχοντας, ὅπως ἔσονται διαφέροντες τῶν ἀρχομένων· φησὶ γὰρ
δεῖν, ὥσπερ ἐξ ἑτέρου τὸ στημόνιον ἐρίου γίνεται τῆς κρόκης,
οὕτω καὶ τοὺς ἄρχοντας ἔχειν δεῖν πρὸς τοὺς ἀρχομένους. ἐπεὶ 15
δὲ τὴν πᾶσαν οὐσίαν ἐφίησι γίνεσθαι μείζονα μέχρι πενταπλασίας, διὰ τί τοῦτ' οὐκ ἂν εἴη ἐπὶ τῆς γῆς μέχρι τινός;
καὶ τὴν τῶν οἰκοπέδων δὲ διαίρεσιν δεῖ σκοπεῖν, μή ποτ' οὐ
συμφέρει πρὸς οἰκονομίαν· δύο γὰρ οἰκόπεδα ἑκάστῳ ἔνειμε
διελὼν χωρίς, χαλεπὸν δὲ οἰκίας δύο οἰκεῖν. ἡ δὲ σύνταξις 16
ὅλη βούλεται μὲν εἶναι μήτε δημοκρατία μήτε ὀλιγαρχία,
μέση δὲ τούτων, ἣν καλοῦσι πολιτείαν· ἐκ γὰρ τῶν ὁπλι-
τευόντων ἐστίν. εἰ μὲν οὖν ὡς κοινοτάτην ταύτην κατασκευά-
ζει ταῖς πόλεσι τῶν ἄλλων πολιτείαν, καλῶς εἴρηκεν ἴσως,
εἰ δ' ὡς ἀρίστην μετὰ τὴν πρώτην πολιτείαν, οὐ καλῶς· τάχα
γὰρ τὴν τῶν Λακώνων ἄν τις ἐπαινέσειε μᾶλλον, ἢ κἂν
ἄλλην τινὰ ἀριστοκρατικωτέραν. ἔνιοι μὲν οὖν λέγουσιν ὡς δεῖ 17
τὴν ἀρίστην πολιτείαν ἐξ ἁπασῶν εἶναι τῶν πολιτειῶν μεμι-
γμένην, διὸ καὶ τὴν τῶν Λακεδαιμονίων ἐπαινοῦσιν· εἶναι
γὰρ αὐτὴν οἱ μὲν ἐξ ὀλιγαρχίας καὶ μοναρχίας καὶ δημοκρατίας φασίν, λέγοντες τὴν μὲν βασιλείαν μοναρχίαν, τὴν
δὲ τῶν γερόντων ἀρχὴν ὀλιγαρχίαν, δημοκρατεῖσθαι δὲ
κατὰ τὴν τῶν ἐφόρων ἀρχὴν διὰ τὸ ἐκ τοῦ δήμου εἶναι τοὺς
ἐφόρους· οἱ δὲ τὴν μὲν ἐφορείαν εἶναι τυραννίδα, δημοκρατεῖσθαι δὲ κατά τε τὰ συσσίτια καὶ τὸν ἄλλον βίον τὸν

18 καθ' ἡμέραν· ἐν δὲ τοῖς νόμοις εἴρηται τούτοις ὡς δέον συγ- 1266 a
κεῖσθαι τὴν ἀρίστην πολιτείαν ἐκ δημοκρατίας καὶ τυραννί-
δος, ἃς ἢ τὸ παράπαν οὐκ ἄν τις θείη πολιτείας ἢ χειρίστας
πασῶν. βέλτιον οὖν λέγουσιν οἱ πλείους μιγνύντες· ἡ γὰρ ἐκ
πλειόνων συγκειμένη πολιτεία βελτίων. ἔπειτα οὐδ' ἔχουσα
φαίνεται μοναρχικὸν οὐδέν, ἀλλ' ὀλιγαρχικὰ καὶ δημοκρα-
τικά· μᾶλλον δ' ἐγκλίνειν βούλεται πρὸς τὴν ὀλιγαρχίαν.
19 δῆλον δὲ ἐκ τῆς τῶν ἀρχόντων καταστάσεως· τὸ μὲν γὰρ
ἐξ αἱρετῶν κληρωτοὺς κοινὸν ἀμφοῖν, τὸ δὲ τοῖς μὲν εὐπορω-
τέροις ἐπάναγκες ἐκκλησιάζειν εἶναι καὶ φέρειν ἄρχοντας
ἤ τι ποιεῖν ἄλλο τῶν πολιτικῶν, τοὺς δ' ἀφεῖσθαι, τοῦτο δ'
ὀλιγαρχικόν, καὶ τὸ πειρᾶσθαι πλείους ἐκ τῶν εὐπόρων εἶναι
τοὺς ἄρχοντας, καὶ τὰς μεγίστας ἐκ τῶν μεγίστων τιμημά-
20 των. ὀλιγαρχικὴν δὲ ποιεῖ καὶ τὴν τῆς βουλῆς αἵρεσιν· αἱροῦνται μὲν γὰρ πάντες ἐπάναγκες, ἀλλ' ἐκ τοῦ πρώτου τιμήματος, εἶτα πάλιν ἴσους ἐκ τοῦ δευτέρου, εἶτ' ἐκ τῶν τρίτων·
πλὴν οὐ πᾶσιν ἐπάναγκες ἦν τοῖς ἐκ τῶν τρίτων ἢ τετάρτων,
ἐκ δὲ [τοῦ τετάρτου] τῶν τετάρτων μόνοις ἐπάναγκες τοῖς πρώ-
21 τοις καὶ τοῖς δευτέροις. εἶτ' ἐκ τούτων ἴσον ἀφ' ἑκάστου τιμήματος ἀποδεῖξαί φησι δεῖν ἀριθμόν. ἔσονται δὴ πλείους οἱ
ἐκ τῶν μεγίστων τιμημάτων καὶ βελτίους διὰ τὸ ἐνίους μὴ
22 αἱρεῖσθαι τῶν δημοτικῶν διὰ τὸ μὴ ἐπάναγκες. ὡς μὲν οὖν
οὐκ ἐκ δημοκρατίας καὶ μοναρχίας δεῖ συνιστάναι τὴν τοιαύτην πολιτείαν, ἐκ τούτων φανερὸν καὶ τῶν ὕστερον ῥηθησομέ-
νων, ὅταν ἐπιβάλλῃ περὶ τῆς τοιαύτης πολιτείας ἡ σκέψις·
ἔχει δὲ καὶ περὶ τὴν αἵρεσιν τῶν ἀρχόντων τὸ ἐξ αἱρετῶν
αἱρετοὺς ἐπικίνδυνον· εἰ γάρ τινες συστῆναι θέλουσι καὶ μέτριοι
τὸ πλῆθος, αἰεὶ κατὰ τὴν τούτων αἱρεθήσονται βούλησιν. τὰ
μὲν οὖν περὶ τὴν πολιτείαν τὴν ἐν τοῖς νόμοις τοῦτον ἔχει
τὸν τρόπον·

Εἰσὶ δέ τινες πολιτεῖαι καὶ ἄλλαι, αἱ μὲν ἰδιωτῶν αἱ 7
δὲ φιλοσόφων καὶ πολιτικῶν, πᾶσαι δὲ τῶν καθεστηκυιῶν
καὶ καθ' ἃς πολιτεύονται νῦν ἐγγύτερόν εἰσι τούτων ἀμφο-

τέρων· οὐδεὶς γὰρ οὔτε τὴν περὶ τὰ τέκνα κοινότητα καὶ τὰς
γυναῖκας ἄλλος κεκαινοτόμηκεν, οὔτε περὶ τὰ συσσίτια τῶν
γυναικῶν, ἀλλ' ἀπὸ τῶν ἀναγκαίων ἄρχονται μᾶλλον.
δοκεῖ γάρ τισι τὸ περὶ τὰς οὐσίας εἶναι μέγιστον τετάχθαι 2
καλῶς· περὶ γὰρ τούτων ποιεῖσθαί φασι τὰς στάσεις πάντας. διὸ Φαλέας ὁ Χαλκηδόνιος τοῦτ' εἰσήνεγκε πρῶτος·
φησὶ γὰρ δεῖν ἴσας εἶναι τὰς κτήσεις τῶν πολιτῶν. τοῦτο 3
1266 b δὲ κατοικιζομέναις μὲν εὐθὺς οὐ χαλεπὸν ᾤετο ποιεῖν, τὰς
δ' ἤδη κατοικουμένας ἐργωδέστερον μέν, ὅμως δὲ τάχιστ' ἂν
ὁμαλισθῆναι τῷ τὰς προῖκας τοὺς μὲν πλουσίους διδόναι μὲν
λαμβάνειν δὲ μή, τοὺς δὲ πένητας μὴ διδόναι μὲν λαμβάνειν δέ. Πλάτων δὲ τοὺς νόμους γράφων μέχρι μέν τινος 4
ᾤετο δεῖν ἐᾶν, πλεῖον δὲ τοῦ πενταπλασίαν εἶναι τῆς ἐλαχίστης μηδενὶ τῶν πολιτῶν ἐξουσίαν εἶναι κτήσασθαι, καθάπερ εἴρηται καὶ πρότερον. δεῖ δὲ μηδὲ τοῦτο λανθάνειν τοὺς 5
οὕτω νομοθετοῦντας, ὃ λανθάνει νῦν, ὅτι τὸ τῆς οὐσίας τάττον-
τας πλῆθος προσήκει καὶ τῶν τέκνων τὸ πλῆθος τάττειν·
ἐὰν γὰρ ὑπεραίρῃ τῆς οὐσίας τὸ μέγεθος ὁ τῶν τέκνων ἀριθ-
μός, ἀνάγκη τόν γε νόμον λύεσθαι, καὶ χωρὶς τῆς λύσεως
φαῦλον τὸ πολλοὺς ἐκ πλουσίων γίνεσθαι πένητας· ἔργον
γὰρ μὴ νεωτεροποιοὺς εἶναι τοὺς τοιούτους. διότι μὲν οὖν ἔχει 6
τινὰ δύναμιν εἰς τὴν πολιτικὴν κοινωνίαν ἡ τῆς οὐσίας ὁμα-
λότης, καὶ τῶν πάλαι τινὲς φαίνονται διεγνωκότες, οἷον καὶ
Σόλων ἐνομοθέτησεν, καὶ παρ' ἄλλοις ἐστὶ νόμος ὃς κωλύει
κτᾶσθαι γῆν ὁπόσην ἂν βούληταί τις· ὁμοίως δὲ καὶ τὴν
οὐσίαν πωλεῖν οἱ νόμοι κωλύουσιν, ὥσπερ ἐν Λοκροῖς νόμος
ἐστὶ μὴ πωλεῖν, ἐὰν μὴ φανερὰν ἀτυχίαν δείξῃ συμβεβη-
κυῖαν· ἔτι δὲ τοὺς παλαιοὺς κλήρους διασώζειν· τοῦτο δὲ λυθὲν 7
καὶ περὶ Λευκάδα δημοτικὴν ἐποίησε λίαν τὴν πολιτείαν
αὐτῶν, οὐ γὰρ ἔτι συνέβαινεν ἀπὸ τῶν ὡρισμένων τιμημάτων εἰς τὰς ἀρχὰς βαδίζειν. ἀλλ' ἔστι τὴν ἰσότητα μὲν
ὑπάρχειν τῆς οὐσίας, ταύτην δὲ ἢ λίαν εἶναι πολλήν, ὥστε
τρυφᾶν, ἢ λίαν ὀλίγην, ὥστε ζῆν γλίσχρως. δῆλον οὖν ὡς

οὐχ ἱκανὸν τὸ τὰς οὐσίας ἴσας ποιῆσαι τὸν νομοθέτην, ἀλλὰ
8 τοῦ μέσου στοχαστέον. ἔτι δ' εἴ τις καὶ τὴν μετρίαν τάξειεν οὐσίαν πᾶσιν, οὐδὲν ὄφελος· μᾶλλον γὰρ δεῖ τὰς ἐπιθυμίας ὁμαλίζειν ἢ τὰς οὐσίας, τοῦτο δ' οὐκ ἔστι μὴ παιδευομένοις ἱκανῶς ὑπὸ τῶν νόμων. ἀλλ' ἴσως ἂν εἴπειεν ὁ Φαλέας ὅτι ταῦτα τυγχάνει λέγων αὐτός· οἴεται γὰρ δυοῖν τούτοιν ἰσότητα δεῖν ὑπάρχειν ταῖς πόλεσιν, κτήσεως καὶ παιδείας.
9 ἀλλὰ τήν τε παιδείαν ἥτις ἔσται δεῖ λέγειν, καὶ τὸ μίαν εἶναι καὶ τὴν αὐτὴν οὐδὲν ὄφελος· ἔστι γὰρ τὴν αὐτὴν μὲν εἶναι καὶ μίαν, ἀλλὰ ταύτην εἶναι τοιαύτην ἐξ ἧς ἔσονται προαιρετικοὶ τοῦ πλεονεκτεῖν ἢ χρημάτων ἢ τιμῆς ἢ συναμ-
10 φοτέρων. ἔτι στασιάζουσιν οὐ μόνον διὰ τὴν ἀνισότητα τῆς κτήσεως, ἀλλὰ καὶ διὰ τὴν τῶν τιμῶν· τοὐναντίον δὲ περὶ ἑκάτερον· οἱ μὲν γὰρ πολλοὶ διὰ τὸ περὶ τὰς κτήσεις ἄνισον, οἱ δὲ χαρίεντες περὶ τῶν τιμῶν, ἐὰν ἴσαι· ὅθεν καὶ "ἐν 1267 a
11 δὲ ἰῇ τιμῇ ἠμὲν κακὸς ἠδὲ καὶ ἐσθλός." οὐ μόνον δ' οἱ ἄνθρωποι διὰ τἀναγκαῖα ἀδικοῦσιν, ὧν ἄκος εἶναι νομίζει τὴν ἰσότητα τῆς οὐσίας, ὥστε μὴ λωποδυτεῖν διὰ τὸ ῥιγοῦν ἢ πεινῆν, ἀλλὰ καὶ ὅπως χαίρωσι καὶ μὴ ἐπιθυμῶσιν· ἐὰν γὰρ μείζω ἔχωσιν ἐπιθυμίαν τῶν ἀναγκαίων, διὰ τὴν
12 ταύτης ἰατρείαν ἀδικήσουσιν· οὐ τοίνυν διὰ ταύτην μόνον, ἀλλὰ καὶ ἂν ἐπιθυμοῖεν, ἵνα χαίρωσι ταῖς ἄνευ λυπῶν ἡδοναῖς. τί οὖν ἄκος τῶν τριῶν τούτων; τοῖς μὲν οὐσία βραχεῖα καὶ ἐργασία, τοῖς δὲ σωφροσύνη· τρίτον δ', εἴ τινες βούλοιντο δι' αὑτῶν χαίρειν, οὐκ ἂν ἐπιζητοῖεν εἰ μὴ παρὰ
13 φιλοσοφίας ἄκος, αἱ γὰρ ἄλλαι ἀνθρώπων δέονται· ἐπεὶ ἀδικοῦσί γε τὰ μέγιστα διὰ τὰς ὑπερβολάς, ἀλλ' οὐ διὰ τὰ ἀναγκαῖα, οἷον τυραννοῦσιν οὐχ ἵνα μὴ ῥιγῶσιν. διὸ καὶ αἱ τιμαὶ μεγάλαι, ἂν ἀποκτείνῃ τις οὐ κλέπτην ἀλλὰ τύραννον. ὥστε πρὸς τὰς μικρὰς ἀδικίας βοηθητικὸς μόνον
14 ὁ τρόπος τῆς Φαλέου πολιτείας. ἔτι τὰ πολλὰ βούλεται κατασκευάζειν ἐξ ὧν τὰ πρὸς αὑτοὺς πολιτεύσονται καλῶς, δεῖ δὲ καὶ πρὸς τοὺς γειτνιῶντας καὶ τοὺς ἔξωθεν πάντας.

ἀναγκαῖον ἄρα τὴν πολιτείαν συντετάχθαι πρὸς τὴν πολεμικὴν ἰσχύν, περὶ ἧς ἐκεῖνος οὐδὲν εἴρηκεν. ὁμοίως δὲ καὶ 15
περὶ τῆς κτήσεως· δεῖ γὰρ οὐ μόνον πρὸς τὰς πολιτικὰς
χρήσεις ἱκανὴν ὑπάρχειν, ἀλλὰ καὶ πρὸς τοὺς ἔξωθεν κιν-
δύνους. διόπερ οὔτε τοσοῦτον δεῖ πλῆθος ὑπάρχειν ὧν οἱ
πλησίον καὶ κρείττους ἐπιθυμήσουσιν, οἱ δὲ ἔχοντες ἀμύνειν
οὐ δυνήσονται τοὺς ἐπιόντας, οὔθ' οὕτως ὀλίγην ὥστε μὴ δύνασθαι πόλεμον ὑπενεγκεῖν μηδὲ τῶν ἴσων καὶ τῶν ὁμοίων.
ἐκεῖνος μὲν οὖν οὐδὲν διώρικεν, δεῖ δὲ τοῦτο μὴ λανθάνειν, ὅτι 16
συμφέρει πλῆθος οὐσίας. ἴσως οὖν ἄριστος ὅρος τὸ μὴ λυσι-
τελεῖν τοῖς κρείττοσι διὰ τὴν ὑπερβολὴν πολεμεῖν, ἀλλ'
οὕτως ὡς ἂν καὶ μὴ ἐχόντων τοσαύτην οὐσίαν. οἷον Εὔβου- 17
λος Αὐτοφραδάτου μέλλοντος Ἀταρνέα πολιορκεῖν ἐκέλευσεν αὐτόν, σκεψάμενον ἐν πόσῳ χρόνῳ λήψεται τὸ χωρίον,
λογίσασθαι τοῦ χρόνου τούτου τὴν δαπάνην· ἐθέλειν γὰρ
ἔλαττον τούτου λαβὼν ἐκλιπεῖν ἤδη τὸν Ἀταρνέα· ταῦτα δ'
εἰπὼν ἐποίησε τὸν Αὐτοφραδάτην σύννουν γενόμενον παύσασ-
θαι τῆς πολιορκίας. ἔστι μὲν οὖν τι τῶν συμφερόντων τὸ 18
τὰς οὐσίας εἶναι ἴσας τοῖς πολίταις πρὸς τὸ μὴ στασιάζειν
πρὸς ἀλλήλους, οὐ μὴν μέγα οὐδὲν ὡς εἰπεῖν. καὶ γὰρ ἂν οἱ
χαρίεντες ἀγανακτοῖεν ἂν ὡς οὐκ ἴσων ὄντες ἄξιοι, διὸ καὶ
φαίνονται πολλάκις ἐπιτιθέμενοι καὶ στασιάζοντες· ἔτι δ' 19
1267 b ἡ πονηρία τῶν ἀνθρώπων ἄπληστον, καὶ τὸ πρῶτον μὲν ἱκανὸν διωβολία μόνον, ὅταν δ' ἤδη τοῦτ' ᾖ πάτριον, ἀεὶ δέονται τοῦ πλείονος, ἕως εἰς ἄπειρον ἔλθωσιν· ἄπειρος γὰρ ἡ
τῆς ἐπιθυμίας φύσις, ἧς πρὸς τὴν ἀναπλήρωσιν οἱ πολλοὶ
ζῶσιν. τῶν οὖν τοιούτων ἀρχή, μᾶλλον τοῦ τὰς οὐσίας ὁμα- 20
λίζειν, τὸ τοὺς μὲν ἐπιεικεῖς τῇ φύσει τοιούτους παρασκευά-
ζειν ὥστε μὴ βούλεσθαι πλεονεκτεῖν, τοὺς δὲ φαύλους ὥστε μὴ
δύνασθαι· τοῦτο δ' ἐστίν, ἂν ἥττους τε ὦσι καὶ μὴ ἀδικῶνται. οὐ καλῶς δὲ οὐδὲ τὴν ἰσότητα τῆς οὐσίας εἴρηκεν· περὶ 21
γὰρ τὴν τῆς γῆς κτῆσιν ἰσάζει μόνον, ἔστι δὲ καὶ δούλων
καὶ βοσκημάτων πλοῦτος καὶ νομίσματος, καὶ κατασκευὴ

πολλὴ τῶν καλουμένων ἐπίπλων. ἢ πάντων οὖν τούτων ἰσό-
12 τητα ζητητέον ἢ τάξιν τινὰ μετρίαν, ἢ πάντα ἐατέον. φαίνεται δ' ἐκ τῆς νομοθεσίας κατασκευάζων τὴν πόλιν μι-
κράν, εἴ γ' οἱ τεχνῖται πάντες δημόσιοι ἔσονται καὶ μὴ
13 πλήρωμά τι παρέξονται τῆς πόλεως. ἀλλ' εἴπερ δεῖ δη-
μοσίους εἶναι τοὺς τὰ κοινὰ ἐργαζομένους, δεῖ καθάπερ ἐν
Ἐπιδάμνῳ τε, καὶ Διόφαντός ποτε κατεσκεύαζεν Ἀθήνησι, τοῦτον ἔχειν τὸν τρόπον. περὶ μὲν οὖν τῆς Φαλέου
πολιτείας σχεδὸν ἐκ τούτων ἄν τις θεωρήσειεν, εἴ τι τυγχάνει
καλῶς εἰρηκὼς ἢ μὴ καλῶς·

Ἱππόδαμος δὲ Εὐρυφῶντος Μιλήσιος, ὃς καὶ τὴν τῶν **8**
πόλεων διαίρεσιν εὗρε καὶ τὸν Πειραιᾶ κατέτεμεν, γενόμενος
καὶ περὶ τὸν ἄλλον βίον περιττότερος διὰ φιλοτιμίαν οὕτως
ὥστε δοκεῖν ἐνίοις ζῆν περιεργότερον τριχῶν τε πλήθει καὶ
κόσμῳ πολυτελεῖ, ἔτι δὲ ἐσθῆτος εὐτελοῦς μὲν ἀλεεινῆς δὲ
οὐκ ἐν τῷ χειμῶνι μόνον ἀλλὰ καὶ περὶ τοὺς θερινοὺς χρόνους, λόγιος δὲ καὶ περὶ τὴν ὅλην φύσιν εἶναι βουλόμενος,
πρῶτος τῶν μὴ πολιτευομένων ἐνεχείρησέ τι περὶ πολιτείας
2 εἰπεῖν τῆς ἀρίστης. κατεσκεύαζε δὲ τὴν πόλιν τῷ πλήθει
μὲν μυρίανδρον, εἰς τρία δὲ μέρη διῃρημένην· ἐποίει γὰρ
ἓν μὲν μέρος τεχνίτας, ἓν δὲ γεωργούς, τρίτον δὲ τὸ προ-
3 πολεμοῦν καὶ τὰ ὅπλα ἔχον. διῄρει δ' εἰς τρία μέρη τὴν
χώραν, τὴν μὲν ἱεράν, τὴν δὲ δημοσίαν, τὴν δ' ἰδίαν· ὅθεν
μὲν τὰ νομιζόμενα ποιήσουσι πρὸς τοὺς θεούς, ἱεράν, ἀφ' ὧν
δ' οἱ προπολεμοῦντες βιώσονται, κοινήν, τὴν δὲ τῶν γεωργῶν
4 ἰδίαν. ᾤετο δ' εἴδη καὶ τῶν νόμων εἶναι τρία μόνον· περὶ
ὧν γὰρ αἱ δίκαι γίνονται, τρία ταῦτ' εἶναι τὸν ἀριθμόν,
ὕβριν βλάβην θάνατον. ἐνομοθέτει δὲ καὶ δικαστήριον ἓν τὸ
κύριον, εἰς ὃ πάσας ἀνάγεσθαι δεῖν τὰς μὴ καλῶς κεκρί-
σθαι δοκούσας δίκας· τοῦτο δὲ κατεσκεύαζεν ἐκ τινῶν γε-
5 ρόντων αἱρετῶν. τὰς δὲ κρίσεις ἐν τοῖς δικαστηρίοις οὐ διὰ 1268 a
ψηφοφορίας ᾤετο γίνεσθαι δεῖν, ἀλλὰ φέρειν ἕκαστον πινάκιον, ἐν ᾧ γράφειν, εἰ καταδικάζοι ἁπλῶς τὴν δίκην, εἰ

δ' ἀπολύοι ἁπλῶς, κενόν· εἰ δὲ τὸ μὲν τὸ δὲ μή, τοῦτο
διορίζειν. νῦν γὰρ οὐκ ᾤετο νενομοθετῆσθαι καλῶς· ἀναγκάζειν γὰρ ἐπιορκεῖν ἢ ταῦτα ἢ ταῦτα δικάζοντας. ἐτίθει δὲ 6
νόμον περὶ τῶν εὑρισκόντων τι τῇ πόλει συμφέρον, ὅπως
τυγχάνωσι τιμῆς, καὶ τοῖς παισὶ τῶν ἐν τῷ πολέμῳ τε-
λευτώντων ἐκ δημοσίου γίνεσθαι τὴν τροφήν, ὡς οὔπω τοῦτο
παρ' ἄλλοις νενομοθετημένον· ἔστι δὲ καὶ ἐν Ἀθήναις οὗτος
ὁ νόμος νῦν καὶ ἐν ἑτέραις τῶν πόλεων. τοὺς δ' ἄρχοντας 7
αἱρετοὺς ὑπὸ τοῦ δήμου εἶναι πάντας· δῆμον δ' ἐποίει τὰ
τρία μέρη τῆς πόλεως· τοὺς δ' αἱρεθέντας ἐπιμελεῖσθαι κοινῶν καὶ ξενικῶν καὶ ὀρφανικῶν. τὰ μὲν οὖν πλεῖστα καὶ
τὰ μάλιστα ἀξιόλογα τῆς Ἱπποδάμου τάξεως ταῦτ' ἐστίν,
ἀπορήσειε δ' ἄν τις πρῶτον μὲν τὴν διαίρεσιν τοῦ πλήθους
τῶν πολιτῶν. οἵ τε γὰρ τεχνῖται καὶ οἱ γεωργοὶ καὶ οἱ 8
τὰ ὅπλα ἔχοντες κοινωνοῦσι τῆς πολιτείας πάντες, οἱ μὲν
γεωργοὶ οὐκ ἔχοντες ὅπλα, οἱ δὲ τεχνῖται οὔτε γῆν οὔτε ὅπλα,
ὥστε γίνονται σχεδὸν δοῦλοι τῶν τὰ ὅπλα κεκτημένων. μετ- 9
έχειν μὲν οὖν πασῶν τῶν τιμῶν ἀδύνατον· ἀνάγκη γὰρ ἐκ
τῶν τὰ ὅπλα ἐχόντων καθίστασθαι καὶ στρατηγοὺς καὶ πολιτοφύλακας καὶ τὰς κυριωτάτας ἀρχὰς ὡς εἰπεῖν· μὴ
μετέχοντας δὲ τῆς πολιτείας πῶς οἷόν τε φιλικῶς ἔχειν
πρὸς τὴν πολιτείαν; ἀλλὰ δεῖ κρείττους εἶναι τοὺς τὰ ὅπλα
γε κεκτημένους ἀμφοτέρων τῶν μερῶν· τοῦτο δ' οὐ ῥᾴδιον μὴ
πολλοὺς ὄντας· εἰ δὲ τοῦτ' ἔσται, τί δεῖ τοὺς ἄλλους μετέχειν 10
τῆς πολιτείας καὶ κυρίους εἶναι τῆς τῶν ἀρχόντων καταστά-
σεως; ἔτι οἱ γεωργοὶ τί χρήσιμοι τῇ πόλει; τεχνίτας μὲν
γὰρ ἀναγκαῖον εἶναι (πᾶσα γὰρ δεῖται πόλις τεχνιτῶν),
καὶ δύνανται διαγίγνεσθαι καθάπερ ἐν ταῖς ἄλλαις πόλεσιν ἀπὸ τῆς τέχνης· οἱ δὲ γεωργοὶ πορίζοντες μὲν τοῖς τὰ
ὅπλα κεκτημένοις τὴν τροφὴν εὐλόγως ἂν ἦσάν τι τῆς
πόλεως μέρος, νῦν δ' ἰδίαν ἔχουσιν, καὶ ταύτην ἰδίᾳ γεωργήσουσιν. ἔτι δὲ τὴν κοινήν, ἀφ' ἧς οἱ προπολεμοῦντες ἕξουσι 11
τὴν τροφήν, εἰ μὲν αὐτοὶ γεωργήσουσιν, οὐκ ἂν εἴη τὸ μά-

χιμον ἕτερον καὶ τὸ γεωργοῦν, βούλεται δ' ὁ νομοθέτης· εἰ
δ' ἕτεροί τινες ἔσονται τῶν τε τὰ ἴδια γεωργούντων καὶ τῶν
μαχίμων, τέταρτον αὖ μόριον ἔσται τοῦτο τῆς πόλεως, οὐδε-
12 νὸς μετέχον, ἀλλὰ ἀλλότριον τῆς πολιτείας. ἀλλὰ μὴν εἴ
τις τοὺς αὐτοὺς θήσει τούς τε τὴν ἰδίαν καὶ τοὺς τὴν κοινὴν
γεωργοῦντας, τό τε πλῆθος ἄπορον ἔσται τῶν καρπῶν ἐξ ὧν
ἕκαστος γεωργήσει δύο οἰκίας, καὶ τίνος ἕνεκεν οὐκ εὐθὺς 1268 b
ἀπὸ τῆς γῆς καὶ τῶν αὐτῶν κλήρων αὑτοῖς τε τὴν τροφὴν
λήψονται καὶ τοῖς μαχίμοις παρέξουσιν; ταῦτα δὴ πάντα
13 πολλὴν ἔχει ταραχήν. οὐ καλῶς δ' οὐδ' ὁ περὶ τῆς κρίσεως
ἔχει νόμος, τὸ κρίνειν ἀξιοῦν διαιροῦντα τῆς δίκης ἁπλῶς
γεγραμμένης, καὶ γίνεσθαι τὸν δικαστὴν διαιτητήν. τοῦτο δ'
ἐν μὲν τῇ διαίτῃ καὶ πλείοσιν ἐνδέχεται (κοινολογοῦνται
γὰρ ἀλλήλοις περὶ τῆς κρίσεως), ἐν δὲ τοῖς δικαστηρίοις οὐκ
ἔστιν, ἀλλὰ καὶ τοὐναντίον τούτῳ τῶν νομοθετῶν οἱ πολλοὶ
παρασκευάζουσιν ὅπως οἱ δικασταὶ μὴ κοινολογῶνται πρὸς
14 ἀλλήλους. ἔπειτα πῶς οὐκ ἔσται ταραχώδης ἡ κρίσις, ὅταν
ὀφείλειν ὁ μὲν δικαστὴς οἴηται, μὴ τοσοῦτον δ' ὅσον ὁ δικαζόμενος; ὁ μὲν γὰρ εἴκοσι μνᾶς, ὁ δὲ δικαστὴς κρινεῖ
δέκα μνᾶς, ἢ ὁ μὲν πλέον, ὁ δ' ἔλασσον, ἄλλος δὲ πέντε,
ὁ δὲ τέτταρας· καὶ τοῦτον δὴ τὸν τρόπον δῆλον ὅτι μεριοῦ-
15 σιν· οἱ δὲ πάντα καταδικάσουσιν, οἱ δ' οὐδέν. τίς οὖν ὁ τρόπος ἔσται τῆς διαλογῆς τῶν ψήφων; ἔτι δ' οὐδεὶς ἐπιορκεῖν
ἀναγκάζει τὸν ἁπλῶς ἀποδικάσαντα ἢ καταδικάσαντα, εἴπερ ἁπλῶς τὸ ἔγκλημα γέγραπται δικαίως· οὐ γὰρ μηδὲν ὀφείλειν ὁ ἀποδικάσας κρίνει, ἀλλὰ τὰς εἴκοσι μνᾶς·
ἀλλ' ἐκεῖνος ἤδη ἐπιορκεῖ ὁ καταδικάσας μὴ νομίζων ὀφεί-
16 λειν τὰς εἴκοσι μνᾶς. περὶ δὲ τοῦ τοῖς εὑρίσκουσί τι τῇ πόλει συμφέρον ὡς δεῖ γίνεσθαί τινα τιμήν, οὐκ ἔστιν ἀσφα-
λὲς τὸ νομοθετεῖν, ἀλλ' εὐόφθαλμον ἀκοῦσαι μόνον· ἔχει
γὰρ συκοφαντίας καὶ κινήσεις, ἂν τύχῃ, πολιτείας. ἐμ-
πίπτει δ' εἰς ἄλλο πρόβλημα καὶ σκέψιν ἑτέραν· ἀποροῦσι
γάρ τινες πότερον βλαβερὸν ἢ συμφέρον ταῖς πόλεσι τὸ

κινεῖν τοὺς πατρίους νόμους, ἂν ᾖ τις ἄλλος βελτίων. διόπερ 17
οὐ ῥᾴδιον τῷ λεχθέντι ταχὺ συγχωρεῖν, εἴπερ μὴ συμφέρει κινεῖν. ἐνδέχεται δ' εἰσηγεῖσθαί τινας νόμων λύσιν ἢ
πολιτείας ὡς κοινὸν ἀγαθόν. ἐπεὶ δὲ πεποιήμεθα μνείαν,
ἔτι μικρὰ περὶ αὐτοῦ διαστείλασθαι βέλτιον. ἔχει γάρ, 18
ὥσπερ εἴπομεν, ἀπορίαν, καὶ δόξειεν ἂν βέλτιον εἶναι τὸ
κινεῖν· ἐπὶ γοῦν τῶν ἄλλων ἐπιστημῶν τοῦτο συνενήνοχεν,
οἷον ἰατρικὴ κινηθεῖσα παρὰ τὰ πάτρια καὶ γυμναστικὴ
καὶ ὅλως αἱ τέχναι πᾶσαι καὶ αἱ δυνάμεις, ὥστ' ἐπεὶ μίαν
τούτων θετέον καὶ τὴν πολιτικήν, δῆλον ὅτι καὶ περὶ ταύτην
ἀναγκαῖον ὁμοίως ἔχειν. σημεῖον δ' ἂν γεγονέναι φαίη τις 19
ἐπ' αὐτῶν τῶν ἔργων· τοὺς γὰρ ἀρχαίους νόμους λίαν ἁπλοῦς
εἶναι καὶ βαρβαρικούς· ἐσιδηροφοροῦντό τε γὰρ οἱ Ἕλληνες, καὶ τὰς γυναῖκας ἐωνοῦντο παρ' ἀλλήλων, ὅσα τε 20
λοιπὰ τῶν ἀρχαίων ἐστί που νομίμων, εὐήθη πάμπαν ἐστίν,
1269 a οἷον ἐν Κύμῃ περὶ τὰ φονικὰ νόμος ἐστίν, ἂν πλῆθός τι
παράσχηται μαρτύρων ὁ διώκων τὸν φόνον τῶν αὑτοῦ συγγενῶν, ἔνοχον εἶναι τῷ φόνῳ τὸν φεύγοντα. ζητοῦσι δὲ 21
ὅλως οὐ τὸ πάτριον ἀλλὰ τἀγαθὸν πάντες· εἰκός τε τοὺς
πρώτους, εἴτε γηγενεῖς ἦσαν εἴτ' ἐκ φθορᾶς τινὸς ἐσώθησαν,
ὁμοίους εἶναι καὶ τοὺς τυχόντας καὶ τοὺς ἀνοήτους, ὥσπερ καὶ
λέγεται κατὰ τῶν γηγενῶν, ὥστε ἄτοπον τὸ μένειν ἐν τοῖς
τούτων δόγμασιν. πρὸς δὲ τούτοις οὐδὲ τοὺς γεγραμμένους ἐᾶν
ἀκινήτους βέλτιον. ὥσπερ γὰρ καὶ περὶ τὰς ἄλλας τέχνας, 22
καὶ τὴν πολιτικὴν τάξιν ἀδύνατον ἀκριβῶς πάντα γραφῆ-
ναι· καθόλου γὰρ ἀναγκαῖον γραφῆναι, αἱ δὲ πράξεις περὶ
τῶν καθ' ἕκαστόν εἰσιν. ἐκ μὲν οὖν τούτων φανερὸν ὅτι κινητέοι καὶ τινὲς καὶ ποτὲ τῶν νόμων εἰσίν, ἄλλον δὲ τρόπον
ἐπισκοποῦσιν εὐλαβείας ἂν δόξειεν εἶναι πολλῆς. ὅταν γὰρ 23
ᾖ τὸ μὲν βέλτιον μικρόν, τὸ δ' ἐθίζειν εὐχερῶς λύειν τοὺς
νόμους φαῦλον, φανερὸν ὡς ἐατέον ἐνίας ἁμαρτίας καὶ τῶν
νομοθετῶν καὶ τῶν ἀρχόντων· οὐ γὰρ τοσοῦτον ὠφελήσεται
κινήσας, ὅσον βλαβήσεται τοῖς ἄρχουσιν ἀπειθεῖν ἐθισθείς.

μνεια - memory, mention
διστελλω - distinguish, determine.
ενοχος - held, liable

24 ψεῦδος δὲ καὶ τὸ παράδειγμα τὸ περὶ τῶν τεχνῶν· οὐ γὰρ
ὅμοιον τὸ κινεῖν τέχνην καὶ νόμον, ὁ γὰρ νόμος ἰσχὺν
οὐδεμίαν ἔχει πρὸς τὸ πείθεσθαι παρὰ τὸ ἔθος, τοῦτο
δ' οὐ γίνεται εἰ μὴ διὰ χρόνου πλῆθος, ὥστε τὸ ῥᾳδίως μεταβάλλειν ἐκ τῶν ὑπαρχόντων νόμων εἰς ἑτέρους νόμους
25 καινοὺς ἀσθενῆ ποιεῖν ἐστὶ τὴν τοῦ νόμου δύναμιν. ἔτι δὲ εἰ
καὶ κινητέοι, πότερον πάντες καὶ ἐν πάσῃ πολιτείᾳ, ἢ
οὔ; καὶ πότερον τῷ τυχόντι ἢ τισίν; ταῦτα γὰρ ἔχει μεγάλην διαφοράν. διὸ νῦν μὲν ἀφῶμεν ταύτην τὴν σκέψιν·
ἄλλων γάρ ἐστι καιρῶν·

Περὶ δὲ τῆς Λακεδαιμονίων πολιτείας καὶ τῆς Κρη- 9
τικῆς, σχεδὸν δὲ καὶ περὶ τῶν ἄλλων πολιτειῶν, δύο εἰσὶν
αἱ σκέψεις, μία μὲν εἴ τι καλῶς ἢ μὴ καλῶς πρὸς τὴν
ἀρίστην νενομοθέτηται τάξιν, ἑτέρα δ' εἴ τι πρὸς τὴν ὑπόθεσιν καὶ τὸν τρόπον ὑπεναντίως τῆς προκειμένης αὐτοῖς
2 πολιτείας. ὅτι μὲν οὖν δεῖ τῇ μελλούσῃ καλῶς πολιτεύεσθαι τὴν τῶν ἀναγκαίων ὑπάρχειν σχολήν, ὁμολογούμενόν
ἐστιν· τίνα δὲ τρόπον ὑπάρχειν, οὐ ῥᾴδιον λαβεῖν. ἥ τε
γὰρ Θετταλῶν πενεστεία πολλάκις ἐπέθετο τοῖς Θετταλοῖς,
ὁμοίως δὲ καὶ τοῖς Λάκωσιν οἱ εἵλωτες (ὥσπερ γὰρ ἐφεδ-
3 ρεύοντες τοῖς ἀτυχήμασι διατελοῦσιν)· περὶ δὲ τοὺς Κρῆτας
οὐδέν πω τοιοῦτον συμβέβηκεν· αἴτιον δ' ἴσως τὸ τὰς γειτνιώ-
σας πόλεις, καίπερ πολεμούσας ἀλλήλαις, μηδεμίαν εἶναι
σύμμαχον τοῖς ἀφισταμένοις διὰ τὸ μὴ συμφέρειν καὶ
αὐταῖς κεκτημέναις περιοίκους· τοῖς δὲ Λάκωσιν οἱ γειτνιῶν-
τες ἐχθροὶ πάντες ἦσαν, Ἀργεῖοι καὶ Μεσσήνιοι καὶ Ἀρ-
κάδες· ἐπεὶ καὶ τοῖς Θετταλοῖς κατ' ἀρχὰς ἀφίσταντο διὰ
τὸ πολεμεῖν ἔτι τοῖς προσχώροις, Ἀχαιοῖς καὶ Περραιβοῖς
4 καὶ Μάγνησιν. ἔοικε δὲ καὶ εἰ μηδὲν ἕτερον, ἀλλὰ τό γε
τῆς ἐπιμελείας ἐργῶδες εἶναι, τίνα δεῖ πρὸς αὐτοὺς ὁμιλῆ-
σαι τρόπον· ἀνιέμενοί τε γὰρ ὑβρίζουσι καὶ τῶν ἴσων ἀξιοῦσιν ἑαυτοὺς τοῖς κυρίοις, καὶ κακοπαθῶς ζῶντες ἐπιβουλεύουσι
καὶ μισοῦσιν. δῆλον οὖν ὡς οὐκ ἐξευρίσκουσι τὸν βέλτιστον

ἐφεδρεύω – sit a rest upon, lie in wait for.

τρόπον, οἷς τοῦτο συμβαίνει περὶ τὴν εἱλωτείαν. ἔτι δὲ ἡ 5
περὶ τὰς γυναῖκας ἄνεσις καὶ πρὸς τὴν προαίρεσιν τῆς πολιτείας βλαβερὰ καὶ πρὸς εὐδαιμονίαν πόλεως. ὥσπερ γὰρ
οἰκίας μέρος ἀνὴρ καὶ γυνή, δῆλον ὅτι καὶ πόλιν ἐγγὺς
τοῦ δίχα διῃρῆσθαι δεῖ νομίζειν εἴς τε τὸ τῶν ἀνδρῶν πλῆθος καὶ τὸ τῶν γυναικῶν, ὥστε ἐν ὅσαις πολιτείαις φαύλως
ἔχει τὸ περὶ τὰς γυναῖκας, τὸ ἥμισυ τῆς πόλεως εἶναι δεῖ
νομίζειν ἀνομοθέτητον. ὅπερ ἐκεῖ συμβέβηκεν· ὅλην γὰρ 6
τὴν πόλιν ὁ νομοθέτης εἶναι βουλόμενος καρτερικήν, κατὰ
μὲν τοὺς ἄνδρας φανερός ἐστι τοιοῦτος ὤν, ἐπὶ δὲ τῶν γυναικῶν ἐξημέληκεν· ζῶσι γὰρ ἀκολάστως πρὸς ἅπασαν ἀκολασίαν καὶ τρυφερῶς. ὥστε ἀναγκαῖον ἐν τῇ τοιαύτῃ πολι- 7
τείᾳ τιμᾶσθαι τὸν πλοῦτον, ἄλλως τε κἂν τύχωσι γυναικοκρατούμενοι, καθάπερ τὰ πολλὰ τῶν στρατιωτικῶν καὶ
πολεμικῶν γενῶν, ἔξω Κελτῶν ἢ κἂν εἴ τινες ἕτεροι φανερῶς τετιμήκασι τὴν πρὸς τοὺς ἄρρενας συνουσίαν. ἔοικε 8
γὰρ ὁ μυθολογήσας πρῶτος οὐκ ἀλόγως συζεῦξαι τὸν Ἄρη
πρὸς τὴν Ἀφροδίτην· ἢ γὰρ πρὸς τὴν τῶν ἀρρένων ὁμιλίαν
ἢ πρὸς τὴν τῶν γυναικῶν φαίνονται κατακώχιμοι πάντες οἱ
τοιοῦτοι. διὸ παρὰ τοῖς Λάκωσι τοῦθ' ὑπῆρχεν, καὶ πολλὰ
διῳκεῖτο ὑπὸ τῶν γυναικῶν ἐπὶ τῆς ἀρχῆς αὐτῶν. καίτοι 9
τί διαφέρει γυναῖκας ἄρχειν ἢ τοὺς ἄρχοντας ὑπὸ τῶν
γυναικῶν ἄρχεσθαι; ταὐτὸ γὰρ συμβαίνει. χρησίμου δ'
οὔσης τῆς θρασύτητος πρὸς οὐδὲν τῶν ἐγκυκλίων, ἀλλ' εἴπερ,
πρὸς τὸν πόλεμον, βλαβερώταται καὶ πρὸς ταῦθ' αἱ τῶν
Λακώνων ἦσαν. ἐδήλωσαν δ' ἐπὶ τῆς Θηβαίων ἐμβολῆς· 10
χρήσιμοι μὲν γὰρ οὐδὲν ἦσαν, ὥσπερ ἐν ἑτέραις πόλεσιν,
θόρυβον δὲ παρεῖχον πλείω τῶν πολεμίων. ἐξ ἀρχῆς μὲν
οὖν ἔοικε συμβεβηκέναι τοῖς Λάκωσιν εὐλόγως ἡ τῶν γυ-
1270 a ναικῶν ἄνεσις· ἔξω γὰρ τῆς οἰκείας διὰ τὰς στρατείας 11
ἀπεξενοῦντο πολὺν χρόνον, πολεμοῦντες τόν τε πρὸς Ἀργείους
πόλεμον καὶ πάλιν τὸν πρὸς Ἀρκάδας καὶ Μεσσηνίους·
σχολάσαντες δὲ αὐτοὺς μὲν παρεῖχον τῷ νομοθέτῃ προω-

κατακωχιμος = κατοκωχιμος – held in possession, held as a pledge, capable of being possessed, inclined.

ἐγκυκλιος – common, ordinary.
ἀποξενοω – drive from house to house, banish, live away from home.
σχολαζω – to be at leisure.

δοπεποιημένους διὰ τὸν στρατιωτικὸν βίον (πολλὰ γὰρ ἔχει
μέρη τῆς ἀρετῆς), τὰς δὲ γυναῖκας φασὶ μὲν ἄγειν ἐπιχειρῆσαι τὸν Λυκοῦργον ἐπὶ τοὺς νόμους, ὡς δ' ἀντέκρουον,
12 ἀποστῆναι πάλιν. αἰτίαι μὲν οὖν εἰσὶν αὗται τῶν γενομένων, ὥστε δῆλον ὅτι καὶ ταύτης τῆς ἁμαρτίας. ἀλλ' ἡμεῖς
οὐ τοῦτο σκοποῦμεν, τίνι δεῖ συγγνώμην ἔχειν ἢ μὴ ἔχειν,
13 ἀλλὰ περὶ τοῦ ὀρθῶς καὶ μὴ ὀρθῶς. τὰ δὲ περὶ τὰς γυναῖκας ἔχοντα μὴ καλῶς ἔοικεν, ὥσπερ ἐλέχθη καὶ πρότερον, οὐ μόνον ἀπρέπειάν τινα ποιεῖν τῆς πολιτείας αὐτῆς
καθ' αὑτήν, ἀλλὰ συμβάλλεσθαί τι πρὸς τὴν φιλοχρηματίαν. μετὰ γὰρ τὰ νῦν ῥηθέντα τοῖς περὶ τὴν ἀνωμα-
14 λίαν τῆς κτήσεως ἐπιτιμήσειεν ἄν τις· τοῖς μὲν γὰρ αὐτῶν
συμβέβηκε κεκτῆσθαι πολλὴν λίαν οὐσίαν, τοῖς δὲ πάμπαν μικράν· διόπερ εἰς ὀλίγους ἧκεν ἡ χώρα. τοῦτο δὲ καὶ
διὰ τῶν νόμων τέτακται φαύλως· ὠνεῖσθαι μὲν γὰρ ἢ
πωλεῖν τὴν ὑπάρχουσαν ἐποίησεν οὐ καλόν, ὀρθῶς ποιήσας,
διδόναι δὲ καὶ καταλείπειν ἐξουσίαν ἔδωκε τοῖς βουλομένοις·
καίτοι ταὐτὸ συμβαίνειν ἀναγκαῖον ἐκείνως τε καὶ οὕτως.
15 ἔστι δὲ καὶ τῶν γυναικῶν σχεδὸν τῆς πάσης χώρας τῶν
πέντε μερῶν τὰ δύο, τῶν τ' ἐπικλήρων πολλῶν γινομένων,
καὶ διὰ τὸ προῖκας διδόναι μεγάλας. καίτοι βέλτιον ἦν
μηδεμίαν ἢ ὀλίγην ἢ καὶ μετρίαν τετάχθαι· νῦν δ' ἔξεστι
δοῦναί τε τὴν ἐπίκληρον ὅτῳ ἂν βούληται· κἂν ἀποθάνῃ
μὴ διαθέμενος, ὃν ἂν καταλίπῃ κληρονόμον, οὗτος ᾧ ἂν
16 θέλῃ δίδωσιν. τοιγαροῦν δυναμένης τῆς χώρας χιλίους ἱπ-
πεῖς τρέφειν καὶ πεντακοσίους καὶ ὁπλίτας τρισμυρίους, οὐδὲ
χίλιοι τὸ πλῆθος ἦσαν. γέγονε δὲ διὰ τῶν ἔργων αὐτῶν
δῆλον ὅτι φαύλως αὐτοῖς εἶχε τὰ περὶ τὴν τάξιν ταύτην·
μίαν γὰρ πληγὴν οὐχ ὑπήνεγκεν ἡ πόλις, ἀλλ' ἀπώλετο
17 διὰ τὴν ὀλιγανθρωπίαν. λέγουσι δ' ὡς ἐπὶ μὲν τῶν προτέ-
ρων βασιλέων μετεδίδοσαν τῆς πολιτείας, ὥστ' οὐ γίνεσθαι
τότε ὀλιγανθρωπίαν πολεμούντων πολὺν χρόνον· καί φασιν
εἶναί ποτε τοῖς Σπαρτιάταις καὶ μυρίους· οὐ μὴν ἀλλ' εἴτ'

προσοδοποιεω – προωδοποιεω – prepare the way.
επικληρος – succeeding to a patrimony, (as subs.) only daughter & heiress

ἐστὶν ἀληθῆ ταῦτα εἴτε μή, βέλτιον τὸ διὰ τῆς κτήσεως
ὡμαλισμένης πληθύειν ἀνδρῶν τὴν πόλιν. ὑπεναντίος δὲ 18
καὶ ὁ περὶ τὴν τεκνοποιίαν νόμος πρὸς ταύτην τὴν διόρθω-
1270 b σιν. βουλόμενος γὰρ ὁ νομοθέτης ὡς πλείστους εἶναι τοὺς
Σπαρτιάτας, προάγεται τοὺς πολίτας ὅτι πλείστους ποιεῖσθαι
παῖδας· ἔστι γὰρ αὐτοῖς νόμος τὸν μὲν γεννήσαντα τρεῖς
υἱοὺς ἄφρουρον εἶναι, τὸν δὲ τέτταρας ἀτελῆ πάντων. καίτοι 19
φανερὸν ὅτι πολλῶν γινομένων, τῆς δὲ χώρας οὕτω διῃρη-
μένης, ἀναγκαῖον πολλοὺς γίνεσθαι πένητας. ἀλλὰ μὴν
καὶ τὰ περὶ τὴν ἐφορείαν ἔχει φαύλως· ἡ γὰρ ἀρχὴ κυρία μὲν αὐτὴ τῶν μεγίστων αὐτοῖς ἐστίν, γίνονται δ' ἐκ τοῦ
δήμου πάντες, ὥστε πολλάκις ἐμπίπτουσιν ἄνθρωποι σφόδρα
πένητες εἰς τὸ ἀρχεῖον, οἳ διὰ τὴν ἀπορίαν ὤνιοι ἦσαν.
ἐδήλωσαν δὲ πολλάκις μὲν καὶ πρότερον, καὶ νῦν δὲ ἐν 20
τοῖς Ἀνδρίοις· διαφθαρέντες γὰρ ἀργυρίῳ τινές, ὅσον ἐφ'
ἑαυτοῖς, ὅλην τὴν πόλιν ἀπώλεσαν. καὶ διὰ τὸ τὴν ἀρχὴν εἶναι λίαν μεγάλην καὶ ἰσοτύραννον δημαγωγεῖν
αὐτοὺς ἠναγκάζοντο καὶ οἱ βασιλεῖς, ὥστε καὶ ταύτῃ συν-
επιβλάπτεσθαι τὴν πολιτείαν· δημοκρατία γὰρ ἐξ ἀριστοκρατίας συνέβαινεν. συνέχει μὲν οὖν τὴν πολιτείαν τὸ ἀρ- 21
χεῖον τοῦτο, ἡσυχάζει γὰρ ὁ δῆμος διὰ τὸ μετέχειν τῆς
μεγίστης ἀρχῆς, ὥστ' εἴτε διὰ τὸν νομοθέτην εἴτε διὰ τύχην τοῦτο συμπέπτωκεν, συμφερόντως ἔχει τοῖς πράγμασιν,
δεῖ γὰρ τὴν πολιτείαν τὴν μέλλουσαν σῴζεσθαι πάντα βού- 22
λεσθαι τὰ μέρη τῆς πόλεως εἶναι καὶ διαμένειν [ταὐτά]·
οἱ μὲν οὖν βασιλεῖς διὰ τὴν αὑτῶν τιμὴν οὕτως ἔχουσιν, οἱ
δὲ καλοὶ κἀγαθοὶ διὰ τὴν γερουσίαν (ἆθλον γὰρ ἡ ἀρχὴ
αὕτη τῆς ἀρετῆς ἐστίν), ὁ δὲ δῆμος διὰ τὴν ἐφορείαν (καθίσταται γὰρ ἐξ ἁπάντων)· ἀλλ' αἱρετὴν ἔδει τὴν ἀρχὴν 23
εἶναι ταύτην ἐξ ἁπάντων μέν, μὴ τὸν τρόπον δὲ τοῦτον ὃν
νῦν· παιδαριώδης γάρ ἐστι λίαν. ἔτι δὲ καὶ κρίσεών εἰσι
μεγάλων κύριοι, ὄντες οἱ τυχόντες, διόπερ οὐκ αὐτογνώμονας βέλτιον κρίνειν ἀλλὰ κατὰ γράμματα καὶ τοὺς

διορθωσις - emendation, reformation.
αυτογνωμων - acting of one's own judgement

24 νόμους. ἔστι δὲ καὶ ἡ δίαιτα τῶν ἐφόρων οὐχ ὁμολογουμένη τῷ βουλήματι τῆς πόλεως· αὐτὴ μὲν γὰρ ἀνειμένη λίαν ἐστίν, ἐν δὲ τοῖς ἄλλοις μᾶλλον ὑπερβάλλει ἐπὶ τὸ σκληρόν, ὥστε μὴ δύνασθαι καρτερεῖν ἀλλὰ λάθρᾳ τὸν νόμον ἀποδιδράσκοντας ἀπολαύειν τῶν σωματικῶν ἡδονῶν. ἔχει δὲ καὶ τὰ περὶ τὴν τῶν γερόντων ἀρχὴν οὐ καλῶς αὐτοῖς· 25 ἐπιεικῶν μὲν γὰρ ὄντων καὶ πεπαιδευμένων ἱκανῶς πρὸς ἀνδραγαθίαν τάχα ἂν εἴπειέ τις συμφέρειν τῇ πόλει· (καίτοι τό γε διὰ βίου κυρίους εἶναι κρίσεων μεγάλων ἀμφισβητήσιμον, ἔστι γάρ, ὥσπερ καὶ σώματος, καὶ διανοίας γῆρας·) τὸν τρόπον δὲ τοῦτον πεπαιδευμένων ὥστε καὶ τὸν νομοθέτην αὐτὸν ἀπιστεῖν ὡς οὐκ ἀγαθοῖς ἀνδράσιν, οὐκ 26 ἀσφαλές. φαίνονται δὲ καὶ καταδωροδοκούμενοι καὶ καταχαριζόμενοι πολλὰ τῶν κοινῶν οἱ κεκοινωνηκότες τῆς ἀρχῆς ταύτης. διόπερ βέλτιον αὐτοὺς μὴ ἀνευθύνους εἶναι· νῦν δ' εἰσίν. δόξειε δ' ἂν ἡ τῶν ἐφόρων ἀρχὴ πάσας εὐθύνειν τὰς ἀρχάς· τοῦτο δὲ τῇ ἐφορείᾳ μέγα λίαν τὸ δῶρον, καὶ τὸν τρόπον οὐ τοῦτον λέγομεν διδόναι δεῖν τὰς εὐθύνας. 27 ἔτι δὲ καὶ τὴν αἵρεσιν ἣν ποιοῦνται τῶν γερόντων, κατά τε τὴν κρίσιν ἐστὶ παιδαριώδης, καὶ τὸ αὐτὸν αἰτεῖσθαι τὸν ἀξιωθησόμενον τῆς ἀρχῆς οὐκ ὀρθῶς ἔχει· δεῖ γὰρ καὶ βουλόμενον καὶ μὴ βουλόμενον ἄρχειν τὸν ἄξιον τῆς ἀρχῆς. 28 νῦν δ' ὅπερ καὶ περὶ τὴν ἄλλην πολιτείαν ὁ νομοθέτης φαίνεται ποιῶν· φιλοτίμους γὰρ κατασκευάζων τοὺς πολίτας τούτῳ κέχρηται πρὸς τὴν αἵρεσιν τῶν γερόντων· οὐδεὶς γὰρ ἂν ἄρχειν αἰτήσαιτο μὴ φιλότιμος ὤν. καίτοι τῶν γ' ἀδικημάτων τῶν ἑκουσίων τὰ πλεῖστα συμβαίνει σχεδὸν 29 διὰ φιλοτιμίαν καὶ διὰ φιλοχρηματίαν τοῖς ἀνθρώποις. περὶ δὲ βασιλείας, εἰ μὲν μὴ βέλτιόν ἐστιν ὑπάρχειν ταῖς πόλεσιν ἢ βέλτιον, ἄλλος ἔστω λόγος· ἀλλὰ μὴν βέλτιόν γε μὴ καθάπερ νῦν, ἀλλὰ κατὰ τὸν αὐτοῦ βίον ἕκαστον 30 κρίνεσθαι τῶν βασιλέων. ὅτι δὲ ὁ νομοθέτης οὐδ' αὐτὸς οἴεται δύνασθαι ποιεῖν καλοὺς κἀγαθούς, δῆλον· ἀπιστεῖ γοῦν ὡς οὐκ

οὖσιν ἱκανῶς ἀγαθοῖς ἀνδράσιν· διόπερ ἐξέπεμπον συμπρεσβευτὰς τοὺς ἐχθρούς, καὶ σωτηρίαν ἐνόμιζον τῇ πόλει εἶναι τὸ στασιάζειν τοὺς βασιλεῖς. οὐ καλῶς δ' οὐδὲ περὶ τὰ συσσίτια τὰ καλούμενα φιδίτια νενομοθέτηται τῷ καταστήσαντι πρῶτον· ἔδει γὰρ ἀπὸ κοινοῦ μᾶλλον εἶναι τὴν σύνοδον καθάπερ ἐν Κρήτῃ· παρὰ δὲ τοῖς Λάκωσιν ἕκαστον δεῖ φέρειν, καὶ σφόδρα πενήτων ἐνίων ὄντων καὶ τοῦτο τὸ ἀνάλωμα οὐ δυναμένων δαπανᾶν, ὥστε συμβαίνει τοὐναντίον τῷ νομοθέτῃ τῆς προαιρέσεως. βούλεται μὲν γὰρ δημοκρατικὸν εἶναι τὸ κατασκεύασμα τῶν συσσιτίων, γίνεται δ' ἥκιστα δημοκρατικὸν οὕτω νενομοθετημένον· μετέχειν μὲν γὰρ οὐ ῥᾴδιον τοῖς λίαν πένησιν, ὅρος δὲ τῆς πολιτείας οὗτός ἐστιν αὐτοῖς ὁ πάτριος, τὸν μὴ δυνάμενον τοῦτο τὸ τέλος φέρειν μὴ μετέχειν αὐτῆς. τῷ δὲ περὶ τοὺς ναυάρχους νόμῳ καὶ ἕτεροί τινες ἐπιτετιμήκασιν, ὀρθῶς ἐπιτιμῶντες, στάσεως γὰρ γίνεται αἴτιος· ἐπὶ γὰρ τοῖς βασιλεῦσιν οὖσι στρατηγοῖς ἀιδίοις ἡ ναυαρχία σχεδὸν ἑτέρα βασιλεία καθέστηκεν. καὶ ὡδὶ δὲ τῇ ὑποθέσει τοῦ νομοθέτου ἐπιτιμή-
1271 b σειεν ἄν τις, ὅπερ καὶ Πλάτων ἐν τοῖς νόμοις ἐπιτετίμηκεν· πρὸς γὰρ μέρος ἀρετῆς ἡ πᾶσα σύνταξις τῶν νόμων ἐστί, τὴν πολεμικήν· αὕτη γὰρ χρησίμη πρὸς τὸ κρατεῖν. τοιγαροῦν ἐσῴζοντο μὲν πολεμοῦντες, ἀπώλλυντο δὲ ἄρξαντες διὰ τὸ μὴ ἐπίστασθαι σχολάζειν μηδὲ ἠσκηκέναι μηδεμίαν ἄσκησιν ἑτέραν κυριωτέραν τῆς πολεμικῆς. τούτου δὲ ἁμάρτημα οὐκ ἔλαττον· νομίζουσι μὲν γὰρ γίνεσθαι τἀγαθὰ τὰ περιμάχητα δι' ἀρετῆς μᾶλλον ἢ κακίας, καὶ τοῦτο μὲν καλῶς, ὅτι μέντοι ταῦτα κρείττω τῆς ἀρετῆς ὑπολαμβάνουσιν, οὐ καλῶς. φαύλως δὲ ἔχει καὶ περὶ τὰ κοινὰ χρήματα τοῖς Σπαρτιάταις· οὔτε γὰρ ἐν τῷ κοινῷ τῆς πόλεώς ἐστιν οὐδὲν πολέμους μεγάλους ἀναγκαζομένοις πολεμεῖν, εἰσφέρουσί τε κακῶς· διὰ γὰρ τὸ τῶν Σπαρτιατῶν εἶναι τὴν πλείστην γῆν οὐκ ἐξετάζουσιν ἀλλήλων τὰς εἰσφοράς. ἀποβέβηκέ τε τοὐναντίον τῷ νομοθέτῃ τοῦ συμ-

φέροντος· τὴν μὲν γὰρ πόλιν πεποίηκεν ἀχρήματον, τοὺς
δ' ἰδιώτας φιλοχρηματους. περὶ μὲν οὖν τῆς Λακεδαιμονίων
πολιτείας ἐπὶ τοσοῦτον εἰρήσθω· ταῦτα γάρ ἐστιν ἃ μάλιστ'
ἄν τις ἐπιτιμήσειεν·

'Η δὲ Κρητικὴ πολιτεία πάρεγγυς μέν ἐστι ταύτης,
ἔχει δὲ μικρὰ μὲν οὐ χεῖρον, τὸ δὲ πλεῖον ἧττον γλαφυρῶς. καὶ γὰρ ἔοικε καὶ λέγεται δὲ τὰ πλεῖστα μεμιμῆσθαι τὴν Κρητικὴν πολιτείαν ἡ τῶν Λακώνων, τὰ δὲ πλεῖ-
2 στα τῶν ἀρχαίων ἧττον διήρθρωται τῶν νεωτέρων. φασὶ
γὰρ τὸν Λυκοῦργον, ὅτε τὴν ἐπιτροπείαν τὴν Χαρίλλου τοῦ
βασιλέως καταλιπὼν ἀπεδήμησεν, τότε τὸν πλεῖστον διατρῖψαι χρόνον περὶ Κρήτην διὰ τὴν συγγένειαν· ἄποικοι γὰρ οἱ Λύκτιοι τῶν Λακώνων ἦσαν, κατέλαβον δ' οἱ
πρὸς τὴν ἀποικίαν ἐλθόντες τὴν τάξιν τῶν νόμων ὑπάρχου-
3 σαν ἐν τοῖς τότε κατοικοῦσιν. διὸ καὶ νῦν οἱ περίοικοι τὸν
αὐτὸν τρόπον χρῶνται αὐτοῖς, ὡς κατασκευάσαντος Μίνω
πρώτου τὴν τάξιν τῶν νόμων. δοκεῖ δ' ἡ νῆσος καὶ πρὸς
τὴν ἀρχὴν τὴν Ἑλληνικὴν πεφυκέναι καὶ κεῖσθαι καλῶς·
πάσῃ γὰρ ἐπίκειται τῇ θαλάσσῃ, σχεδὸν τῶν Ἑλλήνων
ἱδρυμένων περὶ τὴν θάλασσαν πάντων· ἀπέχει γὰρ τῇ μὲν
τῆς Πελοποννήσου μικρόν, τῇ δὲ τῆς Ἀσίας τοῦ περὶ Τριόπιον
4 τόπου καὶ Ῥόδου. διὸ καὶ τὴν τῆς θαλάσσης ἀρχὴν κατέσ-
χεν ὁ Μίνως, καὶ τὰς νήσους τὰς μὲν ἐχειρώσατο τὰς
δ' ᾤκισεν, τέλος δὲ ἐπιθέμενος τῇ Σικελίᾳ τὸν βίον ἐτελεύ-
τησεν ἐκεῖ περὶ Κάμικον. ἔχει δ' ἀνάλογον ἡ Κρητικὴ τά-
5 ξις πρὸς τὴν Λακωνικήν· γεωργοῦσί τε γὰρ τοῖς μὲν εἵλωτες τοῖς δὲ Κρησὶν οἱ περίοικοι, καὶ συσσίτια παρ' ἀμφο- 1272 a
τέροις ἐστίν· καὶ τό γε ἀρχαῖον ἐκάλουν οἱ Λάκωνες οὐ φιδίτια ἀλλὰ ἀνδρεῖα, καθάπερ οἱ Κρῆτες, ᾗ καὶ δῆλον ὅτι
6 ἐκεῖθεν ἐλήλυθεν. ἔτι δὲ τῆς πολιτείας ἡ τάξις· οἱ μὲν
γὰρ ἔφοροι τὴν αὐτὴν ἔχουσι δύναμιν τοῖς ἐν τῇ Κρήτῃ
καλουμένοις κόσμοις, πλὴν οἱ μὲν ἔφοροι πέντε τὸν ἀριθμὸν οἱ δὲ κόσμοι δέκα εἰσίν· οἱ δὲ γέροντες τοῖς γέρουσιν,

οὓς καλοῦσιν οἱ Κρῆτες βουλήν, ἴσοι· βασιλεία δὲ πρότερον
μὲν ἦν, εἶτα κατέλυσαν οἱ Κρῆτες, καὶ τὴν ἡγεμονίαν οἱ
κόσμοι τὴν κατὰ πόλεμον ἔχουσιν· ἐκκλησίας δὲ μετέχουσι 7
πάντες, κυρία δ' οὐδενός ἐστιν ἀλλ' ἢ συνεπιψηφίσαι τὰ δόξαντα τοῖς γέρουσι καὶ τοῖς κόσμοις. τὰ μὲν οὖν τῶν συσσιτίων ἔχει βέλτιον τοῖς Κρησὶν ἢ τοῖς Λάκωσιν· ἐν μὲν
γὰρ Λακεδαίμονι κατὰ κεφαλὴν ἕκαστος εἰσφέρει τὸ τε-
ταγμένον, εἰ δὲ μή, μετέχειν νόμος κωλύει τῆς πολιτείας,
καθάπερ εἴρηται καὶ πρότερον, ἐν δὲ Κρήτῃ κοινοτέρως, 8
ἀπὸ πάντων γὰρ τῶν γινομένων καρπῶν τε καὶ βοσκημάτων ἐκ τῶν δημοσίων καὶ φόρων οὓς φέρουσιν οἱ περίοικοι, τέτακται μέρος τὸ μὲν πρὸς τοὺς θεοὺς καὶ τὰς κοινὰς λειτουργίας, τὸ δὲ τοῖς συσσιτίοις, ὥστ' ἐκ κοινοῦ τρέφεσθαι πάντας, καὶ γυναῖκας καὶ παῖδας καὶ ἄνδρας·
πρὸς δὲ τὴν ὀλιγοσιτίαν ὡς ὠφέλιμον πολλὰ πεφιλο- 9
σόφηκεν ὁ νομοθέτης, καὶ πρὸς τὴν διάζευξιν τῶν γυναικῶν, ἵνα μὴ πολυτεκνῶσι, τὴν πρὸς τοὺς ἄρρενας ποιήσας
ὁμιλίαν, περὶ ἧς εἰ φαύλως ἢ μὴ φαύλως, ἕτερος ἔσται
τοῦ διασκέψασθαι καιρός. ὅτι δὲ τὰ περὶ τὰ συσσίτια βέλτιον τέτακται τοῖς Κρησὶν ἢ τοῖς Λάκωσι, φανερόν. τὰ
δὲ περὶ τοὺς κόσμους ἔτι χεῖρον τῶν ἐφόρων· ὃ μὲν γὰρ 10
ἔχει κακὸν τὸ τῶν ἐφόρων ἀρχεῖον, ὑπάρχει καὶ τούτοις· γίνονται γὰρ οἱ τυχόντες· ὃ δ' ἐκεῖ συμφέρει πρὸς τὴν πολιτείαν, ἐνταῦθα οὐκ ἔστιν. ἐκεῖ μὲν γάρ, διὰ τὸ τὴν αἵρεσιν ἐκ πάντων εἶναι, μετέχων ὁ δῆμος τῆς μεγίστης ἀρχῆς
βούλεται μένειν τὴν πολιτείαν· ἐνταῦθα δ' οὐκ ἐξ ἁπάντων
αἱροῦνται τοὺς κόσμους ἀλλ' ἐκ τινῶν γενῶν, καὶ τοὺς γέρον-
τας ἐκ τῶν κεκοσμηκότων. περὶ ὧν τοὺς αὐτοὺς ἄν τις εἴ- 11
πειε λόγους καὶ περὶ τῶν ἐν Λακεδαίμονι γινομένων· τὸ
γὰρ ἀνυπεύθυνον καὶ τὸ διὰ βίου μεῖζόν ἐστι γέρας τῆς
ἀξίας αὐτοῖς, καὶ τὸ μὴ κατὰ γράμματα ἄρχειν ἀλλ'
αὐτογνώμονας ἐπισφαλές. τὸ δ' ἡσυχάζειν μὴ μετέχοντα 12
τὸν δῆμον οὐδὲν σημεῖον τοῦ τετάχθαι καλῶς· οὐδὲν γὰρ

ἀνυπεύθυνος - not liable to account, irresponsible.

λήμματός τι τοῖς κόσμοις ὥσπερ τοῖς ἐφόροις, πόρρω γ'
13 ἀποικοῦσιν ἐν νήσῳ τῶν διαφθερούντων. ἣν δὲ ποιοῦνται τῆς 1272 b
ἁμαρτίας ταύτης ἰατρείαν, ἄτοπος καὶ οὐ πολιτικὴ ἀλλὰ
δυναστευτική· πολλάκις γὰρ ἐκβάλλουσι συστάντες τινὲς τοὺς
κόσμους ἢ τῶν συναρχόντων αὐτῶν ἢ τῶν ἰδιωτῶν, ἔξεστι
δὲ καὶ μεταξὺ τοῖς κόσμοις ἀπειπεῖν τὴν ἀρχήν. ταῦτα
δὴ πάντα βέλτιον γίνεσθαι κατὰ νόμον ἢ κατ' ἀνθρώπων
14 βούλησιν· οὐ γὰρ ἀσφαλὴς ὁ κανών. πάντων δὲ φαυλότατον τὸ τῆς ἀκοσμίας τῶν δυνατῶν, ἣν καθιστᾶσι πολλάκις
ὅταν μὴ δίκας βούλωνται δοῦναι· ᾗ καὶ δῆλον ὡς ἔχει τι
πολιτείας ἡ τάξις, ἀλλ' οὐ πολιτεία ἐστὶν ἀλλὰ δυναστεία
μᾶλλον. εἰώθασι δὲ διαλαμβάνοντες τὸν δῆμον καὶ τοὺς
φίλους μοναρχίαν ποιεῖν καὶ στασιάζειν καὶ μάχεσθαι πρὸς
15 ἀλλήλους. καίτοι τί διαφέρει τὸ τοιοῦτον ἢ διά τινος χρόνου
μηκέτι πόλιν εἶναι τὴν τοιαύτην, ἀλλὰ λύεσθαι τὴν πολιτικὴν κοινωνίαν; ἔστι δ' ἐπικίνδυνος οὕτως ἔχουσα πόλις,
τῶν βουλομένων ἐπιτίθεσθαι καὶ δυναμένων. ἀλλὰ καθάπερ εἴρηται, σώζεται διὰ τὸν τόπον· ξενηλασίας γὰρ τὸ
16 πόρρω πεποίηκεν. διὸ καὶ τὸ τῶν περιοίκων μένει τοῖς Κρησίν, οἱ δ' εἵλωτες ἀφίστανται πολλάκις· οὔτε γὰρ ἐξωτερι-
κῆς ἀρχῆς κοινωνοῦσιν οἱ Κρῆτες, νεωστί τε πόλεμος ξενικὸς
διαβέβηκεν εἰς τὴν νῆσον, ὃς πεποίηκε φανερὰν τὴν ἀσθέ-
νειαν τῶν ἐκεῖ νόμων. περὶ μὲν οὖν ταύτης εἰρήσθω τοσαῦθ'
ἡμῖν τῆς πολιτείας·

Πολιτεύεσθαι δὲ δοκοῦσι καὶ Καρχηδόνιοι καλῶς καὶ **11**
πολλὰ περιττῶς πρὸς τοὺς ἄλλους, μάλιστα δ' ἔνια παραπλησίως τοῖς Λάκωσιν· αὗται γὰρ αἱ πολιτεῖαι τρεῖς ἀλλήλαις τε σύνεγγύς πώς εἰσι καὶ τῶν ἄλλων πολὺ διαφέρουσιν, ἥ τε Κρητικὴ καὶ ἡ Λακωνικὴ καὶ τρίτη τούτων
ἡ Καρχηδονίων· καὶ πολλὰ τῶν τεταγμένων ἔχει παρ'
2 αὐτοῖς καλῶς. σημεῖον δὲ πολιτείας συντεταγμένης τὸ τὸν
δῆμον ἔχουσαν διαμένειν ἐν τῇ τάξει τῆς πολιτείας, καὶ
μήτε στάσιν, ὅ τι καὶ ἄξιον εἰπεῖν, γεγενῆσθαι μήτε τύ-

ραννον. ἔχει δὲ παραπλήσια τῇ Λακωνικῇ πολιτείᾳ τὰ 3
μὲν συσσίτια τῶν ἑταιριῶν τοῖς φιδιτίοις, τὴν δὲ τῶν ἑκα-
τὸν καὶ τεττάρων ἀρχὴν τοῖς ἐφόροις (πλὴν οὐ χεῖρον· οἱ
μὲν γὰρ ἐκ τῶν τυχόντων εἰσί, ταύτην δ' αἱροῦνται τὴν ἀρχὴν
ἀριστίνδην), τοὺς δὲ βασιλεῖς καὶ τὴν γερουσίαν ἀνάλογον
τοῖς ἐκεῖ βασιλεῦσι καὶ γέρουσιν· καὶ βέλτιον δὲ τοὺς βα- 4
σιλεῖς μήτε κατὰ τὸ αὐτὸ εἶναι γένος, μηδὲ τοῦτο τὸ τυ-
χόν, εἴ τε διαφέρον, ἐκ τούτων αἱρετοὺς μᾶλλον ἢ καθ' ἡλι-
κίαν· μεγάλων γὰρ κύριοι καθεστῶτες, ἂν εὐτελεῖς ὦσι,
1273 a *μεγάλα βλάπτουσι καὶ ἔβλαψαν ἤδη τὴν πόλιν τὴν τῶν*
Λακεδαιμονίων. τὰ μὲν οὖν πλεῖστα τῶν ἐπιτιμηθέντων ἂν 5
διὰ τὰς παρεκβάσεις κοινὰ τυγχάνει πάσαις ὄντα ταῖς
εἰρημέναις πολιτείαις· τῶν δὲ πρὸς τὴν ὑπόθεσιν τῆς ἀρι-
στοκρατίας καὶ τῆς πολιτείας τὰ μὲν εἰς δῆμον ἐκκλίνει
μᾶλλον, τὰ δ' εἰς ὀλιγαρχίαν. τοῦ μὲν γὰρ τὰ μὲν προσ-
άγειν τὰ δὲ μὴ προσάγειν πρὸς τὸν δῆμον οἱ βασιλεῖς
κύριοι μετὰ τῶν γερόντων, ἂν ὁμογνωμονῶσι πάντες· εἰ
δὲ μή, καὶ τούτων ὁ δῆμος· ἃ δ' ἂν εἰσφέρωσιν οὗτοι, οὐ 6
διακοῦσαι μόνον ἀποδιδόασι τῷ δήμῳ τὰ δόξαντα τοῖς ἄρ-
χουσιν, ἀλλὰ κύριοι κρίνειν εἰσὶ καὶ τῷ βουλομένῳ τοῖς
εἰσφερομένοις ἀντειπεῖν ἔξεστιν, ὅπερ ἐν ταῖς ἑτέραις πολι-
τείαις οὐκ ἔστιν. τὸ δὲ τὰς πενταρχίας κυρίας οὔσας πολλῶν 7
καὶ μεγάλων ὑφ' αὑτῶν αἱρετὰς εἶναι, καὶ τὴν τῶν ἑκα-
τὸν ταύτας αἱρεῖσθαι τὴν μεγίστην ἀρχήν, ἔτι δὲ ταύτας
πλείονα ἄρχειν χρόνον τῶν ἄλλων (καὶ γὰρ ἐξεληλυθότες
ἄρχουσι καὶ μέλλοντες) ὀλιγαρχικόν· τὸ δὲ ἀμίσθους καὶ
μὴ κληρωτὰς ἀριστοκρατικὸν θετέον, καὶ εἴ τι τοιοῦτον ἕτε-
ρον, καὶ τὸ τὰς δίκας ὑπὸ τῶν ἀρχείων δικάζεσθαι πά-
σας, καὶ μὴ ἄλλας ὑπ' ἄλλων, καθάπερ ἐν Λακεδαίμονι.
παρεκβαίνει δὲ τῆς ἀριστοκρατίας ἡ τάξις τῶν Καρχηδο- 8
νίων μάλιστα πρὸς τὴν ὀλιγαρχίαν κατά τινα διάνοιαν ᾗ
συνδοκεῖ τοῖς πολλοῖς· οὐ γὰρ μόνον ἀριστίνδην ἀλλὰ καὶ
πλουτίνδην οἴονται δεῖν αἱρεῖσθαι τοὺς ἄρχοντας· ἀδύνατον

9 γὰρ τὸν ἀποροῦντα καλῶς ἄρχειν καὶ σχολάζειν. εἴπερ οὖν
τὸ μὲν αἱρεῖσθαι πλουτίνδην ὀλιγαρχικόν, τὸ δὲ κατ' ἀρετὴν ἀριστοκρατικόν, αὕτη τις ἂν εἴη τάξις τρίτη, καθ' ἥν-
περ συντέτακται καὶ τοῖς Καρχηδονίοις τὰ περὶ τὴν πο-
λιτείαν· αἱροῦνται γὰρ εἰς δύο ταῦτα βλέποντες, καὶ μάλιστα τὰς μεγίστας, τούς τε βασιλεῖς καὶ τοὺς στρατηγούς.
10 δεῖ δὲ νομίζειν ἁμάρτημα νομοθέτου τὴν παρέκβασιν εἶναι
τῆς ἀριστοκρατίας ταύτην· ἐξ ἀρχῆς γὰρ τοῦθ' ὁρᾶν ἐστὶ
τῶν ἀναγκαιοτάτων, ὅπως οἱ βέλτιστοι δύνωνται σχολάζειν
καὶ μηδὲν ἀσχημονεῖν, μὴ μόνον ἄρχοντες ἀλλὰ μηδ'
ἰδιωτεύοντες. εἰ δὲ δεῖ βλέπειν καὶ πρὸς εὐπορίαν χάριν
σχολῆς, φαῦλον τὸ τὰς μεγίστας ὠνητὰς εἶναι τῶν ἀρχῶν,
11 τήν τε βασιλείαν καὶ τὴν στρατηγίαν· ἔντιμον γὰρ ὁ νόμος
οὗτος ποιεῖ τὸν πλοῦτον μᾶλλον τῆς ἀρετῆς, καὶ τὴν πόλιν
ὅλην φιλοχρήματον· ὅτι δ' ἂν ὑπολάβῃ τίμιον εἶναι τὸ
κύριον, ἀνάγκη καὶ τὴν τῶν ἄλλων πολιτῶν δόξαν ἀκολουθεῖν τούτοις· ὅπου δὲ μὴ μάλιστα ἀρετὴ τιμᾶται, ταύτην
12 οὐχ οἷόν τε βεβαίως ἀριστοκρατεῖσθαι τὴν πολιτείαν. ἐθίζεσθαι δ' εὔλογον κερδαίνειν τοὺς ὠνουμένους, ὅταν δαπανή-
σαντες ἄρχωσιν· ἄτοπον γὰρ εἰ πένης μὲν ὢν ἐπιεικὴς δὲ
βουλήσεται κερδαίνειν, φαυλότερος δ' ὢν οὐ βουλήσεται δαπα-
νήσας. διὸ δεῖ τοὺς δυναμένους ἄριστ' ἄρχειν, τούτους ἄρχειν.
βέλτιον δ', εἰ καὶ προεῖτο τὴν εὐπορίαν τῶν ἐπιεικῶν ὁ νομοθέτης, ἀλλὰ ἀρχόντων γε ἐπιμελεῖσθαι τῆς σχολῆς.
13 φαῦλον δ' ἂν δόξειεν εἶναι καὶ τὸ πλείους ἀρχὰς τὸν αὐτὸν
ἄρχειν· ὅπερ εὐδοκιμεῖ παρὰ τοῖς Καρχηδονίοις. ἓν γὰρ
ὑφ' ἑνὸς ἔργον ἄριστ' ἀποτελεῖται. δεῖ δ' ὅπως γίνηται τοῦτο
ὁρᾶν τὸν νομοθέτην, καὶ μὴ προστάττειν τὸν αὐτὸν αὐλεῖν
14 καὶ σκυτοτομεῖν. ὥσθ' ὅπου μὴ μικρὰ πόλις, πολιτικώτερον
πλείονας μετέχειν τῶν ἀρχῶν, καὶ δημοτικώτερον· κοινότερόν τε γάρ, καθάπερ εἴπομεν, καὶ κάλλιον ἕκαστον ἀποτελεῖται τῶν αὐτῶν καὶ θᾶττον. δῆλον δὲ τοῦτο ἐπὶ τῶν
πολεμικῶν καὶ τῶν ναυτικῶν· ἐν τούτοις γὰρ ἀμφοτέροις

διὰ πάντων ὡς εἰπεῖν διελήλυθε τὸ ἄρχειν καὶ τὸ ἄρχεσθαι. ὀλιγαρχικῆς δ' οὔσης τῆς πολιτείας ἄριστα ἐκφεύ- 15
γουσι τῷ πλουτεῖν, αἰεί τι τοῦ δήμου μέρος ἐκπέμποντες ἐπὶ
τὰς πόλεις, τούτῳ γὰρ ἰῶνται καὶ ποιοῦσι μόνιμον τὴν πολιτείαν. ἀλλὰ τουτί ἐστι τύχης ἔργον, δεῖ δὲ ἀστασιάστους
εἶναι διὰ τὸν νομοθέτην. νῦν δέ, ἂν ἀτυχία γένηταί τις 16
καὶ τὸ πλῆθος ἀποστῇ τῶν ἀρχομένων, οὐδέν ἐστι φάρμακον
διὰ τῶν νόμων τῆς ἡσυχίας. περὶ μὲν οὖν τῆς Λακεδαιμονίων
πολιτείας καὶ Κρητικῆς καὶ τῆς Καρχηδονίων, αἵπερ δικαίως
εὐδοκιμοῦσι, τοῦτον ἔχει τὸν τρόπον·

12 Τῶν δὲ ἀποφηναμένων τι περὶ πολιτείας ἔνιοι μὲν οὐκ
ἐκοινώνησαν πράξεων πολιτικῶν οὐδ' ὡντινωνοῦν, ἀλλὰ διετέλεσαν ἰδιωτεύοντες τὸν βίον, περὶ ὧν εἴ τι ἀξιόλογον, εἴρηται σχεδὸν περὶ πάντων, ἔνιοι δὲ νομοθέται γεγόνασιν, οἱ
μὲν ταῖς οἰκείαις πόλεσιν, οἱ δὲ καὶ τῶν ὀθνείων τισί, πολιτευθέντες αὐτοί· καὶ τούτων οἱ μὲν νόμων ἐγένοντο δημιουργοὶ μόνον, οἱ δὲ καὶ πολιτείας, οἷον καὶ Λυκοῦργος καὶ
Σόλων· οὗτοι γὰρ καὶ νόμους καὶ πολιτείας κατέστησαν.
περὶ μὲν οὖν τῆς Λακεδαιμονίων εἴρηται, Σόλωνα δ' ἔνιοι 2
μὲν οἴονται γενέσθαι νομοθέτην σπουδαῖον· ὀλιγαρχίαν τε
γὰρ καταλῦσαι λίαν ἄκρατον οὖσαν, καὶ δουλεύοντα τὸν
δῆμον παῦσαι, καὶ δημοκρατίαν καταστῆσαι τὴν πάτριον,
μίξαντα καλῶς τὴν πολιτείαν· εἶναι γὰρ τὴν μὲν ἐν Ἀρείῳ
πάγῳ βουλὴν ὀλιγαρχικόν, τὸ δὲ τὰς ἀρχὰς αἱρετὰς ἀριστοκρατικόν, τὰ δὲ δικαστήρια δημοτικόν. ἔοικε δὲ Σόλων 3
1274 a ἐκεῖνα μὲν ὑπάρχοντα πρότερον οὐ καταλῦσαι, τήν τε βουλὴν καὶ τὴν τῶν ἀρχῶν αἵρεσιν, τὸν δὲ δῆμον καταστῆσαι,
τὰ δικαστήρια ποιήσας ἐκ πάντων. διὸ καὶ μέμφονταί
τινες αὐτῷ· λῦσαι γὰρ θάτερον, κύριον ποιήσαντα τὸ δικαστήριον πάντων, κληρωτὸν ὄν. ἐπεὶ γὰρ τοῦτ' ἴσχυσεν, ὥσπερ 4
τυράννῳ τῷ δήμῳ χαριζόμενοι τὴν πολιτείαν εἰς τὴν νῦν
δημοκρατίαν κατέστησαν, καὶ τὴν μὲν ἐν Ἀρείῳ πάγῳ βουλὴν Ἐφιάλτης ἐκόλουσε καὶ Περικλῆς, τὰ δὲ δικαστήρια

ὀθνεῖος foreign
Κολουω - dock, clip, curtail.

μισθοφόρα κατέστησε Περικλῆς, καὶ τοῦτον δὴ τὸν τρόπον
ἕκαστος τῶν δημαγωγῶν προήγαγεν αὔξων εἰς τὴν νῦν δη-
5 μοκρατίαν. φαίνεται δὲ οὐ κατὰ τὴν Σόλωνος γενέσθαι τοῦτο
προαίρεσιν, ἀλλὰ μᾶλλον ἀπὸ συμπτώματος (τῆς ναυαρχίας γὰρ ἐν τοῖς Μηδικοῖς ὁ δῆμος αἴτιος γενόμενος ἐφρο-
νηματίσθη, καὶ δημαγωγοὺς ἔλαβε φαύλους ἀντιπολιτευο-
μένων τῶν ἐπιεικῶν), ἐπεὶ Σόλων γε ἔοικε τὴν ἀναγκαιο-
τάτην ἀποδιδόναι τῷ δήμῳ δύναμιν, τὸ τὰς ἀρχὰς αἱρεῖσθαι καὶ εὐθύνειν (μηδὲ γὰρ τούτου κύριος ὢν ὁ δῆμος
6 δοῦλος ἂν εἴη καὶ πολέμιος), τὰς δ' ἀρχὰς ἐκ τῶν γνωρίμων καὶ τῶν εὐπόρων κατέστησε πάσας, ἐκ τῶν πεντακοσιομεδίμνων καὶ ζευγιτῶν καὶ τρίτου τέλους τῆς καλουμένης
ἱππάδος· τὸ δὲ τέταρτον θητικόν, οἷς οὐδεμιᾶς ἀρχῆς μετῆν.
νομοθέται δὲ ἐγένοντο Ζάλευκός τε Λοκροῖς τοῖς ἐπιζεφυ-
ρίοις, καὶ Χαρώνδας ὁ Καταναῖος τοῖς αὐτοῦ πολίταις καὶ
ταῖς ἄλλαις ταῖς Χαλκιδικαῖς πόλεσι ταῖς περὶ Ἰταλίαν
7 καὶ Σικελίαν. πειρῶνται δέ τινες καὶ συνάγειν ὡς Ὀνο-
μακρίτου μὲν γενομένου πρώτου δεινοῦ περὶ νομοθεσίαν, γυμνασθῆναι δ' αὐτὸν ἐν Κρήτῃ Λοκρὸν ὄντα καὶ ἐπιδημοῦντα
κατὰ τέχνην μαντικήν· τούτου δὲ γενέσθαι Θάλητα ἑταῖρον,
Θάλητος δ' ἀκροατὴν Λυκοῦργον καὶ Ζάλευκον, Ζαλεύκου
8 δὲ Χαρώνδαν. ἀλλὰ ταῦτα μὲν λέγουσιν ἀσκεπτότερον τῷ
χρόνῳ λέγοντες, ἐγένετο δὲ καὶ Φιλόλαος ὁ Κορίνθιος νομοθέτης Θηβαίοις. ἦν δ' ὁ Φιλόλαος τὸ μὲν γένος τῶν
Βακχιαδῶν, ἐραστὴς δὲ γενόμενος Διοκλέους τοῦ νικήσαντος
Ὀλυμπίασιν, ὡς ἐκεῖνος τὴν πόλιν ἔλιπε διαμισήσας τὸν
ἔρωτα τὸν τῆς μητρὸς Ἀλκυόνης, ἀπῆλθεν εἰς Θήβας, κἀκεῖ
9 τὸν βίον ἐτελεύτησαν ἀμφότεροι. καὶ νῦν ἔτι δεικνύουσι τοὺς
τάφους αὐτῶν ἀλλήλοις μὲν εὐσυνόπτους ὄντας, πρὸς δὲ τὴν
τῶν Κορινθίων χώραν τοῦ μὲν συνόπτου τοῦ δ' οὐ συνόπτου·
μυθολογοῦσι γὰρ αὐτοὺς οὕτω τάξασθαι τὴν ταφήν, τὸν μὲν
Διοκλέα διὰ τὴν ἀπέχθειαν τοῦ πάθους, ὅπως μὴ ἄποπτος
ἔσται ἡ Κορινθία ἀπὸ τοῦ χώματος, τὸν δὲ Φιλόλαον, ὅπως

1274 b ἄποπτος. ᾤκησαν μὲν οὖν διὰ τὴν τοιαύτην αἰτίαν παρὰ 10
τοῖς Θηβαίοις, νομοθέτης δ' αὐτοῖς ἐγένετο Φιλόλαος περί
τ' ἄλλων τινῶν καὶ περὶ τῆς παιδοποιίας, οὓς καλοῦσιν
ἐκεῖνοι νόμους θετικούς· καὶ τοῦτ' ἐστὶν ἰδίως ὑπ' ἐκείνου νενομοθετημένον, ὅπως ὁ ἀριθμὸς σώζηται τῶν κλήρων. Χα- 11
ρώνδου δ' ἴδιον μὲν οὐδέν ἐστι πλὴν αἱ δίκαι τῶν ψευδομαρτύρων (πρῶτος γὰρ ἐποίησε τὴν ἐπίσκηψιν), τῇ δ' ἀκριβείᾳ
τῶν νόμων ἐστὶ γλαφυρώτερος καὶ τῶν νῦν νομοθετῶν.
[Φαλέου δ' ἴδιον ἡ τῶν οὐσιῶν ἀνομάλωσις, Πλάτωνος δ' ἥ 12
τε τῶν γυναικῶν καὶ παίδων καὶ τῆς οὐσίας κοινότης καὶ
τὰ συσσίτια τῶν γυναικῶν, ἔτι δ' ὁ περὶ τὴν μέθην νόμος,
τὸ τοὺς νήφοντας συμποσιαρχεῖν, καὶ τὴν ἐν τοῖς πολεμικοῖς ἄσκησιν ὅπως ἀμφιδέξιοι γίνωνται κατὰ τὴν μελέτην,
ὡς δέον μὴ τὴν μὲν χρήσιμον εἶναι τοῖν χεροῖν τὴν δὲ
ἄχρηστον]. Δράκοντος δὲ νόμοι μέν εἰσι, πολιτείᾳ δ' ὑπαρ- 13
χούσῃ τοὺς νόμους ἔθηκεν· ἴδιον δ' ἐν τοῖς νόμοις οὐδέν ἐστιν
ὅ τι καὶ μνείας ἄξιον, πλὴν ἡ χαλεπότης διὰ τὸ τῆς ζημίας
μέγεθος. ἐγένετο δὲ καὶ Πιττακὸς νόμων δημιουργὸς ἀλλ'
οὐ πολιτείας· νόμος δ' ἴδιος αὐτοῦ τὸ τοὺς μεθύοντας, ἄν
τι πταίσωσι, πλείω ζημίαν ἀποτίνειν τῶν νηφόντων· διὰ γὰρ
τὸ πλείους ὑβρίζειν μεθύοντας ἢ νήφοντας οὐ πρὸς τὴν συγγνώμην ἀπέβλεψεν, ὅτι δεῖ μεθύουσιν ἔχειν μᾶλλον, ἀλλὰ
πρὸς τὸ συμφέρον. ἐγένετο δὲ καὶ Ἀνδροδάμας Ῥηγῖνος 14
νομοθέτης Χαλκιδεῦσι τοῖς ἐπὶ Θρᾴκης, οὗ περί τε τὰ φονικὰ καὶ τὰς ἐπικλήρους ἐστίν· οὐ μὴν ἀλλὰ ἴδιόν γε οὐδὲν
αὐτοῦ λέγειν ἔχοι τις ἄν. τὰ μὲν οὖν περὶ τὰς πολιτείας,
τάς τε κυρίας καὶ τὰς ὑπὸ τινῶν εἰρημένας, ἔστω τεθεωρημένα τόν τρόπον τοῦτον.

CRITICAL NOTES.

The following notes are intended to be used in conjunction with the *apparatus criticus* of Susemihl's editions, and especially that of 1872. It is in these editions alone that the MSS. and their readings, and also the version of the Vetus Interpres, can be fully studied. In those cases, indeed, in which I have been obliged to choose between a reading supported by the whole of one family of MSS. and one supported by the whole of the other, and the choice was attended with doubt, I have commonly noted the reading which I have not adopted, and I have taken some pains, in dealing with the readings offered by the first family of MSS., to point out the passages in which we are unable to affirm with certainty that Γ agreed with M^s P^1, for perhaps even the third and last of Susemihl's editions hardly makes it clear how numerous they are. The student of Susemihl's *apparatus criticus*, in fact, occasionally finds in it readings which Susemihl does not accept ascribed to Π^2, and may naturally infer that Π^1 (i.e. Γ as well as M^s P^1) support the reading adopted by him. This is, no doubt, frequently the case, but on the other hand it frequently happens that the reading of Γ is not ascertainable, and of course, when this is so, Susemihl's reading rests only on the authority of M^s P^1, for we cannot assume without proof that Γ agreed with M^s P^1 and not with Π^2; on the contrary, Γ often agrees with Π^2 against M^s P^1. Thus the *indubitable* discrepancies between Π^1 and Π^2 prove on examination to be considerably less numerous than might be supposed[1]. I have seldom

[1] Susemihl would seem in the following notes of his third edition, for instance, tacitly or otherwise to attribute to Π^1 a reading which can only be attributed with certainty to M^s P^1:—1252 b 2, *οἱ* om. Π^2: 5, *τὸ* post *καὶ* om. Π^2: 1253 a 32, *ὁ* om. Π^2: 1255 b 23, *ταῖς* post *ἐν* add. Π^1: 26, *ὀψοποιική* Π^2: 1256 b 8, *διδομένη* Π^2: 13, *γενομένοις* Π^2: 1258 b 1, *μεταβλητικῆς* Π^2: 1260 a 31, *ὁ* ante *παῖς* add. Π^2. In 1260 a 21, the reading *ἁπάντων* is ascribed to Π^1, but we cannot tell from Vet. Int. *omnium* whether he found *ἁπάντων* or *πάντων* in his Greek text (see his rendering of 1263 b 17 sq.). These references need not be carried farther than the First Book.

noted variants clearly not supported by the whole of a family, except when I hoped to be able to throw some fresh light on their value. The readings which I have given from O[1] will at any rate serve to illustrate the character of a manuscript which, though belonging to a well-known variety, does not always agree with P[4], the MS. to which it is most nearly allied. I have drawn more largely on the Vetus Interpres, noting freely any renderings which seemed to call for remark. I have sought by a study of his method of translation to contribute to the solution of the important question, in what cases we can safely infer from his renderings a variation in the Greek text used by him. Here and there, but not often, I have noted renderings to which Susemihl has omitted to call attention. I have also occasionally indicated passages in which the text of the translation appears to be by no means certain, and recorded any readings found in the MSS. of it consulted by me which seemed to deserve mention. But my main object in these notes has been to discuss the copious data furnished by Susemihl, and especially to throw light on the characteristics of the MSS. and the Latin translation, in the hope of contributing to the ascertainment of the correct text of the Politics.

My quotations from the Latin translation of Leonardus Aretinus (Lionardo Bruni of Arezzo) are based on a comparison of the beautiful MS. of this translation in the possession of New College, Oxford (MS. 228), which belongs to the middle of the fifteenth century, with a Bodleian MS. (Canon. Class. Lat. 195). I have drawn attention in the following notes to one or two passages in which these MSS. do not support readings ascribed by Susemihl to Aretinus; I do not know what is the cause of this discrepancy, but I may refer to Susemihl's remarks in his first edition of the Politics, p. xxix sq., as to the supposed existence of two versions of Aretinus' translation, for it is possible that the discrepancy is thus to be accounted for.

The conjectures by which scholars have sought to emend the text will be found fully recorded in Susemihl's editions.

I have already (above, p. xlviii, note 1, and p. xlix, note 2) explained the symbols which I have adopted from Susemihl. A full account of the MSS. of the Politics and the Vetus Interpres consulted by Susemihl will be found in the Prolegomena to his first edition (that of 1872), and also a full account of the corrections in P[1], P[2], and P[4]. As to the Vatican Fragments, see the Preface.

I add some remarks on the MSS. consulted by me.

MS. 112 belonging to Corpus Christi College, Oxford (O[1]) is a fifteenth century manuscript containing the Politics together with other writings of Aristotle, or ascribed to him (see for its contents Mr. J. A. Stewart, The English Manuscripts of the Nicomachean Ethics, Anecdota Oxoniensia, vol. i, part i, p. 5), and bearing at the foot of its first page the following inscription:—*Orate pro anima Joannis Claimondi collegii corporis Christi primi presidis, qui hunc librum eidem condonavit.* (Mr. Stewart mentions, p. 6, that Claimond was President of Corpus from 1517 to 1537.) Its text of the Politics is written in a very legible hand, but there are not a few corrections both between the lines and in the margin, and these corrections are made partly by the writer of the MS. himself, partly by a corrector (corr.[1]), whose handwriting is in many cases easily distinguishable from that of the writer of the MS., but in some not so, and especially in those in which the correction is between the lines and consists of a single letter only, or two or three. The ink used by this corrector is often very similar to that of the MS. One or two corrections in the first two books are apparently due to a second corrector. The text of the Politics in O[1] is nearly akin to that of the P[4] of Susemihl (MS. 2025 of the Bibliothèque Nationale at Paris: see as to P[4] Sus.[1], p. xxiii), though neither of these MSS. is copied from the other, but the corrections from a MS. of the first family which lend a special interest and importance to P[4] are wanting in O[1]: the corrections in O[1] which are due to corr.[1] are mostly derived from a MS. of the second family, though a few of them (for instance, the expunged addition of ἀρχόντων καὶ in 1260 a 4) may be derived from the Vetus Interpres or possibly from some gloss. The following passages (to which it would be easy to add indefinitely) will suffice to establish its close kinship with P[4]:—1255 a 24, ἅμα—δικαίαν om. pr. P[4] pr. O[1]: 1256 a 14, μέρος om. P[4] pr. O[1]: 1257 a 13, γέγωνε P[4] O[1]: 32, εἰσάσθαι pr. P[4] pr. O[1]: 1257 b 27, οὐκ—28, τέλος om. P[4] pr. O[1]: 1258 a 14, ἅπαντα δέον om. P[4] pr. O[1]: 16, χρία P[4] O[1]. On the other hand, O[1] often differs from P[4]: thus in 1253 a 7 O[1] omits ἄζυξ ὤν, P[4] only ὤν: in 1253 b 35 O[1] has τοὺς, which P[4] omits: its reading differs from that of P[4] in 1254 a 15 sq.: in 1257 a 33–34 it is free from the blunders found in P[4]: in 1258 a 38 pr. O[1] omits καρπῶν καὶ τῶν, pr. P[4] only καὶ τῶν: in 1259 a 12 pr. O[1] has λόγων, P[4] ὀλίγων: in 1261 a 1 pr. P[4] omits several words, not so O[1]: in 1262 b 13 O[1] has συμφῦναι, not so P[4]. Here and there we find O[1] agreeing with P[2 3] (thus in 1257 a 16 it has δὲ ἐλάττω, in 1263 b 31 πῶς, in 1264 b 14 μῖξαι, in 1271 b 12 ἀναγκαζομένους), or with P[2 3] T[b] (1264 a 35, πενιστείας: 1267 b 28, λόγος); more rarely with M[s] P[1] (as in 1264 b 13, εὐθύς: 1266 a 5, ἔπειτα: 1268 b 15, δηλονότι), or with Ms (as in 1252 b 3, ἀποτελεῖτο: 1263 a 24, ἀγαθῶν).

I pass on to MSS. of the Vetus Interpres. MS. Phillipps 891 (z) is a parchment MS. in quarto form, containing the translation of the Politics together with that of the Oeconomics and an unfinished fragment of the commencement of the translation of the Rhetoric, and written at Zara in Dalmatia[1] in the year 1393. This appears from the following inscription on a blank page at its commencement, which is in the same handwriting as the MS.:—*Liber politicorum et yconomicorum Aristotelis in hoc volumine deputatur (deo volente) ad usum mei Jacobini quondam* [9̄=*condam*] *Alberti de mayn̄tibus* (=*de maynentibus*=dei Maynenti) *de Vīc.* [*Vincentia* or *Vicentia*=Vicenza] *quem scripsi in civitate Jadre* 1393 *cum ibi forem ab illius civitatis communitate pro fisico opere medicine salariatus et habitus. Laus et honor deo.* (For the interpretation of *Vīc.* and of the contraction for *quem scripsi* I am indebted to the kind aid of Mr. F. Madan, Sub-Librarian of the Bodleian Library. The interpretation which I have given above of the symbol 9̄ is that of Mr. E. Maunde Thompson, Keeper of the MSS. in the British Museum, to whom, no less than to Mr. Madan, my best thanks are due for valuable and ready help. Mr. Maunde Thompson explains the meaning of *quondam Alberti* to be 'formerly son of Albertus' or 'son of the late Albertus.' Having found the form *Patricii de Piccolominibus* in the title of a book published in 1485 ('Pontificale A. Patricii de Piccolominibus, Romae, 1485'), I thought it likely that *mayn̄tibus* was a family-name, but the word remained a puzzle, till Mr. Maunde Thompson solved the problem by discovering the name Mainenti in a list of families belonging to Vicenza contained in the 'Historia di Vicenza, by G. Marzari, Venice, 1691.' I shall be glad if the publication of this inscription should lead to the communication of further particulars respecting the writer, Jacobino dei Maynenti.) At the commencement of the MS., prefixed to the translation of the Politics, are the words to which attention has already been called (above, p. xlii); they are in red letters but in the hand of the writer of the MS.:—*Incipit liber politicorum Aristotilis a fratre Guilielmo ordinis praedicatorum de greco in latinum translatus.* At the close of the translation, the words *quod decens* (answering to τὸ πρέπον, 5 (8). 7. 1342 b 34) are not followed either by the sentence—*reliqua huius*

[1] For other MSS. transcribed at Zara, see Schenkl, Ausonius, pp. xxiii, xxvii. I owe this reference to Mr. Robinson Ellis, whom I have also to thank for informing me some years ago of the existence of a MS. of the Vetus Interpres in the Phillipps Library.

operis in greco nondum inveni—which succeeds them in all the MSS. but a, or by the sentences which are here found in a and rec. a (see Sus.[1] *ad loc.*), but simply by the words—*Explicit liber polliticorum Aristotilis*. At the top of the pages of this MS. and in the margins and in a large blank space purposely left at the foot copious annotations are inserted, and the text itself is interspersed with corrections and explanatory additions. Here and there we meet with corrections which are in the same hand and ink as the MS. and have obviously been made by the writer of it, but most of them and all the annotations are in a far smaller hand than that of the MS., and one which, perhaps for this reason, differs a good deal from it. Some, however, of these annotations and corrections are apparently in the same ink as the MS., and as these are in the same handwriting as others which are in a darker ink, it seems probable that all the annotations and corrections were added by the writer of the MS.[1] If so, he was evidently a diligent student of the Politics in William of Moerbeke's Latin Translation. I have given in the following Critical Notes those of the various readings of z in the first two books which seemed to possess most importance, and have added in Appendix C a complete list of its variations in these books from the text printed by Susemihl, with the exception of unimportant errors of spelling. It will be seen that its omissions and blunders are many, and that here and there the original reading has been erased and an incorrect one substituted; nevertheless, it has in not a few passages either alone or in conjunction with a preserved the true reading. It has no doubt likewise done so in the books which I have not as yet collated, for in glancing at a passage in its text of the Seventh (4 (7). 13. 1331 b 31) I found the word ἔκκειται, which is rendered in the other MSS. *latet*, rendered (rightly in all probability) *iacet*. It is worthy of notice that as z was written at Zara in Dalmatia, so the allied MS. a was 'written in Italy' (Sus.[1], p. xxxiv). It is possible that a search among Venetian MSS. of the Vetus Interpres, if such exist, might bring to light other MSS. belonging to the same family and superior to a and z. We might then be less in the dark than we are at present as to the origin of the marked difference between the two families.

MS. 112 belonging to Balliol College, Oxford (o) is ascribed by Susemihl (Sus.[1], p. xxxviii) to the earlier part of the fourteenth century, and is the oldest of the MSS. of the Vetus Interpres yet collated. Its text of the translation of the Politics is evidently

[1] I might be able to speak more positively as to this, if I had read more of these annotations than I have as yet found time to do.

nearly allied to that of Susemihl's c, a far later manuscript, but c is not copied from o.

MS. Bodl. Canon. Class. Lat. 174 (y) is a beautifully written Italian manuscript, belonging to the fourteenth century, and, in Mr. Madan's opinion, to the latter half of it. Each page contains two columns. The text of the translation of the Politics contained in it has been tampered with in places by an ingenious corrector, who has here and there contrived with the aid of a penknife to convert the original reading into an entirely new one: thus in the rendering of 1256 b 13 we find *parientes* over an erasure, the original reading having probably been *pro genitis*, and in 1258 a 7 again we find *iam* over an erasure, the original reading having probably been *non*. These erasures, however, are readily discernible, and they do not seem to occur very often. This MS. is allied, not to a or z, but to the bulk of the MSS. of the translation.

BOOK I.

1252 a 2. ἕνεκεν] 'Only the forms ending in -α are Attic (ἕνεκα, εἵνεκα, οὕνεκα) . . . the form ἕνεκεν does not occur in Attic Inscriptions till after about 300 B.C.' (Meisterhans, Grammatik der attischen Inschriften, p. 103). Aristotle's frequent use of ἕνεκεν deserves notice. **8.** εἶναι om. Γ P^1 pr. M^s; a later hand adds it in M^s after τὸν. Sus. brackets it, and refers (ed. 1) to 7 (5). 12. 1316 b 2, οὐ δίκαιον οἴονται εἶναι ἴσον μετέχειν τῆς πόλεως τοὺς κεκτημένους μηδὲν τοῖς κεκτημένοις, where $P^{1\,6}$ Π^2 read εἶναι and Γ M^s omit it (probably wrongly, as they stand alone), and to 2. 7. 1266 b 1, οὐ χαλεπὸν ᾤετο ποιεῖν, where Γ Π om. εἶναι: he also gives a reference to Schanz, Nov. quaest. Platon. p. 33 sq. The question whether εἶναι should be retained here is a difficult one, for though Π^1 are somewhat prone to omit, and more than once omit εἶναι where it seems to be required (e.g. in 1257 b 7), yet they occasionally omit it where it can be dispensed with (e.g. in 1298 b 36), and Aristotle is well known to be sparing in his use of εἶναι (see Vahlen, Beitr. zu Aristot. Poet. 3. 330, and his edition of the Poetics, p. 243 sqq.: see also Bon. Ind. 239 a 9 sqq.). On the other hand, its omission causes a harshness here, which it does not cause in 1266 b 1. In 1. 9. 1257 a 1, again, the verb is νομίζειν, not οἴεσθαι, and the construction is softened by the use of ὡς. Meteor. 1. 14. 352 a 25, ἀλλὰ τούτου τὴν αἰτίαν οὐ τὴν τοῦ κόσμου γένεσιν οἴεσθαι χρή, however, is a nearer parallel. τὸν αὐτόν] Vet. Int. *idem* (τὸ αὐτό Γ?). **15.** τοὺς om.

pr. O[1] (with Π[3]): it is added in the margin by a corrector. But Π[3] often omit the article—e. g. in 1269 a 7, 1291 a 1, b 3, 1297 a 35. **24.** δὴ] *enim* Vet. Int., but we often find *enim* in Vet. Int. where we expect another word—e.g. in 1253 a 23, 1256 a 31, 1272 a 41. *Enim* does not always stand for γάρ in Vet. Int. (see critical note on 1271 a 23). **25.** ὥσπερ ἐν τοῖς ἄλλοις] Vet. Int. *quemadmodum et in aliis*, but he probably did not find καὶ in his Greek text any more than he found it there in 1335 b 30, where he translates καθάπερ τὰ τῶν νεωτέρων *sicut et iuniorum* (see Busse, p. 30). See also below on 1262 a 29. **26.** συνδυάζεσθαι] y z have *combinare*: I read *obviare* or *obinare* in o, not (with Sus.) *obinari*.

1252 b 2. M[s] P[1] add οἱ before χαλκοτύποι: we cannot tell from *aeris figuratores* what Vet. Int. found in his Greek text: Π[2] omit it, and they may well be right in doing so: see Vahlen, Beitr. zu Aristot. Poet. 3. 340 sq., and Bon. Ind. 109 b 36 sqq. **5.** M[s] P[1] add τὸ before δοῦλον: about the reading of Γ we cannot be certain: a similar difference of reading occurs in 1261 b 25. See on the subject Bon. Ind. 109 b 44 sqq.: Vahlen, Beitr. 4. 409. The reading of Γ being doubtful, it seems better to follow Π[2]. **8.** βαρβάρων δ'] Vet. Int. *barbaris quidem*. But the Vet. Int. occasionally substitutes γε for δὲ (e. g. in 1268 b 16). **14.** Χαρώνδας μὲν] M[s] P[1] ὁ μὲν Χαρώνδας: Vet. Int. *Charondas quidem*, which may represent Χαρώνδας μὲν, the reading of Π[2]. Charondas is nowhere else in the Politics honoured with the prefixed article by any MS. **15.** ὁμοκάπους] ὁμοκάπνους 'Π[1] P[4] L[s] corr. M[b]' (Sus.), also O[1]: as to M[s], however, see Sus.[1] p. xii. note 20. The New College MS. of Ar. has *homotapos*, but Bodl. *homocapnos*. **17.** Vet. Int. *domuum* for οἰκίας, but he probably found οἰκίας, not οἰκιῶν, in his Greek text, for in 1259 a 35 he has *domibus* for οἰκίᾳ. **20.** συνῆλθον om. Γ M[s] pr. P[1]: not so Ar., who has *nam ex hiis qui suberant regno accreverunt*. **28.** ἤδη] ἡ δὴ is the reading of O[1] and of all known MSS. except P[1], which has ἤδη, and two others which have ἡ δὲ (Ar. *quae quidem*): Vet. Int. *iam*. **29.** μὲν οὖν] οὖν om. M[s] P[1], and perhaps Ar. (*constituta quidem gratia vivendi*), but μὲν οὖν is undoubtedly right: it is a common fault in the MSS. to drop out οὖν after μὲν (see 1257 b 3, 1294 b 1, 1300 b 24, 1303 b 15, 1314 a 25). **31.** αὕτη] Vet. Int. *ipsa* (αὐτὴ Γ).

1253 a 1. I follow Π[2] in adding καὶ before τέλος (so O[1]): Π[1] omit it, but the presumption is against this family of MSS. in cases of omission. **2.** M[s] P[1] add ὁ before ἄνθρωπος (Sus.[1]), just as they do in the corresponding passage, 1278 b 19, and in 1253 a 32; we cannot tell whether Vet. Int. found the article in his Greek text or not: Π² omit it in all these passages, probably rightly: see above on 1252 b 2 and the authorities there referred to. **5.** Susemihl omits to call attention to the fact that Vet. Int. has *sceleratus* for ἀνέστιος: Vet. Int. would seem to have misread ἀνέστιος as ἀνόσιος—cp. 1253 a 35, where he translates ἀνοσιώτατον by *scelestissimum*. **6.** ἅτε περ ἄζυξ ὢν ὥσπερ ἐν πεττοῖς] See Susemihl's *apparatus criticus* for the various readings of the MSS. in this passage. O¹ omits ἄζυξ ὤν, leaving however a lacuna where these words should stand. O¹ here differs from P⁴, for pr. P⁴ omits only ὤν. Vet. Int. *sine iugo existens*, which is no doubt a translation of ἄνευ ζυγοῦ τυγχάνων (for τυγχάνειν is often rendered by *existere* in Vet. Int.—e.g. in 1260 b 31, 1269 b 24), and this is probably a gloss explanatory of ἄζυξ ὤν. Ar. does not render ἅτε περ—πεττοῖς, but this does not prove that the clause was wanting in his Greek text; it may well have been imperfect and incomprehensible. All the MSS. may be said to have πεττοῖς (πετοῖς Mᵇ), though πετεινοῖς appears in the margin of P¹ P⁴ and Sᵇ. Vet. Int. *sicut in volatilibus*, but he may possibly be here translating a conjecture added in the margin of the MS. used by him. There can be little doubt that πεττοῖς is the right reading. **10.** τῶν ζῴων] Vet. Int. *supra animalia*, but he seems now and then to add prepositions without finding an equivalent for them in his Greek text—thus in 1263 a 37 he renders ἐφοδίων *pro viaticis*, in 1263 b 41 τοῖς συσσιτίοις *pro conviviis*, in 1316 b 2 τῆς πόλεως *per civitatem*, and in 1273 a 28 τοῖς Καρχηδονίοις *apud Calchedonios*. See also below on 1273 b 15. **12.** For ἐλήλυθε τοῦ ἔχειν αἴσθησιν λυπηροῦ καὶ ἡδέος, the Aldine text has ἐλήλυθεν, P⁴ ⁶ Mᵇ Uᵇ Lˢ (and O¹) προῆλθεν, followed in all these MSS. (which belong to the less good variety of the second family) by ὥστε αἰσθάνεσθαι τοῦ λυπηροῦ καὶ ἡδέος. Compare the deviation of P⁴⁶ Q Mᵇ Uᵇ Lˢ Ald. from the text of other MSS. in 1253 b 2–4, and of P⁴⁶ Q Lˢ in 1258 a 32 sqq., and of P⁴⁶ Uᵇ Lˢ Cᶜ in 1286 b 25, where they read ἀλλ' οὐ καταλείψει τοὺς υἱεῖς διαδόχους ὁ βασιλεὺς ἐπ' ἐξουσίας ἔχων τοῦτο ποιῆσαι (an evident gloss), and of P⁴⁶ Lˢ Ald. in 1260 a 32, where τὸν τέλειον takes the place of τὸ τέλος in these MSS. O¹ agrees with P⁴ in all these passages. In the passage before us, as in some of the others referred to, a gloss seems to be substituted for the text, for it is not likely that we have to do with traces of a double version. See also the readings offered by P⁴⁶ Lˢ Cᶜ in 1301 b 33 and 1309 b 2, and by P⁴⁶ Uᵇ Vᵇ Lˢ in 1302 a 28. **22.** εἴ τις λέγει] Vet. Int. *si quis dicat*, but this is no proof that he found λέγοι (which P² alone has) in his Greek text, for in 1288 b 36 he translates καὶ εἰ τἆλλα λέγουσι καλῶς *et si alia dicant bene.* **23.** πάντα δὲ] All MSS. of Vet. Int. but k have *omnia enim.* **25.** Π[1] omit καὶ before φύσει: P[2] omits καὶ before πρότερον, and most MSS. of Vet. Int. (but not a or z) omit *et* here. Vet. Int. has *prior*, and several of the less good MSS. of the Politics have προτέρα. O[1] (like P[4]) has καὶ φύσει καὶ πρότερα. **28.** μηδὲν δεόμενος] Vet. Int. has *nullo indigens*, but he probably found μηδὲν in his Greek text. **30.** πρῶτος] O[1] has πρῶτον, with ς however superscribed above the final ν—I think by the writer of the MS., though it is difficult to be certain. **32.** M[s] P[1] add ὁ before ἄνθρωπος: we cannot tell whether Vet. Int. found it in his text: see above on 1253 a 2. **36.** πρὸς ἀφροδίσια καὶ ἐδωδήν] Sus.[1]: '*ad* post *venerea et* add. o,' but this *ad* is expunged in o by dots placed beneath it. z adds *ad* here. 'Praepositionem cum plurium nominum casibus copulatam ante unumquodque eorum repetere solet Guilelmus' (Sus.[1], p. xxxiii).

1253 b 2–4. The reading followed in the text is that of the first family of MSS. and the better variety of the second, except that M[s] P[1] read ἡ οἰκία πάλιν in place of πάλιν οἰκία (Vet. Int. *rursum domus*), and that Γ in 3 had οἰκίας in place of οἰκονομίας, unless indeed *domus* is a conjecture due to the translator. The reading of P[4 6] Q M[b] U[b] L[s] (and also of O[1]), on the other hand, is as follows:—ἀνάγκη περὶ οἰκονομίας εἰπεῖν πρότερον· πᾶσα γὰρ πόλις ἐξ οἰκιῶν σύγκειται. οἰκίας δὲ μέρη, ἐξ ὧν αὖθις οἰκία συνίσταται. Bekker follows the reading of these MSS., substituting however ἀναγκαῖον for ἀνάγκη, and in his second edition περὶ οἰκίας for περὶ οἰκονομίας. But see above on 1253 a 12. Οἰκονομίας δὲ μέρη (not οἰκίας δὲ μέρη) appears to be the true reading, for οἰκονομίας here corresponds to οἰκονομίας 2 (which is the reading of all extant MSS. and of Γ) and is confirmed by ἔστι δέ τι μέρος (sc. οἰκονομίας) 12. Besides, if οἰκίας δὲ μέρη be read, the tautology in 3 seems excessive. Cp. also 1. 12. 1259 a 37, ἐπεὶ δὲ τρία μέρη τῆς οἰκονομικῆς ἦν. **17.** δυναίμεθα] δυνάμεθα M[s] P[1] C[4]; Vet. Int. *et utique . . . poterimus*, which represents κἂν . . . δυναίμεθα (the reading of almost all the MSS. of the second family), for in 1252 a 26 Vet. Int. renders θεωρήσειεν ἂν *utique contemplabitur*, in 1253 b 8 σκεπτέον ἂν εἴη *considerandum utique erit*, in 1253 b 26 ἀναγκαῖον ἂν εἴη *necessarium utique erit*, and so generally. In 1253 b 38 οὐδὲν ἂν ἔδει is *nihil utique opus esset*, in 1264 a 3 οὐκ ἂν ἔλαθεν *non utique lateat.* **19.** o y z render πολιτικὴ by *politica* (z *pollitica*), which is preferable to *politia*, the reading adopted by Susemihl. **23.** z adds *manifestum quod* after *pars domus est*, perhaps introducing into the text a conjectural emendation in the margin of its archetype, the object evidently being to obtain an apodosis. **24.** ἀδύνατον καὶ ζῆν] *est* after *impossibile* om. z, perhaps rightly. **25.** ὥσπερ δὲ ταῖς] ὥσπερ ταῖς pr. O[1] (corr.[1] in marg. γρ. ὥσπερ δὲ ἐν), but neither of these readings is probably the correct one, for the former is that of P[4 6] U[b] L[s] Ald. (see as to these MSS. above on 1253 a 12 and 1253 b 2–4), and the latter, though adopted by Bekker, is found only in MSS. of little authority: Ar. (who translates *ut vero in artibus*) perhaps found it in his text. The best MSS. have ὥσπερ δὲ ταῖς. **26.** μέλλει] Vet. Int. *debeat*, but this is no proof that he found μέλλοι in his Greek text (see above on 1253 a 22). **27.** τῶν οἰκονομικῶν] Π[1] τῷ οἰκονομικῷ, but in 1256 b 36 Vet. Int. has *yconomico et politico* (οἰκονομικῶν καὶ πολιτικῶν Π) wrongly beyond a doubt, and perhaps here the three texts of the first family are affected by a similar error. O[1] τῶν οἰκονομικῶν: Ar. *sic etiam in re familiari* (τῶν οἰκονομικῶν?). **33.** 'ὁ om. M[s] del. P[4]' (Sus.). We cannot tell whether Vet. Int. found it in his text. O[1] has ὁ. ἠδύνατο] 'Eta as syllabic augment in βούλομαι, δύναμαι, μέλλω does not appear [in Attic Inscriptions] till after 284 B.C.' (Meisterhans, Grammatik der attischen Inschriften, p. 78). All the MSS. have ἠδύνατο here and ἠβούλετο in 1259 a 16, but in 1307 a 31 M[s] P[1] have ἠδύναντο, the reading of Γ is uncertain, and Π[2] have ἐδύναντο. **37.** δύεσθαι] ὑποδύεσθαι Γ M[s], possibly rightly, for Aristotle may not have preserved the metre in his quotation (compare the various readings in 1328 a 15 and 1338 a 25): O[1] δύεσθαι: Ar. *prodiisse* (δύεσθαι?). οὕτως αἱ κερκίδες ἐκέρκιζον] Vet. Int. *sic si pectines pectinarent*, but it is hardly likely that he found εἰ in his Greek text after οὕτως.

1254 a 5. δ'] z om. *autem* (so M[s]). **6.** Here again Bekker in reading δέονται δ' follows the less good MSS.: the better MSS. of both families have καὶ δέονται. O[1] has δέονται δ', but καὶ has been added above the line with a caret before δέονται, and then crossed out. τὴν αὐτὴν] *hanc* before *eandem* om. z (with a g n), perhaps rightly. **9.** τό τε γὰρ μόριον] *quod quidem enim pars*, the reading of o as well as of several other MSS. of the Vet. Int., may perhaps be correct, and not *quae quidem enim pars* (Sus.), for in 1257 b 28 *quod finis* stands for τὸ τέλος. **10.** ὅλως] Vet. Int. *simpliciter* (i.e. ἁπλῶς, cp. 7 (5). 1. 1301 a 29–33): ἁπλῶς ὅλως M[s] P[1]. See Susemihl's *apparatus criticus*. Susemihl holds in his third edition, in opposition to a marginal remark in P[2], that ὅλως is a gloss on ἁπλῶς and not ἁπλῶς on ὅλως, and that ἁπλῶς is the true reading. It seems strange, however, if that is so, that all the authorities for the text should read ὅλως in 13. **14.** αὐτοῦ] So O[1]. **15.** The reading ἄνθρωπος ὢν Γ M[s] pr. P[1] etc. is supported by Alex. Aphrodis. in

Aristot. Metaph. p. 15, 6 (Bonitz), τὸν γὰρ δοῦλον ἐν τοῖς Πολιτικοῖς εἶναι εἶπεν ὃς ἄνθρωπος ὢν ἄλλου ἐστίν, where, however, the Laurentian MS. of Alexander (L) has τὸν γὰρ δοῦλον ἐν τοῖς Πολιτικοῖς εἶπεν εἶναι τὸν ἄνθρωπον τὸν ἄλλου ὄντα καὶ μὴ ἑαυτοῦ: ἄνθρωπος δέ P^2 and probably P^3 (for there is an erasure here in P^3), and also most of the less good MSS. O^1 has ἄνθρωπος, followed by δὲ expunged by dots placed beneath it, but whether these dots were placed under δὲ by the writer of the MS. or by a corrector, it is impossible to say. Ar., as Sus. notes, probably read δέ, not ὤν, but this is not quite clear, for his rendering is—*qui enim sui ipsius non est secundum naturam, sed* (ἀλλὰ?) *alterius homo, hic natura est servus.* 'Lectio ἄνθρωπος ὢν unice vera videtur, si quidem est natura servus non is, qui quamquam natura alius hominis tamen ipse homo, sed is, qui quamquam homo tamen natura alius hominis est' (Sus. Qu. Crit. p. 341). Passing on to ἄλλου δ' ἐστὶν κ.τ.λ., we find in Vet. Int. *alterius autem est homo, quicunque res possessa aut servus est.* He would therefore appear to have found in his text ὃς ἂν κτῆμα ἢ δοῦλος ᾖ, or perhaps ὃς ἂν κτῆμα ἢ δοῦλος ὤν, which is the reading of M^s: the better MSS. have δοῦλος ὤν, those of less authority ἄνθρωπος ὤν. O^1 has ἀλλ' οὐδ' ἔστιν ἄνθρωπος ὃς ἂν κτῆμα ῇ (i. e. ᾖ, for O^1 is without iotas subscript) δοῦλος ὤν, and in the margin, added by the writer of the MS., γρ. ἄνθρωπος ὤν. Ar. has—*alterius autem est qui possidetur homo existens instrumentum ad acquirendum activum et separabile.* He probably read ἄνθρωπος ὤν. See Susemihl's *apparatus criticus* for the various readings: he adds in his second or explanatory edition—'we must regard either δοῦλος ἐστίν or (which is less probable) ἄνθρωπος ὢν as the reading from which the other readings have arisen, but in either case this reading has proceeded from a mere dittography' (i. e. a repetition of ἄνθρωπος ὢν or δοῦλός ἐστιν in 15). Hence Susemihl reads [δοῦλος ἐστίν]. Busse, however (De praesidiis Aristotelis Politica emendandi, p. 22), attaches little importance to the *est* of the Vet. Int., who, he thinks, found, not δοῦλος ἐστίν, but δοῦλος ὢν (which can hardly be a dittography) in his Greek text, and rendered it freely by *servus est* (compare the renderings noticed above, p. lxv): he holds δοῦλος ὤν, however, to be 'hoc loco omni sensu destitutum,' and falls back on the reading ἄνθρωπος ὤν. This is, as has been said, the reading of the less good MSS., but by adopting it we escape the difficulty of supposing Aristotle to have used the word δοῦλος in his definition of the φύσει δοῦλος. Susemihl's latest remarks on this passage will be found in Qu. Crit. p. 340 sq. (1886). **39.** τῶν γὰρ μοχθηρῶν κ.τ.λ.] Vet. Int. *pestilentium enim et prave* (the equivalent for φαύλως in 1254 b 2) *se habentium*. I know not what *pestilentium* stands for in Vet. Int., but μοχθηρία is rendered in 1303 b 15 by *malitia*, and in 1314 a 14 by *malignitas*. Vet. Int. omits to render ἂν, but this he occasionally seems to do (e. g. in 1256 a 4, 1265 a 30).

1254 b 14. Π[1] add καὶ after χεῖρον, in which they are probably wrong: see below on 1260 a 26. **18.** O[1] (like P[4]) has καὶ τοῦτ' ἔστ' ἐπ' αὐτῶν. **23.** λόγῳ Π[1]. Ar. *nam cetera quidem animalia rationem non sentiunt*: he would seem therefore to have read λόγου, as does O[1]. **34.** γένοιντο is rendered in most MSS. of Vet. Int. by *fiunt*. The reading of o is not *sint* (as Sus. with a query), but *fiunt*.

1255 a 5. καὶ before κατὰ om. Π[1] pr. P[3], etc., and Pseudo-Plutarch De Nobilitate. As to the De Nobilitate, if Volkmann's account of it (Leben Schriften und Philosophie des Plutarch, 1. 118) is correct, no weight can be attached to its testimony. See also Bernays, Dialoge des Aristoteles, pp. 14, 140, and Wyttenbach's notes (Plutarch, Moralia, tom. 5, pars 2, p. 915 sqq.). But in fact the passages quoted from Aristotle were not given in the MS., and were inserted by J. C. Wolf, the first editor of the work (see Volkmann and Wyttenbach), so that the text of them in the De Nobilitate possesses no sort of authority. **14.** z adds *et* before *violentiam pati*, thus giving an equivalent for καὶ βιάζεσθαι, which none of the MSS. of the Vet. Int. known to Sus. appear to do. **16.** Susemihl gives *violentia* as the equivalent in Vet. Int. for τὴν βίαν, but he notes that *violentiam* is found in a: it is also found in o y z and may probably be the correct reading. **29.** ὅταν τοῦτο λέγωσιν] Vet. Int., according to Susemihl's text, *cum hos dicunt*, but o y z have *cum hoc dicunt*. Is *hos* a misprint? **35.** I follow Π[2] (and O[1]), which omit καὶ before ἐλεύθερον: cp. 7 (5). 12. 1316 b 15, ὅτι ἀσωτευόμενοι καταοκιζόμενοι γίνονται πένητες (so Π), and other passages collected by Vahlen, Poet. p. 216 sq. *Et* before *liberum* is omitted in z, but probably through an oversight. **37.** No MS. gives ἔκγονον, except P[1], which removes the iota of ἐκγονοιν (*sic*) by placing a point under it, nor was ἔκγονον found by Vet. Int. in his Greek text. This reading, like some other good ones peculiar to P[1], may well be due, as Susemihl points out (Sus.[3] pp. xiii–xiv), to the emending hand of Demetrius Chalcondylas, the writer of the MS.

1255 b 2. γίνεσθαι] γενέσθαι M[s] P[1 4] O[1], etc.: Vet. Int. *fieri*, which may represent either γίνεσθαι or γενέσθαι (or indeed other forms, as it stands for γεγονέναι in 1268 b 38, and for γεγενῆσθαι in 1272 b 32). **12.** Γ M[s] pr. P[1] add τοῦ σώματος after μέρος: Sus. thinks that this may have been the original position of these two words, but it is possible that they may have been added in the margin to explain *κεχωρισμένον δὲ μέρος*, and then have found their way into the text. Additions which may thus be accounted for occur occasionally in P[4] [6] L[s] (see Susemihl's *apparatus criticus* in 1309 b 2, 1313 b 32, 1316 a 1), and also, though less often, in the first family of MSS. (e. g. in the passage before us, in 1259 b 14, in 1268 a 37, and possibly in 1335 a 37: see also below on 1263 a 12). **14.** *τούτων ἠξιωμένοις* Π: *qui natura tales dignificantur* Vet. Int., but it is doubtful whether he found *τοιούτοις* in his text, for, as Busse remarks (p. 42), he translates *τίνες* by *quales* in 1264 a 38: nevertheless, it is true that in 1284 a 9 he renders *ἀξιούμενοι τῶν ἴσων* *dignificati aequalibus*, and that this is his usual way of rendering phrases of this kind, so that we expect *his* here rather than *tales*. Ar. *quapropter aliquid est quod simul prosit et amicitia servo et domino invicem secundum naturam ita dispositis.* **18.** *ἡ μὲν γὰρ . . . ἡ δὲ*] z *haec quidem enim . . . haec* (or *hoc*) *autem* (not *hic quidem enim . . . hic autem*, like almost all the other MSS.). **24.** M[s] P[1] add *ταῖς* before *Συρακούσαις*: whether Vet. Int. found *ταῖς* in his text, we cannot tell from *in Syracusis*. *ἐπαίδευεν*] So O[1]: M[s] P[1] *ἐπαίδευσεν*: Vet. Int. *erudivit*, which might represent either *ἐπαίδευεν* or *ἐπαίδευσεν*, for in 1267 b 18 *κατεσκεύαζεν* is *constituit*, in 1267 b 30 *construxit*: in 1267 b 31 *ἐποίει* is *fecit*, though in 33 *διῄρει* is *dividebat*. **26.** *πλεῖον* Π: see Bon. Ind. 618 b 13 sqq., and Liddell and Scott, s. v. Meisterhans (Grammatik der attischen Inschriften, p. 68) observes—'before long vowels we find throughout in Attic Inscriptions *-ει* (*πλείων, πλείω, πλείους*): before short vowels in the classical period (till 300 B.C.) *-ε* (*πλέονος, πλεόνων, πλέοσιν*)—in the post-classical period, on the other hand, *-ει* (*πλείονος, πλειόνων, πλείοσιν*): the neuter singular, however, even after 300 B.C. usually retains the simple vowel.' *τῶν τοιούτων*] so Π[2] (and O[1]): Π[1] *τούτων*. *ὀψοπουκὴ*] *ὀψοποιητικὴ* rests only on the authority of M[s] P[1], for it is of course impossible to say whether Vet. Int. found *ὀψοπουκὴ* in his text or *ὀψοποιητικὴ*. O[1] (like P[4]) has *ὀψοποιηκὴ* (or rather *ὀψοποιηκῇ*), which probably points to *ὀψοπουκὴ*, for in 1258 a 37 pr. O[1] has *χρηματιστηκὴ*. The same MSS. which here read *ὀψοπουκή*, read (if we allow for clerical errors) *κερκιδοπουκὴ* in 1256 a 6, where M[s] P[1] (about Γ we cannot be certain) read *κερκιδοποιητικὴ*. All MSS. have *τεκνοποιη-ική* in 1253 b 10. 'In Plato *ὀψοπουκὴ* is now restored from MSS.' (Liddell and Scott). In Eth. Nic. 7. 13. 1153 a 26 and Metaph. E. 2. 1027 a 4 *ὀψοποιητικὴ* is the form used, but in the latter passage the MSS. are not quite unanimous. In Metaph. K. 8.

1064 b 21, Bekker, Bonitz, and Christ read ὀψοποιική, but two MSS. (one of them A^b) have ὀψοποιητική. In Eth. Nic. 1. 1. 1094 a 11 pr. K^b (the best MS.) has χαλινοποιική. **35.** μὴ αὐτοὺς κακοπαθεῖν] Vet. Int. *quod non ipsi malum patiantur*.

1256 a 6. κερκιδοποιική] See above on 1255 b 26. **10.** χαλκόν] So Π² (and O¹): χαλκός Γ P¹ and possibly M^s. See explanatory note on this passage. Corr.² P² (i. e. the writer of P² in darker ink than that of the MS.), followed by Bekk., adds ἡ before οἰκονομική, but Sus.¹ (p. xviii.) says of the corrections thus classed —'maximam partem coniecturas sapiunt, etsi vix eas ex ipsius librari ingenio haustas esse crediderim,' and the erroneous additions of ἡ before οἰκονομική in 1257 b 20, and σκοπεῖν before προσήκει in 1258 a 25, rest on the same authority. **12.** τίς γὰρ] Most MSS. of Vet. Int. *quod enim* (o *quid enim*), but z, like a, has *quae enim*. **16.** πολλὰ] o *multas* rightly: is *multae* (Sus.) a misprint? **23.** z, like a, has *bestiarum et enim*, answering to τῶν τε γὰρ θηρίων. **30.** πολὺ] πολλοὶ pr. O¹ (with P⁴, etc.), πολὺ corr.¹: M^s Π² have the same blunder in 1316 b 1. Vet. Int. *multis*, but he probably found πολλοὶ in his text. **31.** οἱ μὲν οὖν] Vet. Int. *qui quidem enim*: he seems, therefore, to have read οἱ μὲν γάρ, unless *enim* is a blunder, which is very possible. Three MSS. of Vet. Int. om. *enim*. **40.** τοσοῦτοι σχεδόν] z *tot fere*, retaining the order of the Greek text, and *quaecunque* for ὅσοι γε, not *quicunque*, like the MSS. examined by Susemihl.

1256 b 1. πορίζονται] κομίζονται M^s P¹, and Γ if *ferunt* (Vet. Int.) represents κομίζονται, not πορίζονται, which perhaps is the case, for *acquirere* stands for πορίζειν in 1256 b 28, 1268 a 32, etc., though we have *emerunt* for πορίσαι in 1285 b 7. Πορίζεσθαι, however, seems the more probable reading, for we have πορίζοντες τὴν τροφὴν in 1268 a 32, and πορίζεσθαι τὴν τροφὴν occurs in De Gen. An. 3. 1. 749 b 24 and Hist. An. 1. 1. 487 b 1. No instance of κομίζεσθαι τὴν τροφὴν is given in the *Index Aristotelicus* of Bonitz. O¹ πορίζονται. Ar. *sibi praeparant* (= πορίζονται?). **6.** ὡς ἂν ἡ χρεία συναναγκάζῃ] *quocunque modo et oportunitas compellat* o (where *et* may possibly be intended to represent συν- in συναναγκάζῃ). **8.** διδομένη] δεδομένη M^s P¹ and possibly Γ (Vet. Int. *data*), but *data* is just as likely to stand for διδομένη, for *facta* represents γινομένης in 1262 a 38 (cp. 1263 a 12, b 19, 1270 a 24, 1272 a 17), *laudata* ἐπαινουμένης in 1258 a 40, *transmutatum* μεταβαλλόμενον in 1257 b 4, *vocatam* καλουμένου in 1256 b 14. O¹ διδομένη. **9.** τελειωθεῖσιν] Vet. Int. *secundum perfectionem* or *secundum perfectam* (sc. *generationem*), for the reading is doubtful (y z *secundum perfectam*, and, if I am right, o also, not *secundum perfectionem*, as Sus. with a query). Ar. *sic etiam ad perfectionem deductis*. **13.** τοῖς γεννωμένοις] τοῖς γενομένοις Π[2] (O[1]) Bekk.[1]: τοῖς γεννωμένοις M[s] P[1] Bekk.[2] Sus. Most of the MSS. of Vet. Int. have *genitis* (so z), or what probably stands for *genitis*, but Sus. finds *generatis* in two of them (k o): I must confess that after looking at o I feel doubtful whether the contraction found in it stands for *generatis*; still k remains. *Genitis*, however, is probably the true reading; but this may just as well stand for τοῖς γεννωμένοις (cp. 1258 a 35, where *genito* stands for τῷ γεννηθέντι) as for τοῖς γενομένοις or τοῖς γινομένοις. It is not impossible that Ar. found the last-named reading in his Greek text, for his translation is *ad natorum educationem*, and he renders τῶν γινομένων in 1335 b 22 and τὰ γινόμενα in 1336 a 16 by *natos*; but no MS. of the Politics has τοῖς γινομένοις. If we read τοῖς γενομένοις (=τοῖς τέκνοις, as in 4 (7). 16. 1335 b 18), there is a good deal of harshness in the use of γενομένοις in two different senses in 13 and 15, and γενομένοις 15 loses something of its point; it seems probable also that in 1335 b 18 the true reading is τὰ γεννώμενα Π[1], not τὰ γενόμενα Π[2] (so in De Gen. An. 2. 6. 742 a 24 τῷ γενομένῳ has apparently in some MSS. taken the place of the true reading τῷ γεννωμένῳ, which is found in Z and accepted by Aubert and Wimmer). I incline on the whole to adopt the reading which may well be that of Π[1], and to read τοῖς γεννωμένοις. Cp. Menex. 237 E, πᾶν γὰρ τὸ τεκὸν τροφὴν ἔχει ἐπιτηδείαν ᾧ ἂν τέκῃ· ᾧ καὶ γυνὴ δήλη τεκοῦσά τε ἀληθῶς καὶ μή, ἀλλ' ὑποβαλλομένη, ἐὰν μὴ ἔχῃ πηγὰς τροφῆς τῷ γεννωμένῳ. In Plato, Laws 930 D τὸ γενόμενον, τὸ γεννηθέν, and τὸ γεννώμενον are all used close together. **14.** τὴν τοῦ καλουμένου γάλακτος φύσιν] Vet. Int. *vocatam lactis naturam* (τὴν καλουμένην?). **15.** γενομένοις] 'τελειωθεῖσιν Ar. Sus.[1 2] forsitan recte,' Sus.[3], who now places [γενομένοις] in his text; but I find in the New College MS. of Ar., and also in Bodl., *quare similiter est genitis quoque existimandum plantasque animalium esse gratia et cetera animalia hominum causa*. O[1] γενομένοις: Vet. Int. *genitis*. **20.** γίνηται] γένηται M[s] P[1] and possibly also Γ (Vet. Int. *fiant*). **26.** The text of Π[1] and especially of Γ M[s] has suffered here from the intrusion of glosses: see Susemihl's *apparatus criticus*. Vet. Int. *hoc praedativum bellum et primum* (z however omits *et* with M[s] P[1]). Ar. *ut natura id bellum iustum existat*. **28.** o y z have *quarum est* for ὧν ἐστὶ (in agreement with *rerum*). **32.** ἀγαθὴν pr. O[1], but dots are placed under -ὴν and ῶν is written above, probably by corr.[1] **36.** οἰκονομικῶν καὶ πολιτικῶν] οἰκονομικῷ καὶ πολιτικῷ Γ: see note on 1253 b 27. Ar. *multitudo instrumentorum rei familiaris et rei publicae*.

1257 a 3. Vet. Int. either misread ἐκείνης as κειμένη or found κειμένη in his text, for he translates *posita*. Ar. *sed neque est idem neque valde remotum*. He fails to render ἐκείνης, but then he also fails to render τῇ εἰρημένῃ. **6.** κτήματος] χρήματος M[s] and probably also Γ, for Vet. Int. has *rei*, not *rei possessae* (*rei*, however, stands for πράγματος in 8). **10.** Sus.[2] by a misprint omits γὰρ after καὶ. **17.** ᾗ] *qua* o rightly: y z *quare* (with most MSS. of Vet. Int.). **38.** κἂν εἰ] καὶ εἰ P[1], and possibly Γ also (Vet. Int. *et si*); Vet. Int., however, occasionally fails to render ἂν (see above on 1254 a 39). **40.** ἐπιβαλλόντων] ἐπιβαλόντων P[1], Bekk.[2], Sus. (Vet. Int. *imprimentibus* might stand for either reading). For ἀπολύσῃ the MSS. of Vet. Int. have *absolvant*: so y z, and also o, though Susemihl gives its reading (with a query) as *absolvat*.

1257 b 7. εἶναι om. Π[1]: see note on 1252 a 8. Here it can hardly be spared. **11.** καὶ νόμος] O[1] καὶ εἴς νόμον, but the breathing over εἴς has been struck through, and corr.[1] has written something ending in -ος (probably καὶ νόμος) in the inner margin, where the binding partly conceals the correction. See Susemihl's *apparatus criticus* on this passage. **12.** οὔτε] So O[1] (with Π): οὐδὲ Bekk. Sus.: but cp. 6 (4). 6. 1293 a 8, ὥστε πολλάκις οὐ κοινωνοῦσι τῆς ἐκκλησίας οὔτε (so Π: οὐδὲ Bekk. Sus.) τοῦ δικάζειν: 6 (4). 13. 1297 b 7, ἐὰν μὴ (so Π[2] Bekk.: μήτε Π[1] Sus.) ὑβρίζῃ τις αὐτοὺς μήτε ἀφαιρῆται μηδὲν τῆς οὐσίας. **15.** ἀπολεῖται] Vet. Int. *perit*, cp. 1263 b 28, where he renders στερήσονται by *privantur*, and see below on 1262 a 2. **20.** ἡ δὲ καπηλική, ποιητικὴ κ.τ.λ.] Vet. Int. *campsoria autem factiva pecuniarum*, etc., which shews how he interpreted the passage and punctuated it. **21.** ἀλλ' ᾗ] Vet. Int. *sed*, not *sed aut*, as in 1305 b 15, or *nisi*, as in 1272 a 11 and 1286 a 37. **24.** οὗτος om. Π[1]: compare, however, 2. 11. 1273 a 9, where Π[1] om. οὗτοι, 3. 17. 1288 a 29, where Π[1] om. τοῦτον, and 8 (6). 4. 1319 b 11, where Π[1] omit τοῦτο. It is of course possible that Π[2] are wrong in adding these words in the four passages, but the use of οὗτος in the passage before us at any rate, followed by the explanation ὁ ἀπὸ ταύτης τῆς χρηματιστικῆς, is characteristically Aristotelian (cp. 5 (8). 5. 1340 a 32–34: 6 (4). 9. 1294 b 23). See also 1258 b 8. We must bear in mind that Π[1] are prone to omit words. O[1] has οὗτος. **33.** ὁρῶ ΓΠ, and so O[1]: z has *videmus*, but the symbol for *-mus* is over an erasure; y, however, has *videre* (the first two letters of this word in y project slightly into the margin and may have been tampered with), and though o has *video*, the last two letters are over an erasure, the original reading having apparently occupied less space than *video*, for the last letter of this word is in actual contact with the first letter of *accidens*, a perpendicular line being drawn to separate the two words. Possibly therefore the original reading of o was *vide'* (= *videmus*). 'Ορῶ is not perhaps impossible, for we find λέγω, Pol. 3. 13. 1283 b 1: 6 (4). 15. 1299 b 19: τίθημι, Rhet. 1. 10. 1369 b 23: ἔλαβον, Phys. 8. 5. 257 b 22: μοι δοκεῖ σημαίνειν, Meteor. 1. 3. 339 b 23 (where, however, Blass—*Rhein. Mus.* 30. 500—suspects that Aristotle is quoting from one of his own Dialogues): διειλόμην Ms P²³⁶ Qb Vb Ls Ald. (*divisimus* Vet. Int.: διειλόμεθα P¹ Bekk.) in Pol. 6 (4). 3. 1290 a 2, but perhaps Göttling and Sus. (following corr. P¹) are right in reading διείλομεν in this passage, for in 1290 a 24 the MSS. and Vet. Int. agree in reading διείλομεν. The emendation ὁρῶμεν dates as far back as Sepulveda and Victorius, and indeed earlier, for it appears, as we have just seen, in one or two MSS. of Vet. Int.: Bekker adopts it in both his editions, as does also Susemihl, though he brackets the termination. **35.** ἐπαλλάττει] *variatur* z (not *variat*) probably rightly, for *variari*, not *variare*, is the equivalent for ἐπαλλάττειν in the *vetus versio* (cp. 1255 a 13, 1317 a 2). **36.** ἑκατέρα] ἑκατέρας 'vetusta et emendatiora exemplaria' mentioned by Sepulveda (see p. 19 of his translation); three MSS. also of the Vet. Int. (b g h) have *utrique pecuniativae*, and ἑκατέρας is the reading translated by Leonardus Aretinus (*variatur enim usus eiusdem existens utriusque acquisitionis, eiusdem enim est usus acquisitio, sed non secundum idem*); but all known MSS. of the Politics have ἑκατέρα, and most of the MSS. of the Vet. Int. have *uterque* (agreeing with *usus*). z has *uterque*, altered into *utrique*, not, I think, *utrique* altered into *uterque*. If we read ἑκατέρα, two uses of χρηματιστική are referred to, and this seems to suit better with ἐπαλλάττει than ἡ χρῆσις ἑκατέρας τῆς χρηματιστικῆς: if ἑκατέρας, two kinds of χρηματιστική are referred to, whose 'use' (not 'uses') 'overlaps' (ἐπαλλάττει). Perhaps we rather expect to hear of two uses than of one use. Hence on the whole ἑκατέρα seems preferable, but ἑκατέρα might so easily take the place of ἑκατέρας that the true reading is doubtful. **38.** τῆς δ' ἡ αὔξησις] Vet. Int. adds *finis* after *augmentatio*, but probably without any equivalent in his Greek, as Sus. remarks (Sus.¹ p. xxxiv).

1258 a 2. z adds *et* before *ipsius* (answering to καὶ before τοῦ εὖ ζῆν). Sus.¹: '*et* post *autem* librariorum culpa excidisse quam a Guilelmo omissum esse verisimilius duco.' As to *ipsius*, it should be noted that, as Dittmeyer has shown ('Quae ratio inter vetustam Aristotelis Rhetoricorum translationem et Graecos codices intercedat,' p. 34), William of Moerbeke in his translation of the Rhetoric often renders the article by *ipse*—e. g. in Rhet. 1. 6. 1362 b 16, where for ἡδονῆς καὶ τοῦ ζῆν we find *delectationis et ipsius vivere.* **7.** οὔσης] z rightly omits *non* before *existente*: all the MSS. known to Sus. add it: y probably had *non* before *existente* originally, though *iam* occupies its place now over an erasure. **32–34.** Pr. O[1] has here—ἀλλὰ τῆς ἰατρικῆς, οὕτω καὶ περὶ χρηματιστικῆς ἔστι μὲν ὡς τοῦ οἰκονόμου ἔστι δ' ὡς οὔ, ἀλλὰ τῆς κέρδους ὑπηρετικῆς, but corr.[1] adds in the margin γρ. ἀλλὰ τοῦ ἰατροῦ, οὕτω καὶ περὶ τῶν χρημάτων, and κέρδους is expunged by dots placed beneath. For the various readings offered by P[4 6] Q L[s] in this passage, see Susemihl's *apparatus criticus*. See also above on 1253 a 12. These MSS. perhaps follow some gloss or paraphrase.

1258 b 1. μεταβλητικῆς] μεταβολικῆς M[s] P[1], here alone, for in 1257 a 9, 15, 28, 1258 b 21, 29 these MSS. (like Π[2]) have the form μεταβλητική, nor is the word used elsewhere by Aristotle apparently. We cannot tell from *translativa* whether Vet. Int. found μεταβολικῆς or μεταβλητικῆς in his Greek text, for he translates τῆς μεταβλητικῆς in 1258 b 21, 29 by *translativae*. **4.** ἐφ' ὅπερ ἐπορίσθη] So Π[2] (and O[1]) with Ar. (*et non ad quod inductus est*): ἐφ' ᾧπερ ἐπορισάμεθα Π[1] (Vet. Int. *super quo quidem acquisivimus*). **7.** Π[1] add ἐκ before νομίσματος, which Π[2] (and O[1]) omit. **16.** ποίοις] Vet. Int. *quibus*, but he has *quales* for τίνες in 1264 a 38. **27.** τρίτον] τέταρτον Γ M[s] pr. P[1], apparently a mistaken attempt at emendation. **30.** τῶν ἀπὸ γῆς γινομένων] o y *ex a terra genitis*, z *ex altera genitis*. **33.** περὶ ἑκάστου] Here, as Sus. has already noted, o alone among the MSS. of the Vet. Int. has preserved the true reading—*de unoquoque*. **36.** O[1] (with P[4] and some other MSS. which Bekker follows) adds τῆς before τύχης: see below on 1270 b 19. **40.** Χαρητίδῃ] Χάρητι (χάριτι M[s]) δὴ Π Bekk. Many of the MSS. of the Vet. Int., however, and z among them, have *karitide*. Ar. *a carite* (Bodl. *charite*) *pario*.

1259 a 10. In the fourth century B.C. the forms ἐλᾶαι, ἐλάας, ἐλαῶν take the place of ἐλαῖαι, etc., in Attic inscriptions (Meisterhans, Grammatik der attischen Inschriften, p. 14), but here all the MSS. seem to have ἐλαιῶν, as all have Πειραιᾶ in 1303 b 11, though some have πειρεᾶ in 1267 b 23. **13.** Most of the MSS. have ἐλαιουργίων, though some spell or accentuate it wrongly: P[1] has ἐλαιουργείων: P[4] has ἐλαιούργων, O[1] ἐλαιουργῶν, and so Γ apparently, for Vet. Int. has *olivarum cultoribus*. Ἐλαιουργεῖα is the word used in the citation from Hieronymus Rhodius in Diog. Laert. 1. 26, which may possibly be a reproduction of the passage before us, and Liddell and Scott adopt this form of the word (not ἐλαιούργιον). In 1295 b 17 P[2] has διδασκαλίοις, P[3 4] Ald. διδασκαλείοις, Π[1] (probably wrongly) διδασκάλοις. **16.** ἠβούλετο] See above on 1253 b 33. **28.** ἐπέλαβεν] O[1] has ἐπέλαβεν with ά superscribed over έ, apparently by the writer of the MS.: no other MS. gives this reading, which is no doubt wrong: see, however, Schneider *ad loc.* τοῦτον] τοῦτο (Bekk.) is found only in one MS. and that an inferior one. ὁ Διονύσιος] ὁ om. M[s] P[1]: whether Γ omitted it also, it is of course impossible to say. In 1252 b 14 M[s] P[1] give the ὁ to Charondas, which here they deny to Dionysius. **31.** τὸ μέντοι ὅραμα Θάλεω καὶ τοῦτο] Vet. Int. *quod vero visum fuit Thali et huic* (o *quod vero iussum fuerit Thali et huic*). Sus. suspects that the translator found τὸ μέντοι ὅραμα Θάλῃ καὶ τούτῳ in his text: more probably he found τὸ μέντοι ὅραμα Θάλεω καὶ τούτου (unless he misread τοῦτο as τούτου). This is a possible reading, but all MSS. have τοῦτο. See note in Sus.[3], who now reads Θάλεω καὶ τοῦτο. Ὅραμα has been variously emended, but Mitchell (Indices Graecitatis in Orat. Att. 2. 581) gives it as occurring, apparently in a similar sense to that which it bears here, in [Demosth.] Procem. 55. p. 1460, 26, ὅραμα τοῦτο ἐποιεῖτο ὁ δῆμος αὑτοῦ καλόν, ὦ ἄνδρες Ἀθηναῖοι, καὶ λυσιτελὲς τῇ πόλει, and it suits well with κατανόημα 7 and κατανοήσαντα 10. **37.** μέρη om. P[234], etc. (also O[1]). It is not perhaps quite certain that Π[1] are right in adding it. **39.** Almost all MSS. of Vet. Int. (including o y) have *praeest*, but ἄρχειν is undoubtedly right: z has *praeesse*, which appears to be found in only one of the MSS. known to Sus. (b).

1259 b 16. τὸ νεώτερον] z has *iuvenius* rightly: the other MSS. of Vet. Int. *iuvenem*. **28.** σχεδὸν δὲ] The weight of manuscript authority is in favour of δὴ in place of δέ, for of the better MSS. only pr. P[2] has δέ: Vet. Int., however, has *autem*. Δέ seems to be right, answering to μὲν οὖν 21. **31.** καὶ before ἀκόλαστος om. Π[1]. **35.** δέοι ἂν] o *oporteret utique*, but *oportebit utique*, the reading of the other MSS., is probably right (see above on 1253 b 17).

1260 a 3. διαφοράς] διαφορᾶς Γ (Vet. Int. *huius autem esse differentiae*), and so probably pr. O[1], for the accent of διαφοράς is over an erasure: y z have *huius autem differentiae*, omitting *esse* (in z, however, *differentiae* is over an erasure). ὥσπερ καὶ τῶν φύσει ἀρχομένων] Susemihl's text of the Vet. Int. here runs, *quemadmodum et natura principantium et subiectorum*, and he thinks that the Vet. Int. found ἀρχόντων καὶ added in his Greek text between φύσει and ἀρχομένων. But it would seem from the *apparatus criticus* to his text of the Vet. Int. (Sus.[1] p. 53), that of the nine MSS. used by him (a b c g h k l m o), one (o) omits *et natura principantium*, making the passage run *quemadmodum et subiectorum*, and seven (b c g h k l m) read *quemadmodum natura et subiec-*

torum (so y), except that later hands add *principantium* after *natura* in b and the margin of l. Thus the reading adopted by Susemihl was apparently found by him only in a. I have found it, however, in z, which gives the passage thus—*huius autem* (*esse* om. z) *differentiae, quemadmodum et natura principantium et subiectorum.* Whether Vet. Int. found ἀρχόντων καὶ in his Greek text is, however, quite another question. Ar. *quemadmodum in hiis quae natura obediunt.* O[1] has ὥσπερ καὶ τῶν φύσει ἀρχομένων, but corr.[1] has inserted a caret after φύσει and adds in the margin ἀρχόντων καὶ (a dot, however, has been placed under each of these words to expunge it—by whom, it is impossible to say). It is conceivable that Vet. Int. found a similar correction in the margin of the Greek text used by him, and translated it. **4.** ὑφήγηται] ὑφηγεῖται Π[1] (Vet. Int. *exemplificatur : exemplificabitur* a z). **15.** Ar. is said by Sus.[1 2] to add δὲ after ὑποληπτέον, but his translation runs in the New College MS. and in Bodl.—*eodem modo se habere necesse est circa morales virtutes, putandum est omnes participes esse oportere sed non eodem modo, sed quantum cuique opus est.* **20.** ἐστὶν] o z have *est*, in place of *et*, before *moralis* rightly (Susemihl reads *et* and does not mention that o has *est*). **21.** πάντων] M[s] P[1] have ἁπάντων : we cannot tell from Vet. Int. *omnium*, which reading he found in his text. **22.** ᾤετο Σωκράτης] O[1] ὠέτω Σωκράτης (P[4] ᾤετο ὁ Σωκράτης). **26.** ἀρετή] Vet. Int. has *virtute* (= ἀρετῇ, which is the reading of pr. M[s]). τὸ ὀρθοπραγεῖν] I follow P[2 3] S[b] T[b] (z has *est* in place of *aut* after *virtute*, but over an erasure) in omitting ἢ before τὸ ὀρθοποαγεῖν: see Vahlen, Poet. p. 136 and Beitr. zu Aristot. Poet. 1. p. 52, where among other passages the following are referred to—Poet. 8. 1451 a 20, Ἡρακληίδα Θησηίδα καὶ τὰ τοιαῦτα ποιήματα: Rhet. 2. 12. 1388 b 33, ὀργὴν ἐπιθυμίαν καὶ τὰ τοιαῦτα (in the passage before us we have ἢ instead of καὶ). Cp. also 2. 3. 1262 a 12, φράτορα φυλέτην, where Π om. ἢ (see Vahlen, Poet. p. 216): Eth. Nic. 10. 10. 1180 b 34, οἷον ἰατροὶ γραφεῖς (M[b] O[b]): Eth. Nic. 8. 14. 1161 b 23, ὀδοὺς θρὶξ ὁτιοῦν K[b] O[1 3] (θρὶξ ὀδοὺς ὁτιοῦν L[b] O[b]), where other MSS. have ὀδοὺς ἢ θρὶξ ἢ ὁτιοῦν: Pol. 3. 4. 1277 b 10, οἷον ἱππαρχεῖν ἱππαρχηθέντα, στρατηγεῖν στρατηγηθέντα καὶ ταξιαρχήσαντα καὶ λοχαγήσαντα (where no MS. has καὶ before στρατηγεῖν, though Vet. Int. has *et* before his equivalent for it): 6 (4). 4. 1291 b 23–25, where δὲ is absent after πορθμικόν, though Vet. Int. has *autem* : 6 (4). 4. 1292 a 1, where Γ M[s] Π[2] om. δὲ: 7 (5). 8. 1308 b 27, λέγω δ' ἀντικεῖσθαι τοὺς ἐπιεικεῖς τῷ πλήθει, τοὺς ἀπόρους τοῖς εὐπόροις M[s] P[1] (other MSS. add καὶ before τοὺς ἀπόρους). **31.** ὁ παῖς] ὁ om. M[s] P[1] : we have no means of knowing whether Vet. Int. found it in his text. **32.**

τὸν τέλειον καὶ (in place of τὸ τέλος καὶ) P[4 6] L[s] Ald. Ar. (*sed ad perfectum et ducem*) Bekk. O[1] has τὸν τέλειον καὶ, but in the margin, probably added by corr.[1], τὸ τέλος καὶ. See above on 1258 a 32 and 1253 a 12. Here also perhaps these MSS. follow a gloss or paraphrase: Aristotle's language in 1. 12. 1259 b 3 may well have suggested it. **36.** ἐλλείψῃ] O[1] ἐλλείψει (or rather ἐλλείψει), and so too pr. P[3]: all other MSS. apparently have ἐλλείψῃ: Vet. Int. *deficiat*, which may possibly represent ἐλλείψῃ, but we cannot be sure of this, for after *tanta ut* he could use nothing but the subjunctive. Bekk.[1] ἐλλείψῃ: Bekk.[2] Sus. ἐλλείψει. **37.** ἆρα] ἄρα pr. O[1], changed into ἆρα probably by a corrector, for the circumflex is in darker ink than that used in the MS.

1260 b 17. O[1] adds καὶ before τοὺς παῖδας (with Π[2]). **18.** corr.[1] O[1] adds εἶναι in darker ink after γυναῖκας: a m z add *esse* after *mulieres*. **19.** οἱ κοινωνοὶ] Vet. Int. has *dispensatores*: Sus. thinks he found οἰκονόμοι in his text in place of οἱ κοινωνοὶ, and adopts this reading. All MSS., however, have οἱ κοινωνοὶ, and is it not, to say the least, possible that Vet. Int. here as elsewhere has misread the Greek?

BOOK II.

1260 b 27. Ἐπεὶ δὲ] Π[1] om. δέ, but omissions in Π[1] are not infrequent, and δέ, which hardly suits the present ending of Book I., may possibly be a survival from some earlier state of the text. **28.** τίς] ἥ P[2 3] pr. P[4], etc. (so O[1]): τίς M[s] P[1] and possibly Γ (Vet. Int. *quae*). Perhaps ἥ is more likely to have been substituted for τίς here than τίς for ἥ. Cp. Metaph. Z. 1. 1028 b 6, διὸ καὶ ἡμῖν καὶ μάλιστα καὶ πρῶτον καὶ μόνον ὡς εἰπεῖν περὶ τοῦ οὕτως ὄντος θεωρητέον τί ἐστιν. **31.** κἂν εἴ τινες ἕτεραι †τυγχάνωσιν†] καὶ εἰ M[s]: about Γ we cannot be certain, though Vet. Int. has *et si quae aliae existunt*, for he occasionally fails to render ἄν (see above on 1254 a 39). Nor does *existunt* in Vet. Int. enable us to pronounce with certainty that he found τυγχάνουσιν in his Greek text, for in 1270 a 27 he renders κἂν ἀποθάνῃ *et si moritur*. As to τυγχάνωσιν, see explanatory note. **36.** ἐπιβαλέσθαι] So O[1]: ἐπιβάλλεσθαι M[s] P[1]: *inserere* (Vet. Int.) may represent either. **40.** πολιτεία Π: z *civilitas* (with g h l o, y *civilitas* with dots under *li*): most MSS. of Vet. Int. *civitas* (and so Ar.). The same contraction 'may stand for πόλις, πολύς, πόλεμος, πολέμιος, πολίτης, and even πολιτεία, though the last word is most often expressed by another contraction' (Gardthausen, Gr.

Paläographie, pp. 246, 256). This perhaps explains the occasional interchange of πολιτεία, πολίτης, and πόλις: thus πολιτείας takes the place of πόλεως in Π[1] 1294 b 39, πολιτειῶν of πολιτῶν in P[4] etc. 1292 a 9, and πολιτῶν of πολιτειῶν in Γ T[b] 1265 b 34, while in 1318 a 9 Π[1] have πόλει, Π[2] πολιτείᾳ. See Susemihl's *apparatus criticus* in 1326 b 5, 1333 a 11 also. I retain πολιτεία here, though not without hesitation. See explanatory note. Sus.[1 2] πόλις, Sus.[3] πολιτεία. **41.** Here Vet. Int. alone has preserved the true reading εἷς ὁ τῆς (*unus qui unius*): ἰσότης Π (Ar. *paritas*). Only a fraction, however, of the MSS. of Vet. Int. give this reading. Of those used by Sus. only one (g) has *unus* as its original reading (in four, a b k l, a later hand has substituted *unus*): *nullus* pr. a b, *alius* c h and pr. k l, *illius* m. *Qui* again is *quod* in c g h m and pr. k l. Hence it is important to note that z has *unus qui unius* as its original and only reading. The reading of o is *alius quod unius*: in y *eius quid unius* has been first written, but *eius* has been erased by dots placed beneath it and *unus* written above, apparently in the same ink and handwriting as the MS.

1261 a 2. Vet. Int. fails to render πάντων, but see above, p. lxiii, note 12, for other cases in which he omits words or phrases. **6.** ἐν τῇ πολιτείᾳ τῇ Πλάτωνος] So O[1], but τῇ after πολιτείᾳ is added above the line with a caret—whether by the writer of the MS., is uncertain. Vet. Int. *in politia Platonis*. P[2 3 4] have the reading adopted in the text. **11.** δι' ἣν αἰτίαν] z perhaps rightly has *causa*, not *causam*. **15.** ὡς ἄριστον ὂν ὅτι μάλιστα πᾶσαν] So Π[1]: the order is different in Π[2] (and O[1]), which read πᾶσαν ὡς ἄριστον ὅτι μάλιστα in place of ὡς ἄριστον ὂν ὅτι μάλιστα πᾶσαν: the latter order, however, though more rugged, is perhaps more Aristotelian. These MSS. also, as will be noticed, omit ὄν, probably because ἄριστον precedes it, just as M[s] P[1] omit ὄν after δοῦλον in 1252 b 9. **18.** ἐστὶν ἡ πόλις] ἐστὶ πόλις M[s] P[1]: whether Vet. Int. found the article in his text, we cannot say. All MSS., however, have ἡ πόλις in 23. **27.** †ἑλκύσῃ†] ἑλκύσει P[1]: Vet. Int. *quemadmodum utique si pondus amplius trahet*, but it is not by any means certain that *trahet* represents ἑλκύσει. It may represent ἑλκύσειε or ἑλκύσαι (cp. 1253 b 16, where κἂν εἴ τι δυναίμεθα is rendered in Vet. Int. by *et utique si quid poterimus*): on the other hand, in 1263 b 34 ὥσπερ κἂν εἴ τις ποιήσειεν is rendered *quemadmodum utique si quis faciat*. With the exception of P[1] and the possible exception of Γ, all the MSS. here read ἑλκύσῃ, and I have retained it, marking it however as strange, for we look rather for the optative. There is some harshness about ἑλκύσει. Ar. *ceu si pondus magis attrahat*. **30.** γενέσθαι] O[1] γίνεσθαι (Sus.[3], in note, γίνεσθαι ?). **35.** μετέβαλλον] μετέβαλον M[s] P[1]: *quemadmodum utique si transmutarentur* (Vet. Int.) leaves the reading of Γ uncertain.

1261 b 2 sq. Here Π[2] read: ἐν τούτοις δὲ μιμεῖσθαι τὸ ἐν μέρει τοὺς ἴσους εἴκειν (so O[1]: οἰκεῖν two or three MSS.) ὁμοίους (so P[2 3]: ὁμοίως Π[3] C[4] Bekk., also O[1]) τοῖς ἐξ ἀρχῆς. M[s] P[1]: τοῦτο δὲ μιμεῖται τὸ ἐν μέρει τοὺς ἴσους εἴκειν τὸ δ' ὡς ὁμοίους εἶναι ἐξ ἀρχῆς. Vet. Int. *hoc autem imitatur scilicet in parte aequales cedere hoc* (τόδ' Γ) *tanquam similes sint a principio*: *scilicet* here probably represents τὸ, as in 1261 b 16, 1274 a 16, b 12, and it is also probable, though not absolutely certain, that *tanquam similes sint* stands for ὡς ὁμοίους εἶναι. Ar. *et in eo imitari vicissim equales cedendo invicem alios aliis*. See explanatory note. **4.** κατὰ μέρος om. Π[1], but these MSS. are somewhat prone to omit. **5.** καὶ om. Π[2] Bekk. So O[1], which adds τῶν before ἀρχόντων with P[4]. Ar. *eodem modo illorum qui regunt alii alios gerunt* (so New Coll. MS.: *regunt* Bodl.) *magistratus*. **7.** οὐ for οὔτε Π[1]: οὔτε followed by καί occurs, though rarely, in Aristotle—e. g. in De Part. An. 4. 14. 697 b 16 οὔτε is followed by καὶ οὐ. Cp. also Pol. 5 (8). 5. 1339 a 18 sq. Π[1], it must be remembered, are prone to omit, and in 1264 a 1 they have μή for μηδέ, just as in 1265 a 18 M[s] P[1] have μή for μηδὲν and in 1268 b 16 Γ M[s] pr. P[1] have οὔ for οὐδέν. **19.** ὁ om. M[s] P[1] (about Γ we cannot be certain), but wrongly. 'In addition to this passage Socrates is referred to in the Second Book as one of the interlocutors in the "Republic" of Plato 13 times (1261 a 6, 12, 16: b 21: 1262 b 6, 9: 1263 b 30: 1264 a 12, 29: b 7, 24, 37: 1265 a 11), and in not one of these passages is the article absent; its authenticity in 1261 b 19 is thus placed beyond doubt, especially as the reason why it is added is not far to seek; the reference, in fact, is not to the historical Socrates, but to Socrates as one of the *dramatis personae* of the dialogue' (Dittenberger, *Gött. gel. Anz.* Oct. 28, 1874, p. 1359). It is, however, true that all MSS. omit the article in 5 (8). 7. 1342 b 23, where the Platonic Socrates is apparently referred to. **25.** τοῖς om. M[s] P[1]: about Γ we cannot be certain. **35.** πρὸς . . . τοῖς ἄλλοις] Vet. Int. *apud alios* (πρὸς misread παρὰ ?).

1262 a 2. λέγει] Vet. Int. *dicet* (and Ar., following as he often does in his wake, *dicent*), but in 1281 a 19 he has *corrumpet* for φθείρει, and in 1257 b 15 *perit* for ἀπολεῖται, in 1263 b 28 *privantur* for στερήσονται. It is very doubtful whether these variations of tense in Vet. Int. represent variations in Γ (see above, p. lxiii, notes 10 and 11). **3.** τὸν ἀριθμόν] After τὸν ἀριθμὸν Π[1] add ὤν (Bekker and St. Hilaire, but not Sus., also find ὤν in pr. P[2]):

perhaps, however, it may well be dispensed with in the passage before us (compare such phrases as ὁποῖοί τινες ἔτυχον 3. 15. 1286 b 24, and see Bon. Ind. 778 b 4 sqq.). '"Ὢν additum ab aliquo qui Phrynichi praecepta sectabatur: sed vide Lobeck. ad Phryn. p. 277, ad Soph. Aj. 9' (Göttl. p. 311). τοῦ δεῖνος] Vet. Int. *huius filius*, possibly misreading τοῦ δεῖνος as τοῦδε υἱός. **12.** ἕτερον] See explanatory note. As to φράτορα, see Liddell and Scott s. v.: the form used in Attic Inscriptions is φράτηρ, not φράτωρ (Meisterhans, Grammatik der attischen Inschriften, p. 63). Vet. Int. has *aut* before *contribulem*, but see above on 1260a 26. **20.** γενόμενα] O[1] γινόμενα. **21.** καὶ γυναῖκες] *et* (not *etiam*) *femellae* o z. **27.** τοὺς δὲ ἑκουσίους] om. P[2], probably owing to homœoteleuton, and o omits *haec autem voluntaria*, probably from the same cause. **28.** γίνεσθαι is altered to γενέσθαι in O[1] (by whom, I cannot say). **29.** ὥσπερ πρὸς τοὺς ἄποθεν] Most of the MSS. of Vet. Int. have *quemadmodum et eos qui longe*, but a z substitute *et ad* for *et*. For the addition of *et* by Vet. Int., see above on 1252a 25. ἄποθεν M[s] P[14] L[s] Ald.: cp. 1280 b 9, ἄποθεν M[s] P[134] Q[b] T[b] Ald., and 1280 b 18, ἄποθεν Π (the Vatican Palimpsest has απωθε in 9 and αποθεν in 18). "Αποθεν seems to be the reading commonly found in the MSS. of Aristotle, but ἄπωθεν is the Attic, or at least the old Attic, form (Rutherford, New Phrynichus, p. 60: Liddell and Scott, s. v. ἄπωθεν). **30.** ἀλλὰ] ἃ Γ M[s] pr. P[1].

1262 b 7. τε om M[s] P[1]: Vet. Int. *quidem*, which probably represents γε. Ar. has *enim* only, but may well have found τε γὰρ in his Greek text. **8.** ταῖς πόλεσιν] z adds *in* before *civitatibus* (in 1261 b 8 we have μέγιστον ἀγαθὸν ἐν ταῖς πόλεσιν). **13.** συμφυῆναι] συμφῦναι P[2 3] etc. Bekk. (also O[1]), but συμφυῆναι M[s] P[1] (συμφυῆαι pr. P[4], συμφυνῆαι corr. P[4]) may not impossibly be what Aristotle wrote (though Plato in the passage referred to, Symp. 191 A, has of course συμφῦναι), for in Eth. Nic. 7. 5. 1147 a 22 K[b] has συμφυῆναι. Peculiar verbal forms are occasionally used by Aristotle; we have, for instance, προωδοπεποιημένους in 1270 a 4, πιεῖσθαι in Rhet. 1. 11. 1370 b 18. **21.** υἱῶν] So O[1], though P[4] (with Π[1]) has υἱοῦ: Ar. *vel patrem ut filii*. **32.** τοὺς φύλακας] om. M[s] P[1] (so Sus.[2 3]: P[1] only according to Sus.[1]). Vet. Int. places his equivalent for these words (*custodes*) after δοθέντες: *custodes* may of course represent either τοὺς φύλακας or οἱ φύλακες, but it is hardly likely that Vet. Int. found the latter reading in his text. **33.** In reading φύλαξι I follow Π[1]: φύλαξιν εἰς Π[2] Bekk. (and O[1]). Almost all the MSS. of Vet. Int., however, have for καὶ πάλιν οἱ παρὰ τοῖς φύλαξι τοὺς ἄλλους πολίτας *et rursum qui apud alios cives*: Sus. follows a, which adds *custodes* after *apud*, probably rightly (so too z). Ar. translates 31 sqq., οὐ γὰρ ἔτι κ.τ.λ., *nam non amplius appellant custodes fratres et filios et patres et matres qui* (here the New College MS., but not Bodl., adds *ab*) *aliis civibus deduntur et rursus qui ex custodibus aliis civibus.* **40.** χωρὶς κ.τ.λ.] *seorsum ex legum statuto* o, but the last letter of *statuto* is over an erasure.

1263 a 2. πᾶσι] Vet. Int. *omnes*: Ms πασῶν. This variation, like that in 1266 a 4, was probably occasioned by an ambiguous contraction. **12.** Π¹ add ἀλλ' ἀνίσων after ἴσων, and these authorities may possibly be right, for cases of 'abundantia contraria copulandi' are not rare in Aristotle (Vahlen, Aristot. Poet. p. 88), and ἀλλ' ἀνίσων might easily drop out after ἴσων through homœoteleuton, but perhaps it is more likely that ἀλλ' ἀνίσων is a marginal remark which has crept into the text: see above on 1255 b 12 and cp. 1268 a 37, where Γ Ms add ἕτερον εἶναι after βούλεται δ' ὁ νομοθέτης. **13.** πρὸς τοὺς ἀπολαύοντας μὲν [ἢ λαμβάνοντας] πολλὰ] Vet. Int. *ad fruentes quidem, si* (εἰ for ἢ) *accipientes quidem multa*: λαμβάνοντας or λαμβάνοντας μὲν may possibly be an alternative reading which has crept from the margin into the text, together with the ἢ introducing the suggestion (see Vahlen on ἢ ναί, Poet. 4. 1449 a 7). **23.** καὶ before ἐπικοσμηθὲν om. Π¹. ἤθεσι] So O¹ (with Π²), rightly in all probability (see explanatory note): ἔθεσι Π¹. **29.** ἑκάστῳ προσεδρεύοντες Γ Ms Sus. **34.** χρῆται κοινοῖς] Vet. Int. *utitur tanquam communibus.* **36.** κἂν δεηθῶσιν κ.τ.λ.] Vet. Int. *si indigeant pro viaticis in agris per regionem* (a z rec. b *per regionem*: the other MSS. *peregrinationem*, except y which has *peregrinationum*). As to the addition of *pro*, see above on 1253 a 10 and below on 1263 b 41. Vet. Int. appears to read ἂν instead of κἂν, but then he often omits to render καί.

1263 b 4. καὶ τὸν] 'καὶ τὸ P¹ Ar.' (Sus.)—very possibly only a conjectural emendation, like some other readings peculiar to P¹ Ar. (see Sus.³, p. xiv). The rendering in Ar. is *quemadmodum et amatio pecuniarum*, which probably represents καθάπερ καὶ τὸ φιλοχρήματον, or possibly τὸ φιλοχρήματον εἶναι, for τὸ φίλαυτον εἶναι is rendered a line or two above by *amatio sui.* **6.** τῆς κτήσεως . . . οὔσης] a z omit *in* before *possessione* perhaps rightly. **7.** οὐ om. Π¹. **9.** and **11.** τὸ om. Ms P¹: Vet. Int. *temperantiae quidem circa mulieres* (so in 11 *liberalitatis autem circa possessiones*), but we cannot tell from this what he found in his text, for he sometimes renders the article and sometimes does not. **18.** ἄλλως τε καὶ ὅταν] z *aliterque et cum*, answering to the Greek more closely than the reading of Susemihl's MSS. *aliterque cum* (cp. 1269 b 24, where *aliterque et si* stands for ἄλλως τε κἂν). **21.** ψευδομαρτυριῶν] So all MSS. here, though in 1274 b 6 all have ψευδομαρτύρων: even here, however, two MSS. of Vet. Int. (a z) have *falsorum testium*, not *falsorum testimoniorum*. **28.** στερήσονται] Vet. Int. *privantur*: see above on 1262 a 2. **32.** πάντως] Ms pr. P[1] πάντη: Vet. Int. *omnino*, which represents πάντως in 1257 b 21, πάντη in 1302 a 3. **34.** χείρων πόλις] Vet. Int. adds *erit* before *deterior civitas*, and it is perhaps on his authority that Vict. and Bekker read ἔσται χείρων πόλις, but ἔσται is omitted in all the MSS., and, as we have seen (above, p. lxii, note 2), Vet. Int. occasionally adds the auxiliary verb without support from MSS. Aristotle is sparing in its use. **41.** τοῖς συσσιτίοις] Vet. Int. *pro conviviis*: see above on 1253 a 10 and 1263 a 36.

1264 a 1. μηδὲ] μὴ Π[1]: but see above on 1261 b 7. **8.** Susemihl has apparently adopted the form φατρία throughout his third edition, and it is true that in 1300 a 25 and 1309 a 12 all the MSS. examined by him, and in the passage before us nearly all of them, and in 1280 b 37 the best MSS., have this form. So again, in 1319 b 24 all the better MSS. except P[3] have φατρίαι. See however Liddell and Scott s. v. **9.** Vet. Int. adds *et* after his equivalent for ὥστε, but, as Busse points out (p. 29 sq.), he does this in 6 (4). 4. 1292 a 17 also, in both cases probably without warrant. **15.** καὶ before καθ' ἕκαστον is not rendered either by Vet. Int. or by Ar., who translates—*vel proprias singulorum*. **21.** ἐφέντες] Vet. Int. *dimittentes*, which may perhaps stand for ἀφέντες, the reading of some of the less good MSS. ἀπειρήκασι] ἀφηρήκασι Ms P[1]: Vet. Int. *negant*, which perhaps represents ἀπειρήκασι, for ἀπειπεῖν in 1272 b 5 is *abnegare*, and the Vet. Int. occasionally renders the perfect by the present—e. g. in 1273 b 17, 1268 b 38, 1272 b 32, 1266 a 37. If this is so, ἀφηρήκασι has only the authority of Ms P[1] in its favour. Perhaps also ἀπειρήκασι corresponds better to ἐφέντες. **26.** ποιεῖ] Vet. Int. *faciunt*. **38.** τίνες] Vet. Int. *quales*, just as in 1258 b 16 he has *quibus* for ποίοις. **39.** ποιούς τινας] ποίους τινὰς O[1] (so Ms P[1] apparently): Sus.[3] ποίους τινας.

1264 b 7. ἀεὶ Π, not αἰεὶ: so too in 1254 a 25 and 1264 b 13, but αἰεὶ in 1296 a 24, 1299 a 1, 1333 a 21 etc. See Bon. Ind. 11 a 47 sqq. 'The form ἀεί prevails in Attic inscriptions from 361 B.C. onwards' (Meisterhans, Grammatik der attischen Inschriften, pp. 14, 64). **9.** ἤπουθεν δὴ] ἤ πουθεν δὴ O[1]. See explanatory note. **13.** εὐθὺς] So O[1], with Ms pr. P[1]: about Γ we cannot be certain: the rest εὐθύ. 'Εὐθύς is properly used of Time, εὐθύ of Place' (Liddell and Scott). **14.** μῖξαι] So O[1]: 'μῖξαι Ms P[1] Π[3] Bekk., at v. Classen ad Thuc. 2. 84. 5' Sus.[1] Classen's note will be found among his critical notes, Bd. 2, p. 192. **19.** τῶν αὐτῶν] All Susemihl's MSS. of Vet. Int. have *eorum*, not *eorundem*: z, however, has *eorundem* (τῶν αὐτῶν Π). **26.** τὰ is added in Π[1] before περὶ (Vet. Int. here translates the article—*quae circa leges*). **31.** τὴν τάξιν] z (with a and pr. k) has *ordinem* rightly. γὰρ] δὲ Π[1]. **40.** τὸν λόγον is not rendered by Vet. Int., but this may well be an oversight, similar to those pointed out above, p. lxiii, note 12. Ar. also gives no equivalent for it—*cetera vero extraneis peregit sermonibus*. See note in Sus.[3].

1265 a 4. εἰς] So M[s] P[1]: πρὸς O[1] (with Π[2]): Vet. Int. *ad*, which may represent εἰς as in 1265 a 41, b 3, 1270 a 18, but may also represent πρὸς, as in 1254 b 13, etc. Perhaps πρὸς is more likely to have been substituted for εἰς than εἰς for πρὸς. **12.** τὸ is omitted before ζητητικόν in M[s] P[1]: whether it was omitted in Γ also, we cannot tell. **14.** Vet. Int. translates as if he found the words arranged in the following order—χώρας Βαβυλωνίας ἤ τινος ἄλλης ἀπεράντου δεήσει τοῖς τοσούτοις τὸ πλῆθος, but his intention probably is to make it clear that he (wrongly) takes τὸ πλῆθος with τοῖς τοσούτοις: see Busse, p. 14 n. He might have remembered χώρας πλῆθος, 4 (7). 8. 1328 a 28. **16.** περὶ] Vet. Int. almost alone seems to have found παρὰ in his text, for he has *praeter*. For περὶ with the acc. in the sense in which it is used here, cp. 7 (5). 11. 1314 b 25. **21–22.** For the glosses which deform the text of Π[1] here, see Susemihl's *apparatus criticus*. **24.** Almost all the MSS. of Vet. Int. fail to render καὶ before πρὸς: a z alone have *et ad*. **29.** διορίσαι τῷ σαφῶς μᾶλλον] Vet. Int. *determinetur plane magis*, but, as has been pointed out elsewhere, he occasionally substitutes the passive for the active. **30.** ὥσπερ ἂν εἴ τις εἶπεν] Sus. is apparently in error when he says that Π[1] omit εἴ. Vet. Int. has *quemadmodum si quis dicat*. What he omits is ἄν, but this he is rather apt to omit (see above on 1254 a 39). He did not probably find εἴπειεν in his text, but εἶπεν, for *non utique lateat* (1264 a 3) stands for οὐκ ἂν ἔλαθεν. **33–34.** See Susemihl's *apparatus criticus* for the various readings here. Π[1] are not quite unanimous in favour of τῷ μὲν τὸ and τῷ δὲ τὸ, nor indeed are Π[2] in favour of the reading adopted in the text, for P[4] etc. (and O[1]) have τὸ δὲ τὸ in 34 in place of τὸ δὲ τῷ, but Γ Π agree in reading ἑκάτερον: hence it seems probable that the reading in the text is the correct one, as otherwise ἑκάτερον has to be altered without MS. authority to ἑκατέρῳ. τῷ ἐπιπόνως] Vet. Int. adds *vivere* after *laboriose*, but it is very doubtful whether he found an equivalent for it in his Greek text. **35.** ἕξεις αἱρεταὶ] ἕξεις ἀρεταὶ Π (Ar. *virtutes habitus*): Vet. Int. *quoniam* *soli hi habitus sunt virtutes circa habitudinem* (ἕξιν—so Π[1]) *substantiae.* Probably Victorius' conjecture is right and ἀρεταὶ should be αἱρεταί: cp. 1285 a 16, where M[s] Ald. have ἀρεταί for αἱρεταί. **40.** ὁμαλισθησομένην] Vet. Int. *respondentem.* Ὁμαλίζειν is usually represented by *regulare* in Vet. Int. (e.g. in 1266 b 3, 16, 1274 b 9).

1265 b 3. ἀπορεῖ] Vet. Int. *dubitat* (probably only a mistranslation, in which, however, he is followed by Ar.). **4.** παράζυγας] περίζυγας M[s] P[1] and according to Sus. Γ also, but almost all his MSS. of Vet. Int. have *deiectos* (so o y), and we cannot be certain what Greek word this represents: a z have *iugarios* (z in marg. *aliter deiectos*), and this again is hardly a correct rendering either of περίζυγας or παράζυγας. Ar. has *dispares.* **13.** τῶν ἀρχαιοτάτων] Vet. Int. *antiquorum*, but degrees of comparison are often inexactly rendered by Vet. Int. (see below on 1270 b 1, 1271 b 6, 21, 1272 a 8). **19.** ὅπως] πῶς M[s] P[1]: Vet. Int. *quomodo*, which may represent either πῶς or ὅπως. **20.** All Susemihl's MSS. of the Vet. Int. but one (l) have *sit* for γίνεται (so o y): z *fit.* **21.** δεῖν] om. pr. O[1], but it is added above the line with a caret, in darker ink than the MS. but probably by the writer of it. **25.** συμφέρει] For the various readings see Susemihl's *apparatus criticus.* Vet. Int. *expediat*: O[1], with some of the less good MSS., συμφέρῃ. See explanatory note. Ar. has *videndum est . . . ne non prosit.* **30.** πολιτείαν] πολιτειῶν Π[1], possibly rightly. **35.** Sus.[3] 'τῶν om. Π[1]': Π[1], however, would seem to be a misprint for P[1] (see Sus.[1 2]). **39.** ἐφόρων] Vet. Int. *plebeiorum.* In the next line he has *ephoros* for ἐφόρους. Dittmeyer (*op. cit.* p. 36) observes of William of Moerbeke's translation of the Rhetoric—'hic quoque universus interpretis usus respiciendus est: ut verbum Graecum saepe non mutatum versioni inserit, ita idem verbum hic illic sive apto sive inepto vocabulo Latino interpretari conatur.'

1266 a 3. χειρίστας πασῶν] Vet. Int. *pessimas omnibus.* See above on 1263 a 2. **5.** ἔπειτα] So O[1] (with M[s] P[1]). **18.** On τοῦ τετάρτου τῶν τετάρτων, see explanatory note. Here probably two alternative readings have both been admitted into the text, as in some MSS. in 1266 a 37, 1273 a 35, 1254 a 10. In O[1], after ἐκ δὲ τοῦ τετάρτου τῶν τετάρτων, the words ἐκ δὲ τοῦ τετάρτου τῶν τεττάρων are added, but they are crossed through and dots placed beneath them, probably by the writer of the MS. **23.** συνιστάναι] So O[1]: συνεστάναι Π[1] (Vet. Int. *constare*), and also pr. P[3].

1266 b 1. τὰς δ' ἤδη] Vet. Int. *eas autem quae iam habitabantur* (δ' ἤδη Γ?, which Schneider adopts, rightly followed by Bekker and Susemihl), 'δὴ P[1] Π[2], δὲ M[s] Ar.' (Sus.), but it is not perhaps very clear what Ar. found in his text, for his translation is—*postquam vero condita foret, difficilius quidem.* O[1] originally had τὰς δή, but δή has been altered into δέ—by whom, is uncertain. **3.** τὰς om. M[s] P[1]: as to Γ we cannot be certain. **11.** Vet. Int. *multitudinem* for τὸ μέγεθος. **18.** ὁπόσην] ὁπόστην P[23] and some of the less good MSS. (so O[1]): ὅσην M[s] P[1] Sus.: Vet. Int. *quantamcunque*, which leaves it uncertain whether he found ὁπόσην or ὅσην in his text: ὁπόσην Ald. Bekk. **26.** δῆλον οὖν] All the MSS. of Vet. Int. used by Sus. except a have *palam igitur, quod non sufficiens substantias aequales facere erit legislator* (so o y): a z, however, have *legislatori.* **28.** τάξειεν] τάξει M[s] P[1]: Vet. Int. *ordinaverit*, which probably stands for τάξειεν, for in 3. 4. 1277 b 22 εἰ οὕτως ἀνδρεῖος εἴη is rendered by the Vet. Int. *si sic fortis fuerit*, and in 1. 2. 1252 a 24 εἴ τις βλέψειεν is rendered *si quis viderit.* **31.** εἴπειεν is probably the true reading here, as in 1270 b 38, 1272 a 35, 1339 a 14. See Susemihl's *apparatus criticus* on these four passages and Bon. Ind. 222 a 4 sqq.

1267 a 5. ἀλλὰ καὶ] a z *sed etiam* (n *sed et*): the rest wrongly *sed.* **8.** ἀλλὰ καὶ ἂν ἐπιθυμοῖεν] Vet. Int. *sed et si desiderent*, probably a mistranslation of these words. So Ar. *verum etiam si concupiscant ut molestia careant et voluptate fruantur.* See explanatory note on 1267 a 5. **11.** βούλοιντο] Vet. Int. *possint* (δύναιντο M[s]). **17.** βούλεται κατασκευάζειν] Vet. Int. *opus est constitui*, where *constitui* may well stand for κατασκευάζειν, but it is less easy to account for *opus est.* **24.** ὧν] Vet. Int. *quam*, referring to *multitudinem* (πλῆθος). **25.** ἐπιθυμήσουσιν] See Susemihl's *apparatus criticus* for the reading of M[s] P[1]; it finds support in two MSS. of Vet. Int. only (c y), which read *concupiscunt*: most have *concupiscant*, one or two *concupiscent* (so z), either of which, however, may stand for ἐπιθυμήσουσιν—cp. 1268 a 41, where θήσει is rendered by *ponat*, and see below on 1267 b 35. ἀμύνειν] Vet. Int. *sufferre* (=ὑπενεγκεῖν?). **28.** ὅτι 'Γ Π Ar. Bekk.' (so Sus.[2]); but Ar. has *oportet autem neque id latere quantas facultates habere conducat.* Stahr ὅ τι: Sus.[3] [ὅ] τί. **29.** τὸ μὴ λυσιτελεῖν] Vet. Int. *ut non pro levi habeat* (so z and most MSS. of Vet. Int.: o *ut non prae levi habeat*: Sus., however, reads, with g (so also y), *ut non prolem habeat*): in 1279 b 9, on the other hand, τὸ λυσιτελοῦν is rendered *id quod expedit.* Should *ut non pretium habeat* be read (cp. 1258 b 16, where λυσιτελέστατα is *pretiosissima*)? **34.** ἐθέλειν] Vet. Int. *debere* (=μέλλειν or ὀφείλειν?, cp. 1253 b 26, 1268 b 12). **35.** ταῦτα] z has *haec* (*hec*): Susemihl finds *hoc* in his MSS. **40.** ἂν om. Π[1], probably wrongly, just as they are probably wrong in adding ἂν in 8 (6). 8. 1322 a 33 (cp. 3. 13. 1283 b 15, where Π om. ἂν, and see Bon. Ind. 41 b 6 sqq.).

1267 b 1. ἄπληστον] Vet. Int. *irreplebilis.* Sus.[1] 'nonne *irreplebile?*,' and it is true that in 1253 a 37 we find ἡ δὲ δικαιοσύνη πολιτικόν translated by the Vet. Int. *iustitia autem civile*; but see Dittmeyer, *op. cit.* p. 34, who shows that the practice of William of Moerbeke in his translation of the Rhetoric is to make the predicate agree in gender with the subject—thus in Rhet. 1. 3. 1359 a 5 τούτῳ δὲ ὁ μὲν τοιοῦτος θάνατος κάλλιον is rendered *huic autem talis mors pulchrior.* **14.** κατασκευάζων] *constituens* o, perhaps rightly: the other MSS. *construens.* **23.** Πειραιᾶ] πειρεᾶ O[1]. **26.** κόμης (in place of κόσμῳ πολυτελεῖ) Π[1]. Ar. *ornatu sumptuoso.* 'Quibusdam exemplaribus' (i.e. probably MSS., not printed editions: see above on 1257 b 36) 'illud ἔτι δέ, quod in ceteris habetur, abest, ut prolixitas ad capillos, sumptus ad vestem duntaxat referatur' (Sepulveda, p. 51). Ἔτι δὲ is, in fact, omitted in T[b]. **33.** All the better MSS. and some of the inferior ones have here τὸ ὅπλα ἔχον (so O[1]): only one MS., and that of little authority, has τὰ in place of τὸ as its original reading. The phrase commonly is οἱ τὰ ὅπλα ἔχοντες, κεκτημένοι (see e.g. 1268 a 18, 22: 1297 b 2: 1268 a 20, 25), though not quite invariably (see 4 (7). 10. 1329 b 36: 6 (4). 13. 1297 a 29), and here the τὸ seems better away. See explanatory note. **35.** ποιήσουσι] Most of the MSS. of Vet. Int. have *faciant,* and in **36.** for βιώσονται *vivant,* but this does not imply that the translator did not find the future in his Greek text: see above on 1267 a 25. **37.** εἴδη καὶ τῶν νόμων] Vet. Int. *et species legum*: Busse (p. 27) notes a similar change of order in the version given by Vet. Int. of 4 (7). 3. 1325 b 22.

1268 a 3. καταδικάζοι] See Susemihl's *apparatus criticus* here and in the next line. The MSS. which have καταδικάζει seem mostly to have ἀπολύοι in 4. O[1] has καταδικάζοι and ἀπολύθι, the last two letters of ἀπολύθι being however expunged and οι superscribed, probably by the writer of the MS. All the MSS. of Vet. Int. known to Sus. have *condemnetur* for καταδικάζοι (so o y): z, however, has *condempnet*—rightly in all probability, for *absolvat,* not *absolvatur,* follows in all the MSS. Ar. *si condempnaret . . . sin absolveret.* There seems to be little doubt that καταδικάζοι and ἀπολύοι are correct (see Goodwin, Moods and Tenses, § 77). τὴν δίκην om. Π[1], possibly rightly, for the words may be only a gloss, but Π[1] are somewhat given to omitting words. Ar. *si condempnaret simpliciter sententiam.* **12.** αἱρετοὺς εἶναι] Vet. Int. *eligi.* **17.** οἱ before γεωργοὶ om. M[s] P[1] and possibly of course Γ (Vet. Int.

agricolae). **25**. Π[1] add καὶ before κρείττους. **26**. M[s] P[1] om. γε: about Γ we cannot be certain, for Vet. Int. often fails to render γε. **34**. γεωργήσουσιν] Bekker's reading γεωργοῦσιν rests only on the authority of Ar., who has *colunt*. **39**. αὖ] Π[3] οὖν, O[1] οὖν with αὖ superscribed, whether by corr.[1] or by the writer of the MS., is not certain, but very possibly by the latter, for the ink is quite that of the MS., and οὖν is neither expunged by dots placed beneath nor crossed through. Οὖν, though probably not the true reading here, is used in a similar way in Magn. Mor. 2. 9. 1207 b 31 and 2. 11. 1208 b 37, and even in writings of Aristotle (see Bon. Ind. 540 b 32 sqq.).

1268 b 1. γεωργήσει δύο οἰκίας] Vet. Int. *ministrabit duas domos*: hence some have thought that he found ὑπουργήσει δύο οἰκίας in his Greek text, but *ministrare* in Vet. Int. answers to διακονεῖν (cp. 1280 b 5, 1333 a 8). He may here render a marginal gloss. Διαπονήσει would be better than διακονήσει, but see explanatory note. **5**. See explanatory note. διαιροῦντα P[2 3] etc. (so O[1]) seems better than διαιροῦντας Π[1] (cp. τὸν δικάστην 6). On δίκης, see explanatory note. **9**. ἀλλὰ καὶ τοὐναντίον τούτῳ] Vet. Int. *sed contrarium huius*: hence it is probable, though not certain, that Γ omitted καὶ with M[s] and read τούτου with M[s] P[1]. **12**. ὁ μὲν] μὲν ὁ M[s] P[1]: about Γ we cannot be certain, for some MSS. of Vet. Int. have *quidem iudex* (so z), and others (so o y) *iudex quidem*. See explanatory note. **13**. κρινεῖ (Bekk.[2] Sus.) is probably right (cp. 16 καταδικάσουσιν), though Γ Π have κρίνει (so O[1]). **15**. δὴ] O[1] has δὲ with δὴ superscribed, probably, but not certainly, by the writer of the MS. See explanatory note. **19**. Ar. does not render δικαίως (*si simpliciter petatur*). **21**. For the omission of ἤδη here by Π[1], cp. 1288 a 6 and 1336 b 36, where they omit it also. Ar. does not render it. **32**. μικρὰ] μικρὸν Π[1]. **35**. ἰατρικὴ] c o *medicinalis* rightly: the rest *medicinali* (for the reading of z, however, see Appendix C, 112. 3). **40**. ἐσιδηροφοροῦντό τε γὰρ] Vet. Int. *ferrum enim portabant tunc Graeci* (ἐσιδηροφόρουν τότε γὰρ?).

1269 a 11. γραφῆναι] γράφειν Π[1], possibly rightly. **12**. φανερὸν] Vet. Int. *videtur*. **16**. καὶ τῶν νομοθετῶν καὶ τῶν ἀρχόντων] Vet. Int. *et legislatoribus et principibus* (apparently after *sinendum*). Busse (p. 27 note) compares *voluntati* for προαιρέσεως in 1271 a 32. **18**. τις is added in M[s] P[1] before κινήσας: Vet. Int. *qui mutaverit* (perhaps = ὁ κινήσας: see however his version of 1340 b 24): Ar. *qui corrigere perget* (ὁ κινήσας?). See explanatory note. **19**. ψεῦδος δὲ κ.τ.λ.] Vet. Int. *mendax quoque exemplum quod ab artibus* (*ab* probably stands for παρὰ): ψεῦδος, here *mendax*, is *falsum in*

1287 a 33. **21.** πλὴν, which is written in $P^{2\,3}$ over παρὰ, is probably intended as an alternative reading for παρὰ: see 1274 b 9, where φαλέου is written above φιλολάου in $P^{2\,3}$. Bekker, however, reads πλὴν παρὰ in both his editions. **25.** καὶ, which Bekker adds before πάντες, is found in O^1 and in P^4 etc., but not in the best MSS. **38.** οἱ before εἵλωτες is omitted in M^s P^1 L^s: we cannot tell whether Vet. Int. found it in his Greek text or not. **40.** πω] Vet. Int. *unquam*.

1269 b 5. τοῖς Θετταλοῖς] c o om. *a* before *Thessalis* in Vet. Int. **11.** ὡς] *quasi* instead of *quod* o, perhaps rightly, for Vet. Int. takes ἐξευρίσκουσι as a participle. **19.** ἀνομοθέτητον] *inordinatum in lege* o. **21.** φανερός ἐστι τοιοῦτος ὤν] I follow here the reading of Π^2 (which is, except in matters of accent, that of O^1, and also of Ar., who translates—*in viris quidem id fecisse constat*): τοιοῦτος ἐστιν Π^1. The reading of Π^2 appears to me to be probably the true one, especially as in 26 Γ M^s pr. P^1 omit φανερῶς, wrongly, it would seem, cp. 1263 b 9, 1311 a 16. **26.** See note on 21. **28.** Ἄρη] O^1 has ἄρην with M^s $P^{1\,4}$, etc.: we cannot tell which form Vet. Int. found in his text, for he has *Martem*. Ἄρη is the Attic form according to Liddell and Scott. Vahlen reads Ἄρη in Poet. 21. 1457 b 21, where Bekker had read Ἄρην. **30.** κατακώχιμοι] Cp. 5 (8). 7. 1342 a 8. 'Forma κατακώχιμος in duobus Politicorum locis [also in Hist. An. 6. 18. 572 a 32] exhibetur sine varia lectione, Eth. Nic. 10. 10. 1179 b 9 κατοκώχιμον [K^b Ald.] Bekk., sed κατακώχιμον codd. L^b M^b O^b' (Bon. Ind. 371 a 8). I retain the reading of the MSS.: Liddell and Scott, however, remark (s. v. κατοκωχή):—'the corrupt forms κατακωχή, κατακώχιμος, must be corrected, except perhaps in late writers: cf. ἀνοκωχή, συνοκωχή.' **35.** ἀλλ' εἴπερ, πρὸς τὸν πόλεμον] Vet. Int. *nisi ad bellum*. **36.** ταῦθ'] All Susemihl's MSS. of Vet. Int. have *hoc*, but y has *hec* (= *haec*).

1270 a 11. καὶ μὴ ὀρθῶς] Almost all MSS. of Vet. Int. (including z) have *aut* before *non recte*, but *aut* appears to represent καὶ in 1262 a 8. **13.** See Susemihl's *apparatus criticus* for the various readings here: I follow him in reading αὑτῆς καθ' αὑτήν. O^1 has αὐτὴν καθ' αὑτήν. **21.** καταλείπειν] καταλιπεῖν M^s P^1: Vet. Int. *derelinquere*, which may represent either καταλιπεῖν, as in 1252 a 30, or καταλείπειν. **22.** ταὐτὸ] So Π^1 (ταυτὸ P^1): O^1 (with Π^2) and Bekk. τοῦτο less well (cp. 1269 b 34). **27.** τε om. M^s P^1: about Γ we cannot be certain, for the Vet. Int. hardly ever renders τε. κἂν ἀποθάνῃ] Here o agrees with pr. a in omitting (no doubt erroneously) *et si moritur—voluerit*. **28.** ὃν ἂν καταλίπῃ] z *quem utique derelinquat*, perhaps rightly. **37.** Vet. Int. here renders οὐ μὴν ἀλλά by *al-*

tamen, as in 1274 b 25: he often renders it by *quin immo sed* (e.g. in 1262 a 14, 1264 a 11), and οὐ μὴν by *attamen* (e.g. in 1267 a 39).

1270 b 1. βουλόμενος γὰρ κ.τ.λ.] Vet. Int. *volens enim legislator ut plures sint Spartiatae, provocat cives quod plures faciant pueros*: but though *plures* is his rendering, he probably found πλείστους in his text in both places, for he is not always exact in rendering degrees of comparison: see above on 1265 b 13. **3.** ἔστι γὰρ] The MSS. of Vet. Int. have *est autem*, not *est enim*. **8.** αὐτὴ] αὕτη Ar. (*hic enim magistratus*): om. Γ Ms (so Sus.[1 2]: Sus.[3], by a misprint apparently, Ms P[1]). **12.** Ἀνδρίοις] See Susemihl's *apparatus criticus* for the various readings. As to the substitution of τ for δ here in Π[1], it should be noted that this was an error to which Egyptian scribes were especially liable: see Blass, Hyperidis orationes quatuor, praef. p. xvii. I know not whether there are any other indications in Π[1] that the archetype of these MSS. was of Egyptian origin. **14.** δημαγωγεῖν κ.τ.λ.] Vet. Int. *regere populum* (i.e. δημαγωγεῖν, cp. 1274 a 10) *se ipsos cogebant reges*: he evidently does not understand δημαγωγεῖν, and he is quite capable of construing ἠναγκάζοντο *cogebant* (cp. 1269 a 18, where βλαβήσεται is rendered *nocebit*, and 1271 a 22, where κρίνεσθαι is rendered *iudicare*). Perhaps, as Busse remarks (p. 25), Γ had αὑτοὺς in place of αὐτοὺς. All the MSS. read αὐτοὺς ἠναγκάζοντο καὶ οἱ βασιλεῖς. **15.** ταύτῃ] O[1] ταῦτα: ταύτῃ, however, is added in the margin, probably by corr.[1] **19.** On διὰ τύχην see explanatory note. Ms P[1] add τὴν before τύχην, just as in 1332 a 32 they add τῆς before τύχης: as to the reading in Γ we cannot of course be certain. In 1323 b 29 all the MSS. have ἀπὸ τύχης οὐδὲ διὰ τὴν τύχην. **21.** On this passage see explanatory note. **32.** αὐτὴ] αὕτη Π[1], but see explanatory note. **33.** μᾶλλον ὑπερβάλλει] *magis superexcedit* o (perhaps rightly): other MSS. *magis excedit*. **38.** εἴπειέ] Susemihl reads εἴποι, which is, however, apparently only found in P[1], for Ms has εἴπῃ, and the reading of Γ is unknown. See his *apparatus criticus* for the varieties of reading.

1271 a 15. τούτῳ] τούτοις O[1] (with Π[2]). Ar. *illis utitur*. **17.** τῶν after ἀδικημάτων om. Π[2] O[1] Bekk.[1]: Bekk.[2] adds it in brackets. Whether Vet. Int. found this τῶν in his text, it is of course impossible to say; but after ἀδικημάτων it might easily be omitted: cp. 1283 a 11, where in πᾶσαν ἀνισότητα Γ Ms pr. P[1] make ἀνισότητα into ἰσότητα, and 1284 a 3, where in τὸν βίον τὸν κατ' ἀρετὴν two or three MSS. omit the second τόν. **18.** φιλοτιμίαν] o y z have *amorem honorum*: Susemihl's MSS. *amorem honoris*. διὰ] Neither Vet. Int. nor Ar. (*per ambitionem et avaritiam*) renders διὰ before φιλοχρηματίαν, and M[s] omits it. But compare for the repetition of διὰ, 7 (5). 10. 1311 a 25. **19.** In Π[1] μὴ is omitted here and placed between ἢ and βέλτιον (20). **20.** ἀλλὰ μὴν κ.τ.λ.] Vet. Int. *sed et si melius, non sicut nunc, sed per ipsius vitam unumquemque* (o here adds *nunc est*) *iudicare regum* (o z *regnum*). Hence Sus.[3] reads ἀλλὰ κἂν βέλτιον, * * γε μὴ καθάπερ νῦν, ἀλλὰ κ.τ.λ. and supposes a second βέλτιον to have dropped out before γε, or else δεῖ or something similar; but μὴν may easily have been corrupted into κἂν in Γ or misread by the translator. Ar. *attamen melius non ut nunc quidem, sed pro vita cuiusque regis iudicare.* **23.** *Enim* here as elsewhere in the *vetus versio* (1268 b 34, 1280 a 38) represents γοῦν. **27.** φιδίτια] In this passage, probably, as in others, we may ascribe the reading φιλίτια to Π[1], for though almost all the MSS. of Vet. Int. omit the word, two of them (a z) have *amicabilia.* Compare Susemihl's *apparatus criticus* on 1272 a 2, b 34. The form φιλιτείοις occurs in the Herculanean papyri on which the fragmentary remains of the work of Philodemus de Musica are preserved (fragm. 30: p. 18 Kemke). Plutarch, however, it is evident, used the form φιδίτια (see Lycurg. c. 12 *init.*). Dicaearchus, Phylarchus, and Antiphanes (ap. Athen. Deipn. pp. 141, 143) also use either this form or that of φειδίτια (see Meineke on Athen. Deipn. 143 a). Bekker reads φιδίτια both in the Politics and in Rhet. 3. 10. 1411 a 25, though in the latter passage (see Roemer *ad loc.*) no MS. has preserved the true reading, nor yet the Vetus Interpres. So too C. F. Hermann (see Gr. Ant. 1. § 28. 1) and Schömann (Gr. Alterth. 1. 280 n.). **31.** συμβαίνει] So O[1]: Bekker reads συμβαίνειν, but without support from the better MSS. *Quare accidit* in Vet. Int. leaves it uncertain what reading he found in his text. **32.** τῷ νομοθέτῃ τῆς προαιρέσεως] Almost all MSS. of Vet. Int. have *legislatoris voluntati* (a m z have *legislatori voluntati*, y *legumlatori voluntati*). See above on 1269 a 16. **37.** αὐτῆς Π[1] Bekk. Sus. seems to be correct (cp. 1272 a 15, τῆς πολιτείας): for the readings of other MSS. see Susemihl's *apparatus criticus.* O[1] αὐτοῖς. **40.** ἀιδίοις] ἀίδιος Π[2] Ar. (*praefectura illa perpetua*) Bekk. (αἴδιος O[1]). **41.** Vet. Int. does not render καθέστηκεν, but see above, p. lxiii, note 12, for other instances in which he fails to render words. Ar. *fere alterum est imperium.* ὡδὶ] Vet. Int. *hoc.*

1271 b 5. Vet. Int. adds *ad virtutem* after his equivalent for μηδὲ. Similar additions appear in his version in 1254 b 20 and 1287 a 30. Ar. omits these words—*nec quicquam aliud exercere sciebant praestabilius quam rem militarem.* **6.** τούτου] So O[1], though P[4] with some other MSS. has τοῦτο. Vet. Int. would seem to have found τοῦτο in his Greek text, for he has—*hoc autem peccatum non modicum*. He probably found ἔλαττον in his text, though his translation is *modicum*, for he is often inexact in rendering degrees of comparison (see above on 1265 b 13). Ar. *illud quoque erratum non sane minus, quod putant* (om. μὲν with Γ Ms?) *bona illa quae ad bellum pertinent* (he blindly follows Vet. Int. *bona quae circa res bellicas*) *ex virtute magis quam ex vitio fieri*. To omit μὲν with Γ Ms would be a mistake: 'interdum oppositio per particulam μέν indicata et inchoata non accurate continuatur' (Bon. Ind. 454 a 17 sqq.). See Vahlen on Aristot. Poet. 6. 1450 a 3 sqq. and b 16 sqq. (Poet. pp. 118, 127). **21.** τὸ δὲ πλεῖον] Vet. Int. *plurimum autem*, but see above on 1265 b 13, 1271 b 6. **22.** καὶ λέγεται δὲ] Vet. Int. *et dicitur quidem* (καὶ λέγεταί γε?), τε Ms P[1]. **25.** Χαρίλλου Π, but in 7 (5). 12. 1316 a 34 Π have Χαριλάου. This variation may possibly date back to an uncial archetype. See Sus.[1] p. xiv on the confusion of οὐσιῶν and θυσιῶν in 3. 14. 1285 b 10, 16. **27.** ἄποικοι is here rendered by Vet. Int. *domestici*: see above, p. xlv, note 1, for other renderings of the word in Vet. Int. **28.** κατέλαβον] Vet. Int. *susceperunt*. οἱ . . . ἐλθόντες] o *qui venerunt*: other MSS. *qui venerant*. **31.** ὡς κατασκευάσαντος] Vet. Int. *ut instituit*. **34.** ἐπίκειται] Vet. Int. *supponitur* (ὑπόκειται?). **35.** ἀπέχει γὰρ κ.τ.λ.] O[1] ὀλίγον τῆς πελοποννήσου (P[4] ὀλίγον τῆς πελοποννήσου). Vet. Int. *distat enim quidem a Polopo insula modicum, versus Asiam autem ab eo loco qui circa Triopium et a Rhodo* (ῥόδου Π[1], perhaps rightly). Ar. read Ῥόδου. **39.** ἐπιθέμενος τῇ Σικελίᾳ] Vet. Int. *appositus Siciliae*: cp. 1305 a 14, where ἐπιτίθενται is translated *superponuntur*. **40.** Κάμινον is the reading of all the better MSS. (so O[1]) and of Γ (καμινον without accent P[3]): Vict. substituted Κάμικον, and either this or Καμικόν (the true accentuation of the word is, according to Sus., a disputed point) seems to be the correct reading. It is easy to understand how the commoner word took the place of the less common one. **41.** τε om. Ms P[1]: Vet. Int. *agriculturae enim opus faciunt*, but Vet. Int. hardly ever renders τε, hence the reading in Γ is uncertain.

1272 a 3. ἀνδρεῖα] O[1] (with Π[2]) ἄνδρια. Ephorus ap. Strab. p. 480, and Dosiadas and Pyrgion ap. Athen. Deipn. p. 143 have ἀνδρεῖα, not ἄνδρια. C. F. Hermann (Gr. Ant. 1. § 22. 5) is for ἀνδρεῖα. **8.** πρότερον] Vet. Int. *primo*, but see above on 1265 b 13, 1271 b 6, 21. **16.** ἐν δὲ Κρήτῃ κ.τ.λ.] Ar. *at in creta communiter est, ex cunctis enim quae a terra proveniunt vel armentis ex publicis et iis quae afferunt periici* (so New Coll. MS.: Bodl. *perieci*: neither have *periti*, as Schn., Pol. vol. 2. p. 134) *divisio fit*.

Thus Ar. omits, with all the better MSS., the καὶ which Bekker adds before ἐκ τῶν δημοσίων. Most of the MSS. of Vet. Int. omit *et* before *ex publicis*, but a adds it, and so does z. **24.** ποιήσας] a z have *fecit*: the other MSS. of Vet. Int. *facit*. **28.** χεῖρον τῶν ἐφόρων] Vet. Int. *deterius quam quae ephororum*, but whether he found χεῖρον ἢ τὰ τῶν ἐφόρων in his Greek text, may well be doubted. ὁ μὲν γὰρ] Here pr. O[1] (cp. P[4]) has ὁ μὲν γὰρ τὰ περὶ τοὺς κόσμους οὐ καλῶς ἔχει κακὸν τὸ τῶν ἐφόρων ἀρχεῖον ὑπάρχει καὶ τούτων, but corr.[1] adds in the margin—γρ. ὁ μὲν γὰρ ἔχει κακὸν τὸ τῶν ἐφόρων ἀρχεῖον ὑπάρχει καὶ τούτων. Evidently a marginal remark τὰ περὶ τοὺς κόσμους οὐ καλῶς has found its way into the text of these two MSS. **29.** τούτοις] τούτων Π[2] O[1] Bekk., but the genitive seems doubtful (cp. 2. 5. 1264 a 29). Ar. *id est et in illis*, which probably implies that he found τούτων in his text: cp. 1253 b 27, where *sic etiam in re familiari* in Ar. probably stands for οὕτω καὶ τῶν οἰκονομικῶν. **36.** τῶν] ὧν Π, evidently repeated from περὶ ὧν 35. Vet. Int. *de hiis quae in Lacedaemonia fiunt*. **40.** οὐδὲν γὰρ] οὐδὲ γὰρ Γ (Vet. Int. *neque enim*) is adopted by Bekker, but probably wrongly. All the MSS. have οὐδέν. 'Τι secludendum esse ci. Buecheler, μέτεστι Coraes, sufficeret ἔστι, sed nihil mutandum est' Sus.[1]. Οὐδέν τι is common enough used adverbially, but it does not seem to be often used as it is here. **41.** πόρρω γ' ἀποικοῦσιν] Vet. Int. *longe enim peregrinantur*, but, as Susemihl sees in his third edition, this is no proof that Vet. Int. found γὰρ in his Greek text.

1272 b 5. καὶ μεταξὺ] o *etiam* (not *et*) *intermedie*. **8–9.** See explanatory note. δίκας] Vet. Int. *sententias*, as in 7 (5). 3. 1302 b 24. **16.** τοῖς βουλομένοις ἐπιτίθεσθαι καὶ δυναμένοις Π[1]: Sus. adopts this reading in all his editions, but holds in his third that some word is wanting before τοῖς βουλομένοις. Ar. *est autem periculosus hic reipublicae status, si qui velint possintque invadere*. **28.** ἡ before Λακωνικὴ is omitted, not surely by M[s] P[1] only (as Sus.[3] holds), but by Π[1], for Vet. Int. translates—*quae Cretensium et Lacedaemonica et tertia ab hiis quae Calchedoniorum*. **30.** σημεῖον δὲ κ.τ.λ.] Ar. *signum est reipublicae bene institutae quod* (so Bodl.: New Coll. MS. wrongly *quo*) *populus in suo permaneat* (so Bodl.: New Coll. MS. *permanet*) *loco*. Thus he does not render ἔχουσαν, which M[s] P[1] omit, but probably wrongly. **36.** γὰρ after μὲν om. P[2 3] etc., followed by Bekker, but the reading of Π[1] P[4] (and O[1]), which is adopted by Susemihl, seems preferable. Ar. *praeterquam quod non deterior : nam illi ex contingentibus sunt*. The same doubt as to the exclusion or insertion of γὰρ recurs in 1291 a 29 and 1331 b 34, but in 1291 a 29 Π¹ are supported by the Vatican Palimpsest in adding it. **37.** ἀριστίνδην] Vet. Int. *virtuosum*: so again in 1273 a 23, and πλουτίνδην in 1273 a 24 *divitem*. **38.** τοῖς ἐκεῖ βασιλεῦσι] Susemihl's MSS. of Vet. Int. have *hiis quae ibi regibus*: z rightly *hiis qui ibi regibus*. **39.** See explanatory note on 1272 b 38. **40.** εἴ τε] εἴ τι Sus., who takes *si quid* to be the true reading in Vet. Int., but a alone has *si quid* (z *si quod*)—the rest of Susemihl's MSS. having *sed quod, sed quae* (so o), or *se que*—and probably we should read *sique* in Vet. Int., the reading adopted by Susemihl in 5 (8). 4. 1338 b 16: εἶτε O¹, εἴτε M^s Π² Bekk.: Ar. *melius autem quod imperatorem non secundum genus neque ex vili aut precellenti magis eligunt quam secundum virtutem*: εἴ τε is probably right, cp. 1338 b 16.

1273 a 7. τὰ δὲ] τὸ δὲ P²³⁴ etc. Bekk. (so O¹), but the same MSS. have τὰ μὲν in 6, where Bekker's reading τὸ μὲν rests only on a conjecture of Morel's. **9.** οὗτοι om. Π¹, but see above on 1257 b 24. **15.** ταύτας αἱρεῖσθαι] τούτους αἱρεῖσθαι pr. O¹ (so P⁴), but corr.¹ adds ταύτας in the margin. Both O¹ and P⁴ have ταύτας at the end of the line. Vet. Int. has *hos* in both places. **16.** See the various readings for πλείονα in Susemihl, and see above on 1255 b 26. **19.** ὑπὸ τῶν ἀρχείων] Vet. Int. *a principibus* (ὑπὸ τῶν ἀρχόντων?). **22.** ᾗ συνδοκεῖ τοῖς πολλοῖς] Vet. Int. *ut* (ᾗ?) *videtur multis*. **39.** ὅτι δ'] Here z alone among the MSS. of Vet. Int. which have been examined has *enim* (*quicunque enim* instead of *quodcunque autem*), but it has *enim* instead of *igitur* for οὖν in 1273 a 25, and not a few other blunders are to be found in it in this part of the Second Book (δ' Γ Π). Ar. *nam quicquid apud civitatis principes habetur in pretio, necessarium est et aliorum civium opinionem subsequi*: but Ar. has *enim* in 1268 b 6 also, where Γ Π have δ'. It is not likely that Ar. found anything but δὲ in his Greek text in either passage: Sus., however, follows him against Γ Π in both.

1273 b 1. οὐχ οἷόν τε κ.τ.λ.] οὐχ οἷόν τ' εἶναι βεβαίως ἀριστοκρατικὴν πολιτείαν Π² Bekk. See on this reading the explanatory note on 1273 b 1. **5.** ἄριστ' ἄρχειν] ἀρισταρχεῖν ΓΠ Bekk. (a word which occurs nowhere else in Aristotle or perhaps anywhere), ἄριστ' ἄρχειν Spengel, Sus. **6.** προεῖτο] Vet. Int. *praeferret*, but προΐεσθαι is no better translated in 1307 b 4, 1314 a 37 sq. εὐπορίαν] ἀπορίαν Γ M^s, but this kind of mistake often occurs—so in 1278 a 32 Γ M^s have ἀποροῦντες wrongly for εὐποροῦντες, in 1288 a 15 P³ Π³ pr. P² have ἀπόροις wrongly for εὐπόροις: see also the readings in 1300 a 2, 1302 a 2, 1303 a 12. **7.** ἀλλὰ ἀρχόντων γε] Vet. Int.

sed et principantium. Did he read τε for γε, as he seems to have done in 1274 a 15? **15.** τῶν αὐτῶν] Vet. Int. *ab eisdem*, but we have already seen (above on 1253 a 10) that he occasionally inserts prepositions without authority, and here he had a special motive for doing so, for, as Busse (p. 21) points out, he seems to have taken τῶν αὐτῶν with ἀποτελεῖται. **18.** καὶ is added before τῆς πολιτείας in O[1], as in P[4] etc. **25.** Κρητικῆς] M[s] P[1] κρήτης: Vet. Int. *Cretensium.* **27.** τι om. Π[1]. Ar. *eorum autem qui de republica aliquid tradiderunt.* τι is absent in 1. 13. 1260 b 23, in 6 (4). 1. 1288 b 35, and in 5 (8). 5. 1339 a 14 (see Bon. Ind. 88 a 36 sqq.), but we have εἰπεῖν τι in 2. 8. 1267 b 29. **28.** οὐδ' ὡντινωνοῦν] Vet. Int. *nullis.* ἀλλὰ διετέλεσαν κ.τ.λ.] Vet. Int. *sed perseverarunt singulari vita viventes.* **32.** οἱ μὲν—μόνων] οἱ μὲν ἐγένοντο δημιουργοὶ νόμων Π[1]. **39.** μίξαντα] Vet. Int. *miscuisseque*, but this does not prove that he read μίξαι τε: see his rendering of 1259 a 10 sq. εἶναι] Vet. Int. *fuisse.* **41.** τὰ δὲ δικαστήρια] τὸ δὲ δικαστήριον Π[1], which Sus. prefers, comparing 1274 a 4, but we have τὰ δικαστήρια in 1274 a 3.

1274 a 2. τῶν ἀρχῶν] O[1] τῶν ἀρχόντων. **4.** θάτερον O[1], with Π[2] Ar. (*alterum*). **5.** ἴσχυσεν M[s] P[1]: we cannot tell from *invaluit* which reading Vet. Int. found in his text, for he often renders the imperfect by the perfect (e.g. in 1267 b 18, 30, 31). Ἴσχυσεν, however, which Sus. adopts, seems preferable to ἴσχυεν Π[2] O[1] Bekk.: cp. 6 (4). 13. 1297 b 23. **13.** Μηδικοῖς] o *mediis.* See Susemihl's critical note on *Medis* (Sus.[1] p. 145). ἐφρονηματίσθη] Vet. Int. *astute concepit* (the same misapprehension of the meaning of the word appears in his renderings of it in 1284 b 2, 1306 b 28, 1341 a 30). **15.** ἐπεὶ Σόλων γε] Vet. Int. *quoniam et Solon*: see above on 1273 b 7. **19.** O[1] εὐπόρων, but ἐμ is written over the first syllable, probably by the writer of the MS. **21.** Π[1] add τὸ before θητικόν, perhaps rightly (Vet. Int. *quartum autem quod mercenarium*). But I incline to think it is better away: cp. Aristot. Fragm. 350. 1537 a 36 sq. and Pol. 6. (4). 4. 1291 a 4. **24.** ταῖς Χαλκιδικαῖς] Vet. Int. *Chalcidiae* (τῆς Χαλκιδικῆς Γ?). **25.** δέ τινες] δὲ καὶ τινὲς O[1], but καὶ has been expunged by a dot placed beneath it —by whom, is uncertain. Π[2] add καί before τινες. **27.** ἐπιδημοῦντα] Vet. Int. *praefectum populo* (perhaps, however, *praefectus populo*, which I find in o, may be the true reading). **29.** In O[1] δ' is expunged by a dot placed beneath it, and δ' αὖ superscribed—I do not feel certain by whom. **34.** Ὀλυμπίασιν] The true reading of the equivalent for this word in Vet. Int. is probably (as Busse points out, p. 9) that of a and pr. b (also pr. z) *olimpiasem.*

'Guilelmum 'Ὀλυμπίασιν pro nomine a verbo νικήσαντος apto accepisse suspicandum est' (Busse, ibid.). διαμισήσας] Vet. Int. *recordatus.* **40.** ἀπέχθειαν] Vet. Int. *abstinentiam.* 'Απέχθεια is correctly rendered by Vet. Int. in 1305 a 23, 1322 a 2, 17. **41.** ἀπὸ τοῦ χώματος] Vet. Int. *a pulvere.*

1274 b 5. Vet. Int. has *Charondi autem nihil est proprium,* and this is the order of the words in P¹ (and Mˢ?). **6.** μὲν om. O¹ with Π¹ P⁴. ψευδομαρτύρων Γ Π Ar. (*falsorum testium*), ψευδομαρτυριῶν Scaliger, Bentley, Bekk., Sus.: cp., however, Rhet. ad Alex. 16. 1432 a 6, ἐν ἀποφάσει ψευδομαρτυρήσας ψευδομάρτυρος δίκην οὐχ ὑφέξει. In 2. 5. 1263 b 21, where the MSS. of the Politics have ψευδομαρτυριῶν, two MSS. of the Vet. Int. (a z) have *falsorum testium,* not *falsorum testimoniorum.* **7.** ἐπίσκηψιν Scaliger and Bentley, ἐπίσκεψιν Γ Π (Vet. Int. *considerationem*). **9.** On the passage bracketed see explanatory note. All the MSS. (and Vet. Int.) read φιλολάου: P²³, however, have the alternative reading φαλέου superscribed in the same ink, it would seem, as the MS. (Sus.¹, p. xviii). ἀνομάλωσις Bekk., ἀνωμάλωσις Π (Vet. Int. *irregularitas,* which represents ἀνωμαλία in 1270 a 15, and here probably ἀνωμάλωσις). **13.** γίνωνται] So Π¹: pr. O¹ had, I think, γίνονται (with Π²), but it has been dexterously altered into γίνωνται. **14.** τὴν μὲν κ.τ.λ.] Susemihl's MSS. of Vet. Int. have *hac quidem manuum utile esse, hac autem inutile,* but z has *hanc quidem manuum utilem* (*utile* pr. manus?) *esse, hanc autem inutilem.* τοῖν] So O¹ with P²³ etc.: P¹⁴ ταῖν. **20.** τι πταίσωσι, though found only in Lˢ—a manuscript known to Camerarius, however, had τι πταίωσι (Politicorum Interpretationes, p. 109)—is probably right. See Susemihl's *apparatus criticus* for the readings of the other MSS.: most of them read τυπτήσωσι (so O¹). The word used in the law seems to have been ἁμαρτάνειν, which τι πταίσωσι approaches much more nearly than τυπτήσωσι. Camerarius refers to [Plut.] Sept. Sap. Conv. 13, νόμον, ἐν ᾧ γέγραφας, 'Εάν τις ὁτιοῦν μεθύων ἁμάρτῃ, διπλασίαν ἢ τῷ νήφοντι τὴν ζημίαν: to which reference may be added Aristot. Rhet. 2. 25. 1402 b 9 sqq. and Diog. Laert. 1. 76 (ἁμαρτάνειν is the word used in both these passages). Schn. τι πταίωσι (see his note): Bern. Sus. τι πταίσωσι: Bekk. τυπτήσωσι. πλείω ζημίαν] *amplius damnum* (not *damni*) c o z, perhaps rightly. ἀποτίνειν] ἀποτείνειν probably pr. O¹, for after τ there is an erasure leaving a blank, in which ε may once have stood (ἀποτίννειν P², the rest ἀποτείνειν): Vet. Int. *ferre.* 'In the older [Attic] inscriptions τίνω always forms τείσω, ἔτεισα, ἐτείσθην' (Meisterhans, Grammatik der attischen Inschriften, p. 88). Here the ει finds its way into the infinitive ἀποτείνειν. **25.** τὰς ἐπικλήρους] Vet. Int. *heredationes*: his rendering of the word is no better in 1304 a 4, 10, where he translates it *hereditatibus* and *hereditatione*. He certainly does not shine in his version of this twelfth chapter.

NOTES.

BOOK I.

1. THE view that the πόλις is a κοινωνία had an important bearing on Greek political speculation; Plato already asserts it by implication (Rep. 371 B: 462 C: 369 C), but Aristotle seems to have been the first to fix the conception of κοινωνία and to define its meaning. See vol. i. p. 41 sqq. C. 1. 1252 a.

2. ἀγαθοῦ τινός. Cp. Eth. Nic. 1. 1. 1094 a 2, and Pol. 1. 6. 1255 a 15, where the expression recurs, and also Eth. Nic. 3. 5. 1112 b 15, τέλος τι. In Pol. 3. 12. 1282 b 15 we have—ἐπεὶ δ' ἐν πάσαις μὲν ταῖς ἐπιστήμαις καὶ τέχναις ἀγαθὸν (not ἀγαθόν τι) τὸ τέλος. The ends which the various κοινωνίαι seek to attain are described in Eth. Nic. 8. 11. 1160 a 8 sqq. In the passage before us, however, ἀγαθόν τι is explained by τοῦ εἶναι δοκοῦντος ἀγαθοῦ, though in strictness this need not be a good at all. On 'seeming good' as the aim in action, see Eth. Nic. 3. 6 and the commentators. Sepulveda (p. 3) refers to de An. 3. 10. 433 a 27, διὸ ἀεὶ κινεῖ μὲν τὸ ὀρεκτόν, ἀλλὰ τοῦτ' ἐστὶν ἢ τὸ ἀγαθὸν ἢ τὸ φαινόμενον ἀγαθόν· οὐ πᾶν δέ, ἀλλὰ τὸ πρακτὸν ἀγαθόν. Τὸ εἶναι δοκοῦν ἀγαθόν = τὸ ἑκάστῳ εἶναι δοκοῦν ἀγαθόν, or τὸ φαινόμενον ἀγαθόν (Eth. Nic. 3. 6. 1113 a 20–24).

4. πᾶσαι μὲν κ.τ.λ. These words repeat the second of the two premisses (1252 a 2); they do not contain the conclusion. Μέν is 'while,' as in 5 (8). 2. 1337 b 15 and 5. 1340 a 1. Bonitz remarks on Metaph. Θ. 2. 1046 b 15: 'in apodosi duo quidem membra, τὸ μὲν ὑγιεινόν—ψυχρότητα et ὁ δ' ἐπιστήμων ἄμφω, quasi eodem ordine iuxta se posita sunt, sed ipsa apodosis unice in posteriore membro continetur; prius grammatice coordinatum, re vera subiectum est alteri membro. Cf. de hoc abusu partt. μέν—δέ Xen. Cyr. 1. 1. 4 et Bornem. ad h. l.'

Aristotle omits to prove that the aim of κοινωνίαι is not the avoidance or mitigation of evil, which is according to some modern inquirers the end of the State.

μάλιστα, Vict. 'illo "maxime" significatur studium ipsius vehemens in persequendo quod quaerit.' So Bern. Cp. 3. 12. 1282 b 15.

Cp. also Eth. Nic. 10. 4. 1174 b 21–23 and 5. 1175 a 30 sq., referring to which latter passages Teichmüller (Aristoteles Philosophie der Kunst, p. 177) says: 'der Eifer geht immer parallel mit den erstrebten Gütern: je höher das Gut, desto grösser die Bemühung darum.' It is not certain, however, that μάλιστα here means more than 'above all' (Sus. 'ganz vorzugsweise').

5. **κυριωτάτη**, 'most sovereign.' Cp. 2. 9. 1271 b 6.

πάσας περιέχουσα τὰς ἄλλας. Cp. Eth. Nic. 8. 11. 1160 a 8, *αἱ δὲ κοινωνίαι πᾶσαι μορίοις ἐοίκασι τῆς πολιτικῆς*, and 21, *πᾶσαι δ' αὗται (αἱ κοινωνίαι) ὑπὸ τὴν πολιτικὴν ἐοίκασιν εἶναι, οὐ γὰρ τοῦ παρόντος συμφέροντος ἡ πολιτικὴ ἐφίεται, ἀλλ' εἰς ἅπαντα τὸν βίον*, and also Plato, Parmen. 145 B, *πάντα δὲ τὰ μέρη ὑπὸ τοῦ ὅλου περιέχεται.* These passages explain the sense in which the words of the text are used. Aristotle is not thinking of the size of the *κοινωνίαι* here compared, for there were *κοινωνίαι* in Greece, especially of a religious kind—festival-unions, for instance—which extended, as our Churches often do, beyond the limits of the State, but of the more comprehensive end pursued by the *πόλις*—an end as wide as human life—which makes it stand to all other *κοινωνίαι* as a whole stands to its parts. Thus the end of the *πολιτικὴ ἐπιστήμη* is said in Eth. Nic. 1. 1. 1094 b 6 *περιέχειν τὰ τῶν ἄλλων.* See other references given in Bon. Ind. 581 a 41 sqq.

7. The addition of **ἡ κοινωνία ἡ πολιτική** serves to facilitate the transition to the subject discussed in the next sentence.

ὅσοι μὲν οὖν. Socrates (Xen. Mem. 3. 4. 12: 3. 6. 14): Plato (Politicus 259). Aristotle himself had dropped one or two expressions in the last chapter of the Nicomachean Ethics (1180 b 1–2: 1180 b 24), which might be interpreted as lending some countenance to the view that the contrast of household and *πόλις* is a contrast of numbers. Common opinion is said in 4 (7). 2. 1324 b 32 to identify *δεσποτική* and *πολιτική*. It appears to be implied that if the difference lay only in the numbers of those ruled, the four characters would be the same: cp. de Part. An. 1. 4. 644 a 16 sqq., Pol. 3. 8. 1279 b 34, 38 (referred to by Eucken, Methode der Aristotelischen Forschung, p. 50. 4), where a numerical difference is treated as an insufficient basis for a distinction of species, and also Pol. 1. 13. 1259 b 36. *Ὅσοι* 'acerbius dictum est, ut fere nos: "wie gewisse Leute sagen"' (Ideler, Aristot. Meteor. vol. i. p. 363). *Μὲν οὖν* here introduces an inference from what precedes (which is not always the case: see Bon. Ind. 540 b 58 sqq.)—'the *πολιτικὴ κοινωνία* is the supreme *κοινωνία*, and makes the supremest of goods its aim; hence it is a mistake to hold that the *πολιτικός*, βασιλικός, οἰκονομικός, and δεσποτικός are the same.' The μέν seems to be taken up, if at all, by δ' 17, but, owing to the long parenthesis which begins in 9 with πλήθει γάρ, the paragraph is perhaps not completed quite as Aristotle originally intended to complete it.

πολιτικὸν . . . εἶναι τὸν αὐτόν. The Vet. Int., Sepulv., and Lamb. (unlike Vict.) rightly make πολιτικὸν κ.τ.λ. the subject and τὸν αὐτόν the predicate. The article is omitted before πολιτικόν, as in Xen. Mem. 1. 1. 16, τί πολιτικός, to give the word an abstract meaning: cp. also 1. 2. 1252 b 9, ὡς ταὐτὸ φύσει βάρβαρον καὶ δοῦλον ὄν.

11. ὀλίγων, sc. ἄρχη, νομίζουσιν εἶναι. The omission of ἄρχη is quite in the Aristotelian manner. See Bon. Ind. 239 a 52 sqq.

12. ὡς οὐδὲν διαφέρουσαν. On this construction with ὡς, cp. Poet. 20. 1457 a 12 and Vahlen's note, p. 214 of his edition. Plato (Politicus, 259 B) limits his assertion by adding the words πρὸς ἀρχήν, 'in the matter of rule.'

13. καὶ πολιτικὸν δὲ καὶ βασιλικὸν κ.τ.λ. Giph. 'et de politico quidem atque rege,' and so Bern. ('und bezüglich des Verhältnisses zwischen dem verfassungsmässigen Staatsmann und dem Könige')—an interpretation in support of which Eth. Nic. 7. 4. 1146 b 11, καὶ τὸν ἐγκρατῆ καὶ τὸν καρτερικόν, πότερον ὁ αὐτὸς ἢ ἕτερός ἐστιν might be quoted; but perhaps it is more likely that the sentence is framed on the model of that which precedes it (πλήθει γὰρ 9—βασιλικόν 12), and would run, if completed, καὶ πολιτικὸν δὲ καὶ βασιλικὸν [οὐκ εἴδει (or οὕτω?) νομίζουσι διαφέρειν· οἷον] ὅταν μὲν αὐτὸς ἐφεστήκῃ, [νομίζουσιν εἶναι] βασιλικόν. The insertion of διαφέρειν νομίζουσι (Schn.), or of οὕτω διαφέρειν οἴονται (Göttl.), or even of οὐκ εἴδει νομίζουσι διαφέρειν (Rassow, Bemerkungen über einige Stellen der Politik, p. 4, followed by Sus.), does not suffice to complete the sentence. The distinction drawn by the inquirers here referred to between the βασιλικός and the πολιτικός fell short, in Aristotle's opinion, of the truth. They rested the distinction between them on the extent and duration of the authority possessed by them respectively, regarding the βασιλικός as a permanent autocratic ruler and the πολιτικός as one who exchanged his authority from time to time for subjection to rule, and exercised it in subordination to the precepts of the kingly or political science. This distinction between the βασιλικός and the πολιτικός is not, so far as I am aware, to be found *totidem verbis* in the Politicus of Plato, but Aristotle probably gathers it from Polit. 294 A, 300 E sqq., though Plato seems to draw it rather between the ideal βασιλικός and the actual πολιτικός, than between the ideal βασιλικός and the ideal πολιτικός, whom he does not appear to distinguish (300 C). Plato, however, declines in the Politicus (292 E) to refuse the character of βασιλικός to one who, without actually ruling, possesses the kingly science, so that, if the Politicus is referred to here, the reference would seem to be not altogether exact. Aristotle, as has been said, holds that those who distinguished in the way he describes between the βασιλικός and the πολιτικός underrated the difference between them. The βασιλεύς, according to him, differs in nature from those he rules (Pol. 1. 12. 1259 b 14: cp. Eth. Nic. 8. 12. 1160 b 3 sqq.); he is not their equal like the πολιτικός (Pol. 1. 7. 1255 b 18 sqq.). Nor is it the case, in Aristotle's view, that an interchange of ruling and being ruled occurs in all forms of πολιτικὴ ἀρχή (cp. Pol. 1. 12. 1259 b 4, ἐν μὲν οὖν ταῖς πολιτικαῖς ἀρχαῖς ταῖς πλείσταις μεταβάλλει τὸ ἄρχον καὶ τὸ ἀρχόμενον).

14. αὐτὸς (cp. Plato, Rep. 557 E, ἐὰν αὐτῷ σοι ἐπίῃ) here seems to unite the meanings of 'alone' (cp. 5 (8). 4. 1338 b 25) and 'uncontrolled' (cp. 2. 9. 1270 b 8), and to stand in opposition both to κατὰ τοὺς λόγους τῆς ἐπιστήμης τῆς τοιαύτης and to κατὰ μέρος ἄρχων καὶ ἀρχόμενος. So Schn., who however translates 'solus et semper,' which hardly brings out the complete meaning.

ὅταν δὲ κ.τ.λ. Ἐφεστήκῃ should probably be supplied here.

15. κατὰ τοὺς λόγους κ.τ.λ. The ideal king, and indeed the ὄντως πολιτικός (300 C), of the Politicus of Plato rules μετὰ τέχνης (300 E), not in subordination to (κατά) the written precepts of his art (compare the contrast of μετὰ τοῦ ὀρθοῦ λόγου and κατὰ τὸν ὀρθὸν λόγον in Eth. Nic. 6. 13. 1144 b 26 sqq. and Magn. Mor. 1. 35. 1198 a 17 sqq.), just as a training-master who happened to return to his pupils from abroad sooner than he expected, would not feel himself bound by the written directions given them by him for their guidance during his absence (294 D, τὰς τῶν τέχνῃ γυμναζόντων ἐπιτάξεις). The ideal ruler, like the captain of a ship or a physician, should rule over those committed to his charge, 'not in subordination to the laws, but with plenary authority' (299 C, μὴ κατὰ νόμους, ἀλλ' αὐτοκράτορας). Cp. 301 E, θαυμάζομεν δῆτα ἐν ταῖς τοιαύταις πολιτείαις ὅσα ξυμβαίνει γίγνεσθαι κακὰ καὶ ὅσα ξυμβήσεται, τοιαύτης τῆς κρηπῖδος ὑποκειμένης αὐταῖς τῆς κατὰ γράμματα καὶ ἔθη, μὴ μετὰ ἐπιστήμης, πραττούσης τὰς πράξεις; For the expression τοὺς λόγους τῆς ἐπιστήμης τῆς τοιαύτης, cp. Eth. Nic. 7. 5. 1147 a 18, τοὺς λόγους τοὺς ἀπὸ τῆς ἐπιστήμης: Polyb. 1. 32. 7, καὶ τι καὶ κινεῖν τῶν μερῶν ἐν τάξει καὶ παραγγέλλειν κατὰ νόμους ('ex artis legibus iussa dare,' Schweighäuser) ἤρξατο. Cp. also Marc. Antonin. Comment. 6. 35, οὐχ ὁρᾷς, πῶς οἱ βάναυσοι τεχνῖται . . . ἀντέχονται τοῦ λόγου τῆς τέχνης, καὶ τούτου ἀποστῆναι οὐχ ὑπομένουσιν; In de Gen. An. 2. 1. 735 a 1 we have ἡ κίνησις ἡ τῶν ὀργάνων ἔχουσα λόγον τὸν τῆς τέχνης, but the expression perhaps bears a somewhat different meaning in this passage, and also in that last quoted.

τῆς τοιαύτης, i. e. τῆς βασιλικῆς. Rassow (Bemerkungen, p. 3) and Susemihl (Sus.[2], note 3) are probably right in thus explaining τῆς τοιαύτης, which must apparently refer back here as elsewhere to something already mentioned. Plato, as Rassow points out, identifies the βασιλικὴ ἐπιστήμη with the πολιτικὴ ἐπιστήμη (Polit. 259 C).

16. **ταῦτα δ' οὐκ ἔστιν ἀληθῆ**. These words refer to the whole series of opinions described in 9–16, and especially to that which sums them up, that the πολιτικός, βασιλικός, οἰκονομικός, and δεσποτικός do not differ in kind. Compare the still blunter expression used in criticising the Platonic Socrates (7 (5). 12. 1316 b 17), τοῦτο δ' ἐστὶ ψεῦδος.

17. **τὸ λεγόμενον**, i. e. Aristotle's assertion in 9 (repeated in 16), that the doctrine criticised is erroneous. Mr. Congreve, however, and Prof. Tyrrell (*Hermathena*, 12. 22) take the reference to be to 1252 a 3–7. Against this view it may be urged, that (1) it seems more natural to refer τὸ λεγόμενον to that which immediately precedes, especially as otherwise ὅσοι 7—ἀληθῆ 16 becomes a long parenthesis, introduced, strangely enough, by μὲν οὖν, and without any δέ to answer to μὲν οὖν: (2) the word δῆλον has already been applied to the conclusion arrived at in 3–7: (3) if we take τὸ λεγόμενον to refer to the assertion that the πόλις aims at the supreme good, we expect to be told in 21 sqq. that fresh light will be thrown on this subject, not that we shall better understand the nature of the differences existing between the parts of which the πόλις is composed, and it is thus that these scholars explain τούτων 21.

τὴν ὑφηγημένην μέθοδον. Cp. de Gen. An. 3. 9. 758 a 28. 'Camerarius viam et rationem quasi praeeuntem et ducentem ad certam cognitionem interpretatur' (Schn.); we find, however, κατὰ τὸν ὑφηγημένον τρόπον in Pol. 1. 8. 1256 a 2, where the metaphor seems to fall into the background. Still ὑφηγεῖσθαι is probably used in both passages in a middle, and not, as Bonitz takes it (Ind. 807 b 46 sqq.), in a passive sense. The same plan of inquiry—that of dividing a compound whole into its simplest elements and examining these—had been followed in the Nicomachean Ethics in the case of εὐδαιμονία, and so again in the Third Book of the Politics, the πόλις being πολιτῶν τι πλῆθος, the πολίτης is first studied. Cp. de Part. An. 1. 4. 644 a 29, ἡ μὲν γὰρ οὐσία τὸ τῷ εἴδει ἄτομον, κράτιστον, εἴ τις δύναιτο περὶ τῶν καθ' ἕκαστον καὶ ἀτόμων τῷ εἴδει θεωρεῖν χωρίς, ὥσπερ περὶ ἀνθρώπου, οὕτω καὶ περὶ ὄρνιθος, where the best method is said to be to examine the ultimate species separately, but the remark is added that it is better not to apply this method to fishes and birds, for the species under these genera are not far apart (οὐ πολὺ διεστῶτα), and much repetition would result if it were employed in relation to them. So in the de Anima (see de An. 2. 3) it is through studying the δυνάμεις of the soul successively—τὸ θρεπτικόν, τὸ αἰσθητικόν, and so forth—that we obtain a real knowledge of the soul. And so again in the History of Animals Aristotle's first step is to study the parts of which animals are made up, and in the treatise on the Parts of Animals to study the homogeneous parts, which are simpler, before the heterogeneous, which are more complex. The method of rising from the parts to the whole was a tradition from Socrates: see Grote, Plato 1. 384 sq., who refers to Hipp. Maj. 301 B, and notes the objection of Isocrates to it (ad Nicocl. § 52). Cp. also ad Nicoclem, § 9, πρῶτον μὲν οὖν σκεπτέον τί τῶν βασιλευόντων ἔργον ἐστίν· ἐὰν γὰρ ἐν κεφαλαίοις τὴν δύναμιν ὅλου τοῦ πράγματος καλῶς περιλάβωμεν, ἐνταῦθ' ἀποβλέποντες ἄμεινον καὶ περὶ τῶν μερῶν ἐροῦμεν. In de Anima 1. 1. 402 b 9 sqq. we find Aristotle discussing whether it is better to begin with ἡ ὅλη ψυχή or τὰ μόρια or τὰ ἔργα αὐτῶν. His review of the parts of the State in the Politics, indeed, quickly reveals to him its ἔργον.

20 sqq. καὶ πόλιν answers to ἐν τοῖς ἄλλοις, 18. By arriving at the simple elements of the πόλις, which are, as the State consists of households (c. 3. 1253 b 2), the simple elements of the household —husband and wife, father and child, master and slave—we shall not only come to understand the nature of the πόλις, but shall also learn what is the difference between the δεσποτικός, οἰκονομικός, πολιτικός, and βασιλικός, and also how far it is possible to arrive at a scientific account of each of these personages. Some take both τούτων and ἕκαστον τῶν ῥηθέντων to mean 'the parts of which the πόλις is composed,' but if τὸ λεγόμενον 17 refers, as seems probable, to 7–16, we look rather for an inquiry with regard to the δεσποτικός, οἰκονομικός, etc. than for one respecting the parts of which the πόλις is composed. Besides, ἕκαστον τῶν ῥηθέντων reminds us of τούτων ἕκαστον 10, words clearly referring to the δεσποτικός, etc. Sepulveda, on the other hand, takes τούτων to mean 'the parts of which the πόλις is composed,' though he explains ἕκαστον τῶν ῥηθέντων as 'quae pertinent ad regem, ad civilem hominem, ad dominum et patrem familias.' Our attention, however, has been specially drawn in 7–16 to the question as to the nature of the difference existing between the δεσποτικός, οἰκονομικός, and the rest, and it seems likely that διαφέρουσι 21 takes up διαφέρειν 10; perhaps, therefore, on the whole it is most probable that both τούτων and ἕκαστον τῶν ῥηθέντων refer to the δεσποτικός, οἰκονομικός, πολιτικός, and βασιλικός. Cp. 1. 7. 1255 b 16, φανερὸν δὲ καὶ ἐκ τούτων ὅτι οὐ ταὐτόν ἐστι δεσποτεία καὶ πολιτική, οὐδὲ πᾶσαι ἀλλήλαις αἱ ἀρχαί, ὥσπερ τινές φασιν. We shall find that the analysis of the πόλις into its simple elements (which is described in c. 3. 1253 b 1 sq. as completed) does throw light on the difference between the δεσποτικός, the οἰκονομικός, and the ruler of a State, and ultimately to some extent also on the difference between the πολιτικός and the βασιλικός, for we learn to distinguish the rule exercised by the head of the household over his wife, which is a πολιτικὴ ἀρχή, from that which he exercises over his child, which is a βασιλικὴ ἀρχή. As to τεχνικὸν, cp. Eth. Nic. 10. 10. 1180 b 20, οὐδὲν δ' ἧττον ἴσως τῷ γε βουλομένῳ τεχνικῷ γενέσθαι καὶ θεωρητικῷ ἐπὶ τὸ καθόλου βαδιστέον εἶναι δόξειεν ἄν, κἀκεῖνο γνωριστέον ὡς ἐνδέχεται· εἴρηται γὰρ ὅτι περὶ τοῦθ' αἱ ἐπιστῆμαι, and also Pol. 1. 11. 1258 b 33 sqq.: 1259 a 8, 20. For ἐξ ὧν 20 (not ἐκ τίνων), cp. 1. 3. 1253 b 1, ἐπεὶ δὲ φανερὸν ἐξ ὧν μορίων ἡ πόλις συνέστηκεν, and see Jelf, Gr. Gr. 2. § 877. a. Obs. 3, 4.

24. Εἰ δή τις κ.τ.λ. Δή introduces the first step in the inquiry C. 2.
just announced: cp. de An. 1. 2. 403 b 26: Pol. 6 (4). 12. 1296 b 14: 6 (4). 14. 1297 b 37. The first question as to this sentence is, does ὥσπερ ἐν τοῖς ἄλλοις, καὶ ἐν τούτοις form part of the protasis or the apodosis? Bernays connects the words with the protasis. Sepulveda, Vict., and Lamb. take them with the apodosis, and, it would seem, more naturally: cp. above 18–21. Proposals to transfer οὕτω 26 to before καὶ 25 are negatived by the usage of Aristotle (see Bon. Ind. 546 b 18 sqq., who refers among other passages to Eth. Nic. 3. 1. 1110 b 9, εἰ δέ τις τὰ ἡδέα καὶ τὰ καλὰ φαίη βίαια εἶναι (ἀναγκάζειν γὰρ ἔξω ὄντα), πάντα ἂν εἴη οὕτω βίαια), no less than by the intrinsic objections to taking this liberty with the MS. text. The meaning of οὕτω seems to be not 'as follows' (Bern.), but 'by watching the process of growth from the beginning.' Andrew Schott, in some notes appended to D. Heinsius' Paraphrase of the Politics (p. 1042), takes ἐξ ἀρχῆς with φυόμενα, and there is, no doubt, some strangeness in the expression ἐξ ἀρχῆς βλέψειεν: still these words are probably to be taken together. Ἐξ ἀρχῆς means, 'beginning at the beginning': see Waitz on Anal. Post. 2. 8. 93 a 16. For the genetic method here employed, cp. Meteor. 4. 12. 389 b 24 sqq., and Isocr. De Antid. § 180. In

tracing the growth of the πόλις from its earliest moments, Aristotle follows Plato's example both in the Republic (369 A) and in the Laws (678 sqq.). Plato's object, however, is different from Aristotle's. In the Republic his object, or nominal object, is to find justice—in the Laws it is to discover τί καλῶς ἢ μὴ κατῳκίσθη κ.τ.λ. (Laws 683 B); whereas Aristotle's object is to distinguish the δεσποτικός, οἰκονομικός, βασιλικός, and πολιτικός, and still more to prove that the πόλις is by nature and prior to the individual, and the source of αὐτάρκεια to the latter. His substitution of this method of watching the growth of the πόλις from its smallest elements is not a desertion of the method of division (διαιρεῖν, 19) announced just previously; it is, on the contrary, its best application. The same plan is followed in c. 9 to distinguish the sound and the unsound χρηματιστική. The growth of χρηματιστική both within and beyond the limits prescribed by Nature is carefully traced. For τὰ πράγματα, cp. Rhet. 1. 7. 1364 b 8.

26. ἀνάγκη δὴ κ.τ.λ. Society begins in Necessity (that which is necessary always comes first, that which is for well-being afterwards, 4 (7). 10. 1329 b 27), and its earliest form is συνδυασμός, the union in pairs of human beings who are indispensable to each other. Aristotle lays stress on the origin of the household in Necessity and the needs of every day, partly in order to differentiate the οἰκονομικός and the πολιτικός, partly because by tracing the household to Necessity, or in other words Nature, he obtains the means of proving that its outgrowth the πόλις is by Nature. He finds the origin of the Household and the πόλις in Necessity and Nature, not προαίρεσις (for this contrast Bonitz, Ind. 837 a 46, compares de Part. An. 2. 13. 657 a 37, καὶ τοῦτο οὐκ ἐκ προαιρέσεως, ἀλλ' ἡ φύσις ἐποίησε). Plato had seemed in the Republic (369 B: cp. 371) to regard the πόλις as originating in the exchange of products and labour. Even in the Laws, where the household is treated as the germ of the πόλις (680), no such attempt is made to trace its origin and to resolve it into its constituent elements, as is here made by Aristotle. In the view of the latter, human society originates not in the ἀλλακτικὴ κοινωνία (which begins only in the κώμη or Village, c. 9. 1257 a 19 sqq.), but in the relations of husband and wife, and master and slave. The starting-point of the process that gives birth to the πόλις is to be sought in a pair of powerful instinctive desires—that of reproduction, which brings male and female together, and that of self-preservation, which draws the slave to his master, the master also gaining in completeness by having the slave's physical strength placed at his disposal. Elsewhere, however, we are told that human society originates in the aim to live (τοῦ ζῆν ἕνεκεν, c. 2. 1252 b 29: 3. 6. 1278 b 24: cp. Plato, Rep. 369 D) and ultimately to live nobly and well (1252 b 30: 1278 b 21 sqq.), for which purposes men stand in need of ἡ παρ' ἀλλήλων βοήθεια (1278 b 20). This account of the origin of society is set by the side of that which traces it back to the instincts which lead to the formation of the household; we are not taught how to weave them together. There is, besides, a further source of human society—simple ὄρεξις τοῦ συζῆν (3. 6. 1278 b 21): man is so endowed by nature—endowed with speech and perceptions of the good and bad, the just and unjust, the advantageous and disadvantageous—as to seek society irrespective of all needs of βοήθεια: he is, in fact, a πολιτικὸν ζῷον in an especial degree. Without these endowments the instincts of reproduction and self-preservation would not suffice to give birth to the household and the πόλις, for these instincts are possessed by the lower animals, which nevertheless do not form households or πόλεις.

τοὺς ἄνευ ἀλλήλων κ.τ.λ. Cp. de Gen. An. 2. 4. 741 a 3 sq., 2. 5. 741 b 2 sqq., and Menand. Inc. Fab. Fragm. 101:

Οἰκεῖον οὕτως οὐδέν ἐστιν, ὦ Λάχης,
ἐὰν σκοπῇ τις, ὡς ἀνήρ τε καὶ γυνή.

Perhaps τῆς γενέσεως ἕνεκεν 27 is intended to qualify not only συνδυάζεσθαι, but also τοὺς ἄνευ ἀλλήλων μὴ δυναμένους εἶναι. For this purpose they cannot dispense with each other, and for this purpose they must pair.

27. θῆλυ μὲν καὶ ἄρρεν. It would seem from ἐν τοῖς ἄλλοις ζῴοις 29, that in this passage, as occasionally elsewhere (e.g. 1. 13. 1260 a 10, 13), these words are used of the male and female human being.

τῆς γενέσεως ἕνεκεν, the origin, but not, in Aristotle's view, the end of wedlock: see Eth. Nic. 8. 14. 1162 a 19 sqq. The household, like the πόλις, comes into existence for one end, but subsists for another. Γένεσις is a wider term than γέννησις: 'et ipsum τὸ γίγνεσθαι et γεννᾶσθαι significat, et universam eam seriem mutationum complectitur quibus conficitur generatio' (Bon. Ind. 148 b 4).

28. ἀλλ' ὥσπερ . . . ἕτερον. Cp. Democrit. Fragm. 184 (Mullach, Fr. Philos. Gr. 1. 351: Stob. Floril. 76. 17), referred to by Lasaulx (Ehe, p. 91): Aristot. de Anima, 2. 4. 415 a 26, φυσικώτατον γὰρ τῶν ἔργων τοῖς ζῶσιν (all things that partake of life, whether animals or not—de An. 3. 12. 434 a 27), ὅσα τέλεια καὶ μὴ πηρώματα, ἢ τὴν γένεσιν αὐτομάτην ἔχει, τὸ ποιῆσαι ἕτερον οἷον αὐτό, ζῷον μὲν ζῷον, φυτὸν δὲ φυτόν, ἵνα τοῦ ἀεὶ καὶ τοῦ θείου μετέχωσιν ᾗ δύνανται· πάντα γὰρ ἐκείνου ὀρέγεται, κἀκείνου ἕνεκα πράττει ὅσα πράττει κατὰ φύσιν: and the following passages in the de Generatione Animalium—2. 1. 735 a 17 sq.: 2. 1. 731 b 24 sqq.: 1. 23. 731 a 24–b 8: 3. 10. 760 a 35 sqq. (where Nature is said to design that species shall be perpetual). Plato had already pointed to marriage as a mode of attaining immortality (Laws 721 B–C: see Lasaulx, Ehe, p. 93), and the writer of the so-called First Book of the Oeconomics, who is fond of blending the teaching of Aristotle with that of Plato's Laws and the writings of Xenophon, reproduces the view (c. 3. 1343 b 23 sqq.). Eth. Eud. 2. 6. 1222 b 15 sqq. should also be compared with this passage. This impulse of reproduction can hardly be an ὄρεξις, for it is shared by plants, and plants have not τὸ ὀρεκτικόν (de An. 2. 3. 414 a 31 sqq.): it may, however, possibly be an ὁρμή (Pol. 1. 2. 1253 a 29). It seems scarcely to find a place in the enumeration of τὰ ἐν τῇ ψυχῇ γινόμενα (Eth. Nic. 2. 4. 1105 b 19 sq.) as πάθη δυνάμεις ἕξεις, probably because it belongs to τὸ θρεπτικόν, with which an ethical treatise has nothing to do. Aristotle does not enter into the question why the union of man and wife is more than a momentary union, or why it is more lasting than that of male and female among other animals; but his answer may probably be inferred from Eth. Nic. 8. 14. 1162 a 19 sqq., which may be contrasted with Locke on Civil Government, 2. §§ 79, 80.

29. φυτοῖς. There is no assertion in this passage (as Schn. thinks) of a sex in plants. Aristotle, in fact, holds that though plants share in the male and female principle (otherwise they could not be said to live)—de Gen. An. 2. 1. 732 a 11—yet these powers are mingled in them and not separated the one from the other (de Gen. An. 1. 23. 731 a 1). All he says is that plants, like animals, are actuated by an impulse to produce a being like themselves: how this is done, is not here noticed.

30. ἄρχον δὲ κ.τ.λ. Sc. ἀνάγκη συνδυάζεσθαι. Aristotle is probably speaking here only of that form of the relation of ruler and ruled which is exemplified in master and slave. Wherever on one side there is intelligence and on the other brute force only, it is to the interest of both parties to combine, the master supplying what the slave needs and the slave what the master needs. Euripides (Herc. Furens 1235) makes his hero refuse to believe that one god can ever have made a slave of another, as some assert:

> Δεῖται γὰρ ὁ θεός, εἴπερ ἔστ' ὄντως θεός,
> οὐδενός.

Aristotle's theory of natural slavery is already indicated here.

For the thought that it is διάνοια which makes the master, cp. de An. 1. 5. 410 b 12 sq., τῆς δὲ ψυχῆς εἶναί τι κρεῖττον καὶ ἄρχον ἀδύνατον· ἀδυνατώτερον δ' ἔτι τοῦ νοῦ· εὔλογον γὰρ τοῦτον εἶναι προγενέστατον καὶ κύριον κατὰ φύσιν. In 4 (7). 7. 1328 a 6 we read—καὶ τὸ ἄρχον δὲ καὶ τὸ ἐλεύθερον ἀπὸ τῆς δυνάμεως ταύτης ὑπάρχει πᾶσιν, ἀρχικὸν γὰρ καὶ ἀήττητον ὁ θυμός, but yet θυμός by itself and severed from διάνοια confers freedom rather than the capacity to rule others (4 (7). 7. 1327 b 23–33). The slave is throughout regarded by Aristotle as in the main a creature of thew and sinew and nothing more. His function is the use of his body, and this is the best to be got from him, 1. 5. 1254 b 17 sq.: he shares in reason sufficiently to apprehend it, but has it not (1. 5. 1254 b 22): he is wholly without the deliberative faculty (τὸ βουλευτικόν, 1. 13. 1260 a 12), and hence is no partaker in life according to moral choice or happiness (3. 9. 1280 a 33). Plato, on the other hand, had described men possessed of muscular strength and little intelligence as born to be hired labourers (Rep. 371 E).

32. προορᾶν. Cp. Plato, Laws 690 B, τὸ δὲ μέγιστον, ὡς ἔοικεν, ἀξίωμα ἕκτον ἂν γίγνοιτο, ἕπεσθαι μὲν τὸν ἀνεπιστήμονα κελεῦον, τὸν δὲ φρονοῦντα ἡγεῖσθαί τε καὶ ἄρχειν: Isocr. (?) ad Demonicum § 40, πειρῶ τῷ μὲν σώματι εἶναι φιλόπονος, τῇ δὲ ψυχῇ φιλόσοφος, ἵνα τῷ μὲν ἐπιτελεῖν δύνῃ τὰ δόξαντα, τῇ δὲ προορᾶν ἐπίστῃ τὰ συμφέροντα: the same thought recurs in the undoubtedly authentic de Antidosi of Isocrates (§ 180). Cp. also Posidonius ap. Athen. Deipn. 263 c–d, and Democritus ap. Stob. Floril. 44. 14, κρέσσον ἄρχεσθαι τοῖσιν ἀνοήτοισιν ἢ ἄρχειν. Aristotle has evidently in view in his account of master and slave the contrast commonly drawn between soul and body.

33. ταῦτα, 'that which the other has designed.' For a similar roughness in the use of the word, cp. τοῦτο, de Gen. An. 1. 22. 730 b 11.

34. διό, because the one completes the other. Cp. Stob. Ecl. Eth. 2. 6. 17 (tom. 2. p. 92 Meineke), νωθῆ δὲ καὶ καθ' ἑαυτὸν ἀδύνατον διαζῆν, ᾧ τὸ ἄρχεσθαι συμφέρειν. The sketch of the political teaching of the Peripatetics here given (tom. 2. p. 91 sqq. Meineke) deserves study, as being in the main a *résumé*, though a brief one, of the teaching of the Politics.

ταὐτὸ συμφέρει. In the Third Book, on the other hand, the rule of the master is said only accidentally to aim at the advantage of the slave, οὐ γὰρ ἐνδέχεται φθειρομένου τοῦ δούλου σώζεσθαι τὴν δεσποτείαν (3. 6. 1278 b 32). Thus it would seem that even in becoming, as the First Book (c. 13. 1260 b 3) requires him to become, a source of ethical virtue to his slave, the master will have his own interest in view. We are not told this in the First Book.

34-b 9. In mentioning two *κοινωνίαι* and not one, Aristotle has implied that a distinction exists between them, and he now draws attention to the fact, in order that he may remove a difficulty in the way of the acceptance of his view. By nature, then—he in effect says—the female is marked off from the slave (for Nature designed them to serve different purposes), and if this is not so among barbarians, the reason is that among them the element destined by nature for rule is not forthcoming. Μὲν οὖν here, as often elsewhere, introduces a renewed reference to a subject on which increased precision is desirable. Cp. 1253 a 10, where, after the fact has been mentioned that language is peculiar to man, μὲν οὖν introduces an admission that this is not true of voice, and an explanation of the difference between voice and language. The existence of a distinction between women and slaves is implied in Poet. 15. 1454 a 20 sqq. (a reference given in Bon. Ind. 204 b 45). The practice of buying wives, which seems to be referred to in Pol. 2. 8. 1268 b 39 sq. as common among the barbarians, may have often tended to reduce wives to the level of slaves (see Prof. Robertson Smith, Kinship and Marriage in Early Arabia, p. 76 sq.). Plato had remarked already on the treatment of women as slaves in barbarian communities (Laws 805 D–E). Their toils were in some degree compensated by easier child-bearing (Aristot. de Gen. An. 4. 6. 775 a 32 sqq.). Even among the poor of a Hellenic State the true form of the household cannot be quite realized: cp. 8 (6). 8. 1323 a 5, τοῖς γὰρ ἀπόροις ἀνάγκη χρῆσθαι καὶ γυναιξὶ καὶ παισὶν ὥσπερ ἀκολούθοις διὰ τὴν ἀδουλίαν. The fact noted by Plato and Aristotle as to barbarians has been often remarked upon by later writers: so Darwin (Voyage of the Beagle, p. 216) says of the Fuegians, 'the husband is to the wife a brutal master to a laborious slave'; and even as to Montenegro we read—'How can you expect beauty from women who are used as beasts of burden by the men? . . . The well-grown handsome men who are playing at ball before the palace of the Prince are the husbands and brothers of the poor creatures who are carrying wood and water to their homes' (Letter from Montenegro in the *Times*, Oct. 11, 1882). On the other hand, Aristotle elsewhere notes the frequency of γυναικοκρατία among barbarians (2. 9. 1269 b 24 sq.). Both observations are probably true, however we may choose to reconcile them. It should be added that though Aristotle here contrasts that which prevails among the barbarians with that which is natural, he is well aware that legislators may learn much from them (Rhet. 1. 4. 1360 a 33 sqq.); in fact, he occasionally mentions with approval in the Politics practices prevailing among them (for instance, their way of rearing infants, 4 (7). 17. 1336 a 5 sqq.), and often draws attention to their customs (in relation to communism, for example, 2. 5. 1263 a 3 sqq.). Plato had spoken in the passage of the Laws to which reference has been made (805 D–E) of 'the Thracians and many other races,' but Aristotle speaks as if the wife were virtually a slave among the barbarians generally.

1. **οὐδὲν γὰρ κ.τ.λ.** The limits within which this holds good 1252 b. are more fully expressed in de Part. An. 4. 6. 683 a 22, *ὅπου γὰρ ἐνδέχεται χρῆσθαι δυσὶν ἐπὶ δύ' ἔργα καὶ μὴ ἐμποδίζειν πρὸς ἕτερον, οὐδὲν ἡ φύσις εἴωθε ποιεῖν ὥσπερ ἡ χαλκευτικὴ πρὸς εὐτέλειαν ὀβελισκολύχνιον· ἀλλ' ὅπου μὴ ἐνδέχεται, καταχρῆται τῷ αὐτῷ ἐπὶ πλείω ἔργα.* Thus Aristotle says of magistracies in small States, Pol. 6 (4). 15. 1299 b 7, *διόπερ οὐδὲν κωλύει πολλὰς ἐπιμελείας ἅμα προστάττειν, οὐ γὰρ ἐμποδιοῦσιν ἀλλήλαις, καὶ πρὸς τὴν ὀλιγανθρωπίαν ἀναγκαῖον τὰ ἀρχεῖα οἷον ὀβελισκολύχνια ποιεῖν.* For instances in which Nature uses an organ designed for one purpose for certain other side-purposes, see de Part. An. 2. 16. 659 a 20: 3. 1. 662 a 18. There were some conspicuous exceptions in the human economy to the rule of *ἓν πρὸς ἕν*: cp. de Gen. An. 5. 8. 789 b 9, *οἷον γὰρ ἔνια πολύχρηστά ἐστι τῶν περὶ τὰς τέχνας, ὥσπερ ἐν τῇ χαλκευτικῇ ἡ σφύρα καὶ ὁ ἄκμων, οὕτως καὶ τὸ πνεῦμα ἐν τοῖς φύσει συνεστῶσιν*, and de Part. An. 4. 10. 687 a 19, *ἡ δὲ χεὶρ ἔοικεν εἶναι οὐχ ἓν ὄργανον ἀλλὰ πολλά· ἔστι γὰρ ὡσπερεὶ ὄργανον πρὸ ὀργάνων· τῷ οὖν πλείστας δυναμένῳ δέξασθαι τέχνας τὸ ἐπὶ πλεῖστον τῶν ὀργάνων χρήσιμον τὴν χεῖρα ἀποδέδωκεν ἡ φύσις . . . ἡ γὰρ χεὶρ καὶ ὄνυξ καὶ χηλὴ καὶ κέρας γίνεται καὶ δόρυ καὶ ξίφος καὶ ἄλλο ὁποιονοῦν ὅπλον καὶ ὄργανον.* Whether the various uses of the hand interfere with each other, must be left to physiologists to determine.

2. **τὴν Δελφικὴν μάχαιραν.** See Sus.[2], Notes 8 and 1353. Vict. appears to have been the first to draw attention to de Part. An. 4. 6. 683 a 22 sqq. (quoted in the last note) and to the important passage from the comic poet Theopompus quoted by Julius Pollux 10. 118, *τὸ δὲ ὀβελισκολύχνιον στρατιωτικὸν μέντοι* (aliter *μέν τι*) *χρῆμα, εἴρηται δὲ ὑπὸ Θεοπόμπου τοῦ κωμικοῦ ἐν Εἰρήνῃ*—

> *Ἡμᾶς δ' ἀπαλλαχθέντας ἐπ' ἀγαθαῖς τύχαις*
> *ὀβελισκολυχνίου καὶ ξιφομαχαίρας πικρᾶς.*

Vict. says in his note on 6 (4). 15. 1299 b 9 sq., 'Pollux quoque mentionem ipsius fecit, qui narrat militare instrumentum id fuisse. Hoc autem, ut opinor, excogitatum fuerat, ne milites nimis premerentur duobus gravibus instrumentis ferendis, cum ex uno ita conformato valerent eundem fructum capere.' The proverb Δελφικὴ μάχαιρα (Leutsch and Schneidewin, Paroem. Gr. 1. p. 393) seems to throw no light on the passage before us. We see from Athen. Deipn. 173 c sqq. that the Delphians were famous for their knives and their turn for sacrificial feasting and cookery, and they may very well have used and sold to pilgrims nothing loth to avoid expense (683 a 23 sqq.) a knife which might be used not only for killing the victim but also for flaying it and cutting it up. Contrast Eurip. Electr. 743–769 (Bothe), where Aegisthus first kills the victim (a kid) with a σφαγίς, and then Orestes after flaying it with a Dorian κοπίς asks for a large Phthian κοπίς to cut it up. We need not suppose with Göttling (de Machaera Delphica, p. 10) that the Delphic knife was a combination of a knife and a spoon. The passage he quotes from Hesychius—Δελφικὴ μάχαιρα ἀπὸ κατασκευῆς λαμβάνουσα ἔμπροσθεν μέρος σιδηροῦν, ὡς Ἀριστοτέλης—deserves notice, but leaves us much in the dark.

3. **πενιχρῶς.** Vict. 'apte ad usus pauperum'—a rendering probably suggested by πρὸς εὐτέλειαν in the parallel passage from the De Partibus Animalium quoted above (note on 1252 b 1)—but the meaning apparently is 'in a spirit of stint' (Lamb. 'parce tenuiter et anguste').

οὕτω. Cp. 1252 a 24 sqq., though here the clause which explains it, μὴ πολλοῖς ἔργοις ἀλλ' ἑνὶ δουλεῦον, follows and does not precede it. The use of δουλεῦον in the passage before us seems to be a somewhat uncommon one.

ἀποτελοῖτο. Vict. 'effici fabricarique poterit.' Cp. 2. 11. 1273 b 9, ἓν γὰρ ὑφ' ἑνὸς ἔργον ἄριστ' ἀποτελεῖται, and 13, κοινότερόν τε γάρ, καθάπερ εἴπομεν, καὶ κάλλιον ἕκαστον ἀποτελεῖται τῶν αὐτῶν καὶ θᾶττον.

6. **τάξιν.** Cp. Magn. Mor. 1. 34. 1194 b 15, ὅταν ἤδη λάβῃ (ὁ υἱὸς) τὴν τοῦ ἀνδρὸς τάξιν. Vict. compares Virg. Aen. 2. 102:

Si omnes uno ordine habetis Achivos.

τὸ φύσει ἄρχον. What this is appears from 1252 a 31 sq. and 4 (7). 7. 1327 b 23–33. According to Aristotle, the relation between the barbarian husband and wife assumes an unnatural form, because that which is naturally the ruling element is wanting. If the wife is a slave, it is because everybody is so. She is no worse off than her husband. Cp. Eurip. Hel. 246, where Helen says—

Τὰ βαρβάρων γὰρ δοῦλα πάντα πλὴν ἑνός,

and see Hug, Studien aus dem classischen Alterthum, p. 60. When in 4 (7). 7. 1327 b 25 Aristotle speaks of the barbarians of cold climates as tending to be free, he must be referring to political independence.

7. γίνεται, 'comes to be.' See notes on 1264 a 14: 1254 b 31.

ἡ κοινωνία αὐτῶν refers probably to the conjugal union among the barbarians (so Bern. and Sus.).

8. οἱ ποιηταί. Euripides, Iph. Aul. 1266:

> Βαρβάρων δ' Ἕλληνας ἄρχειν εἰκός, ἀλλ' οὐ βαρβάρους,
> μῆτερ, Ἑλλήνων· τὸ μὲν γὰρ δοῦλον, οἱ δ' ἐλεύθεροι.

Lecturers, we are told in Metaph. α. 3. 995 a 7, were often expected by their audience to produce a poet as a witness to the truth of their statements.

9. ἐκ μὲν οὖν κ.τ.λ. The two κοινωνίαι are those of husband and wife, master and slave (the latter being here implied to be a κοινωνία, though the name κοινωνοί is apparently denied to master and slave in 4 (7). 8. 1328 a 28 sqq.). That of father and child arises after the foundation of the household. Translate: 'from these two unions, then, proceeds first the household.' 'Πρώτη is by no means meaningless or pleonastic, for the further societies of the village and State consist of men and women, masters and slaves, but only mediately (mittelbar), inasmuch as they consist of households and households consist of these members. The next paragraph offers a striking analogy (1252 b 15, ἡ δ' ἐκ πλειόνων οἰκιῶν κοινωνία πρώτη χρήσεως ἕνεκεν μὴ ἐφημέρου κώμη): the State also, it is implied, consists of a plurality of households, but only mediately, inasmuch as it is composed of a number of villages which are themselves made up of households' (Dittenberger, *Gött. Gel. Anz.*, Oct. 28, 1874, p. 1373). Some have been tempted to explain οἰκία πρώτη as 'the simplest form of the household' (cp. πρώτη πόλις, 6 (4). 4. 1291 a 17: 4 (7). 4. 1326 b 7), considering the complete form to be realized when children have come into being. But, as Dittenberger observes (p. 1373), there is no confirmatory trace elsewhere in Aristotle's treatment of the household of this distinction between the οἰκία πρώτη and δευτέρα. An οἰκία τέλειος is indeed mentioned in 1. 3. 1253 b 4, but as consisting of slave and free, both of which classes find a place in the household from the first. No doubt, in the third chapter Aristotle adds to the two κοινωνίαι spoken of in 1252 b 10 a third (that which exists between father and child), but the τέλειος οἰκία does not seem to be connected with the appearance of this relation. The parallel of 1252 b 15 also points to the other interpretation, and the absence of any δέ to answer to μὲν οὖν 9 (if indeed the second δέ in 15 does not answer both to μὲν οὖν 12 and to μὲν

οὖν 9) is not uncommon in the Politics (see Sus.[1], Ind. Gramm. μέν), and affords no ground for the surmise of a lacuna after ἐστιν 12.

10. καὶ ὀρθῶς κ.τ.λ. The word πρώτη suggests the quotation from Hesiod, which Aristotle seems to interpret as making the wife and the ox the elements of the household, and thus supporting his own view, for the ox, he says, is the poor man's slave (cp. Aelian, Var. Hist. 5. 14). If the line which follows (Hes. Op. et Dies 406),

Κτητήν, οὐ γαμετήν, ἥτις καὶ βουσὶν ἕποιτο,

is genuine, the meaning which Aristotle attributes to Hesiod is even further from his real meaning than in the contrary case.

13. εἰς πᾶσαν ἡμέραν συνεστηκυῖα κατὰ φύσιν, 'existing by nature for the satisfaction of daily recurring needs,' (compare the phrase which stands in contrast to this, χρήσεως ἕνεκεν μὴ ἐφημέρου, 16). So we have κατά τε τὰ συσσίτια καὶ τὸν ἄλλον βίον τὸν καθ' ἡμέραν (2. 6. 1265 b 41), πρὸς τῷ καθ' ἡμέραν ὄντες (7 (5). 11. 1313 b 20); and τὰ ἐφήμερα are conjoined with τὰ ἀναγκαῖα τοῦ βίου in Strabo 7. p. 311. The κώμη (or γένος), on the contrary, exists to satisfy necessities less incessantly recurring, and as to the πόλις, cp. Eth. Nic. 8. 11. 1160 a 21, οὐ γὰρ τοῦ παρόντος συμφέροντος ἡ πολιτικὴ (κοινωνία) ἐφίεται, ἀλλ' εἰς ἅπαντα τὸν βίον. The view implied here of the aim of the household seems somewhat to differ from that of 1252 a 26–34, where reproduction and self-preservation are said to bring it into being.

14. οἶκος . . . οὗς. Cp. 3. 13. 1283 b 33, τὸ πλῆθος . . οὐχ ὡς καθ' ἕκαστον ἀλλ' ὡς ἀθρόους. Aristotle takes up the word οἶκος from Hesiod in place of the more usual οἰκία. As to the ordinary difference in meaning between οἶκος and οἰκία, see Boeckh, Public Economy of Athens, E. T. p. 142, note 680, and Shilleto on Demosth. de Falsa Legatione, § 279. It is in order to show that the household originates in the needs of daily life that Aristotle adduces the names given to its members by Charondas and Epimenides.

ὁμοσιπύους. The σιπύη was a bread-chest: Vict. refers to Aristoph. Plut. 802.

15. ὁμοκάπους. Κάπη is 'a manger.' Göttling's argument that as Epimenides belonged to Crete, where syssitia prevailed, he would not be likely thus to designate the household, seems of the least possible weight. As Dittenberger says (*ubi supra*, p. 1357), we do not know for certain that the work of Epimenides which Aristotle here quotes was authentic, or that, if it was, he was speaking of Crete. Ὁμοκάπους (with the penult short, at any rate), as Sus.[2] (Note 17) says, would not fit into an hexameter verse, and Epimenides wrote in hexameters, but we learn from Diog. Laert. 1. 112 that a prose treatise on the Cretan Constitution passed under his name, and the term may have occurred in this work. The words κάμματα, κάπτειν, καμματίδες seem to be old-fashioned words used in connexion with the common meals at Sparta (Nicocl. ap. Athen. Deipn. 140 d). For Ζεὺς καπαῖος, see Meineke, Fr. Com. Gr. 3. p. 58: cp. Ζεὺς ἑταιρεῖος, ibid. 4. p. 384. ''Ομοκάπνους is more likely to be a corruption from the less familiar ὁμοκάπους than ὁμοκάπους from it,' observes Mr. Ridgeway (*Trans. Camb. Philol. Soc.* vol. 2. p. 125), who however suggests ὁμοκάπους with the penult long, Dor. for ὁμοκήπους, 'those who have a common plot of ground.' Giphanius, who prefers ὁμοκάπνους, explains ὁμοκάπους in this way (p. 21: Schneider, Pol. vol. 2. p. 9). But perhaps ὁμοκάπους with the penult short better expresses that community in sustenance and in the satisfaction of daily recurring needs to which Aristotle, as Dittenberger remarks (*ubi supra*, p. 1358), points as the characteristic feature of the household. 'Ομέστιος is used in the sense of 'a member of the household' (Polyb. 2. 57. 7, referred to by Vict.), but not ὁμόκαπνος. The word ὁμοκάπους does not necessarily imply that the free and slave members of the household took their meals together, but the practice would be quite in harmony with the simplicity of early Greek life (cp. Theopomp. fragm. 243: Müller, Fr. Hist. Gr. 1. 319).

ἡ δ' ἐκ κ.τ.λ. Πρώτη agrees with κοινωνία: for its position in the sentence, cp. Metaph. I. 3. 1054 b 1, αἱ ἴσαι γραμμαὶ εὐθεῖαι αἱ αὐταί ('are the same'): de Part. An. 2. 14. 658 a 28, καθ' ὅλον τὸ σῶμα πρανές: Phys. 4. 5. 212 b 19: Pol. 2. 8. 1269 a 23: and still nearer, Phys. 4. 4. 212 a 20, τὸ τοῦ περιέχοντος πέρας ἀκίνητον πρῶτον, τοῦτ' ἔστιν ὁ τόπος, where the post-position of the adjectives seems to be for emphasis on the point desired to be pressed, and also to secure the juxtaposition of ἀκίνητον and πρῶτον. Πρώτη in the passage before us qualifies ἐκ πλειόνων οἰκιῶν, and perhaps also χρήσεως ἕνεκεν μὴ ἐφημέρου. 'The first society to be formed out of more households than one, and to exist for the satisfaction of needs not daily recurring, is the village.' See note on 1252 b 9.

16. μάλιστα κ.τ.λ. Vict. 'nec tamen omnem pagum talem esse affirmat, usu namque venire potest, et sane contingit aliquando, ut e variis locis homines non coniuncti inter se sanguine veniant in eandem sedem, atque illic domicilia sibi construant tot numero iam ut pagum ex ipsis conficiant.' For the relation of the κώμη to the deme, see Poet. 3. 1448 a 35 sq. Perhaps the κώμη and the rural deme continued to feel as a *gens*, and to obey a gentile authority, longer than is often supposed, and hence in part the preference of oligarchs and of the Lacedaemonians for village-residence and their dislike of large cities, which had a natural tendency to democracy. The purchaser of land in an Athenian deme to which he did not belong paid something for ἔγκτησις (Boeckh, Publ. Econ. of Athens, E. T. p. 297 n.: Haussoullier, Vie Municipale en Attique, pp. 68, 78): hence the land probably tended, in rural demes at all events, to continue in the hands of the members of the deme. The villages founded by the Teutonic conquerors of Britain were to some extent peopled by kinsmen. 'Harling abode by Harling and Billing by Billing, and each "wick" and "ham" and "stead" and "tun" took its name from the kinsmen who dwelt together in it. In this way the house or "ham" of the Billings was Billingham, and the "tun" or township of the Harlings was Harlington' (Green, The Making of England, p. 188).

17. ἀποικία οἰκίας. A similar expression is used by Plato, Laws 776 A. Cp. also Laws 680 A sqq., a passage which was probably present to Aristotle's mind throughout this part of the second chapter (see vol. 1. p. 37, note 1). Plato appeals to the same passage of Homer as is cited in 22, and for the same purpose, to prove the early prevalence of Patriarchal Kingship, or, as he terms it, δυναστεία. Both Plato and Aristotle regard kingly rule as characteristic of early society and trace it to the government of the household by the father.

οὓς . . . παῖδας. Aristotle's object in mentioning these names for members of the same village is to show by an appeal to the use of language that the village is an extension of the household. He has proved that the household is necessary and natural, and if he can prove that the village is an outgrowth of the household and the πόλις of the village, then the πόλις will be shown to be natural. Cp. Photius, Lexicon (quoted by Sehn.), ὁμογάλακτες, οἱ τοῦ αὐτοῦ γάλακτος, οὓς καὶ γεννήτας ἐκάλουν, and see Liddell and Scott, s. v. Plato had used the expression τοὺς παῖδας καὶ παίδων παῖδας ὃ λέγομεν in the passage of the Laws referred to in the last note (681 B), and Homer before him (Il. 20. 308). Had Cicero the First Book of the Politics in his mind when he wrote (de Offic. 1. 17. 54)—nam cum sit hoc natura commune animantium ut habeant lubidinem procreandi, prima societas in ipso coniugio est; proxima in liberis (in Aristotle master and slave); deinde una domus, communia omnia (cp. 1. 9. 1257 a 21). Id autem est principium urbis et quasi seminarium reipublicae. Sequuntur fratrum coniunctiones, post consobrinorum sobrinorumque, qui cum una domo iam capi non possint in alias domos tanquam in colonias exeunt. Sequuntur connubia et affinitates, ex quibus etiam plures propinqui.

Quae propagatio et soboles origo est rerum publicarum? There is no express mention of the village, however, here, though a reference to it may be intended in the words 'alias domos.' Compare Demosth. in Macart. c. 19, καὶ παῖδες ἐγένοντο αὐτοῖς ἅπασι καὶ παίδων παῖδες, καὶ ἐγένοντο πέντε οἶκοι ἐκ τοῦ Βουσέλου οἴκου ἑνὸς ὄντος.

19. Διὸ . . . ᾤκουν. The fact that the village is an offshoot of the household enables Aristotle to account for the early prevalence of Kingship. Compare with the passage before us a quotation from Theophrastus περὶ βασιλείας in Dion. Hal. Ant. Rom. 5. 73, κατ' ἀρχὰς μὲν γὰρ ἅπασα πόλις Ἑλλὰς ἐβασιλεύετο, πλὴν οὐχ ὥσπερ τὰ βάρβαρα ἔθνη δεσποτικῶς, ἀλλὰ κατὰ νόμους τινὰς καὶ ἐθισμοὺς πατρίους (cp. Pol. 3. 14. 1285 a 16–b 12).

τὰ ἔθνη ('opp. οἱ Ἕλληνες,' Bon. Ind. 216 b 51) are here regarded as preserving the traditions of the village (cp. 1. 9. 1257 a 24: 2. 8. 1268 b 39). The customs of the early Hellenes are thought both by Thucydides (1. 5–6) and by Aristotle (Pol. 2. 8. 1268 b 39) to have had much in common with those of the barbarians of their own day.

20. ἐκ βασιλευομένων γὰρ συνῆλθον, 'for they were formed of persons governed by a king,' i. e. of members of households. Cp. Plato, Laws 680 D, μῶν οὖν οὐκ ἐκ τούτων τῶν κατὰ μίαν οἴκησιν καὶ κατὰ γένος διεσπαρμένων ὑπὸ ἀπορίας τῆς ἐν ταῖς φθοραῖς (sc. τοιαῦται πολιτεῖαι γίγνονται), ἐν αἷς τὸ πρεσβύτατον ἄρχει διὰ τὸ τὴν ἀρχὴν αὐτοῖς ἐκ πατρὸς καὶ μητρὸς γεγονέναι, οἷς ἑπόμενοι καθάπερ ὄρνιθες ἀγέλην μίαν ποιήσουσι, πατρονομούμενοι καὶ βασιλείαν πασῶν δικαιοτάτην βασιλευόμενοι; If συνῆλθον is here said of the ἔθνη as well as the πόλεις, both ἔθνος and πόλις are implied to owe their origin to the household. 'It is worth noting that Aristotle gives us three distinct reasons for the prevalence of kingly rule in early times—here, 3. 15. 1286 b 8 sqq., and '7. 13. 11' (is 4 (7). 14. 1332 b 16 sqq. meant?)—without hinting in any one of the passages that he knew of those specified in the others' (Mr. Postgate, Notes, p. 1). The second of these passages, however, is apparently aporetic; Aristotle is seeing whether the argument in favour of Kingship derivable from the prevalence of it among the men of a former day (οἱ πρότερον) may not be met; may they not have rested content with it, because they had no choice, not many men of high excellence being then forthcoming? We observe, moreover, that almost every discussion in the Politics takes less account of preceding ones, and makes less use of their results, than one might have expected, so that we are not much surprised if Aristotle seems in this passage of the Third Book to forget that he has already accounted otherwise for the prevalence of Kingship in early times. Locke remarks (Civil Government, 2. § 106)—'It is plain that the reason that continued the form of government in a single person was not any regard or respect to paternal authority, since all petty monarchies—that is, almost all monarchies near their original—have been commonly, at least upon occasion, elective.' The etymology of the word 'King,' however, appears to make in favour of Aristotle's view. 'It corresponds with the Sanscrit ganaka. . . . It simply meant father of a family' (Prof. Max Müller, Lectures on the Science of Language, 2. 282, 284, quoted by Dr. Stubbs, Const. Hist. of England, 1. 140).

πᾶσα γὰρ οἰκία κ.τ.λ. Camerarius (Politicorum et Oeconomicorum Aristotelis Interpretationes et Explicationes, p. 25) aptly quotes Hom. Od. 1. 397, where Telemachus says,

Αὐτὰρ ἐγὼν οἴκοιο ἄναξ ἔσομ' ἡμετέροιο
καὶ δμώων, οὕς μοι λῃίσσατο δῖος Ὀδυσσεύς.

21. διὰ τὴν συγγένειαν recurs in 2. 10. 1271 b 24 sq., there also in reference to a colony—*φασὶ γὰρ τὸν Λυκοῦργον . . . τότε τὸν πλεῖστον διατρῖψαι χρόνον περὶ Κρήτην διὰ τὴν συγγένειαν· ἄποικοι γὰρ οἱ Λύκτιοι τῶν Λακώνων ἦσαν.* Just as in that passage the relationship of the Lyctians to the Laconians is referred to, so here the reference probably is to the relationship of the *ἀποικίαι* to the *οἰκία*. So Sus. (Qu. Crit. p. 333): 'propter propinquitatem, id est quia nihil nisi colonia domus sive familia dilatata vicus est.' The words, however, are often explained to refer to the mutual relationship of the members of the *ἀποικίαι*, Kingship being especially in place among relatives (cp. 1. 12. 1259 b 14 sqq.), and this is a possible interpretation.

22. καὶ τοῦτ' ἐστὶν ὃ λέγει Ὅμηρος. What is the meaning of *τοῦτο*? What is the quotation from Homer held by Aristotle to prove? The commentators are not agreed. Giph. 'Homeri versiculus eo pertinere videtur, ut doceat Aristoteles domesticum imperium esse velut regium' (p. 24); he would seem therefore to refer *τοῦτο* to *πᾶσα γὰρ οἰκία βασιλεύεται ὑπὸ τοῦ πρεσβυτάτου* 20
exclusively, as does also Susemihl (Qu. Crit. p. 333). But it is not altogether easy to refer *τοῦτο* to this particular clause only, and we hardly expect Aristotle to appeal to the practice of the Cyclopes in order to justify a general statement respecting the household of all times. The explanation of Vict. is—'utitur etiam auctoritate summi poetae, qui idem ostendit, priscos scilicet, ut ipsis commodum erat, solitos regere suam familiam,' and perhaps it is in some such way as this that we should understand the quotation. Aristotle has been

saying that πόλεις and ἔθνη had their origin in the coming together of human beings who had been previously ruled by kings, and he uses Homer's account of the Cyclopes to prove the existence in the earliest times of a household form of Kingship—a form in which the king was the husband and father, and the subjects were the wives and children. To Plato (cp. Laws 680 D, τὸ ἀρχαῖον αὐτῶν ἐπὶ τὴν ἀγριότητα διὰ μυθολογίας ἐπανενεγκών, and Strabo, p. 592, ταύτας δὴ τὰς διαφορὰς ὑπογράφειν φησὶ τὸν ποιητὴν ὁ Πλάτων, τῆς μὲν πρώτης πολιτείας παράδειγμα τιθέντα τὸν τῶν Κυκλώπων βίον), and probably also to Aristotle (Pol. 1. 2. 1252 b 23, σποράδες γάρ, καὶ οὕτω τὸ ἀρχαῖον ᾤκουν), the Homeric picture of the Cyclopes is a mythical picture of the rude beginnings of human society. Plato had already used the same quotation from Homer in Laws 680 A sqq. to prove that Patriarchal Kingship (which he terms δυναστεία) existed in early times, and the fact that the words with which he prefaces his quotation seem to find an echo in those with which Aristotle prefaces his makes it all the more likely that they quote it for a similar purpose. The passage in the Laws is as follows—ΑΘ. Πολιτείας δέ γε ἤδη καὶ τρόπος ἐστί τις οὗτος. ΚΛ. Τίς; ΑΘ. Δοκοῦσί μοι πάντες τὴν ἐν τούτῳ τῷ χρόνῳ πολιτείαν δυναστείαν καλεῖν, ἣ καὶ νῦν ἔτι πολλαχοῦ καὶ ἐν Ἕλλησι καὶ κατὰ βαρβάρους ἐστί· λέγει δ' αὐτήν που καὶ Ὅμηρος γεγονέναι περὶ τὴν τῶν Κυκλώπων οἴκησιν, εἰπὼν

> τοῖσιν δ' οὔτ' ἀγοραὶ βουληφόροι, οὔτε θέμιστες,
> ἀλλ' οἵ γ' ὑψηλῶν ὀρέων ναίουσι κάρηνα
> ἐν σπέσσι γλαφυροῖσι, θεμιστεύει δὲ ἕκαστος
> παίδων ἠδ' ἀλόχων, οὐδ' ἀλλήλων ἀλέγουσιν.

θεμιστεύει δὲ κ.τ.λ. Odyss. 9. 114. θεμιστεύειν implies kingship: it is used of Minos in Hom. Odyss. 11. 569, quoted by Plato, Gorgias 526 D. The society of the Cyclopes is referred to in Eth. Nic. 10. 10. 1180 a 28, as a typical case of the household standing by itself, not supported or directed by a State. It is in order to account for the independence of the Cyclopic household and its head that Aristotle adds σποράδες γάρ: this would have been clearer, if he had quoted the concluding words of the second line, οὐδ' ἀλλήλων ἀλέγουσιν, but the passage was evidently well-known. Plato also mentions the scattered way in which the habitations were distributed in these early days of human society, and is bold enough to give as the reason for it the difficulty of finding subsistence just after the deluge (ἐκ τούτων τῶν κατὰ μίαν οἴκησιν καὶ κατὰ γένος—cp. the κώμη of Aristotle—διεσπαρμένων ὑπὸ ἀπορίας τῆς ἐν ταῖς φθοραῖς, Laws 680 D), but on this Aristotle is judiciously silent. This 'sporadic' existence of primitive man is also recognized in the myth of Protagoras (Plato, Protag. 322 A) and by Philochorus (Fr. 4: Müller, Fr. Hist. Gr. 1. 384): cp. also Plutarch, Theseus c. 24, and Paus. 2. 15. 5. Some savage races still live thus: '"the Abors, as they themselves say, are like tigers, two cannot dwell in one den," writes Mr. Dalton, "and the houses are scattered singly or in groups of two or three"' (Mr. Herbert Spencer, *Fortn. Rev.* Jan. 1881, p. 5).

24. καὶ τοὺς θεοὺς δὲ κ.τ.λ. 'Nay, the fact that men were at the outset ruled by kings has led them universally to assert that the gods also are so ruled.' Διὰ τοῦτο is explained by ὅτι κ.τ.λ.

26. ἀφομοιοῦσιν. Cp. Metaph. B. 2. 997 b 10: Λ. 8. 1074 b 3 sqq. (where it is said that the gods are sometimes assimilated in form to men, sometimes to certain of the lower animals): Poet. 25. 1460 b 35.

27 sqq. **ἡ δ' ἐκ . . . εὖ ζῆν.** Bonitz (Ind. 751 b 21) and apparently Bernays take τέλειος with πόλις, and a πρώτη πόλις is no doubt mentioned in 6 (4). 4. 1291 a 17 and 4 (7). 4. 1326 b 7, but not in the First Book, unless indeed the village is to be viewed as an imperfect and inchoate πόλις, which is nowhere stated. Nor would the mere union of more villages than one be enough of itself, in Aristotle's view, to constitute a τέλειος πόλις. Τέλειος seems to qualify κοινωνία, not πόλις, and its place in the sentence is explained (see note on 1252 b 15) by the fact that κοινωνία is qualified both by ἐκ πλειόνων κωμῶν and by τέλειος. The fem. form is more often τελεία or τελέα in Aristotle (Bon. Ind. 751 b 56 sqq.).

On μὲν οὖν occurring as it does here in the middle of a sentence, see Vahlen's note on Poet. 22. 1458 a 24 (p. 226 sq. of his edition). He compares (among other passages) the following from the Politics —7 (5). 12. 1316 a 9: 4 (7). 10. 1329 b 2 sq.: 4 (7). 17. 1336 b 6 sqq.: to which 1. 9. 1257 b 2 sqq. (μὲν οὖν, Π[1]) may be added. See also Bon. Ind. 540 b 42 sqq., 'μὲν οὖν saepe usurpatur, ubi notio modo pronunciata amplius explicatur': of this, besides the present passage and 1. 9. 1257 b 2 sq., Poet. 22. 1458 a 23 sqq. is a good instance. Μὲν οὖν thus used seems to introduce a comment on what has just been said, whether by way of modification or confirmation or otherwise. So here, after attributing to the πόλις complete αὐτάρκεια, Aristotle remembers that there is an epoch in its history at which this is not its aim; he therefore slightly corrects what he had just said, but only to confirm it subject to that correction. In de Part. An. 4. 11. 691 a 28, however, μὲν οὖν in the middle of a sentence seems merely intended (in the sense of 'while,' cp. Pol. 2. 6. 1265 a

17) to prepare the way for the sentence introduced by the δέ which follows, and to impart greater emphasis to the latter.

γινομένη τοῦ ζῆν ἕνεκεν. Cp. 3. 6. 1278 b 24: Plato had said the same thing (Rep. 369 D: 371 B). In Aristotle's view the necessary is first sought and then higher things (Pol. 4 (7). 10. 1329 b 27). In Eth. Nic. 8. 11. 1160 a 11 sq., however, the *πόλις* is said to be commonly thought both to be formed and to exist *τοῦ συμφέροντος χάριν*, and in Pol. 3. 6. 1278 b 21 sqq. it seems to be implied that bare existence is not always the aim with which men form it.

πάσης τῆς αὐταρκείας, 'entire self-completeness'—cp. *πᾶς ὁ ὑπηρέτης*, 1. 4. 1253 b 33, and *πᾶσαν τὴν ἀρχήν*, 7 (5). 11. 1313 a 21—both *αὐτάρκεια ἐν τοῖς ἀναγκαίοις*, 4 (7). 4. 1326 b 4, and *αὐτάρκεια* in respect of *τὸ εὖ ζῆν*, 3. 9. 1280 b 34. Cp. also 1. 8. 1256 b 31.

ἤδη, cp. 7 (5). 8. 1308 a 16, *ἔστι γὰρ ὥσπερ δῆμος ἤδη οἱ ὅμοιοι*: Eth. Nic. 6. 10. 1142 b 13, *ἡ δόξα οὐ ζήτησις ἀλλὰ φάσις τις ἤδη* (has, as it were, 'reached the level' of assertion): and cp. also Pol. 2. 2. 1261 b 12, *καὶ βούλεταί γ' ἤδη τότε εἶναι πόλις, ὅταν αὐτάρκη συμβαίνῃ τὴν κοινωνίαν εἶναι τοῦ πλήθους.*

For the attainment of the *πέρας* by the *πόλις* (the third *κοινωνία* in the order of genesis), cp. de Part. An. 2. 1. 646 b 8, *ταῦτα γὰρ ἤδη τὸ τέλος ἔχει καὶ τὸ πέρας, ἐπὶ τοῦ τρίτου λαβόντα τὴν σύστασιν ἀριθμοῦ, καθάπερ ἐπὶ πολλῶν συμβαίνει τελειοῦσθαι τὰς γενέσεις*:- de Gen. An. 3. 10. 760 a 34, *ἐν τῷ τρίτῳ ἀριθμῷ πέρας ἔσχεν ἡ γένεσις*: Probl. 26. 9. 941 a 24, *τελευτᾷ δ' ἐν τρισὶ πάντα*: de Caelo, 1. 1. 268 a 1 sqq.

30. διό, 'because it is the completion of societies existing by nature.'

πᾶσα πόλις. Cp. *οἰκία πᾶσα*, 1. 13. 1260 b 13. Aristotle does not, however, mean that the deviation-forms of State are by nature: they are, indeed, expressly declared to be *παρὰ φύσιν*, 3. 17. 1287 b 39.

αἱ πρῶται κοινωνίαι, i.e. *πρῶται γενέσει.*

34. ἀνθρώπου ἵππου οἰκίας. For the asyndeton, cp. 2. 4. 1262 b 30, *αἰκίας ἔρωτας φόνους*, and see Vahlen's note on Poet. 20. 1457 a 22.

ἔτι . . . 1253 a 1, βέλτιστον. 'Further, that for which things exist and the end is best, and self-completeness, the end of the State, is both the end and best'; hence the State brings that which is best; hence it exists by nature, for nature brings the best. Cp. Eth. Eud. 1. 7. 1218 b 10, *τὸ δ' οὗ ἕνεκα ὡς τέλος ἄριστον καὶ αἴτιον τῶν ὑφ' αὐτὸ καὶ πρῶτον πάντων· ὥστε τοῦτ' ἂν εἴη αὐτὸ τὸ ἀγαθὸν τὸ τέλος τῶν ἀνθρώπῳ πρακτῶν*: 2. 1. 1219 a 9, *φανερὸν τοίνυν ἐκ τούτων ὅτι βέλτιον τὸ ἔργον τῆς ἕξεως· τὸ γὰρ τέλος ἄριστον ὡς τέλος· ὑπόκειται γὰρ τέλος τὸ* βέλτιστον καὶ τὸ ἔσχατον, οὗ ἕνεκα τἆλλα πάντα: Phys. 2. 2. 194 a 32, βούλεται οὐ πᾶν εἶναι τὸ ἔσχατον τέλος, ἀλλὰ τὸ βέλτιστον. A new proof is here adduced of the naturalness of the State, drawn not from the fact that it is the completion of natural societies like the household and village, but from the fact that its end is the best, the end which Nature pursues: cp. de An. Incessu 2. 704 b 15, ἡ φύσις οὐδὲν ποιεῖ μάτην, ἀλλ' ἀεὶ ἐκ τῶν ἐνδεχομένων τῇ οὐσίᾳ περὶ ἕκαστον γένος ζῴου τὸ ἄριστον· διόπερ εἰ βέλτιον ὡδί, οὕτως καὶ ἔχει κατὰ φύσιν.

1253 a. **3. ὁ ἄπολις διὰ φύσιν καὶ οὐ διὰ τύχην.** Aristotle perhaps has in his mind the Μονότροπος of the comic poet Phrynichus. 'Nomen fabulae inditum ab homine tristi et moroso, qui Timonis instar solitariam vitam sequeretur et lucem adspectumque hominum fugeret. . . . Sed quidni ipsum audiamus in loco apud Grammat. Seguer. p. 344 haecce dicentem:

Ὄνομα δέ μοὖστι Μονότροπος * *
* * * ζῶ δὲ Τίμωνος βίον,
ἀπρόσοδον, ὀξύθυμον, ἄγαμον, ἄζυγον,
ἀγέλαστον, ἀδιάλεκτον, ἰδιογνώμονα.'

(Meineke, Historia Critica Comicorum Graecorum, p. 156, who however emends the third line otherwise in Fr. Com. Gr. 2. 587 sq.: the MSS. have

ἄγαμον, ἄζυγον, ὀξύθυμον, ἀπρόσοδον.)

There were, however, Cynics who took for their motto the lines—

Ἄπολις, ἄοικος, πατρίδος ἐστερημένος,
πτωχός, πλανήτης, βίον ἔχων τοὐφ' ἡμέραν

(Diog. Laert. 6. 38: Bernays, Theophrastos' Schrift über Frömmigkeit, p. 162: compare Athen. Deipn. 611 C): these men were ἀπόλιδες by choice, and this saying of Aristotle's would, therefore, reflect on them, whether it was intended to do so or not. Aristippus, again, had said (Xen. Mem. 2. 1. 13, referred to by Camerarius, Interpretationes p. 28)—ἀλλ' ἐγώ τοι . . . οὐδ' εἰς πολιτείαν ἐμαυτὸν κατακλῄω, ἀλλὰ ξένος πανταχοῦ εἰμί. Philoctetes, on the other hand (Soph. Philoct. 1018), was an ἄπολις διὰ τύχην, and so were Themistocles, when Adeimantus applied the epithet to him (Hdt. 8. 61), and Aristotle himself, when Stageira was in ruins. Vict. compares with the passage before us Cic. Philipp. 13. 1: nam nec privatos focos nec publicas leges videtur nec libertatis iura cara habere, quem discordiae, quem caedes civium, quem bellum civile delectat, eumque ex numero hominum eiiciendum, ex finibus humanae naturae exterminandum puto . . . Nihil igitur hoc cive, nihil hoc homine taetrius, si aut civis aut homo habendus est, qui civile bellum concupiscit.

4. ὥσπερ καὶ κ.τ.λ. Il. 9. 63—

Ἀφρήτωρ, ἀθέμιστος, ἀνέστιός ἐστιν ἐκεῖνος,
ὃς πολέμου ἔραται ἐπιδημίου ὀκριόεντος.

The lover of civil war is said by Homer to be 'clanless, lawless, hearthless'; Aristotle, however, seems to conceive him to say that the 'clanless, lawless, hearthless' man is a lover of civil war. But to say of a man that he is a lover of war for the sake of war was, in Aristotle's view, to say that he is either φαῦλος or, like Ares, more than man: compare Eth. Nic. 10. 7. 1177 b 9, οὐδεὶς γὰρ αἱρεῖται τὸ πολεμεῖν τοῦ πολεμεῖν ἕνεκα οὐδὲ παρασκευάζει πόλεμον· δόξαι γὰρ ἂν παντελῶς μιαιφόνος τις εἶναι, εἰ τοὺς φίλους πολεμίους ποιοῖτο, ἵνα μάχαι καὶ φόνοι γίγνοιντο, and the indignant words addressed by Zeus to Ares in Hom. Il. 5. 890 (cp. Polyb. 12. 26). For Mr. Jackson's view of this passage, see *Journ. of Philology*, 7. 1877, p. 236 sqq. I translate ὥσπερ κ.τ.λ. 'like the clanless, lawless, hearthless man reviled by Homer.' It is perfectly true that it is the lover of civil war whom Homer reviles, but Aristotle is often inexact in his use of quotations. Mr. Jackson's proposal to place ὥσπερ—ἐπιθυμητής in a parenthesis and to connect ἅτε περ κ.τ.λ. 6 with the words which precede the parenthesis seems to me to involve an awkward severance of ἅτε περ κ.τ.λ. from the words which this clause is conceived to illustrate, and to be also unnecessary (see below on 6).

6. ἅμα γὰρ κ.τ.λ. Sepulv. 'nam simul ac talis quisque nátura est, bellandi cupidus est': Lamb. 'non enim potest quisquam talis esse, quin uno eodemque tempore sit et belli cupidus.' Prof. Tyrrell (*Hermathena*, 12. 26)—'no sooner is he such (clanless, lawless, hearthless) by nature than his hand is against every man': but is not φύσει τοιοῦτος = φύσει ἄπολις? For the construction, cp. Hyperid. Or. Fun. col. 7. 30 (p. 60 Blass), ἅμα γὰρ εἰς τ[ὸν τό]πον ἀθροισθήσονται καὶ τ[ῆς τού]των ἀρετῆς μνησθήσοντ[αι].

ἅτε περ ἄζυξ ὢν ὥσπερ ἐν πεττοῖς. The term ἄζυξ is used in the well-known epigram of Agathias (Anthol. Pal. 9. 482), where the game described is evidently that which the Romans called 'ludus duodecim scriptorum' (resembling our 'backgammon'): Plato, according to M. Becq de Fouquières (Jeux des Anciens, p. 358), refers to this game in Rep. 604 C. The epigram has been ingeniously explained both by Mr. H. Jackson (*Journ. of Philology, loc. cit.*) and by M. Becq de Fouquières (p. 372 sqq.), but until more light has been thrown on the meaning of line 26, which has been variously emended, we cannot be quite sure that we know the meaning of the term ἄζυξ even in this game, though it would seem to be 'a solitary, unprotected piece'; it is, however, by no means certain that

Aristotle here refers to this particular game. The term *πεττοί* in its wider signification included a variety of games—all games, in fact, in which *πεττοί* were used (Becq de Fouquières, p. 303, 385)—but it was especially applied, in a narrower sense, to a game resembling our 'draughts' (ibid. p. 391), which was played on five lines instead of twelve, and in which each player sought to surround and cut off his antagonist or to reduce him to inactivity (Polyb. 1. 84. 7: Plato, Rep. 487 B—both passages referred to by Becq de Fouquières, p. 397-8). In this game the term *ἄζυξ* may well have borne a different meaning from that which it bore in backgammon, and one more in harmony with its use in the passage before us, but what this meaning was, we can only vaguely conjecture from the connexion in which it is here used. Is *ἄζυξ* an isolated piece pushed by itself far in advance from the 'sacred line' (see Becq de Fouquières, p. 402 sqq.), and therefore alone in the midst of foes? There seems to be no reason for supposing with Becq de Fouquières (p. 398–9) that some game other than the ordinary *πεττεία* is here referred to.

7. διότι. Vict. 'quare,' with many other translators, but as the fact that man is a political animal in a fuller sense than bees or other gregarious animals has not yet been mentioned, it is perhaps better (with Lamb. Bern. and others) to translate it here by 'that.'

8. ἀγελαίου ζῴου. 'His in verbis Platonis *ἀγελαιοτροφική* vel *ἀγελαιοκομική*, quam legimus in Politico, p. 267 B sq., 276 A, significari videtur' (Engelhardt, Loci Platonici, p. 3). The connexion conceived by Plato to exist between this art and *πολιτική* may possibly be here glanced at. In Hist. An. 1. 1. 487 b 34 sqq. man is spoken of as both *ἀγελαῖον* and *μοναδικόν*, and we have the following account of *πολιτικὰ ζῷα* in 488 a 7—*πολιτικὰ δ' ἐστὶν ὧν ἕν τι καὶ κοινὸν γίνεται πάντων τὸ ἔργον· ὅπερ οὐ πάντα ποιεῖ τὰ ἀγελαῖα· ἔστι δὲ τοιοῦτον ἄνθρωπος, μέλιττα, σφήξ, μύρμηξ, γέρανος· καὶ τούτων τὰ μὲν ὑφ' ἡγεμόνα ἐστὶ τὰ δ' ἄναρχα, οἷον γέρανος μὲν καὶ τὸ τῶν μελιττῶν γένος ὑφ' ἡγεμόνα, μύρμηκες δὲ καὶ μυρία ἄλλα ἄναρχα.*

μᾶλλον. For higher faculties are brought by man into the common stock—the power of perceiving that which is good and evil, just and unjust, advantageous and disadvantageous, and of expressing those perceptions—and the higher the faculties brought into the common stock, the fuller the union: cp. Eth. Nic. 9. 9. 1170 b 11, *τοῦτο δὲ γίνοιτ' ἂν ἐν τῷ συζῆν καὶ κοινωνεῖν λόγων καὶ διανοίας· οὕτω γὰρ ἂν δόξειε τὸ συζῆν ἐπὶ τῶν ἀνθρώπων λέγεσθαι, καὶ οὐχ ὥσπερ ἐπὶ τῶν βοσκημάτων τὸ ἐν τῷ αὐτῷ νέμεσθαι.* On language as special to man, cp. Isocr. de Antid.

§§ 253–7 and Nicocl. § 5 sqq., passages which Aristotle perhaps had in view here. Socrates had anticipated Isocrates in speaking of language as the condition of political life (Xen. Mem. 4. 3. 12, τὸ δὲ καὶ ἑρμηνείαν δοῦναι, δι' ἧς πάντων τῶν ἀγαθῶν μεταδίδομέν τε ἀλλήλοις διδάσκοντες καὶ κοινωνοῦμεν καὶ νόμους τιθέμεθα καὶ πολιτευόμεθα ;). According to Plato, Tim. 47 C, λόγος (which he fails to mark off from φωνή) is given us ἕνεκα ἁρμονίας and to regulate the disorderly movements of the soul. It may be questioned whether, as Aristotle seems to imply, language would be useless to a solitary animal.

10. ἄνθρωπος. 'Articulus ubi genus aliquod universum significatur non raro omittitur,' Bon. Ind. 109 b 36 : cp. 1253 a 31, ὥσπερ γὰρ καὶ τελεωθὲν βέλτιστον τῶν ζῴων ἄνθρωπός (so Π²) ἐστιν : on the other hand, all MSS. have ὁ ἄνθρωπος in 1253 a 7, 34.

ἡ μὲν οὖν φωνὴ κ.τ.λ. Language has just been said to be peculiar to man, and μὲν οὖν (' it is true ') introduces an admission that this does not hold of voice, in order that an account of the nature of language may be added. It implies a capacity to form households and πόλεις. As to φωνή, see de Gen. An. 5. 7. 786 b 21, where it is said to be τοῦ λόγου ὕλη, and de An. 2. 8. 420 b 32, σημαντικὸς γὰρ δή τις ψόφος ἐστὶν ἡ φωνή, καὶ οὐ τοῦ ἀναπνεομένου ἀέρος, ὥσπερ ἡ βήξ (contrast Plutarch, de Animae Procreatione in Timaeo, c. 27, p. 1026 A, ὡς δὲ φωνή τις ἐστὶν ἄλογος καὶ ἀσήμαντος, λόγος δὲ λέξις ἐν φωνῇ σημαντικῇ διανοίας): so the words σημεῖον and σημαίνειν are used in 11 and 13 in contrast to δηλοῦν 14 (Vict. 'signa dant, haec enim notio est verbi σημαίνειν : homines autem oratione declarant aperiuntque, hoc enim valet verbum δηλοῦν'). The full force of δηλοῦν appears in Pol. 3. 8. 1279 b 15 : σημεῖα are distinguished from ὁμοιώματα in 5 (8). 5. 1340 a 33. As to the limitation to τὸ λυπηρὸν καὶ ἡδύ, cp. Eth. Nic. 2. 2. 1104 b 30 sqq. and de An. 2. 9. 421 a 10, φαύλως γὰρ ἄνθρωπος ὀσμᾶται καὶ οὐδενὸς ὀσφραίνεται τῶν ὀσφραντῶν ἄνευ τοῦ λυπηροῦ ἢ τοῦ ἡδέος, ὡς οὐκ ὄντος ἀκριβοῦς τοῦ αἰσθητηρίου. Aristotle implies here that animals can only indicate to each other feelings of pleasure and pain (cp. Lucr. 5. 1059 sqq., referred to by Giph.), but in de Part. An. 2. 17. 660 a 35—b 2 and Hist. An. 9. 1. 608 a 17 sqq. he speaks of some of them as receiving μάθησις καὶ διδασκαλία from their likes. See on this subject Dr. Ogle's note 5 on Aristotle's Parts of Animals, 2. 17. Not all animals possess φωνή (Hist. An. 1. 1. 488 a 32).

14. ἐπὶ τῷ δηλοῦν. See Bon. Ind. 268 b 13.

τὸ συμφέρον καὶ τὸ βλαβερόν. Giph. (p. 31) draws attention to the fact that Aristotle denies to the lower animals a sense of the advantageous and the harmful.

15. ὥστε καὶ τὸ δίκαιον. Cp. 3. 12. 1282 b 16, ἔστι δὲ πολιτικὸν ἀγαθὸν τὸ δίκαιον, τοῦτο δ' ἐστὶ τὸ κοινῇ συμφέρον. Epicurus went farther and traced the just back to utility: cp. Diog. Laert. 10. 150 and the well-known line of Horace (Sat. 1. 3. 98) to which Giph. refers:

Atque ipsa utilitas, iusti prope mater et aequi.

16. μόνον is pleonastic, as in 4 (7). 11. 1331 a 11. For the change of number from τοῖς ἀνθρώποις to μόνον, Vahlen (Poet. p. 103) compares τούτῳ διαφέρουσιν (οἱ ἄνθρωποι) τῶν ἄλλων ζῴων ὅτι μιμητικώτατόν ἐστι (sc. τῶν ζῴων), Poet. 4. 1448 b 6. Φρόνησις, however, is allowed by Aristotle to some animals (Hist. An. 9. 1. 608 a 15: Gen. An. 3. 2. 753 a 12: Eth. Nic. 6. 7. 1141 a 26), but in a sense other than that in which it is ascribed to man, as appears from the last-named passage—διὸ καὶ τῶν θηρίων ἔνια φρόνιμά φασιν εἶναι, ὅσα περὶ τὸν αὑτῶν βίον ἔχοντα φαίνεται δύναμιν προνοητικήν.

17. αἴσθησιν. 'Latiore sensu ἔχειν αἴσθησίν τινος idem quod usum habere alicuius rei, novisse aliquid' (Bonitz, Ind. 21 a 1, who compares Eth. Nic. 6. 12. 1143 b 5 and Pol. 3. 11. 1281 b 35, and refers to Zeller, Gr. Ph. 2. 2. 504. 2, ed. 2,=650. 2, ed. 3). See also Zeller, Gr. Ph. 2. 2. 238. 2 (ed. 3), who explains αἴσθησιν in the passage before us by the word 'Bewusstsein,' adding that an immediate kind of knowledge is meant, in contradistinction to ἐπιστήμη. According to Polybius (see above, p. xiii), the ἔννοια τοῦ δικαίου καὶ τοῦ ἀδίκου, τοῦ καλοῦ καὶ τοῦ αἰσχροῦ is the fruit of human society, not that which is prior to human society and makes it possible.

18. ἡ δὲ τούτων κοινωνία. Some translate 'the association of beings possessing these perceptions,' but it seems more natural to take τούτων here as neuter than as masculine, and besides an association of this kind would hardly be said to produce, but rather to be, the household and πόλις. Giph. and Bern. are probably right in translating these words 'community in these things'—i.e. in the good and the bad, the just and the unjust—cp. 3. 9. 1280 b 5, περὶ δ' ἀρετῆς καὶ κακίας πολιτικῆς διασκοποῦσιν ὅσοι φροντίζουσιν εὐνομίας et sqq.: 1. 2. 1253 a 37 sq.: Eth. Nic. 5. 10. 1134 a 31, ἡ γὰρ δίκη κρίσις τοῦ δικαίου καὶ τοῦ ἀδίκου: Plato, Rep. 484 D, τὰ ἐνθάδε νόμιμα καλῶν τε πέρι καὶ δικαίων καὶ ἀγαθῶν: Eth. Nic. 9. 6. 1167 b 2, πολιτικὴ δὲ φιλία φαίνεται ἡ ὁμόνοια . . . περὶ τὰ συμφέροντα γάρ ἐστι καὶ τὰ εἰς τὸν βίον ἀνήκοντα. Some societies are formed for pleasure (Eth. Nic. 8. 11. 1160 a 19), not so the household or the πόλις. These are ethical unities. Cp. also Eth. Nic. 9. 9. 1170 b 4 sqq.: Plato, Politicus 309 C–E: and the myth of Protagoras (Protag. 322 C), in which in answer to the inquiry of Hermes— καὶ δίκην δὴ καὶ αἰδῶ οὕτω θῶ ἐν τοῖς ἀνθρώποις ἢ ἐπὶ πάντας νείμω;—Zeus replies—Ἐπὶ πάντας, καὶ πάντες μετεχόντων· οὐ γὰρ ἂν γένοιντο πόλεις, εἰ ὀλίγοι αὐτῶν μετέχοιεν ὥσπερ ἄλλων τεχνῶν. In 1. 2. 1252 a 26–34 the origin of the household, and therefore of the πόλις, had been traced to instincts common to all animals or even to animals and plants, but here we learn that household and πόλις can only exist for human beings, inasmuch as their existence implies endowments which Nature has given only to man. In 3. 9. 1280 a 31 sq., εἰ δὲ μήτε τοῦ ζῆν μόνον ἕνεκεν ἀλλὰ μᾶλλον τοῦ εὖ ζῆν (καὶ γὰρ ἂν δούλων καὶ τῶν ἄλλων ζῴων ἦν πόλις· νῦν δ' οὐκ ἔστι διὰ τὸ μὴ μετέχειν εὐδαιμονίας μηδὲ τοῦ ζῆν κατὰ προαίρεσιν) κ.τ.λ., a somewhat different reason is given why animals other than man do not form πόλεις.

καὶ πρότερον δή. On καὶ . . . δή see Bon. Ind. 173 a 12 sqq.: conjoined, the two particles seem to indicate a step taken in advance from one point to another by way of inference. Cp. for example Eth. Nic. 4. 1. 1120 a 6 sq. 'Maxime quidem philosophus illa dicendi ratione utitur, si re quadam pertractata significare vult idem quod de ea etiam de alia vel in universum valere' (Eucken, de Partic. usu, p. 44): see 1. 13. 1259 b 32. Aristotle had pointed out that the individual and the household are prior γενέσει to the πόλις; hence he is naturally careful to add that the πόλις is prior φύσει. This is in conformity with the principle—τὸ τῇ γενέσει ὕστερον τῇ φύσει πρότερον (Phys. 8. 7. 261 a 14).

The argument in 18–29 seems to be as follows:—The πόλις is prior to the individual, for the whole is prior to its part. And the whole is prior to its part, because, when severed from the whole, the part loses its capacity to discharge its function, or (which is the same thing) loses its identity. Here Aristotle sums up—we see then, that the πόλις exists by nature and is prior to the individual, for if the individual is not self-complete when severed from the πόλις, he will be posterior to it just as any other part is posterior to its whole, and the individual, if a man and not a god or a brute, is not self-complete when severed from the πόλις. Aristotle might have stopped at the words 'prior to the individual' without adding the words which follow, but he adds these words in order to prove what he assumed in 20, that the individual stands to the πόλις in the same relation of posteriority in which other parts stand to their wholes. In strictness, γὰρ 26 only introduces a proof that the πόλις is prior in nature to the individual, not that it is by nature, but of course, if it is prior by nature to the individual, it exists by nature itself. No proof is given that the πόλις is prior to the household, probably because the same reasoning is applicable both to the household and to the individual. It is possible that here Aristotle has in his mind the verse of Sophocles (Philoct. 1018), in which Philoctetes calls himself

ἄφιλον ἔρημον ἄπολιν ἐν ζῶσιν νεκρόν.

As to the validity of the argument, the fact that the individual is not αὐτάρκης without the πόλις does not prove that he stands to it in the relation of a part to its whole. Man is not αὐτάρκης, for example, without the aid of other communities besides his own; yet he is not necessarily a part of those other communities. And even if we accept the conclusion, it does not follow that all parts of all wholes stand in the same relation to those wholes. A limb stands in a far more intimate relation to the body of which it is a part than a wheel does to a cart, or a portion of a rock does to that rock. The Stoics, in fact, recognized this distinction, for they went on to say that the individual is a limb (μέλος, not μέρος) of the whole to which he belongs. This whole they commonly (cp. Cic. de Nat. Deor. 2. 14. 37 sq.) found in the Universe, but not always, for Epictetus (Arrian 2. 10) speaks of the individual as part of the πόλις. Plato also sometimes found it in the Universe (e. g. in Laws 903). We observe that in the Timaeus (68 E: 69 C) he applies to the Universe similar epithets to those applied by Aristotle to the πόλις (τέλειος, αὐτάρκης, πάσας περιέχουσα τὰς ἄλλας κοινωνίας). The Republic, on the other hand, recognizes the πόλις as the whole of which the individual, or rather perhaps the class, is a part (Rep. 552 A). As to the sense in which a human being is a member of a community, see a letter of Shelley's (dated August 12, 1812), which is published in the *Academy* for July 31, 1886. 'A human being,' he says, 'is a member of the community, not as a limb is a member of the body, or as what is a part of a machine, intended only to contribute to some general joint result. . . . He is an ultimate being, made for his own perfection as his highest end, made to maintain an individual existence, and to serve others only as far as consists with his own virtue and progress.' Aristotle, however, would say that he asks nothing from the individual that would not redound to his own perfection and the perfection of his life.

20. τὸ γὰρ ὅλον κ.τ.λ. No notice is here taken of the principle laid down in Metaph. Z. 10. 1035 b 4 sqq., where some parts—parts of the Essence or Form—are said to be prior to τὸ σύνολον—a principle which, applied to the πόλις, might have suggested a different theory of the relation of some at all events of the individuals composing the πόλις to it—but in other respects there is a close resemblance between the two passages: cp. especially 1035 b

14-25. See also Metaph. Z. 11. 1036 b 30 sqq. and 16. 1040 b 5 sqq. For the account of τὸ πρότερον implied in the passage before us, cp. Phys. 8. 7. 260 b 17, λέγεται δὲ πρότερον, οὗ τε μὴ ὄντος οὐκ ἔσται τἆλλα, ἐκεῖνο δ' ἄνευ τῶν ἄλλων, καὶ τὸ τῷ χρόνῳ, καὶ τὸ κατ' οὐσίαν: Metaph. Δ. 11. 1019 a 1, τὰ μὲν δὴ οὕτω λέγεται πρότερα καὶ ὕστερα, τὰ δὲ κατὰ φύσιν καὶ οὐσίαν, ὅσα ἐνδέχεται εἶναι ἄνευ ἄλλων, ἐκεῖνα δὲ ἄνευ ἐκείνων μή· ᾗ διαιρέσει ἐχρήσατο Πλάτων. Much the same account is given by Aristotle of the ἀρχή (Metaph. K. 1. 1060 a 1, ἀρχὴ γὰρ τὸ συναναιροῦν) or the οὐσία of a thing (de An. 2. 1. 412 b 18 sqq.: cp. Alex. Aphrod. on Metaph. Z. 16. 1040 b 5, οὐσίας ἐκεῖνά φαμεν ὅσα καθ' αὑτὰ ὄντα δύναται τὸ οἰκεῖον ἔργον ἀποτελεῖν· οὐσία γὰρ οὐδὲν ἄλλο ἐστὶν ἢ τὸ ἀφ' οὗ τὸ ἑκάστου ἔργον ἐκπληροῦται). Severance from the Whole, in fact, involves the loss of the Form or οὐσία, and the loss of this involves 'destruction' (cp. διαφθαρεῖσα 22, and φθαρέντα, de Gen. An. 2. 1. 734 b 24 sqq.: 735 a 7 sq.: 1. 19. 726 b 22 sqq.), but a hand destroyed is a hand unfitted to discharge the functions of a hand, or in other words is not a hand at all. Thus we may almost say that in Aristotle's view the πόλις is the οὐσία or ἀρχή of the individual. In the Topics, however, a question is raised (6. 13. 150 a 33), εἰ τῷ ὅλῳ συμφθείρεται τὰ μέρη· ἀνάπαλιν γὰρ δεῖ συμβαίνειν, τῶν μερῶν φθαρέντων, φθείρεσθαι τὸ ὅλον· τοῦ δ' ὅλου φθαρέντος οὐκ ἀναγκαῖον καὶ τὰ μέρη ἐφθάρθαι. But here the object seems merely to be to arm a disputant with a tenable objection.

22. διαφθαρεῖσα γὰρ ἔσται τοιαύτη, 'for a hand when destroyed' (by being severed from the soul, which is its οὐσία) 'will be no better than a stone hand.' Giph. ('haec enim interiit') and others make διαφθαρεῖσα the predicate, but it is clear that τοιαύτη (=probably λιθίνη, not ὁμωνύμως λεχθεῖσα) is the predicate, if we compare de Gen. An. 2. 1. 734 b 24, οὐ γάρ ἐστι πρόσωπον μὴ ἔχον ψυχήν, οὐδὲ σάρξ, ἀλλὰ φθαρέντα ὁμωνύμως λεχθήσεται τὸ μὲν εἶναι πρόσωπον τὸ δὲ σάρξ, ὥσπερ κἂν εἰ ἐγίγνετο λίθινα ἢ ξύλινα: cp. also Meteor. 4. 12. 389 b 31, μᾶλλον γὰρ δῆλον ὅτι ὁ νεκρὸς ἄνθρωπος ὁμωνύμως. οὕτω τοίνυν καὶ χεὶρ τελευτήσαντος ὁμωνύμως, καθάπερ καὶ αὐλοὶ λίθινοι λεχθείησαν. Dr. R. Schöll (Sus. Qu. Crit. p. 334) has anticipated me in calling attention to the above passage of the De Generatione Animalium.

23. πάντα δὲ . . . τῇ δυνάμει. Cp. Meteor. 4. 12. 390 a 10, ἅπαντα δ' ἐστὶν ὡρισμένα τῷ ἔργῳ· τὰ μὲν γὰρ δυνάμενα ποιεῖν τὸ αὑτῶν ἔργον ἀληθῶς ἐστὶν ἕκαστα, οἷον ὁ ὀφθαλμὸς εἰ ὁρᾷ, τὸ δὲ μὴ δυνάμενον ὁμωνύμως, οἷον ὁ τεθνεὼς ἢ ὁ λίθινος: de Gen. An. 1. 2. 716 a 23: Metaph. Z. 10. 1035 b 16, ἕκαστον γοῦν τὸ μέρος ἐὰν ὁρίζηται καλῶς, οὐκ ἄνευ τοῦ ἔργου ὁριεῖται, ὃ οὐχ ὑπάρξει ἄνευ αἰσθήσεως. Plato had already said much the same thing, Soph. 247 D, λέγω δὴ τὸ καὶ ὁποιανοῦν κεκτημένον δύναμιν εἴτ' εἰς τὸ ποιεῖν ἕτερον ὁτιοῦν πεφυκὸς εἴτ' εἰς τὸ παθεῖν καὶ σμικρότατον ὑπὸ τοῦ φαυλοτάτου, κἂν εἰ μόνον εἰσάπαξ, πᾶν τοῦτο ὄντως εἶναι· τίθεμαι γὰρ ὅρον ὁρίζειν τὰ ὄντα, ὡς ἔστιν οὐκ ἄλλο τι πλὴν δύναμις. On the other hand, Aristotle seems in Pol. 3. 3. 1276 b 7 to view τὸ εἶδος τῆς συνθέσεως as constituting the identity of an object, and in de Gen. An. 1. 18. 722 b 30 we read—τὰ μέρη τὰ μὲν δυνάμει τὰ δὲ πάθεσι διώρισται, τὰ μὲν ἀνομοιομερῆ τῷ δύνασθαί τι ποιεῖν, οἷον γλῶττα καὶ χείρ, τὰ δ' ὁμοιομερῆ σκληρότητι καὶ μαλακότητι καὶ τοῖς ἄλλοις τοῖς τοιούτοις πάθεσιν.

24. μηκέτι τοιαῦτα ὄντα, 'if no longer fit for performing their destined work': cp. θάλατταν τοιαύτην, 'fit for fishing,' 1. 8. 1256 a 37, and ὅπως δὲ γίνωνται τοιοῦτοι, 2. 5. 1263 a 39.

25. Μὲν οὖν is here again, as in 1252 b 9, caught up by a second μὲν οὖν before any δέ appears.

27. One would expect here ὁ δὲ αὐτάρκης χωρισθείς, but Aristotle substitutes ὁ δὲ μὴ δυνάμενος κοινωνεῖν ἢ μηδὲν δεόμενος δι' αὐτάρκειαν, as the case of the former, who cannot be called αὐτάρκης and yet does not want the State, occurs to him and, characteristically enough, is kept in view at whatever cost of trimness. Μηδὲν δεόμενος, sc. κοινωνίας or possibly κοινωνεῖν.

29. ἐν πᾶσιν, 'in all human beings.'

30. ὁ δὲ κ.τ.λ. For the turn of the sentence, compare a fragment from the Κναφεύς of Antiphanes (Meineke, Fr. Com. Gr. 3. 66)—

Ὅστις τέχνην κατέδειξε πρῶτος τῶν θεῶν,
οὗτος μέγιστον εὗρεν ἀνθρώποις κακόν.

Cp. also ibid. 4. 75. At Argos men looked back to Phoroneus as having been the first to found a city (Paus. 2. 15. 5). Cicero (De Inventione 1. 2) looks back to some 'magnus vir et sapiens.' Camerarius (p. 31) quotes these two passages, and adds—'Epicurus hoc fortuito factum, ut alia quoque, censet, quemadmodum Lucretius exposuit libro quinto.' The comic poet Athenio makes one of his characters claim the credit for the art of cookery (Meineke, Fr. Com. Gr. 4. 558).

31. On **ὥσπερ καὶ . . . οὕτω καί**, see Sus.[1], Ind. Gramm. ὥσπερ.

τελεωθέν. Aristotle uses both τελεωθέν and τελειωθέν (de Gen. An. 1. 1. 715 a 21), and both τέλεος and τέλειος (see Bon. Ind.). We find both forms together (τελεώτερα, τέλειον) in de Gen. An. 2. 1. 733 b 1 (Bekker). The meaning of τελεωθέν, which is here used in contrast to χωρισθὲν νόμου καὶ δίκης, may be illustrated by Eth. Nic. 2. 1. 1103 a 23, οὔτ' ἄρα φύσει οὔτε παρὰ φύσιν ἐγγίνονται αἱ ἀρεταί, ἀλλὰ πεφυκόσι μὲν ἡμῖν δέξασθαι αὐτάς, τελειουμένοις δὲ διὰ τοῦ ἔθους, and Phys. 7. 3. 246 a 13 sqq. For the gender of τελεωθὲν and χωρισθέν, cp. 4 (7). 13. 1332 b 4, ἄνθρωπος δὲ καὶ λόγῳ, μόνον γὰρ ἔχει λόγον.

33. χείριστον πάντων. Cp. Hesiod, Op. et Dies 275 sqq.: Hdt. 4. 106, Ἀνδροφάγοι δὲ ἀγριώτατα πάντων ἀνθρώπων ἔχουσι ἤθεα, οὔτε δίκην νομίζοντες οὔτε νόμῳ οὐδενὶ χρεώμενοι: Plato, Laws 765 E, ἄνθρωπος δὲ ὥς φαμεν ἥμερον, ὅμως μὴν παιδείας μὲν ὀρθῆς τυχὸν καὶ φύσεως εὐτυχοῦς θειότατον ἡμερώτατόν τε ζῷον γίγνεσθαι φιλεῖ, μὴ ἱκανῶς δὲ ἢ μὴ καλῶς τραφὲν ἀγριώτατον ὁπόσα φύει γῆ: Protag. 327 D–E. See also Eth. Nic. 7. 7. 1150 a 1–5. Plutarch demurs to the saying in the mouth of the Epicurean Colotes (adv. Colot. c. 30), on the ground that in the absence of law men would still be left the teaching of such philosophers as Parmenides, Socrates, Plato, and Heraclitus, and that this would save them from living like beasts.

ἀδικία ἔχουσα ὅπλα. Cp. Rhet. 2. 5. 1382 a 34, καὶ ἀδικία δύναμιν ἔχουσα (is to be dreaded)· τῷ προαιρεῖσθαι γὰρ ὁ ἄδικος ἄδικος. Giph. (p. 37) compares Plutarch, Cicero c. 46, οὕτως ἐξέπεσον ὑπὸ θυμοῦ καὶ λύσσης τῶν ἀνθρωπίνων λογισμῶν, μᾶλλον δ' ἀπέδειξαν ὡς οὐδὲν ἀνθρώπου θηρίον ἐστὶν ἀγριώτερον ἐξουσίαν πάθει προσλαβόντος, which seems to echo Eth. Nic. 7. 7. 1150 a 7, μυριοπλάσια γὰρ ἂν κακὰ ποιήσειεν ἄνθρωπος κακὸς θηρίου.

34. ὁ δὲ ἄνθρωπος κ.τ.λ. Vict. with others explains φρόνησις and ἀρετή as the ὅπλα here referred to, but in that case why have we the dat. φρονήσει καὶ ἀρετῇ and not the acc.? and how can it be said of φρόνησις and ἀρετή that they can be used for opposite purposes? Cp. Rhet. 1. 1. 1355 b 2, εἰ δ' ὅτι μεγάλα βλάψειεν ἂν ὁ χρώμενος ἀδίκως τῇ τοιαύτῃ δυνάμει τῶν λόγων, τοῦτό γε κοινόν ἐστι κατὰ πάντων τῶν ἀγαθῶν πλὴν ἀρετῆς, καὶ μάλιστα κατὰ τῶν χρησιμωτάτων, οἷον ἰσχύος ὑγιείας πλούτου στρατηγίας, and Pol. 3. 10. 1281 a 19. And if it be said that virtue is here used in a lower sense than in these passages, it seems strange that in the very next line (36) it should be used in its ordinary sense. Besides, as Holm (de ethicis Politicorum Aristotelis principiis, p. 39 n.) remarks, 'usitata apud Aristotelem dicendi formula ἀρετὴ καὶ φρόνησις virtutes semper significat ipsas, ethicas et dianoeticas: exempla haec sint—Pol. 3. 11. 1281 b 4: 4 (7). 1. 1323 b 22, 33.' The phrase was known even to the comic poets as one current among philosophers (Meineke, Fragm. Com. Gr. 4. 22). Montecatinus (quoted by Schn.) seems to come much nearer to the truth in rendering these words 'arma homini data sunt ad prudentiam et virtutem'; and so Bern. 'geschaffen mit einer Rüstung zu Einsicht und Tugend,' and Holm (ibid.) 'ad virtutes exercendas.' There is, however, some strangeness in the use of the dative in this sense, and Aristotle does not seem to regard the ὅπλα as means for the attainment of φρόνησις καὶ ἀρετή, or as instruments for their exercise, but rather as powers on which they are to impress a right direction (cp. ἄνευ ἀρετῆς, 36). May not the words mean 'having arms for prudence and virtue to use' (or 'guide in use')? We have had just before ἀδικία ἔχουσα ὅπλα, and it is not surprising to find Prudence and Virtue also spoken of as using arms or guiding their use. As to the dative, cp. Plutarch, Reip. Gerend. Praec. c. 28, δεύτερον δέ, ὅτι πρὸς τοὺς βασκάνους καὶ πονηροὺς ὅπλον ἡ παρὰ τῶν πολλῶν εὔνοια τοῖς ἀγαθοῖς ἐστιν. Ὄργανον, which resembles ὅπλον in meaning and is sometimes conjoined with it (de Part. An. 4. 10. 687 b 2–4), often takes this dative (de Gen. An. 4. 1. 765 b 36: Pol. 1. 4. 1253 b 28). Holm refers to Cic. de Orat. 3. 14. 55 *sub fin.* as supporting his interpretation, but this passage perhaps makes quite as much in favour of that just suggested. The next question is, what are the ὅπλα referred to? Bernays (Wirkung der Tragödie, note 16) quotes Seneca de Ira, 1. 17 (1. 16 Didot): Aristoteles ait adfectus quosdam, si quis illis bene utatur, pro armis esse, quod verum foret, si, velut bellica instrumenta, sumi deponique possent induentis arbitrio. Haec arma, quae Aristoteles virtuti dat, ipsa per se pugnant, non exspectant manum, et habent, non habentur. Hence he explains the ὅπλα here mentioned as 'die Affecte' (the emotions). Aristotle, however, only speaks of 'adfectus quosdam' (he is thinking no doubt especially of anger), and there is nothing to show that these 'adfectus' are viewed by him as the only ὅπλα at the disposal of φρόνησις καὶ ἀρετή. Language, for instance, may well be another. The words 'haec arma quae Aristoteles virtuti dat' (compare those a little lower down, 'rationem ab iracundia petere praesidium') seem to support the view taken in this note of the dative φρονήσει καὶ ἀρετῇ. If, as is probable, the 'adfectus quidam' of the de Ira are among the ὅπλα referred to in this passage, Aristotle, like Seneca himself (de Ira, 1. 3), would appear to have regarded them as peculiar to man.

36. πρὸς ἀφροδίσια . . . χείριστον. Cp. Hist. An. 6. 22. 575 b 30: Plutarch, Gryllus, c. 7. 990 E sqq.: contrast, however, Aristot. de Gen. An. 1. 4. 717 a 23 sqq.

37. ἐδωδήν. Plutarch, ibid. c. 8. Philemon (Fragm. Ἀγύρτης, p. 107 Didot) does not go quite so far as Aristotle, and the good Pheraulas (Xen. Cyrop. 8. 3. 49) is of the opposite opinion.

ἡ δὲ δικαιοσύνη . . . δικαίου κρίσις. Here ἡ δὲ δικαιοσύνη takes up ἄνευ ἀρετῆς, and we have the proof that whoever first instituted the πόλις conferred great benefits on men. He, in fact, gave them virtue. 'Justice is bound up with the State, for adjudication, which is the determination of that which is just, is the ordering of political society.' So Bernays, followed by Susemihl, 'ist nichts als die Ordnung der staatlichen Gemeinschaft.' Sus.[2] (Note 28 c) refers to 3. 10. 1281 a 11–21. Cp. also 8 (6). 8. 1322 a 5, ἀναγκαία δ' ἐστίν, ὅτι οὐδὲν ὄφελος γίνεσθαι μὲν δίκας περὶ τῶν δικαίων, ταύτας δὲ μὴ λαμβάνειν τέλος, ὥστ' εἰ μὴ γιγνομένων κοινωνεῖν ἀδύνατον ἀλλήλοις, καὶ πράξεων μὴ γιγνομένων. In 4 (7). 8. 1328 b 13 judicial institutions are reckoned among those things which are most necessary in a State (πάντων ἀναγκαιότατον). The interpretation just given of the words πολιτικῆς κοινωνίας τάξις is perhaps the one which is most likely to be correct, yet another may be mentioned as possible. These words may mean 'an institution of political society' (cp. 4 (7). 10. 1329 b 5, τῶν συσσιτίων ἡ τάξις). Plato had already said (Laws 937 D)—καὶ δὴ καὶ δίκη ἐν ἀνθρώποις πῶς οὐ καλόν, ὃ πάντα ἡμέρωκε τὰ ἀνθρώπινα; But perhaps Aristotle had a saying of Pindar in his mind: cp. Plutarch, Praec. Reip. Gerend. c. 13. 807 C, ὁ δὲ πολιτικός, ἀριστοτέχνας τις ὢν κατὰ Πίνδαρον, καὶ δημιουργὸς εὐνομίας καὶ δίκης. The words ἡ δὲ δίκη τοῦ δικαίου κρίσις seem to be a necessary link in the reasoning, though some would omit them: similar expressions occur in Eth. Nic. 5. 10. 1134 a 31 and Rhet. 2. 1. 1377 b 22 (cp. Menand. Inc. Fab. Fragm. 56). An αἴσθησις τοῦ δικαίου καὶ τοῦ ἀδίκου is a condition precedent of the πόλις (1253 a 15 sqq.), but this is not the same thing as justice.

2. πρῶτον, i.e. before going on to speak of πολιτεία. Thus we C. 3.
are referred back in 3. 6. 1278 b 17 to the πρῶτοι λόγοι, ἐν οἷς περὶ 1253 b.
οἰκονομίας διωρίσθη καὶ δεσποτείας, and the First Book itself refers forward at its close to τὰ περὶ τὰς πολιτείας (1. 13. 1260 b 12).

3. οἰκονομίας κ.τ.λ. 'The departments into which household management falls are concerned with' (or possibly 'correspond to') 'the parts of which the household is composed.' The ellipse is no doubt considerable, but not more so than that in 1. 11. 1258 b 27, τρίτον δὲ εἶδος χρηματιστικῆς μεταξὺ ταύτης καὶ τῆς πρώτης (ἔχει γὰρ καὶ τῆς κατὰ φύσιν τι μέρος καὶ τῆς μεταβλητικῆς), ὅσα ἀπὸ γῆς καὶ τῶν ἀπὸ γῆς γινομένων . . . οἷον ὑλοτομία τε καὶ πᾶσα μεταλλευτική. See as to constructions of this kind Bon. Ind. 533 b 6–13, and Waitz on Anal. Pr. 1. 46. 52 a 29, to whom Bonitz refers.

4. οἰκία δὲ τέλειος. Lasaulx (Ehe bei den Griechen, p. 7 n.), after referring to δόμος ἡμιτελής (Il. 2. 701), quotes Antipater ap. Stob. Flor. 67. 25, τέλειος οἶκος καὶ βίος οὐκ ἄλλως δύναται γενέσθαι ἢ μετὰ γυναικὸς καὶ τέκνων, and a similar saying of Hierocles, Stob. Flor. 67. 21. Aristotle holds the household to be incomplete without slaves. Contrast Locke, Civil Government, 2. § 86: 'the family is as much a family, and the power of the paterfamilias as great, whether there be any slaves in his family or no.' In 3. 4. 1277 a 7 we find the somewhat careless expression—οἰκία ἐξ ἀνδρὸς καὶ γυναικὸς καὶ κτῆσις ἐκ δεσπότου καὶ δούλου—in, it is true, an aporetic passage: a similar looseness of statement is observable in Eth. Nic. 1. 1. 1094 a 9, where wealth is said to be the end of οἰκονομική, teaching which rather resembles that of the first book (so-called) of the Oeconomics (cp. Oecon. 1. 1. 1343 a 8) than that of the Politics.

7. **περὶ τριῶν τούτων**, 'de his tribus copulis' (Vict.).

8. **τί ἕκαστον καὶ ποῖον δεῖ εἶναι**, 'what each is and how each ought to be constituted.'

9. **δεσποτική**, sc. κοινωνία or some such word.

ἀνώνυμον γὰρ κ.τ.λ. The word ἀνώνυμος is especially used by Aristotle, 'ubi generis alicuius non exstat unum quo contineatur nomen' (Bon. Ind. 69 b 3): hence we read in de An. 2. 7. 418 a 27, ὃ λόγῳ μὲν ἔστιν εἰπεῖν, ἀνώνυμον δὲ τυγχάνει ὄν. Cp. also 10, καὶ γὰρ αὕτη οὐκ ὠνόμασται ἰδίῳ ὀνόματι, i.e. with a name which exactly fits it: see Rhet. 3. 5. 1407 a 31, where τὰ ἴδια ὀνόματα are contrasted with τὰ περιέχοντα. The words γαμική and τεκνοποιητική are probably felt by Aristotle not to describe the nature of the ἀρχή in the same clear way in which the word δεσποτική describes the ἀρχή of the master over his slave. We are told in the de Anima (2. 4. 416 b 23) that 'everything should be named in reference to the end it realizes.' The words γαμική and τεκνοποιητική certainly do not give us this information. Πατρική is substituted for τεκνοποιητική in 1. 12. 1259 a 38.

11. **ἔστωσαν δ' αὗται κ.τ.λ.** 'Let the three relations of which we spoke' as needing to be investigated 'be these' (for the absence of αἱ before τρεῖς, see Bon. Ind. 546 a 51 sqq.); 'but there is a part of Household Management which seems to some to be the whole, and to others the most important part of it, and we must inquire what is the truth about this.' For the imperative ἔστωσαν, which closes the business of naming the three relations and asks content with such terms as are forthcoming, cp. 3. 1. 1275 a 29: Eth. Nic. 2. 7. 1108 a 5 sq.: Metaph. Z. 8. 1033 a 25 sq.: Plato, Soph. 231 A. Aristotle does not at this early point of the discussion think it necessary to mention that the claims of χρηματιστική to be a part of οἰκονομία are open to much question, but, as is often his practice, provisionally adopts a view which he will hereafter reconsider and correct.

12. τοῖς μὲν . . . τοῖς δέ. Who these were, is not known. Xenophon goes some way in this direction (cp. Oecon. 6. 4, *οὐκοῦν, ἔφη ὁ Σωκράτης, ἐπιστήμης μέν τινος ἔδοξεν ἡμῖν ὄνομα εἶναι ἡ οἰκονομία· ἡ δὲ ἐπιστήμη αὕτη ἐφαίνετο ᾗ οἴκους δύνανται αὔξειν ἄνθρωποι· οἶκος δὲ ἡμῖν ἐφαίνετο ὅπερ κτῆσις ἡ σύμπασα*: also Oecon. 7. 15 and 11. 9). He has, however, as great a dislike as Aristotle for most branches of *ἡ καλουμένη χρηματιστική*, and he thinks throughout of husbandry as the vocation of his *οἰκονομικός*.

14. πρῶτον δὲ περὶ δεσπότου κ.τ.λ. Aristotle investigates the relation of master and slave before he examines *χρηματιστική*, probably because he started with the aim of determining whether the *δεσποτικός* is the same as the *οἰκονομικός, πολιτικός*, and *βασιλικός*, but also perhaps because the slave is a part of *κτῆσις* (c. 8. 1256 a 2), and the part should be studied before the whole. The two aims which he proposes to keep in view in studying this subject reappear in c. 11. 1258 b 9, *ἐπεὶ δὲ τὰ πρὸς τὴν γνῶσιν διωρίκαμεν ἱκανῶς, τὰ πρὸς τὴν χρῆσιν δεῖ διελθεῖν*, and in 3. 8. 1279 b 12, *τῷ δὲ περὶ ἑκάστην μέθοδον φιλοσοφοῦντι καὶ μὴ μόνον ἀποβλέποντι πρὸς τὸ πράττειν κ.τ.λ.* So again in 2. 1. 1260 b 32 the aim is *ἵνα τό τ' ὀρθῶς ἔχον ὀφθῇ καὶ τὸ χρήσιμον*: cp. 6 (4). 1. 1288 b 35 sqq. The aim of the Politics is from the first twofold—partly scientific accuracy, partly utility. The eleventh chapter of the First Book is intended to be useful, not only to the *χρηματιστικός* and to the *οἰκονομικός*, but also to the *πολιτικός* (1259 a 33).

15. τὴν ἀναγκαίαν χρείαν. Cp. c. 5. 1254 b 29, *τὴν ἀναγκαίαν χρῆσιν*.

16. κἂν εἰ κ.τ.λ. See Bon. Ind. 41 a 4 sqq. Carry on *ἴδωμεν*.

18. τοῖς μὲν γὰρ κ.τ.λ. Some rate *δεσποτεία* too high, counting it as a science, and identifying the rule of the *δεσπότης* with household management and political and kingly rule (for with *πολιτική* and *βασιλική*—as Bonitz points out, Ind. 614 b 31—*ἀρχή* must be supplied, as in 1. 7. 1255 b 17): language to this effect is put into the mouth of Socrates both by Xenophon in the Oeconomicus and by Plato in the Politicus. This was one extreme. Others go to the other extreme, and regard the distinction of master and slave as resting only on convention, not on nature, and therefore as based on compulsion and consequently unjust. Aristotle here as elsewhere first sets before his reader two or more opposite views, and then seeks a view which will harmonize their contrariety (*λύσει τὰς ἐναντιώσεις*) and make either of them seem to possess a basis of plausibility (*εὐλόγως δοκοῦντα*) by showing that each is in a sense true and in a sense not true: cp. Eth. Eud. 7. 2. 1235 b 13, *ληπτέος* δὴ τρόπος ὅστις ἡμῖν ἅμα τά τε δοκοῦντα περὶ τούτων μάλιστα ἀποδώσει ('plene explicare, explicando exprimere,' Bon. Ind. 80 b 18 sqq.), καὶ τὰς ἀπορίας λύσει καὶ τὰς ἐναντιώσεις· τοῦτο δ' ἔσται ἐὰν εὐλόγως φαίνηται τὰ ἐναντία δοκοῦντα· μάλιστα γὰρ ὁμολογούμενος ὁ τοιοῦτος ἔσται λόγος τοῖς φαινομένοις· συμβαίνει δὲ μένειν τὰς ἐναντιώσεις, ἐὰν ἔστι μὲν ὡς ἀληθὲς ᾖ τὸ λεγόμενον, ἔστι δ' ὡς οὔ. Thus we learn, as the discussion goes on, that there is a δεσποτικὴ ἐπιστήμη (c. 7. 1255 b 22–39), though it has nothing great or impressive about it (1255 b 33), but that the master is not a master by virtue of science but by virtue of character (1255 b 20); he can, in fact, do without the δεσποτικὴ ἐπιστήμη (1255 b 35); it is no part of his essence and therefore no part of his definition. So again, the other side are only partially right (c. 6. 1255 a 3); their objection to slavery holds of one kind of slavery only.

Something has been said already (vol. 1. p. 139 sqq.) as to the question who these objectors to slavery were, who stigmatized it as not based on nature but only on convention, and therefore the offspring of force and consequently unjust. The notions 'conventional,' 'based on force,' and 'unjust' hang together in their contention significantly enough. The connexion which Aristotle traces (Phys. 4. 8. 215 a 3, and often elsewhere) between τὸ βίαιον and τὸ παρὰ φύσιν is inherited by him from Plato (Tim. 64 D) and from still earlier inquirers (cp. Plato, Protag. 337 D, ὁ νόμος, τύραννος ὢν τῶν ἀνθρώπων, πολλὰ παρὰ τὴν φύσιν βιάζεται—the words of the sophist Hippias). So Glaucon in his statement (Rep. 359 C) of the view of Thrasymachus and others about Justice contrasts φύσις with νόμος καὶ βία (ὃ πᾶσα φύσις διώκειν πέφυκεν ὡς ἀγαθόν, νόμῳ δὲ βίᾳ παράγεται ἐπὶ τὴν τοῦ ἴσου τιμήν). On the other hand, we trace the notion of a connexion between force and injustice in a well-known line of Hesiod, Op. et Dies 275—

καί νυ δίκης ἐπάκουε, βίης δ' ἐπιλάθεο πάμπαν,

and in a view referred to by Aristotle, Pol. 4 (7). 2. 1324 a 35—νομίζουσι δ' οἱ μὲν τὸ τῶν πέλας ἄρχειν, δεσποτικῶς μὲν γινόμενον μετ' ἀδικίας τινὸς εἶναι τῆς μεγίστης, πολιτικῶς δὲ τὸ μὲν ἄδικον οὐκ ἔχειν κ.τ.λ.: cp. 3. 3. 1276 a 12, where we find that some constitutions (e.g. tyranny) were popularly contrasted with others (democracy is probably meant) as founded on force, not on the common advantage. So again in 3. 16. 1287 a 10 sqq. that which is by nature and that which is just are tacitly identified. We hear later on (c. 6. 1255 a 8 sq.) that 'many of those versed in laws' impeached enslavement resulting from war, at any rate when based on a bare superiority of Might, but the persons referred to in the passage before us seem to have regarded slavery of all kinds and under all circumstances—even, it would seem, when imposed by Greeks on barbarians—as contrary to nature and unjust. This sweeping protest against slavery is certainly remarkable. We see from Plato, Laws 777 B sqq., how much difficulty was experienced in the practical maintenance and working of the institution.

23. ἐπεὶ οὖν κ.τ.λ. The object of the long sentence which **C. 4.** begins here, and which, like many other long sentences in Aristotle introduced by ἐπεί, is ill-constructed enough, is (as we see from 1254 a 13) to commence an investigation into the nature and function of the slave. It is evident that if Aristotle can show that the slave fills a necessary place in the household as an instrument of household science, raised above and somewhat dissimilar to instruments commonly so called, yet, like them, an instrument and an article of property, he will have gone far to solve the twofold question just raised, whether rule over the slave is the same thing as οἰκονομική, πολιτική, and βασιλικὴ ἀρχή, and whether the slave exists by nature, for the naturalness of the slave will result from his necessity, and rule over the slave will be clearly seen to be a less noble thing than rule over those who are not ὄργανα. Socrates (Xen. Mem. 3. 4. 12), in asserting a close similarity between the management of private and public concerns, had used the following argument —*οὐ γὰρ ἄλλοις τισὶν ἀνθρώποις οἱ τῶν κοινῶν ἐπιμελόμενοι χρῶνται ἢ οἷσπερ οἱ τὰ ἴδια οἰκονομοῦντες.* Aristotle, on the contrary, holds that to rule over slaves is one thing and to rule over freemen is another (c. 7), for slaves, unlike freemen, are mere animate instruments.

ἡ κτῆσις μέρος τῆς οἰκίας κ.τ.λ. As often happens at the outset of an inquiry, Aristotle accepts propositions which he will afterwards correct (see note on 1253 b 11). His definitive view is that property is rather a *sine qua non* (οὗ οὐκ ἄνευ) of the household than a part of it, and that the same is true of the relation of κτητική or χρηματιστική (of the sound sort) to οἰκονομία: cp. c. 10 (which, it would seem, must be taken to correct the passage before us and also c. 8. 1256 b 26–27), and see 4 (7). 8. 1328 a 21 sqq., where property is denied to be part of the πόλις, though necessary to it (1328 a 33 sq.). Not a few translators and commentators—among them, one MS. of the Vet. Int. (z, which inserts 'manifestum quod' before its equivalent for καὶ ἡ κτητική) and Leonardus Aretinus—make καὶ ἡ κτητικὴ κ.τ.λ. an apodosis, but Aristotle often introduces with ἐπεί a long string of protases, and perhaps it is better to begin the apodosis at οὕτω 30 and to avoid interrupting the continuity of the argument, which seems to me to be as follows:—Without necessaries men can neither live nor live well, hence property is essential to the household, and the science of acquiring it is a part of the science of household management, the end of which is life or good life; but instruments, whether animate or inanimate, are also essential to this science: hence an article of property is an instrument for the purpose of living, and property is a mass of instruments, and the slave is an animate article of property [and therefore an animate instrument for the purpose of living]. The proof, however, that articles of property are instruments for the purpose of living seems unsatisfactory, and Aristotle omits to show that the animate instruments of which Household Science stands in need must be, if human beings, slaves and not free. Sus. brackets the words *καὶ ἡ κτητικὴ μέρος τῆς οἰκονομίας* as having no bearing on the conclusion drawn in 30 sqq., but Aristotle's object seems to be to show, first the necessity of Property, and next the necessity of instruments, to Household Science. I am not convinced by Susemihl's arguments (Qu. Crit. p. 339 sqq.), that a rearrangement of the paragraph is called for.

25. ταῖς ὡρισμέναις τέχναις, 'arts with a definite end': Bonitz (Ind. 524 a 29) compares Metaph. M. 10. 1087 a 16, *ἡ μὲν οὖν δύναμις ὡς ὕλη τοῦ καθόλου οὖσα καὶ ἀόριστος τοῦ καθόλου καὶ ἀορίστου ἐστίν, ἡ δ' ἐνέργεια ὡρισμένη καὶ ὡρισμένου τόδε τι οὖσα τοῦδέ τινος*, but Metaph. E. 2. 1027 a 5, *τῶν μὲν γὰρ ἄλλων ἐνίοτε δυνάμεις εἰσὶν αἱ ποιητικαί, τῶν δ' οὐδεμία τέχνη οὐδὲ δύναμις ὡρισμένη· τῶν γὰρ κατὰ συμβεβηκὸς ὄντων ἢ γινομένων καὶ τὸ αἴτιόν ἐστι κατὰ συμβεβηκός* comes still nearer, and here the opposition is between a cause which works for a definite end and one which works *κατὰ συμβεβηκός*—cp. Rhet. 1. 10. 1369 a 32, *ἔστι δ' ἀπὸ τύχης μὲν τὰ τοιαῦτα γιγνόμενα, ὅσων ἥ τε αἰτία ἀόριστος καὶ μὴ ἕνεκά του γίγνεται καὶ μήτε ἀεὶ μήτε ὡς ἐπὶ τὸ πολὺ μήτε τεταγμένως*, and Metaph. E. 2. 1027 a 19, *ὅτι δ' ἐπιστήμη οὐκ ἔστι τοῦ συμβεβηκότος, φανερόν· ἐπιστήμη μὲν γὰρ πᾶσα ἢ τοῦ ἀεὶ ἢ τοῦ ὡς ἐπὶ τὸ πολύ· πῶς γὰρ ἢ μαθήσεται ἢ διδάξει ἄλλον; δεῖ γὰρ ὡρίσθαι ἢ τῷ ἀεὶ ἢ τῷ ὡς ἐπὶ τὸ πολύ, οἷον ὅτι ὠφέλιμον τὸ μελίκρατον τῷ πυρέττοντι ὡς ἐπὶ τὸ πολύ.* It is not clear whether Aristotle regards *οἰκονομική* as *ὡρισμένη*: at any rate it is hardly a *τέχνη*—rather a *πρακτικὴ ἐπιστήμη*, or part of one. For the thought, cp. Plutarch, An Vitiositas ad infelicitiam sufficiat c. 2, *ἡ κακία . . . αὐτοτελής τις οὖσα τῆς κακοδαιμονίας δημιουργός· οὔτε γὰρ ὀργάνων οὔτε ὑπηρετῶν ἔχει χρείαν.*

26. ἀναγκαῖον ἂν εἴη . . . εἰ μέλλει. See Jelf, Gr. Gr. § 853. 2. b.

27. οὕτω καὶ τῶν οἰκονομικῶν. Not to be completed by *τεχνῶν*, nor is *τῶν οἰκονομικῶν* masc., as Göttling, who supplies *τὰ οἰκεῖα ὄργανα*, would make it; the word to be supplied is probably *ὀργάνων*. It comes to the surface, as it were, immediately after in *τῶν δ' ὀργάνων*, and the translation 'the same thing will hold good of the instruments of household science' seems to be justified by the use of the gen. in Phys. 8. 8. 263 a 1, καὶ τῶν κινήσεων ἄρα ὡσαύτως: Pol. 1. 8. 1256 a 29, ὁμοίως δὲ καὶ τῶν ἀνθρώπων ('ebenso ist es nun auch bei den Menschen,' Bern.: cp. 1256 b 6, ὁμοίως δὲ καὶ περὶ τοὺς ἄλλους). Riddell (Plato, Apology p. 126) apparently interprets the passage before us thus, though he does not explain what substantive he would supply.

29. πρῳρεύς. Cp. Plutarch, Agis 1. 3, καθάπερ γὰρ οἱ πρῳρεῖς τὰ ἔμπροσθεν προορώμενοι τῶν κυβερνητῶν ἀφορῶσι πρὸς ἐκείνους καὶ τὸ προστασσόμενον ὑπ' ἐκείνων ποιοῦσιν, οὕτως οἱ πολιτευόμενοι καὶ πρὸς δόξαν ὁρῶντες ὑπηρέται μὲν τῶν πολλῶν εἰσίν, ὄνομα δὲ ἀρχόντων ἔχουσιν: Reipubl. Gerend. Praecepta, c. 15, ὡς οἱ κυβερνῆται τὰ μὲν ταῖς χερσὶ δι' αὑτῶν πράττουσι, τὰ δ' ὀργάνοις ἑτέροις δι' ἑτέρων ἄπωθεν καθήμενοι περιάγουσι καὶ στρέφουσι, χρῶνται δὲ καὶ ναύταις καὶ πρῳρεῦσι καὶ κελευσταῖς . . . οὕτω τῷ πολιτικῷ προσήκει κ.τ.λ.

30. ἐν ὀργάνου εἴδει. See Liddell and Scott s. v. εἶδος.

ταῖς τέχναις. Vict. 'in omni arte, quaecunque illa sit,' and so Bern. Sus. 'für die Künste,' but cp. ταῖς ἄλλαις τέχναις, 1256 b 34.

οὕτω καὶ τὸ κτῆμα. Here at length begins the apodosis. For οὕτω introducing the apodosis after a protasis introduced by ἐπεί, Eucken (de Partic. usu, p. 30) compares 1. 10. 1258 a 31–34.

31. τὸ κτῆμα . . . ὀργάνων ἐστί. Contrast Xenophon's account of κτῆσις in Oecon. 6. 4, κτῆσιν δὲ τοῦτο ἔφαμεν εἶναι ὅ τι ἑκάστῳ ὠφέλιμον εἴη εἰς τὸν βίον, ὠφέλιμα δὲ ὄντα εὑρίσκετο πάντα ὁπόσοις τις ἐπίσταιτο χρῆσθαι—so that friends, for instance (c. 1. 14), come under the head of property, and enemies too, if a man knows how to use friends and enemies. Xenophon's definition seems far too wide. Aristotle avoids this fault by treating property as an appendage of the household and as consisting of ὄργανα, but then there is such a thing as State-property, and his final definition of a κτῆμα in 1254 a 16 as an ὄργανον πρακτικὸν καὶ χωριστόν seems to imply that an ὄργανον ποιητικόν (a shuttle, for example) is not an article of property, so that his definition of κτῆσις appears to be as much too narrow as Xenophon's is too wide. His definition of wealth, however (c. 8. 1256 b 27 sqq.), is not open to these objections.

32. ὥσπερ ὄργανον πρὸ ὀργάνων. For this term cp. de Part. An. 4. 10. 687 a 19 sq., ἡ δὲ χεὶρ ἔοικεν εἶναι οὐχ ἓν ὄργανον ἀλλὰ πολλά, ἔστι γὰρ ὡσπερεὶ ὄργανον πρὸ ὀργάνων (the expression is somewhat unusual, and is therefore introduced by ὡσπερεί, ὥσπερ)· τῷ οὖν πλείστας δυναμένῳ δέξασθαι τέχνας τὸ ἐπὶ πλεῖστον τῶν ὀργάνων χρήσιμον τὴν χεῖρα ἀποδέδωκεν ἡ φύσις. Many have taken ὄργανον πρὸ ὀργάνων in this passage of the De Partibus Animalium as being equivalent in meaning to οὐχ ἓν ὄργανον ἀλλὰ πολλά, but this is not apparently its meaning in the passage before us. In Probl. 30. 5. 955 b 23 sqq. we read ἢ ὅτι ὁ θεὸς ὄργανα ἐν ἑαυτοῖς ἡμῖν δέδωκε δύο, ἐν οἷς χρησόμεθα τοῖς ἐκτὸς ὀργάνοις, σώματι μὲν χεῖρα, ψυχῇ δὲ νοῦν, and in de An. 3. 8. 432 a 1 sq. the soul is said to be like the hand, καὶ γὰρ ἡ χεὶρ ὄργανόν ἐστιν ὀργάνων, καὶ ὁ νοῦς εἶδος εἰδῶν καὶ ἡ αἴσθησις εἶδος αἰσθητῶν, where Trendelenburg explains 'manus, qua tanquam instrumento reliqua instrumenta adhibentur, instrumentum instrumentorum dici potest; eodem fortasse sensu νοῦς εἶδος εἰδῶν, i.e. ea species et forma quae reliquas suscipit, iisque, velut manus instrumentis, utitur.' Cp. also for the relation of the hand to other ὄργανα, de Gen. An. 1. 22. 730 b 15 sqq. Bonitz collects the uses of πρό in Aristotle (Ind. 633 a 34 sqq.), and, like Vict. before him, compares Pol. 1. 7. 1255 b 29, δοῦλος πρὸ δούλου, δεσπότης πρὸ δεσπότου, interpreting πρό both here and in the De Partibus Animalium as meaning 'praeferri alteri alterum.' (So Vict. 'instrumentum quod praestat et antecellit ceteris instrumentis': Lamb. 'instrumentum instrumenta antecedens.') Perhaps, however, something more than this may be meant—'an instrument which is prior to other instruments and without which they are useless.'

33. πᾶς ὁ ὑπηρέτης. Sus. brackets ὁ, following M[s] and corr. P[4], and πᾶς ὑπηρέτης (like πᾶς οἶκος, 1. 7. 1255 b 19) is a commoner expression, but the meaning is 'the class of assistants as a whole'—cp. Eth. Nic. 7. 9. 1150 b 30, ὁ δ' ἀκρατὴς μεταμελητικὸς πᾶς: Pol. 1. 2. 1252 b 28, πάσης τῆς αὐταρκείας: 7 (5). 11. 1313 a 21, πᾶσαν τὴν ἀρχήν. The slave is included under the wider term ὑπηρέτης (1254 a 8: Plato, Politicus 289 C, τὸ δὲ δὴ δούλων καὶ πάντων ὑπηρετῶν λοιπόν).

35. τὰ Δαιδάλου . . . ἢ τοὺς τοῦ Ἡφαίστου τρίποδας. The article is used before Ἡφαίστου, but not before Δαιδάλου. Should we compare the examples collected by Vahlen (Poet. p. 105) in his note on Ἰλιὰς καὶ ἡ Ὀδύσσεια, Poet. 4. 1449 a 1? As to these works of Daedalus, cp. de An. 1. 3. 406 b 18: Plato, Meno 97 D: Euthyphro 11 B: Eurip. Fragm. 373 (Nauck). The poets of the Old Comedy delighted to imagine the utensils of the kitchen and the household themselves doing what they were bidden, the fish cooking himself and so forth, and slaves thus becoming unnecessary. See the lively lines of Crates and others, Athen. Deipn. 267 e. The Greeks, in fact, as appears from these verses, looked back to a golden age when there were no slaves.

36. ὁ ποιητής. Homer (Il. 18. 376). The term, however, is used by Aristotle of others than Homer—Sophocles (Pol. 1. 13. 1260 a 29): an unknown poet (Phys. 2. 2. 194 a 30). Homer refers to them as 'of their own accord entering the assembly of the gods.'

35–37. ὥσπερ . . . οὕτως αἱ κερκίδες. For the construction of this sentence Rassow (Bemerkungen, p. 5) compares 3. 4. 1277 a 5, ἐπεὶ ἐξ ἀνομοίων ἡ πόλις, ὥσπερ ζῷον εὐθὺς ἐκ ψυχῆς καὶ σώματος καὶ ψυχὴ ἐκ λόγου καὶ ὀρέξεως . . . τὸν αὐτὸν τρόπον καὶ πόλις ἐξ ἁπάντων τε τούτων κ.τ.λ., and Sus. adds 3. 15. 1286 a 31, ἔτι μᾶλλον ἀδιάφθορον τὸ πολύ, καθάπερ ὕδωρ τὸ πλεῖον, οὕτω καὶ τὸ πλῆθος τῶν ὀλίγων ἀδιαφθορώτερον. In all these passages, after a similar case or cases have been adduced, the original proposition is reverted to and reasserted, perhaps in more distinct and vigorous language—the whole forming, however cumbrously, an undivided sentence. Neither καὶ before ὥσπερ nor εἰ before αἱ κερκίδες is correct.

37. αὐταί, 'of themselves': cp. 2. 9. 1270 b 8.

38. οὐδὲν ἂν ἔδει. This is in the main true, but slaves might even then be needed as ἀκόλουθοι (8 (6). 8. 1323 a 5 sq.), a purpose for which they were largely used.

1. τὰ μὲν οὖν κ.τ.λ. Aristotle has been speaking of the slave as 1254 a. an ὄργανον πρὸ ὀργάνων made necessary by the inability of shuttles or combs to do their work by themselves, but now he remembers that the word ὄργανον was commonly used of instruments of production; he feels, therefore, that what he has just said may be misleading and may suggest the idea that the slave is a mere instrument of the textile art, a mere complement of the comb, whereas in fact he is a humble auxiliary in life and action, which are higher things than weaving; hence he guards himself by pointing out that the slave is not an ὄργανον in the usual sense of the word—i. e. a ποιητικὸν ὄργανον (cp. Plato, Polit. 287 E, οὐ γὰρ ἐπὶ γενέσεως αἰτίᾳ πήγνυται, καθάπερ ὄργανον)—but a πρακτικὸν ὄργανον, for (1) he is a κτῆμα, (2) he is an ὄργανον πρὸς ζωήν, and life is πρᾶξις, not ποίησις. When he has added the further trait that the slave is, like any other κτῆμα, wholly another's, we know exactly what the slave is, and are prepared to deal with the further question whether a natural slave exists. The slave is a πρακτικόν and ἔμψυχον ὄργανον, and, though a human being, wholly another's. As to the use of μὲν οὖν here, see note on 1253 a 10.

3. ἕτερόν τι . . . παρά. Cp. 6 (4). 15. 1299 a 18.

5. ἔτι δ' ἐπεὶ κ.τ.λ. Aristotle now points out, further, that the difference between ὄργανα of ποίησις and πρᾶξις (and the slave is an ὄργανον of πρᾶξις) is a difference of kind.

8. καὶ ὁ δοῦλος. Cp. *καὶ ταῦτα* 6: life (*βίος*) is action, and the slave is an *ὄργανον πρὸς ζωήν*, 1253 b 31, therefore the slave also (as well as life) has to do with action. Mr. Postgate (Notes on the Politics, p. 1) notices the substitution here of *βίος* for *ζωή*.

τὸ δὲ κτῆμα κ.τ.λ. Cp. 5 (8). 1. 1337 a 27, *ἅμα δὲ οὐδὲ χρὴ νομίζειν αὐτὸν αὑτοῦ τινὰ εἶναι τῶν πολιτῶν, ἀλλὰ πάντας τῆς πόλεως, μόριον γὰρ ἕκαστος τῆς πόλεως*, and Eth. Nic. 5. 10. 1134 b. 10 sq. The slave is also a part of his master (c. 6. 1255 b 11 sq.: Eth. Eud. 7. 9. 1241 b 23).

9. τε γὰρ 'apud Aristot. saepe ita usurpatur, ut particula *τε* manifesto praeparativam vim habeat, eamque sequatur *καί*' (Bon. Ind. 750 a 2). Here *ὁμοίως δὲ* follows.

10. ὅλως, i.e. without the limiting addition of *μόριον*. 'Opponitur *ὅλως* iis formulis, quibus praedicatum aliquod ad angustiorem ambitum restringitur' (Bon. Ind. 506 a 10).

14. φύσει. Vict. 'hoc autem addidit, quia usu venit aliquando ingenuum hominem amittere libertatem, nec suae potestatis esse, cum scilicet capitur ab hostibus: is enim quoque eo tempore non est sui iuris, sed instituto quodam hominum, non natura.' For the definition of the slave here given, cp. Metaph. A. 2. 982 b 25, *ὥσπερ ἄνθρωπός φαμεν ἐλεύθερος ὁ αὑτοῦ ἕνεκα καὶ μὴ ἄλλου ὤν, οὕτω καὶ αὕτη μόνη ἐλευθέρα οὖσα τῶν ἐπιστημῶν· μόνη γὰρ αὐτὴ αὑτῆς ἕνεκέν ἐστιν.* The popular use of language implied quite a different view of freedom and slavery: see Pol. 8 (6). 2. 1317 b 2–13, and contrast the well-known passage, Metaph. Λ. 10. 1075 a 18 sqq.

15. See critical note.

C. 5. **17. πότερον δ' ἐστί τις κ.τ.λ.** Aristotle passes from the question *τί ἐστι* to the question *εἰ ἔστι*: cp. Metaph. E. 1. 1025 b 16 sqq. He has discovered that there is a niche in the household needing to be filled, but he has not yet discovered whether there are any human beings in existence who are gainers by filling it, and whom it is consequently just and in accordance with nature to employ as slaves.

20. οὐ χαλεπὸν δὲ κ.τ.λ. It is not easy to disentangle in what follows the two modes of inquiry, or to mark the point at which the one closes and the other begins. We see that the relation of ruling and being ruled satisfies all tests of that which is natural; it is necessary, and therefore natural (de Gen. An. 1. 4. 717 a 15)—it is for the common advantage, and therefore natural (Pol. 1. 2. 1252 a 34: 1. 5. 1254 b 6, 12: 1. 6. 1255 b 12–14)—the distinction of ruler and ruled, again, appears in some cases immediately after birth (*εὐθὺς ἐκ γενετῆς*), and this is a further evidence of naturalness (Eth. Nic. 6. 13. 1144 b 4–6: Pol. 1. 8. 1256 b 7 sq.: Eth. Eud.

2. 8. 1224 b 31 sqq.). Aristotle continues—'and there are many kinds of ruling and ruled elements, and if one kind of rule is better than another, this is because one kind of ruled element is better than another, for ruler and ruled unite to discharge a function, and the function discharged rises as the level of that which is ruled rises.' Aristotle is careful to point out that the lowness of the rule exercised by the master over the slave is due to the lowness of the person ruled, and that the rule of a natural master over a natural slave no more involves an infraction of nature or justice or the common advantage than the rule of the soul over the body.

21. **καταμαθεῖν** is used of things perceived at a glance without any necessity for reasoning: cp. 3. 14. 1285 a 1. So *ὁρᾶν* is occasionally opposed to *λόγος* (e.g. in Meteor. 1. 6. 343 b 30–33).

23. **ἔνια.** Soul and body, man and brute, male and female.

25. **ἀεὶ κ.τ.λ.** Cp. 7 (5). 11. 1315 b 4, *ἐκ γὰρ τούτων ἀναγκαῖον οὐ μόνον τὴν ἀρχὴν εἶναι καλλίω καὶ ζηλωτοτέραν τῷ βελτιόνων ἄρχειν καὶ μὴ τεταπεινωμένων κ.τ.λ.*

26. **οἷον ἀνθρώπου ἢ θηρίου,** 'as for instance over a man than over a brute.'

27. **ἀπό** is probably used in preference to *ὑπό*, because its signification is more comprehensive—the 'source' (cp. 6 (4). 6. 1293 a 19) rather than the 'agency'—and covers the contribution of the ruled to the common work as well as that of the ruler. 'In the genuine works of Aristotle *ἀπό* is never found in the sense of *ὑπό* with the passive, but all cases in which we find it conjoined with a passive verb may easily be explained by attaching to it its ordinary meaning; in many of the spurious writings, on the other hand, we find passages in which *ἀπό* is used in the sense of *ὑπό*—e.g. Probl. 7. 8. 887 a 22: Rhet. ad Alex. 3. 1424 a 15, 27' (Eucken, Praepositionen, p. 9). See also Bon. Ind. 78 a 9 sqq.

ὅπου δὲ κ.τ.λ. Cp. Hist. An. 1. 1. 488 a 7, *πολιτικὰ δ' ἐστὶ (ζῷα), ὧν ἕν τι καὶ κοινὸν γίνεται πάντων τὸ ἔργον· ὅπερ οὐ πάντα ποιεῖ τὰ ἀγελαῖα.*

28. **ὅσα γὰρ κ.τ.λ.** Camerarius (Interp. p. 35) quotes Cic. De Nat. Deor. 2. 11. 29. *Γὰρ* introduces a proof of the statement in 24 that there are many sorts of ruling elements, and also of ruled, and many kinds of rule. Given the fact of the existence of many compound wholes, each compounded of many constituents, it is not likely that all those constituents will be similarly related to each other and will deserve to be ruled in the same way. Sus. (following Dittenberger, *ubi supra* p. 1376) places *καὶ ἀεὶ βελτίων. . . ἔργον* 28 in a parenthesis, but perhaps *ὅσα γὰρ κ.τ.λ.* is intended to support this assertion as well as that which precedes it, and out of which it grows.

29. ἕν τι κοινόν. See Bon. Ind. 399 a 28 sqq., where Metaph. H. 3. 1043 a 31 is referred to, in which passage τὸ κοινόν is used as equivalent to ἡ σύνθετος οὐσία ἐξ ὕλης καὶ εἴδους, and such a σύνθετος οὐσία may be composed not only of συνεχῆ, but also of διῃρημένα, like τὸ ὅλον in 4 (7). 8. 1328 a 21 sqq. For a definition of τὸ συνεχές Bonitz (Ind. 728 a 33) refers to Phys. 5. 3. 227 a 10–b 2. Vict.: 'sive, inquit, ipsae illae partes continentes sunt, ut contingit in corpore hominis, quod constituunt membra quae sibi haerent, sive seiunctae, partibus non concretis, ut fieri videmus in civitate, quae constat e civibus distinctis, cohorte militum,' etc.

31. καὶ τοῦτ' ἐκ τῆς ἁπάσης φύσεως κ.τ.λ. Bonitz (Ind. 225 b 10) seems inclined to explain ἐκ in this passage as used 'pro genetivo partitivo,' but cp. de Part. An. 1. 1. 641 b 14, αἰτία τοιαύτη ἥν ἔχομεν καθάπερ τὸ θερμὸν καὶ τὸ ψυχρὸν ἐκ τοῦ παντός: 'and this (i.e. ruling and being ruled) comes to things possessed of life from nature as a whole' (ἐκ τῆς ἁπάσης φύσεως, cp. περὶ τὴν ὅλην φύσιν, 2. 8. 1267 b 28). Cp. also de An. 3. 5. 430 a 10, ἐπεὶ δ' ὥσπερ ἐν ἁπάσῃ τῇ φύσει ἐστί τι τὸ μὲν ὕλη ἑκάστῳ γένει (τοῦτο δὲ ὃ πάντα δυνάμει ἐκεῖνα), ἕτερον δὲ τὸ αἴτιον καὶ ποιητικόν, τῷ ποιεῖν πάντα, οἷον ἡ τέχνη πρὸς τὴν ὕλην πέπονθεν, ἀνάγκη καὶ ἐν τῇ ψυχῇ ὑπάρχειν ταύτας τὰς διαφοράς: Plato, Phileb. 30 A: Phaedrus 270 C: Meno 81 C, ἅτε τῆς φύσεως ἁπάσης συγγενοῦς οὔσης. Τὸ ἄψυχον is prior γενέσει, though not οὐσίᾳ, to τὸ ἔμψυχον (Metaph. M. 2. 1077 a 19). Inanimate nature shades off almost imperceptibly into animate (Hist. An. 8. 1. 588 b 4 sqq.).

33. οἷον ἁρμονίας. Bern. 'z. B. in der musikalischen Harmonie'—Sus.[2] 'wie z. B. (die des Grundtons) in einer Tonart': the latter suggests that ἐν ἁρμονίᾳ should be read instead of ἁρμονίας, and certainly, if the word is used in this sense, the genitive seems strange and in need of confirmation from parallel passages. Bonitz, on the other hand (Ind. 106 b 37 sq.), groups this passage with Phys. 1. 5. 188 b 12–16, where ἁρμονία appears to be used in a sense opposed to ἀναρμοστία—διαφέρει οὐδὲν ἐπὶ ἁρμονίας εἰπεῖν ἢ τάξεως ἢ συνθέσεως· φανερὸν γὰρ ὅτι ὁ αὐτὸς λόγος (15–16)—cp. Fragm. Aristot. 41. 1481 b 42: the meaning would thus be 'a rule as of order and system.' But Aristotle may possibly have in his mind the Pythagorean tenet referred to in Metaph. A. 5. 986 a 2, τὸν ὅλον οὐρανὸν ἁρμονίαν εἶναι καὶ ἀριθμόν: cp. Strabo 10. p. 468, καθ' ἁρμονίαν τὸν κόσμον συνεστάναι φασί: Plutarch, Phocion c. 2 *sub fin.*: Plato, Tim. 37 A: Philolaus, Fragm. 3 (Mullach, Fr. Philos. Gr. 2.

1): Plutarch, de Procreatione Animae in Timaeo c. 7. 1015 E, c. 28. 1027 A, c. 33. 1029 E sqq.: Stob. Floril. 103. 26 (p. 555. 27 sq.). Compare also the famous saying of Heraclitus (Fr. 45, ed. Bywater) as to the *παλίντροπος ἁρμονίη* [*κόσμου*] *ὅκωσπερ τόξου καὶ λύρης*. If the Pythagorean views are present to Aristotle's mind, some notion of musical harmony may be included in his meaning.

ἀλλὰ κ.τ.λ. Compare the similar dismissal of a physical parallel in Eth. Nic. 8. 10. 1159 b 23.

34. πρῶτον, 'in the first place.' Cp. 1254 b 2, *ἔστι δ' οὖν, ὥσπερ λέγομεν, πρῶτον ἐν ζῴῳ θεωρῆσαι καὶ δεσποτικὴν ἀρχὴν καὶ πολιτικήν*, and 10, *πάλιν*.

35. ὧν τὸ μὲν κ.τ.λ. Cp. Plato, Phaedo 80 A, and Isocr. De Antid. § 180.

36. δεῖ δὲ σκοπεῖν. Sus. (Qu. Crit. p. 342): 'orationem interrumpendo refellit quae quis de hac re contradicere possit.' For the rule here laid down, cp. Eth. Nic. 9. 9. 1170 a 22 sqq. In the next line *καὶ* before *τὸν βέλτιστα διακείμενον* seems to assert it not only of other things but also of man.

39. τοῦτο, the rule of the soul over the body.

τῶν γὰρ μοχθηρῶν ἢ μοχθηρῶς ἐχόντων. Cp. de An. 3. 4. 429 b 13, *ἢ ἄλλῳ ἢ ἄλλως ἔχοντι*: de An. 3. 4. 429 b 20 sq.: de Gen. An. 1. 18. 725 a 8, *τοῖς κάκιστα διακειμένοις δι' ἡλικίαν ἢ νόσον ἢ ἕξιν* (*ἢ ἕξιν* Z: om. Bekk.)—*ἕξις* being a more permanent and *διάθεσις* a less permanent state (see Mr. Wallace on de An. 2. 5. 417 b 15, who refers to Categ. 8. 8 b 28). *Μοχθηρῶς ἐχόντων* includes both, and relates to individuals who, though not *μοχθηροί*, are, more or less temporarily, in an unsatisfactory state.

3. δ' οὖν seems to be especially used by Aristotle when a transition is made from a disputable assertion to one which cannot be disputed: cp. Eth. Nic. 9. 11. 1171 a 33 (quoted by Vahlen, Beitr. zu Aristot. Poet. 1. 46), *εἰ μὲν οὖν διὰ ταῦτα ἢ δι' ἄλλο τι κουφίζονται, ἀφείσθω· συμβαίνειν δ' οὖν φαίνεται τὸ λεχθέν*. See also Meteor. 1. 13. 350 b 9: Poet. 4. 1449 a 9. 'Be that as it may, at any rate.' 1254 b.

4. ἡ μὲν γὰρ κ.τ.λ. It will be noticed that Aristotle conceives the soul to exercise *δεσποτικὴ ἀρχή* over the body even in the case of the lower animals, at any rate when they are healthily and naturally constituted. Plato (Phaedo 80 A) had already spoken of the soul as ruling the body despotically, and Aristotle follows in his track. We might ask whether Aristotle holds that the soul rules the body primarily for its own advantage, and only accidentally for that of the body (cp. 3. 6. 1278 b 32 sqq.), or whether the disparity which he conceives as existing between a natural master and a natural slave exists between the soul of an insect and its body. Aristotle's meaning, however, is that the body should be the ὄργανον and κτῆμα of the soul. But he does not always draw this sharp line of demarcation between the soul and the body: in Eth. Nic. 10. 8. 1178 a 14, for instance, he relates the body rather closely to the emotions.

5. πολιτικὴν καὶ βασιλικήν. Καὶ perhaps here means 'or,' as in the passages referred to by Bonitz (Ind. 357 b 20). Πολιτική and βασιλικὴ ἀρχή have this in common, that they are exercised over free and willing subjects (cp. 3. 4. 1277 b 7–9: and see notes on 1259 a 39–b 1). Perhaps the word βασιλική is added to enforce the inequality of νοῦς and ὄρεξις, and to exclude the notion that an alternation of rule between νοῦς and ὄρεξις is ever in place, such as is found in most πολιτικαὶ ἀρχαί (1. 12. 1259 b 4: 1. 1. 1252 a 15). For the relation of νοῦς (i. e. ὁ πρακτικὸς νοῦς) and ὄρεξις in moral action, see Eth. Nic. 6. 2. 1139 a 17 sqq. Ὄρεξις does not stand to νοῦς in the relation of a mere ὄργανον—the relation described in Pol. 4 (7). 8. 1328 a 28 sqq.—but is to a certain extent akin to it; see Eth. Nic. 1. 13. 1102 b 30 sqq., and esp. 1103 a 1, εἰ δὲ χρὴ καὶ τοῦτο (sc. τὸ ὀρεκτικόν) φάναι λόγον ἔχειν, διττὸν ἔσται καὶ τὸ λόγον ἔχον, τὸ μὲν κυρίως καὶ ἐν αὑτῷ, τὸ δ' ὥσπερ τοῦ πατρὸς ἀκουστικόν τι, where the relation of ὄρεξις to full reason is conceived as that of a child to its father, and a father, we know (Eth. Nic. 8. 13. 1161 a 10 sqq.), is not far from a king. On the other hand, in Eth. Nic. 5. 15. 1138 b 5 sqq., the relation of the rational to the irrational part of the soul is apparently construed differently, and compared to the relation of a master to his slave or to that of a head of a household to his household; we do not learn how it can be comparable to each of these two dissimilar relations. When Cicero (de Rep. 3. 25. 37) says—nam ut animus corpori dicitur imperare, dicitur etiam libidini, sed corpori ut rex civibus suis aut parens liberis, libidini autem ut servis dominus, quod eam coercet et frangit—he probably means by 'libido' something different from ὄρεξις. His notion of the relation of soul and body contrasts, we see, with Aristotle's.

6. ἐν οἷς. Cp. 1254 a 39, ἐν ᾧ τοῦτο δῆλον: 1254 b 3, ἐν ζῴῳ θεωρῆσαι: 1254 a 36, σκοπεῖν ἐν τοῖς κατὰ φύσιν ἔχουσι: and Plato, Soph. 256 C, περὶ ὧν καὶ ἐν οἷς προὐθέμεθα σκοπεῖν. Ἐν introduces the objects (ψυχή, σῶμα, νοῦς, ὄρεξις) in which the relations are exemplified. Ἐν is sometimes used in the sense of 'as to': see Vahlen, Poet. p. 188 (note on 17. 1455 b 14), who compares (among other passages) Plato, Rep. 2. 376 B, θαρροῦντες τιθῶμεν καὶ ἐν ἀνθρώπῳ . . . φύσει φιλόσοφον αὐτὸν δεῖν εἶναι, but this does not seem to be its meaning here.

8. τῷ παθητικῷ μορίῳ ὑπὸ τοῦ νοῦ καὶ τοῦ μορίου τοῦ λόγον ἔχοντος. That which is usually called *τὸ ὀρεκτικόν* is here termed *τὸ παθητικὸν μόριον*, and the term recurs in 3. 15. 1286 a 17, *κρεῖττον δ' ᾧ μὴ πρόσεστι τὸ παθητικὸν ὅλως ἢ ᾧ συμφυές· τῷ μὲν οὖν νόμῳ τοῦτο οὐχ ὑπάρχει*—cp. 3. 16. 1287 a 32, *ἄνευ ὀρέξεως νοῦς ὁ νόμος ἐστίν*. In the passage before us *τὸ ὀρεκτικόν* is distinguished from *τὸ λόγον ἔχον*, though Aristotle is sometimes not unwilling to treat it as part of *τὸ λόγον ἔχον* (see Eth. Nic. 1. 13. 1103 a 1 sq., quoted in the last note but one), and in the de Anima (3. 9. 432 a 24 sqq.) he speaks of the division of the soul into *τὸ ἄλογον* and *τὸ λόγον ἔχον* as not his own and not satisfactory. He evidently, however, accepts this division in the Politics; this appears still more distinctly in Pol. 1. 13. 1260 a 6 and 4 (7). 15. 1334 b 17 sq. An accurate treatment of psychological questions would in fact be out of place in a political treatise: see Eth. Nic. 1. 13. 1102 a 23 sq. It is not clear whether in the passage before us Aristotle regards *νοῦς* as the *ἕξις* of *τὸ λόγον ἔχον*, as in Pol. 4 (7). 15. 1334 b 17 sqq.

10. ἐν ἀνθρώπῳ καὶ τοῖς ἄλλοις ζῴοις, 'in man taken in conjunction with the other animals.' It is because the relation of ruling and being ruled appears elsewhere than *περὶ ἄνθρωπον*, that Aristotle expressly limits his inquiries in 3. 6. 1278 b 16 to the question, *τῆς ἀρχῆς εἴδη πόσα τῆς περὶ ἄνθρωπον καὶ τὴν κοινωνίαν τῆς ζωῆς*.

11. βελτίω. Cp. 4 (7). 13. 1332 b 3 sq.: Probl. 10. 45. 895 b 23 sqq.: Oecon. 1. 3. 1343 b 15. Being better, their example is to be studied as illustrating the true relation of animals to man (cp. 1254 a 37).

τούτοις δὲ πᾶσι. Vict. 'mansuetis omnibus.' Cp. Theophr. Caus. Plant. 1. 16. 13 (quoted by Zeller, Gr. Ph. 2. 2. 826. 1).

13. ἔτι δὲ κ.τ.λ. *Φύσει* is added because this is not always the case (cp. 1. 12. 1259 b 1). *Κρεῖττον* is probably not 'stronger' (as Sus. and Bern.), but 'better,' as in 3. 15. 1286 a 17: compare as to the relative excellence of male and female de Gen. An. 2. 1. 732 a 5 sqq.: Metaph. A. 6. 988 a 2–7. Aristotle is apparently speaking here, as in 1259 b 1, 1260 a 10, of the male and female human being.

15. ἐπὶ πάντων ἀνθρώπων. Cp. 3. 10. 1281 a 17, *πάλιν τε πάντων ληφθέντων*, where the meaning seems to be 'taking men as a whole, irrespective of wealth and poverty'; so here 'in the case of human beings as a whole, irrespective of sex.'

16. ψυχὴ σώματος καὶ ἄνθρωπος θηρίου. One would expect *ψυχῆς σῶμα καὶ ἀνθρώπου θηρίον*, and Thurot (see Sus.[1]) is inclined to alter the text thus, but the inversion is characteristic: cp. 2. 2. 1261 a 27, where one would expect διοίσει δὲ τῷ τοιούτῳ καὶ ἔθνος πόλεως, instead of ἔθνους πόλις.

18. ἡ τοῦ σώματος χρῆσις. The same criterion of a slave is indicated in 1. 2. 1252 a 31 sqq.: 1. 11. 1258 b 38: 1254 b 25. The slave is here defined by his ἔργον, and in 21 by his δύναμις (like the citizen of the best State, 3. 13. 1284 a 2): cp. 1. 2. 1253 a 23. And the end of a thing is the best to which it can attain (cp. 4 (7). 14. 1333 a 29, αἰεὶ ἑκάστῳ τοῦθ' αἱρετώτατον οὗ τυχεῖν ἔστιν ἀκροτάτου).

19. Μέν seems (as Thurot remarks: see Sus. Qu. Crit. p. 343) to be followed by no δέ. But this often occurs in the Politics (Sus.[1], Ind. Gramm. μέν), and here, as Susemihl observes, 'μέν praeparat quodammodo quaestionem de ceteris servis, qui non item natura sed lege tantum servi sint, sequente demum in capite instituendam.' It is taken up by μὲν τοίνυν, 1254 b 39, and then the δὲ which introduces c. 6 answers this μέν, and consequently in effect μέν 19 also.

οἷς introduces the reason why these are slaves by nature; they are so because it is better for them to be slaves, unlike some who will be mentioned presently. For this pregnant use of the relative, cp. de Part. An. 1. 1. 641 b 22.

20. ταύτην τὴν ἀρχήν, sc. δεσποτικὴν ἀρχήν, for τὰ εἰρημένα seem to be σῶμα and θηρίον (mentioned in 16–17). For (Aristotle in effect continues) the natural slave is very near to a brute in capacity, use, and bodily make, though there is a certain difference between them.

γὰρ (21) justifies what precedes: the slave has just been mentioned as on a level with the brute, and now facts are adduced which show how nearly they approach each other. The natural slave is a being who can be another's, just as any article of property can, but who differs from brutes in this, that he shares in reason to the extent of apprehending it, though he has it not. The slave seems to resemble in this τὸ ὀρεκτικὸν μόριον τῆς ψυχῆς (cp. Eth. Nic. 1. 13. 1103 a 1 sq.), rather than the body, and we are inclined to ask why the rule exercised over him is not to be a kingly rule, like that of νοῦς over ὄρεξις. It is because the slave can apprehend reason that he should be addressed with νουθέτησις (1. 13. 1260 b 5), and not with commands alone, as Plato suggested.

23. τὰ ἄλλα ζῷα. Usually used where ἄνθρωπος has gone before (as in 1254 b 10), but here apparently in contradistinction to δοῦλος, as in 3. 9. 1280 a 32.

αἰσθανόμενα. For the part. in place of the finite verb, cp. 2. 5. 1263 a 18 and 4 (7). 14. 1333 a 18, though it is possible that here some verb should be supplied from ὑπηρετεῖ. Cp. also ὅσοι μήτε πλούσιοι μήτε ἀξίωμα ἔχουσιν ἀρετῆς μηδέν, 3. 11. 1281 b 24, and see Vahlen's note on Poet. 24. 1459 b 7 (p. 243).

24. παθήμασιν. 'Usus Aristotelicus vocis πάθημα ita exponetur, ut appareat inter πάθημα et πάθος non esse certum significationis discrimen, sed eadem fere vi et sensus varietate utrumque nomen, saepius alterum, alterum rarius usurpari' (Bon. Ind. 554 a 56 sqq.). For the expression παθήμασιν ὑπηρετεῖ, cp. 7 (5). 10. 1312 b 30, τοῖς θυμοῖς ἀκολουθεῖν, and for the thought 4 (7). 13. 1332 b 3, τὰ μὲν οὖν ἄλλα τῶν ζῴων μάλιστα μὲν τῇ φύσει ζῇ, μικρὰ δ' ἔνια καὶ τοῖς ἔθεσιν, ἄνθρωπος δὲ καὶ λόγῳ, μόνον γὰρ ἔχει λόγον.

καὶ ἡ χρεία. The use made of the slave, no less than his capacity. The use made of tame animals for food is not taken into account: cp. 1. 8. 1256 b 17, καὶ διὰ τὴν χρῆσιν καὶ διὰ τὴν τροφήν.

παραλλάττει, 'diverges': cp. de Part. An. 2. 9. 655 a 18: de Gen. An. 3. 10. 760 a 16: Probl. 11. 58. 905 b 8. For the thought, cp. Σοφία Σειράχ 30. 24, χορτάσματα καὶ ῥάβδος καὶ φορτία ὄνῳ, ἄρτος καὶ παιδεία καὶ ἔργον οἰκέτῃ: Pol. 1. 2. 1252 b 12, ὁ γὰρ βοῦς ἀντ' οἰκέτου τοῖς πένησίν ἐστιν: and Aeschyl. Fragm. 188 (Nauck).

25. τῷ σώματι, 'with the body,' is to be taken with βοήθεια and not made dependent on τἀναγκαῖα, as Vict. makes it; cp. 1. 2. 1252 a 33: 1. 11. 1258 b 38.

27. βούλεται μὲν οὖν κ.τ.λ. Aristotle has implied in what he has just been saying that there is a difference between the souls of the free and the slave, and now he continues—'Nature's wish, indeed, is to make the bodies also of freemen and slaves different, no less than their souls, but' etc. He evidently feels that he may be asked why the bodies of slaves are not more like those of the domestic animals than they are. He hints in ὀρθὰ 29 that the crouching carriage of slaves marks them off from man, and allies them to the horse or ox. Aristotle attached much importance to the erect attitude of man: cp. de Part. An. 2. 10. 656 a 10, εὐθὺς γὰρ καὶ τὰ φύσει μόρια κατὰ φύσιν ἔχει τούτῳ μόνῳ, καὶ τὸ τούτου ἄνω πρὸς τὸ τοῦ ὅλου ἔχει ἄνω· μόνον γὰρ ὀρθόν ἐστι τῶν ζῴων ἄνθρωπος: 4. 10. 686 a 27, ὀρθὸν μὲν γάρ ἐστι μόνον τῶν ζῴων διὰ τὸ τὴν φύσιν αὐτοῦ καὶ τὴν οὐσίαν εἶναι θείαν· ἔργον δὲ τοῦ θειοτάτου τὸ νοεῖν καὶ φρονεῖν· τοῦτο δ' οὐ ῥᾴδιον πολλοῦ τοῦ ἄνωθεν ἐπικειμένου σώματος· τὸ γὰρ βάρος δυσκίνητον ποιεῖ τὴν διάνοιαν καὶ τὴν κοινὴν αἴσθησιν. As to the failure of nature to give effect to her purposes, perhaps she was thought by Aristotle to miss her mark more often in respect of the body than the soul: cp. de Gen. An. 4. 10. 778 a 4, βούλεται μὲν οὖν ἡ φύσις τοῖς τούτων ἀριθμοῖς ἀριθμεῖν τὰς γενέσεις καὶ τὰς τελευτάς, οὐκ ἀκριβοῖ δὲ διά τε τὴν τῆς ὕλης *ἀοριστίαν καὶ διὰ τὸ γίνεσθαι πολλὰς ἀρχάς, αἱ τὰς γενέσεις τὰς κατὰ φύσιν καὶ τὰς φθορὰς ἐμποδίζουσαι πολλάκις αἴτιαι τῶν παρὰ φύσιν συμπιπτόντων εἰσίν.*

31. If this parenthesis is more than a marginal remark which has crept into the text, it is probably intended to draw out the contrast between *πολιτικὸς βίος* and *ἀναγκαῖαι ἐργασίαι*: the mere mention of all that is implied in the former will suffice to show the unfitness, physical no less than mental, of the slave for it. For **γίνεται διῃρημένος** ('comes to be divided'), see Top. 7. 5. 154 b 11, 22: 155 a 9: Pol. 7 (5). 9. 1310 a 24, and notes on 1252 b 7, 1264 a 14. The contrast of *πολεμικαί* and *εἰρηνικαὶ πράξεις*, as constituting the work of the citizen, is familiar enough to us from 4 (7). 14. 1333 a 30 sq., though *πολεμικαὶ ἀσκήσεις* are distinguished from *πολιτικαί* in 5 (8). 6. 1341 a 8. Cp. [Plutarch] De Liberis Educandis c. 13. 9 c, *δοτέον οὖν τοῖς παισὶν ἀναπνοὴν τῶν συνεχῶν πόνων, ἐνθυμουμένους ὅτι πᾶς ὁ βίος ἡμῶν εἰς ἄνεσιν καὶ σπουδὴν διῄρηται, καὶ διὰ τοῦτο οὐ μόνον ἐγρήγορσις, ἀλλὰ καὶ ὕπνος εὑρέθη, οὐδὲ πόλεμος, ἀλλὰ καὶ εἰρήνη.*

33. τοὺς μὲν . . . ψυχάς. Vict. explains, 'ut servi scilicet natura corpora habeant liberorum hominum, liberi autem animos servorum.' But we can hardly supply 'of slaves' after *τὰς ψυχάς*, and besides, if a freeman had the soul of a slave, that would be no illustration of the failure of Nature to give effect to her purpose in respect of the *bodies* of freemen and slaves, and this alone is in question. Nor would such a freeman be a freeman by nature; yet, as Giphanius says (p. 63), 'de natura et servis et liberis agimus, non de iis qui lege et instituto.' These two latter objections also apply to the translation of *τοὺς μὲν—τοὺς δὲ* as 'some slaves' and 'other slaves.' If a slave had the soul of a freeman, the failure of Nature would be in respect of his soul, not his body, and he would not be a natural slave. Two interpretations seem open to us. 1. We may refer *τοὺς μὲν* to slaves, like *τὰ μὲν* 28, and *τοὺς δὲ* to freemen, like *τὰ δὲ* 29, and translate, 'but the very contrary often comes to pass' (cp. 1. 9. 1257 b 33), 'that (the body does not match the soul, but that) slaves have the bodies of freemen and freemen the souls.' Aristotle might have said 'and freemen the bodies of slaves,' but what he wishes to draw attention to is the occasional disjunction of a freeman's body from a freeman's soul. This resembles the interpretation of Bernays. Or 2. we may adopt the rendering of Sepulveda—'saepe tamen accidit oppositum, ut alii corpora, alii animos ingenuorum habeant'—that one set of people have the bodies of freemen and another the souls, or, in other words, that bodily excellence is parted from excellence of soul. I incline on the whole to the former interpretation. It should be noted that Antisthenes had said that souls are shaped in the likeness of the bodies they dwell in (fr. 33. Mullach, Fr. Philos. Gr. 2. 279, ἐντεῦθεν Ἀντισθένης ὁμοσχήμονάς φησι τὰς ψυχὰς τοῖς περιέχουσι σώμασιν εἶναι): his remark, however, seems to have referred, primarily at any rate, to the souls of the dead.

34. **ἐπεὶ . . . γε** justifies what precedes by pointing out what would result if the contrary were the case (cp. 1255 a 19: Meteor. 1. 4. 342 a 15—if the *γένεσις* of lightning-bolts were not *ἔκκρισις* but *ἔκκαυσις*, they would ascend instead of descending as they do). So here, to prove that Nature sometimes fails to make the bodies of slaves and freemen different, the argument is that 'if it were not so—if all freemen were far superior in physical aspect to slaves—no one would be found to dispute the justice of slavery.' The argument shows how keenly the Greeks appreciated physical excellence and beauty: here the same thing is said of physical excellence as is said of excellence of body and soul together in 4 (7). 14. 1332 b 16 sqq. and Plato, Polit. 301 D–E. We also note that the Greek statues of gods were evidently in respect of physical beauty much above the Greek average: compare Cic. de Nat. Deor. 1. 28. 79, quotus enim quisque formosus est? Athenis cum essem, e gregibus epheborum vix singuli reperiebantur, and see C. F. Hermann, Gr. Antiqq. 3. § 4, who also refers to Dio Chrys. Or. 21. 500 R.

35. **τοὺς ὑπολειπομένους**, 'inferiores': so Bonitz (Ind. 800 a 35), who traces this signification to the simpler one, 'tardius aliis moveri, remanere in via.'

37. **εἰ δ' ἐπὶ κ.τ.λ.** Aristotle wins an unexpected argument in favour of his doctrine of slavery from the appeal which he has just made to Greek sentiment. 'But if this holds good of a difference of body'—i. e. if a vast physical superiority confers the right to hold as slaves those who are less well endowed in this respect—'with much more justice may it be laid down in the case of a difference of soul,' on which Aristotle has rested the distinction of master and slave.

38. For the thought, cp. Eth. Nic. 1. 13. 1102 b 21 sq., and (with Giph.) Plato, Symp. 216 D–217 A: Cic. de Offic. 1. 5. 15. Aristotle hints that as it is not easy to discern superiority of soul, we need not wonder that the right of the natural master should be disputed.

39. **ὅτι μὲν τοίνυν εἰσὶ φύσει τινὲς οἱ μὲν ἐλεύθεροι οἱ δὲ δοῦλοι.** Cp. c. 6. 1255 b 6, *καὶ ὅτι ἔν τισι διώρισται τὸ τοιοῦτον, ὧν συμφέρει τῷ μὲν τὸ δουλεύειν, τῷ δὲ τὸ δεσπόζειν*, a passage which seems to make in favour of the view according to which οἱ μὲν and οἱ δὲ (1255 a 1) are subdivisions of a class designated by τινές. Οἷς, 1255 a 2, is carelessly made to refer to οἱ δὲ only (cp. βιασθεῖσι in 1255 b 15).

C. 6. 1255 a. **3** sqq. The following summary will explain the way in which I incline to interpret the much-disputed passage which follows. The view that slavery is contrary to nature is true τρόπον τινά—i. e. if limited to the enslavement of those who are slaves only by convention. For in fact there are such slaves: the law by which captives of war are accounted the slaves of the victors is nothing but a convention. (Aristotle does not necessarily imply that this was the only way in which slaves by convention came into being. They might evidently come into being in other ways—through descent, through debt, through sale by parents and the like. Into these minutiae he does not enter.) This provision (he proceeds) is dealt with by many who concern themselves with the study of laws, just as any peccant public adviser might be dealt with—they impeach it for unconstitutionality; they exclaim against the idea that anyone who may be overpowered by superior force is to be the slave of the person who happens to possess that superior force. Some are against the law, others are for it, and even accomplished men take different sides. (It appears to me that the πολλοὶ τῶν ἐν τοῖς νόμοις who are here represented as objecting to slavery based on a mere superiority in might must be distinguished from the authorities mentioned in 1253 b 20 as holding that *all* slavery is conventional and contrary to nature. The πολλοὶ τῶν ἐν τοῖς νόμοις do not seem to have objected to slavery based on a superiority of excellence as distinguished from a mere superiority of might. Hence they probably did not object to the enslavement of barbarians in war by Greeks: we see, indeed, that not all the defenders of the law were prepared to defend its application to Greeks. In c. 2. 1252 b 9 the barbarian and the slave, not the conquered person and the slave, are said to be identified by the poets.) Now what is it that alone makes this conflict of view possible? It is that the two contentions 'overlap' in a common principle accepted by both, which affords them a common standing-ground, relates them to each other, and limits their antagonism. They both in fact appeal to the common principle that 'Force is not without Virtue.' Thus they differ only on the question what is just in this matter, not as to the relation between Force and Virtue. The one side pleads that, as Force implies Virtue, Force has a right to enslave: the other side pleads that as Virtue goes with Force and Virtue conciliates good-will, good-will will exist between those who are rightfully masters and slaves. Thus the one side rests just slavery on good-will between master and slave, and condemns slavery resulting from war, when good-will is absent, while the other side rests just slavery simply on the presence of superior Force. (We are not told that those who held slavery resulting from war to be unjust in the absence of good-will between the enslaver and the enslaved also held that good-will must necessarily be absent in all cases of enslavement through war. Their contention rather was that it was not safe to make Force of one, unaccompanied by good-will, the test of just slavery.)

This conflict of opinion is, as has been said, evidently due to the fact that both parties make an appeal to the common principle that 'Force is not without Virtue,' for suppose that they gave up this common standing-ground, ceased to shelter their claims under those of Virtue, and thus came to stand apart in unqualified antagonism, then the other line of argument (ἄτεροι λόγοι) on which they must necessarily fall back—the contention that superiority in virtue confers no claim to rule—is so wholly devoid of weight and plausibility, that no conflict would arise. (Those who connect the right to enslave with superior force, and those who connect it with the existence of mutual good-will between master and slave, are regarded as having two lines of argument open to them: either they may derive the claims of force and good-will to be the justifying ground of slavery from the claims of virtue, and thus shelter themselves under the latter, or they may impugn the claims of virtue; but if they impugn them, their own contentions lose all weight and cease to produce any serious debate.)

We see then that the solid element in this pair of contending views, if we take them in the form which they assume when they possess any weight at all, is to be found in the principle that superiority in virtue confers the right to rule and to rule as a master rules. We shall arrive at exactly the same result if we examine another view on the subject.

We have hitherto had to do with those who discuss the law in question on its merits; but there are those who support slavery arising through war on the broad ground that it is authorized by a law and that that which is so authorized is *ipso facto* just. But a law, though a justifying ground, is not everything in this matter. For the war may be an unjust one, and either on this ground or on grounds personal to himself, the man enslaved through war may be undeserving of his fate: injustices of this kind the law will not avail to make just. In fact, these inquirers admit as much themselves, and contradict their own plea. For they say that Greeks are not to be enslaved, but only barbarians, since barbarians are slaves everywhere (πανταχοῦ δοῦλοι) and Greeks nowhere slaves. They make the same distinction in reference to nobility. They say that Greek nobility is nobility everywhere and in an absolute sense, but barbarian nobility is only local. Thus they hold that there are such beings as πανταχοῦ, ἁπλῶς δοῦλοι—πανταχοῦ, ἁπλῶς ἐλεύθεροι and εὐγενεῖς: Theodectes, in fact, connects the latter quality with descent from the gods. What else then do they do but mark off slave and free by a reference to virtue and its opposite? For descent from the good is, they imply, equivalent to goodness, and so it generally is, though not invariably, since Nature sometimes misses her aim.

3. **οἱ τἀναντία φάσκοντες.** For φάσκειν used of philosophers or others laying down a dogma, cp. c. 13. 1260 b 6.

6. **ὁ γὰρ νόμος κ.τ.λ.** As I understand the passage, it is only this particular law that is here said to be an ὁμολογία. The law enacting the slavery of captives taken in war, ὅταν πολεμούντων πόλις ἁλῷ, is said to be a νόμος ἀΐδιος by Xenophon (Cyrop. 7. 5. 73: cp. Thuc. 1. 76. 2, quoted by Camerarius). Aristotle does not notice the limits commonly imposed on the exercise of this right in wars between Greek States: see as to this C. F. Hermann, Gr. Antiqq. 3. § 12, who notes that, as a rule, captives taken in war were enslaved only when the cities to which they belonged were razed, and that they were commonly reserved by the State which captured them for exchange or ransom. The reference of law to an ὁμολογία seems to have been a commonplace: see Plato, Rep. 359 A: Xen. Mem. 1. 2. 42 (where it is put in the mouth of Pericles): Xen. Mem. 4. 4. 13 (where Socrates adopts the view). Aristotle himself not only reproduces the popular view in Rhet. 1. 15. 1376 b 9, but speaks in Eth. Nic. 8. 14. 1161 b 14 of friendships which rest on ὁμολογία (πολιτικαί, φυλετικαί, συμπλοϊκαί) as appearing to be of a κοινωνική type. In Pol. 3. 9. 1280 b 10, however, we find an emphatic assertion that those theories of the πόλις which reduce it to an alliance, and the law to a συνθήκη, are wrong (cp. Rhet. 1. 13. 1373 b 8, where κοινωνία is tacitly distinguished from συνθήκη). This does not prevent particular laws being based on convention, e.g. that which constitutes a medium of exchange (Eth. Nic. 5. 8. 1133 a 29). The object, it may be added, with which the law enacting enslavement through war is here stated to be an ὁμολογία is to justify the assertion ἔστι γάρ τις καὶ κατὰ νόμον (convention) δοῦλος καὶ δουλεύων, which immediately precedes. For ἐν ᾧ . . . φασιν,

cp. [Plutarch] Sept. Sap. Conv. 13, σὲ γάρ, ὦ Πιττακέ, καὶ τὸν σὸν ἐκεῖνον τὸν χαλεπὸν φοβεῖται νόμον, ἐν ᾧ γέγραφας κ.τ.λ.

7. **τοῦτο . . . τὸ δίκαιον**, 'this plea,' 'this justifying ground of claim': cp. Philip of Macedon's Letter to the Athenians, c. 21 (Demosth. p. 164), ὑπάρχει μοι καὶ τοῦτο τὸ δίκαιον, ἐκπολιορκήσας γὰρ τοὺς ὑμᾶς μὲν ἐκβαλόντας, ὑπὸ Λακεδαιμονίων δὲ κατοικισθέντας, ἔλαβον τὸ χωρίον: Demosth. adv. Androt. c. 70, οὐχὶ προσήγαγε ταὐτὸ δίκαιον τοῦτο: adv. Conon. c. 27, ἐπίστευον τῷ δικαίῳ τούτῳ, and c. 29, καὶ τοῦτο τὸ δίκαιον ἔχων.

8. **τῶν ἐν τοῖς νόμοις.** Cp. Metaph. Θ. 8. 1050 b 35, οἱ ἐν τοῖς λόγοις ('dialecticians,' Grote, Aristotle 2. 366): Rhet. 2. 24. 1401 b 32, οἱ ἐν ταῖς πολιτείαις. Camerarius (Interp. p. 40) quotes Eurip. Hippol. 430, αὐτοί τ' εἰσὶν ἐν μούσαις ἀεί. We see from Plato, Gorgias 484 C–D, with how much favour those who studied the laws were commonly regarded, and how much was thought to be lost by persons who continued to study philosophy after they had attained a certain age, and were thus led to neglect the study of the laws.

ὥσπερ ῥήτορα. Cp. Antiphanes, Σαπφώ Fragm. 1 (Meineke, Fr. Com. Gr. 3. 112)—

πῶς γὰρ γένοιτ' ἄν, ὦ πάτερ, ῥήτωρ * *
ἄφωνος, ἢν μὴ ἁλῷ τρὶς παρανόμων;

10. **κατὰ δύναμιν κρείττονος.** Contrast τὸ βέλτιον κατ' ἀρετήν, 21. Κατὰ δύναμιν is added because κρείττων is sometimes (e. g. in c. 5. 1254 b 14) used in the sense of better. It is, on the other hand, distinguished from βελτίων in 3. 13. 1283 a 41.

11. **καὶ τῶν σοφῶν.** As Sus. points out (Qu. Crit. p. 344), not all of those included under the designation οἱ ἐν τοῖς νόμοις (8) would deserve to be called σοφοί. Σοφοί are constantly contrasted with οἱ πολλοί by Aristotle: philosophers are not perhaps exclusively referred to here, but rather 'accomplished men' generally; even poets would be σοφοί, and it is just possible that there is a reference to Pindar (see note on 1255 a 18). It is still more likely that Aristotle remembers the saying of Heraclitus (Fragm. 44, ed. Bywater)—πόλεμος πάντων μὲν πατήρ ἐστι πάντων δὲ βασιλεύς, καὶ τοὺς μὲν θεοὺς ἔδειξε τοὺς δὲ ἀνθρώπους, τοὺς μὲν δούλους ἐποίησε τοὺς δὲ ἐλευθέρους. So we learn (Plato, Laws 776 C), that there were those who pronounced the Helot slavery of the Lacedaemonian State (ἡ Λακεδαιμονίων εἱλωτεία), which confessedly originated in conquest, to be εὖ γεγονυῖα.

13. **ἐπαλλάττειν.** The following are some of the more prominent uses of this word in the writings of Aristotle. It is used by him (1) of things adjusted to each other, fitting into each other,

dove-tailing—e. g. of teeth that fill each other's intervals, de Part. An. 3. 1. 661 b 21, ἐναλλὰξ ἐμπίπτουσιν (οἱ ὀδόντες), ὅπως μὴ ἀμβλύνωνται τριβόμενοι πρὸς ἀλλήλους, or of two bodies adjusted to one another, de Gen. An. 1. 14. 720 b 10: (2) of two things joined so as to be one, e. g. of hybrid constitutions, Pol. 8 (6). 1. 1317 a 2, where ἐπαλλάττειν is used in connexion with συναγωγαί, συνδυάζεσθαι (so in Plato, Soph. 240 C, ἐπάλλαξις seems used in a similar sense to συμπλοκή): (3) of two or more things united not by joining, but by the possession of a common feature or a common standing-ground, and yet different—things which overlap, or shade off into each other, or are σύνεγγυς to each other. So of a thing which unites attributes of two genera, and in which accordingly these two genera overlap—e. g. the pig, which is both πολυτόκον and yet τελειοτοκοῦν (de Gen. An. 4. 6. 774 b 17, μόνον δὲ πολυτόκον ὂν ἡ ὗς τελειοτοκεῖ, καὶ ἐπαλλάττει τοῦτο μόνον)—or of a thing which possesses many of the attributes of a genus to which it does not belong, as the seal does of fishes (Hist. An. 2. 1. 501 a 21, ἡ δὲ φώκη καρχαρόδουν ἐστὶ πᾶσι τοῖς ὀδοῦσιν ὡς ἐπαλλάττουσα τῷ γένει τῶν ἰχθύων). So here the arguments of those who plead that good-will is a test of just rule and of those who plead that Force by itself without the presence of good-will confers the right to rule are said ἐπαλλάττειν —i. e. to overlap each other (Mr. Heitland, Notes p. 11) and to approach each other—because both start from a common principle though they draw contrary deductions from it. The antithesis to ἐπαλλάττειν comes in διαστάντων χωρὶς τούτων τῶν λόγων 19, where the λόγοι are supposed to draw apart, and no longer to overlap or occupy common ground: cp. κεχώρισται in Περὶ μακροβιότητος καὶ βραχυβιότητος, 1. 464 b 27, ἢ κεχώρισται καὶ τὸ βραχύβιον καὶ τὸ νοσῶδες, ἢ κατ' ἐνίας μὲν νόσους ἐπαλλάττει τὰ νοσώδη τὴν φύσιν σώματα τοῖς βραχυβίοις, κατ' ἐνίας δ' οὐδὲν κωλύει νοσώδεις εἶναι μακροβίους ὄντας. With the use of ἐπαλλάττειν in the passage before us compare its use in Pol. 1. 9. 1257 b 35, where differing uses of the same thing are said ἐπαλλάττειν, or to be σύνεγγυς, because they differ only in not being κατὰ ταὐτόν, and are otherwise identical and of the same thing.

τρόπον τινὰ is used in opposition to κυρίως in de Gen. et Corr. 1. 4. 320 a 2 sqq. (Bon. Ind. 772 b 22) and to ἁπλῶς in Metaph. Θ. 6. 1048 a 29. Is the meaning this, that it is the tendency of Virtue to win willing compliance (Xen. Mem. 1. 2. 10), but that incidentally, when provided with the requisite external means, it has the power of using force with surpassing effect? Cp. Plato, Polit. 294 A, τρόπον μέντοι τινὰ δῆλον ὅτι τῆς βασιλικῆς ἐστὶν ἡ νομοθετική· τὸ δ' ἄριστον οὐ τοὺς νόμους ἐστὶν ἰσχύειν, ἀλλ' ἄνδρα τὸν μετὰ φρονήσεως βασιλικόν, and Pol. 1. 8. 1256 b 23, διὸ καὶ ἡ πολεμικὴ φύσει κτητική πως ἔσται. Whatever may be the exact meaning of τρόπον τινὰ here, it seems, like our phrase 'in a way,' to soften and limit the assertion made, as in de An. 3. 5. 430 a 16, τρόπον γάρ τινα καὶ τὸ φῶς ποιεῖ τὰ δυνάμει ὄντα χρώματα ἐνεργείᾳ χρώματα. For the thought conveyed in this sentence, cp. Solon, Fragm. 36 (Bergk)—

ταῦτα μὲν κράτει,
ὁμοῦ βίην τε καὶ δίκην συναρμόσας,
ἔρεξα:

Aeschyl. Fragm. 372 (Nauck)—

ὅπου γὰρ ἰσχὺς συζυγοῦσι καὶ δίκη,
ποία ξυνωρὶς τῶνδε καρτερωτέρα;

Aristot. Rhet. 2. 5. 1382 a 35, καὶ ἀρετὴ ὑβριζομένη δύναμιν ἔχουσα (is to be dreaded)· δῆλον γὰρ ὅτι προαιρεῖται μέν, ὅταν ὑβρίζηται, ἀεί, δύναται δὲ νῦν: Eth. Nic. 10. 8. 1178 a 32: Pol. 7 (5). 10. 1312 a 17, μάλιστα δὲ διὰ ταύτην τὴν αἰτίαν ἐγχειροῦσιν οἱ τὴν φύσιν μὲν θρασεῖς, τιμὴν δὲ ἔχοντες πολεμικὴν παρὰ τοῖς μονάρχοις· ἀνδρία γὰρ δύναμιν ἔχουσα θράσος ἐστίν, δι' ἃς ἀμφοτέρας, ὡς ῥᾳδίως κρατήσοντες, ποιοῦνται τὰς ἐπιθέσεις. Perhaps also Eth. Nic. 10. 10. 1180 a 21, ὁ δὲ νόμος ἀναγκαστικὴν ἔχει δύναμιν, λόγος ὢν ἀπό τινος φρονήσεως καὶ νοῦ should be compared. Giph. (p. 68) compares Plutarch, Dion c. 1, δεῖ φρονήσει καὶ δικαιοσύνῃ δύναμιν ἐπὶ τὸ αὐτὸ καὶ τύχην συνελθεῖν, ἵνα κάλλος ἅμα καὶ μέγεθος αἱ πολιτικαὶ πράξεις λάβωσιν.

14. καὶ βιάζεσθαι, 'to compel by force as well as to conciliate': cp. Isocr. Philip. § 15, καὶ πλοῦτον καὶ δύναμιν κεκτημένον ὅσην οὐδεὶς τῶν Ἑλλήνων, ἃ μόνα τῶν ὄντων καὶ πείθειν καὶ βιάζεσθαι πέφυκεν—a passage which exhibits the contrast of πείθειν and βιάζεσθαι, and one which Aristotle may possibly intend here tacitly, as is his wont, to correct.

15. ἀγαθοῦ τινός. Cp. 1. 1. 1252 a 2, and 3. 9. 1280 a 9, where δίκαιόν τι is contrasted with τὸ κυρίως δίκαιον. As the ἀγαθόν τι which Force implies may be quite other than ἀρετή (cp. Rhet. 1. 1. 1355 b 4 sq., where τὰ χρησιμώτατα τῶν ἀγαθῶν, such as physical strength, health, etc., are contrasted with ἀρετή), the inference that Force is not without Virtue is incorrect. This appears also from Pol. 3. 10. 1281 a 21–28, where Force is conceived separate from Virtue: cp. 3. 12. 1282 b 23 sqq. Eth. Nic. 4. 8. 1124 a 20–31, again, throws light on the passage before us: men claim respect from others on the strength of any good, κατ' ἀλήθειαν δ' ὁ ἀγαθὸς μόνος τιμητέος.

16. μὴ ἄνευ ἀρετῆς εἶναι τὴν βίαν. It will be observed that the inference drawn is that Force is not without Virtue, which does not necessarily imply that the possessor of superior force is superior in virtue.

ἀλλὰ περὶ τοῦ δικαίου κ.τ.λ. Cp. Eth. Nic. 5. 10. 1135 b 27, *ἔτι δὲ οὐδὲ περὶ τοῦ γενέσθαι ἢ μὴ ἀμφισβητεῖται, ἀλλὰ περὶ τοῦ δικαίου*, and 31, *ὁμολογοῦντες περὶ τοῦ πράγματος, περὶ τοῦ ποτέρως δίκαιον ἀμφισβητοῦσιν*: also Pol. 6 (4). 16. 1300 b 26, *ὅσα ὁμολογεῖται μέν, ἀμφισβητεῖται δὲ περὶ τοῦ δικαίου.* Here it is conceded on both sides that 'force is not without virtue,' and the only subject of dispute is, whether it is just for force to enslave not only the willing but also the unwilling.

17. **διὰ γὰρ τοῦτο κ.τ.λ.** *Διὰ τοῦτο* appears to refer to *ὅτι* 13—*βίαν* 16, and especially to *ὥστε δοκεῖν μὴ ἄνευ ἀρετῆς εἶναι τὴν βίαν.* One side argues from this, that, force being accompanied by virtue, and virtue attracting good-will, slavery is just only where there is good-will between master and slave, and that consequently the indiscriminate enslavement of those conquered in war is unjust; the other side argues that as force implies virtue, wherever there is the force to enslave, there is the right to enslave. For the power which virtue has of attracting good-will, cp. Eth. Nic. 9. 5. 1167 a 18, *ὅλως δ' ἡ εὔνοια δι' ἀρετὴν καὶ ἐπιείκειάν τινα γίνεται, ὅταν τῳ φανῇ καλός τις ἢ ἀνδρεῖος ἤ τι τοιοῦτον, καθάπερ καὶ ἐπὶ τῶν ἀγωνιστῶν εἴπομεν*: Eth. Eud. 7. 1. 1234 b 22, *τῆς τε γὰρ πολιτικῆς ἔργον εἶναι δοκεῖ μάλιστα ποιῆσαι φιλίαν, καὶ τὴν ἀρετὴν διὰ τοῦτό φασιν εἶναι χρήσιμον· οὐ γὰρ ἐνδέχεσθαι φίλους ἑαυτοῖς εἶναι τοὺς ἀδικουμένους ὑπ' ἀλλήλων*: Xen. Mem. 3. 3. 9, *ἐν παντὶ πράγματι οἱ ἄνθρωποι τούτοις μάλιστα ἐθέλουσι πείθεσθαι, οὓς ἂν ἡγῶνται βελτίστους εἶναι.* Those who argued against slavery unaccompanied by good-will between master and slave were probably among those who glorified rule over willing subjects, in contradistinction to rule over unwilling subjects. We trace the idea in Gorgias' praise of rhetoric as the best of all arts—*πάντα γὰρ ὑφ' αὑτῇ δοῦλα δι' ἑκόντων ἀλλ' οὐ διὰ βίας ποιοῖτο* (Plato, Phileb. 58 A–B). The doctrine was perhaps originally Pythagorean: cp. Aristox. Fragm. 18 (Müller, Fr. Hist. Gr. 2. 278), *περὶ δὲ ἀρχόντων καὶ ἀρχομένων οὕτως ἐφρόνουν· τοὺς μὲν γὰρ ἄρχοντας ἔφασκον οὐ μόνον ἐπιστήμονας, ἀλλὰ καὶ φιλανθρώπους δεῖν εἶναι, καὶ τοὺς ἀρχομένους οὐ μόνον πειθηνίους, ἀλλὰ καὶ φιλάρχοντας*, and Cic. de Legibus 3. 2. 5, nec vero solum ut obtemperent oboediantque magistratibus, sed etiam ut eos colant diligantque praescribimus, ut Charondas in suis facit legibus (which shows that what passed for the laws of Charondas in Cicero's day or in that of the authority he here follows had a Pythagorean tinge). Compare also an oracle quoted by Porphyry, de Abstinentia 2. 9 (Bernays, Theophrastos über Frömmigkeit, p. 59):—

οὔ σε θέμις κτείνειν οἴων γένος ἐστὶ βέβαιον [βιαίως Valentinus],
ἔγγονε θειοπρόπων· ὃ δ' ἑκούσιον ἂν κατανεύσῃ
χέρνιβ' ἔπι, θύειν τόδ', Ἐπίσκοπε, φημὶ δικαίως.

Xenophon is especially full of the idea that a ruler should rule so as to win willing obedience from the ruled and so as to make them εὔνους to him (see e.g. Mem. 1. 2. 10: Cyrop. 3. 1. 28: 8. 2. 4). One of the γνῶμαι μονόστιχοι ascribed to Menander (116) runs—Δοῦλος πεφυκὼς εὐνόει τῷ δεσπότῃ: cp. also the words of the attendant in Eurip. Androm. 58 (quoted by Camerarius, p. 42)—

εὔνους δὲ καὶ σοὶ ζῶντί τ' ἦν τῷ σῷ πόσει,

and Plutarch, Cato Censor, c. 20, where we read of Cato's wife—πολλάκις δὲ καὶ τὰ τῶν δούλων παιδάρια τῷ μαστῷ προσιεμένη κατεσκεύαζεν εὔνοιαν ἐκ τῆς συντροφίας πρὸς τὸν υἱόν. But the ruler, it would seem, should also feel εὔνοια for the ruled: cp. Democrit. Fragm. Mor. 246 (Mullach, Fragm. Philos. Gr. 1. 356), τὸν ἄρχοντα δεῖ ἔχειν πρὸς μὲν τοὺς καιροὺς λογισμόν, πρὸς δὲ τοὺς ἐναντίους τόλμαν, πρὸς δὲ τοὺς ὑποτεταγμένους εὔνοιαν: Plutarch, Reip. Gerend. Praecepta, c. 28. 820 F–821 B (where εὔνοια is used both of the ruler and the ruled): and Dio Chrysost. Or. 2. 97 R, where it is implied that the king, unlike the τύραννος, ἄρχει τῶν ὁμοφύλων μετ' εὐνοίας καὶ κηδεμονίας. Aristotle holds that not merely good-will but friendship (c. 6. 1255 b 13) will exist between the natural slave and his natural master, but, unlike these inquirers, he rests natural slavery, not on the existence of mutual good-will, but on the existence of a certain immense disparity of excellence between master and slave. (It is some years since, in writing this commentary, I was led to take the view I have here taken of the meaning of εὔνοια in this passage, and I am glad to find from a note of Mr. Jackson's (*Trans. Camb. Philol. Soc.* vol. ii. p. 115) that he has independently arrived at a nearly similar conclusion. Sepulveda, in his note on 'Quibusdam benevolentia ius esse videtur' (p. 12 b), long ago explained εὔνοια of the good-will of the ruled to their rulers and their willing consent to be ruled, but this escaped my notice till recently. See also Giphanius' note, p. 68 sq.).

18. αὐτό, 'by itself,' without any addition of good-will; cp. 3. 6. 1278 b 24, συνέρχονται δὲ καὶ τοῦ ζῆν ἕνεκεν αὐτοῦ (as contrasted with τὸ ζῆν καλῶς): 1. 9. 1257 a 25, αὐτὰ γὰρ τὰ χρήσιμα πρὸς αὐτὰ καταλλάττονται, ἐπὶ πλέον δ' οὐδέν. Pindar had implied that the rule of the stronger (Plato, Laws 690 B) and of βία (ibid. 714 E: cp. Gorg. 484 B) is in accordance with nature, but is reproved for this by Plato (Laws 690 C). A confusion or identification of the stronger and the better, as Socrates remarks (Gorg. 488 B–D), pervades the address of Callicles in that dialogue (see esp. Gorg. 483 D). It is, in Aristotle's view, from a confusion of this very kind that the doctrines of the advocates of Force derive whatever plausibility they possess. Athens had already, according to Isocrates, learnt that Might is not Right: cp. Isocr. De Pace, § 69, ὅτι μὲν οὖν οὐ δίκαιόν ἐστι τοὺς κρείττους τῶν ἡττόνων ἄρχειν, ἐν ἐκείνοις τε τοῖς χρόνοις τυγχάνομεν ἐγνωκότες, καὶ νῦν ἐπὶ τῆς πολιτείας τῆς παρ' ἡμῖν καθεστηκυίας.

19. ἐπεὶ . . . γε, as in 1254 b 34 (see note), confirms what has been said by introducing a supposition of the contrary: here it confirms διὰ τοῦτο: 'it is owing to the fact that the disputants start from a common principle—the principle that Force is conjoined with Virtue—that a contention between them is possible; for suppose Force and Good-will claimed respectively to be the basis of just slavery, without resting their claims on Virtue, no conflict of opinion would arise; the two claimants would neither of them have a case.' Ἄτεροι λόγοι, 20, I take to be the line of argument which the two contending parties would have to adopt, if they ceased to shelter their claims under the claims of virtue, and argued in effect that not superiority in virtue, but something else (force or good-will) confers the right to rule. If these words meant 'the one of the two views,' one would rather expect ἅτερος λόγος.

διαστάντων . . . χωρὶς τούτων τῶν λόγων, 'severed from the ground which they occupy in common and set opposite the one to the other' (for χωρὶς seems to mean 'apart from each other,' not 'apart from other arguments'), or, in other words, no longer 'overlapping' (ἐπαλλαττόντων): cp. περὶ μακροβιότητος, 1. 464 b 27, where κεχώρισται is used in opposition to ἐπαλλάττει, and Pol. 8 (6). 7. 1321 a 15, where διαστῶσι is opposed to συνδυάζεσθαι, a word used to explain ἐπαλλάττειν in Pol. 8 (6). 1. 1317 a 1.

21. ὅλως seems to qualify δικαίαν in contrast to δικαίου τινός: cp. 3. 9. 1280 a 21, ἔπειτα δὲ καὶ διὰ τὸ λέγειν μέχρι τινὸς ἑκατέρους δίκαιόν τι νομίζουσι δίκαιον λέγειν ἁπλῶς· οἱ μὲν γάρ, ἂν κατά τι ἄνισοι ὦσιν, οἷον χρήμασιν, ὅλως οἴονται ἄνισοι εἶναι, and 3. 9. 1280 a 9, where δίκαιόν τι is contrasted with τὸ κυρίως δίκαιον. Resting on *a* ground of right (for such the law in question is: cp. Eth. Nic. 5. 3. 1129 b 12, and Pindar, Fragm. 146 (Bergk), quoted by Plato, Gorg. 484 B, Laws 714 E), not on τὸ ὅλως δίκαιον, they argue that slavery in war is universally just, but they contradict themselves in the same breath. Ὅλως seems to be placed where it is for the sake of emphasis: for the distance at which it stands from δικαίαν, cp. 2. 2. 1261 a 15, where τὴν πόλιν is similarly severed from πᾶσαν, if we adopt the reading of Π[1], and see below on 1265 b 15.

26. τοὺς εὐγενεστάτους. *Εὐγένεια* was commonly viewed as akin to *ἐλευθερία* and a kind of superlative degree of it (3. 13. 1283 a 33 sq.). Hence the transition here and in 32 from the one to the other.

28. αὐτούς, i.e. Greeks. It is the way with people to do to others what they would not think of allowing to be done to themselves (4 (7). 2. 1324 b 32 sqq.).

32. τὸν αὐτὸν δὲ τρόπον κ.τ.λ. It is interesting to learn from Aristot. Fragm. 82. 1490 a 10 sqq., that the sophist Lycophron had challenged the reality of the distinction between the noble and the ill-born, for the ideas of freedom and nobility lay so close together in the Greek mind, that he or some other sophist may well have gone on to challenge the justifiability of slavery.

34. τοὺς δὲ βαρβάρους οἴκοι μόνον. Cp. Theophrast. Charact. 31 (Tauchnitz), *ἡ μέντοι μήτηρ εὐγενὴς Θρᾷττα ἐστί· τὰς δὲ τοιαύτας φασὶν ἐν τῇ πατρίδι εὐγενεῖς εἶναι*, and contrast the saying which Menander puts in the mouth of one of his characters (Inc. Fab. Fragm. 4: Meineke, Fragm. Com. Gr. 4. 229):—

ὃς ἂν εὖ γεγονὼς ᾖ τῇ φύσει πρὸς τἀγαθά,
κἂν Αἰθίοψ ᾖ, μῆτερ, ἐστὶν εὐγενής·
Σκύθης τις ὄλεθρος; ὁ δ' Ἀνάχαρσις οὐ Σκύθης;

See also Dio Chrysost. Or. 15. 451 R. Isocrates, on the other hand, bluntly refers to the *δυσγένεια* of the Triballi (De Pace, § 50). The contrast between *τὸ ἁπλῶς εὐγενές* and *τὸ ἐν τοῖς βαρβάροις* which the view mentioned by Aristotle implies reminds us of the contrast between natural society and society among the barbarians, which is implied in 1. 2. 1252 a 34–b 6. In 3. 13. 1283 a 35, however, we have *ἡ δ' εὐγένεια παρ' ἑκάστοις οἴκοι τίμιος*, where no difference is made between barbarians and Greeks.

36. καὶ is commonly used when an example is adduced: cp. 1. 12. 1259 b 8, *ὥσπερ καὶ Ἄμασις*.

39. ἀρετῇ καὶ κακίᾳ. A remark of the great Eratosthenes is referred to by Strabo (p. 66) thus: *ἐπὶ τέλει δὲ τοῦ ὑπομνήματος (ὁ Ἐρατοσθένης) οὐκ ἐπαινέσας τοὺς δίχα διαιροῦντας ἅπαν τὸ τῶν ἀνθρώπων πλῆθος εἴς τε Ἕλληνας καὶ βαρβάρους, καὶ τοὺς Ἀλεξάνδρῳ παραινοῦντας τοῖς μὲν Ἕλλησιν ὡς φίλοις χρῆσθαι, τοῖς δὲ βαρβάροις ὡς πολεμίοις, βέλτιον εἶναί φησιν ἀρετῇ καὶ κακίᾳ διαιρεῖν ταῦτα.* This may possibly be a comment on some communication of Aristotle's to Alexander (cp. Plutarch, de Fort. Alexandri 1. 6); but Isocrates had said much the same thing in his address to Philip (§ 154: cp. Panath. § 163). Plato had already (Polit. 262 D) found fault with the division of mankind into Greeks and barbarians, and the passage of the Politics before us shows that Aristotle is really quite at one with Eratosthenes. The fragment of Menander quoted above is in the same spirit. Cp. also Menand. Ἥρως, Fragm. 2 (Meineke, Fragm. Com. Gr. 4. 128),

Ἐχρῆν γὰρ εἶναι τὸ καλὸν εὐγενέστατον,
τοὐλεύθερον δὲ πανταχοῦ φρονεῖν μέγα.

1255 b. **2. ἡ δὲ φύσις κ.τ.λ.** Πολλάκις appears to qualify βούλεται, οὐ μέντοι δύναται, which words hang together and mean 'wishes without succeeding.' See Dittenberger, *Gött. Gel. Anz.* Oct. 28, 1874, p. 1371. We find πολλάκις, however, out of its place in 5 (8). 2. 1337 b 20, if we adopt the reading of Π[1], which is probably the correct one, and it may possibly be simply out of its place here. For the thought, cp. de Gen. An. 4. 4. 770 b 3 sqq.: 4. 3. 767 b 5 sq.: Rhet. 2. 15. 1390 b 22–31: Pol. 1. 2. 1252 a 28 sqq.: 2. 3. 1262 a 21 sqq.: 7 (5). 7. 1306 b 28–30: also Eurip. Fragm. 76, 166, 167 (Nauck), and Plato, Rep. 415 A, ἅτε οὖν ξυγγενεῖς ὄντες πάντες τὸ μὲν πολὺ ὁμοίους ἂν ὑμῖν αὐτοῖς γεννῷτε.

4. ἡ ἀμφισβήτησις. Cp. 1255 a 12, 17.

5. καὶ οὐκ εἰσὶν κ.τ.λ. These words have been interpreted in many different ways. Bern. (followed by Sus. and others) takes the meaning to be that 'not all actual slaves and freemen are so by nature': Mr. Congreve translates—'it is true that some are not by nature slaves, others by nature free, if you interpret aright *the some* and *the others* (οἱ μέν, οἱ δέ).' But does not οἱ μὲν mean 'οἱ ἥττους, as such' (τὸ βιασθέν, 1255 a 11: cp. 1255 b 15, τοῖς κατὰ νόμον καὶ βιασθεῖσι), and οἱ δὲ 'οἱ κρείττους, as such' (cp. τοῦ βιάσασθαι δυναμένου καὶ κατὰ δύναμιν κρείττονος, 1255 a 9)—unless indeed we prefer to explain οἱ μὲν as meaning 'those who are enslaved by force without deserving it,' and οἱ δὲ 'those who enslave others without possessing the superiority of virtue which makes the natural master'?

6. τῷ μὲν . . . τῷ δέ, neut. (as appears from τὸ μὲν . . . τὸ δέ, 7–8).

9. τὸ δὲ κακῶς, sc. δεσπόζειν: 'but a wrongful exercise of this form of rule is disadvantageous to both,' and then follows (τὸ γὰρ αὐτὸ κ.τ.λ.) the reason why both suffer together from a wrongful exercise of it. This is that master and slave stand to each other as whole and part.

11. μέρος τι τοῦ δεσπότου, cp. Eth. Nic. 5. 10. 1134 b 10 sq.

12. διὸ καὶ συμφέρον κ.τ.λ. 'There is something advantageous to both in common,' 'there is a community of interest': cp. 1. 2. 1252 a 34, διὸ δεσπότῃ καὶ δούλῳ ταὐτὸ συμφέρει, and Isocr. Epist. 6. 3, μὴ κοινοῦ δὲ τοῦ συμφέροντος ὄντος, οὐκ οἶδ' ὅπως ἂν ἀμφοτέροις ἀρέσκειν δυνηθείην. The test of τὸ κοινῇ συμφέρον (= τὸ δίκαιον, 3. 12. 1282 b 17), which is here applied to slavery, is the proper test to apply to any political institution, for τὸ κοινῇ συμφέρον is a condition of πολιτικὴ φιλία (Eth. Nic. 9. 6. 1167 b 2 sqq.), and the end of the political union (Eth. Nic. 8. 11. 1160 a 11). Cp. Plato, Rep. 412 D, καὶ μὴν τοῦτό γ' ἂν μάλιστα φιλοῖ, ᾧ ξυμφέρειν ἡγοῖτο τὰ αὐτὰ καὶ ἑαυτῷ, καὶ ὅταν μάλιστα ἐκείνου μὲν εὖ πράττοντος οἴηται ξυμβαίνειν καὶ ἑαυτῷ εὖ πράττειν, μὴ δέ, τοὐναντίον. Plato is perhaps thinking of political rule of a despotic kind, rather than of the private relation of master and slave, when he says (Laws 756 E), δοῦλοι γὰρ ἂν καὶ δεσπόται οὐκ ἄν ποτε γένοιντο φίλοι. Aristotle himself, however, finds some difficulty in explaining in Eth. Nic. 8. 13. 1161 a 32 sqq., how friendship is possible between an animate instrument like the slave and his master, there being no κοινωνία between them (cp. Pol. 4 (7). 8. 1328 a 28 sqq.), but here, in the First Book of the Politics, no notice is taken of this difficulty: on the contrary, in Pol. 1. 13. 1260 a 39 the slave is termed κοινωνὸς ζωῆς (where perhaps ζωή and βίος should be distinguished). Compare with the passage before us Xen. Cyrop. 8. 7. 13, τοὺς πιστοὺς τίθεσθαι δεῖ ἕκαστον ἑαυτῷ· ἡ δὲ κτῆσις αὐτῶν ἔστιν οὐδαμῶς σὺν τῇ βίᾳ, ἀλλὰ μᾶλλον σὺν τῇ εὐεργεσίᾳ.

14. τούτων, i.e. δεσποτείας καὶ δουλείας. Busse (De praesidiis Aristotelis Politica emendandi, p. 42) compares such phrases as ἀξιοῦσθαι τῶν ὁμοίων, τῶν ἴσων (2. 9. 1269 b 9, etc.).

15. βιασθεῖσι. Aristotle has by this time forgotten that his dative plural agrees with δούλῳ καὶ δεσπότῃ, and that βιασθεῖσι, which suits only with δούλοις, should have been replaced by a word which would have applied to δεσπότῃ also.

16. καὶ ἐκ τούτων. The fact had been already proved (cp. 1252 a 17) by tracing the development of κοινωνία: it had already been shown that δεσποτεία and πολιτικὴ ἀρχή belong to different κοινωνίαι: now it is shown that both the ruled and the mode of rule differ in the two cases. C. 7.

17. ἀλλήλαις, sc. ταὐτόν. With his usual economy of words, Aristotle makes ταὐτόν do here, though it fits in somewhat roughly.

19. ἡ μὲν οἰκονομική, sc. ἀρχή. The household seems to be here viewed as under a μοναρχία (the three forms of which are βασιλεία, τυραννίς, αἰσυμνητεία, 3. 14. 1285 a 17, 30: 6 (4). 4. 1292 a 18), because, though the rule of the husband over the wife is a πολιτικὴ ἀρχή (1. 12. 1259 b 1), the rule of the father over the child is a βασιλικὴ ἀρχή (ibid.), and that of the master over the slave is δεσποτική. Perhaps, however (cp. 3. 6. 1278 b 37 sq., where οἰκονομικὴ ἀρχή is distinguished from δεσποτεία), the relation of master and slave may not be included under οἰκονομικὴ ἀρχή. In that case οἰκονομικὴ ἀρχή will be a rule over free persons, but not over free and equal persons, like πολιτικὴ ἀρχή. It must be remembered that the equals over whom πολιτικὴ ἀρχή is said to be exercised are not necessarily ἴσοι κατ' ἀριθμόν, for they may be only ἴσοι κατ' ἀναλογίαν (Eth. Nic. 5. 10. 1134 a 27).

20. ὁ μὲν οὖν κ.τ.λ. Φανερὸν δέ, 16 . . . ἀρχή, 20, is parenthetical, and μὲν οὖν introduces a reaffirmation of what had been already implied in the definition of master and slave (1255 b 6 sqq.) —that a master is a master by virtue of his nature—in order that a transition may be made to δεσποτικὴ ἐπιστήμη and δουλικὴ ἐπιστήμη, and that these sciences, and especially the former, which Plato and Xenophon and Socrates had set on the level of βασιλική, πολιτική, and οἰκονομική, may be replaced on the humble level which is really theirs. Xenophon had said (Oecon. c. 13. 5), ὅστις γάρ τοι ἀρχικοὺς ἀνθρώπων δύναται ποιεῖν, δῆλον ὅτι οὗτος καὶ δεσποτικοὺς ἀνθρώπων δύναται διδάσκειν· ὅστις δὲ δεσποτικούς, δύναται ποιεῖν καὶ βασιλικούς, and again (Oecon. c. 21. 10), ὃν ἂν ἰδόντες [οἱ ἐργάται] κινηθῶσι, καὶ μένος ἑκάστῳ ἐμπέσῃ τῶν ἐργατῶν καὶ φιλονεικία πρὸς ἀλλήλους καὶ φιλοτιμία κρατίστη οὖσα ἑκάστῳ, τοῦτον ἐγὼ φαίην ἂν ἔχειν τι ἤθους βασιλικοῦ. This is just what Aristotle wishes to contest here and elsewhere in the First Book of the Politics. His way is to trace everywhere in Nature the contrast of the conditionally necessary (τὸ ἐξ ὑποθέσεως ἀναγκαῖον) and the noble (τὸ καλόν), and he makes it his business to distinguish carefully between the two. His work on the Parts of Animals is largely taken up with the inquiry, 'what share Necessity and the Final Cause respectively have in their formation' (see Dr. Ogle's translation, p. xxxv). To mix up the δεσποτικὴ ἐπιστήμη with πολιτική or βασιλική is to lose sight of this contrast. The management of slaves has for him nothing of τὸ καλόν (4 (7). 3. 1325 a 25, οὐδὲν γὰρ τό γε δούλῳ, ᾗ δοῦλος, χρῆσθαι σεμνόν· ἡ γὰρ ἐπίταξις ἡ περὶ τῶν ἀναγκαίων οὐδενὸς μετέχει τῶν καλῶν). As to **τῷ τοιόσδε εἶναι**, cp. Eth. Nic. 4. 13. 1127 b 15, κατὰ τὴν ἕξιν γὰρ καὶ τῷ τοιόσδε εἶναι ἀλαζών ἐστιν, and 6. 13. 1143 b 24–28. Aristotle's object is to correct Plato, who had said (Polit. 259 B), ταύτην δὲ (sc. τὴν βασιλικὴν ἐπιστήμην) ὁ κεκτημένος οὐκ, ἄν τε ἄρχων ἄν τε ἰδιώτης ὢν τυγχάνῃ, πάντως κατά γε τὴν τέχνην αὐτὴν βασιλικὸς ὀρθῶς προσρηθήσεται; Δίκαιον γοῦν. Καὶ μὴν οἰκονόμος γε καὶ δεσπότης ταὐτόν. The possession of the science of directing slaves in their work is not of the essence of the master (cp. c. 13. 1260 b 3 sq.), and therefore he is not defined by it. The master may dispense with such knowledge by employing a steward (35).

25. τοὺς παῖδας, 'the slaves.' Camerarius (Interp. p. 45) aptly refers to the Δουλοδιδάσκαλος of the comic poet Pherecrates. 'Ex ea fabulae parte, in qua ministrandi praecepta servo dabantur, petita suspicor quae leguntur apud Athenaeum, xi. p. 408 b—

> νυνὶ δ' ἀπονίζων τὴν κύλικα δὸς ἐμπιεῖν
> ἔγχει τ' ἐπιθεὶς τὸν ἠθμόν,

et xv. p. 699 f—

> ἄνυσόν ποτ' ἐξελθών, σκότος γὰρ γίγνεται,
> καὶ τὸν λυχνοῦχον ἔκφερ' ἐνθεὶς τὸν λύχνον'

(Meineke, Hist. Crit. Com. Graec. p. 82).

εἴη δ' ἂν κ.τ.λ. We rather expect ὀψοποιικῆς καὶ τῶν ἄλλων τῶν τοιούτων γενῶν τῆς διακονίας, but this slight looseness is characteristic. Perhaps with ὀψοποιική we should supply 'might be taught.' The example introduced by οἷον is sometimes put in the nom.—e. g. in 7 (5). 11. 1313 b 12, ἀλλ' εἶναι κατασκόπους, οἷον περὶ Συρακούσας αἱ ποταγωγίδες καλούμεναι. It would seem that the teacher at Syracuse confined his instructions to a portion only of the services needful to the household; Aristotle suggests that other and higher kinds of service should also be taught, such as cooking. For ἐπὶ πλεῖον, see Ast, Lexicon Platon. 3. 113: 'cum v. εἶναι et δύνασθαι est plus valere vel latius patere'—the latter here. Socrates had recognized a right and a wrong in ὀψοποιία (Xen. Mem. 3. 14. 5), but Plato counts ὀψοποιοὶ καὶ μάγειροι among the accompaniments of a φλεγμαίνουσα πόλις (Rep. 373 C): Aristotle's not unfriendly reference to the art in the passage before us illustrates his substitution (4 (7). 5. 1326 b 31: 2. 6. 1265 a 31 sqq.) of σωφρόνως καὶ ἐλευθερίως as the ideal standard of living for the Platonic σωφρόνως. He was himself charged by Timaeus the historian and others with being an epicure (see Polyb. 12. 24. 2, where Timaeus is quoted as saying that writers disclose by the matters on which they dwell frequently, what their favourite inclinations are—τὸν δ' Ἀριστοτέλην, ὀψαρτύοντα πλεονάκις ἐν τοῖς συγγράμμασιν, ὀψοφάγον εἶναι καὶ λίχνον: see also Grote's note, Aristotle 1. 24). Rational ways of living needed to be upheld against the savagery of the Cynics and the asceticism of some other schools. Besides, if the household slave could be taught to cook better, there would be all the less need to have recourse, in accordance with a common Greek practice, to the services of outside professionals. 'With the Macedonian times came in the fashion, continued by the Romans, of having cooks among the slaves of their household, a custom apparently unknown to the earlier Athenians. . . . The reader will here again notice the curious analogy to the history of medicine, for among the late Greeks, and among the Romans, the household physician was always a slave attached to the family' (Mahaffy, Social Life in Greece, p. 287, ed. 1).

27. γὰρ introduces the reason why instruction on these subjects should be extended, as Aristotle suggests.

29. πρό, according to Suidas (Meineke, Fr. Com. Gr. 4. 17) properly meant ἀντί in this proverb, but Aristotle quotes it in a different sense. Another proverb may be compared (Strabo 8. p. 339):—

ἔστι Πύλος πρὸ Πύλοιο· Πύλος γε μέν ἐστι καὶ ἄλλος,

or in a slightly varied form (Leutsch and Schneidewin, Paroemiogr. Gr. 2. 423):—

ἔστι τόκος πρὸ τόκοιο· τόκος γε μέν ἐστι καὶ ἄλλος.

32. τοὺς δούλους, yet in 33 δούλοις: see below on 1259 b 21.

33. οὐδὲν μέγα οὐδὲ σεμνόν. Cp. 4 (7). 3. 1325 a 25 sqq.: 3. 4. 1277 a 33 sqq.: and contrast the tone of the Oeconomicus of Xenophon, who, as we have already seen (above on 1255 b 20), finds in the direction of farm-work, and the winning of cheerful and vigorous service from slaves, a good school of political and even kingly rule (cc. 13, 21).

36. ἐπίτροπος. For the absence of the article, see Bon. Ind. 109 b 36, and cp. Eth. Nic. 1. 4. 1097 a 8, ἄπορον δὲ καὶ τί ὠφεληθήσεται ὑφάντης ἢ τέκτων κ.τ.λ. Vict. compares Magn. Mor. 1. 35. 1198 b 12 sqq., where φρόνησις is described as ἐπίτροπός τις τῆς σοφίας, for the ἐπίτροπος, though managing everything, οὔπω ἄρχει πάντων, ἀλλὰ παρασκευάζει τῷ δεσπότῃ σχολήν, ὅπως ἂν ἐκεῖνος μὴ κωλυόμενος ὑπὸ τῶν ἀναγκαίων ἐκκλείηται τοῦ τῶν καλῶν τι καὶ προσηκόντων πράττειν: cp. also the story of Pheraulas and Sacas (Xen. Cyrop. 8. 3. 39–50). The ἐπίτροπος would be himself a slave ([Aristot.] Oecon. 1. 5. 1344 a 25 sq.), though one would think that it would not be easy to find a φύσει δοῦλος fit for the position. Contrast the tone of this passage with that of Oecon. 1. 6. 1345 a 5, ἐπισκεπτέον οὖν τὰ μὲν αὐτὸν (τὸν δεσπότην), τὰ δὲ τὴν γυναῖκα, ὡς ἑκατέροις διαιρεῖται τὰ ἔργα τῆς οἰκονομίας· καὶ τοῦτο ποιητέον ἐν μικραῖς οἰκονομίαις ὀλιγάκις, ἐν δ' ἐπιτροπευομέναις πολλάκις κ.τ.λ. This is more in Xenophon's tone. For a similar contrast between the teaching of this book of the Politics and the so-called First Book of the Oeconomics, see note on 1256 a 11.

37. ἡ δὲ κτητική, sc. δούλων, takes up ἐν τῷ κτᾶσθαι, 32. **ἀμφοτέρων τούτων,** i. e. δεσποτική and δουλικὴ ἐπιστήμη.

38. οἷον here, as Bonitz points out (Ind. 502 a 7 sqq.), is explanatory (='nempe, nimirum, scilicet'), as in 3. 13. 1283 b 1 and other passages, rather than illustrative by instance or comparison.

ἡ δικαία. Cp. 1. 8. 1256 b 23 sq. and Isocr. Panath. § 163: also 4 (7). 14. 1333 b 38–1334 a 2. The just and natural way of acquiring slaves is by raids of a hunting or campaigning type on φύσει δοῦλοι. Πολεμική τις οὖσα ἢ θηρευτική is added in explanation of ἑτέρα ἀμφοτέρων τούτων, and to show that this science is neither identical with δουλική nor with δεσποτικὴ ἐπιστήμη. Being allied to war and the chase, it is more worthy of a freeman than the other two.

1. χρηματιστικῆς. This word is of frequent occurrence in cc. **C. 8.**
8–10, and also in c. 11, and the sense in which it is used varies **1256 a.**
greatly. Taking cc. 8–10 first, we shall find that, apart from passages in which the word is used in an indeterminate sense (such as 1256 a 1, 1257 b 5, 9, 18), it is used

(1) like κτητική (1256 b 27, 40), in a sense inclusive of both the sound and the unsound form (1257 a 17, b 2, 36, 1258 a 6, 37):

(2) of the unsound form (1257 a 29, 1258 a 8), which is also designated ἡ μάλιστα χρηματιστική (1256 b 40 sq.), ἡ καπηλικὴ χρηματιστική (1257 b 20), ἡ μὴ ἀναγκαία χρηματιστική (1258 a 14), ἡ μεταβλητικὴ χρηματιστική (1258 b 1):

(3) of the sound form (1258 a 20, 28), which is also designated χρηματιστικὴ κατὰ φύσιν (1257 b 19), οἰκονομικὴ χρηματιστική (1257 b 20), ἡ ἀναγκαία χρηματιστική (1258 a 16).

In c. 11, on the other hand, ἡ χρηματιστική is made to include not two forms, but three (1258 b 12 sqq.), and these three forms are—A. ἡ οἰκειοτάτη χρηματιστική (1258 b 20), referred to as ἡ κατὰ φύσιν in 1258 b 28: B. ἡ μεταβλητικὴ χρηματιστική (1258 b 21): C. a kind midway between the two (1258 b 27 sq.). In τοῖς τιμῶσι τὴν χρηματιστικήν (c. 11. 1259 a 5) the word seems to be used in an unfavourable sense.

2. κατὰ τὸν ὑφηγημένον τρόπον. Cp. c. 1. 1252 a 17, τὴν ὑφηγημένην μέθοδον. Either the transition from the slave (the part) to κτῆσις (the whole) is here said to be in conformity with Aristotle's accustomed mode of inquiry, or the plan is foreshadowed by which the nature of κτῆσις and χρηματιστική is ascertained through an analysis of them into their parts (cp. 1256 a 16, ἡ δὲ κτῆσις πολλὰ περιείληφε μέρη καὶ ὁ πλοῦτος), or again the meaning may be that Aristotle will continue to follow τὰ πράγματα φυόμενα, as he in fact does in the sequel. Probably the first of these interpretations is the correct one.

6. ἀνδριαντοποιίᾳ. The *ἀνδριαντοποιός* would appear to be properly a worker in bronze: cp. Eth. Nic. 6. 7. 1141 a 10, *Φειδίαν λιθουργὸν σοφὸν καὶ Πολύκλειτον ἀνδριαντοποιόν.*

8. τὸ ὑποκείμενον. Cp. de Gen. An. 1. 18. 724 b 3, *ἕτερόν τι δεῖ ὑποκεῖσθαι ἐξ οὗ ἔσται πρώτου ἐνυπάρχοντος* (thus it is explained by *πάσχον* in 724 b 6): de Gen. et Corr. 1. 4. 320 a 2, *ἔστι δὲ ὕλη μάλιστα μὲν καὶ κυρίως τὸ ὑποκείμενον γενέσεως καὶ φθορᾶς δεκτικόν, τρόπον δέ τινα καὶ τὸ ταῖς ἄλλαις μεταβολαῖς, ὅτι πάντα δεκτικὰ τὰ ὑποκείμενα ἐναντιώσεών τινων.* But the term is not confined in its application to Matter: cp. Metaph. Z. 13. 1038 b 4, *περὶ τοῦ ὑποκειμένου, ὅτι διχῶς ὑπόκειται, ἢ τόδε τι ὄν, ὥσπερ τὸ ζῷον τοῖς πάθεσιν, ἢ ὡς ἡ ὕλη τῇ ἐντελεχείᾳ.*

10. χαλκόν. Some MSS. have *χαλκός* (for the nom. in sentences introduced by *οἷον*, see above on 1255 b 25).

11. τῆς μὲν γὰρ κ.τ.λ. Contrast Oecon. 1. 1. 1343 a 8, *ὥστε δῆλον ὅτι καὶ τῆς οἰκονομικῆς ἂν εἴη καὶ κτήσασθαι οἶκον καὶ χρήσασθαι αὐτῷ*: Eth. Nic. 1. 1. 1094 a 9, *οἰκονομικῆς δὲ* (*τέλος*) *πλοῦτος*: and indeed Pol. 3. 4. 1277 b 24, *ἐπεὶ καὶ οἰκονομία ἑτέρα ἀνδρὸς καὶ γυναικός· τοῦ μὲν γὰρ κτᾶσθαι, τῆς δὲ φυλάττειν ἔργον ἐστίν*, which agrees with Oecon. 1. 3. 1344 a 2. Probably in these passages of the Nicomachean Ethics and the Politics *οἰκονομία* as it actually is, not as it ought to be, is in view. For Aristotle seems not only here but elsewhere to make 'using' the proper business of *οἰκονομία* (see c. 7. 1255 b 31 sq.: c. 10. 1258 a 21 sq.: 3. 4. 1277 a 35: Sus.[2], Note 68).

13. τοῖς κατὰ τὴν οἰκίαν, 'household things' (Mr. Welldon): cp. 5 (8). 6. 1340 b 27, *ἣν διδόασι τοῖς παιδίοις, ὅπως χρώμενοι ταύτῃ μηδὲν καταγνύωσι τῶν κατὰ τὴν οἰκίαν*: 1. 10. 1258 a 29, *τοὺς κατὰ τὴν οἰκίαν.*

14. ἐστί, sc. *ἡ χρηματιστική.* The change of subject strikes us as strange, but a similar one occurs in Metaph. Γ. 2. 1004 b 22–25, *περὶ μὲν γὰρ τὸ αὐτὸ γένος στρέφεται ἡ σοφιστικὴ καὶ ἡ διαλεκτικὴ τῇ φιλοσοφίᾳ, ἀλλὰ διαφέρει τῆς μὲν τῷ τρόπῳ τῆς δυνάμεως, τῆς δὲ τοῦ βίου τῇ προαιρέσει.* Aristotle reverts to the nominative with which he started (3–4) on his inquiry.

15. εἰ γὰρ κ.τ.λ. Vahlen, in his note on Poet. 6. 1450 b 18, holds that *εἰ γάρ* is here used in the same sense as in Rhet. 3. 17. 1418 a 35, where he reads with the best MS. *λέγων* (not *λέγει*, as Bekker). The meaning will then be—'for this is so' (i.e. 'a dispute may arise on this subject'), 'if, for example,' etc. He therefore places a comma only after *διαμφισβήτησιν.* (For Susemihl's view see Sus.[3] and Qu. Crit. p. 350 sq.) But the passage resembles so closely other passages in Aristotle introduced by *εἰ*, in which a kind of apodosis begins with *ὥστε*, that it seems better to interpret *εἰ γάρ* as commencing a new sentence, and to place a colon or full stop after *διαμφισβήτησιν.*

The following passages will serve as illustrations—Metaph. I. 4. 1055 a 22, ὅλως τε εἰ ἔστιν ἡ ἐναντιότης διαφορά, ἡ δὲ διαφορὰ δυοῖν, ὥστε καὶ ἡ τέλειος: Phys. 6. 1. 232 a 12, εἰ οὖν ἀνάγκη ἢ ἠρεμεῖν ἢ κινεῖσθαι πᾶν, ἠρεμεῖ δὲ καθ' ἕκαστον τῶν ΑΒΓ, ὥστ' ἔσται τι συνεχῶς ἠρεμοῦν ἅμα καὶ κινούμενον. (See Vahlen's note on Poet. 9. 1452 a 10: Bon. Ind. 873 a 31 sqq.: Bonitz, Aristotel. Studien, 3. 106–124. This use of ὥστε may have been common in conversational Greek.) Whichever view we take of the passage, the doubt whether χρηματιστική is a part of οἰκονομική, or something quite different, will be said to arise from the multifariousness of the forms of acquisition falling under χρηματιστική. (This is no doubt more neatly expressed, if with Vahlen we take εἰ γὰρ as = εἴπερ.) It is implied to be easier to imagine χρηματιστική a part of οἰκονομική, if it comprises agriculture and sound modes of acquisition of the same kind, than if it has to do with less natural modes, exclusively or otherwise. This is quite in harmony with the subsequent course of the inquiry, which results in the two-fold conclusion that agriculture and other similar ways of acquiring necessaries do form a part of χρηματιστική, and that this part of χρηματιστική is a part of οἰκονομική (cp. c. 8. 1256 b 26 and 37). To mark off the sound section of χρηματιστική from the unsound is, in fact, the first step towards relating χρηματιστική to οἰκονομική.

17. πρῶτον. Σκεπτέον, or some such word, is dropped. The omission of words which will readily be supplied is characteristic of Aristotle's style.

19. καὶ κτῆσις is added, it would seem, because ἐπιμέλεια does not clearly convey what is meant by κτῆσις τροφῆς. What this is, appears from Eth. Nic. 4. 1. 1120 a 8, χρῆσις δ' εἶναι δοκεῖ χρημάτων δαπάνη καὶ δόσις· ἡ δὲ λῆψις καὶ ἡ φυλακὴ κτῆσις μᾶλλον. We find χρημάτων κτῆσις mentioned in Pol. 1. 9. 1257 b 30.

ἀλλὰ μήν, 'but further there are many kinds of nutriment'—not only many kinds of property (16), but many kinds of nutriment, and articles of subsistence are only one sort of property.

21. ὥστε κ.τ.λ. Cp. Hist. An. 8. 1. 588 a 17 (referred to by Giph.), αἱ δὲ πράξεις καὶ οἱ βίοι (τῶν ζῴων) κατὰ τὰ ἤθη καὶ τὰς τροφὰς διαφέρουσιν, and 8. 2. 590 a 13 sqq.

23. τε γὰρ is here taken up by ὁμοίως δὲ καί, 29, as in 1254 a 9, 2. 9. 1269 a 36 sqq., Hist. An. 8. 1. 588 b 24, etc. See Eucken de Partic. usu, 17–20. The classification here adopted (ζῳοφάγα, καρποφάγα, παμφάγα) is not probably offered as absolutely exhaustive, for in Hist. An. 8. 6. 595 a 13–17 we find ποηφάγα and ῥιζοφάγα ζῷα distinguished in addition to καρποφάγα, and in Hist. An. 1. 1. 488 a

14, in addition to σαρκοφάγα, καρποφάγα, and παμφάγα, we hear of ἰδιότροφα, οἷον τὸ τῶν μελιττῶν γένος καὶ τὸ τῶν ἀραχνῶν. Bernays understands Aristotle to connect gregariousness with an exclusively vegetable diet, and it certainly is not quite clear how he intends to class omnivorous animals. So far as they are carnivorous, we must suppose that they will be solitary. As to carnivorous animals, cp. Hist. An. 1. 1. 488 a 5, γαμψώνυχον δ' οὐδὲν ἀγελαῖον. Vict. remarks—'nam aquilae, si gregatim volarent, longe viserentur, quare aves quibus aluntur se abderent; nunc autem solae, ideoque non conspectae, inopinantes illas capiunt: neque etiam invenirent simul tantos ipsarum greges, ut possent ipsis vesci.' I am informed that 'true as what Aristotle says is upon the whole, still there are many exceptions: e.g. nearly all Canidae, some seals, sand-martins, and some vultures are gregarious and yet carnivorous. Hares and some other rodents are grain-eating but not gregarious.' Fish are often gregarious, yet piscivorous. The carrion-eating condor is 'in a certain degree gregarious' (Darwin, Voyage of the Beagle, p. 183). As to the bearing of the food of animals on the duration of pairing, see Locke, Civil Government, 2. § 79.

26. πρὸς τὰς ῥᾳστώνας, 'ad commoditatem victus' (Bon. Ind. s. v.).

αἵρεσιν is perhaps used here and nowhere else by Aristotle in its simplest sense of 'taking' or 'getting'; it is thus that Bonitz would seem to interpret the word here (Ind. 18 b 38), for he marks off this passage from others in which it bears its usual meaning of 'choice.' Aristotle needed a word applicable at once to ζῷα, καρποί, etc., and he finds it in αἵρεσις. So Vict.: 'Natura tribuit singulis rationem eam, qua commode copioseque vivant, et sumant non magno labore quibus pascantur.' Sepulveda, however, translates—'itaque Natura, prout ratio postulat facile parandi cibum quem genus quodque animantium consectatur, vitas eorum distinxit,' and I do not feel certain that he is wrong (Lamb. 'harum rerum electionem': Giph. 'delectu earum').

τούτων, 'the different kinds of food.'

27. ἑκάστῳ, not 'each individual member of the three classes of animals,' but 'each of the species contained in a class' is probably meant.

28. καὶ αὐτῶν τῶν ζῳοφάγων. Cp. de Part. An. 3. 12. 673 b 16, τό τε γὰρ ἧπαρ τοῖς μὲν πολυσχιδές ἐστι, τοῖς δὲ μονοφυέστερον, πρῶτον αὐτῶν τῶν ἐναίμων καὶ ζῳοτόκων· ἔτι δὲ μᾶλλον καὶ πρὸς ταῦτα καὶ πρὸς ἄλληλα διαφέρει τά τε τῶν ἰχθύων καὶ τετραπόδων καὶ ᾠοτόκων.

29. ὁμοίως δὲ καὶ τῶν ἀνθρώπων. These words apparently answer to τῶν τε γὰρ θηρίων (see above on 23). If so, we have here a further illustration of the remark made in 21–22, αἱ διαφοραὶ τῆς τροφῆς τοὺς βίους πεποιήκασι διαφέροντας τῶν ζῴων. It would indeed be easy to supply οἱ βίοι πρὸς ἄλληλους διεστᾶσιν from the previous sentence, and the tautology of πολὺ γὰρ διαφέρουσιν κ.τ.λ. is not decisive against this, but there are other cases (as has been pointed out above) in which τε γάρ is answered by ὁμοίως δὲ καί, and irrespectively of this it seems likely that the genitive is of the same kind as in 1253 b 27, or in 6 (4). 13. 1297 b 30, δημοκρατία τε γὰρ οὐ μία τὸν ἀριθμόν ἐστι καὶ τῶν ἄλλων ὁμοίως, or in Phys. 8. 8. 263 a 1, καὶ τῶν κινήσεων ἄρα ὡσαύτως: cp. 1256 b 6, ὁμοίως δὲ καὶ περὶ τοὺς ἄλλους. The translation will then be, 'the same thing holds good of men too'—i. e. their mode of life also differs according to the food on which they live. Pastoral nomads live on tame animals (31), hunters on fish or wild birds or beasts, brigands on their booty, whatever it may be, husbandmen on the produce of the soil and the fruits of domesticated plants and trees.

31. οἱ μὲν οὖν ἀργότατοι. Μὲν οὖν (which is taken up by οἱ δ' 35) introduces a confirmation in detail of what has just been said ('saepe usurpatur, ubi notio modo pronunciata amplius explicatur,' Bon. Ind. 540 b 42). For ἀργότατοι, cp. ῥᾳστώνας 26, and Herodotus' account of the Thracians (5. 6, ἀργὸν εἶναι κάλλιστον [κέκριται], γῆς δὲ ἐργάτην ἀτιμότατον· τὸ ζῆν ἀπὸ πολέμου καὶ ληιστύος κάλλιστον). The remark illustrates the effect of men's food on their mode of life. Is there a hint that the nomads live most like the golden race, who are described by Hesiod (Op. et Dies 112 sqq.) as living νόσφιν ἄτερ τε πόνων καὶ ὀϊζύος and ἀκηδέα θυμὸν ἔχοντες (compare the 'table of the sun' among the Ethiopians, Hdt. 3. 18)—most like the infant who simply draws on the stores of nature? It is possible, but it would be rash to assert this. For races are apparently held by Aristotle to take a step in advance, when they exchange the wandering pastoral life for the hard-working life of tillers of the soil (4 (7). 10. 1329 b 14). The leisure of nomad life may be too dearly purchased. On the merits of a pastoral (not nomad) population, see Pol. 8 (6). 4. 1319 a 19 sqq. For the contrast of Aristotle's views as to the natural mode of life with those of Dicaearchus, see vol. i. p. 128, note 2.

32. ἀναγκαίου δὲ κ.τ.λ. Cp. de Part. An. 4. 6. 682 b 6, αὐτῶν δὲ τῶν πτηνῶν ὧν μέν ἐστιν ὁ βίος νομαδικὸς καὶ διὰ τὴν τροφὴν ἀναγκαῖον ἐκτοπίζειν κ.τ.λ. Their way of moving about is enforced on them; their mode of life is none the less on the whole lazy and effortless, because they cannot avoid changing pastures from time to time.

36. ληστείας. In treating ληστεία as a form of hunting (like Plato, Laws 823 B) and a natural way of acquiring food, Aristotle is not thinking of the pickpocket or highwayman of civilized societies —this kind of ληστής is called by him *αἰσχροκερδής* and *ἀνελεύθερος* (Eth. Nic. 4. 3. 1122 a 7) and *ἄδικος* (Eth. Nic. 5. 10. 1134 a 19)— but of ληστεία as he meets with it in the pages of Homer, or of the wild ληστικὰ ἔθνη mentioned by him in Pol. 5 (8). 4. 1338 b 23. The Etruscans were 'even more pirates than traders' (Meltzer, Gesch. der Karthager, 1. 169), and practised piracy not only in the Western Mediterranean but even in the Adriatic (see Dittenberger, Sylloge Inscriptionum Graecarum, vol. i. p. 184) at the very time at which Aristotle was writing. Mr. C. T. Newton (*Contemp. Rev.* Dec. 1876) mentions a bronze plate recording a treaty between two cities of Locris, Oianthe and Chalion, which stipulates that it shall be lawful for the citizens of both States to commit piracy anywhere except within their own or their ally's harbours. 'The date of this inscription,' he adds, 'is probably not earlier than B.C. 431.' Cp. also Cic. de Rep. 3. 9. 15: vitae vero instituta sic distant, ut Cretes et Aetoli latrocinari honestum putent. The Western Mediterranean was a scene of piracy down, probably, even to the time of Aristotle and later (Meltzer, Gesch. der Karthager, 1. 342 sqq.). The Greeks, after all, felt that the robber had something of the warrior about him. Both Plato (Laws 845 C) and Xenophon (de Rep. Lac. 2. 6 sq.) approve the Spartan tolerance of adroit theft of necessaries. Aristotle makes ληστεία a kind of hunting, and hunting a kind of war (1256 b 23). We ourselves look back on the Vikings with admiration; yet, as Mr. Burton says (History of Scotland, 3. 232), the Vikings 'got their capital by force.' It should be noticed, however, that in c. 11 ληστεία is passed over in silence, and indeed θηρευτική in general. Aristotle apparently regards λησταί as plunderers for the sake of subsistence, for in 1256 a 19–b 7 he seems to be concerned with the provision of τροφή: he may perhaps also regard them as in the main appropriators of articles of food—grain, cattle, and the like. He does not explain how a brigand or pirate's mode of life is marked off from others by a difference of nutriment, and it is not clear how it can be called *αὐτόφυτος*.

37. τοιαύτην, 'suitable for fishing': cp. τοιαῦτα 1253 a 24, where the sense is 'possessed of the power of performing their appointed work'—so here 'possessed of the power of supplying fish.' See on τοιοῦτος Riddell, Plato's Apology, p. 137.

39. τῶν ἡμέρων καρπῶν. Aristotle does not include in his enumeration those who live on the fruits of wild trees, like the 'acorn-eating Arcadians' (Hdt. 1. 66: Alcaeus, Fragm. 91) of early days, before Demeter and Dionysus had given men corn and wine (Leutsch and Schneidewin, Paroem. Gr. 1. 42).

40. ὅσοι γε αὐτόφυτον κ.τ.λ. Giph. 'vitae genus quod naturae instinctu agat et actionem habeat naturalem': Bern. 'diejenigen (Lebensweisen), welche auf Ausbeutung von Naturerzeugnissen beruhen': Sus. 'welche eine unmittelbar-natürliche Thätigkeit betreiben.' Vict., however, translates 'vitae quaecunque suam e seque natam culturam habent,' and explains the words in his commentary 'vita quae pariat ipsa vi sua sineque alius auxilio quod alat'; and Liddell and Scott interpret *αὐτόφυτος ἐργασία* here as = *αὐτουργία*, a rendering not far removed from that of Vict., which is probably right—compare such words as *αὐτόποιος* (Soph. O. C. 696), *αὐτοτέλεστος, αὐτογένεθλος*. The meaning will then be 'lives whose work is self-wrought,' and not achieved with the help, or at the expense, of others, like the life of *ἀλλαγὴ καὶ καπηλεία*. Cp. 1. 10. 1258 a 40, *τῆς δὲ μεταβλητικῆς ψεγομένης δικαίως (οὐ γὰρ κατὰ φύσιν ἀλλ' ἀπ' ἀλλήλων ἐστίν*, Rhet. 2. 4. 1381 a 21, *διὸ τοὺς ἐλευθερίους καὶ τοὺς ἀνδρείους τιμῶσι καὶ τοὺς δικαίους· τοιούτους δ' ὑπολαμβάνουσι τοὺς μὴ ἀφ' ἑτέρων ζῶντας· τοιοῦτοι δ' οἱ ἀπὸ τοῦ ἐργάζεσθαι, καὶ τούτων οἱ ἀπὸ γεωργίας καὶ τῶν ἄλλων οἱ αὐτουργοὶ μάλιστα*, and [Plut.] Inst. Lac. c. 12.

41. δι' ἀλλαγῆς καὶ καπηλείας. *Καπηλεία* is perhaps meant to explain and limit *ἀλλαγή*, for *ἀλλαγή* up to a certain point is natural (1257 a 15, 28). Still even the simplest form of *ἀλλαγή* may possibly not deserve the epithet *αὐτόφυτος*.

3. προσαναπληροῦντες κ.τ.λ., 'eking out the shortcomings of one mode of life, where it falls short of completeness of provision, by adding on some other.' The superlative *ἐνδεέστατον* is perhaps used because men may be *ἐνδεεῖς* not only *εἰς τἀναγκαῖα*, as in the case before us, but also *εἰς ὑπεροχὴν ἢ εἰς ἀπόλαυσιν* (Rhet. 1. 12. 1372 b 24 sq.); or else it is used here, as elsewhere by Aristotle (see Bon. Ind. 403 a 3 sqq.), in a sense in which the use of the comparative would seem more natural. *Ἧ τυγχάνει κ.τ.λ.* implies that the added mode of life must be one which will supply the deficiencies of the other: thus when brigandage is added to the nomadic life, or hunting to agriculture, it is because brigandage and hunting fill up gaps which the pastoral and agricultural modes of life leave unfilled. Compare Strabo, p. 833. 27 sqq.: Dio Chrysostom's picture (Or. 7. 224 R) of the life of the rude Eubœan mountaineers, *ζῶμεν δὲ ἀπὸ θήρας ὡς τὸ πολύ, μικρόν τι τῆς γῆς ἐπεργαζόμενοι*: Diodorus' picture of the Ligurians (5. 39. 3, *κυνη-*

1256 b.

γίας δὲ ποιοῦνται συνεχεῖς, ἐν αἷς πολλὰ τῶν θηρίων χειρούμενοι τὴν ἐκ τῶν καρπῶν σπάνιν διορθοῦνται): and Leyden's of the Border people (Scenes of Infancy):—

'The Scott, to rival realms a mighty bar,
Here fixed his mountain home: a wide domain,
And rich the soil, had purple heath been grain;
But what the niggard soil of wealth denied,
From fields more blessed his fearless arm supplied.'

'The Shetlander is a fisherman who has a farm; the Orkneyman a farmer who has a boat' (Tudor's Orkneys and Shetland, quoted in the *Saturday Review* for July 14, 1883).

4. **αὐτάρκης**, i. e. ἐν τοῖς ἀναγκαίοις (cp. 4 (7). 4. 1326 b 4), which is a very different thing from αὐτάρκεια τοῦ εὖ ζῆν (3. 9. 1280 b 34).

6. **συναναγκάζῃ**. Bernays: 'wie das Bedürfniss zum Verbinden verschiedener Lebensweisen treibt' (compels them to combine different modes of life). But if we look back to 1256 a 27, we shall see that it is taste (τὸ ἡδύ) that leads men to select this or that mode of life, though necessity may force them to eke it out with some other: will not the meaning therefore be—'as necessity in conjunction with taste may compel'? Cp. Rhet. 2. 7. 1385 b 2, where it is pointed out that a service may be explained away by the plea that those who rendered it did not render it out of kindness alone, but were in part compelled (συνηναγκάσθησαν): [Demosth.] adv. Aristog. 2. c. 10, ἢ προαιρουμένους ἢ συναναγκαζομένους: and Xen. Hiero 3. 9.

7. **τοιαύτη**, that which is necessary for sustenance, and which is αὐτόφυτος. Cp. Eth. Nic. 3. 13. 1118 b 18, ἀναπλήρωσις γὰρ τῆς ἐνδείας ἡ φυσικὴ ἐπιθυμία.

8. **φαίνεται διδομένη**, 'is evidently given.'

πᾶσιν, here not 'all human beings' (as in 1253 a 30), but 'all animals.'

9. **κατὰ τὴν πρώτην γένεσιν**. We have the proof of this in 10–15, and of **τελειωθεῖσιν** in 15–20, as Prof. Jowett has already remarked. The expression κατὰ τὴν πρώτην ἐν τῇ μητρὶ γένεσιν occurs in Eth. Eud. 1. 5. 1216 a 7.

11. **τοσαύτην . . . ὡς**. Eucken (de Partic. usu, p. 51–52) finds in Aristotle's writings only one other instance of this use of ὡς—Pol. 7 (5). 5. 1305 a 32. He adds—'paullo saepius in libris pseudo-Aristoteleis particula ὡς eo modo usurpatur.'

12. **οἷον ὅσα σκωληκοτοκεῖ ἢ ᾠοτοκεῖ**. Cp. de Gen. An. 2. 1. 732 a 25–32, τῶν δὲ ζῴων τὰ μὲν τελεσιουργεῖ καὶ ἐκπέμπει θύραζε ὅμοιον ἑαυτῷ, οἷον ὅσα ζῳοτοκεῖ εἰς τοὐμφανές, τὰ δὲ ἀδιάρθρωτον ἐκτίκτει καὶ οὐκ ἀπειληφὸς τὴν αὑτοῦ μορφήν· τῶν δὲ τοιούτων τὰ μὲν ἔναιμα ᾠοτοκεῖ, τὰ δ'

ἄναιμα σκωληκοτοκεῖ· διαφέρει δ' ᾠὸν καὶ σκώληξ· ᾠὸν μὲν γάρ ἐστιν ἐξ οὗ γίνεται τὸ γινόμενον ἐκ μέρους, τὸ δὲ λοιπόν ἐστι τροφὴ τῷ γινομένῳ, σκώληξ δ' ἐξ οὗ τὸ γινόμενον ὅλου ὅλον γίνεται. A part of the contents of the egg is intended only to serve as nutriment for the young creature; it is used for that purpose and there is an end of it; the lower part of the σκώληξ, on the contrary, though in Aristotle's view it furnishes in the first place nutriment to the upper and thus aids its growth, begins itself, after it has done this, to grow and receive articulation; and thus no part of the σκώληξ can be said, as a part of the egg can, to be set apart simply and permanently for the sole purpose of nutriment. This is explained in de Gen. An. 3. 11. 763 a 9–16, ποιοῦνται δὲ καὶ τὴν αὔξησιν ὁμοίως τοῖς σκώληξιν· ἐπὶ τὰ ἄνω γὰρ καὶ τὴν ἀρχὴν αὐξάνονται οἱ σκώληκες· ἐν τῷ κάτω γὰρ ἡ τροφὴ τοῖς ἄνω· καὶ τοῦτό γε ὁμοίως ἔχει τοῖς ἐκ τῶν ᾠῶν, πλὴν ἐκεῖνα μὲν καταναλίσκει πᾶν, ἐν δὲ τοῖς σκωληκοτοκουμένοις, ὅταν αὐξηθῇ ἐκ τῆς ἐν τῷ κάτω μορίῳ συστάσεως τὸ ἄνω μόριον, οὕτως ἐκ τοῦ ὑπολοίπου διαρθροῦται τὸ κάτωθεν. On the σκώληξ and τὰ σκωληκοτοκοῦντα (i.e. Insects, Hist. An. 5. 19. 550 b 26), see Dr. Ogle's translation of Aristotle on the Parts of Animals, p. xxvii sqq. I can find space only for the following quotation. 'It has been supposed that Aristotle had in some extraordinary way overlooked the eggs of insects, and fancied that these animals produce primarily grubs or maggots. This, however, was not so. He says that there are two kinds of scolex, one capable of motion, in other words a grub or maggot, the other incapable of motion, and so excessively like an ovum in shape, size, and consistency, as to be indistinguishable from it, excepting by considering its ulterior changes (de Gen. An. 3. 9. 758 b 10 sqq.).' The only difference between the case of σκωληκοτοκοῦντα and ᾠοτοκοῦντα on the one hand and ζῳοτοκοῦντα on the other is, that τὸ λειπόμενον (1258 a 36)—i.e. the surplus material beyond that which is drawn upon in the process of generation—is in the former case severed from the mother, inasmuch as it forms a part of the egg or σκώληξ, while in the case of ζῳοτοκοῦντα it is retained within the person of the mother in the form of milk. Cp. de Gen. An. 3. 2. 752 b 19 sqq., ἡ γὰρ φύσις ἅμα τήν τε τοῦ ζῴου ὕλην ἐν τῷ ᾠῷ τίθησι καὶ τὴν ἱκανὴν τροφὴν πρὸς τὴν αὔξησιν· ἐπεὶ γὰρ οὐ δύναται τελεοῦν ἐν αὑτῇ ἡ ὄρνις, συνεκτίκτει τὴν τροφὴν ἐν τῷ ᾠῷ· τοῖς μὲν γὰρ ζῳοτοκουμένοις ἐν ἄλλῳ μορίῳ γίνεται ἡ τροφή, τὸ καλούμενον γάλα, ἐν τοῖς μαστοῖς· τοῖς δ' ὄρνισι τοῦτο ποιεῖ ἡ φύσις ἐν τοῖς ᾠοῖς, τοὐναντίον μέντοι ἢ οἵ τε ἄνθρωποι οἴονται καὶ Ἀλκμαίων φησὶν ὁ Κροτωνιάτης, οὐ γὰρ τὸ λευκόν ἐστι γάλα, ἀλλὰ τὸ ὠχρόν· τοῦτο γάρ ἐστιν ἡ τροφὴ τοῖς νεοττοῖς. In the case of many kinds of fish, indeed, and among them the Salmonidae, provision is made for the sustenance of the young even after they have left the egg. This has long been known to naturalists. 'When the little fish emerge from the eggs, they have a large bag, the umbilical vesicle, attached to their stomachs; this contains the nourishment which is to serve them for several (three to eight) weeks' subsistence, and they do not commonly take in any food by the mouth until it is absorbed' (from a Paper on Salmon, by F. Day, Esq., F.L.S.). On milk as an evidence of the providence of Nature, see Plutarch de Amore Prolis, c. 3, an interesting passage already noticed in vol. i. p. 30, note 2.

13. τοῖς γεννωμένοις. See critical note.

15. φύσιν. Cp. ἡ φύσις τῶν φλεβῶν, Hist. An. 3. 2. 511 b 20, where 'notio vocis φύσις adeo delitescit, ut meram periphrasin nominis esse putes,' though this is not really quite the case (Bon. Ind. 838 a 9 sq.). Cp. also ὁμοιώματα παρὰ τὰς ἀληθινὰς φύσεις, 5 (8). 5. 1340 a 18. 'Thing' or 'object' seems to approach the sense of φύσις used in this way. So Bern., 'den Stoff, den wir Milch nennen.'

ὥστε. The argument is that if there is a provision of nutriment for the creature in process of birth, it is not likely that nutriment should not be forthcoming for it when past that early stage. Cp. Eth. Eud. 7. 2. 1237 a 29, ὥστ' ἐπεὶ καὶ ἀτελῆ (τὰ ὅμοια ἀλλήλοις χαίρει), δῆλον ὅτι καὶ τελειωθέντα. Aristotle, however, carries his inference further, and argues that not only nutriment but ἄλλα ὄργανα will be forthcoming. We see how large is the superstructure which he raises on the fact that in every species of animal a provision of nutriment is made for the earliest moments of existence.

γενομένοις, which Sus.[3] places within brackets, may well bear somewhat the same meaning as τελειωθεῖσιν, which he substituted for it in his first and second editions (cp. Meteor. 4. 2. 379 b 20, ὅταν γὰρ πεφθῇ, τετελείωταί τε καὶ γέγονεν: Metaph. B. 4. 999 b 11). Γενομένοις may perhaps be used as a more comprehensive term than τελειωθεῖσιν, for γένεσις in the sense of ἡ πρώτη γένεσις 9, or ἡ ἐξ ἀρχῆς γένεσις 10, does not necessarily involve τελειότης. The meaning will be 'when the πρώτη γένεσις is over.' Thus milk is said (de Part. An. 2. 9. 655 b 26 sq.) to be τροφὴ τοῖς γινομένοις: τροφὴ τοῖς γενομένοις is something different. Prof. Jowett quotes Eth. Nic. 8. 14. 1162 a 6, τοῦ γὰρ εἶναι καὶ τραφῆναι αἴτιοι (sc. οἱ γονεῖς) καὶ γενομένοις τοῦ παιδευθῆναι. As to the dative, see Bon. Ind. 166 b 26 sqq.

20. εἰ οὖν ἡ φύσις κ.τ.λ. The inference seems to be as follows—'plants exist for the sake of animals, and the lower animals—all tame ones and most of the wild—for the sake of men; [but the lower animals are made by Nature,] and Nature makes nothing incomplete [in the sense of lacking an end] or in vain, therefore (οὖν) all of them must necessarily be made by Nature for the sake of men.' Αὐτὰ πάντα 22 has been variously interpreted 'all plants and animals,' 'all wild animals' (Sepulv. 'ipsas omnes feras'), and 'all animals.' I have explained the expression in the first of these ways in vol. i. p. 128, but perhaps on the whole the third interpretation is the one most likely to be correct, for plants have just been said to exist for the sake of animals generally, so that they would not be 'in vain' if they did not exist for the sake of men; besides, what Aristotle is here especially concerned to prove (cp. θηρία 24) is that the lower animals are made by Nature for the sake of men; he proceeds, in fact, at once to infer from this, that the kind of war which is waged against wild animals and to compel natural slaves, who differ but little from the lower animals, to submit to enslavement is a natural form of Supply. The interpretation of Sepulveda—'all wild animals'—is a possible interpretation (cp. θηρία 24), though the assertion that Nature has made all wild animals for the sake of men seems strange, if we look back to 18, τῶν δὲ ἀγρίων, εἰ μὴ πάντα, ἀλλὰ τά γε πλεῖστα, where the contrary seems to be implied. It is true, however, that the same assertion is made, though less conspicuously, if we interpret αὐτὰ πάντα 'all animals' or 'all plants and animals.' Aristotle's aim in the passage is to show that just as property in the sense of what is necessary for sustenance is given by Nature to all animals, so the lower animals themselves are made by Nature for the sake of men. Compare Xen. Mem. 4. 3. 10, and Cic. de Nat. Deor. 2. 14 (referred to by Mr. Eaton) and 2. 62–64 (referred to by Giph.). In the last-named passage Cicero argues that as flutes are made for the sake of those who can use them, so the fruits of the soil exist far more for the sake of men than for the sake of the lower animals, 'tantumque abest ut haec bestiarum etiam causa parata sint, ut ipsas bestias hominum gratia generatas esse videamus.' Cp. also Metaph. Λ. 10. 1075 a 16, πάντα δὲ συντέτακταί πως ἀλλ' οὐχ ὁμοίως, καὶ πλωτὰ καὶ πτηνὰ καὶ φυτά· καὶ οὐχ οὕτως ἔχει ὥστε μὴ εἶναι θατέρῳ πρὸς θάτερον μηδέν, ἀλλ' ἐστί τι.

21. ἀτελές. In using this word, is Aristotle referring to man or to the lower animals, which are made for the sake of man? He has often been taken to refer to the state of incompleteness in which man would be left, if he were unprovided with sustenance when past the earliest period of existence. Mr. Welldon translates the passage—'assuming then that none of Nature's products is incomplete or purposeless, [as man requires food and the other animals are suited to his consumption].' But looking to the form of the sentence (ποιεῖ . . . πεποιηκέναι), it seems more likely that Aristotle refers in the protasis as well as in the apodosis, and in ἀτελές as well as in μάτην, to the lower animals. 'Ατελές may in fact bear the meaning 'lacking an end,' and it is thus that Zeller ('ohne Zweck,' Gr. Ph. 2. 2. 565. 6), Bonitz ('οὐκ ἔχον τέλος sive οὗ ἕνεκα,' Ind. 119 a 48), and Susemihl in his translation ('zwecklos') explain it here. Bonitz mentions no other passage in which the word ἀτελής is used in this sense, but perhaps de Gen. An. 1. 1. 715 b 14, ἡ δὲ φύσις φεύγει τὸ ἄπειρον· τὸ μὲν γὰρ ἄπειρον ἀτελές, ἡ δὲ φύσις ἀεὶ ζητεῖ τέλος may be compared: cp. Plato, Phileb. 24 B, ἀεὶ τοίνυν ὁ λόγος ἡμῖν σημαίνει τούτω μὴ τέλος ἔχειν· ἀτελῆ δ' ὄντε δήπου παντάπασιν ἀπείρω γίγνεσθον. But ἀτελής is rarely used in this sense, and I incline on the whole to follow Sepulveda, who translates 'imperfectum' and adds in his note the explanation 'quod non referatur ad aliquem finem, res enim quaeque suo fine perficitur (Metaph. X),' where Metaph. I. 4. 1055 a 12, τέλος γὰρ ἔχει ἡ τελεία διαφορά, ὥσπερ καὶ τἄλλα τῷ τέλος ἔχειν λέγεται τέλεια is probably referred to: cp. Metaph. Δ. 16. 1021 b 23, ἔτι οἷς ὑπάρχει τὸ τέλος σπουδαῖον, ταῦτα λέγεται τέλεια· κατὰ γὰρ τὸ ἔχειν τὸ τέλος τέλεια.

μάτην. Cp. de An. 3. 12. 434 a 30, τὸ δὲ ζῷον ἀναγκαῖον αἴσθησιν ἔχειν, εἰ μηδὲν μάτην ποιεῖ ἡ φύσις· ἕνεκά του γὰρ πάντα ὑπάρχει τὰ φύσει, ἢ συμπτώματα ἔσται τῶν ἕνεκά του. Cp. also de Gen. An. 2. 5. 741 b 2–5: de Animalium Incessu 2. 704 b 15 sq.

ἀναγκαῖον τῶν ἀνθρώπων ἕνεκεν κ.τ.λ. Aristotle is unaware that many animals existed long before man. We are reminded here of the Socratic teleology, according to which the movements of the sun in summer and winter are arranged with a view to the advantage of man (Xen. Mem. 4. 3. 8, καὶ ταῦτα παντάπασιν ἔοικεν ἀνθρώπων ἕνεκα γιγνομένοις). But to Aristotle man is only πως τέλος, not τὸ ἔσχατον τέλος (Phys. 2. 2. 194 a 35). He assumes, it will be noticed, that animal food is necessary to man, and thus incidentally pronounces against those scruples as to its use which can be traced back in Greece to very early days. Orphic teaching forbade it (Plato, Laws 782): Empedocles was against it (see Prof. Campbell, Introduction to the Politicus of Plato, p. xxiii sq.): Democritus seems to have allowed the slaughter only of those animals which injure or wish to injure man (Stob. Floril. 44. 16, quoted by Bernays, Theophrastos' Schrift über Frömmigkeit, p. 149), and in this view he was apparently followed by Theophrastus (Porphyr. de Abstin. 2. 22), who may possibly be alluding to the passage of the Politics before us when he says (ibid. 2. 12), εἰ δὲ λέγοι τις ὅτι οὐχ ἧττον τῶν καρπῶν *καὶ τὰ ζῷα ἡμῖν ὁ θεὸς εἰς χρῆσιν δέδωκεν*—if indeed we are right in ascribing this passage, with Bernays (*op. cit.* p. 61 sqq.), to Theophrastus and not to Porphyry. His contemporary at the head of the Academy, Xenocrates, was also opposed to the use of animal food, though for a different reason (Xenocr. Fragm. 58—Mullach, Fr. Philos. Gr. 3. 127 : Zeller, Gr. Ph. 2. 1. 678. 6, ed. 2). The unhesitating language of Aristotle on this subject is deserving of notice. If there were those in antiquity who ascribed the Politics to Theophrastus, this passage at all events can hardly be from his pen. Observe that Aristotle does not here notice the case of carnivorous animals other than man.

22. αὐτὰ πάντα. See above on 20.

23. διὸ κ.τ.λ. The following extract from Susemihl, Qu. Crit. p. 347, will show how variously this passage has been interpreted. 'Victorium si audimus, cui adstipulati sunt Giphanius, Schneiderus, Boiesenius, *αὐτῆς* et *ᾗ* ad *πολεμικήν* pertinent, ut nihil nisi parenthesis sint *ἡ γὰρ θηρευτικὴ μέρος αὐτῆς*, qua indicetur cur bellum etiam contra bestias geri queat contendi: sin Lambinum, Schnitzerum, Stahrium, Bernaysium, *αὐτῆς* ad *πολεμικήν* et *ᾗ* ad *θηρευτικήν*: sin Garveum, Hampkeum, alios, *αὐτῆς* ad *κτητικήν* et *ᾗ* ad *θηρευτικήν* spectat.' Victorius' commentary refers *ᾗ* to *πολεμική*, but his translation refers it to *θηρευτική* ('studium enim venatorum pars ipsius [artis bellicae] est, quo decet uti,' etc.). Bernays takes *αὐτῆς* as meaning *τῆς πολεμικῆς* and refers *ᾗ* to *ἡ θηρευτική*, and this seems to be the more natural interpretation, looking to the close sequence in which *ᾗ* stands to *θηρευτική*, but then we hardly expect *τοῦτον τὸν πόλεμον* 26, though it is true that hunting has just been brought under the head of war (23: cp. 1255 b 38). Those who refer *ᾗ* to *ἡ πολεμική* will point to the use of the word *πόλεμον* in 26, and may also adduce Isocr. Panath. § 163, *τῶν δὲ πολέμων ὑπελάμβανον ἀναγκαιότατον μὲν εἶναι καὶ δικαιότατον τὸν μετὰ πάντων ἀνθρώπων πρὸς τὴν ἀγριότητα τὴν τῶν θηρίων γιγνόμενον, δεύτερον δὲ τὸν μετὰ τῶν Ἑλλήνων πρὸς τοὺς βαρβάρους τοὺς καὶ φύσει πολεμίους ὄντας καὶ πάντα τὸν χρόνον ἐπιβουλεύοντας ἡμῖν* (cp. Plutarch, Demetrius, c. 8: Porphyr. de Abstin. 1. 14: and Dio Chrysost. Or. 38. 137 R); Isocrates here certainly speaks of war, not hunting. But Aristotle has just said that hunting is a part of war, and the sentence seems to run more naturally if *ᾗ* is referred to *ἡ θηρευτική*. The words *ᾗ δεῖ χρῆσθαι πρός τε τὰ θηρία κ.τ.λ.*, in fact, acquire fresh point, if connected with *ἡ θηρευτική*: *θηρευτική* is not only to be brought to bear against *θηρία*, as the name might suggest, but also against men who are like *θηρία*. The reference of *ᾗ* to *ἡ θηρευτική* is still further supported by two passages of Plato

(Sophist. 222 B–C: Laws 823 B), which seem to be present to Aristotle's memory no less than the passage from the Panathenaic Oration of Isocrates just quoted, for in them Plato speaks of hunting as having to do not only with wild animals but also with men, in language much resembling that of Aristotle here. Διό draws from the fact that animals are made by nature for the service of man, and that their acquisition is natural, the inference that men who are, like animals, made to be ruled, may be acquired without any infraction of the order of nature. Αὐτῆς can hardly mean τῆς κτητικῆς, for the fact that hunting is a part of κτητική is no proof that war is in some sense a part of κτητική, in the absence of a statement that hunting is a part of war. I incline therefore to translate the passage thus: 'hence the art of war also is in some sense' (i. e. so far as one kind of it is concerned) 'by nature a form of κτητική, for of the art of war the art of the chase' (already said in 1256 a 40–b 2 to be a form of κτητική) 'is a part, which ought to be used against both wild animals and such human beings as being intended by nature to be ruled refuse to be ruled, seeing that this kind of war is by nature just.' There were kinds of war which had nothing to do with acquisition (4 (7). 14. 1333 b 38–1334 a 2). The myth of Protagoras had contrasted the art of war with ἡ δημιουργικὴ τέχνη (Plato, Protag. 322 B, ἡ δημιουργικὴ τέχνη αὐτοῖς πρὸς μὲν τροφὴν ἱκανὴ βοηθὸς ἦν, πρὸς δὲ τὸν τῶν θηρίων πόλεμον ἐνδεής· πολιτικὴν γὰρ τέχνην οὔπω εἶχον, ἧς μέρος πολεμική), and Aristotle may wish to point out, in correction of this view, that some kinds of τροφή cannot be obtained without war; he evidently does not agree with Rep. 373 D–E, where the origin of war is traced to the unbounded quest of wealth. On the contrary, he holds that one kind of war (that for the acquisition of φύσει δοῦλοι) falls within the sound or limited χρηματιστική. Columella (de Re Rustica, Lib. 1. Praefat. c. 7) will not admit war to be a laudable form of κτητική: cp. [Aristot.] Oecon. 1. 2. 1343 a 27, ἡ δὲ γεωργικὴ μάλιστα ὅτι δικαία· οὐ γὰρ ἀπ' ἀνθρώπων, οὔθ' ἑκόντων, ὥσπερ καπηλεία καὶ αἱ μισθαρνικαί, οὔτ' ἀκόντων, ὥσπερ αἱ πολεμικαί.

26. ἓν μὲν οὖν κ.τ.λ. The first question which arises as to this much-debated passage relates to κατὰ φύσιν. Sepulv., Vict. ('unam rationem quaerendi rem, illam inquam quae naturam sequitur'), Lamb., and Giph. connect κατὰ φύσιν with κτητικῆς, but this seems hardly possible. Bern., who connects κατὰ φύσιν with μέρος ἐστίν, translates 'is a natural part of Household Science,' but Susemihl and Mr. Welldon are probably right in translating 'is naturally a part.' The remainder of the paragraph (ὃ δεῖ κ.τ.λ.) is thus rendered by Sepulveda—'quae (quaestuaria) vel suppetere debet, vel res ab ipsa comparari, quae condi reponique solent necessariae ad vitam et ad civitatis aut domus societatem tuendam accommodatae'; he adds in his note the following explanation—'aut haec quaestuaria facultas adesse debet patrifamilias atque homini civili, ut per eam res necessariae ab ipsis comparentur, aut certe per eam res necessariae comparari debent ab eo, cuicumque tribuatur.' He evidently refers αὐτήν 28, not to τῆς οἰκονομικῆς 27, to which Bern., Sus., Stahr, and others are probably right in referring it, but to εἶδος κτητικῆς 26. There is much more to be said for his view that χρήματα, the suppressed antecedent of ὧν χρημάτων, is the subject of ὑπάρχῃ. It is thus that both Stahr and Vahlen (Aristotel. Aufsätze, 2. 32) interpret the passage. For the case and position of χρημάτων within the relative sentence, see Vahlen *ubi supra*, who compares 4 (7). 1. 1323 b 15: 6 (4). 4. 1290 b 28: 6 (4). 5. 1292 b 8. If we follow these authorities (as I have done in vol. 1. p. 129), we shall translate—'which (form of the Science of Supply) must either be forthcoming, or Household Science must itself ensure that storeable commodities shall be forthcoming,' etc. This interpretation of the passage, however, is open to the objection that it supplies a different subject with the words ὑπάρχειν and ὑπάρχῃ, whereas the sentence certainly reads as if one and the same subject should be supplied with each. I incline, therefore, on further consideration, to suggest a different interpretation. May not there be an ellipse of 'having to do with' before ὧν ἐστὶ θησαυρισμὸς χρημάτων, just as there is in 1. 3. 1253 b 3, οἰκονομίας δὲ μέρη, ἐξ ὧν πάλιν οἰκία συνέστηκεν, and in 1. 11. 1258 b 27 sqq., τρίτον δὲ εἶδος χρηματιστικῆς . . . ὅσα ἀπὸ γῆς καὶ τῶν ἀπὸ γῆς γινομένων κ.τ.λ. (see above on 1253 b 3)? If we explain the passage thus, ὃ (εἶδος κτητικῆς) will be the subject both of ὑπάρχειν and of ὑπάρχῃ. On Bernays' proposed substitution of καθό for ὅ, see Sus. Qu. Crit. p. 352. For other suggested emendations, and for Susemihl's own view of the passage, see notes 2 and 3 in Sus.[2], vol. 1. p. 116. In strictness the function of οἰκονομική is not τὸ πορίσασθαι τὰ κατὰ τὴν οἰκίαν, but τὸ χρήσασθαι (c. 8. 1256 a 11: cp. διαθεῖναι, c. 10. 1258 a 24); we are told, however, here (cp. μάλιστα, 'if possible,' c. 10. 1258 a 34), that if ἡ κατὰ φύσιν κτητική is not forthcoming from the first, οἰκονομική must see that it is forthcoming. Ἐστὶ θησαυρισμός appears to be added because there are things necessary to human life (e. g. light, air, fire) which cannot be stored. On Storeableness as an attribute of Wealth, see Comte, Social Statics, E. T. p. 131, and J. S. Mill, Principles of Political Economy B. 1. c. 3. § 3.

Are slaves and cattle, however, susceptible of *θησαυρισμός*? and does Aristotle's definition of wealth include wealth in land? For the various kinds of wealth, genuine and other, see 2. 7. 1267 b 10 sq. and Rhet. 1. 5. 1361 a 12 sqq. J. S. Mill defines wealth (Principles of Political Economy, Preliminary Remarks, and B. 1. c. 3. § 3) as 'useful and agreeable things of a material nature, possessing exchange value.' Aristotle says nothing here of exchange value, though his definition of *χρήματα* in Eth. Nic. 4. 1. 1119 b 26 as *πάντα ὅσων ἡ ἀξία νομίσματι μετρεῖται* implies this limitation. How far does his account of wealth in the passage before us agree with his account of *κτήματα* in c. 4. 1254 a 16, where he seems to exclude *ὄργανα ποιητικά* from *κτῆσις*? Such *ὄργανα* are certainly *χρήσιμα εἰς κοινωνίαν πόλεως ἢ οἰκίας*. On Mill's definition, see Prof. H. Sidgwick in the *Fortnightly Review* for Feb. 1879. *Μὲν οὖν* is taken up by *μὲν τοίνυν* 37, and answered by *δὲ* 40.

31. ἐκ τούτων. 'Ἐκ is here used of the 'material' of which wealth is made, the 'elements' which constitute it: cp. 2. 2. 1261 a 22, *ἐκ πλειόνων ἀνθρώπων*.

γάρ, 'for true wealth is not unlimited in quantity (consisting as it does of *ὄργανα*, and no *ὄργανον* being unlimited either in size or quantity), and the wealth of which we speak is not unlimited in quantity.' Just as a very large or very small shuttle, or too many shuttles or too few, would be in the way and ineffective for the end (cp. 4 (7). 4. 1326 a 35 sqq.), so too large or too small a supply of necessary and useful commodities is unfavourable to *ἀγαθὴ ζωή*. This thought was taken up by Epicurus: cp. Porphyr. de Abstin. 1. 49, *ὥρισται γάρ, φησίν, ὁ τῆς φύσεως πλοῦτος καὶ ἔστιν εὐπόριστος, ὁ δὲ τῶν κενῶν δοξῶν ἀόριστός τε ἦν καὶ δυσπόριστος*. Bernays (Theophrastos' Schrift über Frömmigkeit, p. 145) compares also the fourteenth *κυρία δόξα* of Epicurus (Diog. Laert. 10. 144). Cp. also Plutarch de Cupiditate Divitiarum, c. 4. 524 E–F. For *αὐτάρκεια*, cp. c. 9. 1257 a 30.

32. Σόλων. See Fragm. 13. 71 sqq., and Theognis 227 where the lines appear in a slightly altered form. They seem to be present to Isocrates' memory in De Pace § 7.

33. πεφασμένον ἀνδράσι, 'made known to men.'

34. ταῖς ἄλλαις τέχναις, 'in the case of other arts.'

35. οὐδὲν γὰρ ὄργανον κ.τ.λ. Aristippus appears to have met this argument by anticipation; cp. Fragm. 58 (Mullach, Fr. Philos. Gr. 2. 412), *οὐχ ὥσπερ ὑπόδημα τὸ μεῖζον δύσχρηστον, οὕτω καὶ ἡ πλείων κτῆσις· τοῦ μὲν γὰρ ἐν τῇ χρήσει τὸ περιττὸν ἐμποδίζει· τῇ δὲ καὶ ὅλῃ χρῆσθαι κατὰ καιρὸν ἔξεστι καὶ μέρει*.

36. See J. S. Mill, Principles of Political Economy, Preliminary

Remarks, on definitions of wealth which, like that in the text, treat it as 'a mass of instruments.'

38. δι' ἣν αἰτίαν. The reason apparently is that the acquisition of the things assigned by Nature for the service of man is a necessity of human life. For *ἥν*, see above on 1252 a 20, and cp. de An. 2. 7. 419 a 6.

40. ἣν is affected by attraction to *χρηματιστικήν*, though *αὐτὸ* is not: the fem. continues to be used in 41—1257 a 5. C. 9.

41. δι' ἥν. How this happens, we learn in 1. 9. 1257 b 35 sqq.

3. ἐκείνης. 'Pronomen *ἐκεῖνος* ab Aristotele etiam ad proximas voces trahitur' (Busse, de praesidiis Aristotelis Politica emendandi, p. 24, who refers to Pol. 7 (5). 6. 1306 a 10: Meteor. 2. 6. 364 a 8 sq.). 1257 a.

4. δι' ἐμπειρίας. Cp. 1257 b 3.

7. καθ' αὑτό. On predication *καθ' αὑτό*, see Anal. Post. 1. 4. 73 a 34–b 24 and other passages collected in Bon. Ind. 212 a 3 sqq. We have here to do with use *καθ' αὑτό*. A thing is used *καθ' αὑτό*, when it is used as being what it is and nothing else. Thus the term is explained in 12 by *χρῆσθαι τῷ ὑποδήματι ᾗ ὑπόδημα*. The *μεταβλητικὴ χρῆσις* of a shoe is an use of it *καθ' αὑτό*, as much so in fact as the *οἰκεία χρῆσις*, the use of it as an article of wear; it is because the shoe is a shoe that the buyer buys it and the wearer wears it; still the one use is *οἰκεία τοῦ πράγματος* (the use for which the shoe was made) and the other is not. If the shoe were used, on the contrary, for measuring, it would not be used as a shoe, but as being of a certain length. This is explained in Eth. Eud. 3. 4. 1231 b 38 sq., where, however, the writer so far departs from Aristotle's view that he treats the sale of an article as an use of it *κατὰ συμβεβηκός*, not *καθ' αὑτό*. From the use made of commodities in simple exchange must be distinguished the use made of them by the unsound *χρηματιστική*, which aims at the indefinite increase of wealth (c. 9. 1257 b 35 sq.).

14. ἡ μεταβλητική, sc. *χρῆσις*, as in 9, or *τέχνη*? The latter view seems preferable, for we must supply *τέχνη* with *ἡ τοιαύτη μεταβλητική* in 28. Perhaps, however, we may translate simply 'exchange' (Bern. Sus. 'Tauschhandel').

15. μέν has no *δέ* to answer to it, apparently because at *ᾗ καὶ δῆλον* the intended course of the sentence is changed: we expect it to be continued—'but later passing the limit of necessity and nature.'

ἐκ τοῦ κατὰ φύσιν, 'from that which is natural' (Mr. Welldon, 'from natural circumstances').

17. ᾗ καὶ δῆλον κ.τ.λ. Vict. 'quo perspicuum etiam est non constare natura pecuniariae genus cauponarium.' Lamb. (followed by Bernays and Susemihl): 'ex quo licet intelligere cauponariam (seu mercaturam sordidam quam profitentur atque exercent ii qui ab aliis emunt quod pluris revendant) non esse partem artis pecuniae quaerendae natura.' In favour of Vict.'s rendering, cp. Phys. 2. 2. 194 b 2, τῆς ποιητικῆς ἡ ἀρχιτεκτονική, and the statement in 3, ἔστι δ' ἡ μὲν φύσει ἡ δ' οὐ φύσει αὐτῶν: in favour of the other, c. 8. 1256 b 23, διὸ καὶ ἡ πολεμικὴ φύσει κτητική πως ἔσται. The interpretation of Lamb. is probably right. Bern. conjectures τῆς μεταβλητικῆς for τῆς χρηματιστικῆς, looking probably to ἡ μεταβλητικὴ 14, but all the MSS. read τῆς χρηματιστικῆς, and in 1257 b 2 we have θάτερον εἶδος τῆς χρηματιστικῆς . . . τὸ καπηλικόν.

18. ὅσον γὰρ κ.τ.λ. Sepulveda: 'alioquin necesse erat ut quatenus eis satis esset, commutationibus uterentur.' 'For if it were so, those who practise it would necessarily have made use of exchange only to obtain what suffices for themselves [whereas in fact they notoriously purchase not for their own use, but to resell at a profit]. So the commentators generally. Cp. 5 (8). 3. 1337 b 35, οὐ γὰρ δὴ παίζοντας· τέλος γὰρ ἀναγκαῖον εἶναι τοῦ βίου τὴν παιδιὰν ἡμῖν. For the omission of ἂν in phrases like ἀναγκαῖον ἦν, see Jelf, Gr. Gr. § 858. 3. 'Ικανόν takes up τῶν ἱκανῶν. Τὸ κατὰ φύσιν is τὸ ἱκανὸν αὐτοῖς (cp. 30 and 1256 b 11). It is possible, no doubt, to take ἦν historically, and not as = ἦν ἄν, and to translate 'for it was necessary (and therefore natural) to make use of exchange to obtain what suffices for the persons exchanging (which those who practise καπηλική do not do),' and this rendering would suit the paragraph which follows, which is historical in purport; ἀναγκαῖον κ.τ.λ. would also be used in the same sense as four or five lines below (23); but the ordinary interpretation seems on the whole preferable.

19. μὲν οὖν introduces a slight correction of what precedes ('true, exchange is not necessary in the household'). It seems to be answered by ἀλλά, 21: cp. c. 13. 1260 a 13, and see Sus.[1] Ind. Gramm. s. v. μέν.

τῇ πρώτῃ κοινωνίᾳ, i.e. the household, though the union of male and female and that of master and slave are spoken of as κοινωνίαι (c. 2. 1252 b 10), and are of course prior to the household, for the household is formed of them. Cp. αἱ πρῶται κοινωνίαι, c. 2. 1252 b 31.

21. αὐτῆς is taken apparently by Sus. to refer to ἀλλαγὴν 19, but I incline to follow Bern. and Mr. Welldon, who refer it to ἡ μεταβλητικὴ 14 (cp. ἡ μὲν οὖν τοιαύτη μεταβλητική, 28). It is true that in 1257 b 1 the earlier form of μεταβλητικὴ is described as ἡ ἀναγκαία ἀλλαγή, so that the sense is much the same, whichever view we adopt.

πλείονος τῆς κοινωνίας οὔσης, i.e. 'extended,' in opposition to πρώτη (Bon. Ind. 618 b 34): cp. 2. 2. 1261 b 12, καὶ βούλεταί γ' ἤδη τότε εἶναι πόλις, ὅταν αὐτάρκη συμβαίνῃ τὴν κοινωνίαν εἶναι τοῦ πλήθους. 'Η μεταβλητική seems to be regarded as beginning in the κώμη and the πόλις.

οἱ μὲν γὰρ κ.τ.λ. As to the phrase πολλῶν καὶ ἑτέρων, see Bon. Ind. 357 b 8: 'καί interdum duo adiectiva coniungit, quorum alterum definiendo alteri inserviat, non solum ubi prius adiectivum πολύς est (πολλοὶ καὶ παλαιοὶ λέγουσιν, Eth. Nic. 1. 8. 1098 b 27 al.), sed etiam in aliis.' It has been much discussed, on what verb the words πολλῶν καὶ ἑτέρων depend. Schn. would supply ἐδέοντο, while Bern. thinks that no addition is needed, inasmuch as κεχωρισμένοι contains the notion of 'wanting.' For Susemihl's view, see his note. Vict., however, would seem from his commentary to supply ἐκοινώνουν—certainly the most natural course, and that which best agrees with πλείονος τῆς κοινωνίας οὔσης. Aristotle is commonly chary of words, and often expects us to supply a word from a previous clause which is not altogether suitable—e. g. in 3. 16. 1287 b 28 (ἴδοι): 6 (4). 13. 1297 a 40 (πορίζειν): 2. 5. 1264 b 2 (οἰκονομήσει). Cp. also 8 (6). 8. 1322 a 16–18. Both household and village have a certain aggregate of commodities at their disposal, but whereas in the household what one member has all others have, in the village this is not so; on the contrary, some members of the village have corn and no shoes, others shoes and no corn. The members of the village are described as κεχωρισμένοι, i. e. they are no longer ὁμοσίπυοι or ὁμόκαποι, but are parted into a plurality of households. The use of the word κοινωνεῖν in reference both to the household and to the village is of course not fortunate, for the household shares in what it possesses in a different sense from the village.

23. κατὰ τὰς δεήσεις, in contrast to the practice of κάπηλοι.

ποιεῖσθαι τὰς μεταδόσεις . . . κατὰ τὴν ἀλλαγήν. 'Αλλαγή here means 'barter': μετάδοσις is the more comprehensive word, including barter as one of its forms.

24. καί (in place of which Bern. conjectures καὶ νῦν) probably means 'no less than the members of the village.'

26. ἐπὶ πλέον δ' οὐδέν, i. e. no money, which is here contrasted with τὰ χρήσιμα, not that it is not itself one of τὰ χρήσιμα (36), but because it is not directly useful for subsistence, like corn or wine.

29. χρηματιστικῆς, i. e. τῆς μάλιστα χρηματιστικῆς, 1256 b 41.

30. Cp. Eth. Nic. 3. 13. 1118 b 18, ἀναπλήρωσις γὰρ τῆς ἐνδείας ἡ φυσικὴ ἐπιθυμία.

31. κατὰ λόγον, 'in accordance with reason and what one would naturally expect': see the references in Bon. Ind. 368 b 50 sq. It is often used in much the same sense as εὐλόγως (e. g. in Metaph. N. 1. 1088 a 4–6), and the phrase διά τιν' αἰτίαν εὔλογον (de Part. An. 2. 17. 660 b 16) may be compared. In Rhet. ad Alex. 9. 1429 a 28 we have—τὰ μὲν γὰρ τῶν πραγμάτων γίνεται κατὰ λόγον τὰ δὲ παρὰ λόγον.

ξενικωτέρας γὰρ κ.τ.λ. 'For, the supply of men's needs coming to be more drawn from sources external to the State.' Here the origin of money is traced to an increased distance between buyer and seller. Money being more portable than commodities in general, an advantage is found in paying a distant seller in this way. Aristotle perhaps remembers that the Greek coinage had its origin in the commerce of Aegina: cp. Strabo, p. 376, Ἔφορος δ' ἐν Αἰγίνῃ ἄργυρον πρῶτον κοπῆναί φησιν ὑπὸ Φείδωνος· ἐμπόριον γὰρ γενέσθαι. In Eth. Nic. 5. 8, however, the advantages of money in all commercial transactions, whether between parties near to or distant from each other, are recognized. Again, the purchaser may not for the moment need any commodity in return: in this case money serves as an ἐγγυητὴς ὅτι ἔσται ἐὰν δεηθῇ (Eth. Nic. 5. 8. 1133 b 10 sq.). Still all this is quite reconcileable with the view that what first called money into being was its use in distant transactions. Plato (Laws 742 A) seems to regard the payment of wages and of artisans' remuneration as that which makes some sort of money necessary. Giph. (p. 99) refers to Isocr. Paneg. § 42, which is not without resemblances to the passage before us.

32. ὧν ἐνδεεῖς. For the omission of εἶναι and its parts, see Vahlen on Poet. 24. 1459 b 7 (p. 243).

35. διὸ πρὸς τὰς ἀλλαγὰς κ.τ.λ. Cp. 1. 10. 1258 b 4, οὐκ ἐφ' ὅπερ ἐπορίσθη· μεταβολῆς γὰρ ἐγένετο χάριν (τὸ νόμισμα). The selection of the particular commodity was a matter of convention, so that here for the first time convention stepped in; but even then money was for a space dealt with inartificially by weighing, till the measure of its artificiality was made complete by the ingenious addition of a stamp to denote the value of the coin. With συνέθεντο, cp. κατὰ συνθήκην, Eth. Nic. 5. 8. 1133 a 29.

37. εἶχε κ.τ.λ., 'possessed utility of a kind to be easily dealt with and made available for the end of existence'—was, in fact, easily carried, easily stored, easily converted into other commodities, and so forth. Vict. 'unum eorum quae . . . possunt facile deferri ad alios'; but that is only one of the characteristics present to the mind of Aristotle. Lamb. better: 'usum haberet tractabilem ac facilem ad vitam degendam.' For εἶχε τὴν χρείαν (which takes up τῶν χρησίμων), cp. Sosipater (Meineke, Fr. Com. Gr. 4. 483)—

μεγάλην χρείαν τιν' εἰς τὸ πρᾶγμ' ἔχει.

For τὸ ζῆν, cp. 1257 b 41. The Thessalians are said by Isocrates to be ἄνδρες οὐκ εὐμεταχείριστοι (Epist. 2. § 20). Aristotle notices portability and ease in use as characteristics of a satisfactory circulating medium, but not durability or steadiness of value. The last-named characteristic is, however, referred to in Eth. Nic. 5. 8. 1133 b 13 sq.

38. σίδηρος κ.τ.λ. Iron, or the dross of iron—τὸ ἀχρεῖον τοῦ σιδήρου—(by weight) by the Lacedaemonians ([Plato,] Eryxias 400 B): iron coins were also used at Byzantium (see Mr. Ridgeway, *Trans. Cambr. Philol. Society*, vol. 2. p. 131, who refers to Plato Com., Πείσανδρος 3—Meineke, Fr. Com. Gr. 2. 649)—and Ar. Nub. 249): an iron coin of Hermaeus king of Bactria, brought by Sir Douglas Forsyth from the ruined cities of Central Asia, is mentioned in the *Academy*, Nov. 25, 1876 (p. 527). Cp. also Caesar de Bell. Gall. 5. 12: utuntur (Britanni) aut aere aut taleis ferreis ad certum pondus examinatis pro nummo. As to κἂν εἴ τι τοιοῦτον ἕτερον, we find in the Eryxias (399 E sqq.) a description of the leather money of Carthage; but, as Mr. Ridgeway says (ibid.), Aristotle may have in his mind 'some such coinage as the electrum money used at Cyzicus.'

41. ὁ γὰρ χαρακτὴρ κ.τ.λ. The χαρακτήρ varied with the value. 'The tetradrachm of Syracuse is in early times stamped with a quadriga, the didrachm with a pair of horses, the drachm with a single horse with its rider. Thus the number of horses shows at a glance the number of drachms in any piece of Syracusan money. The obol is marked with the wheel of a chariot' (Prof. P. Gardner, Types of Greek Coins, p. 50). 'On the tetrobol of Athens there are two owls; on the diobol the owl has but one head, but two bodies; on the triobol the owl is facing the spectator, and so forth . . . In Thessaly a horseman marks the diobol, a single horse the obol' (ibid. p. 66). But see Mr. Head's remarks, Hist. Numorum, p. lvi.

2. τὸ καπηλικόν. The unsound kind of χρηματιστική is so called, 1257 b.
not because none but κάπηλοι practised it, but because it was exemplified in, and best illustrated by, their way of trading, with which every one was familiar. The κάπηλος did not himself produce what he sold, but bought it of the producer, and bought to sell again,

not to supply his own household needs. His operations were on a smaller scale than those of the ἔμπορος, and, unlike his, were confined within the limits of a particular State (cp. Plato, Polit. 260 C: Rep. 371 D: Sophist. 223 D: and see Büchsenschütz, Besitz und Erwerb, p. 454–6 and notes). This kind of χρηματιστική comes into existence after the appearance of money on the scene, but its existence is in reality due not to money, but to a radically wrong view of the end of human life (1257 b 40 sqq., and esp. 1258 a 5). Money, however, makes it possible,—how, Aristotle does not directly explain; but he probably means that money facilitates sale and re-sale, is easily stored, and the like, and thus meets the spirit of gain half-way. If trade were carried on by barter, the practices of the κάπηλοι would be defeated by the cumbrousness of the operation, and they might suffer more by depreciation of stock. 'The value of money,' says Gibbon (Decline and Fall, c. 9—vol. i. p. 356), 'has been settled by general consent to express our wants and our property, as letters were invented to express our ideas; and both these institutions, by giving a more active energy to the powers and passions of human nature, have contributed to multiply the objects they were designed to represent.' See also the quotation from Xen. de Vectigalibus given in the note on 1257 b 33.

3. μὲν οὖν. See note on 1252 b 27 sqq.

4. τεχνικώτερον. Cp. Isocr. ad Nicocl. § 1.

πόθεν κ.τ.λ. Πόθεν seems to depend on τεχνικώτερον, which itself seems to be adverbial to γινόμενον. But what is the nom. to ποιήσει? Vict. and Bern. make μεταβαλλόμενον passive, the former supplying τὸ νόμισμα, the latter 'etwas' (i.e. a commodity). Lamb. and Giph. explain μεταβαλλόμενον by 'permutando,' apparently making it middle: Bonitz also would seem to take it as middle (Ind. 458 b 15), for he adds 'i.e. ποῖον γένος τῆς μεταβλητικῆς.' Adopting this explanation of πῶς μεταβαλλόμενον, which makes τὸ καπηλικόν nom. to ποιήσει, we are still met by the question, what is the meaning of πόθεν? Does it qualify μεταβαλλόμενον like πῶς, or are the words πῶς μεταβαλλόμενον to be taken together by themselves, so that the meaning will be—'carried on with a more studied skill in devising from what source and by what kind of investment it will win most profit'? Perhaps this is the correct interpretation. Cp. πῶς, c. 11. 1258 b 13.

5. διὸ κ.τ.λ. Aristotle here passes on to describe the effect of the emergence of this kind of χρηματιστική on opinion. It suggests to many the erroneous conclusion that the aim of χρηματιστική is the acquisition of money and of as much money as possible. But then others by a natural reaction refuse to allow that money is wealth, or that this kind of *χρηματιστική* is *χρηματιστική* at all. This conflict of view enables Aristotle to step in, as is his wont, and to say that those who take the latter view are so far right that the *καπηλική χρηματιστική* is not *χρηματιστική κατὰ φύσιν*, nor is money natural wealth. The natural *χρηματιστική* is that which goes hand in hand with the science of household management, and which regards the acquisition of commodities, not as an end, but as a means to *τὸ εὖ ζῆν* rightly understood, and therefore not to be pursued beyond a certain limit of amount.

7. ποιητικὴ γὰρ εἶναι, sc. *δοκεῖ*.

τοῦ πλούτου καὶ χρημάτων. Vahlen (Aristot. Aufsätze, 2. 13 n.) compares 4 (7). 1. 1323 a 37, *πλούτου καὶ χρημάτων*, and 1. 9. 1257 a 1, *πλούτου καὶ κτήσεως*. Here, as often elsewhere (Bon. Ind. 357 b 13), *καί* appears to be used in an explanatory sense, just as it is two lines lower in *τὴν χρηματιστικὴν καὶ τὴν καπηλικήν*, and in *ἀλλαγῆς καὶ καπηλείας*, 1256 a 41. *Χρημάτων* is an ambiguous word, often meaning money and always suggestive of it (cp. Eth. Nic. 4. 1. 1119 b 26, *χρήματα δὲ λέγομεν πάντα ὅσων ἡ ἀξία νομίσματι μετρεῖται*, and [Plato,] Eryxias 403 D, quoted below on 11).

8. καὶ γὰρ τὸν πλοῦτον κ.τ.λ. These words supply an indispensable link in the argument, which seems to be as follows—*χρηματιστική* is *ποιητικὴ τοῦ πλούτου καὶ χρημάτων*, *πλοῦτος* is *νομίσματος πλῆθος*, therefore *χρηματιστική* is *ποιητικὴ νομίσματος πλήθους*, or in other words, its *ἔργον* is *τὸ δύνασθαι θεωρεῖν πόθεν ἔσται πλῆθος χρημάτων*. This word *χρημάτων* might have been *νομίσματος*, but the two words do not lie far apart in meaning. In *καὶ γάρ* somewhat of the force of *καί* perhaps survives: 'they not only misconstrue *χρηματιστική* and take it to be concerned with money (5), but they also misconstrue *πλοῦτος* and take it to be abundance of money.' So we have *τὸν πλοῦτον καὶ τὴν χρηματιστικήν*, 18.

11. νόμος, 'a mere convention': cp. Eth. Nic. 5. 8. 1133 a 30, *καὶ διὰ τοῦτο τοὔνομα ἔχει νόμισμα, ὅτι οὐ φύσει ἀλλὰ νόμῳ ἐστί, καὶ ἐφ' ἡμῖν μεταβαλεῖν καὶ ποιῆσαι ἄχρηστον*: Magn. Mor. 1. 34. 1194 a 21–23: Plato, Laws 889 E: Xen. Mem. 4. 4. 14, *νόμους δ', ἔφη, ὦ Σώκρατες, πῶς ἄν τις ἡγήσαιτο σπουδαῖον πρᾶγμα εἶναι ἢ τὸ πείθεσθαι αὐτοῖς, οὕς γε πολλάκις αὐτοὶ οἱ θέμενοι ἀποδοκιμάσαντες μετατίθενται*; *Νόμος* and *νόμισμα* were both connected in popular etymology with *νομίζω*. Plato had said in Laws 742 E, *πλουσίους δ' αὖ σφόδρα καὶ ἀγαθοὺς ἀδύνατον, οὕς γε δὴ πλουσίους οἱ πολλοὶ καταλέγουσι· λέγουσι δὲ τοὺς κεκτημένους ἐν ὀλίγοις τῶν ἀνθρώπων πλείστου νομίσματος ἄξια κτήματα, ἃ καὶ κακός τις κεκτῆτ' ἄν*: cp. Rep. 521 A, Laws 736 E, and Aristot. Rhet. 1. 5. 1361 a 23 sqq. But it is possible that the Cynics, or some of them, are also here referred to. The Eryxias, which is included among the dialogues ascribed to Plato, appears to treat the subject of money and wealth from a Cynical point of view, and we find in it not indeed the exact arguments here used, but arguments pointing to the same conclusion—e.g. 403 D, τί οὐκ ἐκεῖνον τὸν λόγον διετέλεσας, ὡς τὰ δοκοῦντα οὐκ ἔστι χρήματα, χρυσίον καὶ ἀργύριον καὶ τἆλλα τὰ τοιαῦτα; When we are told (18) that the persons referred to by Aristotle in the passage before us sought wealth and χρηματιστική in something other than the things to which these names were commonly given, we are reminded of Eryxias 403 C, ἐπιστήμην γάρ τινα παραδιδοὺς τῷ ἀνθρώπῳ ἅμα καὶ πλούσιον αὐτὸν πεποίηκε, and Diog. Laert. 6. 68, who says of the Cynic Diogenes—τὴν παιδείαν εἶπε τοῖς μὲν νέοις σωφροσύνην, τοῖς δὲ πρεσβυτέροις παραμυθίαν, τοῖς δὲ πένησι πλοῦτον, τοῖς δὲ πλουσίοις κόσμον εἶναι. The Cynics seem to have made out knowledge how to use things to be real wealth, and its acquisition true χρηματιστική. Compare the doctrine of the Stoics that 'the wise man alone is rich,' and see Cic. Paradoxa Stoicorum 6. 3. 51. Zeno of Citium in his ideal polity, which was much coloured by Cynicism, abolished the use of money altogether (Diog. Laert. 7. 33, νόμισμα δ' οὔτ' ἀλλαγῆς ἕνεκεν οἴεσθαι δεῖν κατασκευάζειν οὔτε ἀποδημίας ἕνεκεν). The arguments used by the inquirers here referred to are far from convincing, though Aristotle does not stop to comment on them: money does not necessarily become valueless when deprived of the character of money (cp. τῶν χρησίμων αὐτὸ ὄν, 1257 a 36), and as Lord Macaulay noted on the margin of his copy of the Politics (*Macmillan's Magazine*, July 1875, p. 220), 'a man who has plenty of clothes and drink may die of hunger, yet you would call clothes and drink wealth.' Aristotle, it is true, speaks (Eth. Nic. 5. 8. 1133 a 31) of money being made 'useless' by demonetization, and he also looks upon articles of subsistence as furnishing the truest type of wealth (ἡ περὶ τὴν τροφήν, 1258 a 17), but he would hardly go so far as the inquirers he refers to here. Things which serve for clothing and as ὄργανα are to him part of true wealth (1256 b 15 sqq.).

οὐδέν. Cp. 5 (8). 6. 1341 b 7: de Gen. An. 4. 4. 771 b 29.

μεταθεμένων. Mr. Welldon: 'give up a currency and adopt another.' For this use of the word, compare Fragm. Aristot. 508. 1561 b 4, ἔλαβεν ὁ Εὔξενος γυναῖκα καὶ συνῴκει μεταθέμενος τοὔνομα Ἀριστοξένην, and the use of the word μεταστήσωσιν in 7 (5). 1. 1301 b 8. Cp. also Plato, Laws 889 E.

12. οὔτε. See critical note.

14. ἀπορήσει. For this use of the third person, see Bon. Ind. 589 b 47 sqq.: 763 a 25 sq.

15. ἀπολεῖται. For the future after τοιοῦτον οὗ, cp. 2. 7. 1266 b 36. Compare also Plato, Euthyd. 299 D–E.

τὸν Μίδαν ἐκεῖνον, sc. ἀπολέσθαι.

20. Bekker reads ἡ δὲ καπηλικὴ ποιητικὴ χρημάτων κ.τ.λ.: thus he evidently, like the Vet. Int., makes ἡ καπηλικὴ the nominative. Susemihl's stopping, however, which I have adopted, seems preferable. With this stopping, the translation will be—'but the other is commercial.' Cp. 1. 10. 1258 a 39.

21. ἀλλ' ᾖ. All MSS. have ἀλλ' ᾗ or ἀλλ' ἡ, none ἀλλά. The sentence would have been regularly constructed, if it had run—οὐ ποιητικὴ χρημάτων ἀλλ' ἢ διὰ χρημάτων μεταβολῆς, or ποιητικὴ χ. οὐ πάντως, ἀλλὰ διὰ χ. μ. μόνον. Instead of adopting either of these forms, Aristotle anticipates in οὐ πάντως the coming exception and employs both οὐ πάντως and ἀλλ' ἤ: cp. Plato, Protag. 354 B, ἢ ἔχετέ τι ἄλλο τέλος λέγειν . . . ἀλλ' ἢ ἡδονάς τε καὶ λύπας, where Riddell (Apol. p. 175) remarks, 'the ἄλλο is anticipatory of the exception, and this is also pleonastic.'

22. καὶ δοκεῖ κ.τ.λ. It is thought to be concerned with money, because it operates through exchange and money is the starting-point and goal of exchange. In reality, however, it deals with κτῆσις (37), the same subject-matter as οἰκονομικὴ χρηματιστικὴ deals with, though with a different aim. Στοιχεῖον, 'id quod est simplicissimum, ex quo reliqua conficiuntur' (Bon. Ind. 702 b 32): cp. πορισθέντος οὖν ἤδη νομίσματος, 1257 a 41. Πέρας, 'quia contenta haec ratio rei quaerendae est cum coacervat nummos, nec aliud sibi proponit' (Vict.). Cp. Hegesipp. Fragm. (Meineke, Fr. Com. Gr. 4. 479),

> Οὔκ, ἀλλὰ τὸ πέρας τῆς μαγειρικῆς, Σύρε,
> εὑρηκέναι πάντων νόμιζε μόνον ἐμέ:

and Posidipp. Fr. (ibid. 4. 521),

> Τῆς τέχνης πέρας
> τοῦτ' ἔστιν.

Aristotle, however, recognizes a kind of exchange which is carried on independently of money and before money comes into being.

23. καὶ . . . δή. See note on 1253 a 18. Here is a further distinction between the καπηλικὴ and the οἰκονομικὴ χρηματιστική. Not only does the former seek wealth by means of exchange alone, but it aims at an unlimited amount. It makes wealth, which is a means, an end, and as all arts pursue their end to an indeterminate extent, it consequently pursues wealth to an indeterminate extent.

25. **εἰς ἄπειρόν ἐστι.** Cp. 1258 a 1, *εἰς ἄπειρον οὖν ἐκείνης τῆς ἐπιθυμίας οὔσης*, and Metaph. Γ. 5. 1010 a 22, *εἶναι εἰς ἄπειρον*, where Bekker conjectures *ἰέναι* without necessity: see Bonitz on the passage.

27. **ἐκεῖνο.** See above on 1257 a 3.

29. **ὁ τοιοῦτος κ.τ.λ.**, i. e. *ὁ χρηματιστικὸς πλοῦτος*—'a mass of *χρήματα*, and especially money, and the quest of this by exchange alone.'

30. **τῆς δ' οἰκονομικῆς κ.τ.λ.** It is natural, looking to *ταύτης τῆς χρηματιστικῆς* 28, to explain *τῆς οἰκονομικῆς* as *τῆς οἰκονομικῆς χρηματιστικῆς*, and with this view to propose the excision of *οὐ*, or the substitution of *αὖ* (Bernays), which the wrong reading of *οὖν* for *αὖ* by Π[3] in 1268 a 39 might well be used to support. But perhaps no change is necessary, for *χρημάτων κτήσεως* is very probably that which we are to supply. Transl.: 'but of house-keeping, not money-making, acquisition of commodities there is a measure, for money-making is not the business of the house-keeping acquisition of commodities.' *Τοῦτο* appears to refer to *ὁ τοιοῦτος πλοῦτος κ.τ.λ.* Contrast 38, *ὥστε δοκεῖ τισὶ τοῦτ' εἶναι τῆς οἰκονομικῆς* [*χρήσεως τῆς χρηματιστικῆς*] *ἔργον*—i. e. *ἡ αὔξησις*.

32. **τῇ μέν.** Vict. 'hac quidem'—'si ita rem attendimus, id est si argumentis ducimur.' The reasoning referred to is that which is set forth in 1257 a 10–31, where we learn that true wealth is that which is necessary to sustenance and for the purposes of the household generally, and that this kind of wealth is limited by the needs of the household (cp. also 1256 b 26–37). Lamb., however, followed by Bernays, translates 'huic quidem'—i. e. for the *οἰκονομικὴ χρηματιστική*—not rightly, as it seems to me.

33. **ἐπὶ δὲ κ.τ.λ.**, 'but we see the opposite occurring in the experience of life.' For *συμβαίνειν ἐπί*, cp. de Gen. An. 2. 5. 741 b 19, *συμβαίνει δ' ἐπὶ πάντων τὸ τελευταῖον γινόμενον πρῶτον ἀπολείπειν, τὸ δὲ πρῶτον τελευταῖον.* Aristotle is met by a contrariety between *ὁ λόγος* and *τὰ γινόμενα* (or *τὰ συμβαίνοντα*), and we might expect that he would apply the famous principle of de Gen. An. 3. 10. 760 b 27 sqq., *ἐκ μὲν οὖν τοῦ λόγου τὰ περὶ τὴν γένεσιν τῶν μελιττῶν τοῦτον ἔχει τὸν τρόπον, καὶ ἐκ τῶν συμβαίνειν δοκούντων περὶ αὐτάς· οὐ μὴν εἴληπταί γε τὰ συμβαίνοντα ἱκανῶς, ἀλλ' ἐάν ποτε ληφθῇ, τότε τῇ αἰσθήσει μᾶλλον ἢ τῷ λόγῳ πιστευτέον, καὶ τοῖς λόγοις, ἐὰν ὁμολογούμενα δεικνύωσι τοῖς φαινομένοις.* But the question here is what ought to be and not what is, and *τὰ γινόμενα* are not as decisive as in a problem of natural history; men's action, as Aristotle proceeds to point out, is in this matter the offspring of mistake.

ὁρῶ(μεν). See critical note.

πάντες γὰρ κ.τ.λ. Cp. Xen. de Vectig. 4. 7, *καὶ γὰρ δὴ ἔπιπλα μέν, ἐπειδὰν ἱκανά τις κτήσηται τῇ οἰκίᾳ, οὐ μάλα ἔτι προσωνοῦνται· ἀργύριον δὲ οὐδείς πω οὕτω πολὺ ἐκτήσατο, ὥστε μὴ ἔτι προσδεῖσθαι.*

35. αἴτιον δὲ κ.τ.λ. What is *αὐτῶν*? I incline to think, not the two kinds of *χρηματιστική*, but the two kinds of *χρημάτων κτῆσις* (30), or in other words, the two uses of *χρηματιστική*. The reason why men act as if wealth were subject to no limit is the mutual proximity and similarity of the two ways of using *χρηματιστική*. 'For either use of *χρηματιστική*, being of the same thing, overlaps the other, so as to seem one and the same; for property—the subject-matter of both (cp. 1. 9. 1257 a 13 sq.)—is applied by both to (or has to do with) the same use, but not with the same aim, the aim of the one mode of using it being its increase and that of the other something quite different.' The two kinds of *χρηματιστική* are, in fact, only two different uses of the same science, or even an identical use, only with a different aim. *'Εκατέρα*, which is the reading of all known MSS., though three MSS. of the Vet. Int. (b g h) have 'utrique pecuniativae,' seems to be placed where it is to bring out the antithesis to *τοῦ αὐτοῦ οὖσα* more sharply. Sepulveda appears to have found *ἑκατέρας* in some MSS. (see critical note on 1257 b 36). There is certainly some strangeness in the immediate sequence of *ἑκατέρα ἡ χρῆσις* and *τῆς αὐτῆς χρήσεως*, and the genitive *τῆς αὐτῆς χρήσεως* is perplexing. But if we accept, with Bern. and Sus., Göttling's emendation *τῆς γὰρ αὐτῆς ἐστι κτήσεως χρῆσις*, we are not quit of our difficulties, for *τῆς αὐτῆς κτήσεως* is not a satisfactory expression. Perhaps the reduction of the two uses of *χρηματιστική* mentioned in 35–36 to the one use not *κατὰ ταὐτόν* of 37 may be no more than the word *ἐπαλλάττει* prepares us for. For the phrase *τῆς γὰρ αὐτῆς ἐστὶ χρήσεως κτῆσις*, Soph. El. 11. 171 b 29 may be compared (the passage also illustrates *οὐ κατὰ ταὐτόν*)—*καὶ τῶν λόγων τῶν αὐτῶν μέν εἰσιν οἱ φιλέριδες καὶ σοφισταί, ἀλλ' οὐ τῶν αὐτῶν ἕνεκεν· καὶ λόγος ὁ αὐτὸς μὲν ἔσται σοφιστικὸς καὶ ἐριστικός, ἀλλ' οὐ κατὰ ταὐτόν, ἀλλ' ᾗ μὲν νίκης φαινομένης, ἐριστικός, ᾗ δὲ σοφίας, σοφιστικός.* Cp. also Pol. 4 (7). 5. 1326 b 33, *ὅταν ὅλως περὶ κτήσεως καὶ τῆς περὶ τὴν οὐσίαν εὐπορίας συμβαίνῃ ποιεῖσθαι μνείαν, πῶς δεῖ καὶ τίνα τρόπον ἔχειν πρὸς τὴν χρῆσιν αὐτήν*; In 7 (5). 2. 1302 a 37 we have *ὧν δύο μέν ἐστι ταὐτὰ τοῖς εἰρημένοις, ἀλλ' οὐχ ὡσαύτως.*

38. ὥστε κ.τ.λ. takes up *ἐπαλλάττει*: the two uses of *χρηματιστική* overlap, and so the end of the *καπηλικὴ χρῆσις*—the increase of property—is taken to be the end of the οἰκονομικὴ χρῆσις (for perhaps it is more natural to supply χρῆσις here than χρηματιστική). Householders are thus led to follow the example of οἱ χρηματιζόμενοι in the use of property and to make its indefinite increase their aim. Aristotle seems, however, after all (40 sqq.) to trace the confusion of the οἰκονομικὴ χρῆσις of property with the καπηλικὴ χρῆσις of it to something more than the ἐπάλλαξις of the two—to a wrong view of the purpose of life and of the nature of τὸ εὖ ζῆν. Either men forget everything else for mere existence (τὸ ζῆν), or they erroneously take τὸ εὖ ζῆν to consist in bodily enjoyment. The same two contrasted classes of misusers of property appear in 4 (7). 5. 1326 b 36 sqq., and in a saying ascribed to Aristotle by Plutarch (de Cupiditate Divit. 8. 527 A), σὺ δὲ οὐκ ἀκούεις, φήσομεν, Ἀριστοτέλους λέγοντος, ὅτι οἱ μὲν οὐ χρῶνται [τοῖς χρήμασιν], οἱ δὲ παραχρῶνται (I owe this quotation to an unpublished essay by the late Mr. R. Shute). As to the former of the two classes, cp. Eth. Nic. 4. 1. 1120 a 2, δοκεῖ δ' ἀπώλειά τις αὐτοῦ εἶναι καὶ ἡ τῆς οὐσίας φθορά, ὡς τοῦ ζῆν διὰ τούτων ὄντος, and Dio Chrysost. Or. 6. 209 R. As to the misapprehension of τὸ εὖ ζῆν by the second, cp. Plato, Rep. 329 A, ἀγανακτοῦσιν ὡς μεγάλων τινῶν ἀπεστερημένοι, καὶ τότε μὲν (while in the enjoyment of the pleasures of youth) εὖ ζῶντες, νῦν δὲ οὐδὲ ζῶντες: Eurip. Fragm. 284. 3–6: Hyperid. Fragm. 209 Blass, μὴ δύνασθαι καλῶς ζῆν, μὴ μαθὼν τὰ καλὰ τὰ ἐν τῷ βίῳ (and these Hyperides notoriously interpreted in this way): Theopomp. Fr. 260. Our own expression 'living well' is, however, illustration enough.

40. τὴν κ.τ.λ., 'their wealth in money': see below on 1259 b 19.

1258 a. **1. εἰς ἄπειρον . . . οὔσης.** See note on 1257 b 25.

2. ὅσοι δὲ καὶ κ.τ.λ., 'and those who do aim at'; or perhaps the sense of καί is 'at all' (see Riddell, Apology of Plato, p. 168).

4. καὶ τοῦτ', i. e. not only τὸ ζῆν, but also τὸ πρὸς τὰς σωματικὰς ἀπολαύσεις.

6. ἐλήλυθεν. For this use of the word, see 8 (6). 2. 1317 b 14 sq. and Bon. Ind. 288 a 52 sq.

10. τῶν δυνάμεων here seems to include not only arts like στρατηγική, but also virtues like ἀνδρία: contrast Eth. Nic. 2. 4. 1105 b 20 sqq. and 5. 1. 1129 a 11 sqq.

οὐ κατὰ φύσιν. Plato (Rep. 346) had already insisted that pay is the end of the art of payment, not of medicine, or building, or navigation (cp. Rep. 342 D, ὡμολόγηται γὰρ ὁ ἀκριβὴς ἰατρὸς σωμάτων εἶναι ἄρχων, ἀλλ' οὐ χρηματιστής). There is perhaps a reminiscence of the passage before us in Magn. Mor. 1. 25. 1192 a 15 sqq., and possibly in Lucian, Cynicus 545.

11. στρατηγικῆς. Generals of the type of Chares (see Theopomp. ap. Athen. Deipn. 532 b sq.) were perhaps present to Aristotle's mind. Aristotle does not refer to the ways of contemporary politicians, but he might well have done so: see Prof. S. H. Butcher, Demosthenes (p. 13), who cites Demosth. Olynth. 3. c. 26 and Isocr. Areopag. § 25. Sophists also used their *φαινομένη σοφία* with a view to *χρηματισμός*, Soph. El. 11. 171 b 27 sqq.

13. τοῦτο, i. e. *τὸ χρηματίζεσθαι*, which must be supplied from *χρηματιστικάς*.

τέλος, 'the end of all these *δυνάμεις*.' Cp. 8 (6). 2. 1317 b 5 sq. for a very similar expression.

15. δι' αἰτίαν τίνα κ.τ.λ. It has been explained (1257 b 40–1258 a 14) that men come to need the unsound kind of *χρηματιστική*, because they live for *τὸ ζῆν* or for *τὸ εὖ ζῆν* wrongly interpreted.

17. ἡ περὶ τὴν τροφήν. The sound form of *χρηματιστική* is, however, concerned with the acquisition of many things besides *τροφή*—e. g. *ἐσθής, ὄργανα, δοῦλοι*, as is explained in c. 8. 1256 b 15 sqq. Still Aristotle viewed articles of subsistence as the type of true wealth, herein apparently following the inquirers referred to in 1257 b 10 sqq., and trifling inexactnesses are not rare in the Politics, so that this one need not disturb us.

19. ἐξ ἀρχῆς, c. 8. 1256 a 4, though there no reference had been **C. 10.** made to *πολιτική*. It was evidently a common view not only that the main function of the head of a household was to add to the household income, but also that the statesman's main business was to provide the State with as large a revenue as possible: cp. c. 11. 1259 a 35, *διόπερ τινὲς καὶ πολιτεύονται τῶν πολιτευομένων ταῦτα μόνον*, and see the account given of the *πολίτης ἀγαθός* in Rhet. ad Alex. 39. 1446 b 33, *ὅστις προσόδους παρασκευάζει πλείστας, τῶν ἰδιωτῶν μηδένα δημεύων*, and Theopompus' picture of Eubulus (Fr. 96: Müller, Fr. Hist. Gr. 1. 293)—*Εὔβουλος . . . δημαγωγὸς ἦν ἐπιφανέστατος, ἐπιμελής τε καὶ φιλόπονος, ἀργύριόν τε συχνὸν πορίζων τοῖς Ἀθηναίοις διένειμε· διὸ καὶ τὴν πόλιν ἐπὶ τῆς τούτου πολιτείας ἀνανδροτάτην καὶ ῥᾳθυμοτάτην συνέβη γενέσθαι*. Aristotle's object here is to correct these erroneous conceptions of the office of the Statesman and the head of a household.

20. οὔ, not *οὐκ*, though preceding *ἀλλά*, as in 1258 a 33 and 3. 14. 1284 b 39. 'Οὐ is used before a vowel without the final κ when it stands at the end of a clause and when it is emphatic: cf. Xen. Hell. 2. 2. 2: Cyr. 2. 3. 8, 5. 5. 31, 8. 1. 5: Mem. 4. 7. 7' (Holden, Oeconomicus of Xenophon, p. 191). For the transition to *ἀλλὰ*, cp. 1258 a 33: 3. 7. 1279 b 1: 6 (4). 8. 1294 a 2.

21. τοῦτο, not probably ἡ χρηματιστική, though this would harmonize well with c. 8. 1256 b 28, but χρήματα as in 35 (μάλιστα δέ, καθάπερ εἴρηται πρότερον, δεῖ φύσει τοῦτο ὑπάρχειν). For the thought that the statesman has not, any more than the weaver, to produce the material on which he exercises his art, cp. 4 (7). 4. 1325 b 40 sqq.: 13. 1332 a 28. Cp. also Plato, Laws 889 A. Aristotle speaks somewhat differently in Phys. 2. 2. 194 b 7, ἐν μὲν οὖν τοῖς κατὰ τέχνην ἡμεῖς ποιοῦμεν τὴν ὕλην τοῦ ἔργου ἕνεκα, ἐν δὲ τοῖς φυσικοῖς ὑπάρχει οὖσα.

ὥσπερ γὰρ καὶ . . . οὕτω καί. See Sus.[1], Ind. Gramm. ὥσπερ.

23. τροφὴν κ.τ.λ. 'So for sustenance nature must make over land or sea or something else.' Cp. Xen. Mem. 4. 3. 5 sq., and Antiphon, Tetral. 3. 1. 2. For a similar use of τροφήν, cp. Xen. Oecon. 17. 14, ἃ ἂν ἐκεῖναι ἐργασάμεναι τροφὴν καταθῶνται. For ἄλλο τι, cp. 8. c. 1256 a 37, λίμνας καὶ ἕλη καὶ ποταμοὺς ἢ θάλατταν τοιαύτην. The food of animals, indeed, is rather that which comes from earth and water, than earth and water (de Gen. An. 3. 11. 762 b 12); earth and water are food rather for plants (ibid.): still food is said to be a mixture of earth and water in de Part. An. 3. 5. 668 b 11.

24. ἐκ δὲ τούτων κ.τ.λ. Schneider, Bonitz (according to Sus. Qu. Crit. p. 356), and Susemihl himself explain ἐκ τούτων here as = μετὰ ταῦτα, and there is much to be said for their view, though perhaps this use of ἐκ τούτων is more common in Xenophon than in Aristotle (as to Plato, see Riddell, Apol. p. 162). This rendering certainly has the merit of softening the harshness of the juxta-position of τούτων and ταῦτα. But I incline on the whole to think that in the context in which it stands ἐκ τούτων means 'starting with this provision.' Ταῦτα must mean 'food,' not 'land, sea, etc.,' for it is the function of οἰκονομική to deal with the former, not the latter; the word is perhaps in the plural because there are many kinds of food—τροφὴ ἐκ γῆς, τροφὴ ἐκ θαλάττης κ.τ.λ.

26. γνῶναι. Cp. Phys. 2. 2. 194 a 36, δύο δὴ αἱ ἄρχουσαι τῆς ὕλης καὶ αἱ γνωρίζουσαι τέχναι, ἥ τε χρωμένη καὶ τῆς ποιητικῆς ἡ ἀρχιτεκτονική. The ship-captain (representing ἡ χρωμένη), ποῖόν τι τὸ εἶδος τοῦ πηδαλίου, γνωρίζει καὶ ἐπιτάττει· ὁ δὲ (the ἀρχιτέκτων who superintends its construction), ἐκ ποίου ξύλου καὶ ποίων κινήσεων ἔσται. The claims of ὁ χρώμενος to be credited with knowledge are also maintained in Pol. 3. 11. 1282 a 17 sq.

27. καὶ γάρ. 'For, if this were not so.'

31. For ἐπεί followed by οὕτω, cp. 1253 b 23–31. The householder must know bad commodities from good, but he need not know even the sound methods of producing or acquiring them. Cp. Cic. de Rep. 5. 3. 5.

33. τῶν χρημάτων. The article is probably added, because the meaning is 'the commodities essential to the household.'

34. The use of the word *μάλιστα* implies that occasionally the means of subsistence may not *φύσει ὑπάρχειν*, in which case the householder must provide them as best he can. The territory of the State may be so infertile and the sea so barren of fish, that a resort to other modes of acquiring sustenance than the obtainment of vegetable and animal food from the soil and sea may be inevitable. Aristotle's meaning may be illustrated by the instance of Aegina: cp. Ephor. ap. Strab. p. 376, *ἐμπόριον γὰρ γενέσθαι, διὰ τὴν λυπρότητα τῆς χώρας τῶν ἀνθρώπων θαλαττουργούντων ἐμπορικῶς.*

πρότερον, 1258 a 23.

35. The proof that it is for Nature to supply the animal once brought into the world with food, is that every creature finds its food in the unexhausted residuum of the matter from which it takes its origin, or in other words receives it from the hands of Nature (c. 8. 1256 b 7 sqq.: see note on 1256 b 12). So we read in de Gen. et Corr. 2. 8. 335 a 10, *ἅπαντα μὲν γὰρ τρέφεται τοῖς αὐτοῖς ἐξ ὧνπερ ἐστίν.* Not only is the earliest food used by an animal born with him and the gift of Nature, but animals subsist throughout life on the products of the earth and water of which they are made (Meteor. 4. 4. 382 a 6 sqq.). Cp. Oecon. I. 2. 1343 a 30, *ἔτι δὲ καὶ τῶν κατὰ φύσιν [ἡ γεωργική]· φύσει γὰρ ἀπὸ τῆς μητρὸς ἡ τροφὴ πᾶσίν ἐστιν, ὥστε καὶ τοῖς ἀνθρώποις ἀπὸ τῆς γῆς*, and Lucr. 2. 1156,

Sed genuit tellus eadem quae nunc alit ex se:

Aristotle, however, would say 'land and water,' and would speak not of the mother, but of the unused residuum as the true source of food. But, if food is always won from land and water, all other commodities, it is implied, should be sought from the same quarter, and the Science of Supply should thus procure them.

38. πᾶσιν. Cp. c. 8. 1256 b 7, *ἡ μὲν οὖν τοιαύτη κτῆσις ὑπ' αὐτῆς φαίνεται τῆς φύσεως διδομένη πᾶσιν* (i. e. *πᾶσι τοῖς ζῴοις*), though here *πᾶσι* seems to mean 'for all human beings,' as in c. 2. 1253 a 30.

2. ἀπ' ἀλλήλων stands in contrast to *ἀπὸ τῶν καρπῶν καὶ τῶν ζῴων.* 1258 b. Cp. Rhet. 2. 4. 1381 a 21, *διὸ τοὺς ἐλευθερίους καὶ τοὺς ἀνδρείους τιμῶσι καὶ τοὺς δικαίους· τοιούτους δ' ὑπολαμβάνουσι τοὺς μὴ ἀφ' ἑτέρων ζῶντας· τοιοῦτοι δ' οἱ ἀπὸ τοῦ ἐργάζεσθαι, καὶ τούτων οἱ ἀπὸ γεωργίας καὶ τῶν ἄλλων οἱ αὐτουργοὶ μάλιστα.* The idea is still further worked out in Oecon. I. 2. 1343 a 27, *ἡ δὲ γεωργικὴ μάλιστα [κτήσεως ἐπιμέλεια] ὅτι δικαία· οὐ γὰρ ἀπ' ἀνθρώπων οὔθ' ἑκόντων, ὥσπερ καπηλεία καὶ αἱ μισθαρνικαί, οὔτ' ἀκόντων, ὥσπερ αἱ πολεμικαί.* Here the writer has before him Plato, Soph. 219 D.

ἡ ὀβολοστατική, 'the trade of a petty usurer' (L. and S.): see also Büchsenschütz, Besitz und Erwerb, p. 501, n. 7, who quotes from Etymolog. Magn. 725. 13, ὀβολοστάτας γοῦν οἱ Ἀττικοὶ τοὺς ὀλίγα δανείζοντας ἔλεγον ὑπερβολικῶς. Aristotle's objection seems to apply as much to lenders of large sums at usury as to lenders of small; but we find τοκισταὶ κατὰ μικρὸν ἐπὶ πολλῷ singled out as objects of obloquy in the Nicomachean Ethics also (4. 3. 1121 b 34). Cp. M. Cato, de Re Rustica, praef.: maiores nostri hoc sic habuerunt, et ita in legibus posuerunt, furem dupli condemnari, feneratorem quadrupli; quanto peiorem civem existimarint feneratorem quam furem, hinc licet existimari. See also Cic. de Offic. 2. 25. 89, and Sandys and Paley on Demosth. contra Steph. 1. c. 70.

3. διὰ τὸ κ.τ.λ., 'because profit is acquired' (literally perhaps, 'the acquisition of profit results': cp. for κτῆσις, 1257 b 30 and 1256 a 19), 'from money taken by itself, and not from exchange, for which money was introduced.' For the ellipse of ἀπὸ τούτου before ἐφ' ὅπερ ἐπορίσθη, cp. 1. 3. 1253 b 3: 5 (8). 5. 1340 a 27: 4 (7). 13. 1332 a 29–30. In usury, according to Aristotle here, the profit comes from money taken by itself, not subjected to any process of exchange, nor converted into corn or any other commodity—the use for which it is intended. It was introduced to serve as a medium of exchange, not to grow, but usury makes it grow. It makes money come out of money, and hence the Greek word for interest (τόκος), for as children are like their parents, so is interest money no less than the principal which begets it. Things, however, should be used for the purpose for which they exist (c. 9. 1258 a 10); hence this mode of acquisition is in an especial degree unnatural. Νόμισμα νομίσματος is perhaps, like Δημοσθένης Δημοσθένους, meant to express a filial relation. The nature of Interest on Money seems to be better understood in c. 11 (see below on 21).

C. 11. 9. We now come to a chapter differing both in matter and manner from the chapters which precede and follow it, and for which we can hardly be said to have been prepared in advance. A friend has expressed to me a doubt of its authenticity, and even if we hold it to be Aristotelian, it might be (as some other passages of the Politics appear to be) a subsequent addition, due either to Aristotle himself or to some succeeding editor. The question deserves examination, and it will be well to notice here a few considerations on either side.

The opening words of c. 8 promise an inquiry into all kinds of property and all forms of the Science of Supply. The question whether the Science of Supply is a part of the Science of Household Management is here indeed singled out as the first question to be discussed, but we gather that other questions also will be treated. Still no reference is made to a division of the inquiry into a part relating to τὰ πρὸς τὴν γνῶσιν and a part relating to τὰ πρὸς τὴν χρῆσιν. C. 11, however, starts with this distinction. Ἐπεὶ δὲ τὰ πρὸς τὴν γνῶσιν διωρίκαμεν ἱκανῶς, τὰ πρὸς τὴν χρῆσιν δεῖ διελθεῖν (c. 11. *init.*). We have learnt—this seems to be the meaning—to distinguish the sound and unsound forms of the Science of Supply. We have also learnt how far the οἰκονομικός has, as such, to concern himself with the Science of Supply; but we have not yet learnt in any degree how to practise this Science, nor which of its branches are most safe or most profitable or most alien to a freeman, nor generally what are the principles of successful money-making. There is nothing un-Aristotelian in giving advice to lovers of money-making (τοῖς τιμῶσι τὴν χρηματιστικήν, c. 11. 1259 a 5), for Aristotle disapproves of the tyranny and the extreme democracy at least as strongly as he disapproves of a money-making spirit, yet he advises both these constitutions how best to secure their own continuance. Besides, States may find the inquiries of this chapter useful (1259 a 33 sq.). And if to us instruction how to farm and trade seems to fall outside the province of a treatise on Household Management and Politics, this was not the view of Aristotle's time, for Xenophon had sketched in his Oeconomicus how a farm was to be managed; the only novelty in this chapter is that it studies the principles of commercial success.

And then again, if Aristotle does not prepare us in c. 8 or elsewhere in the First Book for a consideration of τὰ πρὸς τὴν χρῆσιν in relation to the Science of Supply, it is nevertheless the case that in entering on the question of slavery (c. 3. 1253 b 14 sqq.) he had announced his aim to be not only to arrive at conclusions on the subject better than those commonly held, but also to throw light on the use to be made of the slave (τά τε πρὸς τὴν ἀναγκαίαν χρείαν ἴδωμεν, 1253 b 15), and a similar inquiry respecting χρηματιστική is not unnatural. Throughout the Politics τὸ χρήσιμον, no less than τὸ ὀρθόν, is kept in view (see e.g. 2. 1. 1260 b 32 sq.: 6 (4). 1. 1288 b 35 sqq.).

On the other hand, the account given of χρηματιστική in c. 11 differs in many respects from that given in cc. 8–10. Three kinds of χρηματιστική are now distinguished, not two only as before—the natural kind (or, as it is also now called, ἡ οἰκειοτάτη), ἡ μεταβλητική, and a kind midway between the two of which we have heard nothing in cc. 8–10, and we find labouring for hire (μισθαρνία) and lending money at interest (τοκισμός) ranged under ἡ μεταβλητικὴ χρηματιστική, whereas in cc. 8–10 nothing has been said of μισθαρνία, and ὀβολοστατική has been described as winning money, not from any process of exchange, but from the barren metal itself. The inclusion, however, of the work of the τεχνίτης, as a form of μισθαρνία, under ἡ μεταβλητικὴ χρηματιστική is quite borne out by 1. 13. 1260 b 2, where τεχνῖται are said not to exist by nature, though it does not seem to agree with the recognition of the τεχνίτης elsewhere (4 (7). 8. 1328 b 21: 6 (4). 4. 1291 a 1 sqq.) as one of the necessary elements of a State. The reference to writers on the subject and to τὰ λεγόμενα σποράδην (1258 b 39 sqq.), again, is in accordance with the advice given in Rhet. 1. 4. 1359 b 30 sqq., and this passage of c. 11 may well have been present to the mind of the writer of the so-called Second Book of the Oeconomics, whoever he was (see Oecon. 2. 1346 a 26 sqq.). Hieronymus of Rhodes, as has been observed elsewhere, may possibly have had a passage from this chapter (1259 a 9 sqq.) before him. The writer of the sketch or epitome of the Political Theory of the Peripatetics which is preserved in the Eclogae of Stobaeus (2. 6. 17) would seem to be acquainted with the earlier part of c. 11 down to the notice of μεταλλευτική, for he says, δι' ὃ καὶ πολλῶν ἔμπειρον δεῖν εἶναι τὸν οἰκονομικόν, γεωργίας προβατείας μεταλλείας, ἵνα τοὺς λυσιτελεστάτους ἅμα καὶ δικαιοτάτους καρποὺς διαγινώσκῃ: he may well have been acquainted with the later part also, though he does not mention anything from it. The following passage from the First Book of the Oeconomics may likewise be based on the teaching of c. 11—κτήσεως δὲ πρώτη ἐπιμέλεια ἡ κατὰ φύσιν· κατὰ φύσιν δὲ γεωργικὴ προτέρα, καὶ δεύτεραι ὅσαι ἀπὸ τῆς γῆς, οἷον μεταλλευτικὴ καὶ εἴ τις ἄλλη τοιαύτη (c. 2. 1343 a 25 sqq.).

On the whole, I incline to think that this chapter is Aristotelian, and perhaps coeval with the rest of the First Book.

10. πάντα δὲ τὰ τοιαῦτα κ.τ.λ. Stahr translates: 'auf diesem ganzen Gebiet hat freilich die Theorie freies Spiel, während die Praxis an nothwendige Bedingungen gebunden ist.' Bern. and Sus. follow him in this translation, and Mr. Welldon's version is—'it is to be observed, however, that in all such matters speculation is free, while in practice there are limiting conditions.' Vict. however translates—'cuncta autem huiuscemodi contemplationem habent libero homine dignam, usum vero necessarium'—and I incline to this view of the passage. We have ἐλευθέρα ἀγορά, 4 (7). 12. 1331 a 32: ἐλευθέρα ἐπιστήμη, Metaph. A. 2. 982 b 27.

Prof. Tyrrell (*Hermathena*, 12. 28) 'thinks it will be found that ἐλεύθερος when of two terminations always means "liberalis," not "liber."' The aim of the remark will then be to distinguish between what is liberal and what is not so in relation to these matters—an aim which appears also below, 1258 b 34–39, as well as in the contrast of ἐντιμότερα and ἀναγκαιότερα ἔργα, c. 7. 1255 b 28, and in 5 (8). 2. 1337 b 15 sqq. We are told, in fact, that though speculation about matters relating to the practice of χρηματιστική is liberal, the exercise of the arts which fall under the head of χρηματιστική is not so. So in de Part. An. 1. 5. 645 a 5 sqq. Aristotle tells us that he will treat of Zoology μηδὲν παραλιπὼν εἰς δύναμιν μήτε ἀτιμότερον μήτε τιμιώτερον· καὶ γὰρ ἐν τοῖς μὴ κεχαρισμένοις αὐτῶν (sc. τῶν ζῴων) πρὸς τὴν αἴσθησιν, κατὰ τὴν θεωρίαν ὅμως ἡ δημιουργήσασα φύσις ἀμηχάνους ἡδονὰς παρέχει τοῖς δυναμένοις τὰς αἰτίας γνωρίζειν καὶ φύσει φιλοσόφοις. It appears from Plato, Laws 889 D, that there were those who ranked agriculture very high among the sciences.

12. ἔστι δὲ κ.τ.λ. Varro in his De Re Rustica (lib. 2. praef. 5) gives a similar account of the qualifications which a farmer should possess:—quarum (sc. agriculturae et pastionis) quoniam societas inter se magna . . . qui habet praedium, habere utramque debet disciplinam, et agriculturae et pecoris pascendi, et etiam villaticae pastionis: ex ea enim quoque fructus tolli possunt non mediocres, ex ornithonibus ac leporariis et piscinis. Compare also the opening lines of Virgil's Georgics, and Cicero de Senectute 15. 54. The following passage of Varro, de Re Rustica (2. 1. 16) is very similar to that before us—in qua regione quamque potissimum pascas, et quando, et queis? ut capras in montuosis potius locis et fruticibus, quam in herbidis campis, equas contra; neque eadem loca aestiva et hiberna idonea omnibus ad pascendum. It will be noticed that Aristotle places 'res pecuaria' before 'agricultura,' perhaps because pastoral farming long prevailed more extensively in Greece than agriculture (Büchsenschütz, Besitz und Erwerb, pp. 208 sqq., 313), perhaps because it was more lucrative (cp. Cic. de Offic. 2. 25. 89), perhaps because animals like the horse and ox deserve precedence. We hear nothing from him as to the employment of slaves as a source of profit.

χρήσιμα (cp. 30, ἀκάρπων μὲν χρησίμων δέ) apparently takes up τὰ πρὸς τὴν χρῆσιν and bears probably somewhat the same meaning as in Rhet. 1. 5. 1361 a 15, ταῦτα δὲ πάντα καὶ ἀσφαλῆ καὶ ἐλευθέρια καὶ χρήσιμα· ἔστι δὲ χρήσιμα μὲν μᾶλλον τὰ κάρπιμα, ἐλευθέρια δὲ τὰ πρὸς ἀπόλαυσιν· κάρπιμα δὲ λέγω ἀφ' ὧν αἱ πρόσοδοι, ἀπολαυστικὰ δὲ ἀφ' ὧν μηδὲν παρὰ τὴν χρῆσιν γίγνεται, ὅ τι καὶ ἄξιον.

κτήματα is used in 2. 1. 1261 a 5 in the same sense as κτήσεις, 1261 a 8, but here it seems to be used in a sense exclusive of γεωργία (cp. 17), and the illustrations which follow seem to show that its meaning is 'farm-stock' (Vict. 'pecora'). Horses, oxen, sheep, and some other animals (15) are included under κτήματα, but not, it would appear, the water-animals and birds referred to in 19.

13. πῶς. Vict. 'quomodo habita et curata.'

14. κτῆσις ποία τις, 'what course should be followed in the getting of horses,' so as to secure the maximum of profit. Κτῆσις includes both breeding and purchase: ποία refers to quantity, quality, kind of animal, etc.

15. τῶν λοιπῶν ζῴων, e.g. mules, asses, swine, goats. As to the animals referred to, see above on 12.

πρὸς ἄλληλα. Vict. 'oportet quasi conferre ipsa inter se, videreque ex equorumne gregibus sive armentis boum maiores utilitates capiantur.'

18. ἤδη. Cp. de Gen. An. 2. 6. 742 a 19, τὸ δὲ πρότερον ἤδη πολλαχῶς ἐστίν: ibid. 2. 6. 742 b 33, ἀρχὴ δ' ἐν μὲν τοῖς ἀκινήτοις τὸ τί ἐστιν, ἐν δὲ τοῖς γινομένοις ἤδη πλείους: ibid. 1. 20. 729 a 19, ἐκ δὲ τοῦ συνιστάντος πρώτου ἐξ ἑνὸς ἤδη ἓν γίνεται μόνον. These passages may serve to illustrate the use of ἤδη in the text, though the word does not perhaps bear quite the same meaning in all of them. In the passage before us it may be roughly rendered by 'again.'

ψιλῆς . . . πεφυτευμένης. The distribution of the two kinds of cultivation throughout Greece is well described by Büchsenschütz, Besitz und Erwerb, pp. 293–6. As to Italy, cp. Varro de Re Rustica, 1. 2. 6: contra quid in Italia utensile non modo non nascitur, sed etiam non egregium fit? quod far conferam Campano? quod triticum Appulo? quod vinum Falerno? quod oleum Venafro? Non arboribus consita Italia est, ut tota pomarium videatur? An Phrygia magis vitibus cooperta, quam Homerus appellat ἀμπελόεσσαν, quam haec? aut Argos, quod idem poeta πολύπυρον?

μελιττουργίας. As Vict. points out, honey was of more importance to the ancients than to us. See Büchsenschütz, p. 228 sq., who remarks that 'though sugar was known to the ancients, they used it solely for medical purposes, so that the only material they possessed for sweetening food was honey.' Plato's citizens in the Laws are to be γεωργοὶ καὶ νομεῖς καὶ μελιττουργοί (842 D).

19. καὶ τῶν ἄλλων ζῴων. Should we translate 'and concerning the other animals, whether water-animals or winged,' or should we supply 'the management of' before 'the other animals' from the latter portions of the words γεωργίας, μελιττουργίας? Perhaps we are intended to supply these words. Aristotle seems here to refer, not to fish and fowl in a wild state, but to poultry-houses and fish-preserves. In his time these appurtenances of a farm would be on a simple and moderate scale, wholly unlike that of the 'villatica pastio' in the days when Roman luxury was at its height (Varro, de Re Rustica 3. 3. 6 sqq.). Yet a great ἰχθυοτροφεῖον existed at Agrigentum early in the fifth century before Christ (Diod. 11. 25. 4).

20. τῆς . . . οἰκειοτάτης χρηματιστικῆς, 'of the Science of Supply in its most undistorted form.' The word οἰκεῖος is used by Aristotle in connexion with κύριος and with κατὰ φύσιν, and in contradistinction to βίᾳ (see Bon. Ind. s. v.). Cp. also c. 9. 1257 a 12, οὐ τὴν οἰκείαν χρῆσιν, οὐ γὰρ ἀλλαγῆς ἕνεκεν γέγονεν.

21. ταῦτα μόρια καὶ πρῶτα. Μόρια is sometimes used, like μέρη (Bon. Ind. 455 b 40 sqq.), of 'ea quae naturam alicuius rei constituunt ac distinguunt' (Bon. Ind. 473 b 55 sqq.), and this would seem to be its meaning here. The simplest elements of a thing are often called πρῶτα, as in Pol. 1. 3. 1253 b 5, πρῶτα καὶ ἐλάχιστα μέρη οἰκίας (see Bon. Ind. 652 b 42 sqq.), but here πρῶτα appears rather to mean 'the primary or leading elements' (cp. μέγιστον 22): see Bon. Ind. 653 a 26 sqq., 'πρῶτος significat ipsam per se rei notionem et naturam (ut quae iam a principio sit et rem constituat).' So we have in 28, τῆς πρώτης χρηματιστικῆς (cp. Oecon. 1. 2. 1343 a 25 sqq.), and in de Caelo 1. 3. 270 b 2, τὸ πρῶτον τῶν σωμάτων. The account now given of the various forms of the οἰκειοτάτη χρηματιστική, which is referred to in 28 as ἡ κατὰ φύσιν, is not harmonized with the account given in c. 8 of the βίοι included under the natural χρηματιστική: for instance, we now hear nothing of λῃστεία. Aristotle, however, here mentions only τὰ πρῶτα.

τῆς δὲ μεταβλητικῆς. Already in c. 10. 1258 b 1 the unsound χρηματιστική has been called μεταβλητική, instead of καπηλική, and here the change is especially necessary, for ἐμπορία could hardly be brought under καπηλική without some sense of strangeness. 'Exchanging' comprises, we are told, the transport and sale of commodities (ἐμπορία), and the letting-out of money (τοκισμός) or of labour, skilled or unskilled (μισθαρνία). 'This classification,' says Büchsenschütz (Besitz und Erwerb, p. 455), 'nearly approaches that accepted by modern political economy, inasmuch as the first of the three departments has to do with traffic by way of sale, and the second and third with traffic by way of letting, the object let out being in the one case capital (money, land, etc.), and in the other labour.' Aristotle, however, makes no reference to the letting of land. Büchsenschütz points out that in Plato's Sophist (219 D) μίσθωσις is already brought under μεταβλητική (Besitz und Erwerb, p. 251 n.). He also compares Plato, Rep. 371 E, οἳ δὴ πωλοῦντες τὴν τῆς ἰσχύος χρείαν κέκληνται μισθωτοί. In the passage before us Aristotle regards the work of the βάναυσος τεχνίτης as a form of μισθαρνία: in Pol. 5 (8). 2. 1337 b 12 sqq., however, μισθαρνικαὶ ἐργασίαι are distinguished from βάναυσοι τέχναι.

22. ναυκληρία φορτηγία παράστασις. Sus. and others translate the first two words, 'maritime trade,' 'inland trade'; but Büchsenschütz (p. 456 and note 1) explains them otherwise. According to him, ἐμπορία is here resolved into the three elements—the provision of a ship, the conveyance of cargo, and exposure for sale. The ναύκληρος lets out a ship, sometimes (Xen. Mem. 3. 9. 11) himself taking passage in it; the merchant transports goods from point to point; and the salesman, wholesale or retail, sets out goods for sale. Ἐμπορία is thus made to include the work of the κάπηλος, if this interpretation is correct. That φορτηγία does not refer exclusively to land-trade, appears from C. F. Hermann, Griech. Antiqq. 3. § 45. 6 (ed. 2). According to Büchsenschütz (p. 458), the transport of commodities was effected in Greece almost entirely by sea. It should be added that the same individual might often be ναύκληρος, φορτηγός, and wholesale salesman in one.

23. παράστασις would probably be safer and less remunerative than ναυκληρία and φορτηγία. As to the chances of ναυκληρία, see Eth. Eud. 7. 14. 1247 a 21 sqq., and for the general ὅρος ἀσφαλείας, Rhet. 1. 5. 1361 a 19 sqq. A shield-manufactory was safer than a bank (see Sandys and Paley on Demosth. Pro Phorm. c. 11). The remark in the text is interposed to give useful guidance in the practice of χρηματιστική (cp. τὰ πρὸς τὴν χρῆσιν δεῖ διελθεῖν, 1258 b 9): we find a similar hint in Oecon. 1. 6. 1344 b 28 sqq.

26. τῶν ἀτέχνων κ.τ.λ. is masc. There is no need to alter τεχνῶν to τεχνιτῶν. Similar transitions occur in 1. 10. 1258 a 33–34 (τοῦ οἰκονόμου . . . τῆς ὑπηρετικῆς) and 3. 1. 1275 a 23–26. As the labour of the θής is of a purely physical kind, he is nearly akin to the slave: cp. 1258 b 38 and 5 (8). 2. 1337 b 21, θητικὸν καὶ δουλικόν.

27. τρίτον δὲ εἶδος κ.τ.λ. How can this kind be said to possess any of the characteristics of μεταβλητική? Probably because, though the commodities it acquires are acquired from the earth, it does not seek wealth ἀπὸ τῶν καρπῶν καὶ τῶν ζῴων (1258 a 38), but seeks it from things ἄκαρπα μὲν χρήσιμα δέ, such as timber-trees, just as μεταβλητική seeks it ἀπ' ἀλλήλων or from money.

29. ὅσα κ.τ.λ. '(Having to do with) things won from the earth and from products of the earth not yielding fruit, but still useful.' For the ellipse, see notes on 1253 b 3, 1256 b 26. Of commodities won ἀπὸ γῆς marble or chalk may serve as an example: timber is an instance of a commodity won ἀπὸ τῶν ἀπὸ γῆς γινομένων ἀκάρπων μὲν χρησίμων δέ. Metals probably fall under the former head, notwithstanding that they are called, together with some other mineral products, τὰ ἐν τῇ γῇ γινόμενα (Meteor. 3. 6. 378 a 19 sqq.).

32. ἤδη, 'again' (see above on 18). The indifferent use of γένος and εἶδος should be noted here. Cp. Rhet. 1. 2–3, 1358 a 33–36.

35. φορτικόν. Cp. Rhet. 3. 1. 1403 b 35, οὔπω δὲ σύγκειται τέχνη περὶ αὐτῶν, ἐπεὶ καὶ τὸ περὶ τὴν λέξιν ὀψὲ προῆλθεν· καὶ δοκεῖ φορτικὸν εἶναι, καλῶς ὑπολαμβανόμενον. To overdo the illustration of one's meaning is φορτικόν (Poet. 26. 1461 b 27 sqq.). And those who pay too much attention to τὸ χρήσιμον especially merit the epithet (4 (7). 14. 1333 b 9: 5 (8). 3. 1338 b 2). Cp. also 7 (5). 11. 1315 a 40, περίεργον δὲ τὸ λέγειν καθ' ἕκαστον τῶν τοιούτων: Metaph. α. 3. 995 a 8 sqq.

εἰσὶ δὲ . . . 39. ἀρετῆς. These remarks come in with singular abruptness, and it is not clear that they are not an interpolation. On the other hand, there is something not quite satisfactory in the sequence, if we omit them and place ἐπεὶ δ' ἐστὶν ἐνίοις κ.τ.λ. immediately after φορτικὸν δὲ τὸ ἐνδιατρίβειν. Susemihl places περὶ ἑκάστου δὲ τούτων 33—τὸ ἐνδιατρίβειν 35 after, instead of before, εἰσὶ δὲ—ἀρετῆς, but τούτων 33 is thus robbed of its significance and not much is gained in any way. There is this to be said for the passage, that a somewhat similar reference to the varying dignity of different kinds of slave-work is to be found in c. 7. 1255 b 27 sqq.

36. τεχνικώταται. According to Eth. Eud. 7. 14. 1247 a 5, στρατηγία and κυβερνητική are instances of arts in which τέχνη ἐστί, πολὺ μέντοι καὶ τύχης ἐνυπάρχει. Agathon, on the other hand, traced a relation between Art and Fortune in the well-known line, quoted in Eth. Nic. 6. 4. 1140 a 19, τέχνη τύχην ἔστερξε καὶ τύχη τέχνην.

37. βαναυσόταται. Those pursuits also are βάναυσοι which deteriorate the character or the intelligence (τὴν ψυχὴν ἢ τὴν διάνοιαν, 5 (8). 2. 1337 b 8 sqq.), but this does not conflict with what is said here.

λωβῶνται. For the third person plural after τὰ σώματα, see Bon. Ind. 490 a 44 sqq.

38. δουλικώταται. Cp. 1. 2. 1252 a 33: 1. 5. 1254 b 18.

39. προσδεῖ, i.e. in addition to technical skill (cp. Eth. Nic. 10. 10. 1181 a 12).

ἐπεὶ δ' ἐστὶν κ.τ.λ. According to Varro de Re Rustica 1. 1. 8, and Columella 1. 1. 7, both Aristotle and Theophrastus wrote on agriculture. See Menage on Diog. Laert. 5. 50. They probably refer to the Γεωργικά, which the list of Aristotle's works given by the Anonymus of Menage names as spurious (No. 189), though in the Arabic list based on Ptolemaeus (No. 72) it is accounted genuine. See Aristot. Fragm. 255 sq., 1525 b 1 sqq., and Zeller, Gr. Ph. 2. 2. 100. n. 1, who adds—'that Aristotle did not write on agriculture and the cognate subjects, appears from Pol. 1. 11. 1258 b 33, 39.' The Γεωργικά are thus probably spurious. Is it possible that Charetides of Paros is the same as the Chartodras, whose opinions as to manures are referred to by Theophrastus in Hist. Plant. 2. 7. 4? A Messenian named Charetidas figures in an inscription (Dittenberger, Sylloge Inscr. Graec. 240. 5, vol. i. p. 346). Apollodorus of Lemnos is mentioned by Varro and Pliny (see Dict. of Greek and Roman Biography, s. v.).

1259 a. 3. ἐκ τούτων, 'with the aid of their writings': cp. Eth. Nic. 10. 10. 1181 b 17: Rhet. 1. 4. 1359 b 30 sq.: de Gen. An. 1. 11. 719 a 10: de Part. An. 2. 16. 660 a 7. As to the collection of scattered notices of instances of commercial sagacity and success, cp. 2. 5. 1264 a 3, πάντα γὰρ σχεδὸν εὕρηται μέν, ἀλλὰ τὰ μὲν οὐ συνῆκται, τοῖς δ' οὐ χρῶνται γινώσκοντες, and Rhet. 1. 4. 1359 b 30 sq. An attempt to act on this suggestion appears to be made in the so-called Second Book of the Oeconomics: see Oecon. 2. 1346 a 26 sqq.

6. οἷον κ.τ.λ. 'such as the feat told of Thales.' Cp. Plato, Rep. 600 A, ἀλλ' οἷα δὴ εἰς τὰ ἔργα σοφοῦ ἀνδρὸς πολλαὶ ἐπίνοιαι καὶ εὐμήχανοι εἰς τέχνας ἤ τινας ἄλλας πράξεις λέγονται, ὥσπερ αὖ Θάλεώ τε πέρι τοῦ Μιλησίου καὶ Ἀναχάρσιος τοῦ Σκύθου; Καί here as elsewhere serves to introduce an example. It is not quite clear whether οἷον κ.τ.λ. is adduced in illustration of the sentence immediately preceding or of ἔτι δὲ . . . συλλέγειν. Perhaps Sus. is right in taking the former view of the passage—cp. τοῦτο γάρ ἐστι κατανόημά τι χρηματιστικόν, which seems to take up πάντα γὰρ ὠφέλιμα ταῦτ' ἐστὶ τοῖς τιμῶσι τὴν χρηματιστικήν, and also 1259 a 33, χρήσιμον δὲ γνωρίζειν ταῦτα καὶ τοῖς πολιτικοῖς, which seems to refer back to the same words. The passage also gains in point when taken in this way, for it conveys a hint that Aristotle is aware how paradoxical the idea of χρηματιστικοί learning anything from Thales

will appear to his readers. **Τοῦ Μιλησίου** is added to distinguish him from the Cretan Thales mentioned in 2. 12. 1274 a 28. His ingenuity was proverbial (Aristoph. Aves 946); yet there was also a popular impression that he was *σοφός*, but not *φρόνιμος* (Eth. Nic. 6. 7. 1141 b 3 sqq.).

8. τὴν σοφίαν. Cp. Diog. Laert. 1. 22, *καὶ πρῶτος σοφὸς ὠνομάσθη (ὁ Θαλῆς) ἄρχοντος Ἀθήνησι Δαμασίου, καθ' ὃν καὶ οἱ ἑπτὰ σοφοὶ ἐκλήθησαν.*

τυγχάνει δὲ καθόλου τι ὄν, i.e. not confined to philosophers like Thales, but generally applicable in commercial transactions. We have not here a *σοφός* devising a novel subtlety, but rather an instance of the use of a recognized weapon from the armoury of *χρηματιστική*.

9. ὀνειδιζόντων γὰρ κ.τ.λ. For the construction, cp. 2. 12. 1274 a 25. The charge against philosophers was a commonplace (Anaxippus ap. Athen. Deipn. 610 f: Plato, Gorg. 484 C sqq.: Isocr. adv. Sophist. §§ 7–8: Eth. Eud. 7. 14. 1247 a 17 sqq.).

11. ἐκ τῆς ἀστρολογίας. The Egyptian priests claimed to be able to predict *καρπῶν φθορὰς ἢ τοὐναντίον πολυκαρπίας* by means of their observation of the stars (Diod. 1. 81. 5).

12. εὐπορήσαντα, cp. Plutarch, Sulla c. 26, *εὐπορήσαντα τῶν ἀντιγράφων.*

ὀλίγων. The point of the story lies in the smallness of the capital. Thales only paid down the earnest-money of the rent of the olive-presses which he hired, trusting to his future profit to pay the rest. If we compare Cic. de Divin. 1. 49. 111, non plus quam Milesium Thalem, qui ut obiurgatores suos convinceret ostenderetque etiam philosophum, si ei commodum esset, pecuniam facere posse, omnem oleam, antequam florere coepisset, in agro Milesio coemisse dicitur, we shall see that though this passage is very similar to the passage before us, Cicero's version of the story, nevertheless, as Vict. remarks, misses the point, for only a large capitalist could have done what Thales is described as doing. Cicero can hardly have had this passage of the Politics before him; still less can Pliny, who tells the story of Democritus (Hist. Nat. 18. 28). The version of Hieronymus of Rhodes, though abbreviated, is nearer to the Politics—*φησὶ καὶ ὁ Ῥόδιος Ἱερώνυμος ἐν τῷ δευτέρῳ τῶν σποράδην ὑπομνημάτων, ὅτι βουλόμενος δεῖξαι [ὁ Θαλῆς] ῥᾷον εἶναι πλουτεῖν, φορᾶς μελλούσης ἐλαιῶν ἔσεσθαι, προνοήσας ἐμισθώσατο τὰ ἐλαιουργεῖα καὶ πάμπλειστα συνεῖλε χρήματα* (Diog. Laert. 1. 26). We cannot, however, be certain that Aristotle and he were not drawing from some common source. If the story is true, it would seem that a citizen of Miletus was legally capable of renting olive-presses in Chios. Chios and Miletus both belonged to the Ionic Confederacy, and a special friendship seems to have existed between the two States (Hdt. 1. 18 : 6. 5). This may have made the thing easier.

διαδοῦναι is used because the owners of the presses were many.

13. **τ'** is displaced as elsewhere by being added 'ei vocabulo quod utrique membro commune est,' Bon. Ind. 749 b 44 sqq.: cp. *μεταξύ τε τῶν εἰδῶν καὶ τῶν αἰσθητῶν*, Metaph. K. 1. 1059 b 6: *ἀλλὰ μὴν οὐδὲ διαγωγήν τε παισὶν ἁρμόττει καὶ ταῖς ἡλικίαις ἀποδιδόναι ταῖς τοιαύταις*, Pol. 5 (8). 5. 1339 a 29: *νομίζοντες τόν τε τοῦ ἐλευθέρου βίον ἕτερόν τινα εἶναι τοῦ πολιτικοῦ καὶ πάντων αἱρετώτατον*, Pol. 4 (7). 3. 1325 a 19.

15. For the two participles *ἐκμισθοῦντα, συλλέξαντα*, cp. 8 (6). 5. 1320 b 8, *διαλαμβάνοντας τοὺς ἀπόρους ἀφορμὰς διδόντας τρέπειν ἐπ' ἐργασίας*, and Plato, Rep. 465 C, *τὰ δὲ πάντως ποριζόμενοι θέμενοι παρὰ γυναῖκάς τε καὶ οἰκέτας, ταμιεύειν παραδόντες.* But here the participles are in different tenses.

17. **πλουτεῖν**, 'to become rich,' as in 8 (6). 4. 1318 b 20.

18. **μὲν οὖν** ('so then') is here used as in c. 2. 1252 a 34.

19. **ἐπίδειξιν . . . τῆς σοφίας.** Cp. Plato, Hippias Minor, 368 C, *σοφίας πλείστης ἐπίδειγμα.*

'But, as we said, the plan adopted by Thales—that of trying to secure oneself a monopoly—is a general principle of the science of money-making.' Τὸ τοιοῦτον is explained by *ἐάν τις . . . κατασκευάζειν*: compare the use of *ἐάν* in Rhet. 3. 5. 1407 b 19, and of *ὅταν* in Metaph. M. 1. 1076 a 30.

21. **διό.** Having said that this plan is not confined to philosophers but embodies a broad principle of money-making science (*χρηματιστικόν* 20), Aristotle points out that some States practise it, when they are in want of money (*χρημάτων* 22). See on the subject of State-monopolies in Greece Büchsenschütz, Besitz und Erwerb, p. 547 sqq., who traces them at Selymbria (Oecon. 2. 1348 b 33 sqq.), Byzantium (1346 b 25 sq.), and Lampsacus (1347 a 32 sqq.), and refers to the scheme of Pythocles at Athens (1353 a 15 sqq.) and to the measures of Cleomenes, the governor of Egypt (1352 b 14 sqq.). 'There is no evidence,' he adds, 'that monopolies were anywhere used in Greece, as they have often been in modern States, as a permanent source of revenue.' 'Nay,' Aristotle continues, 'in Sicily an individual with whom a sum of money had been deposited'—he seems to have had a larger amount at his disposal than Thales—'resorted to a similar device, but he found that his success aroused the jealousy of the ruler of the State.' Thus the story incidentally bears out the assertion made in 21–23, that States occasionally seek revenue from sources of this kind. The hero of this story may probably have been a τραπεζίτης: cp. Demosth. Pro Phorm. c. 11, ἡ δ' ἐργασία (of banking) προσόδους ἔχουσα ἐπικινδύνους ἀπὸ χρημάτων ἀλλοτρίων, and see Büchsenschütz, p. 502.

24. συνεπρίατο. Compare the use of συνωνεῖσθαι in Theopomp. Fr. 219 and Plutarch, de Cupiditate Divitiarum c. 3. 524 B.

25. τῶν σιδηρείων. Bern. 'iron-mines': Sus. 'iron-works.' The latter rendering is perhaps the more likely to be correct, as the metal would come from smelting-works, even if the ore was obtained in Sicilian mines, which may possibly have been the case, for iron-ore is still 'found in the mountains of Sicily' (A. K. Johnston, Dict. of Geography, art. Sicily). Aetna and the Lipari islands were famed in myth as the scene of the labours of Hephaestus and the Cyclopes (Virg. Georg. 4. 170 sqq.: Aen. 3. 675 sqq.: 8. 416 sqq.: Ovid, Fasti 4. 287 sq.).

ἐμπορίων. The merchants are conceived as sojourning at the ἐμπόρια (cp. 4 (7). 6. 1327 a 11 sqq.), which would usually be on the seacoast or not far from it, like the Peiraeus or Naucratis (τῆς Αἰγύπτου τὸ ἐμπόριον, Aristot. Fragm. 161. 1505 a 14). Not every city was an ἐμπόριον.

26. ἐπώλει. Note the tense.

27. τῆς τιμῆς, i. e. the usual price charged for iron. His winnings appear to have been due, in part to the advance on the usual price, which though small mounted up in proportion to the large quantity of iron sold, in part to the large returns which even the usual price brought to the merchants.

ἐπὶ τοῖς πεντήκοντα ταλάντοις ἐπέλαβεν ἑκατόν. Cp. Matth. 25. 20, Κύριε, πέντε τάλαντά μοι παρέδωκας· ἴδε, ἄλλα πέντε τάλαντα ἐκέρδησα ἐπ' αὐτοῖς, and Strabo p. 701, ὧν τινα κοινὰ καὶ ἄλλοις Ἰνδοῖς ἱστόρηται, ὡς τὸ μακρόβιον ὥστε καὶ τριάκοντα ἐπὶ τοῖς ἑκατὸν προσλαμβάνειν. The article may be prefixed to πεντήκοντα ταλάντοις because the sum originally invested was fifty talents, or it may be added for the same reason for which it is prefixed to δέκα in Xen. Oecon. 20. 16, ῥᾳδίως γὰρ ἀνὴρ εἷς παρὰ τοὺς δέκα διαφέρει τῷ ἐν ὥρᾳ ἐργάζεσθαι, on which passage Dr. Holden remarks, 'where parts of a whole are stated in numbers, the article is sometimes prefixed to the numeral "to denote the definiteness of the relation" (Madvig, § 11, Rem. 6).' Bernays translates, 'he gained a hundred talents in addition to the fifty which he had laid out': Mr. Welldon, 'he realized 200 per cent. on all his outlay.' Perhaps the passage quoted from St. Matthew makes in favour of Bernays' interpretation, though the article is probably to be explained in the same way as in the passage of Xenophon.

28. τοῦτον μὲν οὖν κ.τ.λ. This man brought on himself expulsion from the State, while Thales won applause for his wisdom, but yet the two men proceeded on the same principle. Μὲν οὖν is answered by *μέντοι* 31.

31. ἀσυμφόρους. Cp. 2. 9. 1270 b 20, *συμφερόντως ἔχει τοῖς πράγμασιν*. Dionysius probably objected to the whole available supply of a commodity so important both in war and peace as iron finding its way into the hands of a single private individual and coming to be obtainable only at an enhanced price. He would also hold that a private person had no business with a monopoly; monopolies would in his view be for the State. Besides, tyrants usually sought to keep their subjects poor (7 (5). 11. 1313 b 18) and distrusted the rich (7 (5). 10. 1311 a 15 sqq.).

33. καὶ τοῖς πολιτικοῖς, i.e. to statesmen as well as to heads of households (cp. c. 8. 1256 b 37, *ὅτι μὲν τοίνυν ἔστι τις κτητικὴ κατὰ φύσιν τοῖς οἰκονόμοις καὶ τοῖς πολιτικοῖς*, and Eth. Nic. 6. 5. 1140 b 10) and to those who hold the science of money-making in high esteem (1259 a 5). For *χρήσιμον γνωρίζειν*, cp. 8 (6). 1. 1317 a 33, *χρήσιμον δ' ἕκαστον αὐτῶν γνωρίζειν*.

34. πολλαῖς γὰρ πόλεσι κ.τ.λ. A large revenue was essential to the working of the extreme democracy (Pol. 6 (4). 6. 1293 a 1 sq.); States frequently at war were also bound to have plenty of money at command (2. 9. 1271 b 11). Households stand less in need of exceptional sources of income.

35. τινὲς καὶ πολιτεύονται, i.e. in addition to those who pursue these aims in private life. See Schneider's note, vol. 2. p. 65, on the *πορισταί* at Athens, but Eubulus is probably referred to—cp. Plutarch, Reip. Gerend. Praecepta, c. 15 *sub fin.*, and Theopomp. Fr. 96 (Müller, Fr. Hist. Gr. 1. 293). See also Plato, Laws 742 D, and the account of the good citizen given in Rhet. ad Alex. 39. 1446 b 33.

For **ταῦτα** as the object of *πολιτεύονται*, cp. 2. 7. 1267 a 18.

C. 12. **37. Ἐπεὶ δὲ κ.τ.λ.** 'Since we distinguished' (in 1. 3. 1253 b 3 sqq.) 'three parts of *οἰκονομική*' (for *ἦν*, cp. Metaph. Λ. 6. 1071 b 3, *ἐπεὶ δ' ἦσαν τρεῖς οὐσίαι*, and de Caelo 1. 3. 269 b 33), the question arises, with which of them is *οἰκονομική* most concerned? We have seen that the *οἰκονομικός* as such can hardly be said to be directly concerned with χρηματιστική: but with which of the three relations that make up the household—γαμική, πατρική, δεσποτική—is he most concerned? This is the question which Aristotle apparently intends to raise here (compare the solution given at the beginning of c. 13), but his articulation of it is in unusual disarray. He has no sooner enumerated the three parts of οἰκονομική, than he proceeds to refer to the account which he has already given of δεσποτική, and to distinguish the rule exercised by the husband over his wife from the rule exercised by the father over his children, with the object apparently of showing that the two latter relations represent a higher kind of rule (πολιτική or βασιλική) than the former—the result being that οἰκονομική is more concerned with πατρική and γαμική than with δεσποτική (cp. 1. 5. 1254 a 25, ἀεὶ βελτίων ἡ ἀρχὴ ἡ τῶν βελτιόνων ἀρχομένων, and 4 (7). 14. 1333 b 27, τοῦ γὰρ δεσποτικῶς ἄρχειν ἡ τῶν ἐλευθέρων ἀρχὴ καλλίων καὶ μᾶλλον μετ' ἀρετῆς), and that it is more concerned with δεσποτική than with χρηματιστική.

39. καὶ γάρ. Vict. 'statim autem causam affert, cur distinxerit copulam patris ac liberorum a copula viri et uxoris; docet enim illa imperia diversa esse.'

ἄρχειν, sc. ἔφαμεν (latent in ἦν, 37) τὸν οἰκονόμον. The reference would seem to be to c. 3. 1253 b 4 sq.

ὡς ἐλευθέρων μὲν ἀμφοῖν, i.e. τοῦ ἀρχομένου χάριν (4 (7). 14. 1333 a 3 sqq.), or perhaps for the common good of ruler and ruled (3. 6. 1278 b 37 sqq.). Contrast δεσποτικὴ ἀρχή, 3. 6. 1278 b 32 sqq. Πολιτική, βασιλική (3. 7. 1279 a 33), and ἀριστοκρατικὴ ἀρχή (3. 17. 1288 a 11) are forms of ἡ τῶν ἐλευθέρων ἀρχή. It may be questioned whether it is quite an adequate idea of ἡ τῶν ἐλευθέρων ἀρχή to make it consist simply in ruling for the benefit of the ruled; Marcus Aurelius (Comment. 1. 14) seems to understand it otherwise.

1. πολιτικῶς, 'as a citizen-ruler rules over his fellow-citizens.' 1259 b.
Πολιτικὴ ἀρχή is said in 3. 4. 1277 b 7 to be the kind of rule which is exercised over τῶν ὁμοίων τῷ γένει καὶ τῶν ἐλευθέρων, but this account seems too wide, for the rule of a father over a child would then fall under πολιτικὴ ἀρχή: in 1. 7. 1255 b 20 it is explained as ἐλευθέρων καὶ ἴσων ἀρχή, and this seems more exact, but we must bear in mind that under ἴσων are included proportionate, as well as absolute, equals. Πολιτικὴ ἀρχή usually implies an interchange of ruling and being ruled (cp. 3. 6. 1279 a 8 sqq.), but it does not necessarily do so (cp. c. 1. 1252 a 15)—it does not do so in the case of the wife, nor does it do so in the case of the rule of

νοῦς over ὄρεξις, which is πολιτικὴ καὶ βασιλική (1. 5. 1254 b 5). The relation of husband and wife is elsewhere described as ἀριστοκρατική (Eth. Nic. 8. 12. 1160 b 32 sqq.: 8. 13. 1161 a 22 sqq.), because it should be such as to assign τὸ ἁρμόζον ἑκάστῳ (cp. Pol. 6 (4). 8. 1294 a 9, δοκεῖ δὲ ἀριστοκρατία μὲν εἶναι μάλιστα τὸ τὰς τιμὰς νενεμῆσθαι κατ' ἀρετήν). Aristotle holds that though on the whole and as a rule the man is superior to the woman, there is nevertheless work which she can do better than he, and that account should be taken of this fact in determining the position of the wife in the household.

2. εἰ μή που κ.τ.λ. Sus. 'was nicht ausschliesst, dass das Verhältniss sich hie und da auch wider die Natur gestaltet,' and so Mr. Welldon: 'wherever the union is not unnaturally constituted.' Sepulveda, on the other hand, supplies as the nom. to συνέστηκε, not ἡ κοινωνία, but 'mas et femina,' translating 'nisi ubi praeter naturam constiterunt,' and Lambinus 'mas,' translating 'nisi forte ita comparatus est, ut a natura desciverit.' I incline, however, to take συνέστηκε as impersonal and to translate 'except where there is a contravention of nature.' See Bon. Ind. 342 b 20 sqq., and for συνέστηκε παρὰ φύσιν, ibid. 731 a 20–27. As to the impersonal use of verbs in Greek, see Riddell, Apology of Plato, p. 155 sqq. The following epigram on James I is quoted by the late Mr. Mark Pattison in his copy of Stahr's edition of the Politics (1839):

'Rex fuit Elisabeth, nunc est regina Iacobus.'

4. ἐν μὲν οὖν κ.τ.λ. Μὲν οὖν appears to be answered by δ' 9. In most cases of political rule, indeed, there is an interchange of ruling and being ruled, which does not occur in the case of husband and wife. Free and equal citizens, in fact, aim at being equal in nature and differing in nothing. (I take τὸ ἄρχον καὶ τὸ ἀρχόμενον to be the nom. to βούλεται.) Yet even here differences do not wholly vanish, for the holders of office seek for the time of their magistracy to have their position marked by a distinctive aspect and bearing, a distinctive mode of address and marks of respect; thus if there is an equality of nature, there is a temporary inequality in externals even among like and equal citizens. The relation in which the citizen-ruler stands to those over whom he rules during his term of office is that in which the male permanently stands to the female. (Cp. 2. 2. 1261 a 30 sqq., where the same idea appears that even ἐλεύθεροι καὶ ἴσοι are differentiated by the fact of their holding or not holding office.) The husband, we learn, rules his wife as a citizen-ruler rules his fellow-citizens; he is marked off from his wife less by a difference in nature than by a difference σχήμασι καὶ λόγοις καὶ τιμαῖς. The father, on the contrary, is different in nature from his child (1259 b 14). Aristotle does not, perhaps, always abide by this view of the relation of husband and wife; thus in Eth. Nic. 5. 10. 1134 a 26 sqq., τὸ πολιτικὸν δίκαιον, which obtains ἐπὶ κοινωνῶν βίου πρὸς τὸ εἶναι αὐτάρκειαν, ἐλευθέρων καὶ ἴσων ἢ κατ' ἀναλογίαν ἢ κατ' ἀριθμόν, is said not to obtain even between husband and wife, though the conjugal relation comes nearer to realizing it than any other household relation, but only τὸ οἰκονομικὸν δίκαιον—indeed in this very book of the Politics (c. 13. 1260 a 29) he requires from the wife a submissive silence before her husband.

7. ὅταν, 'for the time during which.'

ζητεῖ, sc. τὸ ἄρχον. The claim made by a ruler (Amasis) is mentioned in illustration. Cp. 6 (4). 14. 1298 a 10, τὴν τοιαύτην γὰρ ἰσότητα ζητεῖ ὁ δῆμος: 7 (5). 8. 1308 a 11, ὁ γὰρ ἐπὶ τοῦ πλήθους ζητοῦσιν οἱ δημοτικοὶ τὸ ἴσον: 8 (6). 3. 1318 b 4, ἀεὶ γὰρ ζητοῦσι τὸ ἴσον καὶ τὸ δίκαιον οἱ ἥττους, οἱ δὲ κρατοῦντες οὐδὲν φροντίζουσιν.

8. σχήμασι. Lamb. 'vestitu,' Bern. 'die Tracht,' but ἐσθῆτι and σχήματι are distinguished in Eth. Nic. 4. 9. 1125 a 30 (cp. Rhet. 2. 8. 1386 a 32, if ἐσθῆτι is the right reading in this passage). Sepulv. and Giph. 'ornatu:' Vict. 'vestibus.' Perhaps 'aspect and bearing.' See Bon. Ind. 739 b 59–740 a 5.

λόγοις, 'mode and matter of address.'

καὶ (before Ἄμασις) as elsewhere introduces an instance. Amasis is an instance of 'that which rules after being ruled.' He had been a subject and was now a ruler. He claimed that, like the utensil referred to, which had been recast to form the image of a god and now was an object of veneration to the Egyptians, he should be treated for what he was, not what he had once been. Cp. Hdt. 2. 172. A somewhat similar metaphor is used by Themistocles in Aelian. V. H. 13. 39.

9. ἀεὶ . . . τοῦτον ἔχει τὸν τρόπον, 'at all times, not merely for a term, stands to the female in this relation.'

11. τὸ γὰρ γεννῆσαν. Γεννᾶν is used of the female as well as the male (cp. 4 (7). 16. 1334 b 36: de Gen. An. 2. 5. 741 b 3), but Aristotle is here evidently thinking of the father, not the mother.

ἄρχον ἐστίν, cp. Metaph. Λ. 7. 1072 b 10, ἐξ ἀνάγκης ἄρα ἐστὶν ὄν, and Pol. 2. 6. 1265 b 19, ἔσονται διαφέροντες. It is not identical with ἄρχει: the participle is used in an adjectival sense, 'a permanent quality being predicated of the subject' (Holden, Oeconomicus of Xenophon, Index p. 36 *).

12. βασιλικῆς εἶδος ἀρχῆς, 'the specific nature of royal rule.' Sus. 'was denn eben die Form einer königlichen Gewalt ergiebt.' Cp. Eth. Nic. 8. 12. 1160 b 24, ἡ μὲν γὰρ πατρὸς πρὸς υἱεῖς κοινωνία

βασιλείας ἔχει σχῆμα, Pol. 1. 4. 1253 b 30, ἐν ὀργάνου εἴδει, and 3. 15. 1286 a 2 sq.

14. τὸν βασιλέα τούτων ἁπάντων. Cp. Eth. Nic. 8. 12. 1160 b 24–27, ἡ μὲν γὰρ πατρὸς πρὸς υἱεῖς κοινωνία βασιλείας ἔχει σχῆμα, τῶν τέκνων γὰρ τῷ πατρὶ μέλει· ἐντεῦθεν δὲ καὶ Ὅμηρος τὸν Δία πατέρα προσαγορεύει, πατρικὴ γὰρ ἀρχὴ βούλεται ἡ βασιλεία εἶναι. Homer is praised for using the words 'father of gods and men' to designate the Kingship of Zeus over gods and men. For, Aristotle proceeds, the father is the truest type of a King. The King, like the father, 'should surpass those he rules in nature' ('indole,' Bon. Ind. 837 a 52, cp. Pol. 2. 2. 1261 a 39, διὰ τὸ τὴν φύσιν ἴσους εἶναι πάντας), 'but be one with them in race.'

15. μέν should logically have followed φύσει, but, as Bonitz observes (Ind. 454 a 20), who compares 6 (4). 5. 1292 b 12 sqq., 'interdum non ei additur vocabulo in quo vis oppositionis cernitur.'

C. 13. **18. Φανερὸν τοίνυν.** So far as the protasis introduced by ἐπεί in 1259 a 37 survives the long series of considerations which break in upon it in 1259 a 39–b 17, it here finds its apodosis, which is introduced by τοίνυν, as elsewhere by ὥστε (Bon. Ind. 873 a 31 sqq.) or possibly διό (Bonitz, Aristotel. Stud. 3. 122 sqq.). For the connexion of the whole, see note on 1259 a 37. Xenophon in the Oeconomicus had described with much zest the mixture of vigilance and geniality with which the thrifty Ischomachus gets everybody connected with his farm, from his wife and his steward downwards, to strain every nerve for the increase of his substance, which is, according to him, the aim of οἰκονομία (cp. Oecon. c. 6. 4, ἡ δὲ ἐπιστήμη αὕτη—i. e. ἡ οἰκονομία—ἐφαίνετο ᾗ οἴκους δύνανται αὔξειν ἄνθρωποι). In tacit opposition to Xenophon, Aristotle here presses the consequences of the principle which he has established in the foregoing chapters, that χρηματιστική, and even its soundest part, is in strictness no part of οἰκονομία, but only an auxiliary art (ὑπηρετική), and that though οἰκονομία will not be indifferent to the goodness or badness of the property it uses (1258 a 26), its business is nevertheless rather to care for the excellence of the human beings with whom it has to deal, and for that of the free rather than the slave. The original propounder of this view may well have been Socrates (Cleitophon 407 A sq.: see Wyttenbach on [Plutarch] de Liberis Educandis c. 7. 4 E), but traces of it appear in Plato, Politicus 261 C and Laws 743 E, and we find doctrines of a similar kind ascribed to Cynics like Diogenes (Aelian, V. H. 12. 56: cp. Diog. Laert. 6. 41). The views of Crassus, who was not unacquainted with the teaching of Aristotle (Plutarch, Crassus c. 3), may possibly have been influenced by the passage before us (see the account of them given in Crassus c. 2. and above, p. xvii). Cato the Censor is praised by Plutarch (Cato Censor, c. 20) for combining with keenness as an economist care for the welfare of his wife and children. For the relation of the Stoic and Epicurean conceptions of οἰκονομία to those of Plato and Aristotle, see Schömann, Opusc. Acad. 3. 234 sqq.

19. τὴν τῶν ἀψύχων κτῆσιν, 'inanimate property.' Cp. 2. 7. 1267 b 10, τὴν τῆς γῆς κτῆσιν, and 1. 9. 1257 b 40, τὴν τοῦ νομίσματος οὐσίαν.

20. τὴν τῆς κτήσεως, ὃν καλοῦμεν πλοῦτον. Sus. 'als diesen' (inanimate property) 'in den tüchtigen Stand zu setzen, den man Reichthum und Wohlhabenheit nennt,' ὃν καλοῦμεν πλοῦτον being explanatory of ἀρετὴ κτήσεως, cp. Rhet. 1. 6. 1362 b 18, πλοῦτος· ἀρετὴ γὰρ κτήσεως καὶ ποιητικὸν πολλῶν [ἀγαθῶν.]

21. τῶν ἐλευθέρων μᾶλλον ἢ δούλων. For the addition of the article before ἐλευθέρων and its absence before δούλων, see Vahlen's note on Poet. 4. 1449 a 1, where Rhet. 2. 13. 1390 a 16, μᾶλλον ζῶσι κατὰ λογισμὸν ἢ κατὰ τὸ ἦθος is quoted. It is, however, possible that a slightly depreciatory significance attaches to the omission of the article before δούλων, as in Agesil. 11. 4, ἤσκει δὲ ἐξομιλεῖν μὲν παντοδαποῖς, χρῆσθαι δὲ τοῖς ἀγαθοῖς. Cp. 1. 7. 1255 b 32–33.

πρῶτον μὲν οὖν κ.τ.λ. Μὲν οὖν here as often elsewhere is introductory to a clearer definition of what has just been said. (The μέν is apparently answered by δέ 28.) Aristotle has spoken in the preceding sentence of an ἀρετὴ δούλων, and the thought occurs to him that there are two senses of ἀρετή, and that he may be understood merely to inculcate on the master the communication of technical excellence to the slave (cp. 1260 b 3 sqq.). He therefore loses no time in raising the question, what the virtue is in the case of slaves, which he has said the householder is to care for and promote: is it merely ὀργανικὴ καὶ διακονικὴ ἀρετή, or are they capable of ἠθικὴ ἀρετή? (For the terms in which the question is raised, cp. 5 (8). 5. 1339 b 42, οὐ μὴν ἀλλὰ ζητητέον μή ποτε τοῦτο μὲν συμβέβηκε, τιμιωτέρα δ' αὐτῆς ἡ φύσις ἐστὶν ἢ κατὰ τὴν εἰρημένην χρείαν.) Aristotle had defined the natural slave in the words, ὅσων ἐστὶν ἔργον ἡ τοῦ σώματος χρῆσις, καὶ τοῦτ' ἔστ' ἀπ' αὐτῶν βέλτιστον, 1. 5. 1254 b 17—words which went farther even than the well-known saying in Homer (Ody. 17. 322), that Zeus in taking away a man's freedom takes away half his virtue—and he feels that a doubt may well be raised whether a slave is capable of moral virtue. The course of the argument on this subject seems to be as follows: —'The answer is not easy, for if the slave has moral virtue, how does he differ from a freeman? Yet if he has it not, the fact is surprising, seeing that he is a man and shares in reason. The same question, however, arises as to the wife and child, and it is better to put the question in its most comprehensive form—is the virtue of that which by nature rules the same as the virtue of that which by nature is ruled, or different? (It will be seen that Aristotle abstains for the present from raising any question as to that which neither naturally rules nor naturally is ruled.) If we say that both have complete virtue, why should the one rule and the other be ruled? If again we say that their virtue differs in degree, the same question arises, for between ruling and being ruled there is a difference not of degree, but of kind. If, on the other hand, we say that one has virtue and the other not, how can the ruler rule well, or the ruled obey well, without virtue? Both, it is clear, must have virtue, and virtue must have different kinds, just as there are different kinds of that which is by nature ruled. We are familiar with this in the case of the soul; in the soul there is a part which naturally rules and another which naturally is ruled, and to each of these two parts we attribute a virtue of its own. But if these two parts, related to each other as naturally ruling and ruled, exist by nature, then other pairs also, destined by nature to rule and be ruled respectively, exist by nature—the master and slave, the husband and wife, the father and child—and each member of these three pairs has a virtue of its own varying according to the constitution of the soul in each and the work each has to perform.' We must bear in mind that in the Meno of Plato Socrates is made to assert the identity of the temperance and other virtues of women and men, in opposition to the sophist Gorgias, and that Aristotle's object here is to show that virtue varies with social function, the virtue of the ruled not being the same as the virtue of the ruler. It is, however, also his object to show, in opposition to those who confined virtue to the ruler (3. 4. 1277 a 20), that τὸ φύσει ἀρχόμενον, whether wife, child, or slave, is not without moral virtue, but has a sort of virtue varying with its psychical constitution and the function it discharges. Here therefore, as elsewhere, Aristotle steers a midway course between two extremes—the view of those who denied virtue to the ruled, and the view of those who identified the virtue of women and men.

24. σωφροσύνη κ.τ.λ. These virtues are instanced as those most likely to be found in slaves, more likely than μεγαλοψυχία, φρόνησις, or σοφία.

τῶν ἕξεων. For this use of the gen., Susemihl rightly compares 1. 13. 1260 b 2 (already referred to by Schn., vol. 2. p. 68): 3. 5. 1278 a 27: 3. 13. 1284 b 11 (if $Π^2$ are wrong): 5 (8). 4. 1338 b 30.

26. ἔχει . . . ἀμφοτέρως. 'For whichever alternative we adopt, difficult questions arise' (Lamb. 'dubitationem habet, utrumcunque dixeris'). Ἔχει is probably here impersonal; see Bon. Ind. 305 b 31 sqq., and Riddell, Apology of Plato, p. 155 sq.

εἴτε γὰρ ἔστι, sc. *ἀρετή τις δούλου*.

32. καὶ . . . δή. See note on 1. 2. 1253 a 18.

33. πότερον . . . ἑτέρα. This is not exactly the same question as had been raised about the woman and child just before; perhaps it is already felt to be paradoxical to deny to the *ἀρχόμενον φύσει* the possession of any kind of moral virtue. Besides, the question now raised is that which Socrates had raised (1260 a 22), and Aristotle is much preoccupied with his view on the subject.

34. γάρ justifies *ἐπισκεπτέον* by adducing difficulties which arise.

καλοκἀγαθίας. The question is put as paradoxically as possible, for *καλοκἀγαθία* is precisely the type of virtue from which slaves and women and children are furthest removed: see L. Schmidt, Ethik der alten Griechen 1. 333 sq., who refers to Xen. Mem. 1. 1. 16, *περὶ τῶν ἄλλων (διελέγετο Σωκράτης), ἃ τοὺς μὲν εἰδότας ἡγεῖτο καλοὺς κἀγαθοὺς εἶναι, τοὺς δ' ἀγνοοῦντας ἀνδραποδώδεις ἂν δικαίως κεκλῆσθαι.* *Καλοκἀγαθία* is the virtue of knights and hoplites (Xen. Mem. 3. 5. 18 sqq.). Cp. also Eth. Nic. 4. 7. 1124 a 1, *ἔοικε μὲν οὖν ἡ μεγαλοψυχία οἷον κόσμος τις εἶναι τῶν ἀρετῶν· μείζους γὰρ αὐτὰς ποιεῖ καὶ οὐ γίνεται ἄνευ ἐκείνων· διὰ τοῦτο χαλεπὸν τῇ ἀληθείᾳ μεγαλόψυχον εἶναι· οὐ γὰρ οἷόν τε ἄνευ καλοκἀγαθίας*: Magn. Mor. 2. 9. 1207 b 20 sqq.: Eth. Nic. 10. 10. 1179 b 10 sqq. The conception of *καλοκἀγαθία* is still further worked out in Eth. Eud. 7. 15.

37. τὸ δὲ κ.τ.λ. Cp. 1. 1. 1252 a 9.

38. οὐδέν, 'not at all,' as in Probl. 10. 35. 894 b 13.

40. ἀρχθήσεται. The fut. med. *ἄρξονται* occurs in a passive sense in 8 (6). 4. 1318 b 36.

1. δειλός. Cp. Plato, Laws 901 E, *δειλίας γὰρ ἔκγονος ἔν γε ἡμῖν* 1260 a.
ἀργία: Aristot. Eth. Nic. 9. 4. 1166 b 10, *διὰ δειλίαν καὶ ἀργίαν*, and below 1260 a 36.

3. ταύτης δ' . . . ἀρχομένων. These words are often translated—'and that there are different forms of virtue corresponding to the differences between the naturally ruled.' But then hitherto, as Susemihl remarks (*Hermes* (1884), Bd. 19. Heft 4), Aristotle has been dwelling on the difference between ruler and ruled, not on the differences between various ruled elements, and if *ὥσπερ* here means 'corresponding to,' we certainly expect *ὥσπερ καὶ τοῦ φύσει ἄρχοντος καὶ ἀρχομένου*. Not *ὥσπερ καὶ τῶν φύσει ἀρχόντων καὶ ἀρχομένων*, the reading to which the rendering found in two MSS. (a, z) of the *vetus versio* points—'quemadmodum et natura principantium et subiectorum'—for hitherto, as Sus. sees, though he accepts this reading, no stress has been laid on the fact of the existence of different forms of ἄρχοντα and ἀρχόμενα: on the contrary, it is on the difference between τὸ ἄρχον and τὸ ἀρχόμενον and their respective ἔργα that the existence of different forms of virtue has been rested. Perhaps, however, ὥσπερ does not here mean 'corresponding to,' but simply 'as indeed'—so that our rendering will run 'and that different types of virtue exist, as indeed differences also exist between the naturally ruled.' Compare the use of ὥσπερ in 1. 11. 1259 a 35, πολλαῖς γὰρ πόλεσι δεῖ χρηματισμοῦ, ὥσπερ οἰκίᾳ, μᾶλλον δέ. Aristotle's meaning will then be, that there is nothing more surprising in the fact of ruler and ruled having different types of virtue than there is in the fact of the naturally ruled differing in character. He has already said in 1. 5. 1254 a 24, καὶ εἴδη πολλὰ καὶ ἀρχόντων καὶ ἀρχομένων ἐστίν, καὶ ἀεὶ βελτίων ἡ ἀρχὴ ἡ τῶν βελτιόνων ἀρχομένων. Perhaps, however, τῆς ἀρετῆς should be supplied before τῶν φύσει ἀρχομένων, and the translation should be—'as indeed differences also exist between the virtue of one naturally ruled element and that of another.' Those who take ὥσπερ in the sense of 'corresponding to' will be much tempted to read ὥσπερ καὶ τῶν φύσει ἀρχόντων καὶ ἀρχομένων, but this reading rests, as has been said, only on the authority of one or two MSS. of the *vetus versio*, the rendering found in which may represent nothing more than a conjectural emendation. This change of reading might, indeed, be dispensed with, if an ellipse of πρὸς τὸ φύσει ἄρχον or πρὸς τὰ φύσει ἄρχοντα could be supposed between ὥσπερ καὶ and τῶν φύσει ἀρχομένων (compare the ellipse of πρὸς τὴν ψυχήν in 5 (8). 5. 1340 b 17). But ὥσπερ need not mean 'corresponding to,' and probably does not. (Since writing the foregoing note, I have become acquainted with the following annotation by the late Mr. Mark Pattison in the copy of Stahr's Politics already referred to (above on 1259 b 2). Stahr translates in this edition—'diese aber ihre Verschiedenheiten hat, so gut wie die, welche von Natur zum Beherrschtwerden und zum Herrschen bestimmt sind.' The annotation is—'if the words [ἀρχόντων καὶ] are to form part of the text, surely the meaning is, not "so gut wie die," but "have differences corresponding to the differences between the natural ruler and the natural ruled." But all the MSS. appear to omit them, and the meaning is—"and in the same way as there are differences between the virtues of the ruler and those of the ruled, so there are differences between the virtues of the different species of the ruled."')

4. καὶ τοῦτο κ.τ.λ. I take the literal rendering to be—'and this has at once led the way for us in the case of the soul' ('this' being 'the existence of a natural ruler and a natural ruled, each with a virtue of its own'). For ὑφήγηται in this sense, compare Plato, Lysis 217 A, ἆρ' οὖν καὶ καλῶς . . . ὑφηγεῖται ἡμῖν τὸ νῦν λεγόμενον; and the use of the word προοδοποιεῖσθαι in de Gen. An. 4. 4. 770 b 3. Περὶ τὴν ψυχήν is perhaps not far removed in meaning from ἐν τῇ ψυχῇ (cp. Bon. Ind. 579 a 29 sqq.). The soul is one of the things that lie nearest to us, and on examining it the phenomenon of which we are in quest appears, and thus we are guided to detect it in other cases also. Cp. Plutarch, de Fraterno Amore c. 2 *init.*, καίτοι τὸ παράδειγμα τῆς χρήσεως τῶν ἀδελφῶν ἡ φύσις οὐ μακρὰν ἔθηκεν, ἀλλ' ἐν αὐτῷ τῷ σώματι τὰ πλεῖστα τῶν ἀναγκαίων διττὰ καὶ ἀδελφὰ καὶ δίδυμα μηχανησαμένη, χεῖρας, πόδας, ὄμματα, ὦτα, ῥῖνας, ἐδίδαξεν ὅτι κ.τ.λ. The perfect ὑφήγηται may be defended, either as referring to the previous assertion of the existence of a ruling and a ruled element within the soul (1. 5. 1254 b 5), or as implying that the soul affords an already forthcoming and familiar example of the fact—cp. de Part. An. 1. 3. 643 b 10, δεῖ πειρᾶσθαι λαμβάνειν κατὰ γένη τὰ ζῷα, ὡς ὑφήγηνθ' οἱ πολλοὶ διορίσαντες ὄρνιθος γένος καὶ ἰχθύος. Schütz' conjectural addition of τὰ before περὶ τὴν ψυχήν simplifies the passage, but is perhaps unnecessary. It should be added that Vict. takes ὑφήγηται in a passive sense ('incoeptum est'), and that Bonitz also (Ind. 807 b 46) gives it a passive meaning. The correctness of this view, however, is open to doubt. For the thought, cp. 4 (7). 14. 1333 a 16 sqq.

6. οἷον does not seem here to exemplify but to explain, as in 3. 13. 1283 b 1.

8. τῶν ἄλλων, 'other things besides the rational and irrational elements of the soul.'

ὥστε κ.τ.λ. Thurot (Études, p. 18), with most others, translates the words ὥστε φύσει τὰ πλείω ἄρχοντα καὶ ἀρχόμενα 'de sorte que la plupart des êtres commandent ou obéissent par nature,' and fails, not without reason, to find a satisfactory meaning in the words when thus translated, adding 'du moins la leçon vulgaire ne se lie pas avec ce qui suit immédiatement.' Hence he proposes to read ὥστε πλείω τὰ φύσει ἄρχοντα καὶ ἀρχόμενα. But is not another interpretation of τὰ πλείω possible? May not the meaning of the passage be as follows—'so that not only is this one case of a ruling element and a ruled natural, but the plurality of cases of the same thing which we observe are natural too—I say "plurality," for the free rules the slave in one way, and the male the female in another, and the man the child in a third, and while (μὲν) the parts of the soul exist in all these, they exist differently in each.' The first conclusion drawn is, that in a plurality of cases we find a ruling element and a ruled, both existing by nature. The reason for proving their naturalness is that only τὰ φύσει ἄρχοντα καὶ ἀρχόμενα have a moral virtue of their own; thus the τεχνίτης, being neither φύσει nor fully a slave, has not a moral virtue of his own, except so far as he is a slave. From this first inference Aristotle passes on to a second—that of a diversity of psychological constitution and of moral virtue in every ruling and ruled element subsisting by nature, according as the function discharged in each case is absolute and complete (τὸ ἁπλῶς ἔργον) or falls in various degrees short of being so. For τὰ πλείω ἄρχοντα καὶ ἀρχόμενα, cp. de Gen. An. 2. 7. 746 a 12, ἐπεὶ δὲ τὰ μὲν μονοτόκα, τὰ δὲ πολυτόκα τῶν τοιούτων ἐστὶ ζῴων, καὶ τὰ πλείω τῶν ἐμβρύων ('mehreren Embryen,' Aubert and Wimmer) τὸν αὐτὸν ἔχει τρόπον τῷ ἑνί: de Caelo 1. 8. 276 b 19, ἐν τοῖς πλείοσιν οὐρανοῖς ('in den mehreren Himmelsgebäuden,' Prantl). So we have οἱ πολλοὶ σύνδεσμοι ('a multiplicity of conjunctions') in Rhet. 3. 5. 1407 b 12, and οἱ πολλοὶ θεράποντες in Pol. 2. 3. 1261 b 37: cp. also Dio Chrys. Or. 1. 50 R, τἆλλα οὕτως ἀγαπᾷ τὰ ἀρχόμενα τοὺς ἄρχοντας. Thurot, as has been said, would read ὥστε πλείω τὰ φύσει ἄρχοντα καὶ ἀρχόμενα, but this conclusion seems hardly to be that to which the preceding words point. Bernays avoids this objection in his rewriting of 8–17, as does also Susemihl in his still more sweeping reconstruction of 8–20 (Qu. Crit. p. 359: *Hermes* 19. 588 sqq.), but no MS. gives them any support, nor am I convinced that any change is necessary.

11. τὰ μόρια τῆς ψυχῆς, i. e. τὸ ἄλογον and τὸ λόγον ἔχον: cp. de Gen. An. 2. 4. 741 a 2, τὰ δ' ἄλλα μόρια τῆς ψυχῆς (other than ἡ γεννῶσα καὶ θρεπτικὴ ψυχή) τοῖς μὲν ὑπάρχει, τοῖς δ' οὐχ ὑπάρχει τῶν ζῴων. To give the slave τὸ λόγον ἔχον, τὸ παθητικόν must be counted here (as in Eth. Nic. 1. 6. 1098 a 3 and 1. 13. 1103 a 2) as part of τὸ λόγον ἔχον, not of τὸ ἄλογον, for he has not the more indubitable element of τὸ λόγον ἔχον, τὸ βουλευτικόν (1260 a 12: cp. 3. 9. 1280 a 32 sqq.), which is apparently identical with that which is called τὸ λογιστικόν in Eth. Nic. 6. 2. 1139 a 12. Thus in 1. 5. 1254 b 22, he is said κοινωνεῖν λόγου τοσοῦτον ὅσον αἰσθάνεσθαι ἀλλὰ μὴ ἔχειν.

13. ἄκυρον, 'imperfect in authority,' 'imperfectly obeyed'—cp. Eth. Nic. 7. 10. 1151 b 15, λυποῦνται, ἐὰν ἄκυρα τὰ αὐτῶν ᾖ ὥσπερ ψηφίσματα. In women τὸ βουλευτικόν is there, but often does not get its own way.

14. ἀτελές. Cp. Plato, Laws 808 D, ὅσῳ γὰρ μάλιστα [ὁ παῖς] ἔχει πηγὴν τοῦ φρονεῖν μήπω κατηρτυμένην, and Rep. 441 A–B. Cp. also Aristot. Phys. 7. 3. 247 b 18 sqq., where the child is described as in a state of φυσικὴ ταραχή, which must settle down before it can become φρόνιμον καὶ ἐπιστῆμον. In Eth. Nic. 3. 4. 1111 b 8 προαίρεσις, and in Eth. Nic. 6. 13. 1144 b 8 νοῦς, are denied to the child, who is said in Eth. Nic. 3. 15. 1119 b 5 to live κατ' ἐπιθυμίαν.

ὁμοίως κ.τ.λ., i. e. the moral virtues, like the parts of the soul, exist in all, but differently. The construction of this sentence seems to be—ὑποληπτέον τοίνυν ἀναγκαῖον (εἶναι) ὁμοίως ἔχειν καὶ περὶ τὰς ἠθικὰς ἀρετάς, δεῖν μὲν κ.τ.λ. For the omission of εἶναι, see Bon. Ind. 43 a 6, 239 a 9 sqq., and cp. c. 9. 1257 b 32. A somewhat similarly constructed sentence occurs in Magn. Mor. 1. 18. 1190 a 15 sq.: cp. also 28, διὸ δεῖ, ὥσπερ ὁ ποιητὴς εἴρηκε περὶ γυναικός, οὕτω νομίζειν ἔχειν περὶ πάντων. Bekker and Sus., however, begin a fresh sentence with ὑποληπτέον.

16. ὅσον κ.τ.λ. Ἐπιβάλλει or some such word needs to be supplied here, but Aristotle follows pretty closely the language of Meno in Plato, Meno 72 A, καθ' ἑκάστην γὰρ τῶν πράξεων καὶ τῶν ἡλικιῶν πρὸς ἕκαστον ἔργον ἑκάστῳ ἡμῶν ἡ ἀρετή ἐστιν. Compare also for the thought Plato, Rep. 601 D.

17. διὸ κ.τ.λ. 'Hence the ruler must possess moral virtue in its complete rational form, for any function taken absolutely and in its fullness belongs to [and demands] a master-hand, and reason is such a master-hand.' The function of healing, for instance, is predicated ἁπλῶς of the physician who directs and superintends the process, and only in a qualified way (πως) of the subordinate who carries his directions into effect: cp. 4 (7). 3. 1325 b 21, μάλιστα δὲ καὶ πράττειν λέγομεν κυρίως καὶ τῶν ἐξωτερικῶν πράξεων τοὺς ταῖς διανοίαις ἀρχιτέκτονας. Cp. also Eth. Nic. 7. 12. 1152 b 1, περὶ δὲ ἡδονῆς καὶ λύπης θεωρῆσαι τοῦ τὴν πολιτικὴν φιλοσοφοῦντος· οὗτος γὰρ τοῦ τέλους ἀρχιτέκτων, πρὸς ὃ βλέποντες ἕκαστον τὸ μὲν κακὸν τὸ δ' ἀγαθὸν ἁπλῶς λέγομεν, and Marc. Antonin. Comment. 6. 35. As to τελέαν . . . τὴν ἠθικὴν ἀρετήν, cp. Magn. Mor. 2. 3. 1200 a 3, ἡ τελεία ἀρετὴ ὑπάρξει, ἣν ἔφαμεν μετὰ φρονήσεως εἶναι: Eth. Nic. 10. 8. 1178 a 18, τὸ δ' ὀρθὸν τῶν ἠθικῶν (ἀρετῶν) κατὰ τὴν φρόνησιν: Pol. 3. 4. 1277 b 18 sqq. (especially ἡ δὲ φρόνησις ἄρχοντος ἴδιος ἀρετὴ μόνη, 25).

21. οὐχ ἡ αὐτὴ κ.τ.λ. Cp. 3. 4. 1277 b 20 sqq. This teaching is anticipated in Eth. Nic. 8. 14. 1162 a 26, ἔστι γὰρ ἑκατέρου ἀρετή (i. e. ἀνδρὸς καὶ γυναικός).

22. Σωκράτης. Cp. Plato, Meno 71–73, though the absence of the article before Σωκράτης seems to imply that Aristotle is speaking of the historical Socrates, not of the interlocutor in the Meno. Antisthenes agreed with Socrates (Diog. Laert. 6. 12). On the views of Socrates and Plato respectively as to the unity of virtue, see Zeller, Plato, E. T. p. 448 sqq. Plutarch seeks to prove in his De Virtute Muliebri, that though there are differences between the virtue of men and that of women, just as there are differences between the same virtue in different men (e.g. the courage of Ajax and Achilles), yet the virtues of women are not specifically different from those of men.

24. τὰς ἄλλας, sc. ἀρετάς, i.e. σωφροσύνη καὶ δικαιοσύνη. The word ἀρετή is so easily supplied that it is often suppressed—e.g. in 3. 5. 1278 b 1 and 5 (8). 4. 1338 b 15.

τοῦτο, i.e. the conclusion stated in 20–24. This had been reached through premisses relating to the virtue of φύσει ἄρχοντα and ἀρχόμενα in general, but it might also have been reached by examining the subject more in detail, as for instance by examining the virtue of women, children, and slaves separately and successively (κατὰ μέρος μᾶλλον ἐπισκοποῦσιν). This seems from what Meno says (Plato, Meno 71 E) to have been the method followed by Gorgias.

25. καθόλου. For the place of καθόλου, see Vahlen's note on Poet. 17. 1455 a 24 (p. 184). The thought is too characteristic of Aristotle and recurs too often in his writings to need much illustration, but reference may be made to Eth. Nic. 2. 7. 1107 a 28 sqq.: Pol. 2. 6. 1265 a 31: Rhet. 2. 19. 1393 a 16 sqq.

26. τὸ εὖ ἔχειν τὴν ψυχήν. Plato had said this in Rep. 444 D, ἀρετὴ μὲν ἄρα, ὡς ἔοικεν, ὑγίειά τέ τις ἂν εἴη καὶ κάλλος καὶ εὐεξία ψυχῆς.

τὸ ὀρθοπραγεῖν. As to the omission of ἤ, see critical note. For this definition of virtue, cp. Plato, Charmides 172 A: Meno 97.

27. ἐξαριθμοῦντες, as in Plato, Meno 71 E, πρῶτον μέν, εἰ βούλει ἀνδρὸς ἀρετήν . . . εἰ δὲ βούλει γυναικὸς ἀρετήν . . . καὶ ἄλλη ἐστὶ παιδὸς ἀρετή, καὶ θηλείας καὶ ἄρρενος, καὶ πρεσβυτέρου ἀνδρός, εἰ μὲν βούλει, ἐλευθέρου, εἰ δὲ βούλει, δούλου: cp. also 77 A.

28. διό seems to introduce an inference from the general tenour of 17–24.

29. ὁ ποιητής, here Sophocles (Ajax 293). Cp. Athen. Deipn. 559 a, where the following lines are quoted from the Ὕπνος of Xenarchus:

Εἶτ' εἰσὶν οἱ τέττιγες οὐκ εὐδαίμονες,
ὧν ταῖς γυναιξὶν οὐδ' ὁτιοῦν φωνῆς ἔνι;

30. πάντων, slaves, children, and women. For the thought, cp. Xen. Rep. Lac. 3. 4 sq.

For the asyndeton at γυναικί, compare the somewhat similar examples adduced by Vahlen in his note on Poet. 25. 1460 b 23 (p. 261 sqq.).

31. οὐκέτι. Cp. de Gen. et Corr. 1. 2. 315 b 3.

32. πρὸς τὸ τέλος καὶ τὸν ἡγούμενον, 'relative to the fully developed human being' (contrasted with *ἀτελής*: cp. 1. 2. 1252 b 31, *τέλος γὰρ αὕτη ἐκείνων*) 'and to his guiding authority.' The child is apparently regarded as finding in his father the fully developed type of manhood which he himself is designed ultimately to realize and as accepting guidance from him. Cp. Eth. Eud. 7. 15. 1249 b 6, *δεῖ δή, ὥσπερ καὶ ἐν τοῖς ἄλλοις, πρὸς τὸ ἄρχον ζῆν καὶ πρὸς τὴν ἕξιν κατὰ τὴν ἐνέργειαν τὴν τοῦ ἄρχοντος, οἷον δοῦλον πρὸς δεσπότου καὶ ἕκαστον πρὸς τὴν ἑκάστου καθήκουσαν ἀρχήν*: Eth. Nic. 3. 15. 1119 b 7, and 3. 5. 1113 a 5 sqq.

33. ὁμοίως δὲ κ.τ.λ. For the thought, cp. Menander, Inc. Fab. Fragm. 56:

> *Ἐμοὶ πόλις ἐστὶ καὶ καταφυγὴ καὶ νόμος*
> *καὶ τοῦ δικαίου τοῦ τ' ἀδίκου παντὸς κριτὴς*
> *ὁ δεσπότης· πρὸς τοῦτον ἕνα δεῖ ζῆν ἐμέ,*

and Fragm. 150:

> *Ἐλεύθερος πᾶς ἑνὶ δεδούλωται, νόμῳ,*
> *δυσὶν δὲ δοῦλος, καὶ νόμῳ καὶ δεσπότῃ.*

ἔθεμεν, e.g. in c. 5. 1254 b 25.

35. The construction of *τοσοῦτος* with *ὅπως* does not seem to be very common. See with respect to it Weber, Die Absichtssätze bei Aristoteles, p. 33, who compares Oecon. 1. 6. 1344 b 29, *καὶ τὰς ἐργασίας (δεῖ) οὕτω νενεμῆσθαι ὅπως μὴ ἅμα κινδυνεύσωσιν ἅπασιν.*

36. ἐλλείψῃ. Eucken (de Partic. usu, p. 54) compares 7 (5). 1. 1301 b 7: 4 (7). 14. 1334 a 5.

ἀπορήσειε δ' ἄν τις κ.τ.λ. It would be possible to take *ἆρα* (37) and *ἤ* (39) as in the same construction, and the whole sentence *ἆρα—πλεῖστον* as dependent on *ἀπορήσειε* (for *ἆρα* followed by *ἤ* in indirect interrogations, see Vahlen, Beitr. zu Aristot. Poet. 1. 43 sq., and on Poet. 4. 1449 a 7), but *ἢ διαφέρει τοῦτο πλεῖστον* is probably not a part of the question raised: it is rather Aristotle's own solution of the *ἀπορία* (see Bon. Ind. 313 a 7 sqq., and compare the very similar passage, 7 (5). 9. 1309 b 8–11). The difficulty raised is—'if we allow the existence of an *ἀρετὴ δούλου*, because the slave needs to possess it, must we not also allow the existence of an *ἀρετὴ τεχνίτου*?'

40. κοινωνὸς ζωῆς, 'is a sharer with his master in a common existence': cp. 3. 6. 1278 b 16, *τῆς ἀρχῆς εἴδη πόσα τῆς περὶ ἄνθρωπον καὶ τὴν κοινωνίαν τῆς ζωῆς*, and other similar phrases collected by Lasaulx, Ehe bei den Griechen (p. 13, note 22). It was only of *φύσει ἀρχόμενα* that the possession of a form of moral virtue was proved in 1259 b 32 sqq. Cp. Plin. Epist. 8. 16: servis respublica quaedam et quasi civitas domus est.

πορρώτερον, 'less closely attached to the master.' Cp. 3. 5. 1278 a 11, *τῶν δ' ἀναγκαίων οἱ μὲν ἑνὶ λειτουργοῦντες τὰ τοιαῦτα δοῦλοι, οἱ δὲ κοινοὶ βάναυσοι καὶ θῆτες.*

1260 b. **1. ἀφωρισμένην τινὰ ἔχει δουλείαν.** Sepulveda translates 'determinatae cuidam servituti addictus est,' and explains in his note that the *βάναυσος τεχνίτης* is not a slave for all purposes, but only for the performance of a definite servile task. The extent of his slavery is determined by his *ἔργον*: cp. 6 (4). 15. 1300 a 15, *ἢ ἐκ πάντων ἢ ἐκ τινῶν ἀφωρισμένων, οἷον ἢ τιμήματι ἢ γένει ἢ ἀρετῇ ἢ τινι τοιούτῳ ἄλλῳ*, and Eth. Nic. 8. 11. 1159 b 33.

καὶ ὁ μὲν δοῦλος κ.τ.λ. The artisan is not only rather an adjunct of the household than one of its ruled members, but he is also not by nature. He is not a *φύσει ἀρχόμενον*, and all that has been proved in the foregoing is that *φύσει ἀρχόμενα* possess a moral virtue of their own. Nature has indeed provided men with materials for dress and consequently for shoemaking (1. 8. 1256 b 20), but the shoemaker works for hire and practises *μισθαρνία*, which was brought under the unnatural form of *χρηματιστική* in 1. 11. 1258 b 25. Yet in 4 (7). 8. 1328 b 6 and 6 (4). 4. 1291 a 1 sq. artisans are admitted to be a necessary element in a State; it seems strange then that they are not by nature.

2. τῶν ἄλλων τεχνιτῶν. For the gen., see note on 1259 b 24.

3. φανερὸν τοίνυν κ.τ.λ. The reasoning is—we have seen that the slave possesses a certain ministerial form of moral virtue over and above his technical excellences, and that his moral virtue is relative to his master, who is his end and guiding authority; hence it is from the master *qua* master, and not from the master as possessing the *δεσποτικὴ ἐπιστήμη*, that the slave must derive the kind of moral virtue which he ought to possess. The concluding part of the sentence, if it were complete, would apparently run—*τελέαν ἔχοντα τὴν ἠθικὴν ἀρετήν, ἀλλ' οὐ τὴν διδασκαλικὴν ἔχοντα τῶν ἔργων δεσποτικήν.* Nothing is gained, as it seems to me, by introducing *τὸν* (with Bern. Sus. and others) before *τὴν διδασκαλικήν*. The point insisted on by Aristotle appears to be that the master should be the source of moral virtue (in a subordinate and ministerial form) to the slave *qua* master, and as possessing complete moral virtue and reason, not as possessing the *δεσποτικὴ ἐπιστήμη*: it is not, that the master and nobody else is to be the source of moral virtue to the slave. Aristotle had said at the commencement of the chapter (1259 b 20), that the householder should care for the virtue of his slaves, and he has now made it clear what sort of virtue he should seek to produce in them. In 1. 7. 1255 b 30 sqq. (cp. 4 (7). 3. 1325 a 23 sqq.) the δεσποτικὴ ἐπιστήμη has already been said to be nothing great and to be in no way of the essence of the master. Socrates and Plato, who had denied the name of δεσπότης to any one not possessed of the science of δεσποτική, are here glanced at; Aristotle perhaps also remembers the picture of the δεσπότης in Xenophon's Oeconomicus, himself training his slaves to be efficient servants. Xenophon, however, had already in the same work depicted the householder as teaching his slaves justice (πειρῶμαι ἐμβιβάζειν εἰς τὴν δικαιοσύνην τοὺς οἰκέτας, Oecon. 14. 4: compare his account of the training of a housekeeper, ibid. 9. 13), and in this Aristotle is thoroughly with him.

5. **διὸ λέγουσιν οὐ καλῶς οἱ λόγου τοὺς δούλους ἀποστεροῦντες κ.τ.λ.** When Aristotle speaks of ἐπίταξις in connexion with the master of slaves, he has in his mind ἐπίταξις περὶ τὰ ἀναγκαῖα: cp. 4 (7). 3. 1325 a 25, οὐδὲν γὰρ τό γε δούλῳ, ᾗ δοῦλος, χρῆσθαι σεμνόν· ἡ γὰρ ἐπίταξις ἡ περὶ τῶν ἀναγκαίων οὐδενὸς μετέχει τῶν καλῶν, and 1. 7. 1255 b 33, ἔστι δ' αὕτη ἡ ἐπιστήμη οὐδὲν μέγα ἔχουσα οὐδὲ σεμνόν, ἃ γὰρ τὸν δοῦλον ἐπίστασθαι δεῖ ποιεῖν, ἐκεῖνον δεῖ ταῦτα ἐπίστασθαι ἐπιτάττειν. The drift of the passage before us, therefore, seems to be—'the master should be the source of moral virtue to the slave, hence he should not confine himself to commands relating to the slave's discharge of his servile functions.' But then comes the question—what is the meaning of οἱ λόγου τοὺς δούλους ἀποστεροῦντες? Bern. and Sus. translate 'those who forbid converse with slaves'—Stahr, 'those who withdraw rational admonition (die vernünftige Zurechtweisung) from slaves' (cp. Xen. Oecon. 13. 9, ἀνθρώπους δ' ἔστι πιθανωτέρους ποιεῖν καὶ λόγῳ, ἐπιδεικνύοντα ὡς συμφέρει αὐτοῖς πείθεσθαι); but I incline on the whole, following Bonitz (Ind. 436 b 50) and the earlier commentators, to explain λόγου here as 'reason' (cp. 1260 a 17–19 and Eth. Nic. 1. 13. 1102 b 33, ὅτι δὲ πείθεταί πως ὑπὸ λόγου τὸ ἄλογον, μηνύει καὶ ἡ νουθέτησις καὶ πᾶσα ἐπιτίμησίς τε καὶ παράκλησις), though it should be borne in mind that the two senses of the word λόγος, 'reason' and 'reasoning,' often tend to pass into each other. We still have to ask, however, what is the meaning of οἱ λόγου ἀποστεροῦντες. The earlier commentators explain the words 'those who deny that slaves partake in reason' (cp. 3. 1. 1275 a 28, καίτοι γελοῖον τοὺς κυριωτάτους ἀποστερεῖν ἀρχῆς), but perhaps their meaning rather is 'those who withhold reason from the slave' (by withholding the reasoning which is its source, 1. 5. 1254 b 22). For the relation of λόγος to the moral virtues, see Eth. Nic. 6. 1. With

the teaching of the passage before us may be compared that of Eth. Nic. 9. 9. 1170 b 10, *συναισθάνεσθαι ἄρα δεῖ καὶ τοῦ φίλου ὅτι ἔστιν, τοῦτο δὲ γίνοιτ' ἂν ἐν τῷ συζῆν καὶ κοινωνεῖν λόγων καὶ διανοίας· οὕτω γὰρ ἂν δόξειε τὸ συζῆν ἐπὶ τῶν ἀνθρώπων λέγεσθαι, καὶ οὐχ ὥσπερ ἐπὶ τῶν βοσκημάτων τὸ ἐν τῷ αὐτῷ νέμεσθαι.* What is here said of the intercourse of two friends may hold to a certain extent of the intercourse between master and slave. The reference in *οἱ λόγου τοὺς δούλους ἀποστεροῦντες κ.τ.λ.* is to Plato, Laws 777 E: cp. also 720 B sqq. Pallas, one of the favourite freedmen of the Emperor Claudius, 'would not deign even to speak to his slaves, but gave them his commands by gestures, or, if that was not enough, by written orders' (Capes, Early Roman Empire, p. 87). According to Clement of Alexandria (Aristot. Fragm. 179. 1508 b 7 sqq.), *οὐδὲ προσγελᾶν δούλοις Ἀριστοτέλης εἴα.* Is not this writer thinking of what Plato had said in the Laws?

6. **φάσκοντες.** 'Infinitives following certain verbs (of saying, thinking, etc.) sometimes contain a Dictative force . . . The governing verb gets a different and a stronger meaning: to "say" becomes to "recommend" or to "pray"' (Riddell, Apology of Plato, p. 148). *Φάσκειν* is used of philosophers setting forth a dogma.

7. **νουθετητέον γὰρ κ.τ.λ.** Aristotle does not say why (Vict. wishes that he had), but his reason probably is that the slave's one chance of sharing in reason is to receive it in reasoning from outside. The child (1260 a 13) has *τὸ βουλευτικόν* already, though as yet imperfect, whereas the slave has it not; all he has is the power of recognizing reason when set before him by another. One of Menander's characters says, in a fragment which perhaps belongs to the *Ἀδελφοί* (fr. 2: Meineke, Fr. Com. Gr. 4. 69)—

Οὐ λυποῦντα δεῖ
παιδάριον ὀρθοῦν, ἀλλὰ καὶ πείθοντά τι.

Aristotle's view would probably strike his contemporaries as a decided paradox, for Pseudo-Plutarch, de Liberis Educandis c. 12. 8 F, most likely expresses the view commonly taken—*κἀκεῖνό φημι, δεῖν τοὺς παῖδας ἐπὶ τὰ καλὰ τῶν ἐπιτηδευμάτων ἄγειν παραινέσεσι καὶ λόγοις, μὴ μὰ Δία πληγαῖς μηδ' αἰκισμοῖς. Δοκεῖ γάρ που ταῦτα τοῖς δούλοις μᾶλλον ἢ τοῖς ἐλευθέροις πρέπειν· ἀποναρκῶσι γὰρ καὶ φρίττουσι πρὸς τοὺς πόνους, τὰ μὲν διὰ τὰς ἀλγηδόνας τῶν πληγῶν, τὰ δὲ καὶ διὰ τὰς ὕβρεις*: cp. also Ecclesiasticus 33. 28.

8. **περὶ δ' ἀνδρὸς κ.τ.λ.** Nothing of this kind appears in the Politics; its inquiries, in fact, seldom assume this delicate ethical character. There are a few words as to the mutual behaviour of

husband and wife in Oecon. 1. 4. 1344 a 13 sq. which may possibly reproduce some part of Aristotle's teaching. See also the Latin translation of a fragment on this subject (which can hardly be from the pen of Aristotle) in Val. Rose, Aristoteles Pseudepigraphus, p. 644 sqq.

11. **τὸ καλῶς.** See Bon. Ind. 291 b 25 sqq.

12. **ἐν τοῖς περὶ τὰς πολιτείας.** The First Book (*οἱ πρῶτοι λόγοι, ἐν οἷς περὶ οἰκονομίας διωρίσθη καὶ δεσποτείας*, 3. 6. 1278 b 17) is here marked off from *τὰ περὶ τὰς πολιτείας*: cp. *ἡ πρώτη μέθοδος περὶ τῶν πολιτειῶν*, 6 (4). 2. 1289 a 26. So in Rhet. 2. 24. 1401 b 32, the phrase *οἱ ἐν ταῖς πολιτείαις* occurs, and Plato's Republic seems to have been sometimes spoken of as *αἱ πολιτεῖαι* (cp. 6 (4). 7. 1293 b 1, *ὥσπερ Πλάτων ἐν ταῖς πολιτείαις*: see for other instances Henkel, Studien, p. 10).

14. **ταῦτα,** i. e. *ἀνὴρ καὶ γυνή, τέκνα καὶ πατήρ*, though only *παῖδες* and *γυναῖκες* are mentioned in 16; it is perhaps taken for granted that the training of the head of the household will be relative to the constitution.

τὴν δὲ τοῦ μέρους κ.τ.λ. Cp. 5 (8). 1. 1337 a 29, *μόριον γὰρ ἕκαστος τῆς πόλεως· ἡ δ' ἐπιμέλεια πέφυκεν ἑκάστου μορίου βλέπειν πρὸς τὴν τοῦ ὅλου ἐπιμέλειαν.*

15. **πρὸς τὴν πολιτείαν.** The virtue of the part must be adjusted to the virtue of the whole; hence the virtue of the woman and the child must be adjusted to the constitution, for the constitution is the standard of virtue in the *πόλις*, the whole to which they belong. Cp. 7 (5). 9. 1310 a 12 sqq.: 5 (8). 1. 1337 a 11 sqq. The course followed in 4 (7). 14. 1332 b 12 sqq. is quite in conformity with this principle, though we are concerned there only with the children, or probably the sons, not with the women; *δῆλον γὰρ* (says Aristotle in that passage), *ὡς ἀκολουθεῖν δεήσει καὶ τὴν παιδείαν κατὰ τὴν διαίρεσιν ταύτην* (i. e. the decision whether the same persons are always to be rulers or not).

18. **αἱ μὲν γὰρ κ.τ.λ.** Cp. Plato, Laws 781 A sq.

19. **οἱ κοινωνοὶ τῆς πολιτείας.** Cp. 3. 3. 1276 b 1, *ἔστι δὲ (ἡ πόλις) κοινωνία πολιτῶν πολιτείας*, and 8 (6). 6. 1320 b 28, *ἀεὶ δὲ δεῖ παραλαμβάνειν ἐκ τοῦ βελτίονος δήμου τοὺς κοινωνούς.*

20. **ὥστ' ἐπεὶ κ.τ.λ.** Birt (Das antike Buchwesen, p. 459. 3) holds that 'these last five lines are evidently added by the "redaction" to form a transition to the Second Book.' The opening paragraph of the Second Book, however, accords but ill with the close of the First (see note on 1260 b 27); in fact, *καὶ πρῶτον* 23 . . *τῆς ἀρίστης* 24 would be better away, though it certainly is the case that the designers of 'best constitutions' are criticised in the Second Book before actual constitutions like the Lacedaemonian, etc., are criticised. It is possible that the closing words of the First Book were added by a bungling editor, but it is also possible that Aristotle himself may be in fault. The opening paragraph of the investigations which now constitute the Second Book of the Politics may have been imperfectly harmonized by him with the closing sentence of τὰ περὶ οἰκονομίας καὶ δεσποτείας, just as the sequence of the Third and Fourth (Seventh) Books is not absolutely perfect, and the programme of the Politics given at the close of the Nicomachean Ethics is departed from to a large extent in the Politics itself. Or again the opening paragraph of the Second Book may have been an after-thought of Aristotle's, and the book may have originally begun Ἀρχὴν δὲ πρῶτον ποιητέον κ.τ.λ. This is perhaps less probable, as ταύτης τῆς σκέψεως 37 seems to refer back to θεωρῆσαι περὶ τῆς κοινωνίας τῆς πολιτικῆς 27. It is impossible to penetrate these secrets of the workshop; one thing, however, should be borne in mind, that the component parts of the Politics are not as closely welded together as they might be, and often look as though they were more or less separate works. This makes defects of 'callida iunctura' less surprising.

BOOK II.

C. 1. **27. Ἐπεὶ δὲ κ.τ.λ.** The First Book ends, καὶ πρῶτον ἐπισκεψώμεθα
1260 b. περὶ τῶν ἀποφηναμένων περὶ τῆς πολιτείας τῆς ἀρίστης. The Second begins by premising that Aristotle's aim is to inquire what form of political union is best for those most favourably circumstanced—a fact which had not been stated before—and then proceeds to argue that this involves a preliminary review of 'other constitutions than that to be propounded by Aristotle' (τὰς ἄλλας πολιτείας), whether actual working constitutions (termed κύριαι in 2. 12. 1274 b 27) held to be well-ordered, or schemes in good repute put forward by individual inquirers. The two passages are evidently not in strict sequence. The opening paragraph of the Second Book is not perhaps absolutely inconsistent with the closing words of the First, inasmuch as all that is said at the close of the latter book is that those who have put forward views with regard to the best constitution will be first dealt with, but it appears to ignore them. In c. 12. 1273 b 27 sqq. the plan of the book is still further extended to include a notice of οἱ ἀποφηνάμενοί τι περὶ πολιτείας generally, and even of those

who were the authors of laws only and not of constitutions. Isocrates (Nicocl. § 24) refers to the Lacedaemonians and Carthaginians as admittedly possessing good constitutions; Polybius (6. 43) adds Crete and Mantineia, and in the opinion of some, Athens and Thebes. Plato (Laws 638 B) speaks of Ceos and the Italian Locri as well-governed. Cp. also Plato, Rep. 599 E and Crito 52 E.

29. τὰς ἄλλας πολιτείας, 'others than that which I am about to set forth': cp. *παρ' αὐτὰς ἕτερον*, 33. It is possible that these words may be used in the same sense ('other than my own') in 4 (7). 4. 1325 b 34.

31. † τυγχάνωσιν †. In eleven passages at least of the genuine writings of Aristotle, if the MSS. are to be trusted, we find *εἰ* followed by the subjunctive. These are as follows:—30 b 14, 66 b 9, 636 b 29, 1261 a 27, 136 a 20, 27, 179 b 22, 343 b 33, 1279 b 22 (*συμβαινηι*, Vat. Palimpsest), 1447 a 24, and the passage before us. (In 1132 a 11 K^b has the subjunctive after *κἂν εἰ*: see also 322 b 28, 326 a 6, 645 b 31, and Susemihl's *apparatus criticus* on 1323 a 2.) In the first four of these passages the subjunctive is used with *καὶ εἰ*, *εἰ*, *οὐδ' ἂν εἰ*, and *ὥσπερ ἂν εἰ*: in the remainder with *κἂν εἰ*. See Vahlen, Beitr. zu Aristot. Poet. 1. 35 sqq., Bon. Ind. 217 a 31 sqq. and 41 a 26 sq., and Eucken, de Partic. Usu p. 59 sqq. All the MSS. but pr. P^3 and possibly Γ have *τυγχάνωσιν* here, and all except P^1 and possibly Γ have *ἑλκύσῃ* in 1261 a 27. Vahlen's instructive discussion of the question as to the construction of *κἂν εἰ* with the subjunctive in Aristotle's writings results in the conclusion that its use is 'very doubtful' and in Poet. 1. 1447 a 24 he substitutes *κἂν εἰ τυγχάνουσιν* for *κἂν εἰ τυγχάνωσιν*, which is the reading of the one authoritative MS. of the Poetics. Bonitz would emend all the passages referred to above, so as to expel from Aristotle's writings the use of *εἰ* with the subjunctive. Eucken remarks (*ubi supra*, p. 63), that *τυγχάνωσιν* here, *συμβαίνῃ* in 3. 8. 1279 b 22, and *τυγχάνωσιν* in Poet. 1. 1447 a 25 may very easily have arisen from *τυγχάνουσιν*, *συμβαίνει*, and *τυγχάνουσιν*, and that it is only in passages 'ubi minima mutatione ex indicativo nasci potuit' that the subjunctive is found after *κἂν εἰ* in Aristotle's writings. It is easy, however, to lay too much stress on arguments of this kind (see Blass as to Dawes' Canon, Handbuch der klass. Alterthums-Wissenschaft, 1. 252). In Plato, Rep. 579 D the MSS. have *κἂν εἰ μή τῳ δοκῇ*, and in Thuc. 6. 21 an 'indubitable' instance of *εἰ* with the subjunctive occurs (Classen *ad loc.*). See Stallbaum's note on Laws 958 C, where other instances of the occurrence of this construction in Attic writers are noticed. Aristotle is not a strictly Attic writer, and the fact should be noted for what it is worth that there are other passages of the Politics in which either the one family of MSS. or the other gives the subjunctive where we expect the indicative or else the subjunctive with ἄν: thus in 1301 a 38 Π² have τυγχάνωσιν, and in 1307 a 37 ὅτῳ θέλωσι, while in 1313 a 20 Π¹ have ὅσῳ γὰρ ἐλαττόνων ὦσι κύριοι. On the whole, I have contented myself with indicating by obeli the grave doubts which attach to the inculpated readings—τυγχάνωσιν here and ἑλκύσῃ in 1261 a 27.

32. ἵνα κ.τ.λ. There is a considerable resemblance between the passage before us and de An. 1. 2. 403 b 20 sqq. With regard to τὸ ὀρθῶς ἔχον and τὸ χρήσιμον as the two ends of inquiry in the Politics, cp. 1. 3. 1253 b 15 sq. and 6 (4). 1. 1288 b 35 sq.

33. τὸ ζητεῖν τι παρ' αὐτὰς ἕτερον very probably refers to Isocr. de Antidosi § 83, οὐδὲν γὰρ αὐτοὺς δεῖ ζητεῖν ἑτέρους [νόμους], ἀλλὰ τοὺς παρὰ τοῖς ἄλλοις εὐδοκιμοῦντας πειραθῆναι συναγαγεῖν, ὃ ῥᾳδίως ὅστις ἂν οὖν βουληθεὶς ποιήσειε. It is precisely this view that the Second Book is intended to disprove. See the opinion of Isocrates on this subject, de Antid. §§ 79–83. Πάντως probably goes with σοφίζεσθαι βουλομένων in the sense of 'at all hazards.'

35. τὰς νῦν ὑπαρχούσας. Vict. 'significat, ut arbitror, utrumque genus rerumpublicarum (id est, et usurpatas ab aliquibus civitatibus et literarum monimentis proditas), etsi id nomen magis convenire videtur receptis iam, verius enim hae ὑπάρχειν dicuntur.'

διὰ τοῦτο. Bonitz (Ind. 546 a 47) compares for this use of τοῦτο, in which 'per ubertatem quandam dicendi quae antea exponuntur postea epanaleptice comprehenduntur,' Categ. 5. 2 b 17: de An. 3. 3. 427 b 8–11. Cp. also c. 11. 1273 b 5.

36. ἀρχὴν δὲ κ.τ.λ. The natural starting-point of an inquiry περὶ τῆς κοινωνίας τῆς πολιτικῆς (1260 b 27) is the question, in what and how much is there to be κοινωνία? The question put by Protagoras (Plato, Protag. 324 E) reminds us in form of that raised here, but Protagoras is there thinking of virtue as the thing shared.

40. πολιτεία. Cp. 3. 4. 1276 b 29, κοινωνία δ' ἐστὶν ἡ πολιτεία, where the meaning of πολιτεία is evidently 'constitution'; thus Bonitz (Ind. 612 b 15) is apparently right in rendering the word here as 'civitatis forma et ordo'; otherwise we might be tempted by τοὺς πολίτας 38 and οἱ πολῖται 1261 a 1 to explain it here, as in some other passages (see Bon. Ind. 612 b 10 sqq.), as = 'the citizen-body,' especially as in 3. 3. 1276 b 2 the πολιτεία is spoken of rather as the thing shared, than the κοινωνία—a term more usually applied to the πόλις.

41. Citizenship implies membership of the same city, and membership of the same city implies residence in the same locality. Still residence in the same locality does not amount to much: cp. Eth. Nic. 9. 9. 1170 b 11, *τοῦτο δὲ γίνοιτ' ἂν ἐν τῷ συζῆν καὶ κοινωνεῖν λόγων καὶ διανοίας· οὕτω γὰρ ἂν δόξειε τὸ συζῆν ἐπὶ τῶν ἀνθρώπων λέγεσθαι, καὶ οὐχ ὥσπερ ἐπὶ τῶν βοσκημάτων τὸ ἐν τῷ αὐτῷ νέμεσθαι.*

2. πότερον κ.τ.λ. The question is raised in very similar language to the question about Kingship, 3. 14. 1284 b 37. This is worth remarking, as these correspondences show a certain continuity of treatment. **1261 a.**

ὅσων. What are the objects which it is implied cannot be shared? This appears from Plato, Rep. 464 D, *διὰ τὸ μηδένα ἴδιον ἐκτῆσθαι πλὴν τὸ σῶμα, τὰ δ' ἄλλα κοινά.* In the Laws (739 C) Plato insists with humorous exaggeration, that even hands ears and eyes are to be common.

9 sqq. 'Community in women involves both many other difficulties, and this especially, that the object for the sake of which Socrates recommends its establishment by legislation evidently is not borne out (proved to be a desirable object) by the arguments he uses, and then again as a means to the end which he marks out for the State, the scheme set forth in the dialogue is impracticable; yet how it should be limited and qualified, is nowhere definitely explained.' Socrates fails to make out that the aim with which he pleads for a community in women—that of rendering the State as far as possible one—is a correct aim; and the means which he adopts for the realization of his end are—apart from qualifications and limitations of which we hear nothing from him—impossible. The first of these two allegations is developed in c. 2 and the second in c. 3. The Platonic Socrates anticipates a reception of this kind for his suggestion of community in women and children; cp. Rep. 450 C, *καὶ γὰρ ὡς δυνατὰ λέγεται, ἀπιστοῖτ' ἄν, καὶ εἰ ὅτι μάλιστα γένοιτο, ὡς ἄριστ' ἂν εἴη ταῦτα, καὶ ταύτῃ ἀπιστήσεται.* Aristotle's criticisms on the Lacedaemonian and other constitutions are grouped under two heads (c. 9. 1269 a 30) in a not very dissimilar way. As to *ἀδύνατον*, cp. c. 3. 1261 b 30, *διὸ ἐστὶ τὸ πάντας τὸ αὐτὸ λέγειν ὡδὶ μὲν καλόν, ἀλλ' οὐ δυνατόν, ὡδὶ δ' οὐδὲν ὁμονοητικόν*, and 1262 a 14 sqq. As to *δι' ἣν αἰτίαν*, cp. c. 4. 1262 b 5 sq. For *οὐ φαίνεται συμβαῖνον* in the sense of 'evidently does not result,' cp. 2. 6. 1266 a 5, *οὐδ' ἔχουσα φαίνεται*, and see Bon. Ind. 808 b 40 sqq. For *συμβαῖνον ἐκ τῶν λόγων*, cp. Top. 8. 1. 156 b 38 (Bon. Ind. 713 b 16), and de Caelo 1. 3. 270 b 11. It seems **C. 2.**

better to interpret these words as 'borne out by the arguments used' than with Thurot (Études sur Aristote, p. 19) to explain, 'la communauté n'atteint pas le résultat, en vue duquel Platon établit cette legislation.' The sentence ὡς μὲν εἴρηται νῦν appears to be the nom. to ἐστί, which we must supply with ἀδύνατον: cp. c. 5. 1263 a 22, ὃν δὲ νῦν τρόπον ἔχει . . . οὐ μικρὸν ἂν διενέγκαι. As to πρός, cp. 2. 4. 1262 b 3: 3. 13. 1284 a 1: 4 (7). 17. 1336 b 31 sq.: 5 (8). 3. 1338 a 42. For διελεῖν ('explicare,' Bon. Ind. 180 a 23, 29), cp. Eth. Nic. 6. 1. 1138 b 20 sqq., and 9. 8. 1168 b 12, ἴσως οὖν τοὺς τοιούτους δεῖ τῶν λόγων διαιρεῖν καὶ διορίζειν, ἐφ' ὅσον ἑκάτεροι καὶ πῇ ἀληθεύουσιν: also Metaph. A. 9. 992 b 18 sq.

15. **ὅτι μάλιστα** qualifies μίαν (cp. 1261 b 16, and τελέως, 1261 b 20).

16. **ταύτην ὑπόθεσιν**, 'this as his fundamental aim.' For this use of οὗτος, see Bon. Ind. 546 a 51 sqq. For the gender—ταύτην, not τοῦτο—cp. 5 (8). 3. 1337 b 32: 4 (7). 7. 1327 b 41.

καίτοι κ.τ.λ. For the argument, compare 7 (5). 9. 1309 b 21 sqq.

18. **πλῆθος . . . τι.** Cp. 3. 1. 1274 b 41: 1275 b 20: 4 (7). 8. 1328 b 16—passages which explain the addition of τι. Plato had said in Rep. 462 C, καὶ ἥτις δὴ ἐγγύτατα ἑνὸς ἀνθρώπου ἔχει (αὕτη ἡ πόλις ἄριστα διοικεῖται), but his meaning is that the hurt of one member of the community is to be felt as a hurt by all, just as the hurt of a finger is felt as a hurt by the whole man. He knows well that the State consists both ἐκ πλειόνων ἀνθρώπων and ἐξ εἴδει διαφερόντων (Polit. 308 C). Nevertheless there was a real difference of opinion between Aristotle and Plato on this subject. The State is less of a σύμφυσις (2. 4. 1262 b 14 sqq.) to Aristotle than to Plato; the individual counts for more with him, and is less lost and swallowed up in the State.

22. **ἀναιρήσει γὰρ τὴν πόλιν.** Cp. 1261 b 8 sq. For the future, cp. 2. 5. 1264 a 5, μάλιστα δ' ἂν γένοιτο φανερόν, εἴ τις τοῖς ἔργοις ἴδοι τὴν τοιαύτην πολιτείαν κατασκευαζομένην· οὐ γὰρ δυνήσεται κ.τ.λ.

23. **ἐξ εἴδει διαφερόντων.** Cp. 3. 4. 1277 a 5 sq., and the enumeration of the different γένη of the πόλις in 4 (7). 8. 1328 b 20 sq. and 6 (4). 4. Especially the broad distinction of rulers and ruled is referred to (cp. 4 (7). 14. 1332 b 12); but even among rulers there will be differences (1261 b 5). When we are told in 6 (4). 11. 1295 b 25 that ἡ πόλις βούλεται ἐξ ἴσων εἶναι καὶ ὁμοίων ὅτι μάλιστα, the word πόλις appears to include only the citizens, as in the phrase ἡ πόλις πολιτῶν τι πλῆθός ἐστιν, 3. 1. 1274 b 41. But even like and equal citizens can only be 'as far as possible' like and equal, for some of them will be rulers and others ruled.

25. μέν is answered by δέ 29. For the thought expressed in 24–27, cp. Xen. de Vectig. c. 4. 32, ὥσπερ σύμμαχοι, ὅσῳ ἂν πλείους συνιῶσιν, ἰσχυροτέρους ἀλλήλους ποιοῦσιν.

27. ὥσπερ ἂν εἰ κ.τ.λ. It is not quite clear whether the meaning is 'just as a greater weight of anything is more useful than a less,' or 'just as a greater weight depresses the scale more.' Giph. takes the words in the former way, Vict. in the latter. Ὥσπερ ἂν εἰ does not always imply an ellipse after ὥσπερ ἄν (see Bon. Ind. 872 b 55 sqq. and Eucken, de Partic. Usu, p. 60), but it may perhaps do so here, and we may be right in translating (with Giph.)—'just as would be the case, if a weight were to depress the scale more.'

† ἑλκύσῃ †. See critical note on this word, and also above on 1260 b 31.

διοίσει δὲ κ.τ.λ. The first of the many questions which arise as to this passage is, what is the meaning of τῷ τοιούτῳ? Here as elsewhere it seems to mean 'in the before-mentioned respect,' but it is not quite clear whether it should be explained as = τῷ ἐξ εἴδει διαφερόντων εἶναι, or 'in being all the stronger for being larger, even though its components are identical.' Probably the latter explanation is the correct one. Κεχωρισμένοι κατὰ κώμας, again, may mean either 'scattered (sundered from each other) in villages' (cp. 1. 9. 1257 a 22, οἱ δὲ κεχωρισμένοι πολλῶν πάλιν καὶ ἑτέρων, and Hdt. 1. 96), or 'distributed in villages' (cp. 2. 5. 1264 a 6, οὐ γὰρ δυνήσεται μὴ μερίζων αὐτὰ καὶ χωρίζων ποιῆσαι τὴν πόλιν, and Eth. Nic. 4. 3. 1121 b 19). The two interpretations do not lie far apart, but perhaps the former of them is the more likely to be correct (see Liddell and Scott s. v. κώμη). Passing on to discuss the meaning of the passage as a whole, we find that ὅταν μὴ—Ἀρκάδες has been taken by some to be explanatory of πόλις, and has been rendered 'when the members of the πόλις are not scattered in villages, but are concentrated in a city, like the Arcadians (after the foundation of Megalopolis),' but it seems strange that 'the Arcadians' should be selected to serve as an example of a πόλις. It is far more likely that ὅταν μὴ—Ἀρκάδες refers to the members of the ἔθνος, and is intended to explain under what circumstances the difference alleged to exist between the πόλις and the ἔθνος does really exist. But then comes the question, what is the meaning of οἷον Ἀρκάδες? Sepulveda explains, 'gens quae non per castella et vicos distributa est, ut divisos habeat magistratus, sed sparsas per agros domos habitat, ut olim Arcades,' and Lamb., Ramus, and others follow in his track, but Aristotle does not indicate in any way that he is not referring to the Arcadians of his own day, who had long ceased to live in this fashion. Dittenberger, on the other hand, whose able discussion of the passage in *Gött. gel. Anz.* 1874, p. 1376 sqq. (see an extract from it in Sus.[2], Note 132) deserves careful perusal, explains the passage thus (p. 1383)—'provided, that is to say, that the nation is not distributed, like most barbarian nations, into non-independent (unselbständige) villages, but, like the Arcadian for instance, into a number of independent (selbständiger) City-States.' He holds that a distinction is drawn in the passage between 'nations forming a political unity (commonly with a monarchical constitution)' and nations composed of a number of City-States. This is a possible view of it, but it must not be forgotten that in Aristotle's day the Arcadians were a confederacy of City-States, and that a general assembly of the nation met at Megalopolis: cp. Aristot. Fragm. 442. 1550 b 6 (Harpocr. p. 280), μύριοι ἐν Μεγάλῃ πόλει . . . συνέδριόν ἐστι κοινὸν Ἀρκάδων ἁπάντων, οὗ πολλάκις μνημονεύουσιν οἱ ἱστορικοί· διείλεκται δὲ περὶ αὐτῶν καὶ Ἀριστοτέλης ἐν τῇ κοινῇ Ἀρκάδων πολιτείᾳ ἀρχόμενος τοῦ βιβλίου, and see Müller, Fr. Hist. Gr. 2. 134, who refers to Diod. 15. 59, περὶ δὲ τοὺς αὐτοὺς χρόνους Λυκομήδης ὁ Τεγεάτης ἔπεισε τοὺς Ἀρκάδας εἰς μίαν συντέλειαν ταχθῆναι καὶ κοινὴν ἔχειν σύνοδον συνεστῶσαν ἐξ ἀνδρῶν μυρίων, καὶ τούτους ἐξουσίαν ἔχειν περὶ πολέμου καὶ εἰρήνης βουλεύεσθαι, as well as to Paus. 8. 27 and some other passages. Cp. also Hyperid. adv. Demosth. col. 16. 14 (p. 10 Blass), τοὺς κοινοὺς συλλόγους Ἀχαιῶν τε καὶ Ἀρκάδων. It is to this confederation that Müller (*ubi supra*) takes Aristotle here to allude, and the writer of some valuable remarks on the passage in the *Guardian* newspaper for Jan. 27, 1886, explains it in the same way. Is it not likely that Aristotle's meaning is—'a nation also differs from a City-State in being all the stronger for being larger, even though its components are identical, whenever at least the nation is not scattered in villages, as some nations are, but united in a confederacy, like the Arcadian'? It will then be implied that the addition of fresh villages to an uncompacted mass of villages brings no accession of strength, whereas the addition of fresh City-States to a confederacy like the Arcadian does so. An ἔθνος 'sundered in villages' seems, indeed, to have been little better than a rope of sand: cp. Diod. 5. 6, οἱ δ' οὖν Σικανοὶ τὸ παλαιὸν κωμηδὸν ᾤκουν, ἐπὶ τῶν ὀχυρωτάτων λόφων τὰς πόλεις κατασκευάζοντες διὰ τοὺς λῃστάς· οὐ γὰρ ἦσαν ὑπὸ μίαν ἡγεμονίαν βασιλέως τεταγμένοι, κατὰ πόλιν δὲ ἑκάστην εἷς ἦν ὁ δυναστεύων: Hdt. 1. 96: Dion. Hal., Ant. Rom. 1. 9. Pollux, it may be noted, speaks as if the ἔθνος were always composed of πόλεις —καὶ αἱ μὲν πολλαὶ πόλεις εἰς ἓν συντελοῦσαι ἔθνος, αἱ δὲ πολλαὶ κῶμαι εἰς ἓν συμφέρουσαι ὄνομα πόλις (9. 27, quoted by C. F. Hermann, Gr.

Antiqq. 1. § 11. 10)—but this evidently was not the case. As to the position of καί before πόλις, Dittenberger remarks that though it is surprising, it is not more surprising than much else in Aristotle's collocation of words. See note on 1254 b 16. Certainly καὶ ἔθνους πόλις would be more natural, but perhaps the idea uppermost in Aristotle's mind is, that there is another pair of things between which a similar contrast exists, and he places καί before both these two things. Compare the displacement of the negative noticed in Bon. Ind. 539 a 14 sqq.

29. ἕν. The State is a κοινωνία ἐξ ἧς ἕν τι τὸ γένος, 4 (7). 8. 1328 a 25: cp. 1. 5. 1254 a 28 sqq. For the various kinds of unity, see Metaph. Δ. 6. 1016 b 31 sqq. Aristotle inherits the thought expressed in this passage to some extent from earlier inquirers—from the Pythagoreans, from Heraclitus (Eth. Nic. 8. 2. 1155 b 4 sq.), and from Plato (Polit. 308 C: Laws 773 C sqq.). Of course he also holds the complementary truth that there should be an unity of ethical conviction as to τὰ ποιητικὰ εὐδαιμονίας in the minds of the citizens (4 (7). 8. 1328 a 37 sqq.).

30. διόπερ κ.τ.λ. For other passages in the Politics in which τὰ ἠθικά are referred to, see Bon. Ind. 101 b 19 sqq. It is the reciprocal rendering of an equivalent amount of dissimilar things, not the receipt of an equal amount of the same thing, that holds the State together (σώζει τὰς πόλεις, cp. 1261 b 9 and 3. 12. 1282 b 16 sq.). Cp. Eth. Nic. 5. 8. 1132 b 33, τῷ ἀντιποιεῖν γὰρ ἀνάλογον συμμένει ἡ πόλις: 9. 1. 1163 b 32 sqq.: Eth. Eud. 7. 10. 1243 b 29 sqq. and 1242 b 22 sqq. (In the first of these passages Aristotle includes under ἀνταπόδοσις a return of ill for ill, as well as of good for good, and thus takes a wider view of it than he does in the passage before us: ἀνταπόδοσις is made to include the return of ill for ill, and further (1133 a 4 sq.) the return not only of service for service, but of favour for favour.) The fact that the State rests on τὸ ἴσον τὸ ἀντιπεπονθός, and not on the other kind of equality, serves to show that it is composed of unlikes, for if all the members of the State were likes (e. g. shoemakers), there would be no question of equivalence; an absolutely equal share of the one product would be assignable. As it is, the ruler renders to the ruled the offices of a good ruler, and the ruled repay him with the offices of good subjects. It is thus that the State holds together, and that friendship is maintained between its members (Eth. Nic. 8. 8. 1158 b 11 sqq.). This is true even of free and equal citizens, among whom one would least expect any difference in kind to exist, for though here there is no intrinsic difference, yet the impossibility of all ruling at the same time leads to an 'imitation' of, or approximation to, such difference, and breaks them into rulers and ruled, two classes different in kind, even though they interchange their positions from time to time. Hence here too *τὸ ἴσον τὸ ἀντιπεπονθός* is in place.

33. κατ' ἐνιαυτόν, 'year by year,' cp. 7 (5). 8. 1308 a 40, *ἐν ὅσαις μὲν πόλεσι τιμῶνται κατ' ἐνιαυτόν, ἐν δὲ ταῖς μείζοσι διὰ τριετηρίδος ἢ πενταετηρίδος*. Mr. Welldon: 'they must follow a system of yearly rotation.' Vict. 'hoc igitur pacto solum id administrari potest, si interposito spatio anni unius id fiet.'

ἢ κατά τινα ἄλλην τάξιν ἢ χρόνον, 'or by some other order of succession' (Bern. 'Abfolge') 'or official period.'

34. καὶ . . . δή, see note on 1. 2. 1253 a 18. For *συμβαίνειν ὥστε* Bonitz compares Pol. 6 (4). 5. 1292 b 12. Cp. also de Sensu 2. 437 b 8.

35. ὥσπερ ἂν εἰ κ.τ.λ., 'as all would be shoemakers and carpenters, if' etc. So Giph. p. 154.

37 sqq. **οὕτως**. Sepulv. 'ut nunc sese res habet in sutoribus et fabris, ut iidem semper sint sutores, iidem fabri.' Since it is better that the same men should always rule (cp. for the thought Isocr. Busiris § 16: Nicocl. §§ 17–18: Aristot. Pol. 4 (7). 14. 1332 b 16 sqq. and 6 (4). 2. 1289 a 39 sq.: Eth. Eud. 7. 10. 1242 b 27 sq.: and contrast Pol. 6 (4). 11. 1295 b 25), and that there should be a permanent difference between rulers and ruled, men seek, where this is out of the question, to get as near to this state of things as possible (*μιμεῖται*), and by alternation of office to create two different classes, rulers and ruled, thus conjuring up a difference where it can hardly be said to exist. For *ἐν οἷς δὲ . . . τοῦτο δέ*, see Bonitz (Ind. 166 b 58–167 a 12), who points out that in this passage there is not (as in 6 (4). 12. 1296 b 32: 4 (7). 9. 1329 a 11) any preceding sentence introduced by *μέν* for the first *δέ* of the two to answer. The same thing appears in Rhet. 1. 4. 1359 a 32 sqq. and other passages adduced by Bonitz.

1261 b. **1. εἴτ' ἀγαθὸν εἴτε φαῦλον τὸ ἄρχειν.** Camerarius (p. 76) refers to Plato, Rep. 345 E sqq.: 346 E sqq. Cp. also Pol. 3. 6. 1279 a 8 sqq.

2. † τοῦτο δὲ μιμεῖται τὸ ἐν μέρει τοὺς ἴσους εἴκειν τὸ δ' ὡς ὁμοίους εἶναι ἐξ ἀρχῆς †. I place in the text the reading of the first family of MSS., for though it is obviously untenable as it stands, it probably approaches the true reading far more closely than that of the second. See Susemihl's able note on this passage in Qu. Crit. p. 360. He reads *ἀνομοίους* for *δ' ὡς ὁμοίους*, and this conjecture may be correct, but it is of course only a conjecture. *Ἐν τούτοις δὲ* (Π^2)

might perhaps with advantage take the place of τοῦτο δὲ (Π[1]), but μιμεῖται (Π[1]) appears to suit better with οἱ μὲν γὰρ ἄρχονται κ.τ.λ. than μιμεῖσθαι (Π[2]), with which βέλτιον must be supplied, for, as Thurot says (Études, p. 24), 'Aristote constate un fait, mais ne donne pas un précepte.' A. Schott, in Heinsius' Paraphrase of the Politics (p. 1044) conjectures τῷ in place of τὸ 3, and Sus. adopts this conjecture, which certainly simplifies the passage if τοῦτο δὲ is read or if the reading of the second family is adopted, but if we read ἐν τούτοις δὲ μιμεῖται τὸ ἐν μέρει τοὺς ἴσους εἴκειν τὸ ἀνομοίους εἶναι ἐξ ἀρχῆς, τὸ—εἴκειν will be the nom. to μιμεῖται, and the translation will be, 'in the case of these the alternation of ruling and being ruled imitates an original inequality.' So Thurot (Études, p. 23), 'là où les membres de l'État sont naturellement égaux, l'inégalité naturelle est imitée par l'alternative dans l'exercice du pouvoir et dans l'obéissance. Les citoyens commandent et obéissent tour à tour, comme s'ils devenaient d'autres hommes, c'est-à-dire comme s'ils étaient inégaux.' Cp. 1. 12. 1259 b 7, ὅταν τὸ μὲν ἄρχῃ τὸ δ' ἄρχηται, ζητεῖ διαφορὰν εἶναι κ.τ.λ. For μιμεῖται in the sense in which it is used here, cp. Isocr. Archid. § 81, ἢν οὖν εἰλικρινὲς τοῦτο ποιήσωμεν, ὃ μιμησαμένοις ἡμῖν συνήνεγκεν, οὐκ ἄδηλον ὅτι ῥᾳδίως τῶν πολεμίων ἐπικρατήσομεν, and Plato, Polit. 293 E, 301 A. Εἴκειν appears to occur extremely rarely in Aristotle: Bonitz (Ind. 219 b 18) gives no other instance of the pres. infinitive.

5. **καὶ τὸν αὐτὸν δὴ τρόπον κ.τ.λ.** 'And in the same way, again, even when they rule, one man holds one office and another another [just as if there were a difference between them].' So inseparable is differentiation from the State, that when its members are alike and equal, differences are conjured up not only between rulers and ruled, but even among rulers. It is thus that I incline to understand the passage; I add, however, Mr. Welldon's translation of it—'the same principle [of alternation] during the period of their rule regulates the distribution of the different offices among different persons.'

7. On **οὔτε**, see critical note. As to **πέφυκε**, see Vahlen's note on Poet. 6. 1450 a 2.

οὕτως. Cp. c. 5. 1263 b 31, δεῖ μὲν γὰρ εἶναί πως μίαν καὶ τὴν οἰκίαν καὶ τὴν πόλιν, ἀλλ' οὐ πάντως κ.τ.λ.: 1261 a 15, b 16, ὅτι μάλιστα: 1261 b 20, τελέως: 1261 b 10, λίαν.

8. **τὸ λεχθὲν ὡς μέγιστον ἀγαθόν.** Cp. Rep. 462 A. For the pleonastic use of ὅτι, cp. Phys. 8. 7. 260 a 25 and the passages collected in Bon. Ind. 538 b 33 sqq. We have ἐν ταῖς πόλεσιν here, but ἐν is absent in the similar passage, c. 4. 1262 b 8.

10. καὶ κατ' ἄλλον τρόπον, i. e. by asking, not how the State is composed, but what is most desirable.

12. καὶ βούλεταί γ' ἤδη κ.τ.λ. Cp. 4 (7). 4. 1326 b 7 sqq.

C. 3. **16. Ἀλλὰ μὴν κ.τ.λ.** Here Aristotle seems to pass to his second point (1261 a 12 sq.), that saying mine and not-mine of the same thing is not a means to the unity of the State. The unity of the State is not 'indicated' (*ἀποδείκνυσθαι*, cp. *σημεῖον εἶναι*, 19) by men's saying mine and not-mine of the same thing.

18. κατὰ τὸν λόγον, 'in connexion with' (or 'in') 'the expression,' i. e. *τὸ λέγειν πάντας ἅμα τὸ ἐμὸν καὶ τὸ μὴ ἐμόν*.

28. τὸ γὰρ πάντες κ.τ.λ. For the ambiguity of *περιττὰ καὶ ἄρτια*, cp. c. 5. 1264 b 20 sqq.: de Soph. El. 4. 166 a 33 sqq. As to *πάντες*, cp. 7 (5). 8. 1307 b 35 sqq.: 4 (7). 13. 1332 a 36 sq.

29. καὶ ἐν τοῖς λόγοις takes up and justifies *παραλογισμός*: not only do ambiguous terms such as these cause contention in practical life, but in discussions also they generate contentious syllogisms. Cp. Top. 8. 11. 162 a 16, *σόφισμα δὲ συλλογισμὸς ἐριστικός*: 12. 162 b 3, *ψευδὴς δὲ λόγος καλεῖται τετραχῶς, ἕνα μὲν τρόπον ὅταν φαίνηται συμπεραίνεσθαι μὴ συμπεραινόμενος, ὃς καλεῖται ἐριστικὸς συλλογισμός*. Cp. also Metaph. *α*. 3. 995 a 10, *ἔχει γάρ τι τὸ ἀκριβὲς τοιοῦτον, ὥστε, καθάπερ ἐπὶ τῶν συμβολαίων, καὶ ἐπὶ τῶν λόγων ἀνελεύθερον εἶναί τισι δοκεῖ*: Isocr. adv. Soph. § 7, *τὰς ἐναντιώσεις ἐπὶ μὲν τῶν λόγων τηροῦντας, ἐπὶ δὲ τῶν ἔργων μὴ καθορῶντας* (also § 14): Plato, Polit. 306 A, *τοῖς περὶ λόγους ἀμφισβητητικοῖς*. Thurot (Études, p. 24) refers to Waitz, Top. 8. 3. 159 a 1 and An. Post. 1. 1. 71 a 5. Perhaps Pol. 4 (7). 7. 1328 a 19, *οὐ γὰρ τὴν αὐτὴν ἀκρίβειαν δεῖ ζητεῖν διά τε τῶν λόγων καὶ τῶν γιγνομένων διὰ τῆς αἰσθήσεως* should also be mentioned.

31. οὐ δυνατόν. 'Iurisconsulti negant fieri posse ut eiusdem rei duo in solidum sint domini; hoc tantum permittunt, ut rei communis dominum quisque se vocare possit, sed pro parte indivisa, non in solidum' (Giph.). Cp. *ἀδύνατον*, 1261 a 14.

32. τὸ λεγόμενον, i. e. (probably) *τὸ πάντας τὸ αὐτὸ λέγειν ἐμὸν καὶ μὴ ἐμόν*.

34. φροντίζουσιν, 'men care for': cp. 6 (4). 11. 1295 b 24, *βούλονται*: 8 (6). 8. 1321 b 25, *καθιστᾶσιν*. Plato had claimed (Rep. 463 C–D), that his plan of an extended application of the names of brother, sister, father, mother, son, and daughter would not impair the fulfilment of the duties implied by such relationship. With this Aristotle does not agree.

35. ἢ ὅσον ἑκάστῳ ἐπιβάλλει. Vict. 'aut quantum suas partes postulare putant.' Men care for matters of common interest less, or at any rate only to the extent to which they are personally concerned in them.

πρὸς γὰρ τοῖς ἄλλοις is added to explain this limitation of attention. Even where there is no other cause for inattention, men may well think that some one else is looking after the matter. Camerarius (p. 78) compares Xen. Cyrop. 5. 3. 49 sq.

38. The argument is—each of the citizens has a thousand sons, and these not exclusively his, for every son is as much the son of one citizen as he is of another; hence all the fathers will alike neglect the sons. The indefiniteness of the relation between father and child and the neglect to which this will lead is here insisted on, as in the next paragraph the fractional character of this relationship and the consequent diminution of *οἰκειότης*. Cp. Rep. 463 C, *παντὶ γάρ, ᾧ ἂν ἐντυγχάνῃ τις, ἢ ὡς ἀδελφῷ ἢ ὡς ἀδελφῇ ἢ ὡς πατρὶ ἢ ὡς μητρὶ ἢ υἱεῖ ἢ θυγατρὶ ἢ τούτων ἐκγόνοις ἢ προγόνοις νομιεῖ ἐντυγχάνειν.*

γίνονται, 'every citizen comes to have.' Cp. *γίνεται*, c. 5. 1264 a 14: 8 (6). 1. 1317 a 24: 7 (5). 4. 1304 b 5.

πολιτῶν must be taken here in a sense exclusive of the third class of the Republic, though this class also is included by Plato within the citizen-body.

1. ἔτι κ.τ.λ. Here Aristotle seems to pass from the point of 1262 a.
neglect and defect of attention to that of defective *οἰκειότης*. Plato had claimed (Rep. 462 B sqq.) that all the citizens of his State would feel as one man, and would sympathize as keenly with any one of their number who might happen to meet with good or ill fortune, as the physical frame responds to pain or pleasure affecting a limb. Aristotle contends, on the contrary, that they will be connected with any given member of their body only by a fractional relationship varying with the size of the State, and will feel only a fractional joy or sorrow at his prosperity or adversity, nor will they feel even that without doubt and uncertainty, for they will not know whether they ever had a child, much less whether it has survived.

2. οὕτως, i. e. 'fractionally,' or in other words, with the feeling that he has a thousandth share in him, not the whole; *οὕτως* is explained by *ὁπόστος τυγχάνει τὸν ἀριθμόν*, as *οὕτω* 6 is explained by *τὸ αὐτὸ μὲν προσαγορεύοντας*: cp. Metaph. B. 4. 999 b 33, *τὸ γὰρ ἀριθμῷ ἓν ἢ τὸ καθ' ἕκαστον λέγειν διαφέρει οὐδέν· οὕτω γὰρ λέγομεν τὸ καθ' ἕκαστον τὸ ἀριθμῷ ἕν*, where *τὸ ἀριθμῷ ἓν* explains *οὕτω* (see Bonitz' note on the passage).

3. οἷον ἐμὸς ἢ τοῦ δεῖνος κ.τ.λ., 'i. e. he will say he is my son, or so and so's, naming in this way each of the thousand fathers or more who are comprised in the State.' For the case of ἐμός, Göttl. compares Soph. Antig. 567, ἀλλ' ἥδε μέντοι μὴ λέγε. Cp. also Metaph. Θ. 8. 1049 b 5. The Latin idiom is the same: cp. Cic. de Legibus 1. 21. 54: ergo adsentiris Antiocho familiari meo—magistro enim non audeo dicere.

4. **καθ' ἕκαστον τῶν χιλίων.** Κατά is not 'of' here, for then we should have καθ' ἑκάστου (cp. 7 (5). 7. 1307 b 2, εἴρηται κατὰ πασῶν τῶν πολιτειῶν): we must take καθ' ἕκαστον as one word (= singulos): cp. Eth. Nic. 1. 4. 1097 a 13, καθ' ἕκαστον γὰρ ἰατρεύει, and see Bon. Ind. 226 a 25 sqq. See also Ast, Lexicon Platon. 2. p. 145.

6. **καίτοι πότερον κ.τ.λ.** Δισχιλίων καὶ ('vi non multum ab ἤ distans,' Bon. Ind. 357 b 20) μυρίων is probably gen. after ἕκαστον, which is the subject of λέγειν. Plato had hoped that when the whole of the citizens spoke of the same person or thing as 'mine,' the State would be pervaded with a feeling of friendliness and brotherhood. Μέν has nothing to answer to it, but instances of this are by no means rare: see for example 3. 13. 1284 b 13. On μέν *solitarium* see Holden, Oeconomicus of Xenophon, Index p. 80*. In the passage before us the reason why μέν has nothing to answer to it probably is that Aristotle in his eagerness hurries on to ἢ μᾶλλον κ.τ.λ. without pausing to add 'but though using the same name, not feeling any clear sentiment of relationship.'

9. The words **αὑτοῦ . . . αὑτοῦ** are emphatic: cp. ἴδιον ἀνεψιόν, 13, and Plutarch de Esu Carnium 2. 5. 998 D, υἱὸν αὑτοῦ τὸν κείμενον ἢ ἀδελφὸν αὑτοῦ. Though A, B, C, and D call the same man severally by a different name, they nevertheless have that keen sense of something ἴδιον in connexion with him which, in Aristotle's view, the change proposed by Plato would take away or seriously diminish.

11. **οἰκειότητα,** here included under συγγένεια, while in the Rhetoric (2. 4. 1381 b 33 sq.) οἰκειότης and συγγένεια figure as two distinct forms of φιλία.

12. **ἢ τῶν αὑτοῦ.** Giph. 'ut si frater uxorem ducat.'

πρὸς δὲ τούτοις ἕτερον. All the MSS. read ἕτερον, but Bern. conjectures ἕτεροι, and Thurot (followed by Sus.) ἕτερος (Études sur Aristote, p. 26). '"Ετερος,' says Thurot, 'est opposé à πρὸς τούτοις, aux parents considérés comme faisant une seule classe: cf. 3. 14. 1285 a 29.' We then have ὁ μὲν—ὁ δὲ—ὁ δὲ—πρὸς δὲ τούτοις ἕτερος, and the sentence gains in neatness. And even if we take τούτοις not as masc. (with Thurot), but as neut. (cp. πρὸς δὲ τούτοις, 1261 b 32: 3. 14. 1285 b 10: 6 (4). 11. 1295 b 13, and often elsewhere), and make πρὸς τούτοις mean 'besides' or 'again,' the change of *ἕτερον* into *ἕτερος* or *ἕτεροι* is attractive. But all the MSS. are against it, and perhaps the point which Aristotle is pressing is not so much the number of persons related to one man as the number of appellatives indicating definite relationship in ordinary use under the actual system. *Ἕτερον*, if we retain it, will be added, because the person hitherto spoken of would not be called *φράτωρ* or *φυλέτης* by his relatives. It is not quite clear whether *πρὸς τούτοις* should be translated 'in addition to these appellatives,' or simply 'again.' It is to be noticed that Aristotle in defending the family defends also not only the more distant degrees of relationship, but the phratric and tribal relations, which in modern societies do not exist. Cp. 2. 5. 1264 a 8, and the mention of phratries in 3. 9. 1280 b 37.

φράτορα φυλέτην. For the omission of *ἤ*, see critical note on 1260 a 26.

14 sqq. Women had the credit in Greece of being especially quick in noticing resemblances between parents and children (Athen. Deipn. 5. 190 e). Athenaeus makes the remark in commenting on Helen's recognition (Odyss. 4. 141 sqq.) of Telemachus' likeness to his father, and this passage of the Odyssey may well be present to Aristotle's memory here.

16. κατὰ γὰρ τὰς ὁμοιότητας. Cp. *κατὰ τὰς ὁμοιότητας*, 21. *Λαμβάνειν τὰς πίστεις* is more usually followed by *ἐκ* or *διά*, but these resemblances are referred to here rather as the standard by which conclusions as to parentage are arrived at, than as the source from which they are drawn. Compare the use of *κατά* in 4 (7). 14. 1332 b 15, *δῆλον γὰρ ὡς ἀκολουθεῖν δεήσει καὶ τὴν παιδείαν κατὰ τὴν διαίρεσιν ταύτην.*

18. καί, 'in fact.' Not only is it likely to happen, but it does happen. Cp. de Gen. An. 1. 20. 729 a 31, *ὅπερ καὶ φαίνεται συμβαῖνον.*

19. τὰς τῆς γῆς περιόδους. Aristotle dwells in Rhet. 1. 4. 1360 a 33 sq. on the utility of these works in discussions about legislation, and here we have an instance of it. Hdt. 4. 180 is probably Aristotle's authority in this passage, though the Auseans, of whom Herodotus is here speaking, are said by him to be *παραθαλάσσιοι* (c. 181: see Camerarius, p. 79). Aristotle refers to Herodotus less respectfully in de Gen. An. 3. 5. 756 b 6 (*Ἡρόδοτος ὁ μυθολόγος*), and in Hist. An. 6. 31. 579 b 2. Meltzer (Geschichte der Karthager 1. 69) holds that the Libyans were as a rule monogamists, and that the customs here and elsewhere (4. 172, 176) ascribed to Libyan races by Herodotus were exceptional among them.

21. εἰσὶ δέ τινες κ.τ.λ. Vet. Int. 'sunt autem quaedam etiam femellae etiam aliorum animalium'; thus he takes γυναῖκες here as = 'females,' as do Lambinus and many other translators and commentators after him, including Susemihl (also Liddell and Scott, s.v.). Sepulveda however translates, 'sunt autem mulieres quaedam et in aliis animantium generibus foeminae,' and Bernays, 'wirklich giebt es Frauen und auch Thierweibchen.' Γυναῖκες is not often used by Aristotle in the sense of 'females,' and I incline to follow the rendering of Sepulveda and Bernays, especially as the word seems to bear its ordinary meaning in the very similar passage from the History of Animals quoted in the next note.

23. τοῖς γονεῦσιν. Cp. Hist. An. 7. 6. 586 a 12, *εἰσὶ δὲ καὶ γυναῖκες ἐοικότα αὐταῖς γεννῶσαι, αἱ δὲ τῷ ἀνδρί, ὥσπερ ἡ ἐν Φαρσάλῳ ἵππος ἡ Δικαία καλουμένη*, and Plin. Nat. Hist. 7. 12. 51. Vict. 'ea de causa Iusta appellata fuit, quasi fideliter semper redderet quod acceperat.' Giph. 'quasi suum cuique redderet, Iusta vulgo dicta fuit.' Vict. is probably right: compare the language of Pheraulas in Xen. Cyrop. 8. 3. 38, *μάλα μικρὸν γήδιον, οὐ μέντοι πονηρόν γε, ἀλλὰ πάντων δικαιότατον· ὅ τι γὰρ λάβοι σπέρμα, καλῶς καὶ δικαίως ἀπεδίδου αὐτό τε καὶ τόκον οὐδέν τι πολύν· ἤδη δέ ποτε ὑπὸ γενναιότητος καὶ διπλάσια ἀπέδωκεν ὧν ἔλαβεν*, and Fragm. 4 of Menander's Γεωργός (Meineke, Fr. Com. Gr. 4. 97), together with Meineke's comments:

> *Ἀγρὸν εὐσεβέστερον γεωργεῖν οὐδένα*
> *οἶμαι· φέρει γὰρ ὅσα θεοῖς ἄνθη καλά,*
> *κιττόν, δάφνην· κριθὰς δ' ἐὰν σπείρω, πάνυ*
> *δίκαιος ὢν ἀπέδωχ' ὅσας ἂν καταβάλω.*

In the land of the just (Hesiod, Opera et Dies, 225–237), as Mr. Evelyn Abbott has pointed out to me,

> *Τίκτουσιν . . . γυναῖκες ἐοικότα τέκνα τοκεῦσι.*

Mr. Bywater adds a reference to Hor. Od. 4. 5. 23:

> Laudantur simili prole puerperae.

C. 4. **26. ταύτην τὴν κοινωνίαν.** Cp. 1262 b 15, *διὰ τὴν κοινωνίαν τὴν τοιαύτην*.

27. τοὺς δὲ ἑκουσίους. Cp. *ἐλεγειοποιοὺς τοὺς δὲ ἐποποιοὺς ὀνομάζουσιν*, Poet. 1. 1447 b 14, and see Vahlen on this passage (Poet. p. 91), who collects other instances. See also Shilleto on Demosth. de Falsa Legatione c. 200. Aristotle refers to involuntary homicides, and then it occurs to him to add—'and voluntary ones.' Plato hoped to prevent outrages of the kind referred to here by his regulations as to relationship (Rep. 461 D: cp. 465 A–B); he holds that younger men in his State will not do violence to seniors, because they will regard them as their fathers. But Aristotle does not think that they will be restrained by consideration for a fatherhood which he accounts unreal, and if they are not, then their violence may chance to fall on their real father or other near relative, and thus they may unwittingly sin against the divine ordinances.

28. ὅσιον. 'Herodotus often uses the epithets οὐχ ὅσιος and ἀνόσιος of violations of duty to near relatives, e.g. in 3. 19: 3. 65: 4. 154' (L. Schmidt, Ethik der alten Griechen, 1. 400). Aristotle does not neglect in the Politics considerations of τὸ ὅσιον: cp. 4 (7). 16. 1335 b 25. He writes as a Hellene animated by the religious feelings of his race and time. In his view, ignorance and absence of intention would not remove the lamentableness or even perhaps the guilt of these crimes. Nor would it excuse the absence of λύσεις. So Plato (Laws 865 A–866 B) enforces on the involuntary homicide not only purification but a temporary exile. His procedure in cases of homicide is largely copied from the Attic (Grote, Plato 3. 404–5). See as to the Attic Law on the subject Gilbert, Gr. Staatsalt. 1. 368 sq. In the Hercules Furens of Euripides, the hero, though his murder of his wife and children has been committed in the unconsciousness of raving madness, still veils his face before Theseus in order to save him the pollution inseparable from the sight of even an involuntary homicide (1050 sqq.). See also Prof. Jebb's note on Soph. O. T. 1415. It appears from the Liber Poenitentialis of Theodore, 3. 14 (Thorpe, Ancient Laws of England, 2. 5, cp. Capitula et Fragmenta Theodori, ibid. 2. 74) and from that of Egbert, 2. 1 (Thorpe 2. 183), that even justifiable or unwilling homicide was regarded by the Church as needing to be expiated by penance. So again, under the laws of King Alfred, 'even in the case of unintentional homicide, it was *prima facie* lawful and even proper to slay the slayer' (Sir J. Stephen, History of the Criminal Law in England, 3. 24). Plato, however, set little store by λύσεις (Rep. 364 E), so far as ἀδικήματα are concerned; those to which Aristotle here refers, therefore, would in his view only avail in the case of an ἀκούσιον ἁμάρτημα (Laws 860 sqq.). Indeed, if Bernays is right (Theophrastos über Frömmigkeit, p. 106), the Peripatetics thought little of expiatory sacrifice, so that Aristotle may here be speaking somewhat exoterically.

30. καί does not mean 'both' probably, but emphasizes πλεῖον.

31. τῶν μὲν γνωριζόντων, gen. after λύσεις.

32. ἄτοπον δέ. Cp. Plato, Rep. 403 A sq.

35. πατρὶ πρὸς υἱόν. Cp. Plato, Rep. 403 B, ἅπτεσθαι ὥσπερ υἱέος παιδικῶν ἐραστήν.

38. ὡς λίαν δὲ κ.τ.λ. Cp. Plato, Rep. 403 A sq.

40. τοῖς γεωργοῖς is in the dative not after *χρήσιμον*, but after *κοινάς*, unless indeed we should compare the use of the dative in c. 7. 1267 a 37, *τὸ τὰς οὐσίας εἶναι ἴσας τοῖς πολίταις.*

1262 b. **2. τοιούτους**, i. e. *ἧττον φίλους*: cp. 4 (7). 10. 1330 a 26 sqq.

3. ὅλως δὲ κ.τ.λ. Aristotle has been making a number of objections to this or that feature of the proposed law, and the last of them (*ἧττον ἔσται φιλία*, 1) leads up now to a broad impeachment of the law as a whole. 'Broadly, the law is a bad one; it brings about results the very opposite of those which a law should bring about.' Compare the transition in Metaph. M. 2. 1077 a 14. For the thought that affection is the end of *πολιτική*, cp. Eth. Eud. 7. 1. 1234 b 22.

5. καὶ δι' ἣν αἰτίαν, 'and of that on account of which.'

7. φιλίαν κ.τ.λ. For the thought, cp. Eth. Nic. 8. 1. 1155 a 22 sqq. and Xen. Mem. 4. 4. 16, *ὁμόνοια μέγιστον ἀγαθὸν δοκεῖ ταῖς πόλεσιν εἶναι.*

τε γάρ is here duly followed by *καί*.

11. ἐν τοῖς ἐρωτικοῖς λόγοις. Cp. Plato, Symp. 191 A: 192 D sq.: 'in the discourses on the subject of love' contained in the Symposion of Plato. It is not necessary to suppose that Aristotle means to designate the dialogue by this as a second title. See Sus.², Note 148.

12. For this construction with *λέγειν*, cp. 6 (4). 9. 1294 b 20: Polyb. 6. 46. 9.

13. ἀμφοτέρους ἕνα. Cp. for the contrast of *ἀμφότεροι* and *εἷς*, 3. 4. 1277 a 30, *ἀμφότερα καὶ οὐ ταὐτά*, and St. Paul, Ephes. 2. 14, *ὁ ποιήσας τὰ ἀμφότερα ἕν.*

14. ἐνταῦθα μὲν οὖν κ.τ.λ. In this case *τὸ σφόδρα φιλεῖν* is present and the persons are only two in number (contrast *μικρὸν γλυκὺ εἰς πολὺ ὕδωρ μιχθέν*): here therefore a close unity results which involves the absorption and disappearance of the two persons or one of them (cp. *μία ψυχή*, Eth. Nic. 9. 8. 1168 b 7). The case is, in fact, that of a *σύμφυσις*: cp. *συμφυῆναι* 13 (Plato, Symp. 191 A, had already used the word *συμφῦναι*), and Phys. 4. 5. 213 a 9, *σύμφυσις δέ, ὅταν ἄμφω ἐνεργείᾳ ἓν γένωνται.* But the measure which Plato is for applying to the State will not produce *τὸ σφόδρα φιλεῖν*, but only a weak and watery kind of affection, and this watery sentiment will be spread over a whole State. For both these reasons no *σύμφυσις* will result. Plato's idea was not entirely novel (cp. Hdt. 4. 104), and it survived him, not only in the *πολιτεία* of Zeno of Citium (cp. Diog. Laert. 7. 131, and Athen. Deipn. 561 c quoted by Henkel, Studien p. 27), but far later (see Plutarch's account of the proposition of Hortensius, Cato Minor, c. 25). For τὸν ἕνα in the sense of τὸν ἕτερον, cp. τῷ ἑνὶ παιᾶνι ('the one form of paean') Rhet. 3. 8. 1409 a 10.

17. **γλυκύ**, probably the γλυκὺς ἄκρατος οἶνος of Diog. Laert. 7. 184. The γλυκύ is φιλία, the ὕδωρ the κοινωνία, here the large κοινωνία of the State. A similar comparison recurs in de Gen. et Corr. 1. 10. 328 a 23 sqq., and in an illustration by Chrysippus of the nature of a κρᾶσις (Diog. Laert. 7. 151).

18. **οὕτω κ.τ.λ.** This sentence may be construed in two ways at least: either we may (with Sus. and others) place a comma after τούτων 20 and supply ἀναίσθητον εἶναι with τὴν οἰκειότητα κ.τ.λ., taking διαφροντίζειν ἥκιστα ἀναγκαῖον ὂν κ.τ.λ. as an acc. absolute, or we may with Bonitz (Ind. 192 b 61) make διαφροντίζειν govern τὴν οἰκειότητα. Συμβαίνει ἥκιστα ἀναγκαῖον ὂν will then go together (cp. οὐδὲν ἄλλο συμβήσεται νενομοθετημένον, 2. 5. 1264 a 9). If we adopt the latter interpretation, the question will arise, how the genitives in ἢ πατέρα ὡς υἱῶν, ἢ υἱὸν ὡς πατρός, ἢ ὡς ἀδελφοὺς ἀλλήλων are to be explained. On this subject see Mr. Ridgeway (*Trans. Camb. Philol. Soc.*, vol. 2. p. 132), who compares Metaph. M. 5. 1079 b 34, εἶδος ὡς γένους ('an εἶδος viewed in relation to a genus') and Pol. 7 (5). 11. 1314 b 17, ταμίαν ὡς κοινῶν (he would however read ἀδελφοὺς ὡς ἀλλήλων); but perhaps Susemihl's interpretation, which is certainly simpler, is also more likely to be correct. For the acc. absol. with the participle of εἰμί and its compounds, see Dr. Holden's note on Xen. Oecon. 20. 10, ῥᾴδιον ὂν πολλὴν ποιεῖν, and Jelf, Gr. Gr. § 700. I take ἥκιστα with ἀναγκαῖον, not with διαφροντίζειν. It is probably in order to avoid the repetition involved in ἀδελφὸν ὡς ἀδελφοῦ, that Aristotle writes ὡς ἀδελφοὺς ἀλλήλων.

23. **τὸ ἴδιον** is that which belongs to oneself, exclusively of all others: τὸ ἀγαπητόν 'carum valet ... idque significare voluit Catullus cum inquit "si quid carius est oculis," quo uno se aliquis consolatur, in quo omnem spem suorum gaudiorum collocatam habet, quo impetrato ac retento contentus vivere potest' (Vict. on Rhet. 1. 7. 1365 b 16, quoted by Mr. Cope in his note on this passage, which should be consulted).

24 sqq. Cp. Plato, Rep. 415 B sq.

27. **πολλὴν ἔχει ταραχήν**, 'perplexity': cp. c. 8. 1268 b 3. For the use of ἔχει, cp. Eth. Nic. 8. 15. 1163 a 10.

28. **γινώσκειν ἀναγκαῖον.** Susemihl asks (Sus.², Note 152) 'what harm will there be in this, so far as the displaced children of guardians are concerned?' Mr. Welldon's explanatory addition may well be correct—'and hence a child cannot be absolutely separated from the class to which he belongs.' Aristotle may also hint that persons incorporated with one class and conscious of being related to the members of another will find themselves in an equivocal position, being neither quite the one thing nor the other.

29. **πάλαι**, above in 1262 a 24 sqq.: so *τὸν πάλαι λόγον* in 3. 11. 1282 a 15 refers to 1281 a 39–b 21.

33. If with Vet. Int. M^s and pr. P^1 we read *φύλαξι τοὺς ἄλλους πολίτας* in place of *φύλαξιν εἰς τοὺς ἄλλους πολίτας*, which the sense seems to oblige us to do, we must translate *οἱ παρὰ τοῖς φύλαξι* 'those placed among the guardians' (placed among them, but not born among them).

34. **ὥστε κ.τ.λ.** is connected, not with the whole of the preceding clause, but with the word *προσαγορεύουσιν* in it.

C. 5. **38.** **κατασκευάζεσθαι**, probably passive.

πολιτεύεσθαι τὴν ἀρίστην πολιτείαν. Cp. Plato, Laws 676 C, (*πόλεις*) *πεπολιτευμέναι πάσας πολιτείας.*

40. **τοῦτο δ' ἄν τις κ.τ.λ.** *Τοῦτο* clearly refers to *πότερον κοινὴν ἢ μὴ κοινὴν εἶναι τὴν κτῆσιν*, but in explaining it (*λέγω δὲ κ.τ.λ.*) Aristotle does not, as we expect, repeat these words; he substitutes a slightly different topic of inquiry, i. e. whether both property and use ought to be common. He wisely decides to treat the question of community of property apart from that of community in women and children: experience has confirmed his view that the two questions are separable. His feeling appears to be—(1) that a decision in favour of severalty as respects women and children does not necessitate a similar decision as to property; (2) that alternatives present themselves for consideration in reference to property which had not presented themselves in reference to women and children. For instance, the ownership of property may be several and its use common, or the ownership common and the use several, or both ownership and use may be common. He thus prepares the way for his own solution, which is, if we take into account the conclusions of the Fourth Book, that while part of the land is to be *κοινή* and to be set apart for the supply of the common meals and for the service of the gods, other property is to be owned in severalty and yet made common in use.

41. **λέγω δὲ κ.τ.λ.**, 'and I mean that as to what relates to property (one may inquire) whether,' etc. Susemihl brackets *τὰ περὶ τὴν κτῆσιν* (see his remarks, Qu. Crit. p. 365), and these words may certainly be a marginal note which has crept into the text (see critical note on 1272 a 28 for an instance of this), but the expression *λέγω δέ*, which, as Sus. allows, often introduces matter of a somewhat superfluous kind (see Vahlen on Poet. 13. 1453 a 4), here perhaps applies to the whole of the succeeding sentence, and not to *τὰ περὶ τὴν κτῆσιν* exclusively.

1. ἐκεῖνα, i.e. *τὰ τέκνα καὶ αἱ γυναῖκες*. For the gender, cp. *αὐτά*, c. 5. 1264 a 7. 1263 a.

2. πᾶσι 'commode opponitur iis quae sequuntur, *ὅπερ ἔνια ποιεῖ τῶν ἐθνῶν*, et *λέγονται δέ τινες καὶ τοῦτον τὸν τρόπον κοινωνεῖν τῶν βαρβάρων*' (Busse, De praesidiis Aristotelis Politica emendandi, p. 23). Yet the Libyans referred to in 1262 a 19 sq. had women in common (for other instances, see below on 1266 a 34). Πᾶσι, however, probably goes with *ἔχει*, and not with what follows, as Sus. thinks.

3. The words *τάς τε κτήσεις . . . χρήσεις* imply that there is a doubt whether *κτῆσις* and *χρῆσις* need be treated in the same way, and *οἷον* takes up this unexpressed doubt and instances a way (not the only one, nor indeed Aristotle's own) in which *κτῆσις* may be made several and *χρῆσις* common. We might have expected that *καὶ τὰ γήπεδα καὶ τοὺς καρποὺς κοινούς*, 8, would have been the first alternative introduced by *οἷον*, but while it suits better the expressed thought of *τάς τε κτήσεις—χρήσεις*, the hint contained in these words that it is better to make a distinction between *κτῆσις* and *χρῆσις* would not have been taken up. Spengel's proposed insertion of *τὰς κτήσεις ἢ τὰς χρήσεις ἢ* (or *τὰς χρήσεις ἢ τὰς κτήσεις ἢ*) before *τάς τε κτήσεις* seems to me unnecessary.

χωρίς, sc. *εἶναι*. For the change of subject to *ἀναλίσκειν*, cp. 5, *εἶναι . . . γεωργεῖν*: 4 (7). 5. 1326 b 29, *τὸ γὰρ πάντα ὑπάρχειν καὶ δεῖσθαι μηδενὸς αὔταρκες*: and 3. 11. 1281 b 28. See Riddell, Apology of Plato, p. 210.

5. τῶν ἐθνῶν, Vict. 'intelligit autem barbaras nationes': this appears from *καὶ τοῦτον τὸν τρόπον*, 7. For *τὰ ἔθνη* in this sense, cp. 1. 2. 1252 b 19: 5 (8). 2. 1324 b 10. Diodorus (5. 34. 3) says of the Vaccaei of Spain—*οὗτοι καθ' ἕκαστον ἔτος διαιρούμενοι τὴν χώραν γεωργοῦσι, καὶ τοὺς καρποὺς κοινοποιούμενοι μεταδιδόασιν ἑκάστῳ τὸ μέρος, καὶ τοῖς νοσφισαμένοις τι γεωργοῖς θάνατον τὸ πρόστιμον τεθείκασι.* Aristotle, however, will hardly have been acquainted with the Vaccaei. He may possibly have the Itali in his mind (4 (7). 10. 1329 b 5 sqq.), and other races practising the custom of common meals (cp. 1263 b 40, *ὥσπερ τὰ περὶ τὰς κτήσεις ἐν Λακεδαίμονι καὶ Κρήτῃ τοῖς συσσιτίοις ὁ νομοθέτης ἐκοίνωσεν*). Κοινῇ ἀναλίσκειν is used in Rep. 464 C of Plato's guardians, who, we know, had common meals (Rep. 458 C). Cp. also Diod. 5. 9. 4, *τὰς οὐσίας κοινὰς ποιησάμενοι καὶ ζῶντες κατὰ συσσίτια*, and Strabo, p. 701 *sub fin.* Aristotle instances only barbarians; we find, however, an approach to the system he describes in Crete, where the men, women, and children received their maintenance from the State (ὥστ' ἐκ κοινοῦ τρέφεσθαι πάντας, 2. 10. 1272 a 20). 'Les Syssities existent de nos jours dans les communes kabyles sous le nom de *Thimecheret*' (Jannet, Les institutions sociales à Sparte, who refers to Hanoteau et Letourneux, La Kabylie 2. 82 sqq.).

ἢ τοὐναντίον κ.τ.λ. For γεωργεῖν κοινῇ, cp. Plato, Laws 739 E, νειμάσθων μὲν δὴ πρῶτον γῆν τε καὶ οἰκίας, καὶ μὴ κοινῇ γεωργούντων. In this scheme the land would be common and cultivation common —i.e. the cultivators would act under the control of some central authority, and their labour would not be confined to a particular piece of land, but applicable promiscuously to the whole cultivable area belonging to the community. This system is hardly less unlike than the preceding one to that of the Teutonic village-community (see for a description of it Sir H. Maine's work on Village Communities, p. 79 sq.). 'In some Russian communes the meadow portion of the communal land is mown by all the peasants in common, and the hay afterwards distributed by lot among the families' (Wallace, Russia 1. 208). No mention is made by Aristotle of any barbarian races which treated both land and produce as common, but the partly Greek population of the Liparaean islands appears to have done so for a time; see the remarkable passage of Diodorus (5. 9. 4 sq.) referred to in the last note.

8. ἑτέρων, 'others than the citizens,' not, I incline to think, 'others than the owners,' though the two meanings do not lie far apart. Aristotle is considering the question in the interest of οἱ μέλλοντες πολιτεύεσθαι τὴν ἀρίστην πολιτείαν (1262 b 38). For the contrast between ἑτέρων ὄντων τῶν γεωργούντων and αὐτῶν αὑτοῖς διαπονούντων, cp. c. 8. 1268 a 36 sqq. If those who till the soil are not citizens but a separate and subordinate class, like the Helots or the tillers of the soil in Aristotle's own ideal community (4 (7). 10. 1330 a 25 sqq.), disagreements would be less likely to result from the citizens holding property in common, for, as the citizens would not work themselves, individual citizens would not be in a position to compare their own hard work and small recompense with the easy work and large recompense of others, and thus one main source of disagreement among the citizens would be removed. If this observation is intended as a criticism of Plato's arrangements in the Republic, it seems to miss its mark, for the guardians cannot be said αὐτοὶ αὑτοῖς διαπονεῖν, and though the γεωργοί are made citizens by Plato, they are not intended to hold property in

common. It is true, however, that in Laws 739 E Plato uses the expression *κοινῇ γεωργεῖν* in reference to the Republic.

9. ἄλλος ἂν εἴη τρόπος καὶ ῥᾴων. Vict. 'alia erit ratio et minus molestiae in se continebit.' *Κοινωνίας* should probably be supplied with *τρόπος* (cp. 7), or else *τῶν περὶ τὰς κτήσεις* (cp. 10).

10. αὐτῶν, i. e. *τῶν πολιτῶν*—not, as it seems to me, *τῶν γεωργούντων*, though this interpretation has the high authority of Bonitz (Ind. 187 a 57) in its favour.

τὰ περὶ τὰς κτήσεις, not (as Lamb.) acc. after *διαπονούντων*, but nom. to *παρέχοι*.

11. καὶ γὰρ κ.τ.λ. Cp. Eth. Nic. 9. 6. 1167 b 9 sqq.

13. [ἢ λαμβάνοντας]. See critical note. Congreve omits *ἢ λαμβάνοντας πολλά*: Sus. brackets *ἢ λαμβάνοντας*.

15. ὅλως δέ, 'but indeed we may say broadly that,' etc. Apart from all intensifying circumstances, living together and sharing in everything is in itself enough to give rise to troubles.

καί introduces a limitation and explanation of *τὸ συζῆν*: see Bon. Ind. 357 b 13 sqq., and cp. c. 2. 1261 a 17, *προϊοῦσα καὶ γινομένη μία μᾶλλον*. The article is omitted before *κοινωνεῖν*, as it is omitted before *βοηθῆσαι* in 1263 b 5, *τὸ χαρίσασθαι καὶ βοηθῆσαι* (cp. also 7 (5). 10. 1311 a 13 sq., 15 sq.: 7 (5). 11. 1313 a 40—b 18).

τῶν ἀνθρωπικῶν πάντων. Bonitz (Ind. 57 b 43) gives a reference to Eth. Nic. 3. 5. 1112 a 28, *ἀλλ' οὐδὲ περὶ τῶν ἀνθρωπικῶν πάντων* (*βουλεύονται*).

16. τῶν τοιούτων, 'the things of which we have spoken,' i. e. property, which, it is evident from what follows, is classed by Aristotle with *ἐγκύκλια*, cp. 18, *τῶν ἐν ποσὶ . . . μικρῶν*, and 21, *ἐγκυκλίους*. So in c. 7. 1266 a 36 sq. *τὸ περὶ τὰς οὐσίας* explains *ἀπὸ τῶν ἀναγκαίων*. Aristotle appears to think that quarrels are more likely to arise over questions relating to *ἀναγκαῖα* and *τὰ καθ' ἡμέραν* than over greater matters.

17. τῶν συναποδήμων. Fellow-travellers are perhaps conceived here, as Bernays implies by his translation, to be sharers in a common purse, but this is not quite certain, for the next illustration is taken from a master and his servants, who would not have a common purse. It is enough to cause quarrels, if men *κοινωνοῦσι τῶν ἐγκυκλίων*.

18. διαφερόμενοι, not **διαφέρονται.** Sus.[1] (Ind. Gramm. s. v. Participium) compares 1. 5. 1254 b 23. Cp. also 4 (7). 14. 1333 a 18, and see note on 1259 b 11. The participle expresses a habitual fixed characteristic, and means rather more than the indicative.

ἐκ τῶν ἐν ποσὶ . . . ἀλλήλοις explains how their differences arise.

ἐκ μικρῶν. Cp. 7 (5). 4. 1303 b 18.

20. προσχρώμεθα seems here to be used in a sense ('utor in aliquam rem': see Ast, Lex. Platon. 3. p. 213) more common in Plato than in Aristotle.

τὰς διακονίας τὰς ἐγκυκλίους. Cp. c. 3. 1261 b 36, *ἐν ταῖς οἰκετικαῖς διακονίαις*, and Plato, Theaet. 175 E, *ᾧ ἀνεμέσητον εὐήθει δοκεῖν καὶ οὐδενὶ εἶναι, ὅταν εἰς δουλικὰ ἐμπέσῃ διακονήματα, οἷον στρωματόδεσμον μὴ ἐπιστάμενος συσκευάσασθαι μηδὲ ὄψον ἡδῦναι ἢ θῶπας λόγους.*

22. For **ὃν δὲ νῦν τρόπον κ.τ.λ.** as the subject of *διενέγκαι*, cp. c. 2. 1261 a 13. But why is *ἐπικοσμηθέν* neut.? Does it agree with some neut. latent in *ὃν . . . ἔχει*, perhaps *τὸ μὴ κοινὰς εἶναι τὰς κτήσεις*?

23. καί before *ἐπικοσμηθέν* (add. Π²) implies that severalty of property is not enough without *ἤθη κ.τ.λ.* The use of *καί* is somewhat similar in 6 (4). 16. 1300 b 22, *πέμπτον τὸ περὶ τῶν ἰδίων συναλλαγμάτων καὶ ἐχόντων μέγεθος.* We have in 1263 b 39 *τοῖς ἔθεσι καὶ τῇ φιλοσοφίᾳ καὶ τοῖς νόμοις*, and Π¹ read *ἔθεσι* here, but *ἤθεσι* (Π²) is in all probability the correct reading—cp. Plato, Laws 751 C, *ἔπειτα αὖ τοὺς μέλλοντας αἱρήσεσθαι τεθράφθαι τε ἐν ἤθεσι νόμων εὖ πεπαιδευμένους πρὸς τὸ κ.τ.λ.*: Rep. 557 C, *πᾶσιν ἤθεσι πεποικιλμένη πολιτεία*: Ephor. ap. Strab. p. 302, *τῶν δικαιοτάτοις ἤθεσι χρωμένων.*

24. ἕξει γὰρ κ.τ.λ. This implies that there is good in community of property. What this is, is not distinctly stated, but Aristotle probably means that it ensures every one having what he needs. See 4 (7). 10. 1330 a 2 sqq.

26. πῶς, i.e. *κατὰ τὴν χρῆσιν.*

ὅλως, 'broadly, on the whole.'

27. αἱ μὲν γὰρ κ.τ.λ. 'For when every one has a separate province, one main source of disputes will be removed, and work will prosper all the more, because each man will feel that he is applying himself to business of his own.' *Γάρ* explains and justifies the preceding sentence. *Τὰ ἐγκλήματα*, i.e. those mentioned in 12. *Αἱ ἐπιμέλειαι* appears to be nom. to *ἐπιδώσουσι* (Bon. Ind. 271 a 43). Cp. Soph. El. 33. 183 b 19 sqq., Xen. Hiero 9. 7, *ἡ γεωργία αὐτὴ ἂν πολὺ ἐπιδοίη*, and Pol. 6 (4). 15. 1299 a 38, *καὶ βέλτιον ἕκαστον ἔργον τυγχάνει τῆς ἐπιμελείας μονοπραγματούσης ἢ πολυπραγματούσης.*

29. δι' ἀρετήν is here emphatic (cp. *δι' ἀρετήν*, 5 (8). 2. 1337 b 19, where the antithesis is *δι' ἄλλους*, which is not far removed in meaning from *ἐξ ἀνάγκης*, 1263 b 10, *ἔργον γὰρ καλὸν ἀλλοτρίας οὔσης ἀπέχεσθαι διὰ σωφροσύνην*, and 22, *ὧν οὐδὲν γίνεται διὰ τὴν ἀκοινωνησίαν ἀλλὰ διὰ τὴν μοχθηρίαν*): *δέ* answers to *μέν* 27. 'And on the other hand it will be owing to virtue, that according to the proverb, "friends' goods" will be "common goods."' Virtue will be called forth for the accomplishment of this result, and this will be a gain. Pythagoras was, it would seem, the original author of the saying (Diog. Laert. 8. 10), but Zeller doubts whether he meant it as an injunction to practise communism (Gr. Ph. 1. 291. 3). The addition here of πρὸς τὸ χρῆσθαι (cp. ἐπὶ τὴν χρῆσιν, 8 (6). 5. 1320 b 10) perhaps looks as if Aristotle so understood it. Epicurus certainly did so: cp. Diog. Laert. 10. 11, τόν τε Ἐπίκουρον μὴ ἀξιοῦν εἰς τὸ κοινὸν κατατίθεσθαι τὰς οὐσίας, καθάπερ τὸν Πυθαγόραν κοινὰ τὰ φίλων λέγοντα· ἀπιστούντων γὰρ εἶναι τὸ τοιοῦτον, εἰ δ' ἀπίστων, οὐδὲ φίλων.

31. ἐνίαις πόλεσιν. Tarentum (8 (6). 5. 1320 b 9 sqq.): Carthage (8 (6). 5. 1320 b 4 sqq.): the Lacedaemonian and Cretan States (1263 b 40 sq.): Rhodes (Strabo, p. 652). Compare also Isocrates' picture of the earlier Athens (Areopag. § 35). For the appeal here made to the practice of existing States, cp. Rhet. 1. 1. 1354 a 18, εἰ περὶ πάσας ἦν τὰς κρίσεις καθάπερ ἐν ἐνίαις τε νῦν ἐστὶ τῶν πόλεων καὶ μάλιστα ταῖς εὐνομουμέναις, οὐδὲν ἂν εἶχον ὅ τι λέγωσιν.

ὑπογεγραμμένον. For the meaning of this word, cp. de Gen. An. 2. 6. 743 b 20–25, esp. οἱ γραφεῖς ὑπογράψαντες ταῖς γραμμαῖς οὕτως ἐναλείφουσι τοῖς χρώμασι τὸ ζῷον: it explains τύπῳ διορίζειν in de An. 2. 1. 413 a 10. The fact that the institution of property assumes here and there in outline the form which Aristotle wishes it to assume is taken as an indication that this form is not impracticable.

34. τὰ μὲν χρήσιμα ποιεῖ τοῖς φίλοις. Vict. 'copiam quorundam ipsorum faciunt amicis, relinquuntque ipsis ea utenda.' Cp. Xen. Mem. 2. 6. 23, τὸν δὲ φθόνον παντάπασιν ἀφαιροῦσιν (οἱ καλοὶ κἀγαθοί), τὰ μὲν ἑαυτῶν ἀγαθὰ τοῖς φίλοις οἰκεῖα παρέχοντες, τὰ δὲ τῶν φίλων ἑαυτῶν νομίζοντες.

χρῆται κοινοῖς. For the absence of ὡς, cp. 36, ἰδίοις: c. 3. 1261 b 24, οἱ κοιναῖς χρώμενοι ταῖς γυναιξί: Isocr. Paneg. § 181 (quoted in Aristot. Rhet. 3. 9. 1410 a 14). Plutarch, speaking of brothers (De Fraterno Amore, c. 1), uses the expression, καὶ τὸ χρῆσθαι κοινῶς τοῖς πατρῴοις χρήμασι καὶ φίλοις καὶ δούλοις: cp. ibid. c. 11, χρῆσιν δὲ καὶ κτῆσιν ἐν μέσῳ κεῖσθαι κοινὴν καὶ ἀνέμητον ἁπάντων.

35. ἐν Λακεδαίμονι. See Xen. de Rep. Lac. 6 as to this Lacedaemonian practice. As to slaves, Xenophon there says, ἐποίησε δὲ (ὁ Λυκοῦργος) καὶ οἰκέταις, εἴ τις δεηθείη, χρῆσθαι καὶ τοῖς ἀλλοτρίοις, and he adds the same thing of dogs and horses. The expression ἐν Λακεδαίμονι frequently recurs in the Politics (see Bon. Ind. 421 b 7 sqq.). Λακεδαίμων is used by Xenophon (Sturz, Lexic. Xenophont. s. v.) and other writers to designate both the city of Sparta and Laconia. Aristotle perhaps uses ἐν Λακεδαίμονι here as he uses ἐν Ἀθήναις in 2. 8. 1268 a 10, ἔστι δὲ καὶ ἐν Ἀθήναις οὗτος ὁ νόμος νῦν καὶ ἐν ἑτέραις τῶν πόλεων, where the name of the city seems to stand for the State. He does not seem to intend to contrast ἐν Λακεδαίμονι with ἐν τοῖς ἀγροῖς κατὰ τὴν χώραν, or to suggest that it was only in the city that men placed their slaves, horses, and dogs at each other's service. Nothing of the kind is said by Xenophon in the passage of the de Rep. Lac. (6. 3 sq.) which Aristotle seems to have before him here.

36. κἂν δεηθῶσιν ἐφοδίων, i. e. καὶ ἐφοδίοις, ἂν δεηθῶσι (cp. Xen. Rep. Lac. 6. 4, ὅπου γὰρ ἂν ὑπὸ θήρας ὀψισθέντες δεηθῶσι τῶν ἐπιτηδείων). The word ἐφοδίοις is caught into the construction of the conditional clause and must be supplied from it: cp. χρημάτων, 1. 8. 1256 b 29.

37. ἐν τοῖς ἀγροῖς κατὰ τὴν χώραν. This seems at first sight tautological, and many emendations have been suggested: see Susemihl's critical note (Sus.[2], vol. i. p. 170). Both Busse (Sus.[3]) and Mr. Welldon suggest, ingeniously enough, the substitution of ἐν ταῖς ἄγραις for ἐν τοῖς ἀγροῖς—a change which agrees well with the passage of Xenophon de Rep. Lac. part of which has been quoted in the last note, for Xenophon makes no mention of ἀγροί and does use the words ὑπὸ θήρας ὀψισθέντες. The passage concludes—τοιγαροῦν οὕτως μεταδιδόντες ἀλλήλοις καὶ οἱ τὰ μικρὰ ἔχοντες μετέχουσι πάντων τῶν ἐν τῇ χώρᾳ, ὁπόταν τινὸς δεηθῶσιν. But we find ἐν ἀγρῷ in the very similar passage, [Plutarch] Inst. Lac. c. 23, and the meaning of ἐν τοῖς ἀγροῖς κατὰ τὴν χώραν may not improbably be 'in the farms throughout the territory.' Sturz (Lexicon Xenophont. s. v. ἀγρός) collects many passages of Xenophon in which ἀγροί = 'praedia.' The word may possibly bear this meaning in Pol. 7 (5). 5. 1305 a 19, ἐπὶ τῶν ἀγρῶν οἰκεῖν τὸν δῆμον ἄσχολον ὄντα πρὸς τοῖς ἔργοις. In Plato, Laws 881 C, however, we have κατ' ἀγροὺς τῆς χώρας που, so that there is nothing strange in the conjunction of the two words. The χώρα, or district attached to the city, included villages or even towns, as well as woods, fields, and the like (cp. Xen. Hiero 9. 7, κατ' ἀγροὺς ἢ κατὰ κώμας).

38. For the change of subject from **εἶναι** to **ποιεῖν**, see note on 1263 a 3. As to the thought, Plato himself had said, Laws 740 A (while giving up community of property as impracticable in the absence of a complete reform of marriage, rearing, and education)—νεμέσθων δ' οὖν τοιᾷδε διανοίᾳ πως, ὡς ἄρα δεῖ τὸν λαχόντα τὴν λῆξιν ταύτην νομίζειν μὲν κοινὴν αὐτὴν τῆς πόλεως ξυμπάσης κ.τ.λ. But the expression used by Aristotle appears to be derived from Isocrates

(Areopag. § 35)—κεφάλαιον δὲ τοῦ καλῶς ἀλλήλοις ὁμιλεῖν· αἱ μὲν γὰρ κτήσεις ἀσφαλεῖς ἦσαν, οἷσπερ κατὰ τὸ δίκαιον ὑπῆρχον, αἱ δὲ χρήσεις κοιναὶ πᾶσι τοῖς δεομένοις τῶν πολιτῶν. Cp. also Xen. Mem. 2. 6. 23, τὸν δὲ φθόνον παντάπασιν ἀφαιροῦσιν (οἱ καλοὶ κἀγαθοί), τὰ μὲν ἑαυτῶν ἀγαθὰ τοῖς φίλοις οἰκεῖα παρέχοντες, τὰ δὲ τῶν φίλων ἑαυτῶν νομίζοντες.

39. τοιοῦτοι, sc. ὥστε τῇ χρήσει ποιεῖν κοινὰς τὰς κτήσεις. For the thought, cp. 4 (7). 13. 1332 a 31 sqq.

40. καὶ πρὸς ἡδονήν, as well as in relation to virtue, cp. 29. But how does the fact that a reasonable degree of self-love is natural prove that to regard something as one's own adds greatly to human pleasure? Perhaps the link is supplied by Rhet. 1. 11. 1370 a 3, ἀνάγκη οὖν ἡδὺ εἶναι τό τε εἰς τὸ κατὰ φύσιν ἰέναι ὡς ἐπὶ τὸ πολύ, where we learn that pleasure arises from the satisfaction of nature, and Pol. 5 (8). 7. 1342 a 25, ποιεῖ δὲ τὴν ἡδονὴν ἑκάστοις τὸ κατὰ φύσιν οἰκεῖον (cp. 5 (8). 5. 1340 a 3, ἔχει γὰρ ἡ μουσικὴ τὴν ἡδονὴν φυσικήν, διὸ πάσαις ἡλικίαις καὶ πᾶσιν ἤθεσιν ἡ χρῆσις αὐτῆς ἐστὶ προσφιλής). If so, the complete argument will be 'for the satisfaction of a natural craving brings pleasure, and is not self-love in moderation natural'? Compare also Rhet. 1. 11. 1371 b 18 sq., and Hist. An. 8. 1. 589 a 8, τὸ δὲ κατὰ φύσιν ἡδύ· διώκει δὲ πάντα τὴν κατὰ φύσιν ἡδονήν. Or should we complete the ellipse thus—'for is there not a purpose, namely pleasure, for which we are so constituted as to feel love for ourselves, and is not this an ordinance of nature'? Or again—'yes, and natural pleasure too, for is not self-love implanted in us for a purpose and natural'? The first of these ways of completing the ellipse is probably the correct one.

41. νομίζειν ἴδιόν τι, 'to regard a thing as one's own,' for νομίζειν will hardly be used here in the sense which it bears in 3. 1. 1275 b 7, οὐδ' ἐκκλησίαν νομίζουσιν ἀλλὰ συγκλήτους.

μὴ γὰρ κ.τ.λ. See on this use of μή, Bon. Ind. 464 b 43 sqq. ('dubitanter et modestius affirmantis est'). Eucken (de Partic. Usu p. 57) would read ἔχῃ for ἔχει in b 1, because Aristotle sometimes uses the subjunctive in this construction (e.g. in 6 (4). 4. 1291 a 9, where all the MSS. have the subjunctive: Eth. Nic. 10. 2. 1172 b 36: 10. 10. 1179 b 24), and 'in eodem libro ad eandem sententiam significandam modo coniunctivum, modo indicativum adhibuisse minime verisimile sit.' But the indicative is found under similar circumstances (without various reading) in Eth. Nic. 10. 1. 1172 a 34 and 10. 2. 1173 a 23, and Bekker, whom Susemihl follows, is probably right in retaining this variation of mood.

1263 b. **2. τὸ δὲ κ.τ.λ.** The connexion just established between affection for oneself and Nature reminds Aristotle of a fact which seems to conflict with it, that φιλαυτία is blamed and justly so, and he proceeds to explain that the epithet φίλαυτος is applied to those who are fonder of themselves than they should be. Herein he follows Plato, Laws 731 E sqq. (cp. 732 B, διὸ πάντα ἄνθρωπον χρὴ φεύγειν τὸ σφόδρα φιλεῖν αὑτόν), and he repeats the same view in Eth. Nic. 4. 10. 1125 b 16 (cp. 3. 13. 1118 b 22 sqq.: 2. 7. 1107 b 28 sq.: 4. 10. 1125 b 9 sqq.). In Eth. Nic. 9. 8. 1168 b 15–23 and 1169 a 20 sq. the unfavourable use of the word is connected rather with the preference of money, honour, and τὰ περιμάχητα ἀγαθά generally to τὸ καλόν: so too in Magn. Mor. 2. 13. 1212 b 2–6. Affection for oneself is implied in Pol. 7 (5). 9. 1309 b 12 to be to a certain extent a preservative against ἀκρασία, though not a complete preservative like virtue.

3. If here we read, with all the MSS. except P[1], καθάπερ καὶ τὸν φιλοχρήματον, we must explain 'as it is for this that we blame the money-lover,' ψέγομεν being supplied from ψέγεται 2. To read τό for τόν undoubtedly makes the sentence far less rugged: its meaning will then be—'as to be a money-lover is to be fonder of money than one ought to be.' Cp. Plato, Rep. 347 B, ἢ οὐκ οἶσθα, ὅτι τὸ φιλότιμόν τε καὶ φιλάργυρον εἶναι ὄνειδος λέγεταί τε καὶ ἔστιν;

4. **ἐπεὶ κ.τ.λ.**, 'and it cannot be intended to blame men for loving what all love' seems to be here suppressed. Cp. ὃ πᾶσι δοκεῖ τοῦτ' εἶναί φαμεν, Eth. Nic. 10. 2. 1172 b 36, and Pol. 2. 8. 1269 a 3.

6. For the absence of the article before **βοηθῆσαι**, see above on 1263 a 15.

ἑταίροις, Π[2] rightly: cp. Rhet. 2. 4. 1381 b 34. For the thought, cp. Eth. Nic. 9. 9. 1169 b 10 sqq.: 8. 1. 1155 a 7, τί γὰρ ὄφελος τῆς τοιαύτης εὐετηρίας, ἀφαιρεθείσης εὐεργεσίας, ἣ γίγνεται μάλιστα καὶ ἐπαινετωτάτη πρὸς φίλους; Aristotle possibly has in his mind some lines of Antiphanes (Inc. Fab. Fragm. 4: Meineke, Fr. Com. Gr. 3. 133).

ὃ γίνεται κ.τ.λ. shows that χαρίσασθαι, βοηθῆσαι must be used in reference to goods or money, for it would still be possible to help and confer favours on friends in other ways, even though property were common.

7. **ταῦτα**, if we read οὐ συμβαίνει, appears to refer to τὸ νομίζειν ἴδιόν τι and τὸ χαρίσασθαι καὶ βοηθῆσαι φίλοις—'these things do not come to pass for those who' etc.: cp. 2. 9. 1269 b 39 sq., and Xen. Mem. 1. 2. 11, καὶ φονεύειν δὲ τοῖς τοιούτοις ἥκιστα συμβαίνει.

8. **ἔργα δυοῖν ἀρεταῖν.** Cp. Isocr. Nicocl. § 41, σωφροσύνης ἔργα καὶ δικαιοσύνης. It would seem from Eth. Nic. 10. 8. 1178 a 21–b 1 that both προαίρεσις and πράξεις are necessary to perfect virtue. But the passage before us does not raise this subtle question; it appears to imply (cp. Magn. Mor. 1. 19. 1190 b 1 sqq.: Eth. Eud. 2. 1. 1219 b 11: 2. 11. 1228 a 16), that men may be virtuous without being able to evidence their virtue.

9. φανερῶς, 'undisguisedly' or 'visibly and unmistakably'? Probably the latter (cp. φανεράν, c. 7. 1266 b 20).

τὸ περὶ τὰς γυναῖκας, sc. ἔργον, which comes to the surface in the parenthesis.

10. καλόν, and therefore a work of virtue (cp. 4 (7). 14. 1333 b 28.)

ἀλλοτρίας is emphatic: no woman, it is implied, would be another's in the State described in the Republic.

11. ἔσται. For the suppression of the subject, cp. de Part. An. 1. 3. 643 b 17: Metaph. Z. 12. 1038 a 13.

13. ἐν τῇ γάρ. For the place of γὰρ (ἐν γὰρ τῇ, Ald.), cp. διὰ τὸ ἀντὶ πτερόνης γάρ, de Part. An. 2. 6. 652 a 18: ἐν τοῖς δεξιοῖς γάρ, de Part. An. 3. 9. 671 b 35. As to the thought here expressed, cp. Eth. Nic. 4. 2. 1120 b 27 sqq., where we find that ἐλευθεριότης has to do both with δόσις and λῆψις, though more with the former than with the latter (4. 1. 1119 b 25).

15. μέν here seems to have no δέ to answer to it, because the structure of the sentence is altered at ὧν, 22. If the sentence had been more regularly constructed, it would apparently have run—'hence, while legislation of the kind proposed wears a plausible look, it will in reality fail to remove the evils which it is designed to remove, it will involve the loss of many goods, and it will require men to live a life which cannot be lived by man.'

ἡ τοιαύτη νομοθεσία. Cp. c. 4. 1262 b 20, ἐν τῇ πολιτείᾳ τῇ τοιαύτῃ, and c. 5. 1264 a 6, τὴν τοιαύτην πολιτείαν.

16. ὁ γὰρ ἀκροώμενος κ.τ.λ. Aristotle is probably thinking here of communism in relation to property: cp. τὴν οὐσίαν, 20. Yet Ephorus seems, if we may judge by his eulogistic remarks on some Scythian races which had women children and property in common, to have been, in their case at all events, well pleased with the institution (Strabo, p. 302), to say nothing of Cynics and half-Cynics, like Diogenes of Sinope and Zeno of Citium (Diog. Laert. 6. 72: 7. 33, 131). Plato had not been sanguine of support (Rep. 450).

18. ὅταν κ.τ.λ. So Plato, Rep. 464 D–465 C.

19. ἐν ταῖς πολιτείαις. Cp. 5 (8). 1. 1337 a 13, βλάπτει τὰς πολιτείας.

21. περὶ συμβολαίων. Compare Strabo p. 702, quoted below on 1267 b 37. These suits would be brought within narrow limits in the State of the Laws (742 C: cp. Rep. 556 A); there were indeed some actual States in which they were not permitted (Eth. Nic. 9. 1. 1164 b 13 sqq.). Theophrastus recommended the registration of property and of contracts (*συμβόλαια*) in the hope of avoiding suits on this subject or diminishing their number (Fr. 97). Such a register appears to have existed in some States (see C. F. Hermann, Gr. Ant. 3. § 49. 10). Zeno of Citium, the founder of Stoicism, was for getting rid of law-courts altogether in his ideal State (Diog. Laert. 7. 33). It is evident that Greek society had more than enough of litigation. As to actions for false evidence, it is obvious that the adoption of community of property would remove only one of their occasions.

23. καὶ τοὺς κοινὰ κεκτημένους κ.τ.λ. Sus. 'dass gerade Leute welche Etwas gemeinschaftlich besitzen und benutzen . . .' Here *καί* is perhaps rightly rendered by 'gerade': 'it is just those who possess and enjoy things in common, whom' etc. Among the cases referred to here would be that of brothers holding undivided property, which seems to have been not uncommon at Athens (see Caillemer, Succession légitime à Athènes, p. 34 sqq.) and elsewhere (Jannet, Les institutions sociales à Sparte, p. 88 sqq.). 'Les enfants, après la mort de leur père, au lieu de partager entre eux sa fortune, restaient quelquefois dans l'indivision' (Caillemer, *ubi supra*). See C. F. Hermann, Gr. Ant. (ed. Thalheim), Rechtsalt. p. 54. 2.

25. ἀλλὰ θεωροῦμεν κ.τ.λ. '*Θεωρεῖν* is here synonymous with *ὁρᾶν*' (Bon. Ind. 328 a 36). 'But those who fall out in consequence of owning common property look to us to be few in number, because we compare them with the large number of those who own property in severalty.'

28. στερήσονται. The fut. med. of *στερέω*, like that of several other verbs (*θρέψονται*, c. 6. 1265 a 16: *ἄρξονται*, 8 (6). 4. 1318 b 36), is often used in a passive sense.

κοινωνήσαντες (cp. *κοινωνοῦντας*, 23), 'having made common stock': so we have *χρημάτων κοινωνήσαντας*, Xen. Oecon. 6. 3. For the tense, see below on 1270 a 4 and 1271 b 4.

29. Vict. 'tot autem tantaque sunt (bona quibus spoliantur), ut plane cognoscatur non posse ullo pacto vitam traduci illa lege.' The life which the members of Plato's State are to live is in such flagrant opposition to well-ascertained tendencies of human nature—so starved and poor in pleasure, affection, and virtue, and so wanting in concord—that it will be unliveable.

30. παρακρούσεως is usually rendered 'error,' but perhaps Liddell and Scott, who compare Soph. El. 17. 175 b 1, are right in rendering it 'fallacy.'

31 sqq. Compare the argument in 7 (5). 9. 1309 b 21 sqq.

33. προϊοῦσα. Cp. c. 2. 1261 a 17, *προϊοῦσα καὶ γινομένη μία μᾶλλον.*

33 sq. Cp. 8 (6). 1. 1317 a 27, *οὐ μόνον διαφέρει τῷ βελτίω καὶ χείρω γίνεσθαι τὴν δημοκρατίαν, ἀλλὰ καὶ τῷ μὴ τὴν αὐτήν.*

34. ὥσπερ κἂν εἰ κ.τ.λ. 'Just as you would spoil a harmony or a rhythm, if' (Mr. Welldon).

35. τὸν ῥυθμὸν βάσιν μίαν. The unit of a rhythm—the *ἀσύνθετον* of which it is composed—is the *βάσις* or else the syllable (Metaph. N. 1. 1087 b 36). The *βάσις* is in dancing the 'step,' in verse the metrical foot. Thus to make the State absolutely and in every way one is here compared to dwarfing a long rhythm to one single *βάσις*, i.e. to one of its component parts: cp. c. 2. 1261 a 19, *οἰκία ἐκ πόλεως, ἄνθρωπος δ' ἐξ οἰκίας*, where *ἄνθρωπος* answers to *βάσις*.

36. πρότερον, c. 2. 1261 a 18.

διὰ τὴν παιδείαν. Eucken (Praep. p. 39) explains *διά* with the acc. here 'by means of' ('durch, vermittelst'), comparing de Caelo 3. 2. 301 a 18, *σύγκρισιν δὲ ποιῶν διὰ τὴν φιλότητα*: Meteor. 2. 8. 366 b 5: Phys. 4. 11. 219 b 29, cp. b 23 sq. So Bonitz remarks (Ind. 177 a 45), '*διά* cum acc. coniunctum legitur, ubi genetivum exspectes,' instancing this passage and referring to *διὰ ταύτης*, 38.

37. κοινὴν καὶ μίαν. Bern. 'zum einigen und Einen Staat machen:' Sus. 'zur Gemeinschaft und Einheit gestalten.' Perhaps the latter translation comes nearest to the sense. There is no English word which adequately represents *κοινήν*: 'to make it social and so one' is an approach to the meaning of the words.

38. διὰ ταύτης. Cp. 4 (7). 13. 1332 b 31 sqq.

39. τοῖς τοιούτοις, i.e. 'by the measures which we have described,' measures which do not unite the State by improving the character of the citizens.

40. τῇ φιλοσοφίᾳ, distinguished here from *τοῖς ἔθεσι*, as from *ἀνδρία, καρτερία*, and other ethical virtues in 4 (7). 15. 1334 a 23, 32, where Bonitz (Ind. 821 a 6) explains the meaning of the word to be 'virtus intellectualis': cp. Eth. Nic. 2. 1. 1103 a 17, *ἡ δ' ἠθικὴ ἀρετὴ ἐξ ἔθους περιγίνεται.* Here perhaps 'intellectual culture' (Mr. Welldon) is the meaning.

41. τοῖς συσσιτίοις, adduced apparently as an instance of a law acting on the character. Compare Aristotle's language as to syssitia in 4 (7). 10. 1330 a 1 sqq.

1264 a. 1. τοῦτο αὐτό, 'this by itself': cp. αὐτὸ τοῦτο, 1. 6. 1255 a 18.

2. τῷ πολλῷ χρόνῳ κ.τ.λ. Plato himself appeals (Rep. 376 E) to the testimony of Time in favour of γυμναστική and μουσική. For ἔτεσιν Bernays (Gesammelte Abhandlungen 1. 177) conjectures ἔθνεσιν (comparing Simonides Ceus, Fragm. 193 Bergk: he might have added to his citations Plato, Laws 638 E, ἐπειδὴ καὶ μυρία ἐπὶ μυρίοις ἔθνη περὶ αὐτῶν ἀμφισβητοῦντα ὑμῖν πόλεσι δυεῖν τῷ λόγῳ διαμάχοιτ' ἄν, for the saying of Simonides appears to be present to Plato's mind in this passage of the Laws), and the suggestion of a reminiscence of this bit of Simonides here is brilliant and ingenious, but we find ἐκ πολλῶν ἐτῶν καὶ παλαιοῦ χρόνου in Aristot. Fragm. 40. 1481 a 41, and tautological expressions are not rare in Aristotle's writings (see Vahlen, Poet. p. 87, on Poet. 1. 1447 a 17, ἑτέρως καὶ μὴ τὸν αὐτὸν τρόπον): besides, ἐν οἷς suits ἔτεσιν better than ἔθνεσιν.

4. εὕρηται. Cp. 4 (7). 10. 1329 b 25, σχεδὸν μὲν οὖν καὶ τὰ ἄλλα δεῖ νομίζειν εὑρῆσθαι πολλάκις ἐν τῷ πολλῷ χρόνῳ, μᾶλλον δ' ἀπειράκις. Aristotle held that the world existed from everlasting (Zeller, Gr. Ph. 2. 2. 432 sq.) and mankind too (ibid. 508. 1), and that in the infinity of past time everything has been discovered, and, if lost, discovered over again. Hence he advises inquirers rather to avail themselves of what has been already made out and to investigate what has been insufficiently investigated, than to seek to strike out something altogether new (4 (7). 10. 1329 b 33 sq.). There seem, however, to have been subjects on which Aristotle claims to have inherited little or nothing from his predecessors (see Eucken, Methode d. Aristot. Forschung, p. 5, who refers to Phys. 4. 1. 208 a 34: de Gen. et Corr. 1. 2. 315 a 34: Meteor. 1. 13. 349 a 14).

συνῆκται, 'gathered together for scientific use': cp. Metaph. A. 9. 991 a 18 and 5. 986 a 3, ὅσα εἶχον ὁμολογούμενα δεικνύναι ἔν τε τοῖς ἀριθμοῖς καὶ ταῖς ἁρμονίαις πρὸς τὰ τοῦ οὐρανοῦ πάθη καὶ μέρη καὶ πρὸς τὴν ὅλην διακόσμησιν, ταῦτα συνάγοντες ἐφήρμοττον. The word is already used by Isocrates, de Antid. §§ 83, 45.

5. μάλιστα δ' ἂν κ.τ.λ. Thurot (Études, p. 28) would supply 'l'impossibilité de l'unité sociale, telle que la veut Platon,' but perhaps it is more natural to supply εἰ ταῦτα καλῶς ἔχει from 3.

7. δυνήσεται. For this use of the third person 'non addito τὶς,' see Bon. Ind. 589 b 47. For the future, see above on 1261 a 22. According to Dionysius of Halicarnassus (Ant. Rom. 2. 7) Romulus' first step was to effect divisions of the kind here referred to. Cp. also Xen. Hiero c. 9. 5, διῄρηνται μὲν γὰρ ἅπασαι αἱ πόλεις αἱ μὲν

κατὰ φυλάς, αἱ δὲ κατὰ μόρας, αἱ δὲ κατὰ λόχους. Aristotle probably remembers Nestor's advice (Il. 2. 362)—

> *Κρῖν' ἄνδρας κατὰ φῦλα, κατὰ φρήτρας, Ἀγάμεμνον,*
> *ὡς φρήτρη φρήτρηφιν ἀρήγῃ, φῦλα δὲ φύλοις,*

and the line (Il. 9. 63) which associates the *ἀφρήτωρ* with the *ἀθέμιστος* and the *ἀνέστιος.*

αὐτά = 'cives,' Sus.[1], Ind. Gramm. s. v. (who however doubts the correctness of the reading), or perhaps in a somewhat vaguer sense 'the materials of the State': so Camerarius (Schn. 2. 88) 'ea quae Socraticis rationibus contrahuntur et fiunt unum.' For the neuter, cp. *ἐκεῖνα*, 1263 a 1.

χωρίζων. Bonitz (Ind. 860 a 10) compares Eth. Nic. 4. 3. 1121 b 19.

8. τὰ μὲν . . . τὰ δέ, 'on the one hand'—'on the other.' Plato, in fact, adopts syssitia in the Republic (416 E: cp. 458 C), and syssitia (Laws 842 B), phratries (785 A), and tribes (745 E) in the Laws. Syssitia differ from phratries and tribes in not being based on relationship: Herodotus also regards them as belonging to *τὰ ἐς πόλεμον ἔχοντα* (1. 65: see Trieber, Forschungen zur spartanischen Verfassungsgeschichte, pp. 15, 18 sqq.). Dosiadas (ap. Athen. Deipn. 143 b) says of Lyctus in Crete, *διήρηνται δ' οἱ πολῖται πάντες καθ' ἑταιρίας, καλοῦσι δὲ ταύτας ἀνδρεῖα* (= *συσσίτια*).

9. ὥστε κ.τ.λ. *Ὥστε* with the indicative ('and so') draws an emphatic conclusion: cp. c. 8. 1268 a 20. Plato will not succeed in making his guardians an undivided unity; he will only succeed in forbidding them to cultivate the soil. But this is nothing new (cp. Pol. 4 (7). 10. 1329 a 40 sqq.). Thus what is new in Plato's scheme is not practicable, and what is practicable is not new. The mention of the prohibition of agriculture to the guardians reminds Aristotle that two classes will exist in Plato's State, guardians and cultivators, and he now turns to consider their mutual relations.

10. καὶ νῦν, 'as it is.'

Λακεδαιμόνιοι. For the absence of the article, see Meisterhans, Grammatik der attischen Inschriften, p. 90, who remarks that the article is commonly absent in Attic Inscriptions before names of peoples in the plural, though exceptions to this rule occur even in inscriptions of an early date. Aristotle sometimes omits and sometimes adds the article (see, for instance, 1264 a 20, and c. 9. 1269 a 29—b 7). The references given in the Index Aristotelicus suggest the view that Aristotle uses the word *Λακεδαιμόνιοι* of the Lacedaemonians in their public capacity as constituting a State, while he uses Λάκωνες both of the State (as in 7 (5). 7. 1307 b 23, οἱ δὲ Λάκωνες τοὺς δήμους κατέλυον) and of the people, but more often of the latter. See Gilbert, Gr. Staatsalt. 1. 40. 1.

ἐπιχειροῦσιν, 'attempt to bring about.' Schiller (Sclaverei, p. 21, n. 72) remarks on this word. Some Spartans were probably compelled by need to till the soil. Cp. 2. 9. 1270 b 6, πολλοὺς πένητας, and Plutarch, Agis 5. 3, πενία ἀσχολίαν τῶν καλῶν καὶ ἀνελευθερίαν ἐπιφέρουσα. Prof. Jowett points out that ἐπιχειρεῖν is often used pleonastically by Plato, though he does not adopt the view that it is pleonastic here, but translates 'try to enforce.' Cp. c. 9. 1270 a 6, ἄγειν ἐπιχειρῆσαι.

11. οὐ μὴν ἀλλά. Why 'not but that'? How is this sentence in opposition to that which precedes? Perhaps Aristotle's meaning is—'but indeed it is not only in this respect that the constitution is in fault, for the whole scheme of it is hard to make out.'

ὁ τρόπος κ.τ.λ., i.e. the whole σύνθεσις of guardians and cultivators, as distinguished from the arrangements as to the guardians with which Aristotle has hitherto been occupied. Cp. c. 7. 1267 a 17, ὁ τρόπος τῆς Φαλέου πολιτείας, c. 9. 1271 b 2, ἡ πᾶσα σύνταξις τῶν νόμων, and Polyb. 4. 20. 7, τὴν ὅλην πολιτείαν. Much pains have been taken to secure the internal unity of the guardians, but none to secure the harmony of the whole State, which includes the third class as well as the two upper ones. Cp. Plato, Rep. 421 A, ἀλλὰ τῶν μὲν ἄλλων ἐλάττων λόγος κ.τ.λ.

12. τοῖς κοινωνοῦσιν, i.e. τοῖς πολίταις: cp. 1. 13. 1260 b 19, οἱ κοινωνοὶ τῆς πολιτείας. Bern. 'für alle Angehörigen eines solchen Staates.'

13. τό γε πλῆθος. Cp. Rep. 442 C, τῷ σμικρῷ μέρει: 428 D–E, τῷ σμικροτάτῳ ἔθνει καὶ μέρει ἑαυτῆς.

14. γίνεται, 'results in being,' cp. 1. 2. 1252 b 7: Rhet. 3. 9. 1409 b 26: Strabo, p. 653, εἰ δ' . . . ἐξ Ἄργους καὶ Τίρυνθος ἀπῆρεν ὁ Τληπόλεμος, οὐδ' οὕτω Δωρικὴ γίνεται ἡ ἐκεῖθεν ἀποικία.

περὶ ὧν κ.τ.λ. 'Immemor fuit Aristoteles locorum, quales sunt de Rep. iii. p. 417 A: iv. p. 419, quibus certe possessiones eorum non constituendas esse communes disertis verbis dixit Plato, et profecto per se satis superque apparet uxorum, liberorum, possessionum communionem ex eius sententia propriam esse debere custodum,' Sus.[1] (cp. Sus.[2], Note 170). See also Tim. 18 B. As Susemihl remarks, Aristotle seems to take it for granted above, c. 4. 1262 a 40, that community of women and children is to be confined to the guardians.

15. ἢ καί often means 'or even' (e.g. in Plato, Phileb. 61 A):

elsewhere, however, and perhaps here, it seems to mean 'or also,' 'or again' (e.g. in de Gen. An. 1. 18. 723 a 29, *ἐν τῷ σύμμετρον ἢ ἀσύμμετρον εἶναι ἢ καὶ δι' ἄλλην τινὰ τοιαύτην αἰτίαν*: ibid. 1. 18. 724 b 5, *πότερον ὡς ὕλην καὶ πάσχον ἢ ὡς εἶδός τι καὶ ποιοῦν, ἢ καὶ ἄμφω*).

17. εἰ μὲν γὰρ κ.τ.λ. Three alternatives are considered: 1. the case of the *γεωργοί* having women, children, and property in common (17–22): 2. the opposite case (22–40): 3. the case of their having women and children in common but not property (40 sq.). The other case of property being common and women and children not so, is not considered.

18. τί διοίσουσιν κ.τ.λ. Cp. c. 4. 1262 a 40 sqq. If a community in women, children, and property produces close friendship, it will do so among the cultivators no less than among the guardians. The two classes will be, it is implied, on a par in point of unity, and in whatever excellence flows from community in these things. Yet rulers ought to differ from those they rule (cp. c. 6. 1265 b 18), and this is the opinion of Plato. Evidently, however, it does not follow, if women, children, and property are common in both classes, that the two will be absolutely alike, as Aristotle's argument implies.

ἢ τί πλεῖον κ.τ.λ. The argument seems to be that if the cultivators are in no way dissimilar to the guardians, the former will gain nothing by obeying the latter. In Aristotle's view, the ruled, if inferior to the ruler, profit by their obedience: so the slave, 1. 2. 1252 a 30 sqq.—domestic animals, 1. 5. 1254 b 10 sqq.—the subjects of the *παμβασιλεύς*, 3. 13. 1284 b 33. Bernays omits *ἢ—αὐτῶν*, but this clause seems to be in place, and not superfluous.

19. ἢ τί μαθόντες κ.τ.λ. 'Or what is to make them' etc.? The use of *τί μαθόντες* perhaps implies that their submission to *ὅμοιοι* would be a mistake. '*Τί μαθών* signifies an intentionally, *τί παθών* an accidentally, wrong action,' Jelf, Greek Grammar, § 872. 2 k.

21. τἆλλα ταὐτὰ κ.τ.λ. Cp. c. 6. 1265 a 5, *τὰ ἄλλα ταὐτὰ ἀποδίδωσιν.*

For **ἐφέντες**, cp. c. 6. 1265 b 22, *ἐφίησι.*

Τοῖς δούλοις probably includes those elsewhere called *περίοικοι* by Aristotle (e.g. in c. 10. 1272 b 18), though a distinction seems to be made between the terms *δοῦλος* and *περίοικος* in 4 (7). 10. 1330 a 25 sqq. Aristotle's account of the status of the Cretan slaves is confirmed by the tenour of the recently discovered inscription containing a portion of the laws of Gortyna. See Bücheler und Zitelmann, Das Recht von Gortyn, p. 64: 'their legal status appears to have been good . . . they have property of their own (col. 3. 42), a well-developed family-law, are capable of marriage with free women (col. 7. 3): nay, they even have a remote and contingent right of succession to the property of their master' (col. 5. 27: see also Bücheler und Zitelmann, p. 144).

ἀπειρήκασι. Compare the well-known scolion of Hybrias the Cretan (Bergk, Poet. Lyr. Gr.):

Ἔστι μοι πλοῦτος μέγας δόρυ καὶ ξίφος
καὶ τὸ καλὸν λαισήϊον, πρόβλημα χρωτός·
* * *
τούτῳ δεσπότας μνοίας κέκλημαι.
Τοὶ δὲ μὴ τολμῶντ' ἔχειν δόρυ καὶ ξίφος
καὶ τὸ καλὸν λαισήϊον, πρόβλημα χρωτός,
πάντες γόνυ πεπτηῶτες ἀμὸν
. . . . . (προσ)κυνεῦντί (με) δεσπόταν
καὶ μέγαν βασιλέα φωνέοντες.

Compare also 6 (4). 13. 1297 a 29 sqq., and what Xenophon says of Cyrus (Cyrop. 8. 1. 43)—*οὓς δ' αὖ κατεσκεύαζεν εἰς τὸ δουλεύειν, τούτους οὔτε μελετᾶν τῶν ἐλευθερίων πόνων οὐδένα παρώρμα οὔθ' ὅπλα κεκτῆσθαι ἐπέτρεπεν· ἐπεμέλετο δὲ ὅπως μήτε ἄσιτοι μήτε ἄποτοί ποτε ἔσοιντο ἐλευθερίων ἕνεκα μελετημάτων.* Plato (Laws 625 D) speaks of bows and arrows as the arms most suitable to Crete, but he no doubt does not intend to imply that the Cretans did not possess and use *ὅπλα* of a heavier kind.

22. εἰ δέ, καθάπερ κ.τ.λ. Sepulv. 'sin autem eodem modo, quo in aliis civitatibus, haec' (i.e. households and property) 'fuerint apud ipsos constituta, qui erit communitatis modus?' It should be noted that the expression, *τίς ὁ τρόπος τῆς κοινωνίας*, is used by Adeimantus in Rep. 449 C, though in reference to the guardians alone.

25. δύο πόλεις. Aristotle retorts on Plato the charge which he had brought (Rep. 422 E sqq.) against most large States of his own day.

26. ποιεῖ γὰρ κ.τ.λ. Cp. Rep. 419: 415 D–417 B: 543 B–C. Φυλακή was a common euphemism at Athens for the garrison of a dependent city (Plutarch, Solon c. 15): cp. 7 (5). 11. 1314 b 16 sqq. Yet the term *φύλακες* must have had a somewhat unpleasant sound in the ears of Greeks, for the Athenians gave this name to the officials whom the Lacedaemonians called harmosts (Theophr. Fragm. 129 Wimmer: Boeckh, Public Economy of Athens E. T. p. 156). Πολίτας, 27, is the predicate.

29. καὶ τούτοις, to the cultivators and artisans who are the real citizens of Plato's State, no less than to the citizens of actual States.

ὁ **Σωκράτης**, Rep. 425 C–D.

32. ἀποδιδούς. Vict. 'cum tamen tribuerit': cp. 1265 a 3, *βουλόμενος*. *Μόνον* qualifies *τοῖς φύλαξιν*.

ἔτι δὲ κ.τ.λ. Rep. 464 B, *οὔτε οἰκίας οὔτε γῆν οὔτε τι κτῆμα*.

33. ἀποφορά is the technical term for 'the money which slaves let out to hire paid to their master' (Liddell and Scott): see Büchsenschütz, Besitz und Erwerb p. 195. The contribution in kind which the Helots rendered to their masters went by this name (Plutarch, Lycurg. c. 8: Inst. Lac. c. 40). Plato's designation for the contribution of *οἱ ἄλλοι πολῖται* to the support of the guardians is, however, not *ἀποφορά* (for this would imply that they were slaves), but *μισθὸς τῆς φυλακῆς* (Rep. 416 E).

34. πολὺ μᾶλλον, because they are free and citizens, and have the land in their hands.

35. εἱλωτείας, 'bodies of Helots,' just as *πολιτεία* is used by Aristotle occasionally (Bon. Ind. 612 b 10 sqq.) in the sense of 'a body of citizens.' So *δουλείας*, 36: cp. Thuc. 5. 23, *ἢν ἡ δουλεία ἐπανιστῆται*.

36. 'Whether a definite settlement of the question as to property and the family is as necessary in relation to the cultivators as it is in relation to the guardians or not, at present at all events nothing definite has been laid down.'

37. καί, 'nor.'

38. τε here as elsewhere 'ei vocabulo additur, quod utrique membro commune est,' Bon. Ind. 749 b 44 sqq. The meaning of **πολιτεία** here is not absolutely certain; it might possibly be 'participation in political power'—cp. 4 (7). 9. 1329 a 13, *ἀμφοτέροις ἀποδιδόναι τὴν πολιτείαν ταύτην* ('hanc partem reipublicae administrandae,' Bon. Ind. 612 b 47). See Bon. Ind. 612 b 38 sqq. in illustration of the sense 'ius civitatis, potestas in civitate.' But Bonitz does not appear to attach this sense to the word in this passage; and perhaps the ordinary meaning of 'political constitution' is more probable here. Aristotle has been speaking of this class as a separate *πόλις* (24), and he would like to know what its *πολιτεία* is to be, because it is essential that its character should be suitable to its position, and the *πολιτεία* is a main determinant of character.

ἔστι δ' . . . ῥᾴδιον, sc. *τίς ἡ τούτων τε πολιτεία κ.τ.λ.*

39. οὔτε . . . κοινωνίαν. 'Nor is their character of slight importance in relation to the preservation of the guardians' society.' For the construction, cp. Eryxias 394 D, *ἡ τῆς μὲν οἰκίας ἥ τε χρῆσις πολλὴ τυγχάνει οὖσα καὶ ἀναγκαία, καὶ μεγάλα τῷ ἀνθρώπῳ τὰ διαφέροντα τὰ πρὸς* τὸν βίον ἐν τῇ τοιαύτῃ οἰκίᾳ οἰκεῖν μᾶλλον ἢ ἐν σμικρῷ καὶ φαύλῳ οἰκιδίῳ· τῆς δὲ σοφίας ἥ τε χρεία ὀλίγου ἀξία καὶ τὰ διαφέροντα σμικρὰ ἢ σοφῷ ἢ ἀμαθεῖ εἶναι περὶ τῶν μεγίστων; In the passage before us we have τὸ ποιούς τινας εἶναι τούτους instead of the simple infinitive οἰκεῖν. Ποιούς τινας (cp. 5 (8). 5. 1340 a 7, 8: 5 (8). 6. 1341 b 18) includes what is often expressed by two alternatives, as (e.g.) in Rhet. 3. 1. 1404 a 9, διαφέρει γάρ τι πρὸς τὸ δηλῶσαι ὡδὶ ἢ ὡδὶ εἰπεῖν.

1264 b. **2. τὰ ἐπὶ τῶν ἀγρῶν.** A verb must be supplied from οἰκονομήσει (see above on 1257 a 21 and 1258 b 19); perhaps, however, οἰκονομήσει itself will do (cp. 3. 18. 1288 a 34).

3. κἂν εἰ . . . γυναῖκες. 'And who will keep house, if . . . ?' This clause has much exercised the commentators ('secluserunt Sylburgius, Bekkerus, ante τίς 2 traiecerunt Schneiderus et Coraes, lacunam post haec verba statuit ante Sus. iam Thurotus' Sus.[1]), but a similarly constructed sentence is to be found in Phys. 8. 3. 254 a 27, εἴπερ οὖν ἐστὶ δόξα ψευδὴς ἢ ὅλως δόξα, καὶ κίνησίς ἐστι, κἂν εἰ φαντασία, κἂν εἰ ὁτὲ μὲν οὕτως δοκεῖ εἶναι ὁτὲ δ' ἑτέρως. Göttling: 'Deinde verba κἂν εἰ κοιναὶ κ.τ.λ. sic intelligenda sunt: καὶ τὸ αὐτὸ ἀπορήσειεν ἄν τις (sc. τίς οἰκονομήσει αὐτῶν;), εἰ κοιναὶ αἱ κτήσεις καὶ αἱ τῶν γεωργῶν γυναῖκές εἰσιν.' So Vict. 'idem etiam incommodum illic nascetur, si' etc. But no fresh apodosis need be supplied: τίς οἰκονομήσει is the common apodosis of the whole sentence. (If in the much-debated passage, Soph. O. T. 227–8, we retain the reading of all the MSS. ὑπεξελὼν αὐτὸς καθ' αὑτοῦ, the apodosis (κελεύω πάντα σημαίνειν ἐμοί) must be obtained from the preceding line (226) in much the same way as in the passage before us and in the passage just quoted from the Physics.) If women are common, the question will arise who is to keep house, whether property is also common or not, for 'nulla certam aut suam domum habebit' (Giph. p. 187). Whether Aristotle's objection holds, is another matter.

4. ἄτοπον δὲ κ.τ.λ. Cp. Rep. 451 D. In the Laws, however (804 E), Plato appeals to the example of the women of the Sauromatae to show that women's pursuits should be the same as men's. Still Plutarch (de Amore Prolis, c. 1) found men even in his day inclined to regard the lower animals as furnishing a standard of that which is natural in matters relating to marriage and the begetting and rearing of offspring; he himself seems to think that they follow nature more closely than man. This short treatise is well worth reading even in the abbreviated and imperfect form in which we have it.

6. οἷς probably refers to θηρίων: Bonitz, however (Ind. 500 b 22), refers it to ἀνδράσιν. Οἷς is here used in a pregnant sense, as in 1. 5. 1254 b 19, and Isocr. Paneg. § 123.

7. **τοὺς αὐτούς**, i. e. as Vict. points out, not 'eosdem homines,' but 'eundem ordinem.'

8. **στάσεως αἴτιον.** Cp. 4 (7). 9. 1329 a 9 sqq. Sus.[2] (Note 182) explains the difference between the schemes of Plato and Aristotle in regard to this matter.

9. **ἀξίωμα.** Cp. Eth. Nic. 3. 11. 1117 a 22, *ἀνδρεῖοι δὲ φαίνονται καὶ οἱ ἀγνοοῦντες, καί εἰσιν οὐ πόρρω τῶν εὐελπίδων, χείρους δ' ὅσῳ ἀξίωμα οὐδὲν ἔχουσιν* (i. e. *οὐδενὸς ἑαυτοὺς ἀξιοῦσιν*, Bon. Ind. 70 a 43), *ἐκεῖνοι δέ*.

ἤπουθεν δή. So Π, except that accentuation varies and Vet. Int. with M[s] reads *εἴπουθεν δή*. *Ἠ πού γε δὴ* Bekk.[1] (following Vict. Schn. Cor. with some differences of accentuation): *ἤπουθεν δὴ* Bekk.[2]. *Ἤπουθεν δή* does not appear to occur elsewhere, though *ἤπού νυν . . . δή* occurs in Eurip. Troad. 59, and *ἤπου δή* ibid. 158, and Thucydides has *ἤπου δή* 1. 142. 3, and *ἤπού γε δή*, 6. 37. 2, and Aeschines de Falsa Legatione, § 88, *ἤπου . . . γε*. The particle *ἤ* is nowhere found in Aristotle, if we except this passage (Eucken de Partic. Usu p. 69). *Δήπουθεν* is common enough, though it is not found apparently in Aristotle.

θυμοειδέσι καὶ πολεμικοῖς. The members of the second class of Plato's Republic are referred to, who are thus designated in Rep. 375 A, 376 C (Eaton).

11. **ἄλλοις** is governed by *μέμικται*: *ταῖς ψυχαῖς* is added to give the place of mingling: cp. Rep. 415 B, *ὅ τι αὐτοῖς τούτων ἐν ταῖς ψυχαῖς παραμέμικται*.

13. **φησί**, Rep. 415 A.

εὐθὺς γινομένοις, cp. Rep. 415 A, *ἐν τῇ γενέσει*.

14. **μίξαι**, sc. *τὸν θεόν*.

15. **καὶ τὴν εὐδαιμονίαν**, 'even the happiness of the guardians' (Sus. 'selbst die Glückseligkeit der Wächter'). Is the meaning, 'not only wives children and property, but even happiness'? Or is it 'even their happiness, which is the last thing one would expect him to take away'?

16. **φησί**, 'Rep. iv. p. 419 sq., at immemor fuit Aristoteles alterius loci v. p. 465 sq. neque respexit quae Plato docuit ix. p. 580–592 B, et sic haud intellexit non eam quam ei tribuit, sed plane contrariam esse veram Platonis sententiam' (Sus.[1]). There is, however, as Zeller observes (Gr. Ph. 2. 2. 698. 2) a real difference between the views of Plato and Aristotle on this point, 'for Plato is in principle opposed to the contention of Aristotle that the happiness of the individual as such is to be a decisive consideration in framing the institutions of the State, and he insists

for precisely this reason (Rep. 420 B sqq.) that the individual must find his highest happiness in a self-forgetting (selbstlosen) devotion to the Whole.'

17. ἀδύνατον δὲ κ.τ.λ. Cp. 4 (7). 9. 1329 a 23, *εὐδαίμονα δὲ πόλιν οὐκ εἰς μέρος τι βλέψαντας δεῖ λέγειν αὐτῆς, ἀλλ' εἰς πάντας τοὺς πολίτας*, and 4 (7). 13. 1332 a 36, *καὶ γὰρ εἰ πάντας ἐνδέχεται σπουδαίους εἶναι, μὴ καθ' ἕκαστον δὲ τῶν πολιτῶν, οὕτως αἱρετώτερον.*

18. μὴ τῶν πλείστων κ.τ.λ. One expects *μὴ πάντων ἢ τῶν πλείστων ἢ τινῶν*, but a not very dissimilar displacement occurs in 4 (7). 11. 1330 b 37, *ἐπεὶ δὲ καὶ συμβαίνει καὶ ἐνδέχεται κ.τ.λ.*: cp. also Magn. Mor. 1. 20. 1190 b 19, *λέγω δὲ ἃ οἱ πολλοὶ φοβοῦνται ἢ οἱ πάντες.* Zeller (Gr. Ph. 2. 2. 698. 2) would like to get rid of the second *μή*, but cp. Laws 766 A, *μὴ ἱκανῶς δὲ ἢ μὴ καλῶς τραφὲν κ.τ.λ.*

19. οὐ γὰρ κ.τ.λ. Cp. 7 (5). 8. 1307 b 35, *παραλογίζεται γὰρ ἡ διάνοια ὑπ' αὐτῶν, ὥσπερ ὁ σοφιστικὸς λόγος· εἰ ἕκαστον μικρόν, καὶ πάντα. τοῦτο δ' ἔστι μὲν ὥς, ἔστι δ' ὡς οὔ· τὸ γὰρ ὅλον καὶ τὰ πάντα οὐ μικρόν, ἀλλὰ σύγκειται ἐκ μικρῶν*, and also Plato, Protag. 349 C.

24. ἡ μὲν οὖν πολιτεία (cp. *ἐν τῇ πολιτείᾳ*, 28) gives the title of Plato's *Πολιτεία* (mistranslated 'Republic') as we have it: so *τοὺς νόμους* 26 agrees with the title of the Laws. Aristotle's testimony supports not only the authenticity of both dialogues, but also that of their titles: cp. Athen. Deipn. 507 f, *οἱ δὲ συντεθέντες ὑπ' αὐτοῦ νόμοι καὶ τούτων ἔτι πρότερον ἡ πολιτεία τί πεποιήκασιν;* The plural, *αἱ πολιτεῖαι*, seems, however, to have been sometimes used: see note on 1260 b 12. The object of the criticisms on the Republic which we have been perusing is, we see from this sentence, in the main to point out *ἀπορίαι* enough in connexion with the work to show that there is still room for another attempt to depict a 'best constitution' (cp. 2. 1. 1260 b 32 sqq.). The same may be said of the somewhat grumbling criticism of the Laws which follows. Aristotle's real opinion of the two works must be gathered from the Politics as a whole; we shall best be able to gather it, if we note, as we have sought to do in vol. i, the points in which his political teaching and method depart from those of Plato.

C. 6. **26. Σχεδὸν δὲ παραπλησίως κ.τ.λ. . . . διό.** Giph. 'Reddit initio rationem, cur et in secundam Platonis Rempublicam disserat hanc: quia ut primae, item et secundae sua sint vitia et incommoda.' To study the rocks on which other voyagers have been wrecked is the best means of avoiding similar disasters. A further reason seems to be introduced by *καὶ γάρ* 28.

31. τῆς πολιτείας τὴν τάξιν. Probably not after *περί*, but acc. after *διώρικεν*. The expression seems to refer especially to the distribution of political power (cp. 2. 10. 1272 a 4: 3. 11. 1281 b 39: 7 (5). 7. 1307 b 18); thus in what follows we are told in what hands Plato has placed the supreme authority of the State.

33. τρίτον δ' ἐκ τούτων, 'and third recruited from these last' (i. e. from τὸ προπολεμοῦν μέρος): cp. Plato, Rep. 412 D, ἐκλεκτέον ἄρ' ἐκ τῶν ἄλλων φυλάκων τοιούτους ἄνδρας, οἳ ἂν κ.τ.λ. For the expression, cp. de Part. An. 2. 1. 646 a 20, δευτέρα δὲ σύστασις ἐκ τῶν πρώτων ἡ τῶν ὁμοιομερῶν φύσις: Plato, Laws 891 C, ψυχὴν δὲ ἐκ τούτων (earth, air, fire, and water) ὕστερον: Phileb. 27 B, πρῶτον μὲν τοίνυν ἄπειρον λέγω, δεύτερον δὲ πέρας, ἔπειτ' ἐκ τούτων τρίτον μικτὴν καὶ γεγενημένην οὐσίαν. For the identification of τὸ βουλευόμενον and τὸ κύριον, cp. 6 (4). 14. 1299 a 1.

34. περὶ δὲ . . . μή. 'Reapse haec non praetermissa esse a Platone invitus ipse testatur Aristoteles 6–10 et 31–34' (Sus.[1]). But perhaps the recognition of the first class as ἄρχοντες and of the second as τὸ προπολεμοῦν μέρος does not absolutely involve the denial of all office and all share in military service to the third class. That Aristotle did not understand Plato to have pronounced clearly for the denial of ὅπλα to the third class appears from c. 5. 1264 a 20 sq.

37. τὰς μὲν γυναῖκας κ.τ.λ. Plato, Rep. 451 E–452 A. Aristotle hints his surprise that Plato should say so little about the γεωργοί and τεχνῖται, and so much about the women.

39. τὰ δ' ἄλλα κ.τ.λ., 'but for the rest' (for τὰ ἄλλα, cp. 7 (5). 11. 1314 a 39: Plato, Rep. 403 B: Laws 763 E), 'we find that he has filled the dialogue with extraneous discussions' (cp. Demosth. de Cor. c. 9), 'and with discourse about the education of the guardians.' A somewhat similarly constructed sentence occurs in c. 11. 1273 a 9, ἃ δ' ἂν εἰσφέρωσιν οὗτοι, οὐ διακοῦσαι μόνον ἀποδιδόασι τῷ δήμῳ τὰ δόξαντα τοῖς ἄρχουσιν. What extraneous matters are here referred to? Among other things perhaps, as Sus. conjectures, 'illa quae 608 C–621 D de animorum immortalitate proponuntur,' but also probably the ethical discussions, such as that on justice, which Aristotle himself deals with in a separate treatise (cp. 4 (7). 1. 1323 b 39, ἑτέρας γάρ ἐστιν ἔργον σχολῆς ταῦτα). The same complaint as to extraneous matter in the Republic is made by Dio Chrysostom, Or. 7. 267 R. The juxtaposition of λόγοις and τὸν λόγον here is awkward, but not much more so than that of λέγεται and λεχθῆναι in de Gen. An. 2. 7. 746 b 7 sqq.

3. ταύτην βουλόμενος κ.τ.λ. 'Though wishing': cp. c. 5. 1265 a
1264 a 32. Κοινοτέραν ταῖς πόλεσι probably means, not 'having

more affinity to existing States,' but 'more suitable to them' or 'more within their reach': cp. 6 (4). 1. 1288 b 38, where (as Bonitz points out, Ind. 399 b 15 sqq.) *τὴν ῥᾴω καὶ κοινοτέραν ἁπάσαις* (*ταῖς πόλεσι πολιτείαν*) is apparently used in the same sense as *τὴν μάλιστα πάσαις ταῖς πόλεσιν ἁρμόττουσαν* 34. For the fact, cp. Laws 739 E.

4. εἰς. Cp. 3. 3. 1276 b 14, *ὅταν εἰς ἑτέραν μεταβάλλῃ πολιτείαν ἡ πόλις*, and 7 (5). 1. 1301 b 14 sq.

6. ἀποδίδωσιν. Cp. 6 (4). 11. 1296 a 40, *ταύτην ἀποδοῦναι τὴν τάξιν* (sc. *ταῖς πόλεσιν*): 2. 11. 1273 a 10: 2. 12. 1274 a 15 sq.

7. παιδείαν τὴν αὐτήν. The subjects of education prescribed in the two dialogues are much the same—*γυμναστική*, *μουσική*, arithmetic, geometry, astronomy; even dialectic reappears, for this study seems to be required in the Laws (965 B sqq.) of the members of the Nocturnal Council, as it is required of select individuals in the Republic. 'The main principles of education are essentially the same as in the Republic' (Zeller, Plato E. T. p. 542). But as the education prescribed in the Laws is in the main designed for the whole body of citizens and not for a few of them only, like that of the Republic, it must probably be intended by Plato to be less arduous and exacting.

τὸ . . . ζῆν. 'Plat. Legg. 741 E: 806 D–807 D: 842 D: 846 D: 919 D sq.' (Sus.[1]).

8. καὶ . . . γυναικῶν. 'Plat. Legg. 780 D sqq.: 806 E: cf. 842 B' (Sus.[1]). We are not expressly told in the Republic that women are to take part in the syssitia, though, as Sus. remarks (Sus.[2], Note 153), they are probably intended to do so, but in the Laws this is distinctly insisted upon. Giph., however (p. 194), takes Aristotle's meaning to be, that while in the Republic men and women are intended to take their meals at the same tables, in the Laws separate mess-tables are instituted for women. The notion of syssitia for women would be all the more surprising to Greeks, as one name for the syssitia was Andreia and the institution was regarded as an essentially military one (Hdt. 1. 65).

9. τὴν μέν. 'He makes to consist' seems to be suppressed, unless we suppose *φησὶ δεῖν εἶναι* to be carried on, which is perhaps less likely.

χιλίων. Cp. Rep. 423 A, *ὡς ἀληθῶς μεγίστη, καὶ ἐὰν μόνον ᾖ χιλίων τῶν προπολεμούντων*. For the total of the citizens of the Republic, the number of the first class and that of the third (far the largest) must be added.

10. πεντακισχιλίων. 'Accuratius *πεντακισχιλίων καὶ τετταράκοντα*, v. Plat. Legg. 737 E: 740 C sq.: 745 B sqq. etc.' (Sus.[1]).

μὲν οὖν, 'it is true that,' as in 17. We pass with *μὲν οὖν* from description to criticism, as in c. 10. 1272 a 12.

11. περιττόν, 'uncommon, out of the common,' but no English word adequately translates it. The epithet suggests an aspiring wisdom which follows paths of its own—which has something of greatness, but also of superfluity: cp. 5 (8). 2. 1337 a 42, 2. 8. 1267 b 24, and *περιεργότερον*, 25. So *περιττὴ τῶν ἄλλων*, Poet. 24. 1459 b 36 seems to be represented by *σεμνὸν καὶ αὔθαδες*, Rhet. 3. 3. 1406 b 3 (Vahlen, Beitr. zu Poet. 3. 291: Bon. Ind. 585 a 59). *Περιττός* is often joined with *ἴδιος*, but is less wide and more subtle in meaning.

τοῦ Σωκράτους. Aristotle identifies with Socrates the *Ἀθηναῖος ξένος* of the Laws. Grote (Plato 3. 301 n.) conjectures that the latter name was preferred by Plato to avoid the difficulty of implying the presence of Socrates in Crete. In c. 7. 1266 b 5 we have *Πλάτων δὲ τοὺς νόμους γράφων*, and in c. 9. 1271 b 1, *ὅπερ καὶ Πλάτων ἐν τοῖς νόμοις ἐπιτετίμηκεν*.

12. κομψόν, 'clever,' opposed to *ἁπλουστέρως* in de Caelo 3. 5. 304 a 13: to *ἱκανῶς* in Pol. 6 (4). 4. 1291 a 11.

καινοτόμον, 'novelty of view,' cp. c. 7. 1266 a 35.

ζητητικόν, 'the spirit of inquiry'—love of inquiry and keenness in inquiry.

καλῶς δὲ πάντα, sc. *ἔχειν*: see Bon. Ind. 306 a 16.

13. καί introduces an instance of *πάντα*: cp. *ὥσπερ καὶ Ἄμασις*, 1. 12. 1259 b 8.

πλῆθος. For the acc. cp. c. 9. 1271 a 9, and see Dr. Holden's note on Xen. Oecon. 13. 3, *τὰ ἔργα μάθῃ ὡς ἔστιν ἐργαστέα*. In the criticisms on constitutions contained in the Second Book Aristotle commonly notices first, or at any rate before he has gone very far, their arrangements with respect to what he terms in the Fourth Book the *ὑποθέσεις* of the State—the number of the citizens and the extent of the territory (cp. 4 (7). 4. 1325 b 38, *διὸ δεῖ πολλὰ προϋποτεθεῖσθαι καθάπερ εὐχομένους, εἶναι μέντοι μηδὲν τούτων ἀδύνατον· λέγω δὲ οἷον περί τε πλήθους πολιτῶν καὶ χώρας*).

14. Βαβυλωνίας. Cp. 3. 3. 1276 a 28.

15. Yet the territory of the Spartans (is Aristotle thinking of his own time, when Messenia had been lost?) is said in 2. 9. 1270 a 29 to be capable of supporting 30,000 hoplites and 1500 horsemen, who, if Spartans, would be *ἀργοί*. But perhaps this is not present to Aristotle's mind. He does not probably mean to assert that it would be capable of supporting 31,500 *ἀργοί*. See note on 1270 a 29.

16. θρέψονται. See note on *στερήσονται*, 1263 b 28.

17. μὲν οὖν (here answered by *μέντοι*, as in 1257 a 28 and 1259 a 28) prepares the way for and helps to emphasize the correction introduced by *μέντοι*. 'True, it is right to presuppose freely, but one must not presuppose anything impossible.' Plato had, in effect, said much the same thing (Laws 709 D: 742 E: Rep. 456 C). Aristotle repeats this remark in 4 (7). 4. 1325 b 38, without any indication that he is conscious of the repetition.

18. λέγεται. 'Expressis quidem verbis hoc non fit in Legibus Platonicis, sed recte hanc sententiam e iv. p. 704–709 et v. p. 747 D eruere potuit Aristoteles' (Sus.[1]). Add 625 C sqq. and 842 C–E. In Laws 705 D–E the Cretan laws are censured for looking only to war (i. e. *πρὸς τοὺς γειτνιῶντας τόπους*), whereas the Athenian Stranger claims that he legislates looking to nothing but the virtue of his citizens. For this reason he dispenses with a fleet. Aristotle does not approve of this (cp. 4 (7). 6. 1327 a 21 sqq.). If, as Susemihl following Schlosser points out (Sus.[2], Note 204), Plato pays regard to considerations of defence against neighbours in fixing the number of the citizens (Laws 737 C–D: cp. 628 D), Aristotle would no doubt ask why he does not keep them in view when dealing with other matters. See also c. 7. 1267 a 17 sqq. and 6 (4). 4. 1291 a 6–22.

22. πολιτικόν, i. e. a life of intercourse with other States: cp. 4 (7). 6. 1327 b 3 sqq., where we have *ἡγεμονικὸν καὶ πολιτικὸν βίον*.

τοιούτοις . . . ἅ. Cp. c. 7. 1266 b 36: 1267 a 24.

23. ὅπλοις. Is there not a reference here to Plato, Laws 625 C sqq., where the Cretan lawgiver is said to have chosen for the Cretans such arms as were most suitable to swift runners in a hilly country like Crete—bows and arrows, in fact? Aristotle urges that the arms used by a nation should be such as to enable it not only to cope with its foes in its own territory, but also to retaliate on them in theirs, which bows and arrows would not enable it to do. He dwells elsewhere on the importance of a fleet for this purpose (4 (7). 6. 1327 a 23 sqq.).

28. καὶ τὸ πλῆθος δὲ κ.τ.λ. The connexion of this with what precedes is illustrated by the similar sequence of topics in c. 7. 1267 a 17–27. The amount of the collective wealth, no less than the nature of the *ὅπλα* at the command of the State, must be fixed in relation to perils from without. The verb after *μήποτε* is suppressed and 'must be supplied in the indicative, not the subjunctive, as the idea of "warding off" (Abwehr) is here absent' (Weber, Die Absichtssätze bei Aristoteles, p. 17).

29. βέλτιον κ.τ.λ. Τῷ σαφῶς μᾶλλον explains ἑτέρως—'in a way which differs through being clearer': cp. de Part. An. 4. 5. 681 a 18, ἕτερα τοιαῦτ' ἐν τῇ θαλάττῃ μικρὸν διαφέρει τούτων τῷ ἀπολελύσθαι. Lamb. 'aliter definire, hoc est, planius atque apertius.' Bern. however seems to take it as explaining βέλτιον: 'ob nicht vielleicht eine andere Begrenzung besser, weil deutlicher, ist.'

30. φησι. Cp. Laws 737 D. Ephorus also (ap. Strab. p. 480) had praised the Cretans for living σωφρόνως καὶ λιτῶς. I do not feel the difficulty which Susemihl follows others in raising (see Sus.[2], Critical Note, and Qu. Crit. p. 368 sq.) with regard to τοῦτο—ζῆν at all as strongly as he does. Aristotle makes two objections to Plato's ὅρος—1. that it is too vague and fails to enlighten: 2. that it tends to mislead. For other instances in which μᾶλλον is used in the sense of λίαν, see Bon. Ind. 445 a 1 sqq. In de Gen. An. 2. 8. 748 a 7 we have, οὗτος μὲν οὖν ὁ λόγος καθόλου λίαν καὶ κενός. Τοῦτο—ζῆν gives the reason for Aristotle's suggestion in 28 sq. that a clearer definition should be substituted.

33. σωφρόνως καὶ ἐλευθερίως. Cp. 4 (7). 5. 1326 b 30 sqq., a passage which shows that Aristotle intended fully to discuss in a later part of his work the question of the true mode of using property.

χωρὶς γὰρ κ.τ.λ., 'for if we part the one from the other, liberal living will accompany luxurious life, and temperate living a life of hardship.' For ἀκολουθεῖν as here used, Bonitz (Ind. 26 a 44) compares 3. 13. 1285 a 39 and Eth. Eud. 3. 5. 1232 a 31. Cp. also Theopomp. fragm. 110 (Müller, Fr. Hist. Gr. 1. 295), τῶν ἀγαθῶν καὶ τῶν κακῶν οὐδὲν αὐτὸ καθ' αὑτὸ παραγίγνεται τοῖς ἀνθρώποις, ἀλλὰ συντέτακται καὶ συνακολουθεῖ τοῖς μὲν πλούτοις καὶ ταῖς δυναστείαις ἄνοια, καὶ μετὰ ταύτην ἀκολασία, ταῖς δ' ἐνδείαις καὶ ταῖς ταπεινότησι σωφροσύνη καὶ μετριότης. In c. 7. 1266 b 26 and in 4 (7). 5. 1326 b 37 sqq. the alternative to τρυφᾶν is γλίσχρως, not ἐπιπόνως, ζῆν.

34. τῷ ἐπιπόνως, sc. ζῆν, suppressed as already implicitly expressed in τρυφᾶν (cp. 1. 11. 1258 b 19).

35. ἕξεις αἱρεταί (see critical note and cp. Eth. Nic. 6. 13. 1144 a 1 sq.) is a wider term than ἀρεταί: ἐγκράτεια (e.g.) is a σπουδαία ἕξις, but not an ἀρετή in the strict sense of the word (see the references in Zeller, Gr. Ph. 2. 2. 627. 2). Those who reject Victorius' conjecture of αἱρεταί for ἀρεταί, which is the reading of all the MSS., and prefer to strike out one of the two words ἕξεις and ἀρεταί, should probably strike out the former, for the illustrations which follow (35 sq.) show that good ἕξεις are alone referred to.

37. τὰς χρήσεις, i. e. τὰς ἐνεργείας, in contradistinction to τὰς ἕξεις (see Bon. Ind. 854 b 37 sqq. for instances of this use of the word). Here also Aristotle would seem to refer to commendable χρήσεις only.

38. τὰς κτήσεις, 'landed property,' as in 4 (7). 9. 1329 a 18. Plato does not equalize all kinds of property (cp. 1265 b 22). The lots of land, however, are evidently intended by him to be equal or virtually equal (Laws 737).

39. κατασκευάζειν, 'de placitis philosophicis (cf. ποιεῖν, τίθεσθαι) dicitur,' Bon. Ind. 374 b 17 sq.

ἀφεῖναι κ.τ.λ. It is not the case that Plato trusts to ἀτεκνία alone to maintain the numbers of his citizen-body unaltered: see Laws 740 D–E, 923 D. Aristotle, however, desires a limitation of τεκνοποιία: he wishes the State to fix a definite number of children, not to be exceeded, in the case of every marriage (4 (7). 16. 1335 b 22). Aristotle must be quite aware that Plato intends to fix the number of citizens in the Laws, but he appears to think that Plato takes no effectual means to secure that the number named shall not be exceeded.

40. ἂν ὁμαλισθησομένην. On ἂν with the Future Participle, see Goodwin, Moods and Tenses, § 41. 4. Madvig (Adversaria Critica 1. 463) would read ἀνομαλισθησομένην, but this verb appears only to occur elsewhere in a single passage, Rhet. 3. 11. 1412 a 16, καὶ τὸ ἀνωμαλίσθαι τὰς πόλεις.

41. διὰ τὰς ἀτεκνίας, 'by means of': see note on 1263 b 36.

1265 b. **1. ὅτι δοκεῖ κ.τ.λ.** Plato does not give this reason. The fact mentioned by Aristotle is interesting.

δεῖ δὲ κ.τ.λ., 'this stationariness of numbers will need to be maintained with greater accuracy in the State of the Laws than it is now,' for in this State those over the right number will be starved, which now is not the case. This remark was perhaps suggested by an observation in the Laws (928 E)—ἐν μὲν οὖν ἄλλῃ πολιτείᾳ παῖς ἀποκεκηρυγμένος οὐκ ἂν ἐξ ἀνάγκης ἄπολις εἴη, ταύτης δέ, ἧς οἵδε οἱ νόμοι ἔσονται, ἀναγκαίως ἔχει εἰς ἄλλην χώραν ἐξοικίζεσθαι τὸν ἀπάτορα· πρὸς γὰρ τοῖς τετταράκοντα καὶ πεντακισχιλίοις οἴκοις οὐκ ἔστιν ἕνα προσγενέσθαι.

3. ἀπορεῖ, 'is destitute' (cp. μηδὲν ἔχειν 5).

For **μερίζεσθαι τὰς οὐσίας εἰς ὁποσονοῦν πλῆθος**, where εἰς seems to be used of the recipients, cp. c. 9. 1270 a 18, εἰς ὀλίγους ἧκεν ἡ χώρα, and de Part. An. 3. 3. 664 a 27 sq.

4. ἀδιαιρέτων, indivisible by testation (Laws 740 B): by sale (741 B): in other ways (742 C): not divisible even by the action of the State (855 A sq.: 856 D–E: 909 C sq.: 877 D).

τοὺς παράζυγας, 'eos qui praeter numerum et extra ordinem accessissent' Lamb. (cp. *τοῖς περιγενομένοις*, Laws 740 D).

7. τὴν τεκνοποιίαν, 'reproductive intercourse.' Compare on this subject 4 (7). 16. 1335 b 22 sq.

10. τῶν ἄλλων, i.e. other than *τῶν γεννησάντων* implied in *τῶν γεννηθέντων*.

If with P[1] Π[2] Bekk. we read **ταῖς πλείσταις**, we must infer that in some States a check of some kind on the procreation of children existed. Aristotle's suggestion in 7–10 much resembles that of Plato, Rep. 460 A, *τὸ δὲ πλῆθος τῶν γάμων ἐπὶ τοῖς ἄρχουσι ποιήσομεν, ἵν' ὡς μάλιστα διασῴζωσι τὸν αὐτὸν ἀριθμὸν τῶν ἀνδρῶν, πρὸς πολέμους τε καὶ νόσους καὶ πάντα τὰ τοιαῦτα ἀποσκοποῦντες*.

12. κακουργίαν. Vict. 'alii autem in minutioribus rebus exercent malitiam suam, qui multis locis in his libris vocantur ab ipso *κακοῦργοι*, id est, fraudulenti.' *Κακοῦργοι* and *μικροπόνηροι* are conjoined, it is true, in 6 (4). 11. 1295 b 10, and contrasted with *ὑβρισταὶ καὶ μεγαλοπόνηροι* (cp. Rhet. 2. 16. 1391 a 18), but in Pol. 7 (5). 8. 1308 a 19 the malpractices ending in tyranny which long terms of office favour are spoken of by this name, and these cannot be said to be 'in minutioribus rebus.' 'Knavery' perhaps comes near the meaning. For the thought here expressed, Sus.[2] compares c. 7. 1266 b 13 (cp. also Isocr. Areopag. § 44); yet Aristotle seems to make less of this danger in 7 (5). 12. 1316 b 18 sqq.

Φείδων μὲν οὖν κ.τ.λ. 'Pheidon, in fact.' Here, as in *ἔνιοι μὲν οὖν*, 1265 b 33 sqq., and also in 3. 5. 1278 a 6 sq., *μὲν οὖν* introduces a confirmation of what has preceded, in order to emphasize the sentence introduced by *δέ*. The arrangements of the Laws are said to be the opposite of those of Pheidon, because Pheidon, though careless as to the equality of the lots, fixed for ever both the number of households in his city and the number of citizens, whereas Plato equalizes the lots and fixes the number of households, but does not effectually fix the number of citizens (cp. 1265 a 38, *ἄτοπον δὲ καὶ τὸ τὰς κτήσεις ἰσάζοντα τὸ περὶ τὸ πλῆθος τῶν πολιτῶν μὴ κατασκευάζειν, ἀλλ' ἀφεῖναι τὴν τεκνοποιίαν ἀόριστον*). Under Pheidon's scheme no pauper citizens would exist: Plato, on the contrary, takes no effectual means for preventing their existence. Is Pheidon's early date mentioned to indicate surprise that Plato took no better means than he did of preventing the existence of paupers within the citizen-body? If Pheidon legislated for Corinth, we can understand how it came to send forth so many colonies in early days. Aristotle would go farther, however, than Pheidon; he would not be content with excluding the over-plus from citizenship, but would prevent it from coming into existence. Ὁ Κορίνθιος is probably added to distinguish this Pheidon from the better known tyrant of Argos (7 (5). 10. 1310 b 26). Compare with the aims of Pheidon those of Philolaus, who also was a Corinthian (c. 12. 1274 b 4 sq.). We learn from Isaeus de Apollodori Hereditate § 30 (quoted by Caillemer, Succession légitime à Athènes, p. 133), that the Attic law required the Archon to take care that no house was left without a representative (*καὶ οὐ μόνον ἰδίᾳ ταῦτα γινώσκουσιν, ἀλλὰ καὶ δημοσίᾳ τὸ κοινὸν τῆς πόλεως οὕτω ταῦτ' ἔγνωκε· νόμῳ γὰρ τῷ ἄρχοντι τῶν οἴκων, ὅπως ἂν μὴ ἐξερημῶνται, προστάττει τὴν ἐπιμέλειαν*). But Pheidon went much further than this; he fixed not only the number of households, but also the number of the lots and the number of the citizens. Lycurgus is conceived to have fixed the number of households and lots in Plutarch, Agis 5. 1.

13. ὢν νομοθέτης τῶν ἀρχαιοτάτων. For the gen. see Jelf, Gr. Gr. § 533. 1.

14. οἴκους, used of households especially as owning property: see Boeckh, Public Economy of Athens, E. T. p. 142 n. (who refers to Xen. Oecon. 1. 4–5), and Holden's Index to the Oeconomicus, p. 95*. Here perhaps something of this meaning is present; elsewhere, however, e.g. in 1. 7. 1255 b 19 and 1. 2. 1252 b 14, the difference between *οἶκος* and *οἰκία* seems hardly traceable.

ἴσους, 'as they originally were'? or 'at their original number'? If the former, the primitive distribution of property, as well as the primitive number of households, would be stereotyped; if the latter, only the primitive number of households. Perhaps this is all that is meant.

15. ἀνίσους . . . κατὰ μέγεθος. For the severance, cp. de Part. An. 4. 8. 683 b 28, *τούτων δ' ἑκάστου πλείω εἴδη ἐστὶ διαφέροντα οὐ μόνον κατὰ τὴν μορφὴν ἀλλὰ καὶ κατὰ τὸ μέγεθος πολύ*, and see below on 1265 b 29.

16. τοῖς νόμοις τούτοις recurs in 18, and also in 1266 a 1.

τοὐναντίον. See above on 12.

17. ὕστερον, 4 (7). 10. 1330 a 2–23: 4 (7). 16. 1335 b 19–26 (Sus.[3]).

18. ἐλλέλειπται δὲ κ.τ.λ. At first sight it seems surprising that Aristotle digresses here to the subject of *οἱ ἄρχοντες* from that of the property and numbers of the citizens, with which he has been dealing, for he returns to the subject of their property in 21, but the reason for this is that he has just been mentioning an omission (a 38–b 17), the omission to regulate *τεκνοποιία*, and now he has another omission to mention, the omission to explain distinctly in what way the rulers are to be different from the ruled. Hence the *καί* before *τὰ περὶ τοὺς ἄρχοντας*.

19. ὅπως. So Π² Bekk.: Ms P¹ *πῶς*. In either case 'how' will be the translation. Giph. (p. 201): 'hoc tantum Plato ... magistratus privatis antecellere et meliores esse debere, universe et confuse, similitudine suo more adhibita, monuit.' Aristotle would have been glad if Plato had spoken more definitely and in detail on this subject.

ἔσονται διαφέροντες. See above on 1259 b 11.

φησί. 'Plato, Legg. 734 E: non tamen prorsus neglegere debuit Aristoteles quae Plato disseruit 961 A sq.: 951 E sqq.' (Sus.¹). Some few of the citizens are to receive a more scientific training in arithmetic, geometry, and astronomy than the rest (Laws 818 A). In 632 C we find the guardians of the State described as of two kinds—*φύλακας ἐπιστήσει, τοὺς μὲν διὰ φρονήσεως, τοὺς δὲ δι' ἀληθοῦς δόξης ἰόντας*—so that even the 'warp' of the State will apparently be of two textures, and this is confirmed by 961 A sq. and 951 E sqq.

20. τῆς κρόκης, called *ἐφυφή* in Laws 734 E.

21. For the repetition of **δεῖν**, compare the repetition of *δῆλον* in 3. 13. 1283 b 16 sqq., of *ἔργον* in 8 (6). 5. 1319 b 33 sqq., and the addition of *ἅτερος* in 7 (5). 4. 1304 a 16 and *ἐκεῖνον* in 7 (5). 10. 1312 b 17. See also above on 1261 b 8.

22. πενταπλασίας. Sepulv. p. 43 b—'mirum est Aristotelem ad quintuplum dicere, cum in libro quinto de legibus Plato ad quadruplum dicat, nisi forte, quod suspicor, vitio librariorum factum est ut in Aristotelicis exemplaribus *πενταπλασίας* scriptum sit pro *τετραπλασίας*': Sus.¹—'immo *τετραπλασίας*, v. Plat. Legg. 744 E, cf. 754 D sqq.: errorem ipsius Aristotelis esse, non librariorum, inde apparet quod idem repetitur 7. 1266 b 5 sqq.' Plato's words, Laws 744 E, are—*μέτρον δὲ αὐτὸν* (i. e. *τὸν ὅρον* = *τὴν τοῦ κλήρου τιμήν*) *θέμενος ὁ νομοθέτης διπλάσιον ἐάσει τούτου κτᾶσθαι καὶ τριπλάσιον καὶ μέχρι τετραπλασίου*. He would seem therefore, as Prof. Jowett points out (Politics of Aristotle 2. 1. 63), to permit the acquisition of property four times the value of the lot in addition to the lot, so that the richest man in the State would be, as Aristotle says (c. 7. 1266 b 5 sqq.), five times as rich as the poorest, who has nothing but the lot. The passage 754 D sqq., to which Sus. refers, does not seem to bear on the subject, if Stallbaum's interpretation of it is correct. **Μείζονα** 22 appears (cp. *τῆς ἐλαχίστης*, 1266 b 6) to mean 'greater than the minimum with which every citizen starts' (i. e. the lot).

23. διὰ τί κ.τ.λ. 'Why should not an increase be allowed in respect of land up to a certain point?' The answer is 'because if a citizen were allowed to add to his landed property, what he gains other citizens must lose; their lots must pass from them or be diminished, and thus, besides an infraction of the laws, the main security against pauperism within the citizen-body, itself. not complete (cp. 1265 b 4 sq.), would be still further weakened.'

25. συμφέρει. Eucken de Partic. Usu p. 58: 'particula ita adhibita (i. e. in oratione obliqua) vulgo cum indicativo construitur, ita ut μή indicet eum qui dicat expectare ut affirmetur sententia, μὴ οὐ ut negetur—cf. Pol. 5 (8). 5. 1339 b 42: Phys. 8. 6. 259 b 3: Eth. Nic. 8. 9. 1159 a 6.' Some MSS. (not the best) have συμφέρῃ, and it is possible that the Vet. Int. ('ne forte non expediat') found it in his Greek text. The subjunctive occurs in this construction in only four other passages of Aristotle, if we exclude the Rhetorica ad Alexandrum: these are Rhet. 2. 20. 1393 b 19: Top. 6. 9. 147 a 21: Metaph. M. 4. 1079 b 6: Metaph. N. 3. 1090 b 8 (Weber, Die Absichtssätze bei Aristoteles, p. 16: see also Eucken, *ubi supra*).

ἔνειμε. 'Plat. Legg. 745 E: 775 E sqq., cf. 848: at mirum est hoc loco idem in Platone ab Aristotele reprehendi, quod ipse instituit, 4 (7). 10. 1330 a 14 sqq.' (Sus.[1]). But Aristotle's words in that passage are δύο κλήρων ἑκάστῳ νεμηθέντων—two lots, not necessarily two houses. The object of Plato in this arrangement seems to have been to provide a means of settling the married son in a separate household of his own (Laws 776 A). Aristotle would probably approve the separation, but perhaps in his State there would be little need for the arrangement, for if the father were 37 years of age when he married, and the son waited to marry till he was 37, he would not be very likely to marry in his father's lifetime. At any rate, Aristotle does not provide for the contingency in what we have of the Politics.

26. διελὼν χωρίς. Vict. 'distinctas separatasque.'

χαλεπὸν δὲ οἰκίας δύο οἰκεῖν. Cp. Demosth. in Boeot. de Nomine, c. 26, εἰ γὰρ οὕτω δαπανηρὸς ἦν ὥστε γάμῳ γεγαμηκὼς τὴν ἐμὴν μητέρα ἑτέραν εἶχε γυναῖκα, ἧς ὑμεῖς ἐστέ, καὶ δύ' οἰκίας ᾤκει, πῶς ἂν ἀργύριον τοιοῦτος ὢν κατέλιπεν;

26 sqq. Here Aristotle passes from the subject of the citizens, their numbers and property, to that of the constitution. His objections to the constitution described in the Laws are as follows. It is not the next best after that which Plato places first, for it aims at being a polity, which is a constitution compounded of two constitutions, whereas an ἀριστοκρατία like the Lacedaemonian, which is compounded of three, is better. Nor again (1266 a 5 sqq.) does it answer to Plato's own account of the best constitution, for this is compounded, according to him, of monarchy and democracy, whereas the constitution of the Laws is a mixture of oligarchy and democracy and leans rather to oligarchy.

27. βούλεται μέν. This μέν appears to emphasize βούλεται and to imply that success is not attained; we see, however, from 1266 a 7, μᾶλλον δ' ἐγκλίνειν βούλεται πρὸς τὴν ὀλιγαρχίαν, that, in Aristotle's view, the constitution of the Laws hardly remains true even in aim to a midway course between oligarchy and democracy.

28. ἐκ γὰρ κ.τ.λ. Cp. 3. 7. 1279 b 1. See Laws 753 B. Ἐστίν, sc. ἡ σύνταξις ὅλη.

29. εἰ μὲν οὖν κ.τ.λ. Μὲν οὖν ('now while') here introduces an admission which does not exclude, but rather lends fresh emphasis to, a coming criticism introduced by δέ. Translate: 'now while, if his view in constructing (1265 a 39) this constitution is that it is the constitution most readily attainable by States.' Ὡς κοινοτάτην must be taken with ταῖς πόλεσι and with πολιτείαν. For the severance of πολιτείαν from ὡς κοινοτάτην, cp. 2. 2. 1261 a 15, and see above on 1255 a 21. For κοινοτάτην τῶν ἄλλων, see Bon. Ind. 403 a 3 sq. ('superlativus comparativi vim in se continet, ita ut vel ipse coniungatur cum genetivo comparativo').

31. εἰ δ' ὡς κ.τ.λ. This is Plato's meaning (Laws 739 E, ἀθανασίας ἐγγύτατα καὶ ἡ μία δευτέρως). 'Ita tamen cum Platone agit Aristoteles, ut videatur id compertum se non habere; hoc autem facit, ut aequior ipsi videatur' (Vict.). For τὴν πρώτην πολιτείαν, cp. Laws 739 B.

33. ἀριστοκρατικωτέραν, 'more aristocratic than the State of the Laws' is probably the meaning, not than the Lacedaemonian State. Aristotle is inclined to regard the State of the Laws as leaning too much to oligarchy (1266 a 7).

ἔνιοι μὲν οὖν, 'some, in fact': see note on 1265 b 12. Who these inquirers were, is not known; they seem to have recognized only three constitutions, monarchy, oligarchy, and democracy; neither Socrates nor Plato, therefore, can well be referred to, though Plato (Laws 691 C–693 E: cp. 773 C–D) praises the Lacedaemonian constitution for tempering the 'strong wine' of royalty with a senate representing age and sobriety, and with the Ephorate representing the democratic principle of the lot or something like it. There is a nearer approach to the views of these ἔνιοι in the doubt expressed by Megillus, the Spartan interlocutor in the Laws (712 D), whether to call the Lacedaemonian constitution a tyranny (because of the Ephorate) or a democracy or an aristocracy or a kingship. On the difference between their conception of mixed government and that of Aristotle something has already been said, vol. i. p. 264, and above, p. xiii. Whether Aristotle agrees with them in regarding the senate as an oligarchical element in the constitution, is not quite clear, for though in 7 (5). 6. 1306 a 18 sq. he describes the mode of electing the senators as *δυναστευτική*, he elsewhere says of the senate, *ἆθλον ἡ ἀρχὴ αὕτη τῆς ἀρετῆς ἐστίν* (2. 9. 1270 b 24). He clearly, however, did not agree with them in their view that the Lacedaemonian constitution was a mixture of monarchy, oligarchy, and democracy, for he speaks of it as a mixture of virtue (or aristocracy) and democracy in 6 (4). 7. 1293 b 16 sq. With the passage before us 6 (4). 9. 1294 b 18–34 should be compared, where other grounds for finding a democratical and an oligarchical element in this constitution are mentioned.

38. δημοκρατεῖσθαι. Bonitz remarks on this passage (Ind. 174 b 54), 'ubi subiectum non additur, *δημοκρατεῖσθαι* non multum differt a *δημοκρατίαν εἶναι*,' and he refers to 40 and to 7 (5). 1. 1301 b 16. It is not, however, quite certain that *τὴν πολιτείαν* should not be supplied: cp. 2. 11. 1273 a 41, where Π[1] are probably right in reading *ταύτην οὐχ οἷόν τε βεβαίως ἀριστοκρατεῖσθαι τὴν πολιτείαν*, and 7 (5). 1. 1301 b 14 sqq.

39. κατά, 'in respect of': cp. *τῶν κατ' ἀρετὴν ἡγεμονικῶν*, 3. 17. 1288 a 11.

ἐκ τοῦ δήμου. For this mention of a demos in the Lacedaemonian State, cp. c. 9. 1270 b 8, 18, 25: 6 (4). 9. 1294 b 30. It is not meant that the ephors were always taken from the demos, but that all citizens were eligible (cp. c. 9. 1270 b 25, *καθίσταται γὰρ ἐξ ἁπάντων*). As to the distinction between 'people' (or *οἱ τυχόντες*, c. 9. 1270 b 29) and *καλοὶ κἀγαθοί* (1270 b 24), see Schömann, Opusc. Acad. 1. 108 sqq.: 'non Homoeos illis qui *ὑπομείονες* erant opponit, sed in ipsis Homoeis alios *καλοὺς κἀγαθοὺς* esse innuit, alios autem in quos haec appellatio non conveniat . . . Dignitatis tantum atque existimationis discrimen est' (p. 138). See 6 (4) 9. 1294 b 29 sq.

40. δημοκρατεῖσθαι δέ. Cp. c. 9. 1271 a 32: 6 (4). 9. 1294 b 19 sqq.: 6 (4). 5. 1292 b 11 sqq. Cp. also Isocr. Areopag. § 61: Thuc. 1. 6. 4.

1266 a. **1. ἐν δὲ κ.τ.λ.** 'Aristotle understands this last principle' (that the best constitution should be a compound of monarchy and democracy) 'somewhat differently from what Plato seems to have intended' (Grote, Plato 3. 363 n.). Plato says (Laws 693 D) that μοναρχία (not τυραννίς) and δημοκρατία are the two mother-forms of constitution, Persia being an extreme example of the former, and Athens of the latter: δεῖ δὴ οὖν καὶ ἀναγκαῖον μεταλαβεῖν ἀμφοῖν τούτοιν, εἴπερ ἐλευθερία τ' ἔσται καὶ φιλία μετὰ φρονήσεως: that is to say, a good constitution should partake of each of the two mother-forms (not of their extreme phases), or as he expresses it in 692 A, the fiery self-willed strength of birth (ἡ κατὰ γένος αὐθάδης ῥώμη) must be tempered by the sobriety of age and checked by an approach to the principle of the lot. In other words, the force of authoritative hereditary government and the tempering element of freedom ought to find a place in every good State. It is doubtful from the sequel whether Plato intended to represent monarchy, even in its milder form, as an essential ingredient. Thus in Laws 756 E he describes his scheme for the election of councillors as 'a mode of election midway between monarchy and democracy,' though it is hard to see anything in it which could in strictness be called monarchical. He certainly never meant that a good State must be an union of tyranny and extreme democracy, of which forms alone it could be said that they are the worst of constitutions or not constitutions at all. Aristotle here seems to confound democracy with extreme democracy, for he elsewhere speaks of democracy in general as the least bad of the παρεκβάσεις (Eth. Nic. 8. 12. 1160 b 19: Pol. 6 (4). 2. 1289 b 4 sqq.).

δέον. It is possible that ἐστί should be supplied with δέον here, as in Eth. Nic. 2. 7. 1107 a 32 and 7. 3. 1145 b 28. Bonitz, however, is apparently inclined to emend the latter passage and to adopt a different reading from that of Bekker in the former (see Ind. 168 a 50 sqq.).

3. As to tyranny, cp. 6 (4). 8. 1293 b 28 sq.: 6 (4). 2. 1289 b 2. Aristotle must refer, as has been said already, to the extreme democracy (cp. 6 (4). 14. 1298 a 31: 7 (5). 10. 1312 b 36), which is called in 6 (4). 14. 1298 b 14 ἡ μάλιστ' εἶναι δοκοῦσα δημοκρατία, but he nowhere else seems to treat the extreme democracy as worse than the extreme oligarchy: both are διαιρεταὶ τυραννίδες, 7 (5). 10. 1312 b 37.

4. ἡ γὰρ κ.τ.λ. The ἀριστοκρατία, which is a mixture of οἱ εὔποροι, οἱ ἄποροι, and οἱ καλοὶ κἀγαθοί, or of πλοῦτος, ἐλευθερία, and ἀρετή, is superior to the polity, which combines only οἱ εὔποροι and οἱ ἄποροι (πλοῦτος and ἐλευθερία): cp. 6 (4). 8. 1294 a 15: 7 (5). 7. 1307 a 7 sqq. Each of the three elements—πλοῦτος, ἐλευθερία, ἀρετή—is the ὅρος of a constitution (1294 a 10): hence the ἀριστοκρατία may be said to combine three constitutions. It is true that a constitution combining only two of the three elements is admitted (6 (4). 7. 1293 b 16) to be ἀριστοκρατική, but this is not Aristotle's usual account of the ἀριστοκρατία. Susemihl, following Riese, brackets ἡ γὰρ—βελτίων: he is inclined, indeed, to question with Schmidt the authenticity of the whole passage 1265 b 29, εἰ—1266 a 6, δημοκρατικά (Qu. Crit. p. 370). His reason for bracketing ἡ γὰρ—βελτίων is that the view expressed in this clause cannot have been held by Aristotle, who would regard, for instance, a combination of aristocracy and democracy, or even of oligarchy and democracy, as better than a combination of oligarchy, democracy, and tyranny (Sus.[2], Note 222). The clause seems certainly open to this objection, but perhaps the contrast present to Aristotle's mind is that which he has just drawn between an ἀριστοκρατία like the Lacedaemonian and a polity like that of Plato's Laws.

5. οὐδ' ἔχουσα φαίνεται. See note on 1261 a 9.

7. τὴν ὀλιγαρχίαν, as in c. 11. 1273 a 22 (contrast 1273 a 6).

9. ἐξ αἱρετῶν κληρωτούς. 'In the appointment of members of the Boulê, of the astynomi, and of the judges of competitions, Laws 756 B–E: 763 D sq.: 765 B–D' (Sus.[2], Note 223). As to κοινὸν ἀμφοῖν, cp. 6 (4). 9. 1294 b 6 sqq.

10. ἐκκλησιάζειν. 'Plato, Legg. 764 A,' Sus.[1]—compulsory for the first and second classes only. See 6 (4). 13. 1297 a 17 sqq., where provisions of this nature are reckoned among ὀλιγαρχικὰ σοφίσματα τῆς νομοθεσίας.

φέρειν ἄρχοντας. 'In reality, only in the election of the judges of gymnastic competitions (Laws 765 C), and also of the Boulê (Laws 756 B–E), and Aristotle has not yet come to the subject of the Boulê' (Sus.[2], Note 225).

11. τοῦτο δέ takes up τὸ δὲ κ.τ.λ.: see Bon. Ind. 166 b 58 sqq.

12. καὶ τὸ πειρᾶσθαι κ.τ.λ. So the astynomi and agoranomi must belong to the first or second class (763 D–E); the three hundred names from which the Nomophylakes are selected are to be chosen by those who are serving or have served in war as hoplites or horse-soldiers, and hoplites and horse-soldiers were well-to-do, substantial people (753 B sq.); the superintendent of education is to be chosen by the magistrates out of the Nomophylakes (766 B); the select judges are to be chosen by the magistrates out of their own number (767 C–D). As to the Nocturnal Council, see 951 D–E.

13. καὶ τὰς μεγίστας κ.τ.λ. 'Haec falsa sunt, v. Plat. Legg. 753 B sqq.: 755 B sqq.: 766 A sq.: 945 E sqq.' (Sus.[1]). It is true that selection from the two highest classes is enforced only in the cases of the astynomi and the agoranomi, but Plato probably counted on his arrangements proving adequate to secure the same result as to the Nomophylakes (for these needed at least as much as the Astynomi to be at leisure to attend to public affairs—cp. καὶ τούτους, 763 D), and therefore as to the superintendent of education, the select judges, and the Nocturnal Council. On the other hand, the emphasis with which Plato insists on high excellence in his magistrates, especially in reference to the superintendent of education (ἄριστος εἰς πάντα, 766 A) and the priests of Apollo (πάντῃ ἄριστον, 946 A), seems to negative Aristotle's charge that the constitution approaches oligarchy. Still, in Aristotle's view, an ἀριστοκρατία selects the best ἐκ πάντων, not ἐκ τινῶν ἀφωρισμένων (6 (4). 5. 1292 b 2–4).

14. καί, 'as well as the choice of ἄρχοντες.' The distinction between membership of the Boulê and ἀρχή is not always maintained: cp. 7 (5). 6. 1306 b 8. As to the election of members of the Boulê, see Laws 756 B sqq.

15. ἀλλ' seems to answer to μὲν (see Sus.[1], Ind. Gramm. s. v. μέν). It introduces a limitation of what has just been said, as in Eth. Nic. 10. 5. 1176 a 21, ἡδέα δ' οὐκ ἔστιν, ἀλλὰ τούτοις καὶ οὕτω διακειμένοις: cp. Rhet. 2. 24. 1402 a 27.

16. ἐκ τῶν τρίτων. Should we supply τιμημάτων here with Mr. Eaton, or is τῶν τρίτων masc.? The same question arises with regard to τῶν τρίτων ἢ τετάρτων, 17, and τοῖς πρώτοις καὶ τοῖς δευτέροις, 18. In the passage of the Laws, the substance of which Aristotle is here reproducing (756 B sqq.), Plato has ἐκ τῶν μεγίστων τιμημάτων, ἐκ τῶν δευτέρων τιμημάτων, ἐκ τῶν τρίτων τιμημάτων, and lastly ἐκ τοῦ τετάρτου τιμήματος, and if he changes without apparent cause from the plural to the singular, it is possible that Aristotle, who has hitherto used the singular (τοῦ πρώτου τιμήματος, τοῦ δευτέρου τιμήματος, 15 sq.), may change from the singular to the plural. It is, however, also possible that τῶν τρίτων may be masc., and mean 'the members of the third class.'

17. πλὴν οὐ πᾶσιν ἐπάναγκες ἦν τοῖς ἐκ τῶν τρίτων ἢ τετάρτων. Here again the doubt arises whether τιμημάτων should be supplied with τῶν τρίτων ἢ τετάρτων, or whether these words are of the masculine gender. Πᾶσιν has universally been taken to agree with τοῖς ἐκ τῶν τρίτων ἢ τετάρτων, and if we thus take it, τιμημάτων must be supplied, and the meaning of the sentence will be, 'but Plato did not make voting compulsory [in elections from the third class] on all the members of the third and fourth classes.' This is a strange way of expressing the fact that Plato compelled the three higher classes alone to vote in elections from the third, and it is not surprising that extensive alterations have been suggested in the MS. text. But is it absolutely certain that πᾶσιν agrees with τοῖς ἐκ τῶν τρίτων ἢ τετάρτων? May not the meaning of the passage be—'but Plato did not make voting compulsory on all in the case of those elected from the thirds or fourths,' or, if we supply τιμημάτων, 'from the third or fourth classes'? For the dative τοῖς ἐκ τῶν τρίτων ἢ τετάρτων, if we understand it thus, cp. 1. 8. 1256 b 34, ταῖς ἄλλαις τέχναις ('in the case of other arts'), and [Xen.] Rep. Ath. 1. 5, ἐνίοις τῶν ἀνθρώπων, and see Bon. Ind. 166 b 26–38. Πᾶσιν is no more bound to be in agreement with τοῖς κ.τ.λ. than ταύτης with τῆς ἡγεμονίας in 7 (5). 4. 1304 a 22–23: see for other instances of the same thing de Part. An. 4. 9. 685 a 9: 3. 1. 662 a 9. If, however, the interpretation of τοῖς ἐκ τῶν τρίτων ἢ τετάρτων which I have ventured to suggest should be thought inadmissible, I would propose the omission of τοῖς: αἱρεῖσθαι will then need to be supplied, as in the next sentence. See Susemihl's *apparatus criticus*, and Qu. Crit. p. 370 sqq., for the emendations which have been already proposed. As to ἦν, cp. 1. 12. 1259 a 37.

18. ἐκ δὲ [τοῦ τετάρτου] τῶν τετάρτων. The probability is that τοῦ τετάρτου and τῶν τετάρτων are alternative readings, which have been by some misadventure admitted together into the text. See critical note for other instances of the same thing. It is hardly conceivable that Aristotle wrote 'from the fourth class of the fourths,' and the only remaining alternative is to adopt Victorius' conjecture of τῶν τεττάρων, which Sepulveda found in some MSS.—there also probably a conjectural emendation.

19. ἐκ τούτων, 'from the persons so elected.'

20. οἱ ἐκ τῶν μεγίστων τιμημάτων καὶ βελτίους. These words seem to go together as the subject of the sentence. For οἱ ἐκ τ. μ. τιμημάτων, cp. Plato, Laws 756 D, τὸν ἐκ τοῦ τετάρτου καὶ τρίτου τιμήματος . . . τὸν δ' ἐκ τοῦ δευτέρου καὶ πρώτου. Βελτίους, 'the more respectable': cp. 3. 13. 1283 a 36. That these words refer not to the elected but to the electors, is evident from Plato's use of them; besides, the μέγιστα τιμήματα (i.e. the first and second, 13) will number in the Boulê exactly as many representatives as the third and fourth. Not only most of the magistrates will belong to the well-to-do classes (1266 a 12), but also most of the voters in the election of members of the Boulê.

23. τὴν τοιαύτην πολιτείαν, 'the constitution of which we have spoken,' i. e. τὴν ἀρίστην, 1266 a 2. The conclusion here arrived at is considered by Aristotle to be established, partly by what he has said in 1266 a 3, and partly by the failure of Plato to construct his State in the way in which he had announced that it ought to be constructed. We need not infer from 1266 a 4, that the best constitution of Aristotle will be a compound of more constitutions than two; all that Aristotle says is, that a constitution compounded of more than two is better than a constitution compounded of two only. It is evident from the passage before us, as well as from the commencement of the Second Book, that Aristotle is looking forward to an inquiry as to the best constitution.

26. καὶ περὶ τὴν αἵρεσιν τῶν ἀρχόντων, i. e. as well as in the election of members of the Boulê. For in the election of the Boulê, though Aristotle has not fully described it in the passage before us, the process laid down by Plato is threefold (Laws 756 B sqq.):—first, an equal number of individuals is to be nominated by election from each class in the manner he prescribes: next, all the citizens are to select out of those thus nominated 180 persons from each class: thirdly, half of these are to be taken by lot. Thus Plato's scheme for the election of the Boulê is one which involves *τὸ ἐξ αἱρετῶν αἱρετούς*, and Aristotle implies by *καί* that this is a perilous way of electing a Boulê. Plato employs the same method in the selection of the Nomophylakes, Laws 753.

27. ἔχει ἐπικίνδυνον, cp. 4 (7). 2. 1324 a 38, *ἐμπόδιον ἔχειν*. Cp. also de Gen. et Corr. 1. 7. 323 b 30, *ὅσα ἢ ἐναντία ἐστὶν ἢ ἐναντίωσιν ἔχει*. Observe that Aristotle's objection is to *ἐξ αἱρετῶν αἱρετοί*, not to *κληρωτοὶ ἐκ προκρίτων*, an arrangement which suits a polity (6 (4). 14. 1298 b 9).

29. τὴν πολιτείαν τὴν ἐν τοῖς νόμοις. Aristotle does not meddle with the laws which occupy so large a part of the dialogue (1265 a 1), because his aim is to show that the constitution sketched in it is unsatisfactory, and that there is still room for an effort to suggest a better.

31. πολιτεῖαι. Bern. 'Verfassungsentwürfe.' Aristotle refers to **C. 7.** constitutional schemes, not to actual constitutions like those of Solon and Lycurgus.

The word **ἰδιώτης** is used by Aristotle both in contrast with such terms as *ἄρχων* (6 (4). 16. 1300 b 21) or *οἱ τὰ κοινὰ πράττοντες καὶ πολιτευόμενοι* (4 (7). 2. 1324 b 1), and in contrast with *οἱ εἰδότες* (3. 11. 1282 a 11: cp. Plato, Soph. 221 C, Protag. 322 C). Here both these contrasts seem to be combined: we find the former of the two in c. 11. 1273 a 35 and c. 12. 1273 b 29. The distinction of the *ἰδιώτης* and the philosopher survives in Cicero (Vict. quotes pro Sestio 51. 110) and in Epictetus (Arrian, Epictet. 3. 19)—see Grote, Plato 3. 130 n.

33. καὶ καθ' ἃς κ.τ.λ. Vict. 'est quasi declaratio antecedentis illius nominis.'

34. οὐδεὶς γὰρ κ.τ.λ. We read of the Cynic Diogenes in Diog. Laert. 6. 72, ἔλεγε δὲ καὶ κοινὰς εἶναι δεῖν τὰς γυναῖκας, γάμον μηδένα νομίζων, ἀλλὰ τὸν πείσαντα τῇ πεισάσῃ (πεισθείσῃ conj. H. Stephanus) συνεῖναι· κοινοὺς δὲ διὰ τοῦτο καὶ τοὺς υἱέας: but if this view was expressed in the Πολιτεία which passed under his name (Diog. L. 6. 80: Henkel, Studien p. 9), Aristotle knows nothing of it. The work must either have been spurious or of a later date than this passage. Zeno of Citium taught a community of women among the wise in his Πολιτεία (Diog. L. 7. 131), and was followed by Chrysippus (ibid.), but this would be after the time of Aristotle. The Ecclesiazusae of Aristophanes was not a πολιτεία. Aristotle, however, mentions in 2. 3. 1262 a 19 sqq. that some Libyans had women in common, and he might have mentioned other instances of this, just as he notices the customs of some barbarous tribes in relation to community of property (c. 5. 1263 a 1 sqq.): see for instance Hdt. 4. 104, and Strabo's report (p. 302) of the stories of Ephorus about some Scythian tribes—εἶτ' αἰτιολογεῖ διότι ταῖς διαίταις εὐτελεῖς ὄντες καὶ οὐ χρηματισταὶ πρός τε ἀλλήλους εὐνομοῦνται, κοινὰ πάντα ἔχοντες τά τε ἄλλα καὶ τὰς γυναῖκας καὶ τέκνα καὶ τὴν ὅλην συγγένειαν, πρός τε τοὺς ἐκτὸς ἄμαχοί εἰσι καὶ ἀνίκητοι, οὐδὲν ἔχοντες ὑπὲρ οὗ δουλεύσουσι. Cp. also Ephor. Fr. 53 and Strabo p. 775. Euripides in the Protesilaus (Fr. 655 Nauck) had made one of his characters say,

Κοινὸν γὰρ εἶναι χρῆν γυναικεῖον λέχος:

indeed, we are told by Polybius, that among the Lacedaemonians καὶ πάτριον ἦν καὶ σύνηθες τρεῖς ἄνδρας ἔχειν τὴν γυναῖκα καὶ τέτταρας, τοτὲ δὲ καὶ πλείους ἀδελφοὺς ὄντας, καὶ τὰ τέκνα τούτων εἶναι κοινά (12. 6^b. 8 Hultsch). In c. 12. 1274 b 9, the plan of a community in property as well as in women and children is spoken of as special (ἴδιον) to Plato; here only the latter.

36. ἀπὸ τῶν ἀναγκαίων ἄρχονται. The authors of constitutional schemes before the time of Plato seem to have made their special care the supply of the necessary wants of their citizens. (It is not clear how far this is true of Hippodamus.) Plato, though he too attaches great importance to questions relating to property (Laws 736 C sqq.), did not lose sight of higher things. Cp. 4 (7). 10. 1329 b 27, where τὰ ἀναγκαῖα are contrasted with τὰ εἰς εὐσχημοσύνην καὶ περιουσίαν and are said to be attended to first. Plato has some remarks in Laws 630 E on the way in which the legislators of his own day approached their task. For *ἄρχονται*, cp. de Sensu 1. 436 a 19–b 1: Top. 1. 14. 105 b 12–15. Their starting-point was also their main point, as the next sentence shows. Cp. Isocr. Areopag. §§ 44–45.

38. ποιεῖσθαι. We have *ποιοῦσι στάσιν*, 7 (5). 4. 1304 b 4, but *ποιοῦνται τὰς ἐπιθέσεις*, 7 (5). 10. 1312 a 20, and *στασιωτικῶς πεποιημένων τὴν κόλασιν*, 7 (5). 6. 1306 a 38. See on phrases of this kind Shilleto, Demosth. de Falsa Legatione § 103, where he says—'any verb in Greek may be resolved into the cognate substantive with *ποιεῖσθαι*.'

39. τοῦτ' perhaps means the regulation of property with a view to prevent civil discord. Bern. 'dahin zielende Vorschläge.' Others, who must probably be earlier in date than Phaleas (for he is contrasted with *τῶν πάλαι τινές* in 1266 b 16), e. g. Pheidon the Corinthian (c. 6. 1265 b 12), had sought to regulate property. According to Henkel, Studien p. 36, who refers to Roscher, Thucydides p. 247, Anm. 1, Phaleas was an older contemporary of Plato.

40. τὰς κτήσεις, 'landed property' (1267 b 9), as in c. 6. 1265 a 38 and 4 (7). 9. 1329 a 18.

1. κατοικιζομέναις is probably not to be taken with *χαλεπόν*, but rather in the sense of 'for,' or possibly 'in the case of.' 1266 b.

οὐ χαλεπὸν ᾤετο. It would seem from this that even in the foundation of colonies unequal lots of land were often given. Πόλεσι must be supplied here and *πόλεις* in the next line. This is a word which Aristotle often omits: thus *πόλει* has to be supplied in c. 9. 1269 a 34: *τὴν πόλιν* in c. 11. 1272 b 31: *πόλεσι* in 8 (6). 4. 1319 a 37 and 3. 6. 1278 b 12.

τὰς δ' ἤδη κατοικουμένας, sc. *πόλεις ὁμαλίζειν.* Cp. for this phrase Rhet. 3. 11. 1412 a 16, *καὶ τὸ ἀνωμαλίσθαι τὰς πόλεις.*

3. τῷ τὰς προῖκας κ.τ.λ. Rich men were to give dowries when their daughters married poor men, but not to accept them from the parents of the bride, if poor, when they or their sons married. Poor men were never to give dowries, but only to receive them. Aristotle does not criticise this regulation, but it appears to make it the interest of rich fathers to marry their daughters to rich men; thus it tends to defeat its own object. An additional regulation compelling rich families to intermarry with poor ones would seem to be needed. This scheme of equalizing landed property by regulations as to dowries implies that dowries were often given in land, and also that they were often large, as we know from other sources that they were. We see also that poor fathers commonly gave dowries as well as rich ones. Plato abolishes dowries altogether in the Laws (742 C: 774 C). Vict. remarks, 'in mentem hoc etiam venit Megadoro Plautino,' and quotes Plaut. Aulul. 3. 5. 4:

> Nam meo quidem animo, si idem faciant ceteri
> Opulentiores, pauperiorum filias
> Ut indotatas ducant uxores domum:
> Et multo fiat civitas concordior
> Et invidia nos minore utamur quam utimur,
> Et illae malam rem metuant, quam metuunt, magis,
> Et nos minore sumptu simus quam sumus.

The absence of a dowry, however, would be much felt by the wife, owing to the facility of divorce in Greece: cp. Menand. Sentent. 371, *νύμφη δ' ἄπροικος οὐκ ἔχει παρρησίαν*, and see C. F. Hermann, Gr. Antiqq. 3. § 30. 16, who quotes this line. See also vol. i. p. 171 sq.

6. ἐᾶν, sc. *τὸ τῆς οὐσίας πλῆθος* (cp. *ἐατέον*, 1267 b 13). Plato, however, would seem, no less than Phaleas, to have equalized the landed property of his citizens (Laws 737 C, *τήν τε γῆν καὶ τὰς οἰκήσεις ὅτι μάλιστα ἴσας ἐπινεμητέον*). Phaleas himself did not meddle with anything but land (1267 b 9 sq.), but this may well have been an oversight, for his views clearly pointed to an equality in all kinds of property. If so, he went, in intention at all events, farther than Plato.

πλεῖον δὲ κ.τ.λ. Literally, 'to acquire to a larger extent than would leave his property five times the size of the smallest.' As to *πενταπλασίαν*, see note on 1265 b 22, the passage referred to in *πρότερον*.

12. ἀνάγκη κ.τ.λ., 'the abrogation of the law must of necessity follow': 'neque enim pati poterunt patres filios suos esurire' (Vict.). Some render *λύεσθαι* 'be broken,' but the following passages, collected by Bonitz (Ind. 439 a 5)—2. 8. 1269 a 15: 7 (5). 7. 1307 b 10: 6 (4). 14. 1298 b 31—seem to point rather to 'abrogation' as the meaning. Cp. also c. 8. 1268 b 30, *νόμων λύσιν ἢ πολιτείας*, and 1269 a 15, *τὸ δ' ἐθίζειν εὐχερῶς λύειν τοὺς νόμους φαῦλον*.

13. ἔργον γὰρ κ.τ.λ. Cp. Plato, Rep. 552. Yet contrast Pol. 7 (5). 12. 1316 b 18, *ὅταν μὲν τῶν ἡγεμόνων τινὲς ἀπολέσωσι τὰς οὐσίας, καινοτομοῦσιν, ὅταν δὲ τῶν ἄλλων, οὐδὲν γίγνεται δεινόν*.

14. διότι, 'that.'

μὲν οὖν here, as in 1265 b 29 and elsewhere, introduces an admission which lends emphasis to the criticism introduced by *ἀλλά*, 24. What the main value of equality of property is, appears from c. 9. 1270 a 38. Another useful effect of laws of this kind is mentioned in 8 (6). 4. 1319 a 6 sqq.

ἔχει τινὰ δύναμιν εἰς τὴν πολιτικὴν κοινωνίαν. For this use of *εἰς*, cp. 6 (4). 16. 1300 b 20, *ὅσα εἰς τὴν πολιτείαν φέρει.*

16. φαίνονται διεγνωκότες, 'clearly have recognized': see note on 1261 a 9.

17. Σόλων. To what law of Solon's does this refer? C. F. Hermann (Gr. Antiqq. 1. § 106. 12) and E. Curtius (Gr. Hist. 1. 329 E. T.) take it as referring to some law fixing a maximum limit to the acquisition of land, but Grote (Gr. Hist. 3. 182, ed. 3) thinks that 'the passage does not bear out such an opinion.' He seems to hold that Aristotle here only refers to Solon's 'annulment of the previous mortgages,' and to the Seisachtheia generally. The former view is probably correct, but in any case Solon's legislation is evidently conceived by Aristotle to have tended to an equality of property. It is deserving of notice that no mention is made of the equality of landed property which Lycurgus is alleged by some authorities to have instituted.

παρ' ἄλλοις. Laws of this nature appear at one time to have existed at Thurii (7 (5). 7. 1307 a 29 sq.) and elsewhere (8 (6). 4. 1319 a 6 sqq.). On the other hand, Polybius remarks as to Crete (6. 46. 1, quoted by C. F. Hermann, Gr. Antiqq. 3. § 63. 16), *τήν τε γὰρ χώραν κατὰ δύναμιν αὐτοῖς ἐφιᾶσιν οἱ νόμοι, τὸ δὴ λεγόμενον, εἰς ἄπειρον κτᾶσθαι.* The Licinian Law at Rome probably imposed a limit only on the occupation (*possessio*) of the public land.

19. Λοκροῖς. According to Büchsenschütz, Besitz und Erwerb, p. 32 n., the Italian Locrians are meant, and the law was probably among those ascribed to Zaleucus. It appears, unlike the rest, to have applied to property generally (*οὐσία*), and not merely to land.

21. ἔτι δὲ κ.τ.λ. It seems better to supply *νόμος ἐστί* from 17, 19 with *διασώζειν* than to supply some word from *κωλύουσιν* (19) with the opposite meaning of 'enjoin.' Cp. 8 (6). 4. 1319 a 10, *ἦν δὲ τό γε ἀρχαῖον ἐν πολλαῖς πόλεσι νενομοθετημένον μηδὲ πωλεῖν ἐξεῖναι τοὺς πρώτους κλήρους.* A special protection was given in the Lacedaemonian State to the 'original share,' if we may trust Heraclid. Pont. de Rebuspublicis 2. 7, *πωλεῖν δὲ γῆν Λακεδαιμονίοις αἰσχρὸν νενόμισται· τῆς δ' ἀρχαίας μοίρας οὐδὲ ἔξεστιν.* Aristotle approves the discouragement by the Lacedaemonian lawgiver of the sale of landed property (if that is the meaning of *ἡ ὑπάρχουσα* [*γῆ*?], c. 9. 1270 a 20: cp. 8 (6). 4. 1319 a 13, *τὸ μὴ δανείζειν εἴς τι μέρος τῆς ὑπαρχούσης ἑκάστῳ γῆς*). Pheidon the Corinthian, again, had sought to keep the number of landowners the same. These legislators appear to have endeavoured, like Plato in the Laws, to secure each household in the possession of the original lot. The motive probably was partly a wish to prevent the impoverishment of old-established households and the civil troubles which were apt to follow, partly a wish to prop up an oligarchical *régime*, for Plato (Rep. 552 A, 556 A) notices prohibitions of alienation as a means, though one too rarely resorted to, of preserving oligarchies, concentration of wealth in a few hands being regarded by him as commonly the cause of their displacement by democracies.

22. καὶ περὶ Λευκάδα, i. e. 'at Leucas to name one instance,' as in 1. 12. 1259 b 8. As to *περὶ Λευκάδα*, see Bon. Ind. 579 a 29 sqq.

23. οὐ γὰρ κ.τ.λ. The meaning apparently is that men became admissible to office on the strength of half a lot or less, an arrangement suitable enough to an agricultural democracy like Aphytis (8 (6). 4. 1319 a 14 sqq.), but not suitable to an oligarchy, because poor men came to hold office.

29. μᾶλλον γὰρ κ.τ.λ. Cp. Plutarch, Demetr. c. 32, *λαμπρὰν τῷ Πλάτωνι μαρτυρίαν διδοὺς διακελευομένῳ μὴ τὴν οὐσίαν πλείω, τὴν δὲ ἀπληστίαν ποιεῖν ἐλάσσω τόν γε βουλόμενον ὡς ἀληθῶς εἶναι πλούσιον, ὡς ὅ γε μὴ παύων φιλοπλουτίαν οὗτος οὔτε πενίας οὔτε ἀπορίας ἀπήλλακται.* Plutarch evidently refers to Plato, Laws 736 E: cp. 742 E and Rep. 521 A. Cp. also Sen. Epist. 2, non qui parum habet, sed qui plus cupit, pauper est.

33. παιδείας. A remarkable view, probably suggested by Spartan precedents: cp. 6 (4). 9. 1294 b 21, *οἷον πρῶτον τὸ περὶ τὴν τροφὴν τῶν παίδων· ὁμοίως γὰρ οἱ τῶν πλουσίων τρέφονται τοῖς τῶν πενήτων, καὶ παιδεύονται τὸν τρόπον τοῦτον ὃν ἂν δύναιντο καὶ τῶν πενήτων οἱ παῖδες· ὁμοίως δὲ καὶ ἐπὶ τῆς ἐχομένης ἡλικίας, καὶ ὅταν ἄνδρες γένωνται, τὸν αὐτὸν τρόπον, οὐδὲν γὰρ διάδηλος ὁ πλούσιος καὶ ὁ πένης.* Aristotle is quite with him in this matter (5 (8). 1. 1337 a 21 sqq.).

36. τοιαύτην ἐξ ἧς. See above on 1257 b 15, and cp. 1267 a 24.

38. ἔτι, for which Spengel and Sus.[2] would read *ἐπεὶ*, Sus.[3] *ὅτι ?*, seems defensible. The meaning is—'besides, you need to deal with office in addition to equalizing property, for *στάσις* is occasioned not only, as Phaleas and his school think, by questions about property, but also by questions about office. It is as great a trial to a man of high capacity to have to share office equally with his inferiors as it is to a poor man to be starved.' Compare Jason's saying (3. 4. 1277 a 24), that it was starvation to him not to be a tyrant. Cp. also Stob. Flor. 45. 21, *ἐκ τῶν κοινῶν Ἀριστοτέλους διατριβῶν· αἱ πλεῖσται στάσεις διὰ φιλοτιμίαν ἐν ταῖς πόλεσι γίγνονται, περὶ τιμῆς γὰρ οὐχ οἱ τυχόντες, ἀλλ' οἱ δυνατώτατοι διαμφισβητοῦσι.*

1267 a. **1. οἱ δὲ χαρίεντες**, 'men of education': cp. 1267 a 39, and see L. Schmidt, Ethik der alten Griechen 1. 334 sq. Cp. also Eth. Nic.

1. 3. 1095 b 22, οἱ δὲ χαρίεντες καὶ πρακτικοὶ τιμὴν [προαιροῦνται], and Pol. 6 (4). 13. 1297 b 9, where this quality in the rulers is treated as a security that they will not plunder or outrage the ruled.

ἐν δὲ ἰῇ κ.τ.λ. Hom. Il. 9. 319 is quoted to support by the authority of Homer what has just been said as to the feeling of οἱ χαρίεντες. Cp. Plato, Laws 756 E, δοῦλοι γὰρ ἂν καὶ δεσπόται οὐκ ἄν ποτε γένοιντο φίλοι, οὐδὲ ἐν ἴσαις τιμαῖς διαγορευόμενοι φαῦλοι καὶ σπουδαῖοι: Eth. Eud. 2. 3. 1221 b 1: and the remarks on constitutions placed by Isocrates in the mouth of Nicocles (Isocr. Nicocles § 14 sqq.).

2. οὐ μόνον δ'. Here there is a transition from στασιάζουσιν, 1266 b 38 to ἀδικοῦσιν, 3—from men as citizens to men as moral beings. As inequality of property is not the only cause of civil discord, so neither is it the only cause of ἀδικία. Aristippus had apparently anticipated a part of what Aristotle says in the passage which follows: see Plutarch, de Cupiditate Divitiarum, c. 3. 524 A sqq., a passage which I do not notice in Mullach's collection of the Sententiae et Apophthegmata of Aristippus in the Fragmenta Philosophorum Graecorum. Compare also Cic. de Offic. 1. 7. 24–1. 8. 26 (referred to by Giph. p. 217).

3. διὰ τἀναγκαῖα ἀδικοῦσιν, ὧν ἄκος. '"Ακος τινός, genetivo vel id significatur quod avertitur, Pol. 7 (5). 8. 1308 b 26, vel id quod expetitur, Pol. 2. 7. 1267 a 3, 9: 7 (5). 5. 1305 a 32' (Bon. Ind. 26 b 50 sq.). For this second meaning of the word ἄκος ('a means of obtaining'), see Liddell and Scott s. v., and cp. 7 (5). 5. 1305 a 32, ἄκος δὲ τοῦ ἢ μὴ γίνεσθαι ἢ τοῦ γίνεσθαι ἧττον τὸ τὰς φυλὰς φέρειν τοὺς ἄρχοντας, and 2. 11. 1273 b 23, φάρμακον τῆς ἡσυχίας. Bonitz, it will be seen, explains ἄκος as 'a means of obtaining' both here and in 9, and there is much to be said for this view. But on the whole I incline, with the commentators generally, to give it in these two passages its more usual meaning of 'remedy' (Sus. 'Gegenmittel'). Ὧν will then refer, not to τῶν ἀναγκαίων, but to ἀδικημάτων, which must be supplied from ἀδικοῦσιν. The view of Phaleas was probably shared by many: cp. 6 (4). 8. 1293 b 38 sq. and [Xen.] Rep. Ath. 1. 5.

4. ὥστε . . . πεινῆν explains ὧν ἄκος: 'the result being that no one will be driven to steal clothes by cold and hunger.'

5. ὅπως . . . ἐπιθυμῶσιν. Χαίρωσι is introduced here and not before, because when a man satisfies an absolute need, though he feels pleasure (see de Part. An. 4. 11. 690 b 26–691 a 5), yet pleasure is not his aim. Compare the distinction drawn between μὴ ἀλγεῖν and χαίρειν in Eth. Eud. 2. 8. 1225 a 24: cp. also Rhet.

1. 12. 1372 b 24, ἀδικοῦσι δὲ τοὺς τοιούτους καὶ τὰ τοιαῦτα τοὺς ἔχοντας ὧν αὐτοὶ ἐνδεεῖς ἢ εἰς τἀναγκαῖα ἢ εἰς ὑπεροχὴν ἢ εἰς ἀπόλαυσιν.

ἐὰν γὰρ κ.τ.λ. This passage would be much simplified, if ἀδικοῖεν were substituted for ἐπιθυμοῖεν in 8, but it is perhaps possible to elicit a satisfactory sense from it as it stands. Taking it as it stands, I incline to translate as follows—'for if men have a desire going beyond mere necessaries, they will commit wrongful acts to cure it: nay, not only to cure a desire of this nature, for they may desire superfluities with a view to experiencing painless pleasures.' I follow Lamb. and Bern. in my rendering of διὰ ταύτην. Sepulveda translates these words 'medendi gratia,' apparently interpreting ταύτην as = ἰατρείαν, not τὴν ταύτης ἰατρείαν: it would also be possible to supply τὴν ἐπιθυμίαν with ταύτην. For μείζω ἐπιθυμίαν τῶν ἀναγκαίων (i. e. μείζω ἐπιθυμίαν τῆς ἐπιθυμίας τῶν ἀναγκαίων), cp. c. 10. 1272 a 28, χεῖρον τῶν ἐφόρων (i. e. χεῖρον ἢ τὰ τῶν ἐφόρων), and see Jelf, Gr. Gr. § 781 d. For οὐ τοίνυν, cp. Xen. Anab. 7. 6. 19, συνεπόμνυμι μηδὲ ἃ οἱ ἄλλοι στρατηγοὶ ἔλαβον εἰληφέναι, μὴ τοίνυν μηδὲ ὅσα τῶν λοχαγῶν ἔνιοι, and Demosth. de Cor. cc. 107, 244. What pleasures are meant by 'painless pleasures,' appears from Eth. Nic. 10. 2. 1173 b 16, ἄλυποι γάρ εἰσιν αἵ τε μαθηματικαὶ καὶ τῶν κατὰ τὰς αἰσθήσεις αἱ διὰ τῆς ὀσφρήσεως, καὶ ἀκροάματα δὲ καὶ ὁράματα πολλὰ καὶ μνῆμαι καὶ ἐλπίδες and de Part. An. 1. 5. 645 a 7 sq. Isocrates (ad Demon. §§ 46–47) is already acquainted with the distinction. It has long been noticed that painless pleasures are elsewhere said by Aristotle not to be accompanied by desire (Eth. Nic. 7. 13. 1152 b 36, ἐπεὶ καὶ ἄνευ λύπης καὶ ἐπιθυμίας εἰσὶν ἡδοναί, οἷον αἱ τοῦ θεωρεῖν ἐνέργειαι, τῆς φύσεως οὐκ ἐνδεοῦς οὔσης: 3. 14. 1119 a 4, μετὰ λύπης ἡ ἐπιθυμία: Eth. Eud. 2. 10. 1225 b 30, ἔτι ἐπιθυμία μὲν καὶ θυμὸς ἀεὶ μετὰ λύπης). Still an ἐπιθυμία τοῦ θεάσασθαι is spoken of in Rhet. 1. 11. 1370 a 25 sq., and an ἐπιθυμία μαθήσεως in Eth. Nic. 3. 3. 1111 a 31. But here perhaps the question hardly arises, even if we retain ἐπιθυμοῖεν, for the desire spoken of in the passage before us is not a desire for the painless pleasures themselves, but for the superfluities through which men sometimes mistakenly seek them. If this is so, it would seem to be unnecessary to adopt any of the emendations of the words καὶ ἂν ἐπιθυμοῖεν which have been suggested with the view of meeting this difficulty, among which may be noticed that of Schneider, καὶ ἂν μὴ ἐπιθυμῶσιν, that of Bojesen, whom Sus. follows, καὶ ἄνευ ἐπιθυμιῶν or καὶ ἀνεπιθύμητοι (cp. Clem. Al. Strom. vii. p. 742 A, B), and that of Bernays, who omits ἂν ἐπιθυμοῖεν. With the account here given of the motives of ἀδικία, compare (in addition to the passage from the Rhetoric quoted above) Pol. 2. 9. 1271 a 16 sq.: 6 (4). 11. 1295 b 10 sq.: Isocr. de Antidosi, § 217 (cp. Aristot. Rhet. 2. 23. 1398 a 29 sqq.): Plato, Laws 870: Cic. de Rep. 2. 41. 68. 8.

9. τί οὖν ἄκος τῶν τριῶν τούτων; For Bonitz' interpretation of ἄκος, see above on 3. The last three words have been translated in many different ways. Lamb. supplies 'malorum,' Vict. 'fomitum,' Sepulv. and Giph. 'cupiditatum.' Susemihl translates, 'in allen diesen drei Fällen': Bernays, 'für diese drei Klassen.' Others supply ἀδικημάτων, and, I incline to think, rightly (cp. 16, πρὸς τὰς μικρὰς ἀδικίας βοηθητικός). If we take this view, the translation will be, 'what then is the remedy for these three kinds of wrong-doing?' The three are (1) wrong-doing for the sake of absolute necessaries; (2) wrong-doing for the sake of superfluities with a view to curing painful desire and obtaining pleasure; (3) wrong-doing for the sake of superfluities with a view to obtaining painless pleasure.

11. δι' αὑτῶν χαίρειν. We expect, not δι' αὑτῶν χαίρειν, but χαίρειν ταῖς ἄνευ λυπῶν ἡδοναῖς: Aristotle, however, seems to say that those seekers for painless pleasure who desire to be independent of others for their enjoyment will ask the aid of philosophy, for all other pleasures save that of philosophy (αἱ ἄλλαι, 12) presuppose the assistance of other human beings. He does not absolutely deny that ὑπερβολαί are a means to some sorts of painless pleasure; a tyrant, for instance, may use his power over other men to provide himself with exquisite sculpture or music; but those seekers after painless pleasure who desire to be independent of others will go to philosophy for it (cp. Eth. Nic. 10. 7. 1177 a 27 sqq.).

12. ἐπεὶ ἀδικοῦσί γε κ.τ.λ. 'Other remedies, in short, besides that of Phaleas, are necessary, for ...' For ἐπεὶ ... γε, cp. 1. 5. 1254 b 34: 1. 6. 1255 a 19. In the passage before us ἐπεὶ ... γε introduces an evident fact adduced in support of the unexpressed conclusion to which the preceding sentences point—the conclusion that to remove the occasions of ἀδικία something more than a due supply of the necessaries of life is requisite—training, in fact, both moral and intellectual. Both these kinds of training tend to wean the mind from the pursuit of excess—τὰς ὑπερβολάς, i. e. an excess of wealth, power, glory, and the like (4 (7). 1. 1323 a 37–38), or an excess of other goods such as wine and good living (Eth. Nic. 7. 14. 1154 a 15 sqq., referred to by Congreve)—the one by limiting the desires, the other by affording pleasures attainable without command over other human beings; and it is through a craving for excess that men come to commit the worst offences. Men become tyrants, for instance, when they are not content with the honours and emoluments of citizen-rulers (Eth. Nic. 5. 10. 1134 b 7); and how great the tyrant's crime is may be gathered from the high honours paid to the tyrannicide.

14. **καὶ αἱ τιμαί**, 'the honours, as well as the crime the punishment of which they reward.'

15. For the place of **οὐ**, see Bon. Ind. 539 a 5 sqq.

17. **ὁ τρόπος τῆς Φαλέου πολιτείας.** Cp. c. 5. 1264 a 11.

ἔτι κ.τ.λ. Compare the criticism passed on Plato's Laws in c. 6. 1265 a 18 sqq. Ephorus had already insisted that it is as necessary for a State to possess the qualities which enable it to repel attacks from without as the internal concord (ὁμόνοια) which secures it from στάσις (Diod. 7. 14. 3–4: cp. Ephor. ap. Strab. p. 480), and Aristotle in a similar spirit (cp. Pol. 6 (4). 4. 1291 a 6 sqq.) now goes on to point out that it is necessary to take considerations of national security into account, not only in framing the constitution, but also in reference to the question of the amount of property to be possessed by the members of the State, for if this is too small—and perhaps Aristotle imputes to Phaleas a leaning in this direction, though the latter had said nothing definite—the State will hardly be a match for States similar to itself, while, if the amount is too large, States superior to it in power may well be tempted to attack it. (It is interesting to notice that a Greek State might be too poor to resist attack. In Aristotle's day (4 (7). 11. 1331 a 1 sqq.) the *matériel* of war had become elaborate and costly.) Thus an ὅρος τῆς οὐσίας is necessary, as he had already said in 1266 b 27; he returns, in fact, to this point, reasserting it on grounds of national security, whereas in the intervening passage, 1266 b 28–1267 a 17, his aim had been to show the insufficiency of even a correct ὅρος τῆς οὐσίας without a correct education. Down to 1267 a 37 Aristotle in criticising Phaleas seeks in the main to point out the latter's errors of omission—he ought to have regulated τεκνοποιία, to have fixed an ὅρος τῆς οὐσίας, to have satisfied the Few as well as the Many, to have instituted a given kind of education, to have taken the security of the State into account: in 1267 a 37–1267 b 9, on the other hand, he deals directly with Phaleas' panacea for στάσις, and points out how small is its value, indicating at the same time the true remedy. Thus the passage 1267 a 17–37 finds an appropriate place where it stands in the text: to place 1267 a 37–b 13 before it (with Susemihl) as an alternative version of 1266 b 38–1267 a 17 (which it does not seem to me to be) is, surely, to disturb the sequence of the criticisms contained in this chapter. For τὰ πρὸς αὐτοὺς πολιτεύσονται καλῶς, cp. Polyb. 6. 46. 8, ᾗ καὶ Λακεδαιμονίους . . . κάλλιστα τῶν Ἑλλήνων τὰ πρὸς σφᾶς αὐτοὺς πολιτεύεσθαι καὶ συμφρονεῖν.

19. For the contrast implied in καὶ πρὸς τοὺς γειτνιῶντας καὶ τοὺς ἔξωθεν πάντας, cp. 4 (7). 11. 1330 b 35 sqq. and Thuc. 1. 80. 3.

22. τὰς πολιτικὰς χρήσεις. Vict. 'domesticos usus': cp. 5 (8). 6. 1341 a 8, where, as here, it is contrasted with πολεμικάς (the sense of πολιτικόν in c. 6. 1265 a 22 is quite different). Here (cp. 18) the political activities of fellow-citizens in relation to each other are referred to. The citizens of a State must possess a due amount of property (3. 12. 1283 a 17: cp. also 2. 11. 1273 a 24).

24. τοσοῦτον . . . ὤν. See Vahlen, Aristotel. Aufsätze 2. 21 n., and cp. 1266 b 36. Thasos was a case in point. As to its wealth, see Boeckh, Public Economy of Athens E.T. p. 311. 'The Thasians were compelled to defend their gold mines on the continent from the cupidity of Athens, which perhaps claimed them as a conquest won from the Persians' (Thirlwall, Hist. of Greece, 3. 6). Samos also suffered for its fertility in a similar way (Strabo, p. 637).

οἱ πλησίον καὶ κρείττους. Cp. 1266 a 20, οἱ ἐκ τῶν μεγίστων τιμημάτων καὶ βελτίους, and 1263 b 5, τὸ χαρίσασθαι καὶ βοηθῆσαι.

25. ἀμύνειν with the acc. seems to occur but rarely in the writings of Aristotle (see Bon. Ind. s.v. and Mr. Ridgeway, *Camb. Philol. Trans.* 2. 132), but it is less infrequent in those of Plato (see Ast, Lexicon Platon. s.v.).

28. μὲν οὖν ('it is true,' as in 1265 a 17) prepares the way for, and lends increased emphasis to, δεῖ δὲ κ.τ.λ. I take the meaning of the passage to be—'Abundant wealth is advantageous' (why it is so, we learn from 1267 a 22–24: cp. 3. 12. 1283 a 17 sq.: 6 (4). 4. 1291 a 33): 'therefore, let us ask abundant wealth for the State, only stopping short of that excessive amount which suffices of itself to attract attack on the part of stronger States, apart from any other causes of war.' Cp. Poet. 7. 1451 a 3, ὥστε δεῖ καθάπερ ἐπὶ τῶν σωμάτων καὶ ἐπὶ τῶν ζῴων ἔχειν μὲν μέγεθος, τοῦτο δὲ εὐσύνοπτον εἶναι, οὕτω καὶ ἐπὶ τῶν μύθων ἔχειν μὲν μῆκος, τοῦτο δ' εὐμνημόνευτον εἶναι.

31. οὕτως ὡς ἂν κ.τ.λ., 'but only under circumstances under which they would go to war, even if' etc. In the anecdote which follows Aristotle's principle finds illustration and confirmation. The wealth of Atarneus was not out of proportion to its defensibility. It was not considerable enough to lead stronger States, not influenced by other motives for attacking it, to attack it in the hope of gain, for a long continuance of costly operations would be necessary for its reduction. Atarneus was a renowned stronghold, like Pergamon in the same region. As to Eubulus, see Boeckh, Hermias von Atarneus (Ges. Kl. Schriften, 6. 183 sqq.), and Sus.[2], Note 247. He was a wealthy Bithynian money-changer, who had got possession of two strong places on the coast of Asia Minor, Atarneus and Assos, at a time when the Persian Empire was falling to pieces. The crisis in his fortunes referred to here must have occurred before he was succeeded—about 352 B.C. according to Boeckh, but certainly not later than 347 B.C.—by Hermias. Boeckh places it as early as 359 B.C. (Ol. 105. 1), when the Persians under Autophradates were operating in this region against the revolted satrap Artabazus. Aristotle, being a friend of Hermias, would be well acquainted with the history of Eubulus, and also with the neighbourhood of Atarneus. For other illustrations derived from this part of the world, see the references in Bon. Ind. 662 b 61 sqq. Autophradates remained a conspicuous Persian leader till 332 B.C., when he disappears from the scene (A. Schäfer, Demosthenes und seine Zeit, 3. 169).

35. ἤδη, 'on the spot.'

37. ἔστι μὲν οὖν κ.τ.λ. Μὲν οὖν, which is here answered by οὐ μήν, introduces a summing up on the merits of Phaleas' scheme, which is no longer criticised for not being accompanied by other measures, but considered in itself. Susemihl regards ἔστι, 37–ἀδικῶνται, 1267 b 8, as a repetition or alternative version of 1266 b 38–1267 a 17, but it hardly seems to repeat 1267 a 2–17, for this passage refers to ἀδικία, not to στάσις, and its teaching does not agree with 1266 b 38–1267 a 2, for there we are led to infer that equality of property would be a remedy for στάσις, so far as the mass of men are concerned, whereas here we are told that the desires of the many are boundless and that a mere sufficiency will fail permanently to satisfy them.

39. ἂν . . . ἄν. See Bon. Ind. 41 a 59 sq., who compares 3. 9. 1280 a 36: 6 (4). 4. 1290 b 4. The doubled ἄν gives emphasis: see Prof. Jebb on Soph. Oed. Tyr. 862, 1438.

40. καὶ φαίνονται. Not only are the χαρίεντες likely to feel irritation, but as a matter of fact they visibly make attacks, etc. (cp. c. 3. 1262 a 18).

1267 b. **1. ἄπληστον.** Cp. Isocr. de Pace, § 7, where Solon, Fragm. 13. 71 sqq. is in the writer's mind.

2. διωβολία. The form found in Attic Inscriptions is διωβελία (so too ἐπωβελία, ἡμιωβέλιον, ὀβελίσκος, ὀβελεία), though they have τριώβολον, πεντώβολον, δεκώβολον, and the old form ὀβελός only once (and that before B.C. 444) takes the place of the usual ὀβολός (Meisterhans,

Grammatik der attischen Inschriften, p. 9). All the MSS., however, have διωβολία here. See Boeckh, Public Econ. of Athens E. T. p. 216 sqq., where the fact noticed by Aristotle is fully illustrated. Here, as is often the case in the Politics, Athens is glanced at without being referred to by name.

πάτριον, 'a settled, traditional thing.'

3. For ἕως without ἄν with the subj., see Bon. Ind. 307 b 38.

5. τῶν τοιούτων, 'the before-mentioned things': i.e. τοῦ μὴ στασιάζειν πρὸς ἀλλήλους καὶ τοῦ μὴ ἀεὶ δεῖσθαι τοῦ πλείονος (or τοῦ μὴ πλεονεκτεῖν, 7). Ἀρχή, which has called forth many emendations, seems to be used in the sense of 'source': cp. 7 (5). 1. 1301 b 4: 7 (5). 7. 1307 a 7: Meteor. 1. 14. 351 a 26, ἀρχὴ δὲ τούτων καὶ αἴτιον κ.τ.λ. For the thought, cp. 8 (6). 4. 1319 a 1 sqq.: 6 (4). 13. 1297 b 6 sqq. Compare also Isocr. ad Nicocl. § 16, and the answer of the Pythia to Lycurgus, when he enquired, 'by the establishment of what kind of usages (ποῖα νόμιμα) he would most benefit the Spartans'—ἐὰν τοὺς μὲν καλῶς ἡγεῖσθαι τοὺς δὲ πειθαρχεῖν νομοθετήσῃ (Diod. 7. 14. 2).

6. ἐπιεικεῖς . . . φαύλους. Vict. 'honestiores et humiliores.'

13. ἢ ('aut certe,' Bon. Ind. 313 a 26) **τάξιν τινὰ μετρίαν**, 'some moderate maximum.'

14. Is ἐκ to be taken with φαίνεται (as Vict. takes it) or with κατασκευάζων (as Bern.)? Probably with the former. 'It is evident from the legislation of Phaleas that he constructs his State (or citizen-body) on a small scale': cp. Meteor. 2. 2. 354 b 15, ἐκ ταύτης δὴ τῆς ἀπορίας καὶ ἀρχὴ τῶν ὑγρῶν ἔδοξεν εἶναι καὶ τοῦ παντὸς ὕδατος ἡ θάλαττα. For τὴν πόλιν (Vict. 'ordo civium'), cp. c. 8. 1267 b 30 and 3. 1. 1274 b 41.

15. Phaleas seems to have been as unfavourable to the τεχνῖται —a far wider term than our 'artisans,' for we hear of τεχνῖται who were favourites of tyrants, 7 (5). 11. 1314 b 4—as Hippodamus was the reverse. Hippodamus, himself one of the class, brings them within the citizen-body (c. 8. 1267 b 32); Phaleas makes them public slaves. The βάναυσοι τεχνῖται, as we learn from 3. 5. 1278 a 6 sq., were in early times in not a few States either slaves or aliens, and this continued to be the case to a large extent down to the time of Aristotle. But Phaleas wished them to be public slaves. We do not learn why he proposed this. When Xenophon proposed in the De Vectigalibus (4. 23) that the Athenian State should invest in 1200 public slaves, and let them out for service in the mines of Laurium, his aim was to increase the revenue of the State. The scheme of Phaleas would obviously have this effect, for it would secure the State a monopoly of skilled labour, but whether the object of Phaleas was to enrich the State, is perhaps doubtful. More probably, he wished to keep down an aspiring class, the members of which often acquired considerable wealth (3. 5. 1278 a 24) and would be likely to overshadow or even to buy up his cherished class of small landowners, to say nothing of the difficulty of fixing a maximum to their income. Aristotle, we see, recoils from the strong measure of making all τεχνῖται public slaves, but he seems to be willing that οἱ τὰ κοινὰ ἐργαζόμενοι (cp. 8 (6). 7. 1321 a 36, κατασκευάζειν τι τῶν κοινῶν) should be so. Does this mean 'all workers on public land, buildings, and property' or 'all τεχνῖται employed on public property'? It is not clear: perhaps the latter is the more probable interpretation, though, as a matter of fact, Aristotle does make the cultivators of the public land in his own ideal State public slaves (4 (7). 10. 1330 a 31). In any case he adds the proviso that even this measure must be carried into effect in a certain way, if it is to have his approval. Diodorus describes (11. 25. 2 sqq.) how the cities of Sicily, and especially Agrigentum, employed the multitude of Libyan and Carthaginian captives taken after Gelon's victory at Himera in all sorts of public works (αἱ δὲ πόλεις εἰς πέδας κατέστησαν τοὺς διαιρεθέντας αἰχμαλώτους καὶ τὰ δημόσια τῶν ἔργων διὰ τούτων ἐπεσκεύαζον κ.τ.λ.). The work was no doubt cheaply executed, and this would be one of the advantages of employing public slaves for this purpose. Another would be that work would be executed more rapidly and efficiently than if, in accordance with the usual method, a contractor (ἐργολάβος) was employed: see C. F. Hermann, Gr. Ant. 3. § 42. 8 (ed. 2). Plato, it may be noted, includes ἐργολάβοι among the indications of a φλεγμαίνουσα πόλις (Rep. 373 B). On the system of ἐργολαβεία or ἐργωνία, see C. F. Hermann, Gr. Ant. 3. § 69. 15 (ed. 2), or in the later edition by Thalheim, Rechtsalt. p. 99. 1, and Dittenberger, Sylloge Inscr. Gr. 2. 481 sqq., 507 sqq. (inscr. 353, 367). The scheme of Diophantus would no doubt be unpopular with the many citizens of Athens who were τεχνῖται (Büchsenschütz, Besitz und Erwerb, pp. 325–8), and it probably came to nothing (κατεσκεύαζεν, 18). Whether the Diophantus here referred to is the well-known Athenian statesman of the time of Demosthenes (as to whom, see A. Schäfer, Demosthenes und seine Zeit, 1. 11. 1: 1. 182), is quite uncertain. Schömann (Griech. Alterth. 1. 365) thinks not.

16. ἀλλ' εἴπερ κ.τ.λ. I see no cause for any change in the text. Ὡς, which Bekker, following Morel, inserts before Διόφαντος, 18,

rests on no MS. authority and can probably be dispensed with. Aristotle's intention perhaps was to make the sentence run *καθάπερ ἐν Ἐπιδάμνῳ τε καὶ Ἀθήνησι*, but then he remembered that the scheme of Diophantus remained unexecuted.

22. Ἱππόδαμος δὲ Εὐρυφῶντος Μιλήσιος. Hesychius calls him *Εὐρυβόοντος παῖς*: Photius, *Εὐρυκόοντος Μιλήσιος ἢ Θούριος* (C. F. Hermann, de Hippodamo Milesio, p. 4 sq.). He was one of the colonists of Thurii. We notice that the name of Hippodamus' father is here mentioned, whereas in c. 7. 1266 a 39 Phaleas is simply described as *Φαλέας ὁ Χαλκηδόνιος*. Were there other Milesians who bore the name Hippodamus? **C. 8.**

τὴν τῶν πόλεων διαίρεσιν, 'the division of cities into streets' or 'quarters': Bern. 'den Städtebau mit getheilten Quartieren.' Diodorus thus describes the laying-out of Thurii, which was done under the direction of Hippodamus—*τὴν δὲ πόλιν διελόμενοι κατὰ μὲν μῆκος εἰς τέτταρας πλατείας . . . κατὰ δὲ τὸ πλάτος διεῖλον εἰς τρεῖς πλατείας . . . ὑπὸ δὲ τούτων τῶν στενωπῶν πεπληρωμένων ταῖς οἰκίαις ἡ πόλις ἐφαίνετο καλῶς κατεσκευάσθαι* (Diod. 12. 10. 7). For the use of the word *πλατεῖα* here, compare the phrase *ξενικὴ ὁδός* (Hoeck, Kreta 3. 452), which Hoeck explains as 'a strangers' quarter.' C. F. Hermann (de Hippodamo Milesio, p. 52) thinks that when Meton is made in the Aves of Aristophanes (941 sq.) to design an agora at the centre of his city with straight streets converging on it from every point, he reproduces the Hippodameian agora at the Peiraeus, but this seems doubtful, for then Meton's scheme would be nothing new, and much of the point would be lost. Besides, Thurii was not thus laid out.

23. κατέτεμεν. See C. F. Hermann, ibid. p. 47. The word is used of 'cutting up' a surface with roads, trenches, or mines: so Strabo (p. 793) says of Alexandria, *ἅπασα μὲν οὖν ὁδοῖς κατατέτμηται ἱππηλάτοις καὶ ἁρματηλάτοις*. In the passage before us *ὁδοῖς* is not expressed. A city laid out in Hippodamus' fashion with straight roads was said to be *εὔτομος*, 4 (7). 11. 1330 b 23, 30. This laying out of Peiraeus is not to be confounded with its fortification by Themistocles; it is probably to be referred to the time of Pericles.

24. καὶ περὶ τὸν ἄλλον βίον, 'as well as in his architectural innovations.'

περιττότερος, see note on 1265 a 11. Hippodamus belonged to the stirring generation, active in striking out fresh paths (5 (8). 6. 1341 a 30 sq.), which followed the Persian Wars.

25. περιεργότερον, 'in too studied and overdone a way.' The meaning of the word is well illustrated by its use in a fragment of

Dicaearchus (Fragm. 33 a: Müller, Fr. Hist. Gr. 2. 246), *περίεργος γὰρ ἡ τοιαύτη σχηματοποιία καὶ προσποίητος κ.τ.λ.* Cp. also Isocr. ad Demon. § 27, *εἶναι βούλου τὰ περὶ τὴν ἐσθῆτα φιλόκαλος, ἀλλὰ μὴ καλλωπιστής· ἔστι δὲ φιλοκάλου μὲν τὸ μεγαλοπρεπές, καλλωπιστοῦ δὲ τὸ περίεργον.* Hippodamus was probably influenced, as will be shown presently, by the teaching of Ion of Chios, who was himself perhaps influenced by Pythagoreanism; but his peculiarities of dress, etc., seem to be characteristic rather of the individual than of any school of opinion, political or philosophical. The Pythagoreans of Hippodamus' day do not seem to have worn long hair: Diodorus of Aspendus, who apparently lived at and after the time of Aristotle, is said to have been the first Pythagorean to wear it after the fashion of the Cynics (Athen. Deipn. 163 c–164 a, *τῶν πρὸ αὐτοῦ πυθαγορικῶν λαμπρᾷ τε ἐσθῆτι ἀμφιεννυμένων καὶ λουτροῖς καὶ ἀλείμμασι κουρᾷ τε τῇ συνήθει χρωμένων*). Long hair was in Hippodamus' day a mark of Laconism, and it does not surprise us in a Thurian (cp. Philostrat. Vita Apollon. 3. 15, quoted by C. F. Hermann, de Hippodamo p. 20 n., *κομᾶν δὲ ἐπιτηδεύουσιν, ὥσπερ Λακεδαιμόνιοι πάλαι καὶ Θούριοι Ταραντῖνοί τε καὶ Μήλιοι καὶ ὁπόσοις τὸ λακωνίζειν ἦν ἐν λόγῳ*), but the expensive adornment of the long hair of Hippodamus points perhaps rather to his Ionic extraction (cp. Thuc. 1. 6. 3), if it does not remind us of the *Θουριομάντεις, ἰατροτέχνας, σφραγιδονυχαργοκομήτας* of Aristoph. Nub. 326. His abundant and expensively ornamented robes would recall the Persian costume (Sext. Emp. Pyrrh. Hyp. 1. 148, *καὶ Πέρσαι μὲν ἀνθοβαφεῖ ἐσθῆτι καὶ ποδήρει χρῆσθαι νομίζουσιν εὐπρεπὲς εἶναι, ἡμεῖς δὲ ἀπρεπές*), or the Ionian (Tim. Fr. 62: Müller, Fr. Hist. Gr. 1. 206), or the garment which Zeuxis, a resident at Ephesus, wore at the Olympic festival, into the fabric of which his name was woven in gold letters (Plin. Nat. Hist. 35. 62), were it not that they were of cheap material and that he made a point of wearing warm clothing in summer as well as winter, notwithstanding the current proverb, *ἐν θέρει τὴν χλαῖναν κατατρίβεις* (Leutsch und Schneidewin, Paroemiogr. Gr. 1. 74). This would seem to have been a purely individual whim, comparable to that of the Sophist Hippias, who would only wear things which he had made himself (Hippias Minor, 368 B sqq.), for if the Cynic Crates (Philemon, Inc. Fab. Fragm. 53, ap. Diog. Laert. 6. 87)

> *Τοῦ θέρους μὲν εἶχεν ἱμάτιον δασύ,*
> *ἵν' ἐγκρατὴς ᾖ, τοῦ δὲ χειμῶνος ῥάκος,*

his crotchet is far more comprehensible than that of Hippodamus. Perhaps, however, like Protagoras (Plato, Protag. 321 A), he held that the thick shaggy hides of animals served them as a defence not only against the cold of winter, but also against the heat of summer, and sought to protect himself in a similar way. Be this as it may, Aristotle had little patience with affectation even in a man like Xenocrates (Athen. Deipn. 530 d, quoted by Bernays, Phokion p. 119), and what he thought of one of these whims of Hippodamus may probably be gathered from Rhet. 3. 7. 1408 a 11, τὸ δ' ἀνάλογόν ἐστιν, ἐὰν μήτε περὶ εὐόγκων αὐτοκαβδάλως λέγηται μήτε περὶ εὐτελῶν σεμνῶς, μηδ' ἐπὶ τῷ εὐτελεῖ ὀνόματι ἐπῇ κόσμος· εἰ δὲ μή, κωμῳδία φαίνεται, οἷον ποιεῖ Κλεοφῶν· ὁμοίως γὰρ ἔνια ἔλεγε καὶ εἰ εἴπειεν ἂν "πότνια συκῆ." (Compare the quotation from Strattis in Athen. Deipn. 160 b,

Παραινέσαι δὲ σφῷν τι βούλομαι σοφόν·
ὅταν φακῆν ἕψητε, μὴ 'πιχεῖν μύρον,

and the whole following passage in Athenaeus, and see Meineke, Fr. Com. Gr. 2. 780.) There was a saying about the people of Miletus—Μιλήσιοι ἀξύνετοι μὲν οὐκ εἰσίν, δρῶσι δ' οἷάπερ οἱ ἀξύνετοι (Eth. Nic. 7. 9. 1151 a 9)—which the eccentricities of Hippodamus recall (cp. also Ephor. Fr. 92 Müller). Aristotle must have obtained these details about Hippodamus from some earlier source, but I do not think that there is much reason for doubting the authenticity of the passage. The Greeks were vigilant observers and keen critics of things which seem to us personal trifles (see Mr. Sandys' note on Demosth. contra Steph. 1. c. 68). Hermippus took the trouble to record that Theocritus of Chios criticised the dress of Anaximenes as ἀπαίδευτος (Athen. Deipn. 21 C), and we also hear in the same passage that the grammarian Callistratus in one of his writings found fault with his great contemporary, the Homeric critic Aristarchus, ἐπὶ τῷ μὴ εὐρύθμως ἀμπέχεσθαι, φέροντός τι καὶ τοῦ τοιούτου πρὸς παιδείας ἐξέτασιν. The Socratic Aeschines seems to have been very severe on the dress of Telauges in one of his dialogues (Athen. Deipn. 220 a sqq.). Plato himself reckons it as one of the merits of μουσική (Rep. 425 B), that it teaches men how to dress and wear their hair and carry themselves. Aristotle's object in this curious paragraph probably is in part to prepare the reader for the fancifulness of Hippodamus' constitution, but he also regarded a man's life and character as to some extent a guide to the value of his speculations, in practical philosophy at all events; thus Eudoxus' view that Pleasure is the greatest good gained support from his remarkable temperance (Eth. Nic. 10. 2. 1172 b 15 sqq.: cp. 10. 9. 1179 a 17 sqq., and Rhet. 1. 2. 1356 a 5 sqq.).

26. ἐσθῆτος I incline to make dependent on πλήθει καὶ κόσμῳ πολυτελεῖ. C. F. Hermann makes it depend on πλήθει only (de Hippodamo, p. 21 n.), but it seems more natural to carry on both πλήθει and κόσμῳ πολυτελεῖ. The combination of costly ornament with clothing of a cheap material is quite in harmony with the other eccentricities attributed to Hippodamus in this passage.

28. λόγιος δὲ καὶ περὶ τὴν ὅλην φύσιν, 'learned in Physics also' (Zeller, Gr. Ph. 1. 963. 5), as well as about the laying out of cities: 'learned about Nature as a whole also.' As to the word λόγιος, see Rutherford, New Phrynichus, p. 284. For τὴν ὅλην φύσιν, cp. τῆς ἁπάσης φύσεως, 1. 5. 1254 a 31: τῆς ὅλης φύσεως, Metaph. A. 6. 987 b 2 (opp. τὰ ἠθικά): Metaph. Λ. 8. 1074 b 3, περιέχει τὸ θεῖον τὴν ὅλην φύσιν (cp. Pol. 4 (7). 4. 1326 a 32). To Aristotle the meddling of Hippodamus with ἡ ὅλη φύσις was probably a further sign of περιεργία: cp. de Respir. 21. 480 b 26, τῶν τε γὰρ ἰατρῶν ὅσοι κομψοὶ ἢ περίεργοι, λέγουσί τι περὶ φύσεως καὶ τὰς ἀρχὰς ἐκεῖθεν ἀξιοῦσι λαμβάνειν. Was Plato thinking of men like Hippodamus, when he speaks (Rep. 495 C sq.) of ἀνθρωπίσκοι who ἐκ τῶν τεχνῶν ἐκπηδῶσιν εἰς τὴν φιλοσοφίαν, οἳ ἂν κομψότατοι ὄντες τυγχάνωσι περὶ τὸ αὑτῶν τεχνίον?

30. κατεσκεύαζε. The imperfect is used with reference to Hippodamus' plans, as being nothing more than plans.

31. μυρίανδρον, 'of ten thousand citizens.' Isocrates contrasts Sparta with αἱ μυρίανδροι πόλεις, Panath. § 257. Hippodamus evidently wished his State to be large for a Greek State, but not so large as Athens, which had 20,000 citizens.

τρία. In this view of Hippodamus, which may have suggested Plato's classification in the Republic, we can perhaps trace the influence of Egypt: cp. 4 (7). 10. 1329 a 40 sqq.: Plato, Tim. 24 A sqq.: Isocr. Busiris, § 15 sq. Compare also the three classes into which the population of Attica was divided—Eupatridae, Geomori, and Demiurgi. But Hippodamus evidently had a passion for threefold divisions, inherited very probably from Ion of Chios: cp. Isocr. de Antidosi § 268, ὧν (sc. τῶν παλαιῶν σοφιστῶν) ὁ μὲν ἄπειρον τὸ πλῆθος ἔφησεν εἶναι τῶν ὄντων, Ἐμπεδοκλῆς δὲ τέτταρα, καὶ νεῖκος καὶ φιλίαν ἐν αὐτοῖς, Ἴων δ' οὐ πλείω τριῶν. See vol. i. p. 381 n. and Zeller, Gr. Ph. 1. 450. 1. This leaning to the threefold was also Pythagorean: cp. de Caelo 1. 1. 268 a 10, καθάπερ γάρ φασι καὶ οἱ Πυθαγόρειοι, τὸ πᾶν καὶ τὰ πάντα τοῖς τρισὶν ὥρισται, and the whole passage down to 268 a 29. That which was divisible into three was held by them to be perfect and continuous. Aristotle himself is inclined to say, τελευτᾷ δ' ἐν τρισὶ πάντα: see note on 1252 b 27 sqq., and cp. Meteor. 3. 4. 374 b 33 sqq. He would not, however, agree that there are only three μέρη πόλεως, or that these are γεωργοί, τεχνῖται, and τὸ προπολεμοῦν: contrast his own enumerations in 4 (7). 8–9 and 6 (4). 4.

33. **καί** explains and limits *τὸ προπολεμοῦν*. See note on 1263 a 15.

τὴν χώραν. In most Greek States there was sacred, public, and private land. This was so in Crete, in the Lacedaemonian State (Thirlwall, Hist. of Greece, 1. 305), at Athens, etc. Aristotle divides the land of his 'best State' into public (including sacred) and private land, his public land being set apart for the support of the syssitia and the worship of the gods, not for the support of the military force, like that of Hippodamus. The public land, here termed *δημοσία*, is called *κοινή* in 36 (cp. 4 (7). 10. 1330 a 10), because it was to be the property of the community (Sus. 'Staatsacker'), and not of private individuals. We are not told why Hippodamus made the soldiers' land public land; perhaps he did so, wishing to keep it more under the control of the State than private land would be—to prevent its alienation, for instance, or its passing into other hands than those of soldiers.

34. **ἰδίαν.** In 3. 4. 1277 b 26 the fem. *ἴδιος* is used.

37. It would seem that Hippodamus regarded the office of law as measurable by the action of the law-courts; if the law-courts only checked mutual wrong, law did no more. This would not satisfy Plato or Aristotle, who, unlike the Sophist Lycophron (3. 9. 1280 b 10 sq.), expected law to do something more than protect men from mutual wrong—required it, in fact, to aim at making them good and just. As to the classification of offences here given, C. F. Hermann (Gr. Ant. 3. §§ 61–62) traces in Attic law a classification under the three heads of *ὕβρις*, *κακουργία*, and *φόνος*. As to *ὕβρις*, see Rhet. 2. 2. 1378 b 23 sqq. and Rhet. 1. 13. 1374 a 13 sq., where its nature is explained: see also the remarks of Hug, Studien aus dem classischen Alterthum, p. 61. As to the *δίκη βλάβης*, which included all damage, direct or indirect, not falling under some recognized category of offence, see C. F. Hermann, Gr. Ant. 3. § 70 and note 9. Mr. Pattison, in his copy of Stahr's edition of the Politics, quotes Strabo, p. 702, where Onesicritus, in recording the customs of the Indians of Musicanus' territory, says—*δίκην δὲ μὴ εἶναι πλὴν φόνου καὶ ὕβρεως· οὐκ ἐπ' αὐτῷ γὰρ τὸ μὴ παθεῖν ταῦτα, τὰ δ' ἐν τοῖς συμβολαίοις ἐπ' αὐτῷ ἑκάστῳ, ὥστε ἀνέχεσθαι δεῖ ἐάν τις παραβῇ τὴν πίστιν, ἀλλὰ καὶ προσέχειν ὅτῳ πιστευτέον, καὶ μὴ δικῶν πληροῦν τὴν πόλιν.* Compare with this Pol. 2. 5. 1263 b 20, and note on 1263 b 21. C. F. Hermann (de Hippodamo, p. 29) regards offences against the State and against religion as omitted in Hippodamus' classification, and it would seem that if they are to be included, they must be brought under one or other of his three heads. A different classification of the subject-matter of laws will be found in Demosth. contra Timocr. c. 192, where οἱ περὶ τῶν ἰδίων νόμοι are distinguished from οἱ περὶ τῶν πρὸς τὸ δημόσιον (see Hug, Studien, p. 81). Aristotle's own classification of δικαστήρια, which is given in 6 (4). 16. 1300 b 18 sqq., throws light on his views as to this subject.

39. ἐνομοθέτει δὲ κ.τ.λ. See as to this Supreme Court, vol. i. p. 382 sqq. That a few should judge, as this court would do, of all matters, is treated as an oligarchical arrangement in 6 (4). 16. 1301 a 12: an aristocracy or polity would commit some subjects to all the citizens, others to a few, but here the few were to judge (in appeals at any rate) on all subjects.

1268 a. **2. φέρειν,** sc. ᾤετο δεῖν. 'Deposit' is probably the meaning (Bern. 'einreichen')—cp. ψηφοφορίας, and Plato, Laws 753 C—not 'ferri domo' (Vict.), or 'dari unicuique' (Lamb.).

3. γράφειν is in the same construction as φέρειν. This proposal implies that most people of the class to which dicasts belonged could write. The regulations as to the Ostracism suggest the same conclusion. But then it must be remembered that in either case only a word or two would have to be written, and that in the Ostracism at all events persons unable to write would be allowed to get others to write for them.

τὴν δίκην, cp. ἐρήμην καταδικάζεσθαι [sc. τὴν δίκην], de Caelo 1. 10. 279 b 10.

4. κενόν, sc. φέρειν πινάκιον.

τὸ μὲν τὸ δὲ μή, 'wished partly to acquit, partly to condemn.'

τοῦτο διορίζειν, 'to particularize this.'

5. ἀναγκάζειν. We see from οὐδείς in 1268 b 17, that the unexpressed subject of ἀναγκάζειν probably is a person or persons, but it is not clear whether we should supply τὸν νομοθέτην or interpret with Bern. 'people compel them.'

9. γίνεσθαι is dependent on νόμον ἐτίθει = ἐνομοθέτει.

ὡς οὔπω κ.τ.λ. See on this passage Dittenberger, *Gött. gel. Anz.*, Oct. 28. 1874, p. 1369 sqq. With him I take Aristotle to mean that Hippodamus proposed this law as a novelty (compare the importance attached to τὸ ἴδιον in c. 12), whereas, in reality (νῦν, i.e. 'in Wirklichkeit'), says Aristotle, it exists in several States. I do not think Aristotle means that Hippodamus' suggestion may be taken as an indication that no such law then existed, whereas in his own day it existed in several States, for his remark would then possess merely an antiquarian interest and would be out of place where it stands. Besides, the other interpretation suits better with the use of ὡς with the participle. On νῦν in the sense of 'id quod in re ac veritate est,' see Bon. Ind. 492 a 60 sqq. As to the existence of this law at Athens, see A. Schäfer, Demosthenes und seine Zeit 3. 2. 33, who compares Aristot. Fragm. 428. 1549 a 5 sqq.: Aeschin. in Ctes. c. 154: Isocr. de Pace § 82. It is noticed as a wise law in democratic States in Rhet. ad Alex. 3. 1424 a 34 sqq. It is not clear how if all the fighting class was supported by public land together (doubtless) with its offspring, there should be any need in Hippodamus' State for a separate enactment securing to the children of those slain in war sustenance from the State.

10. παρ' ἄλλοις, 'in other States than that designed by him.'

12. αἱρετούς, 'elected,' not taken by lot—a sign of oligarchy (6 (4). 9. 1294 b 8 sq.). Cp., however, 2. 11. 1273 a 26 sq.

δῆμον δ' ἐποίει κ.τ.λ. This is added, because the word is often used of the poor only, as in c. 6. 1265 b 39 and c. 9. 1270 b 25. Hippodamus might well have meant by it only the γεωργοί and τεχνῖται.

13. κοινῶν καὶ ξενικῶν καὶ ὀρφανικῶν, 'public matters, matters relating to aliens, and matters relating to orphans.' For ξενικῶν, Bonitz (Ind. 493 a 42) compares 3. 5. 1278 a 7. Hippodamus would seem to have contemplated the sojourn of aliens in his State —contrast the Lacedaemonian ξενηλασία (C. F. Hermann, Gr. Ant. 1. § 27. 14)—and to have provided for magistrates like the Polemarch at Athens (Aristot. Fragm. 388. 1542 b 14 sqq.), charged with their supervision. Ὀρφανοφύλακες and ὀρφανισταί (in the Law of Gortyna, col. 12. 21, ὀρπανοδικασταί) were also known to Greek States (C. F. Hermann, Gr. Ant., ed. Thalheim, Rechtsalt. p. 14. 3), and orphan heiresses were especially cared for (Hdt. 6. 57). Hippodamus' classification, however, brings the supervision of aliens and orphans into unusual prominence: contrast Aristotle's treatment of the subject of magisterial competence in 6 (4). 15. 1299 b 10 sqq. and 8 (6). 8. C. F. Hermann notices the omission of 'res sacrae,' but they are probably included under 'public matters': Hippodamus made a liberal provision for worship (1267 b 35).

16. πρῶτον μέν seems either not to be taken up at all, or not till οὐ καλῶς δ', 1268 b 4.

τὴν διαίρεσιν. For the acc. after ἀπορῆσαι, cp. Meteor. 2. 2. 355 b 24.

20. γίνονται, i. e. those without arms, the cultivators and artisans. We see from the scolion of Hybrias the Cretan, that the possessor of arms was the lord and master of those who had them not. But the enslavement of one part of the citizen-body to another is a constitutional solecism: cp. c. 12. 1273 b 37 and 6 (4). 11. 1295 b 25, *βούλεται ἡ πόλις ἐξ ἴσων εἶναι καὶ ὁμοίων ὅτι μάλιστα.*

21. **μὲν οὖν**, I incline to think, introduces, not a correction of *ὥστε γίνονται σχεδὸν δοῦλοι τῶν τὰ ὅπλα κεκτημένων*, but an inference, as in 1. 1. 1252 a 7: each of the two words retains its own meaning, *μέν* being answered by *δέ*, 24.

22. **πολιτοφύλακας.** A magistracy bearing this name existed at Larissa (7 (5). 6. 1305 b 29). Its main duty probably was to guard the city against external, and possibly also internal, foes: see Aen. Tact. Comment. Poliorc. 1. 3 and 22. 7, where the words *πολιτοφυλακεῖν* and *πολιτοφυλακία* are used. The mention of *στρατηγούς* just before supports the view that this was a military office (see also Pol. 8 (6). 8. 1322 a 30–b 1). Sepulveda suggests (p. 51 b) that *πολιτοφύλακες* were to exist in the State of Hippodamus, and it is possible that strategi also found a place in it.

23. **μὴ μετέχοντας δὲ τῆς πολιτείας κ.τ.λ.** On the phrase *μετέχειν τῆς πολιτείας*, see the references in Bon. Ind. 462 b 26 sqq. It is here used in contradistinction to *κοινωνεῖν τῆς πολιτείας*, though in 27, four lines lower down, it appears to be used in the same sense as this phrase. In line 23 it is implied that, while those who elect to magistracies *κοινωνοῦσι τῆς πολιτείας*, only those who are eligible to the supreme magistracies can truly be said *μετέχειν τῆς πολιτείας*. In 6 (4). 6. 1293 a 3 sqq., however, the distinction between the two expressions is differently drawn, for in that passage *οἱ μετέχοντες τῆς πολιτείας* are those who possess, *οἱ κοινωνοῦντες* those who actually exercise political privileges. The contrast between the Lacedaemonian constitution and that of Hippodamus is probably present to Aristotle's mind, for under the former the ephorship was open to the people, and this helped to recommend the constitution to them (6 (4). 9. 1294 b 29 sqq.). Yet at Carthage the demos was propitiated, not in this way, but in another (2. 11. 1273 b 18 sqq.), and the constitution of Solon, the merits of which are often acknowledged by Aristotle, though it opened the dicasteries to all, excluded a large portion of the citizens from office. Even under the fully developed democracy, the Athenian demos seems to have willingly left some offices of the highest importance to be filled by those who were fittest to fill them ([Xen.] Rep. Ath. 1. 3).

25. **ἀλλά** introduces a rejoinder from some imagined defender of Hippodamus' scheme, and *τοῦτο δ'* 26 Aristotle's comment in reply.

29. **ἔτι κ.τ.λ.** Hippodamus probably intended, as Vict. suggests, that the cultivators should sell food, etc. to the artisans: this would be a sufficient *raison d'être* for them. This implies, no doubt, that the cultivators will produce enough from their lots to supply both themselves and the artisans, whereas Aristotle questions (42) whether two households could be supported even from the cultivators' and warriors' land together. Still, how else are the artisans to be maintained?

31. καθάπερ, i. e. in the State of Hippodamus (where they have no land) as in others.

33. εὐλόγως, because any social element that contributes to the existence of the State is in a broad sense a part of the State (6 (4). 4. 1290 b 39 sqq.).

34. ἰδίᾳ, 'for themselves.'

36. γεωργήσουσιν, 'are to till the soil': see on this use of the future (cp. *ἔσονται*, 38) Bon. Ind. 754 b 17 sq.

40. ἀλλότριον, 'alien to the constitution,' and in all likelihood hostile to it (cp. 23 sq.). Hippodamus, however, probably meant the public land to be cultivated by slaves. Aristotle, we notice, does not raise any question as to the mode of cultivating the sacred land, though the same difficulty might arise here also.

42. τό τε πλῆθος κ.τ.λ. 'It will be a difficult matter to produce enough to enable each of them to support as a cultivator two households, and then again, why are not the cultivators to derive directly from their own farms and from the same lots of land at once sustenance for themselves and a supply of food for the fighting class?' *Εὐθύς* means 'without any preliminary distinction between public and private land.' *Ἄπορον* seems to be used in the same sense as in Metaph. Z. 3. 1029 a 33 and Eth. Nic. 1. 4. 1097 a 8, or perhaps as in Plato, Rep. 378 A and 453 D, though Bonitz would appear to explain it as 'deficient,' to judge by the passages with which he groups the passage before us (Ind. 85 b 20). Vict., Lamb., Giph., Sepulveda, and others also translate the word 'too small.' I have rendered *γεωργήσει δύο οἰκίας* 'support as a cultivator two households,' because this rendering seems to be required by the sense, but it is difficult to extract it from the words. Stahr translates 'zwei Haushaltungen zu bestreiten,' but this translation is open to the same objection. *Γεωργήσει* does not suit well with *καρπῶν*: Spengel, in fact, conjectures *πόνων* in place of *καρπῶν* (Aristot. Studien 3. 15), but *γεωργήσει* appears to be the doubtful word. The expression *γεωργήσει δύο οἰκίας* has long been felt to be a very strange one: we fail to find a real parallel to it in such phrases as *χορεύειν Φοῖβον*, Pind. Isthm. 1. 7 (cp. Soph. Antig. 1151), and if we retain the reading *γεωργήσει* (see critical note), we must probably seek an explanation of the construction in the use of the cognate accusative. We have οἰκεῖν δύο οἰκίας in c. 6. 1265 b 26, and it is possible that Aristotle here substitutes γεωργεῖν for οἰκεῖν seeing that the phrase οἰκεῖν δύο οἰκίας (or even διοικεῖν δύο οἰκίας, 4 (7). 10. 1330 a 7) would obviously be inapplicable to the cultivator of whom he is speaking. In 6 (4). 1. 1289 a 1 sqq. we find, if the reading of Π² is correct, τάξιν ἣν ῥᾳδίως δυνήσονται κοινωνεῖν. For ἀπὸ τῆς γῆς = ἀπὸ τοῦ γηπέδου, see Liddell and Scott s. v. γῆ and Bon. Ind. 154 a 39 sq. Or do the words mean 'from the land as a whole'? Bern. would omit καί and read ἀπὸ τῆς γῆς τῶν αὐτῶν κλήρων, where however τῆς γῆς seems superfluous. As to the thought, Comte, on the contrary (Social Statics E. T. p. 130), 'assumes as an average that, under all conditions which are not very unfavourable, the labour of every agricultural family can support at least one other as numerous as itself, if not two or three.' It will be observed that Aristotle takes it for granted that the cultivators will be equal in number to the warriors in the State of Hippodamus, for if the former were more numerous than the latter, one cultivator would not have to maintain two households, and the difficulty anticipated by Aristotle would not arise.

1268 b. **5. τὸ κρίνειν ἀξιοῦν.** So Π, and though Vet. Int. has 'lex iudicare dignificans,' there is no doubt of the correctness of this reading: cp. 2. 12. 1274 b 11, ὁ περὶ τὴν μέθην νόμος, τὸ τοὺς νήφοντας συμποσιαρχεῖν, and 1274 b 19–20. Ἀξιοῦν is 'to prescribe' (cp. φάσκειν, 1. 13. 1260 b 6), as in 4 (7). 11. 1331 a 3, where it answers to φάσκοντες, 1330 b 32.

τῆς δίκης ἁπλῶς γεγραμμένης. Π² read κρίσεως: Π¹ δίκης, which Sus. adopts. In 18 we have εἴπερ ἁπλῶς τὸ ἔγκλημα γέγραπται δικαίως. If we read κρίσεως (and perhaps we thus get some additional point from the more marked contrast with κρίνειν διαιροῦντα), we cannot well attach to it a different sense from that which it bears in the preceding line, where it seems to mean 'adjudication' or 'judicial decision.' We cannot well interpret the first κρίσεως thus, and the second (with Bonitz, Ind. 409 b 60) 'causa,' 'the action.' But if we translate the second κρίσεως also as 'the decision,' we must apparently take 'the decision' here as meaning 'the charge to be adjudicated upon.' This is awkward, and it seems better to adopt the reading of Π¹. Κρίσεως may well have been repeated by mistake from the preceding line.

ἁπλῶς, 'in absolute terms,' without saying τὸ μὲν τὸ δὲ μή, 1268 a 4, or πῶς μὲν ἔστι πῶς δ' οὔ. For this was, as is implied here, the special province of the διαιτητής (τὸ διαιρεῖν): cp. Phys. 3. 6. 206 a 12, ὅταν δὲ διωρισμένων οὕτως μηδετέρως φαίνηται ἐνδέχεσθαι, διαιτητοῦ δεῖ, καὶ δῆλον ὅτι πῶς μέν ἐστι πῶς δ' οὔ, and Rhet. 1. 13. 1374 b 19 sq.

6. τοῦτο δ' ἐν κ.τ.λ., 'for this (τὸ κρίνειν διαιροῦντα) is possible in an arbitration, even if there are more arbitrators than one.'

10. μὴ κοινολογῶνται. Vict. 'arbitror, cum verba auctoris attendo, ipsum ostendere voluisse illos nomothetas praecepisse sedilia ipsorum ita aedificari, ut si vellent capita conferre, non possent, communicareque opiniones inter se.' But perhaps we need not go quite so far as this. The object of the prohibition of communication between jurors seems to have been to preserve the secrecy of suffrage (see Shilleto on Demosth. de Falsa Legatione § 265, p. 192 of his edition, and C. F. Hermann, Gr. Ant. 1. § 143. 1, who compares Plato, Laws 876 A, ἐν πόλει, ἐν ᾗ δικαστήρια φαῦλα καὶ ἄφωνα, κλέπτοντα τὰς αὐτῶν δόξας, κρύβδην τὰς κρίσεις διαδικάζει). In τιμητοὶ δίκαι, however, where the jurors were left to fix the penalty, communication must have been unavoidable (see C. F. Hermann, Gr. Ant. 1. § 143. 11), to say nothing of the 'shouting dicasteries' censured by Plato in the Laws (876 B), the members of which must soon have come to know the opinion of their fellows.

11. ταραχώδης, 'full of perplexity': cp. 5 (8). 2. 1337 a 40, and πολλὴν ἔχει ταραχήν ('involves much perplexity'), 1268 b 4.

12. ὁ μέν, Π²: other MSS. μὲν ὁ, a more logical order, but for the displacement of μέν, see Bon. Ind. 454 a 20 sqq.

ὁ δικαζόμενος, 'he who brings the action, the plaintiff,' as in 3. 1. 1275 a 9.

14. ἢ ὁ μὲν πλέον, ὁ δ' ἔλασσον. These words have been variously interpreted. Bernays translates them 'or whatever larger sum one may select for the plaintiff and whatever smaller sum for the juror': others 'or one juror more than ten and another less.' Susemihl now apparently adopts the rendering of Bernays (Qu. Crit. p. 375). The meaning of the words is doubtful, but perhaps on the whole Bernays' view, which makes them parenthetical, is the one most likely to be correct.

15. καὶ τοῦτον δή is right, though Π³ have δέ instead of δή, for here we have, as in 1. 13. 1259 b 32 and 2. 3. 1261 b 23, a transition from particular statements to an universal statement.

μεριοῦσιν, 'divident sententias,' Lamb. followed by Bonitz (Ind. 454 b 30). Is it not rather 'split up the amount' (Schn. 'summam pecuniae divident')? Those who vote part of the amount claimed are apparently contrasted with those who vote all or none. Cp. Philemon, Στρατιώτης (Meineke, Fr. Com. Gr. 4. 27),

Οἱ μὲν ἥρπασάν τι γάρ,
οἱ δ' οὐδέν, οἱ δὲ πάντα.

18. εἴπερ . . . δικαίως, 'if the charge has been duly brought in an unqualified form': i. e. if the question which ought to be raised is really an unqualified one. 'Duly,' not 'truly,' for of course if the unqualified charge were true, no one could suppose that the juror who decided that it was so would perjure himself, and the denial of perjury would apply only to a case in which perjury obviously would not occur. For *δικαίως* in the sense of 'properly,' cp. Eth. Eud. 3. 1. 1229 b 34. Aristotle seems to admit by implication that if the charge has been brought in an unqualified form not duly, but otherwise, then the juror, if compelled to give an unqualified verdict, may have to break his oath; he ascribes, however, the perjury thus necessitated, not to the plan of requiring an unqualified verdict from the jury, but to the putting of an improper question.

19. οὐ γὰρ κ.τ.λ. No doubt; and Hippodamus would say at once that the case adduced by Aristotle is not one of those which would create the difficulty he foresees. The kind of case in which he anticipates difficulty is that in which the charge is partially true and partially false (*τὸ μὲν τὸ δὲ μή*, 1268 a 4), and this is not so where a debt of 20 minae is untruly alleged. It is possible that Hippodamus had in view cases in which the issue put to the jury included more charges than one. The indictment of Socrates was of this nature: it ran (Diog. Laert. 2. 40: Xen. Mem. 1. 1)—*Ἀδικεῖ Σωκράτης οὓς μὲν ἡ πόλις νομίζει θεοὺς οὐ νομίζων, ἕτερα δὲ καινὰ δαιμόνια εἰσηγούμενος· ἀδικεῖ δὲ καὶ τοὺς νέους διαφθείρων· τίμημα θάνατος.* Suppose that a juror thought that one of these charges was true, but the rest not: was he to say Yes or No to the indictment? The latter would probably be the correct course, yet some might think it not wholly satisfactory. In Socrates' case the three questions ought to have been put separately to the jury, and then the difficulty would not have arisen; but the same evil may well have occasionally assumed subtler forms. No doubt, however, there is much force in Aristotle's plea that the fault lay in the question put to the jury, not in expecting the jury to give an absolute answer. The Roman plan of a 'non liquet' verdict would not have met Hippodamus' difficulty; nor would the form of verdict which the Emperor Augustus adopted in one case (Suet. Aug. c. 33: et cum de falso testamento ageretur, omnesque signatores lege Cornelia tenerentur, non tantum duas tabellas, damnatoriam et absolutoriam, simul cognoscentibus dedit, sed tertiam quoque, qua ignosceretur iis quos fraude ad signandum vel errore inductos constitisset).

21. ἀλλ' ἐκεῖνος ἤδη ἐπιορκεῖ. For the use of *ἤδη* in this passage, cp. Xen. Hell. 5. 1. 4, *τοῦτο γὰρ ἤδη . . . ἀξιολογώτατον ἀνδρὸς ἔργον ἐστίν*, and Plato, Gorg. 485 C, *ὅταν δὲ δὴ πρεσβύτερον ἴδω ἔτι φιλοσοφοῦντα καὶ μὴ ἀπαλλαττόμενον, πληγῶν μοι δοκεῖ ἤδη δεῖσθαι . . . οὗτος ὁ ἀνήρ*. In the passage from Xenophon Sturz, Lex. Xenoph. s.v., translates *ἤδη* by 'utique' or 'quidem,' but perhaps in all three passages something of the usual meaning of *ἤδη* is traceable, and we may render that before us 'in him we do arrive at a man who perjures himself.'

22. Athens already awarded special honours to persons who had done great service to the State and their descendants, and even to victors at the four great games (Demosth. in Lept. c. 105 sqq.: see also R. Schöll in *Hermes* 6. 32 sqq.), and Aristotle makes no objection to this; he is himself quite willing to award honours for integrity in office (7 (5). 8. 1309 a 13); but he disapproves of the proposition to award honours to those who claimed to have discovered something advantageous to the State. False accusations, he thought, would thus be encouraged—accusations, for instance, directed against persons deemed to be withholding money from the State or otherwise damaging it. Eubulus appears to have risen to power at Athens by repeated exposures of men who detained or embezzled public money (Schäfer, Demosthenes 1. 175). Aristotle thinks that legislation of the kind desired by Hippodamus might even result in changes of the constitution: thus Theramenes according to Lysias (contra Eratosthen. cc. 68, 70) overthrew the Athenian democracy and laid Athens at the feet of her foes under cover of an assurance that he had made a great and valuable discovery (*φάσκων πρᾶγμα εὑρηκέναι μέγα καὶ πολλοῦ ἄξιον*). The recommendations of Simonides in Xen. Hiero c. 9 (esp. § 9, *εἰ δὲ φανερὸν γένοιτο ὅτι καὶ ὁ πρόσοδόν τινα ἄλυπον ἐξευρίσκων τῇ πόλει τιμήσεται, οὐδ' αὕτη ἂν ἡ σκέψις ἀργοῖτο*, cp. § 10, *ὁ ἀγαθόν τι εἰσηγούμενος*) recall this one of Hippodamus, and are perhaps present to Aristotle's mind. Contrast the view of Diodotus (Thuc. 3. 42. 7) —*τὴν δὲ σώφρονα πόλιν [χρὴ] τῷ τε πλεῖστα εὖ βουλεύοντι μὴ προστιθέναι τιμήν, ἀλλὰ μηδ' ἐλασσοῦν τῆς ὑπαρχούσης*.

24. ἔχει. Cp. Isocr. Philip. § 68, *τὰ μὲν γὰρ τοιαῦτα τῶν ἔργων φθόνον ἔχει καὶ δυσμένειαν καὶ πολλὰς βλασφημίας*.

26. ἄλλο . . . ἑτέραν. See Bon. Ind. 34 b 34 sq.

27. τινες. Very possibly Pythagoreans, for this school held, according to Aristox. Fragm. 19 (Müller, Fr. Hist. Gr. 2. 278), that it was better *μένειν τοῖς πατρίοις ἔθεσί τε καὶ νόμοις, εἰ καὶ μικρῷ χείρω τῶν ἑτέρων εἴη*. It was a charge against tyrants that they altered time-honoured laws (Hdt. 3. 80). The fact, however, that the Greeks used the same word (κινεῖν) for the alteration of a law and the development of an art or science, tended to disguise the difference between the two things, and thus Isocrates had said (Evagoras § 7), ἐπειδὴ καὶ τὰς ἐπιδόσεις ἴσμεν γιγνομένας καὶ τῶν τεχνῶν καὶ τῶν ἄλλων ἁπάντων οὐ διὰ τοὺς ἐμμένοντας τοῖς καθεστῶσιν, ἀλλὰ διὰ τοὺς ἐπανορθοῦντας καὶ τολμῶντας ἀεί τι κινεῖν τῶν μὴ καλῶς ἐχόντων (compare the remark of the Corinthian orator to the Lacedaemonians in Thuc. 1. 71. 3, ἀνάγκη δ' ὥσπερ τέχνης ἀεὶ τὰ ἐπιγιγνόμενα κρατεῖν, καὶ ἡσυχαζούσῃ μὲν πόλει τὰ ἀκίνητα νόμιμα ἄριστα, πρὸς πολλὰ δὲ ἀναγκαζομένοις ἰέναι πολλῆς καὶ τῆς ἐπιτεχνήσεως δεῖ, which may possibly be in Aristotle's memory here: compare also the view ascribed to Charondas in Diod. 12. 16, to Zaleucus in Stob. Floril. 44. 21, p. 280). Plato provides for the improvement, in course of time, of his legislation in the Laws (769 D), but subject to strict conditions (772 A–D) which almost exclude the possibility of serious changes. See also Polit. 298 E–299 E.

30. ἐνδέχεται δ'. Sus., after Spengel, reads γάρ in place of δέ without MS. authority, but Aristotle occasionally uses δέ where we rather expect γάρ (e.g. in 3. 9. 1280 a 15, σχεδὸν δ' οἱ πλεῖστοι φαῦλοι κριταὶ περὶ τῶν οἰκείων, where we expect σχεδὸν γάρ, and in 8 (6). 7. 1321 a 19, where ταύτῃ γάρ might well take the place of ταύτῃ δέ). Perhaps he adds the words—'and it is not impossible that changes in the laws or constitution may be proposed as a common good'—to anticipate an objection that no revolutionist would proceed in this way (compare the use of δέ in 1. 5. 1254 a 36); for it was only those who claimed to have discovered something for the advantage of the community that it was proposed to reward. Theramenes had, in fact, done exactly what Aristotle here says might be done: see note on 22 above.

35. ἰατρική, i.e. has improved. This must be elicited from συνενήνοχεν.

36. αἱ τέχναι πᾶσαι καὶ αἱ δυνάμεις. For the difference between an art, or ποιητικὴ ἐπιστήμη, and a 'faculty,' see Cope on Rhet. 1. 4. § 6. 1359 b 12 sqq., where ῥητορική and διαλεκτική are said to be not ἐπιστῆμαι but δυνάμεις. It is implied in what follows that if ἡ πολιτικὴ κινεῖται, this will involve τὸ κινεῖν τοὺς νόμους, which are ἔργα τῆς πολιτικῆς (Eth. Nic. 10. 10. 1181 a 23).

39. ἐπ' αὐτῶν τῶν ἔργων. For this use of ἐπί, see Bon. Ind. 268 a 31 sqq.

νόμους. Perhaps unwritten: cp. 1269 a 8. In 42 νομίμων is the word used, apparently in the same sense as νόμοι here: these words are interchanged, as Bonitz points out (Ind. 488 a 16 sqq.), in 4 (7). 2. 1324 b 5, 7 also. Much the same thing is said by Thucydides (1. 6. 7, πολλὰ δ' ἂν καὶ ἄλλα τις ἀποδείξειε τὸ παλαιὸν Ἑλληνικὸν ὁμοιότροπα τῷ νῦν βαρβαρικῷ διαιτώμενον). Popular sentiment, however, with which Isocrates appears to agree (de Antid. § 82), praised most highly the oldest laws, and Aristotle himself often counts the antiquity of an institution or opinion as a point in its favour.

40. ἐσιδηροφοροῦντο. Cp. Thuc. 1. 5 sq. where we find both the active and the middle. As to the contrast of Hellenic and barbarian practice in this matter, see Lucian, Anacharsis c. 34.

41. τὰς γυναῖκας, i.e. brides, not wives. This custom existed among the Thracians (Hdt. 5. 6). Thirlwall remarks (Hist. of Greece, 1. 175) with respect to Homeric Greece, that 'it does not seem that the marriage contract was commonly regarded in the light of a bargain and sale,' but he adds in a note—'compare, however, Od. 15. 367 and 18. 279 with the constant epithet ἀλφεσίβοιαι.' Plato (Laws 841 D) seems to recognize the purchase of brides—ταῖς μετὰ θεῶν καὶ ἱερῶν γάμων ἐλθούσαις εἰς τὴν οἰκίαν, ὠνηταῖς εἴτε ἄλλῳ ὁτῳοῦν τρόπῳ κτηταῖς.

42. λοιπά, 'still in existence.'

1. Κύμῃ. Which of the cities of this name is meant, is unknown, 1269 a.
as also in 7 (5). 5. 1305 a 1.

πλῆθός τι, 'a definite number,' as in 3. 1. 1274 b 41. **Τῶν αὑτοῦ συγγενῶν** is to be taken with μαρτύρων—'witnesses from the number of his own kinsmen.' We are reminded of the practice of compurgation, but compurgators were called by both parties to the suit, they 'swore to the purity and honesty of the oath of their principal,' and they had to be 'possessed of qualities and legal qualifications which should secure their credibility' (Stubbs, Const. Hist. of England 1. 610–1). Some traces of a not very dissimilar custom to that mentioned by Aristotle have been thought to be discoverable in the law of Gortyna—see the recently discovered Gortyna Inscription, col. 2. 37 sqq.: 3. 51: 4. 8, and the comments of Zitelmann (Bücheler und Zitelmann, Das Recht von Gortyn, p. 76–77).

3. ζητοῦσι δὲ . . . πάντες. Cp. 1. 1. 1252 a 2: 2. 5. 1263 b 4: Eth. Nic. 10. 2. 1172 b 36, ὃ πᾶσι δοκεῖ, τοῦτ' εἶναί φαμεν.

4. τοὺς πρώτους, 'the earliest human beings': cp. Polyb. 4. 20. 7, τοὺς πρώτους Ἀρκάδων ('priscos Arcades'): Plato, Tim. 22 A, Φορωνέως τοῦ πρώτου λεχθέντος: Antiphon, Tetral. 3. 1. 2, τοὺς πρῶτον γενομένους ἡμῶν.

5. εἴτε γηγενεῖς ἦσαν εἴτ' ἐκ φθορᾶς τινὸς ἐσώθησαν. Here two current views as to the human race are grouped together—the former enshrined in Greek poetry and literature (Pindar, Nem. 6. 1: Hesiod, Op. et Dies, 108: Plato, Menex. 237 D), and taught by Anaximander (Zeller, Gr. Ph. 1. 209 sq.)—the latter adopted by Plato in the Laws (676 sqq.) and the Timaeus (22 B sqq.). Euripides had already dealt a blow at the 'earth-born' myth of man's origin in his Ion, where Ion says (482), *γῆς ἄρ' ἐκπέφυκα μητρός*, and Xuthus rejoins, *οὐ πέδον τίκτει τέκνα*: and Plato (Laws 781 E sqq.) holds that 'the human race either had no beginning at all and will never have an end, but always will be and has been, or had a beginning an immense time ago' (Prof. Jowett's translation). Aristotle himself believed that not only the world (Zeller, Gr. Ph. 2. 2. 432 sq.), but also mankind (ibid. 508. 1) had existed from everlasting. (See on this subject Dicaearch. Fragm. 3 and 4 (Müller, Fr. Hist. Gr. 2. 234 sq.), and Bernays, Theophrastos über Frömmigkeit, p. 44 sqq., and Über die unter Philon's Werken stehende Schrift über die Unzerstörbarkeit des Weltalls, p. 58 sqq.) Thus Aristotle cannot have believed in the 'earth-born' theory of man's origin, though in de Gen. An. 3. 11. 762 b 28 sqq. he thinks it worth while to inquire how *γηγενεῖς* can have come into being. The other view, that the earliest known men were the survivors of some vast *φθορά* was more reconcilable with the doctrine of the eternity of the human race, but Aristotle does not seem to admit universal, or nearly universal, *φθοραί*. The *φθοραί* he recognizes are quite partial, arising from some local excess of moisture or aridity (see the interesting discussion of the subject in Meteor. 1. 14). As to the Stoical view, see Zeller, Stoics E. T. pp. 155-160.

6. **ὁμοίους κ.τ.λ.** For *ὁμοίους καί*, see Bon. Ind. 511 a 21: Vahlen, Beitr. zu Poet. 3. 314: Sus.[1], Ind. Gramm. s. v., who compares 4 (7). 11. 1331 a 3. 'Similar to ordinary or even' (Bon. Ind. 357 b 20 sqq.) 'weak-minded people nowadays.' Why *οἱ πρῶτοι* should be so, Aristotle does not explain; but as to the *γηγενεῖς*, cp. de Part. An. 2. 4. 650 b 18, *συμβαίνει δ' ἔνιά γε καὶ γλαφυρωτέραν ἔχειν τὴν διάνοιαν τῶν τοιούτων, οὐ διὰ τὴν ψυχρότητα τοῦ αἵματος, ἀλλὰ διὰ τὴν λεπτότητα μᾶλλον καὶ διὰ τὸ καθαρὸν εἶναι· τὸ γὰρ γεῶδες οὐδέτερον ἔχει τούτων*, and Dio Chrys. Or. 21. 507 R, *παντελῶς σκληροὶ καὶ ἄγριοι, τῆς γῆς τὰ τέκνα*. As to the survivors of the *φθορά*, he probably conceived the *φθορά* as entailing a wholesale destruction of knowledge (cp. Aristot. Fragm. 2. 1474 b 6, [*αἱ παροιμίαι*] *παλαιᾶς εἰσὶ φιλοσοφίας ἐν ταῖς μεγίσταις ἀνθρώπων φθοραῖς ἀπολομένης ἐγκαταλείμματα περισωθέντα διὰ συντομίαν καὶ δεξιότητα*: and Metaph. Λ. 8. 1074 b 10 sq.): he also ascribes the progress of the arts to the

favouring influence of time (Eth. Nic. 1. 7. 1098 a 23 sq.: Poet. 4. 1449 a 9–15). Plato had already said that the remnant left by the deluge (in Greece, at all events—Tim. 22 D) would be hill-shepherds or herdsmen ignorant of the arts which flourish in cities (Laws 677 B–678 B), though he draws a favourable picture of their morals and social state (678 E–679 E). Contrast the opposite view of some of the later Stoics: *τῶν δὲ νεωτέρων στωικῶν φασί τινες τοὺς πρώτους καὶ γηγενεῖς τῶν ἀνθρώπων κατὰ πολὺ τῶν νῦν συνέσει διαφέροντας γεγονέναι* (Sext. Empir. adv. Phys. 1. 28).

9. ὥσπερ γὰρ κ.τ.λ. 'For, as in relation to the other arts, so in relation to the political [art, and its product, the political] organization it is impossible that everything should be written down with complete precision.' As to *αἱ ἄλλαι τέχναι*, cp. *τὸ κατὰ γράμματα ἰατρεύεσθαι φαῦλον*, Pol. 3. 16. 1287 a 33. It seems to be implied that as written law is necessarily couched in general terms, and human action, which it seeks to guide, is concerned with particulars, it is unlikely that the first form of a law will be as *ἀκριβής* (cp. Eth. Nic. 2. 2. 1104 a 1 sqq.) as it may be rendered by revision after fuller experience (cp. Plato, Laws 769 D, a passage probably present to Aristotle's mind here: Aristot. Pol. 3. 16. 1287 a 27: Eth. Nic. 1. 7. 1098 a 20, *περιγεγράφθω μὲν οὖν τἀγαθὸν ταύτῃ· δεῖ γὰρ ἴσως ὑποτυπῶσαι πρῶτον, εἶθ' ὕστερον ἀναγράψαι* et sqq.: Soph. El. 33. 183 b 17 sqq.: Rhet. 1. 1. 1354 b 2). For the omission of *περί* before *τὴν πολιτικὴν τάξιν*, Bonitz (Ind. 630 b 2) compares 7 (5). 10. 1311 b 37: Rhet. 2. 18. 1391 b 15, 17: see also below on 1274 b 12. *Ἡ πολιτικὴ τάξις* seems here to include not the *πολιτεία* only but also laws; it means something more, therefore, than *ἡ τάξις τῆς πολιτείας* means in Pol. 7 (5). 7. 1307 b 18, and elsewhere (cp. c. 10. 1271 b 40, where *ἡ Κρητικὴ τάξις* is used in a different sense from *τῆς πολιτείας ἡ τάξις*, 1272 a 4).

13. ἄλλον . . . τρόπον, i. e. looking not to cases where the law is antiquated and absurd, but to cases where changing it brings little gain and tends to weaken men's respect for law. It appears from 17, that Aristotle feels the same reluctance to disturb measures adopted by magistrates of the State.

17. ὠφελήσεται. See note on 1263 b 28. For the omission of the subject (M^s P^1 wrongly supply *τις*), see note on 1268 a 5.

19. ψεῦδος δὲ κ.τ.λ. Cp. 3. 16. 1287 a 32 sqq.

21. παρὰ τὸ ἔθος. If we adopt this reading (which is that of the better MSS.) instead of *πλὴν παρὰ τὸ ἔθος* Bekk., *παρά* will mean 'other than,' or 'except' (cp. 6 (4). 15. 1299 a 18, *ἕτερόν τι παρὰ τὰς πολιτικὰς ἀρχάς*, and 1. 13. 1259 b 25), and the *ἔθος* will be viewed as a kind of ἰσχύς: cp. 3. 15. 1286 b 29, ἰσχύν τινα περὶ αὑτὸν ᾗ δυνήσεται βιάζεσθαι τοὺς μὴ βουλομένους πειθαρχεῖν. For the thought, cp. 7 (5). 9. 1310 a 14 sqq.

τοῦτο, i.e. τὸ ἔθος. Cp. Rhet. 1. 10. 1369 b 6, ἔθει δὲ (γίνεται), ὅσα διὰ τὸ πολλάκις πεποιηκέναι ποιοῦσιν.

23. ἑτέρους νόμους καινούς. For the order, cp. 1. 2. 1252 b 15–16: de Part. An. 2. 14. 658 a 28, καθ' ὅλον τὸ σῶμα πρανές: Pol. 2. 11. 1272 b 26, αὗται αἱ πολιτεῖαι τρεῖς. We have, however, in the indictment of Socrates (Xen. Mem. 1. 1: Diog. Laert. 2. 40) ἕτερα καινὰ δαιμόνια (though in the version of the same indictment given by Plato, Apol. 24 B, ἕτερα δαιμόνια καινά). So we find in de Gen. An. 3. 2. 752 b 6, στόλον μικρὸν ὀμφαλώδη. In each case, probably, a reason can be discerned for the order in which the words are placed.

24. εἰ καὶ κινητέοι, 'if in fact it is allowable to change them': see Riddell, Apology of Plato, p. 168, and compare the use of εἰ καί in 2. 2. 1261 a 21 and 2. 11. 1273 b 6.

25. Should the laws which embody the constitution be changed? Or sacred laws? Or unwritten laws, such as are referred to in 3. 16. 1287 b 5? Should laws be allowed to be changed even in the case of the best constitution? And is anybody to be permitted to propose a change, or only selected persons? Plato had held (Laws 634 D–E) that only old men should be allowed to draw attention to defects in the laws. Aristotle is, however, perhaps thinking of assigning the right of proposing a change to a specially constituted magistracy.

26. ταῦτα γὰρ ἔχει μεγάλην διαφοράν. 'For there is a great difference between these various alternatives.' (See for this expression Bon. Ind. 192 b 13 sqq.) Hence the discussion of the question is likely to take time, and Aristotle drops it.

C. 9. **29.** Aristotle speaks in 4 (7). 14. 1333 b 18 sq. of 'the writers on the Lacedaemonian Constitution' as if there were not a few of them, and describes them as 'admiring the lawgiver because he had trained his citizens to face perils and thus enabled the State to win a wide supremacy.' He names only one of them, Thibron, but Xenophon's work on the subject is also probably present to his mind (see Sus.[2], Note 911[ab], who refers to Xen. Rep. Lac. 1. 1), besides others which, like that of Critias, have not come down to us. Ephorus had treated of the Lacedaemonian constitution in his history, and he too may possibly be referred to. Aristotle mentions in the chapter before us (1271 a 37) that he was not the first to criticise the arrangements respecting the Admiralship, but it is not certain whether he means that writers on the constitution had done so. The grounds on which the Lacedaemonian constitution was approved were very various. Hippodamus, like others after him, would praise it for the distinction which it drew between soldiers on the one hand and cultivators and artisans on the other, but it seems to have been commonly commended mainly for two reasons—first, because the system of training which it enforced had given the State empire, and secondly, because it harmonized the claims of the Few and the Many. It was held to be a skilful mixture of all constitutions (2. 6. 1265 b 33 sqq.), and especially of two, democracy and oligarchy (6 (4). 9. 1294 b 14 sqq.). At Sparta rich and poor received the same education in childhood, they dressed alike and fared alike at the public mess-tables. This would please both Phaleas (c. 7. 1266 b 31 sqq.) and Ephorus (ap. Strab. p. 480). Oligarchs and democrats, soldiers and philosophers all found something to commend at Sparta. Socrates commended the obedience to law which gave the State happiness in peace and irresistible strength in war (Xen. Mem. 4. 4. 15). On the other hand, opinions were much divided as to the Helotage (Plato, Laws 776 C sqq.), and other weak points in Lacedaemonian institutions were well known to Thucydides and Isocrates. Aristotle would no doubt be fully acquainted with what had been said on the subject, but he is especially influenced by the views of Plato. Plato is perhaps more favourable to the Lacedaemonian constitution in the Republic than in the Laws. In the Republic he ranks it (with the Cretan) next to the ideal constitution, whereas in the Laws he assigns this place to the constitution described in the dialogue, which differs much from the Lacedaemonian, and if it is true that in the Laws a new merit is discovered in the Lacedaemonian constitution—its mixed and tempered character—it is also true that much is borrowed in this dialogue from Attic legislation.

If we turn to Aristotle's criticisms in the chapter before us, we note first of all that his object is mainly to point out defects, not to give a complete estimate of the constitution. His admiration for Lycurgus is sufficiently proved by his reference to him in 6 (4). 11. 1296 a 20, and by the remark which Plutarch reproduces from the Polities—*δι' ὅπερ καὶ Ἀριστοτέλης ἐλάττονας σχεῖν φησι τιμὰς ἢ προσῆκον ἦν αὐτὸν ἔχειν ἐν Λακεδαίμονι, καίπερ ἔχοντα τὰς μεγίστας· ἱερόν τε γάρ ἐστιν αὐτοῦ, καὶ θύουσι καθ' ἕκαστον ἐνιαυτὸν ὡς θεῷ* (Lycurg. c. 31). In criticising the constitution he takes the word *πολιτεία* in its widest sense and examines the whole social and political organization of the State. Plato had tested the Lacedaemonian constitution by comparing it either with the ideal constitution or with other actual constitutions of Greece, whereas Aristotle also inquires how far its arrangements fulfil the design of the lawgiver, which was to found an ἀριστοκρατία. This was perhaps the most novel feature of his criticisms. He had included a notice of the Lacedaemonian constitution in his Polities—indeed, he probably repeats in the chapter before us not a little of what he had said in that work—and his studies must have given him an unrivalled knowledge of the subject, but his grasp of the details must not lead us to forget how often he repeats previous criticisms of Plato. Plato had already said that the Lacedaemonian laws aimed only at the production of a single kind of virtue, warlike prowess (Laws 626 A sqq., etc.)—that the Spartans valued external goods such as wealth and honour more than virtue (Rep. 548)—that the Helot type of slavery was wrong (Rep. 469 B sq.: Laws 776 sqq.)—that the lives of the Spartan women were left unregulated by law (Laws 780 E). He so far anticipated in the Laws Aristotle's account of the causes which had thinned the ranks of the Spartan citizens that he makes the lots of land in his State inalienable and indivisible (740 B sqq.), forbids dowries (742 C), restricts the right of bequest (922 E sqq.), and asserts the claims of relatives both in relation to inheritances and in the disposal of orphan heiresses (924 D sqq.). On the other hand, his attention does not seem to have been called to the mischievousness of the Lacedaemonian law by which the enjoyment of political rights was made dependent on the payment of a quota to the syssitia. Nor does he criticise the Lacedaemonian Kingship, Senate, and Ephorate, though we observe that he does not seem to adopt any of these institutions in the Laws.

30. δύο. The organization of slavery in the Lacedaemonian State is apparently criticised in what follows as being by no means the best possible; the γυναικῶν ἄνεσις, on the other hand, as not only wrong from an ideal point of view but also as not in accordance with the spirit of the constitution (1269 b 12–14). The δίαιτα τῶν ἐφόρων (1270 b 31) and the φιδίτια (1271 a 31) are criticised on the latter ground. In 1271 a 41 sqq. we find a criticism of the ὑπόθεσις of the constitution which may perhaps be brought under the first of the two heads, though the ὑπόθεσις itself can hardly be said νενομοθετῆσθαι (32). What does Aristotle consider the ὑπόθεσις of the Lacedaemonian constitution to be? Probably he views it as an ἀριστοκρατία (i. e. as a mixture of ἀρετή and δῆμος) organized πρὸς τὸ κρατεῖν: cp. 1269 b 19–20: 1271 b 2–3: 4 (7). 2. 1324 b 7 sqq.: 2. 11. 1273 a 4, πρὸς τὴν ὑπόθεσιν τῆς ἀριστοκρατίας καὶ τῆς πολιτείας: 6 (4).

7. 1293 b 15 sqq. Yet, as Sus.[2] (Note 1262) points out, Aristotle seems to speak in 6 (4). 9. 1294 b 14 sqq. as if the Lacedaemonian constitution were a polity, i. e. a combination of oligarchical and democratic elements. As in the chapter on Phaleas, so here Aristotle begins with subjects connected with the primary elements of the State—slavery, the household, property, population, and the like—and passes on from them to constitutional questions.

34. For the omission of *πόλει*, see note on 1266 b 1. We see from Plato, Laws 831 C sqq., that something more than slavery—freedom from the spirit of money-getting—is necessary to secure leisure to a State. In illustration of the difficulty of determining how the citizens of a State may best be secured leisure from necessary work, Aristotle refers to three slave-systems, in two of which the slaves had attacked their masters, while in the third, according to him, a similar catastrophe was only warded off by fortuitous circumstances. These three slave-systems were especially conspicuous and famous (Plato himself refers to two of them in entering on the subject of slavery, Laws 776 C sqq., a passage present to Aristotle's mind here); and it is perhaps for this reason that Aristotle regards their failure as proving the difficulty of the subject. It is not impossible, however, that they enjoyed a good deal of credit in some quarters: we see from the passage of the Laws just referred to, that even the Helotage of the Lacedaemonian State had its defenders. Many Greeks may have preferred serfage to slavery, and in all the three systems referred to, the slaves were only half enslaved (*μεταξὺ ἐλευθέρων καὶ δούλων*, Pollux 3. 83, quoted by Büchsenschütz, Besitz und Erwerb, p. 127: *δοῦλοι ἐπὶ τακτοῖς τισιν*, Strab. p. 365, cp. p. 701: *θητεύοντες*, Strab. p. 542). Aristotle, however, holds that serfs of the type of the Helots and Penestae (c. 5. 1264 a 34 sq.: 4 (7). 10. 1330 a 25 sqq.) are dangerous inmates in a State, especially if neighbouring States are not withheld, as in Crete, by their own interest from making common cause with the revolted serfs of their antagonist. Where this is not the case, war with neighbours commonly brings in its train risings of the serfs. As to the importance of the attitude of neighbours in this matter, see Plato, Rep. 579 A–B. In c. 10. 1272 b 18 sqq. another reason is given for the quiescence of the Cretan serfs—the distance of Crete from the rest of Greece, together with the fact that it possessed no dependencies outside the island to tempt interference, and was for a very long time exempt from invasion. They probably were not as purely Hellenic as the Helots; they do not seem to have been employed as hoplites in the wars (c. 5. 1264 a 21), and their freer and more satisfactory position (1264 a 21) may, as Oncken suggests (Sus.[2], Note 281), have made them more manageable. Aristotle's language in this passage seems to imply that the Argives, Messenians, and Arcadians had no class corresponding to the Helots; yet περίοικοι (serfs) are mentioned at Argos in 7 (5). 3. 1303 a 8 (Herodotus speaks of slaves in 6. 83), and it would seem that the Gymnesii or Gymnetes of Argos answered in some degree to the Helots (see Sus.[2], Note 1518, and Gilbert, Gr. Staatsalt. 2. 74). It is to be noticed that Aristotle in constructing his best State (4 (7). 10. 1330 a 25 sqq.) prefers slaves to serfs, and insists that, if serfs there are to be, they shall be non-Hellenic (βάρβαροι). The Mariandynian serfs of the Pontic Heracleia (Strabo, p. 542) were non-Hellenic, but we know not whether Aristotle would regard this race as sufficiently submissive (1330 a 26).

35. τὴν τῶν ἀναγκαίων σχολήν, 'leisure from necessary things' (i.e. necessary work): cp. Plato, Tim. 18 B, *τῶν ἄλλων ἐπιτηδευμάτων ἄγοντας σχολήν*, and Plut. Agis 5. 3, *πενία ἀσχολίαν τῶν καλῶν καὶ ἀνελευθερίαν ἐπιφέρουσα* (see Schömann's note on this passage). Cp. also [Plut.] Inst. Lac. c. 40, *ἓν δέ τι τῶν καλῶν καὶ μακαρίων ἐδόκει παρεσκευακέναι τοῖς πολίταις ὁ Λυκοῦργος, ἀφθονίαν σχολῆς· τέχνης μὲν γὰρ ἅψασθαι βαναύσου τὸ παράπαν οὐκ ἔξεστι . . . οἱ δὲ εἵλωτες αὐτοῖς εἰργάζοντο τὴν γῆν.*

1269 b. **3. τοῖς δὲ Λάκωσιν κ.τ.λ.** Cp. Isocr. Philip. § 51, *πολεμοῦσι μὲν γὰρ ['Αργεῖοι], ἐξ οὗ περ τὴν πόλιν οἰκοῦσι, πρὸς τοὺς ὁμόρους, ὥσπερ Λακεδαιμόνιοι, τοσοῦτον δὲ διαφέρουσιν ὅσον ἐκεῖνοι μὲν πρὸς ἥττους αὑτῶν, οὗτοι δὲ πρὸς κρείττους*, and § 74. Does *ἦσαν* mean 'at the time when the Helots first revolted'? Possibly, but the past tense recurs frequently throughout the chapter: see below on 1269 b 31.

5. ἐπεί adduces a proof that the cause assigned for the troubles of the Lacedaemonian State and the exemption of Crete is the true one.

7. καὶ εἰ μηδὲν ἕτερον, such as (e.g.) self-defence against their attacks. So Vict. 'si nihil periculi impenderet reipublicae ab hoc genere colonorum, relicto hoc malo.'

8. αὐτούς, 'serfs such as the Helots.' Aristotle gives a promise in 4 (7). 10. 1330 a 31 sq. to consider the question how slaves are to be treated. He would offer ultimate emancipation to slaves as a reward for good conduct. This is just what the Spartan owner had no power to do (Strabo, p. 365, *κριθῆναι δούλους ἐπὶ τακτοῖς τισιν, ὥστε τὸν ἔχοντα μήτ' ἐλευθεροῦν ἐξεῖναι μήτε πωλεῖν ἔξω τῶν* ὅρων τούτους). Plato (Rep. 549 A) seems to regard the Spartans as erring on the side of severity, for in his description of the timocratical man, the type of character corresponding to a timocracy like the Lacedaemonian and Cretan constitutions (544 C), he speaks of him as δούλοις ἄγριος, οὐ καταφρονῶν δούλων, ὥσπερ ὁ ἱκανῶς πεπαιδευμένος, and Aristotle himself is said by Plutarch to have ascribed the institution of the Crypteia to Lycurgus (Aristot. Fragm. 495. 1558 b 19 sqq.). But the Spartans may have had occasional fits of leniency.

12. τρόπον, probably 'mode of organization,' referring to τρόπον, 1269 a 36, not to τρόπον, 1269 b 9, for Aristotle is concerned rather with the organization than the administration of the State, and he is opposed to slave-organizations like the Lacedaemonian, not merely to the way in which the Spartans behaved to their slaves.

τοῦτο συμβαίνει (cp. 1269 a 40, οὐδέν πω τοιοῦτον συμβέβηκεν) probably refers to 1269 a 38 sq., and also to 1269 b 7 sqq.

13. προαίρεσιν. Cp. 19–22.

14. πρὸς εὐδαιμονίαν πόλεως. Aristotle adopts this phrase from Plato, Laws 781 B, a passage relating to the subject here discussed. But Mr. Congreve is probably right in explaining it here as = πρὸς τὴν ἀρίστην τάξιν, 1269 a 31 (see Sus.[2], Note 284).

ὥσπερ γὰρ κ.τ.λ. For μέρος, not μέρη, cp. Eth. Nic. 5. 10. 1134 b 10, τὸ δὲ κτῆμα καὶ τὸ τέκνον, ἕως ἂν ᾖ πηλίκον καὶ μὴ χωρισθῇ, ὥσπερ μέρος αὐτοῦ. In 3. 4. 1277 a 7 man and wife are said to be the component parts of the household, and perhaps the same thing is said here, though on the other hand Mr. Welldon may be right in translating μέρος, not 'the constituent elements,' but 'constituent elements.' For though man and wife are the most important parts of the household, others are mentioned in 1. 3. 1253 b 4–7. Plato thinks that, as women are inferior to men in excellence, and therefore need more legislation, the lawgiver who omits to legislate for them leaves far more than half his work undone. See on this subject Plato, Laws 781 A sq.: 806 C: Aristot. Rhet. 1. 5. 1361 a 10 sqq. The Spartan girls were trained both in gymnastic and music (Plato, Laws 806 A: cp. Plutarch, Lyc. c. 14), and marriage and the education of children were controlled by the State, but Aristotle looked to the State to do something more than this—to exercise a control over the life of women inside and outside the household and to develope in them, as well as in children (1. 13. 1260 b 13 sqq.), the moral virtues which they need to possess.

15. δῆλον ὅτι κ.τ.λ. What is the construction of this sentence? Vict. translates, 'ita prope accedere civitatem ut bifariam dissecta sit . . . existimandum est,' apparently making the sentence run *δῆλον ὅτι δεῖ νομίζειν καὶ πόλιν* (*εἶναι*) *ἐγγὺς τοῦ δίχα διῃρῆσθαι*, but the translators and commentators generally take *ἐγγὺς τοῦ δίχα* as an adverb meaning 'nearly equally.' Probably the latter view is correct, though adverbs thus formed do not seem to be by any means common.

19. ὅλην τὴν πόλιν. See below on 1273 a 38.

20. καρτερικήν. Compare the description of the Lacedaemonian training given by the Lacedaemonian interlocutor of the Laws in Laws 633 B sqq., where the expressions *καρτερήσεις τῶν ἀλγηδόνων, πολύπονος πρὸς τὰς καρτερήσεις, δειναὶ καρτερήσεις* are used.

22. ἐξημέληκεν, 'has wholly neglected to apply his principle.'

ζῶσι γὰρ κ.τ.λ. An old indictment (Eurip. Androm. 575 sqq.: Ibycus ap. Plutarch. Num. et Lycurg. inter se comp. c. 3: Dionys. Hal. Ant. Rom. 2. 24, *οὔτε ἀφῆκαν, ὥσπερ Λακεδαιμόνιοι, τὰς τῶν γυναικῶν φυλακάς*) stated in exceptionally strong language. What the charge amounts to, we see from Eth. Eud. 3. 2. 1231 a 19, *οἰνοφλυγία γὰρ καὶ γαστριμαργία καὶ λαγνεία καὶ ὀψοφαγία καὶ πάντα τὰ τοιαῦτα περὶ τὰς εἰρημένας ἐστὶν αἰσθήσεις, εἰς ἅπερ μόρια ἡ ἀκολασία διαιρεῖται* (cp. *πᾶσαν ἀκολασίαν*, Theopomp. Fragm. 178: Müller, Fr. Hist. Gr. 1. 308). Plato (Rep. 548 B) speaks of the Spartan women as the objects of extravagant expenditure; but in Laws 806 A we get a more favourable impression of their life, and we see from Plutarch's Lives of Agis and Cleomenes that even in the corruptest period there were noble exceptions. According to [Plutarch,] Apophth. Lac. Lycurg. 20, men looked back to a time when adultery was unknown at Sparta. *Πρός*, Bon. Ind. 641 b 46 sqq.

23. ὥστε ἀναγκαῖον κ.τ.λ. The necessity of this is explained by what is said in 1. 9. 1258 a 2 sqq. *Ἐν τῇ τοιαύτῃ πολιτείᾳ* means 'in a constitution of the kind we have just described' (cp. 17, *ἐν ὅσαις πολιτείαις φαύλως ἔχει τὸ περὶ τὰς γυναῖκας*, as well as c. 4. 1262 b 20 and c. 5. 1264 a 6). In a constitution which allows half the population to live a dissolute life, wealth as the means to dissoluteness must be honoured, especially if the dissolute half of the population bears virtual sway. In [Plutarch,] Apophth. Lac. Lycurg. 20, a Spartan of the 'good old days' asks, *πῶς ἂν μοιχὸς ἐν Σπάρτῃ γένοιτο, ἐν ᾗ πλοῦτος καὶ τρυφὴ καὶ καλλωπισμὸς ἀτιμάζονται;*

25. καθάπερ κ.τ.λ. We may gather from 4 (7). 2. 1324 b 9–21, what nations are referred to. Cp. Ephor. Fragm. 78 (Müller, Fr. Hist. Gr. 1. 258), or rather Scymnus Chius (888 sq.),

Ἐφ' οἷς ἐπεκλήθησαν Γυναικοκρατούμενοι οἱ Σαυρομάται.

Contrast 1. 2. 1252 b 5, ἐν δὲ τοῖς βαρβάροις τὸ θῆλυ καὶ δοῦλον τὴν αὐτὴν ἔχει τάξιν. It would seem, therefore, that the more warlike barbarian races allowed at all events some of their women to gain ascendency over them; but it does not follow that many or most of the sex were not made drudges. These nations were strong in θυμός, and θυμός, we learn from Pol. 4 (7). 7. 1327 b 40, is the seat of the affections as well as the source of military spirit.

τῶν στρατιωτικῶν καὶ πολεμικῶν γενῶν. For γένος in this sense, cp. Isocr. Paneg. § 67, ἔστι γὰρ ἀρχικώτατα μὲν τῶν γενῶν καὶ μεγίστας δυναστείας ἔχοντα Σκύθαι καὶ Θρᾷκες καὶ Πέρσαι. The word στρατιωτικός ('soldierlike') is not a common one, but it recurs in 1270 a 5. Compare the contrast of πολεμικός and στρατηγικός in [Plut.] Inst. Lac. c. 25.

26. Κελτῶν. The commentators refer to Athen. Deipn. p. 603 a (see Sus.[2], Note 287). See also Diod. 5. 32. 7 and Strabo 4. p. 199, who probably draw from the same source as Athenaeus. Sextus Empiricus speaks in similar terms of the Germani (Pyrrhon. Hyp. 3. 199) and of the Persians (ibid. 1. 152). 'Aristotle, like the earlier Greeks generally, appears to make no distinction between the Celts and the Germans' (Sus.[2], whose notes 287, 722, 953 should be consulted). From the sources of the Danube in the mountain Pyrene (the Pyrenees?) the Celts seem to have extended to the sea (Meteor. 1. 13. 350 a 36 sqq.: Eth. Nic. 3. 10. 1115 b 26 sqq.). There were, besides, Celts at this time 'settled in the neighbourhood of the Ionian Gulf,' an embassy from whom reached Alexander after he had crossed the Danube (Arrian, Anab. 1. 4. 6). Ephorus appears to have given a great extension to the designation (Strabo 4. p. 199, ὑπερβάλλουσαν τῷ μεγέθει λέγει τὴν Κελτικήν, ὥστε ἥσπερ νῦν Ἰβηρίας καλοῦμεν ἐκείνοις τὰ πλεῖστα προσνέμειν μέχρι Γαδείρων). As to φανερῶς, cp. Polyb. 6. 56. 4, παρὰ μὲν Καρχηδονίοις δῶρα φανερῶς διδόντες λαμβάνουσι τὰς ἀρχάς, and perhaps we should also compare the language of Plutarch, Pelopid. c. 19, with regard to the lawgivers of Thebes—λαμπρὸν δὲ τὸν ἔρωτα ταῖς παλαίστραις ἐνεθρέψαντο συγκεραννύντες τὰ ἤθη τῶν νέων. If Aristotle is not thinking exclusively of barbarian races, he may allude to the Thebans here, and also to the Cretans (cp. c. 10. 1272 a 24) and Chalcidians (Aristot. Fragm. 93. 1492 b 22 sqq.).

28. ὁ μυθολογήσας πρῶτος. Sus.[2] (Note 288) points out that just as Aristotle traces the πόλις to a 'first constructor' (1. 2. 1253 a 30), so here he speaks of ὁ μυθολογήσας πρῶτος. For a similar hint of the truth in myth, see 5 (8). 6. 1341 b 2. The myths are conceived by Aristotle to embody fragments of truth saved from the wreck of previous periods of greatness in philosophy and art (Metaph. Λ. 8. 1074 b 1–14). Cp. Plato, Theaet. 180 C. What age, however, he ascribes to the myth here mentioned does not appear.

συζεῦξαι, 'paired,' as in 4 (7). 16. 1335 a 16 ('join in wedlock'). Cp. Lucret. 1. 31–40. The two deities are often named together: see Tümpel, Ares und Aphrodite (Teubner, 1880), who illustrates their association in local worships (esp. at Thebes, Aeschyl. Sept. c. Theb. 135 sqq.: cp. Hes. Theog. 933 sqq.)—in poetry (Pind. Pyth. 4. 155: Simonides, Fragm. 43 Bergk: Aeschyl. Suppl. 664 sq.)—and in art. The Ares of the Villa Ludovisi has an Eros at his feet and may perhaps have formed a group with Aphrodite: the Venus of Milo is thought by some to have formed part of a similar group. Tümpel points out that the tradition passed to Rome, where it did the Julian house the service of bringing Venus Victrix, its foundress, into close union with the national god Mars, and thus consecrated the rule of the Caesars. So on silver coins of Augustus we see the Julian Venus looking down at a helmet in her hand, the symbol of Mars (Tümpel, p. 677 n.): compare the couplet ascribed to Petronius Arbiter (Fragm. 46 Buecheler):—

Militis in galea nidum fecere columbae:
Adparet, Marti quam sit amica Venus.

The lines of Rutilius Namatianus (De Reditu Suo, 1. 67 sq.) may also be quoted—

Auctorem generis Venerem Martemque fatemur,
Aeneadum matrem Romulidumque patrem.

Sulla, indeed, had already inscribed on his trophies *Ἄρη καὶ Νίκην καὶ Ἀφροδίτην* (Plut. Sulla c. 19), and the month sacred to Venus at Rome (April) came next to that sacred to Mars (Plut. Numa c. 19). Compare also the Chalcidian song, Aristot. Fragm. 93. 1492 b 30, *σὺν γὰρ ἀνδρείᾳ καὶ ὁ λυσιμελὴς Ἔρως ἐπὶ Χαλκιδέων θάλλει πόλεσιν*. Aphrodite is, however, occasionally conjoined with Dionysus, as in Probl. 30. 953 b 31, *ὀρθῶς Διόνυσος καὶ Ἀφροδίτη λέγονται μετ' ἀλλήλων εἶναι*, but this is quite comprehensible, as is also the statement of the Scholiast on Aristophanes, Ranae 315, *συνίδρυται τῇ Δήμητρι ὁ Διόνυσος*.

30. **κατακώχιμοι**. See critical note.

31. **τοῦθ'**, 'the latter.' Cp. Plut. Agis c. 7, *ἅτε δὴ τοὺς Λακεδαιμονίους ἐπισταμένας κατηκόους ὄντας ἀεὶ τῶν γυναικῶν καὶ πλεῖον ἐκείναις τῶν δημοσίων ἢ τῶν ἰδίων αὐτοῖς πολυπραγμονεῖν διδόντας*, and Lycurg. c. 14,

καὶ διὰ τοῦτο μᾶλλον τοῦ προσήκοντος αὐτὰς ἐθεράπευον καὶ δεσποίνας προσηγόρευον.

ὑπῆρχεν. We have already had *ἦσαν* in 1269 b 4, and the past tense recurs in 1269 b 37, 1270 a 18, 31, 32, though we find the present in 1270 a 23. Aristotle appears to look back to the days of Lacedaemonian greatness, wishing perhaps to make his criticism of the constitution apply to the time when its apparent success was greatest.

32. ἐπὶ τῆς ἀρχῆς αὐτῶν, 'at the time when they held the empire of Hellas': cp. c. 10. 1271 b 33, *τὴν ἀρχὴν τὴν Ἑλληνικήν*, and Xen. Cyrop. 8. 7. 1, *ἐπὶ τῆς αὐτοῦ ἀρχῆς*. Aristotle probably refers to the time between the close of the Peloponnesian War and the battle of Leuctra (cp. Xen. Anab. 6. 6. 12 sq., and Diod. 14. 10).

καίτοι κ.τ.λ. The meaning is—'and yet if the rulers of the State are ruled by women, how does this differ from women holding office themselves, of which of course the Spartans would not dream?' Aristotle's words recall the remark addressed to Gorgo the wife of Leonidas (Plut. Lycurg. c. 14)—*εἰπούσης γάρ τινος, ὡς ἔοικε, ξένης πρὸς αὐτὴν ὡς "μόναι τῶν ἀνδρῶν ἄρχετε ὑμεῖς αἱ Λάκαιναι," "μόναι γάρ," ἔφη, "τίκτομεν ἄνδρας."* For the construction of *διαφέρειν* with *ἤ*, cp. c. 10. 1272 b 13 and Xen. Hell. 3. 4. 19.

35. ἀλλ' εἴπερ, 'but if for any purpose whatever': cp. 7 (5). 11. 1315 a 9, and see Bon. Ind. 217 a 55 sqq.

36. ταῦθ', i.e. *τὰ τοῦ πολέμου.*

37. ἐδήλωσαν δ'. Cp. Xen. Hell. 6. 5. 28: Plutarch, Agesilaus c. 31. Plato may possibly have this circumstance in view in Laws 813 E–814 B. Theopompus seems to have mentioned the fact (Fragm. 291: Müller, Fr. Hist. Gr. 1. 327). As Vict. says (note on 4 (7). 11. 1330 b 32), the Spartan women appear to have behaved far better during the defence of Sparta against Pyrrhus in 272 B.C. (Plutarch, Pyrrhus c. 27).

38. Sus. translates—'for they were of no use any more than women in other States are on similar occasions.' But there is probably a reference to 34, *χρησίμου δ' οὔσης τῆς θρασύτητος πρὸς οὐδὲν τῶν ἐγκυκλίων*, and I take the meaning to be—'for they were not at all useful, as women are in other States' (i.e. *πρὸς τὰ ἐγκύκλια*). Cp. c. 10. 1272 a 40, *οὐδὲν γὰρ λήμματός τι τοῖς κόσμοις, ὥσπερ τοῖς ἐφόροις.* Women have often been useful in their own sphere in times of peril from war; for instance, there were 110 baking-women with the force blockaded in Plataea (Thuc. 2. 78).

39. θόρυβον δὲ κ.τ.λ. Lamb. 'sed trepidationem et tumultum civitati incusserunt maiorem quam hostes.'

μὲν οὖν, 'indeed' or 'true,' taken up by μὲν οὖν, 1270 a 8, and then answered by ἀλλά, 9. Aristotle here seeks to account for the error of the Lacedaemonian lawgiver, whose name he mentions (perhaps out of respect) only once in this chapter (1270 a 7), though oftener in later ones (c. 10. 1271 b 25: c. 12. 1273 b 33, 1274 a 29: also in 6 (4). 11. 1296 a 20). He often seeks to account for the errors he corrects (e. g. in 1. 9. 1257 b 40 sqq.), and explains his reason for doing so in Eth. Nic. 7. 15. 1154 a 22 sqq.

1270 a. **2. ἀπεξενοῦντο.** Giph. (p. 245) refers as to the Messenian war to Justin 3. 4, where however Ephorus is the original source (fragm. 53: Müller, Fr. Hist. Gr. 1. 247). Cp. also Aristot. Fragm. 504. 1560 b 17 sqq.

Ἀργείους. Πάλιν (3) seems to imply that the war with Argos preceded the other wars (see Bon. Ind. 559 b 5 sqq.).

4. σχολάσαντες. For the tense, see note on 1271 b 4, ἄρξαντες.

Ὁ νομοθέτης does not always, apparently, in this chapter mean Lycurgus (e. g. in 1270 b 19 the reference would seem to be to Theopompus, for it is to him that Aristotle ascribes the establishment of the ephorate in 7 (5). 11. 1313 a 26 sqq.); but here Lycurgus is referred to, as is evident from 1270 a 7. Thus the passage before us would seem to place the date of Lycurgus' legislation after the close of, at all events, the first Messenian War—i. e. according to the ordinary chronology, after B.C. 723. Yet Aristotle makes Lycurgus the guardian of Charilaus, whom the ordinary chronology places about 880 B.C. Trieber (Forschungen zur spartanischen Verfassungsgeschichte, pp. 44–65) illustrates the contradictions in the testimony of the authorities as to the date of Lycurgus, without, however, referring to this passage. Plutarch, indeed, already notes the fact (Lycurg. c. 1). The remarks of Plato (Laws 780–1, esp. 780 B and 781 A) are probably present to Aristotle's mind here. Plato speaks of Lycurgus as having given way in the matter of the women (εἴξαντος τοῦ νομοθέτου, 781 A). The following passage from Plutarch's Life of Lycurgus (c. 14) deserves to be quoted in full—*οὐ γάρ, ὥς Ἀριστοτέλης φησίν, ἐπιχειρήσας σωφρονίζειν τὰς γυναῖκας ἐπαύστοα μὴ κρατῶν τῆς πολλῆς ἀνέσεως καὶ γυναικοκρατίας διὰ τὰς πολλὰς στρατείας τῶν ἀνδρῶν, ἐν αἷς ἠναγκάζοντο κυρίας ἀπολείπειν ἐκείνας, καὶ διὰ τοῦτο μᾶλλον τοῦ προσήκοντος αὐτὰς ἐθεράπευον καὶ δεσποίνας προσηγόρευον· ἀλλὰ καὶ τούτων τὴν ἐνδεχομένην ἐπιμέλειαν ἐποιήσατο.* Is Plutarch here commenting on the passage of the Politics before us? It is quite possible that he is, for though he connects the γυναικοκρατία with the prolonged absence of the husbands on campaigns far more distinctly than Aristotle does, and though Aristotle says nothing about the title δέσποιναι, there is a great resemblance between what he makes Aristotle say and this passage of the Politics. Perhaps, however, it is more likely that Plutarch is commenting on a passage of the Polities, for Aristotle may have used this work here, as he seems to have done elsewhere in the Politics (see above, p. xviii sq.)

προωδοπεποιημένους. The form προωδοποιημένη, προωδοποίηται is elsewhere used by Aristotle (see Bon. Ind. s.v.), and Liddell and Scott (s.v.) would read προωδοποιημένους here. Προωδοπεποίηκε, however, as these authorities remark, occurs in Probl. 30. 1. 954 b 12. See Göttling's note on προῳκονόμηται in his edition of [Aristotle,] Oeconomica, p. 74.

5. **διὰ τὸν στρατιωτικὸν βίον.** Cp. c. 5. 1263 b 36, διὰ τὴν παιδείαν.

ἔχει. Sus. 'zur Entwicklung bringt': rather, perhaps, 'brings with it'—cp. Xen. Oecon. 4. 3, καὶ ἀσχολίας δὲ μάλιστα ἔχουσι καὶ φίλων καὶ πόλεως συνεπιμελεῖσθαι αἱ βαναυσικαὶ καλούμεναι [τέχναι].

6. **μέρη**, i.e. εἴδη, Bon. Ind. 455 b 46 sqq. (cp. 1271 b 2).

ἄγειν ἐπὶ τοὺς νόμους. Bonitz (Ind. 5 a 47) groups this expression with 7 (5). 11. 1313 a 19, ἄγειν τὰς βασιλείας ἐπὶ τὸ μετριώτερον. In Demosth. adv. Timocr. c. 31 we have ἄγετ' αὐτοὺς ὑπὸ τοὺς νόμους.

8. **αἰτίαι μὲν οὖν εἰσὶν αὗται τῶν γενομένων.** 'The causes then of what happened are these': for the omission of the article before αἰτίαι, see above on 1. 3. 1253 b 11. The causes referred to are the long absence of the husbands and the fact that the women had not been prepared by previous experience to submit to the lawgiver's yoke.

9. **ἡμεῖς.** See Vahlen, Beitr. zu Aristot. Poet. 2. 37, and Aristot. Aufs. 2. 17, where in commenting on 4 (7). 1. 1323 a 38 Vahlen refers among other passages to Pol. 4. (7). 3. 1325 a 16 sqq. and 6 (4). 2. 1289 b 9.

10. **τίνι** is probably neuter, like τοῦ ὀρθῶς καὶ μὴ ὀρθῶς in the next line, not masculine. Cp. Eth. Nic. 7. 3. 1146 a 2 sqq.

12. **πρότερον**, 1269 b 23 sq.: 1269 b 12–14.

13. **οὐ μόνον κ.τ.λ.**, i.e. not only spoils the harmony of the constitution taken by itself, but also spoils its influence and has an ill effect on character. The negligence of the lawgiver in relation to women is not only inconsistent with the ὑπόθεσις of the constitution, but also unfavourable to virtue: cp. 1269 b 12, ἔτι δ' ἡ περὶ τὰς γυναῖκας ἄνεσις καὶ πρὸς τὴν προαίρεσιν τῆς πολιτείας βλαβερὰ καὶ πρὸς εὐδαιμονίαν πόλεως. I incline to the reading αὐτῆς καθ' αὑτήν, not αὐτὴν καθ' αὑτήν, though the latter is the reading both of M^s and Π^2.

Τὴν φιλοχρηματίαν, because the Spartan fondness for money was well-known: cp. ἁ φιλοχρηματία Σπάρταν ὀλεῖ, ἄλλο δὲ οὐδέν (Aristot. Fragm. 501. 1559 b 27 sqq.), and Eurip. Androm. 446. For an instance of Spartan φιλοχρηματία, see Theopomp. Fr. 258 (Müller, Fr. Hist. Gr. 1. 322).

15. γάρ. 'I draw attention to this now, for the arrangements of the State respecting property are my next topic.'

τοῖς περὶ τὴν ἀνωμαλίαν τῆς κτήσεως. Cp. 1270 b 7, τὰ περὶ τὴν ἐφορείαν.

18. διόπερ. Property in general falling into a few hands, land did so too. For the fact, cp. Oecon. 1. 6. 1344 b 30, πρὸς δὲ φυλακὴν τοῖς τε Περσικοῖς συμφέρει χρῆσθαι καὶ τοῖς Λακωνικοῖς, on which Schömann (Opusc. Acad. 3. 223–4) remarks, that both the Persian and the Laconian methods referred to are designed for 'latifundia.' In what follows (18 sqq.) the unequal distribution of landed property in the Lacedaemonian State is traced in part to the freedom of gift (especially on marriage) and of bequest. But nothing here said excludes the operation of another cause, to which the inequality of wealth in this State is ascribed in 7 (5). 7. 1307 a 34, ἔτι διὰ τὸ πάσας τὰς ἀριστοκρατικὰς πολιτείας ὀλιγαρχικὰς εἶναι μᾶλλον πλεονεκτοῦσιν οἱ γνώριμοι, οἷον καὶ ἐν Λακεδαίμονι εἰς ὀλίγους αἱ οὐσίαι ἔρχονται. For this use of εἰς, compare also Plut. Agis c. 5, τῆς εὐπορίας εἰς ὀλίγους συρρυείσης, Pol. 6 (4). 15. 1299 b 1 sq., and 7 (5). 6. 1305 b 11, ἐξ ἐλαττόνων εἰς ἑξακοσίους ἦλθεν, and see Bon. Ind. 222 b 17 sqq.

τοῦτο δὲ κ.τ.λ. 'This matter'—i.e. probably τὰ περὶ τὴν ἀνωμαλίαν τῆς κτήσεως, though it is evident from what follows (τῆς πάσης χώρας, 23: τῆς χώρας, 29) that the faulty distribution of the land is uppermost in Aristotle's mind. Cp. 32, φαύλως αὐτοῖς εἶχε τὰ περὶ τὴν τάξιν ταύτην, and 38, βέλτιον τὸ διὰ τῆς κτήσεως ὡμαλισμένης πληθύειν ἀνδρῶν τὴν πόλιν, passages which serve to explain that before us. Aristotle is bound to trace the evil in some degree to the lawgiver, because he is occupied in the Second Book with a criticism of constitutions and lawgivers, and if the faulty distribution of property in the Lacedaemonian State had been due not to ill-conceived laws, but to some other cause, its mention would not have been in place in an attempt to show that the laws of the State were not wholly satisfactory (cp. 2. 1. 1260 b 34, διὰ τὸ μὴ καλῶς ἔχειν ταύτας τὰς νῦν ὑπαρχούσας, διὰ τοῦτο ταύτην δοκῶμεν ἐπιβαλέσθαι τὴν μέθοδον). The remarks which follow (18–39) are interesting, especially because they indicate to some extent how Aristotle intended to deal with the question of property in his 'best State.' We learn from his comments here what we do not learn from the Fourth Book, that he was in favour of making the citizens' lots of land inalienable and of regulating, or perhaps putting an end to, gift and bequest. He would abolish dowries or limit their amount, and would not allow either a father or his heir to give an heiress in marriage to any one they pleased. See below on 21. We do not learn whether he was, like Plato, in favour of Unigeniture.

19. ὠνεῖσθαι μὲν γὰρ κ.τ.λ. Μέν here = 'while.' The nom. ὁ νομοθέτης must be supplied from τῶν νόμων: cp. c. 8. 1268 a 5, if τὸν νομοθέτην is to be supplied there. Is οὐσίαν or γῆν to be supplied here with τὴν ὑπάρχουσαν? Probably the latter: cp. 8 (6). 4. 1319 a 13, τὸ μὴ δανείζειν εἴς τι μέρος τῆς ὑπαρχούσης ἑκάστῳ γῆς, and 10, ἦν δὲ τό γε ἀρχαῖον ἐν πολλαῖς πόλεσι νενομοθετημένον μηδὲ πωλεῖν ἐξεῖναι τοὺς πρώτους κλήρους, and the regulations of Plato in Laws 741 B: cp. also Heraclid. Pont. de Rebuspublicis 2. 7, πωλεῖν δὲ γῆν Λακεδαιμονίοις αἰσχρὸν νενόμισται· τῆς δ' ἀρχαίας μοίρας οὐδὲ ἔξεστιν: and [Plutarch,] Inst. Lac. c. 22 (quoted by Gilbert, Studien, p. 163–5), ἔνιοι δ' ἔφασαν ὅτι καὶ τῶν ξένων ὃς ἂν ὑπομείνῃ ταύτην τὴν ἄσκησιν τῆς πολιτείας κατὰ τὸ βούλημα τοῦ Λυκούργου μετεῖχε τῆς ἀρχῆθεν διατεταγμένης μοίρας· πωλεῖν δ' οὐκ ἐξῆν. Aristotle says nothing here about the 'original share': on the other hand, we see that the purchaser no less than the seller lay under a ban. Polybius (6. 45–46) implies that not only had the land been at the outset divided equally among the citizens, but that this equality of landed property was enforced by law; he also holds in the same passage that all ambition to make money was thoroughly and successfully discountenanced by the Lacedaemonian constitution. In all these contentions he is altogether at issue with Aristotle, who can hardly have credited Lycurgus with an equal division of the land belonging to the citizens, or he would have mentioned the fact in c. 7. 1266 b 14 sqq. and here, and who certainly does not hold that an equality of landed property was enforced by law, or the love of money discouraged. Aristotle, however, would evidently have attached but little value to an equal division of the land unsupported by checks on population and by laws making the lot inalienable and regulating gift and bequest. He refers to the subject of population in 1270 a 39 sqq.: here he dwells on the lawgiver's omission to regulate gift and bequest, and traces the inequality of property in part to this cause. Was this criticism of Aristotle's (or possibly a similar criticism in the Polities) known to the writer whom Plutarch follows in his life of Agis (c. 5)? For here the inequality of property in the Lacedaemonian State is traced to precisely the same cause—the freedom of gift and bequest—though the error is not ascribed to the original lawgiver, but to an ephor named Epitadeus in the fourth century, who is said to have effected a change in the law, of which Aristotle does not seem to be cognisant (ἐφορεύσας δέ τις ἀνὴρ δυνατός, αὐθάδης δὲ καὶ χαλεπὸς τὸν τρόπον, Ἐπιτάδευς ὄνομα, πρὸς τὸν υἱὸν αὐτῷ γενομένης διαφορᾶς ῥήτραν ἔγραψεν ἐξεῖναι τὸν οἶκον αὐτοῦ καὶ τὸν κλῆρον ᾧ τις ἐθέλοι καὶ ζῶντα δοῦναι καὶ καταλιπεῖν διατιθέμενον). There were evidently two views current in Greece as to the cause of the decline of the Lacedaemonian State: many (e. g. the writer of the fourteenth chapter of Xenophon's treatise de Republica Lacedaemoniorum and of [Plutarch,] Inst. Lac. c. 42) ascribed it to a departure from the laws of Lycurgus; Aristotle, on the contrary, ascribed it to faults in his laws (cp. 4 (7). 14. 1333 b 23, ἔτι δὲ τοῦτο γελοῖον, εἰ μένοντες ἐν τοῖς νόμοις αὐτοῦ, καὶ μηδενὸς ἐμποδίζοντος πρὸς τὸ χρῆσθαι τοῖς νόμοις, ἀποβεβλήκασι τὸ ζῆν καλῶς). Is it not, to say the least, possible that the writer whom Plutarch follows in this chapter of his Life of Agis, belonged to the former school, and was anxious to save the credit of Lycurgus from the criticism passed on him by Aristotle here or in the Polities? He in effect replies to Aristotle, that Lycurgus was not in fault; the fault was that of Epitadeus and the degenerate Spartans of his day. In just the same way Plutarch (Lycurgus c. 28) will not believe that Lycurgus can have had anything to do with the Crypteia, which Aristotle had attributed to him, or with the illtreatment of the Helots generally, and in another chapter of the same life (c. 14), as we have seen (note on 1270 a 4), will not admit that Lycurgus failed to subject the women to his laws.

21. διδόναι δὲ καὶ καταλείπειν κ.τ.λ. We must here again supply τὴν ὑπάρχουσαν γῆν. Vict. 'non vidit idem incommodum nasci ex utroque facto, non minus enim usu venit ut aliqui locupletiores quam oporteat fiant posteriore hoc modo quam priore.' A man might impoverish himself and his family and enrich others by giving and bequeathing as easily as by selling. He might, for instance, give or bequeath more than he ought to a favourite son and so leave his other sons poorly off, or he might give or bequeath to some flatterer or legacy-hunter (Plato, Laws 923 B: cp. Aristot. Pol. 2. 5. 1263 b 21 sq.) property which ought to have descended to his own children, but Aristotle probably refers especially to the giving and bequeathing of dowries to daughters (cp. 25). If these were large, as they often were at Sparta, the father might impoverish both himself and his sons and enrich husbands perhaps already sufficiently wealthy, while his own sons, if impoverished, would be little likely to receive large dowries with their brides. Thus the rich would become richer and the poor poorer. The Spartan father, however, seems from what follows to have had not only full power to give and bequeath dowries, but also full power to give and bequeath an ἐπίκληρος or heiress to any one he pleased. The Attic law also gave this power to the father, though his exercise of the right to bequeath an ἐπίκληρος was often, it would appear, contested by the relatives, if his will interfered with their claims to her hand (C. F. Hermann, Gr. Ant., ed. Thalheim, Rechtsalt. p. 57. 1). The Lacedaemonian law, however, seems to have gone further than the Attic, for if the father died leaving an ἐπίκληρος and without having disposed of her hand by will, the person who inherited the ἐπίκληρος had full power to give her in marriage to any one he pleased. He was not bound to give her in marriage to a relative; he might give her away to an entire stranger, possibly to a man already rich. In this way again the rich would become richer and the poor poorer. Under the Attic law an ἐπίκληρος who had not been given or bequeathed in marriage by her father descended to the nearest male relative, who would be entitled to marry her if he chose, but if he did not, would have no right to give her in marriage to any one he pleased: the right to marry her would in fact pass from him to the male relative next in succession. 'If the person entitled to marry a rich ἐπίκληρος waived his claim, he left the field open to the claims of less near relatives (Isaeus 3. 74, p. 45, and 10. 5, p. 80), while in the case of a poor ἐπίκληρος (θῆσσα) the Attic law required the nearest relative to marry her or to give her a dowry' (Hermann-Thalheim, p. 57. 1). Aristotle holds that property stands a better chance of being evenly distributed when inheritances pass, not by gift or bequest, but by descent, and he recommends oligarchies to adopt this system of succession (7 (5). 8. 1309 a 23 sqq.). Thus, though he would prefer the provisions of the Attic law to those of the Lacedaemonian, he would evidently wish to go far beyond them. He is clearly unwilling to allow even a father to give or bequeath an ἐπίκληρος to any one he pleased, and he may well have been in favour of abolishing the right of bequest altogether, or at any rate of imposing severe restrictions on it. Plato had adopted the latter course in the Laws (922 E sqq.), where he confines the discretion of testators within narrow limits and exhorts them to remember that their property belongs not to themselves alone, but to their family (γένος) and to the whole State (contrast the language of Plutarch as to Solon's law περὶ διαθηκῶν, Solon c. 21), while he prescribes that in the disposal of heiresses not bequeathed in marriage by their fathers regard shall be had to nearness of relationship and to the preservation of the lot, and in fact gives the relatives in a fixed order of succession the right to marry the heiress, thus withholding from the inheritor of the ἐπίκληρος the prerogative which he possessed at Sparta of giving her in marriage to any one he pleased. In the time of Herodotus, if the father had not betrothed his ἐπίκληρος before he died, it fell to the Lacedaemonian King to determine to whom she was to be married (Hdt. 6. 57), but possibly only in case there were more claimants than one for her hand; it would seem, however, that by the time of Aristotle the inheritor of the ἐπίκληρος had come to have the same right to dispose of her hand as her father. There were some who asserted that Lycurgus forbade dowries (see C. F. Hermann, De vestigiis institutorum veterum per Platonis de Legibus libros indagandis, p. 24, n. 78, who refers to Hermippus ap. Athen. Deipn. p. 555 C, Aelian, Var. Hist. 6. 6, and Justin 3. 3. 8). In Crete dowries were fixed in amount by law at half a son's share: this had been mentioned by Ephorus (ap. Strab. p. 482) and was probably known to Aristotle. Compare the Gortyna Inscription, col. 4. 48, and see Bücheler und Zitelmann, Das Recht von Gortyn, p. 116. The law of Gortyna also placed a maximum limit on gifts (Bücheler und Zitelmann, pp. 125–9), which seem usually to have been left uncontrolled by Greek legislation (Hermann-Thalheim, p. 64). Under the Attic law there was no right of bequest if there were sons (Isaeus 3. 68, p. 45), but if the story of Epitadeus, as Plutarch tells it, is true, testators at Sparta would appear not to have been subject to this restriction, for Epitadeus' object in introducing the right of bequest is implied to have been to disinherit his own son.

23. καὶ τῶν γυναικῶν, i.e. not only belongs to a few but to women. For the fact, cp. Plutarch, Agis c. 4, τῆς τε μητρὸς Ἀγησιστράτας καὶ τῆς μάμμης Ἀρχιδαμίας, αἳ πλεῖστα χρήματα Λακεδαιμονίων ἐκέκτηντο: and c. 7, ἦν δὲ τότε τῶν Λακωνικῶν πλούτων ἐν ταῖς γυναιξὶ τὸ πλεῖστον.

24. γινομένων. The tense indicates a continued occurrence of the circumstance: cp. 1270 b 5.

25. ἦν. For the suppression of ἄν, see Goodwin, Moods and Tenses, § 49. 2.

26. ἢ καί, here apparently 'or even': see note on 1264 a 15.

νῦν δ' ἔξεστι, 'but, as it is, so far from that being the case . . .' I do not think, with Bücheler, Sus. (see Sus.[2], Note 304), and others, that we are obliged to suppose a lacuna after τετάχθαι. The law, says Aristotle, ought to fix some limit to the amount of dowries, but, as it is, so far from doing so, it actually allows the father or his representative to give an heiress in marriage to any one they please, or, in other words, to dispose as they like of an entire inheritance. It goes, in fact, quite into an extreme in its complaisance. We often find a contrast between what ought to be and what is drawn, as here, by means of *βέλτιον* or *δεῖ* followed by *νῦν δέ* (e. g. in 1271 a 11–14 and 1273 b 21 sqq.).

27. ὅτῳ ἂν βούληται. According to Plutarch, Lysand. c. 30 (cp. Stob. Floril. 67. 16), there was a form of action at Sparta (*κακογαμίου δίκη*) available against those who looked to the wealth rather than the virtue of a family in marriage (cp. Plutarch, Apophth. Lac., Lysand. 15. 230 A). But of this Aristotle seems to know nothing.

28. μὴ διαθέμενος, 'without having disposed of her hand by will.'

ὃν ἂν καταλίπῃ κληρονόμον. For the phrase, cp. Plato, Laws 740 B. Camerarius (p. 99) asks, 'qui autem est heres iste alius praeter illam *ἐπίκληρον*?' and Coray in his edition of the Politics (p. 276) quotes Harpocration's explanation of *ἐπίκληρος*—*ὀρφανὴ ἐπὶ παντὶ τῷ κλήρῳ καταλελειμμένη, μὴ ὄντος αὐτῇ ἀδελφοῦ.* If all the property of the father passed to the *ἐπίκληρος*, how would it be possible for him to leave a *κληρονόμος* in addition to the *ἐπίκληρος*? (It may be noted that Harpocration's account seems not to be literally correct, for there might be more *ἐπίκληροι* than one (C. F. Hermann, Gr. Ant. 3. § 64. 11), but that does not concern us here.) The explanation of the enigma probably is, that the *κληρονόμος* referred to in the passage before us is the *κληρονόμος τῆς ἐπικλήρου*, the person who inherits the *ἐπίκληρος*: cp. Demosth. contra Eubulid. c. 41, *ἐπικλήρου δὲ κληρονομήσας εὐπόρου*, and Heraclid. Pont. de Rebuspubl. 28, *καὶ ἀποθανόντος τοῦ ἀνδρός, ὥσπερ τἄλλα, οὕτω καὶ τὰς γυναῖκας κληρονομοῦσιν.* C. F. Hermann (Gr. Ant. 3. § 64. 10) quotes Gans, Erbrecht, 1. 339—'diesen' (i. e. this recognition of the *ἐπίκληρος*) 'liegt durchaus nicht der Begriff zu Grunde, dass sie selbst als Erbende auftreten, sondern dass sie mit dem Vermögen von den Collateralen ererbt werden.' So too Caillemer (Droit de succession à Athènes, p. 40) says that in an *ἐπιδικασία* for an heiress 'les formes de procédure ressemblaient beaucoup à celles que le législateur avait établies pour les démandes d'envoi en possession d'un heredité.' The *κληρονόμος* would be 'the nearest adult male relative, or if there should be more than one equally near, the eldest of them' (Sus.², Note 305), for we need hardly concern ourselves with the unlikely case of the father naming a *κληρονόμος* without disposing of his daughter's hand.

29. τοιγαροῦν κ.τ.λ. As the land found its way into fewer and fewer hands, the number of citizens would dwindle, especially as in the Lacedaemonian State the citizen who could not pay his quota to the syssitia lost his political rights. As to the extent of the territory, cp. Isocr. Panath. § 45, (Λακεδαιμόνιοι) ἔχοντες πόλιν ἀλλοτρίαν καὶ χώραν οὐ μόνον ἱκανήν, ἀλλ' ὅσην οὐδεμία πόλις τῶν Ἑλληνίδων. Does Aristotle mean by τῆς χώρας the territory belonging to Spartan citizens both in Laconia and in Messenia, or in Laconia alone, for Messenia had long been lost to the Lacedaemonians, when he wrote? He is probably speaking of the time before Leuctra (cp. ἦσαν, 31), and, if so, he refers to Laconia and Messenia together. It is perhaps not necessary to suppose that he means 31,500 ἀργοί, though, as a matter of fact, the Spartans were ἀργοί. If he does, he need not have gone so far as to Babylon to find a parallel to the extent of the State-territory in Plato's Laws. See note on 1265 a 15. As the women who owned land would be married to Spartans, the military strength of the State can hardly have been impaired, however large the number of households may have been in which the family property was derived from the wife, and not from the husband. The evil appears rather to have lain in the concentration of landed property in a few hands, than in its frequent devolution to females. It is, however, no doubt true that female landowners, even when they were free from the vices which Aristotle ascribes to the Spartan women, might be less inclined to use their property for the good of the State than male landowners trained from their earliest years to live for the discharge of their duties as citizens. It does not seem that the feudal plan of proportioning the amount of military service due from the holder of land on military tenure to the amount of land held occurred to the Lacedaemonian lawgiver or to the lawgiver of any other Greek community. If there were no males in the family of the owner, no military service was rendered: the owner was not bound to supply hired military service. Yet the land, whether owned by women or by men, might have been made subject to the burden of supplying a given number of soldiers. It is true that hired military service, though not unknown to the Lacedaemonians, would not have been as satisfactory, or as politically safe, as that of citizens.

31. αὐτῶν, 'by themselves,' apart from any reasoning.

32. φαύλως, an epithet frequently applied in this book of the Politics to defective social and political arrangements (e.g. in 1271 b 10, c. 10. 1272 b 7, c. 11. 1273 a 36, b 8). Οὐ καλῶς (1271 a 26, etc.) is a somewhat milder expression.

33. μίαν γὰρ κ.τ.λ. Leuctra, of course, is meant. Cp. Isocr. Archid. § 56, *τίνας γὰρ ἴσμεν, ὧν καὶ ποιήσασθαι μνείαν ἄξιόν ἐστιν, οἵτινες ἅπαξ ἡττηθέντες καὶ μιᾶς εἰσβολῆς γενομένης, οὕτως ἀνάνδρως ὡμολόγησαν πάντα τὰ προσταττόμενα ποιήσειν*; and Polyb. 4. 81. 12. The power of Carthage, Athens, and Syracuse had survived several defeats.

34. τὴν ὀλιγανθρωπίαν, 'its paucity of citizens,' or possibly 'its well-known paucity of citizens': for the meaning of *ὀλιγανθρωπία*, see 3. 5. 1278 a 31. Xenophon (Rep. Lac. c. 1) had already spoken of Sparta as *τῶν ὀλιγανθρωποτάτων πόλεων οὖσα*: cp. also Isocr. Panath. §§ 255, 257.

λέγουσι δ' ὡς κ.τ.λ. On *μέν* not followed by *δέ*, see above on 1262 a 6. The suppressed clause evidently is, 'but that now they do not,' or rather perhaps, 'though they do not now.' Sus.[2] (Note 310) thinks that the Aegeidae and Talthybiadae, old families of non-Doric extraction, are referred to. The case of the Epeunacti, as to whom see Theopomp. Fragm. 190 (Müller, Fr. Hist. Gr. 1. 310), is, however, also to the point. Trieber (Forschungen, p. 101) suggests that Aristotle here has in view the statement of Ephorus (ap. Strab. p. 364 *sub fin.*), *τὴν δὲ Σπάρτην (Εὐρυσθένη καὶ Προκλῆ) βασίλειον ἀποφῆναι σφίσιν αὐτοῖς· εἰς δὲ τὰς ἄλλας πέμψαι βασιλέας, ἐπιτρέψαντας δέχεσθαι συνοίκους τοὺς βουλομένους τῶν ξένων διὰ τὴν λειπανδρίαν*: but this seems to refer to the Perioecic cities, not to Sparta. Alcman the Lydian is said to have become a Spartan in an epigram which is given in Anth. Pal. 7. 709 and in Plutarch, de Exilio c. 2. Herodotus, on the other hand, knows only of two men, Tisamenus and Hegias, who were ever made Spartan citizens (9. 35).

35. On **ὥστ' οὐ γίνεσθαι,** see Appendix B to Shilleto's edition of Demosthenes de Falsa Legatione.

36. πολεμούντων, 'though engaged in war': cp. 1271 b 12 and c. 5. 1264 a 32.

καί φασιν κ.τ.λ. *Τοῖς Σπαρτιάταις*, cp. 1271 b 10, *φαύλως δὲ ἔχει καὶ περὶ τὰ κοινὰ χρήματα τοῖς Σπαρτιάταις*, and 1270 b 8, *αὐτοῖς*. Demaratus (Hdt. 7. 234) makes Sparta a city of 8000 citizens at the time of the invasion of Xerxes. Nine thousand lots are said by Plutarch (Lyc. c. 8) to have been assigned to Spartans by Lycurgus. Isocrates, on the contrary, puts their number at 2000 only even in the earliest times (Panath. § 255), and contrasts Sparta with *αἱ μυρίανδροι πόλεις* (§ 257).

38. βέλτιον, i.e. better than populousness obtained by the admission of strangers to citizenship: cp. Plutarch, Agis c. 6, *καλὸν ὁ Ἆγις, ὥσπερ ἦν, ποιούμενος ἐξισῶσαι καὶ ἀναπληρῶσαι τὴν πόλιν.*

40. ταύτην τὴν διόρθωσιν, i.e. the correction of ὀλιγανθρωπία by means of an equalization of property. For, though this law tends to promote an increase of population, it does nothing to equalize property; on the contrary, it tends to increase the number of pauper citizens and to add to their poverty, thus intensifying the existing disparities of wealth. It encourages parents to bring off-spring into the world for whose maintenance no land is available. Plato may possibly have this Lacedaemonian law before him, when he says (Laws 740 D), *μηχαναὶ δ' εἰσὶ πολλαί· καὶ γὰρ ἐπισχέσεις γενέσεως οἷς ἂν εὔρους ᾖ γένεσις, καὶ τοὐναντίον ἐπιμέλειαι καὶ σπουδαὶ πλήθους γεννημάτων εἰσὶ τιμαῖς τε καὶ ἀτιμίαις καὶ νουθετήσεσι πρεσβυτῶν περὶ νέους κ.τ.λ.*

1270 b. **2. προάγεται.** Spengel (Aristotelische Studien 3. 16): 'imo *προάγει*.' The middle does not seem to be used in this sense by Aristotle elsewhere (see Bon. Ind. s. v.), but a reference to Liddell and Scott will show that it is thus used by other authors.

3. νόμος, 'a law': cp. c. 10. 1272 a 15, *εἰ δὲ μή, μετέχειν νόμος κωλύει τῆς πολιτείας*, and Isaeus De Apollodor. Hered. § 30, *καὶ οὐ μόνον ἰδίᾳ ταῦτα γινώσκουσιν, ἀλλὰ καὶ δημοσίᾳ τὸ κοινὸν τῆς πόλεως οὕτω ταῦτ' ἔγνωκε· νόμῳ γὰρ τῷ ἄρχοντι τῶν οἴκων, ὅπως ἂν μὴ ἐξερημῶνται, προστάττει τὴν ἐπιμέλειαν.* Νόμος takes up *ὁ νομοθέτης*.

4. ἄφρουρον. '*Φρουράν* Lacones dicebant *τὴν στρατείαν*, ut in nota illa formula *οἱ ἔφοροι ἔφηναν φρουράν*, Xen. Hell. 5. 4. 59' (Schn.).

6. πολλοὺς γίνεσθαι πένητας. Sus. 'many poor must come into being': Mr. Welldon, 'there will inevitably be a large body of poor': but I incline to translate (with Prof. Jowett) 'many must necessarily fall into poverty' (cp. c. 7. 1266 b 13, *φαῦλον τὸ πολλοὺς ἐκ πλουσίων γίνεσθαι πένητας*). The father of several sons would be likely to become a poor man, and the sons still poorer.

ἀλλὰ μὴν κ.τ.λ. This subject naturally follows. There being many poor men among the citizens, and all being eligible for the ephorship, the corruption of the ephorship followed from the unequal distribution of property.

8. αὐτή, 'by itself': cp. *αὐτογνώμονας*, 29.

αὐτοῖς. Bernays connects *αὐτοῖς* with *τῶν μεγίστων*, translating 'über die wichtigsten Angelegenheiten Sparta's' (Mr. Welldon, 'issues of the highest importance to the Lacedaemonian State'), but perhaps *αὐτοῖς* should be connected with the sentence generally and translated 'amongst them' or 'in the Lacedaemonian State' (cp. 1271 a 35, *ὅρος δὲ τῆς πολιτείας οὗτός ἐστιν αὐτοῖς ὁ πάτριος*, and c. 10. 1272 a 27, *τοῖς Κρησὶν ἢ τοῖς Λάκωσι*).

γίνονται κ.τ.λ. As to the nature of the distinction between the demos and the καλοὶ κἀγαθοί in the Lacedaemonian State, see Schömann, Opusc. Acad. 1. 138. It is not necessarily implied here that none but members of the demos ever became ephors; the meaning is, that all the seats in the college of ephors were as open to the demos as to anybody else (cp. 25, καθίστανται ἐξ ἁπάντων, and c. 6. 1265 b 39). It appears from 1271 a 3, however, that the senators also, though presumably καλοὶ κἀγαθοί, were often bribeable.

10. ἦσαν. The tense is noticeable. Is it used because Aristotle is speaking here, as elsewhere in this chapter, of the time of the Lacedaemonian empire, or because he looks back to definite instances of corruption arising from poverty?

11. ἐδήλωσαν. Vict. 'sc. se esse tales ut muneribus facile labefactari possint': cp. ἐδήλωσαν δέ, 1269 b 37.

ἐν τοῖς Ἀνδρίοις, 'in the events at Andros,' 'in the Andros business': cp. 7 (5). 3. 1303 a 38, μετὰ τὰ τυραννικά: Isocr. περὶ τοῦ ζεύγους § 25, τὴν δ' εὔνοιαν ἣν εἶχον εἰς τὸ πλῆθος, ἐν τοῖς τυραννικοῖς ἐπεδείξαντο· συγγενεῖς γὰρ ὄντες Πεισιστράτου κ.τ.λ.: and τὰ Κύπρια, the subject of an Epic poem, Aristot. Poet. 23. 1459 b 1. It is quite unknown to what Aristotle here refers, but I venture to suggest whether it is not possible that certain events of the year 333 B.C. are referred to. In that year the Persian fleet under Pharnabazus and Autophradates advanced from Chios first to Andros and then to Siphnos (nearer to Laconia), with the object of bringing about a rising in Greece against Macedon, and thus effecting a diversion in favour of Persia at the critical moment when Alexander was commonly thought to be 'caught and cooped up in Cilicia' (Grote, Hist. of Greece, 12. 157 n.). We have, indeed, no record of any negotiations between the ephors and the Persian admirals while the fleet was at Andros, though we know from Diodorus (17. 29) that the Lacedaemonians were already on the side of Persia, and that Memnon had won over many of the Greeks by means of bribes; but at Siphnos King Agis made his appearance in a single trireme, and commenced negotiations for a subsidy and for the despatch of a fleet and an army to his aid in the war which he was contemplating with Macedon. The news of Issus, however, arrived in the midst of these communications and nipped the project in the bud (see A. Schäfer, Demosthenes und seine Zeit, 3. 1. 163, who refers to Arrian 2. 13. 4 sq.: Curt. 4. 1. 37). If, as is probable, the ephors sent Agis on this errand, Aristotle may well have thought that they came near to ruining their country. Τὴν πόλιν, 13, in any case probably means the Lacedaemonian State, not Andros, for the fact that the corruptness of the Ephors nearly ruined Andros would not be to the point: Aristotle has to prove that it was perilous to their own State. If events of 333 B.C. are really referred to, the circumstance would be interesting, because it would show that this passage was added to, if not written, subsequently to that date. I mention the hypothesis for what it is worth.

14. ἰσοτύραννον. Cp. c. 6. 1265 b 40: Plato, Laws 712 D: Xen. Rep. Lac. 8. 3–4.

δημαγωγεῖν. Cp. 7 (5). 6. 1305 b 24 sqq. According to Plutarch, Agesilaus was fined by the ephors on one occasion for seeking to court the senators (De Fraterno Amore, c. 9, οἱ μὲν γὰρ ἔφοροι, τοῦ Ἀγησιλάου τῶν ἀποδεικνυμένων ἀεὶ γερόντων ἑκάστῳ βοῦν ἀριστεῖον πέμποντος, ἐζημίωσαν αὐτὸν αἰτίαν ὑπειπόντες, ὅτι τοὺς κοινοὺς ἰδίους κτᾶται δημαγωγῶν καὶ χαριζόμενος).

15. ὥστε κ.τ.λ., 'so that, together with the kingship itself, the constitution received injury in this way also' (i.e. it suffered not only through the venality of the ephors, but also through the kings being forced to court them).

16. δημοκρατία γὰρ κ.τ.λ. Sepulv. 'nam ex optimatum imperio in principatum popularem mutabatur' (sc. respublica), and so Sus. and others, but the expression ἡ πολιτεία συνέβαινε δημοκρατία seems a strange one, and it is possible that δημοκρατία is the subject, not the predicate: cp. Plato, Rep. 545 C, τίνα τρόπον τιμοκρατία γένοιτ' ἂν ἐξ ἀριστοκρατίας. For συνέβαινεν, cp. 2. 7. 1266 b 23.

17. For **συνέχει τὴν πολιτείαν**, cp. Demosth. adv. Timocr. c. 2, ἃ δοκεῖ συνέχειν τὴν πολιτείαν, τὰ δικαστήρια.

μὲν οὖν, 'true' or 'indeed,' answered by ἀλλά, 26. Aristotle has just been saying that the organization of the ephorate was such as to injure the constitution, and he now admits its value in holding the constitution together, only to reaffirm (ἀλλ' αἱρετὴν ἔδει κ.τ.λ., 26) his statement respecting its defects of organization.

19. διὰ τὸν νομοθέτην, 'owing to the lawgiver': cp. c. 11. 1273 b 22, and δι' ἀρετήν, c. 5. 1263 a 29. It would seem that Theopompus must be referred to here: cp. 7 (5). 11. 1313 a 26 sqq. 'Plerumque γίγνεσθαι ἀπὸ τύχης dicitur, sed etiam διὰ τύχην, Phys. 2. 4. 195 b 32: Rhet. 1. 10. 1368 b 34' (Bon. Ind. 780 b 40 sq.). See critical note.

21. δεῖ γὰρ κ.τ.λ. All the MSS. have the word ταὐτά after διαμένειν, except P^1 O^1, which have ταυτά, and P^4, which has ταῦτα (Vet. Int. 'has'). Ar. has 'oportet enim rempublicam quae duratura sit velle ut omnes civitatis partes constent atque in statu suo permaneant': he therefore probably read ταὐτά. But if we retain this word, τὴν πολιτείαν must, it would seem, be the subject of βούλεσθαι. The next sentence (23–26), however, certainly reads as if, not τὴν πολιτείαν, but πάντα τὰ μέρη were the subject of βούλεσθαι, and this impression will be confirmed, if we compare c. 10. 1272 a 32 sq.: c. 8. 1268 a 23 sqq.: 6 (4). 9. 1294 b 36 sqq.: 8 (6). 5. 1320 a 14 sqq., especially as εἶναι καὶ διαμένειν is used of constitutions in 7 (5). 9. 1309 b 38–40, οὐδετέραν μὲν γὰρ ἐνδέχεται αὐτῶν (i. e. democracy and oligarchy) εἶναι καὶ διαμένειν ἄνευ τῶν εὐπόρων καὶ τοῦ πλήθους (cp. Eth. Nic. 8. 11. 1160 a 12). It is true that we gather from 6 (4). 12. 1296 b 15 and 7 (5). 9. 1309 b 16 sqq. that the safety of a constitution is sufficiently secured, if the stronger section of the elements of the State, not necessarily all of them, desire its preservation, but nevertheless I incline on the whole to think that ταὐτά should be omitted. It may have been added by some one who deemed it necessary for the completion of the sentence, or it may be a blundered dittography of πάντα, 21: a dittography of τὰ ἄλλα occurs in 1. 8. 1256 b 18, where Π[1] appear to repeat these words from 16 (see Susemihl's *apparatus criticus*). Schneider would omit ταὐτά or read τὴν αὐτήν in place of it; Bernays would read κατὰ ταὐτά. On the phrase μέρη τῆς πόλεως, which comes to Aristotle from Plato, Rep. 552 A, see vol. i. Appendix A. The 'parts of the State' are here βασιλεῖς, καλοὶ κἀγαθοί, and δῆμος—quite a different enumeration from those given in 4 (7). 8 and 6 (4). 4.

23. μὲν οὖν, 'saepe usurpatur ubi notio modo pronunciata amplius explicatur' (Bon. Ind. 540 b 42): so here πάντα τὰ μέρη are successively taken up and considered separately: a similar use of μὲν οὖν occurs in Soph. El. 6. 169 a 18 sqq.

τιμήν. Aristotle occasionally applies the term ἀρχή to a Kingship (e. g. in 7 (5). 10. 1313 a 8 and 2. 11. 1273 a 30).

24. ἆθλον. Cp. Xen. Rep. Lac. 10. 1–3, and Demosth. in Lept. c. 107. In the latter passage the very same words, τῆς ἀρετῆς ἆθλον, are used of the Lacedaemonian γερουσία (cp. Plutarch, Lycurg. c. 26, νικητήριον τῆς ἀρετῆς).

28. παιδαριώδης. The same thing is said in 1271 a 9 sq. of the κρίσις in the election of senators. Susemihl has already pointed out (Sus.[2], Note 324) that the condemnation here passed on the method of electing ephors is not thus limited. We learn from Plutarch, Lyc. c. 26, how elections to the γερουσία were decided. The test was the comparative loudness of the shouts of approval evoked on the appearance in the popular assembly of the different candidates. Plato's language as to the ephorate—

ἐγγὺς τῆς κληρωτῆς ἀγαγὼν δυνάμεως (Laws 692 A: cp. 690 C)—has led to the conjecture that the election of the ephors was in some way or other determined by auspices. See Sus.², Note 324, and Schömann, Gr. Alterth. 1. 247. Schömann suggests that the people may have designated a certain number of persons for the ephorate, and that five of those designated may have been selected for the office by taking the auspices. The language of Aristotle in 6 (4). 9. 1294 b 29 sq. has been held to imply that the people did not elect to the ephorate, and the passage before us does not expressly say that they did, though it implies that the office was in some sense an elective one (cp. Isocr. Panath. § 154). In c. 10. 1272 a 31 sqq. we have ἐνταῦθα δ' (in Crete) οὐκ ἐξ ἁπάντων αἱροῦνται τοὺς κόσμους, and as Aristotle is here contrasting the election of the cosmi with that of the ephors, his language might be taken to imply that the Lacedaemonians elected the ephors, if it were certain that we should supply οἱ Κρῆτες with αἱροῦνται. But in c. 11. 1272 b 36 αἱροῦνται is used of the election of the Hundred and Four at Carthage, who were not elected by the people, if they were identical with the Hundred, for the Hundred were elected by the Pentarchies (c. 11. 1273 a 14). All we can be sure about, therefore, is that the ephors were elected in a way which Aristotle regarded as 'very childish.' He evidently thinks that the office might safely remain open to all, if the mode of election were improved. He seems, in fact, to hold that the 'very poor' and 'venal' men of whom he speaks (1270 b 9 sq.) would not then be elected ephors.

κρίσεων . . . μεγάλων. Sus.² compares 3. 1. 1275 b 9, οἷον ἐν Λακεδαίμονι τὰς τῶν συμβολαίων δικάζει τῶν ἐφόρων ἄλλος ἄλλας. Add 8 (6). 2. 1317 b 26, περὶ τῶν πλείστων καὶ τῶν μεγίστων καὶ τῶν κυριωτάτων, οἷον περὶ εὐθυνῶν καὶ πολιτείας καὶ τῶν ἰδίων συναλλαγμάτων.

30. κατὰ γράμματα καὶ τοὺς νόμους. For the omission of the article before γράμματα, see Bon. Ind. 109 b 44 sqq. Καί is explanatory, as in c. 5. 1263 a 15. The recently discovered Inscription containing a portion of the laws of Gortyna refers to its own provisions as τάδε τὰ γράμματα (col. 12. 17), or τὰ ἐγραμένα (col. 1. 54).

31. καὶ ἡ δίαιτα. Their mode of life as well as their powers, which in effect turn an ἀριστοκρατία into a democracy, 16. Cp. Isocr. ad Nicocl. § 31. Plato (Laws 674 A sq.) forbids wine to magistrates during their year of office. He does not seem, however, to have been aware of any excesses on the part of the ephors: see Laws 637 A. The ephors did not take their meals at the public mess-tables, but had a συσσίτιον of their own (see Gilbert, Gr. Staatsalt. 1. 57, who refers to Plutarch, Cleom. c. 8).

32. τῷ βουλήματι τῆς πόλεως, 'the aim of the State.' We expect rather *τοῦ νομοθέτου* (cp. Eth. Nic. 2. 1. 1103 b 4), or *τῆς πολιτείας* (Scaliger), and the words *πόλις* and *πολιτεία* are often interchanged in the MSS.: still *τῆς πόλεως* is possible.

αὐτὴ μὲν γάρ, 'for that' etc.: compare the use of *αὐτά* in 4 (7). 12. 1331 a 21, and see Vahlen on Poet. 15. 1454 b 17.

33. τοῖς ἄλλοις, sc. *πολίταις* (Coray).

μᾶλλον, 'rather than in the opposite direction,' as in c. 11. 1273 a 6, or = *λίαν*, as in c. 6. 1265 a 31? Probably the former.

ὑπερβάλλει, sc. *ἡ δίαιτα* (Bon. Ind. 684 a 39). For the fact, cp. 5 (8). 4. 1338 b 12 sqq.

34. λάθρᾳ τὸν νόμον ἀποδιδράσκοντας. Aristotle has here in his mind the language of Plato about the Spartans in Rep. 548 B, *λάθρᾳ τὰς ἡδονὰς καρπούμενοι, ὥσπερ παῖδες πατέρα, τὸν νόμον ἀποδιδράσκοντες*. The expression, however, was perhaps first used by Alcibiades: see Aelian, Var. Hist. 13. 37. Lysander was said to be one of these recreants (Aelian, Var. Hist. 13. 8). Dercyllidas also liked to live away from Sparta (Xen. Hell. 4. 3. 2: cp. Plut. Lycurg. c. 15). As to the Spartan Archidamus, see Theopomp. Fr. 259 (Müller, Fr. Hist. Gr. 1. 322).

37. ἐπιεικῶν μὲν γὰρ κ.τ.λ. Xenophon had adduced the arrangements respecting the senate in proof of the care taken by the lawgiver of the State to encourage *καλοκἀγαθία* even in old age (de Rep. Lac. c. 10. 1); he had already dwelt (c. 4) on the lawgiver's skill in developing *ἀνδραγαθία* in the young (c. 4. 1–2). *Ἀνδραγαθία* is rather a Xenophontic than an Aristotelian word (Aristotle would seem from Bonitz' Index to use it nowhere else), and perhaps the aim of this passage is to controvert the opinion of Xenophon. As to the meaning of *ἀνδραγαθία*, see L. Schmidt, Ethik der alten Griechen 1. 301 sq. Xenophon, according to him, used it in much the same sense as *ἀρετή*, to denote 'moral perfection.' *Συμφέρειν*, sc. *ταύτην τὴν ἀρχήν*.

39. Aristotle seems to have held that judges of important causes should not retain their office after a certain age, for there is an old age of the mind as well as of the body. The view is noticeable, for we are familiar with the opposite practice. He apparently would not approve the life-long tenure of the members of the Athenian Areopagus. The best men in his own ideal State become priests in advanced life. Plato is of much the same opinion (Laws 755 A: 923 B): extreme old age in parents is for reverence rather than for use (Laws 931). The *γέροντες* of the Lacedaemonian State tried cases of homicide (3. 1. 1275 b 10). As to *διανοίας γῆρας*, however, contrast de An. 1. 4. 408 b 19 sqq., though this passage may perhaps be only aporetic (see Wallace *ad loc.*), and compare Rhet. 2. 13. Giph. compares Lucr. 3. 445 sqq. For *ὥσπερ καί* answered by *καί*, Sus.[1] (Ind. Gramm. s. v. *ὥσπερ*) compares c. 8. 1269 a 9 sq.

1271 a. **2. ἀπιστεῖν**, cp. 23 sqq. Contrast Polyb. 6. 10. 9, *τῶν γερόντων, οἳ κατ' ἐκλογὴν ἀριστίνδην κεκριμένοι πάντες ἔμελλον ἀεὶ τῷ δικαίῳ προσνέμειν ἑαυτούς.*

3. φαίνονται δὲ κ.τ.λ. 'And it is evident that those who have enjoyed this dignity have often been led by bribery and favouritism to deal recklessly with the public interests.' I have ventured (with Lamb. and others) to connect *πολλὰ τῶν κοινῶν* not only with *καταχαριζόμενοι* but also with *καταδωροδοκούμενοι*, though this use of *καταδωροδοκεῖσθαι* (med.) is uncommon and hardly finds a complete parallel in Demosth. de Falsa Legatione § 377, *ὅτι γὰρ ταῦθ' ἁπλῶς δεδωροδόκηνται καὶ τιμὴν ἔχουσιν ἁπάντων τούτων οὗτοι* ('they have done this because they have been bribed,' Shilleto), for the acc. here is of the thing done, not of the thing betrayed. Sepulv., Vict., Bern., and Sus., in fact, take *πολλὰ τῶν κοινῶν* with *καταχαριζόμενοι* only. They may be right, but the sentence seems to read rather the other way.

5. ἀνευθύνους. *'Ανυπεύθυνος* is common in Aristotle: *ἀνεύθυνος* occurs only here, according to Bonitz' Index.

6. δόξειε δ' ἂν κ.τ.λ. Cp. Xen. Rep. Lac. 8. 4, *ἔφοροι οὖν ἱκανοὶ μέν εἰσι ζημιοῦν ὃν ἂν βούλωνται, κύριοι δ' ἐκπράττειν παραχρῆμα, κύριοι δὲ καὶ ἄρχοντας μεταξὺ καταπαῦσαι καὶ εἶρξαί γε καὶ περὶ τῆς ψυχῆς εἰς ἀγῶνα καταστῆσαι*: they have also the power to inflict immediate punishment on elected magistrates for any infraction of the laws, as tyrants and the superintendents of the great festivals have. Aristotle does not approve this mode of exacting an account. He regards the power of the ephors as *ἰσοτύραννος* (1270 b 14) and probably wishes it to be regulated by law (cp. c. 10. 1272 b 5–7). The Athenian plan of requiring a public account from the magistrate at the close of his term of office would evidently be inapplicable or unsatisfactory in the case of magistracies held for life. It would seem from Rhet. 3. 18. 1419 a 31 that the ephors held office subject to accountability.

8. οὐ τοῦτον. 'Ad augendam oppositionis vim negatio, quae poterat ad universum enunciatum referri, ipsi nomini negato praeponitur, veluti 6 (4). 5. 1292 b 6: 2. 7. 1267 a 15' etc. (Bon. Ind. 539 a 5).

9. τὴν αἵρεσιν. For the acc. cp. c. 6. 1265 a 13. The subject of approaching comment is first mentioned (in the acc.), and then the comment follows. The regulation which determines who may become candidates is distinguished from the selection (κρίσις), both being incidents of ἡ αἵρεσις. Perhaps κρίσις was the technical term: at all events both Xenophon (de Rep. Lac. 10. 1, 3) and Plutarch (Lyc. c. 26) use it in referring to the election of the senators at Sparta. This election was, in fact, an ἀγών, in which the prize was awarded to the best and most temperate of the candidates (see Xenophon and Plutarch, *ubi supra*). Plutarch describes the process, which seems, as Sus.[2] (Note 333) says, to be a peculiar development of the rude old-fashioned method of voting by 'cry.' In 7 (5). 6. 1306 a 18 the process of choosing senators at Elis is said to be δυναστευτική, and similar to the same process in the Lacedaemonian State. Thus the childish method followed in the latter State seems somehow to have favoured the predominance of a few wealthy families. Contrast with Aristotle's account of the election of the Lacedaemonian senate those of Isocrates (Panath. § 154) and Polybius (6. 10. 9).

10. αἰτεῖσθαι, 'ask to be elected,' 'offer himself for election.' I do not think that the making of 'a personal canvass' (Mr. Welldon) is necessarily implied.

11. δεῖ γὰρ κ.τ.λ. Cp. Plato, Rep. 557 E, τὸ δὲ μηδεμίαν ἀνάγκην, εἶπον, εἶναι ἄρχειν ἐν ταύτῃ τῇ πόλει, μηδ' ἂν ᾖς ἱκανὸς ἄρχειν.

13. νῦν δ' ὅπερ κ.τ.λ. We have just been told what ought to be: now we are told what is: compare for the contrast of δεῖ and νῦν δέ 1270 a 25 sq. and c. 11. 1273 b 21 sqq.

14. φιλοτίμους γὰρ κ.τ.λ. Sepulveda (who seems to read τούτῳ) translates (p. 55): 'ut enim cives ambitiosos redderet, hanc senatores deligendi rationem inivit, cum nemo non ambitiosus imperio se praefici petat.' Mr. Welldon also reads τούτῳ and translates in much the same way. It seems to me that this view of the passage is the right one, and that τούτῳ (cp. c. 11. 1273 b 20 and 3. 5. 1278 a 31 sq.), not τούτοις, is the true reading: I translate, therefore, 'for it is in his anxiety to make his citizens emulous of distinction, that he has adopted this regulation for the election of senators'—the regulation that the future senator must ask to be elected—'for' etc. To require men to ask to be elected is to make φιλοτιμία a condition of the attainment of the highest honours, and so to encourage the citizens to be φιλότιμοι. Sus. and others read τούτῳ but explain it as = τῷ φιλοτίμῳ. If τούτοις is read (with Π[2] Bekk.), then we must translate, 'for in his anxiety to make his citizens emulous of distinction, he makes use of men of this type in filling vacancies in the senate'; but τούτοις κέχρηται πρὸς τὴν αἵρεσιν τῶν γερόντων is an awkward way of expressing this.

16. τῶν γ' ἀδικημάτων τῶν ἑκουσίων. Π² Bekk.[1] read τῶν γ' ἀδικημάτων ἑκουσίων, and it is not impossible that instances might be found of a similar displacement of the adjective when emphatic (compare, for instance, Plato, Laws 713 D, ταὐτὸν δὴ καὶ ὁ θεὸς ἄρα φιλάνθρωπος ὢν τὸ γένος ἄμεινον ἡμῶν ἐφίστη τὸ τῶν δαιμόνων: Theopomp. Fr. 143 (Müller, Fr. Hist. Gr. 1. 302), ὅταν περὶ τὸν ἄροτον τρίτον καὶ σπόρον ἡ ὥρα ᾖ), but the probability here is that, ἀδικημάτων immediately preceding τῶν, the latter word was omitted in copying by a natural and frequent error of copyists. The words imply that ἀδικήματα ἀκούσια are possible: contrast Eth. Nic. 5. 10. 1135 a 15–23. For the view expressed in this passage, cp. Plato, Laws 870: Eth. Nic. 5. 10. 1134 b 7. 'I would rather,' said Dr. Johnson, 'have the rod to be the general terror to all to make them learn, than tell a child, if you do thus or thus, you will be more esteemed than your brothers and sisters.' For other accounts in the Politics and elsewhere of the causes of ἀδικία, see note on 1267 a 5. Plato says of the timocratic State (Rep. 548 C)—διαφανέστατον δ' ἐν αὐτῇ ἐστὶν ἕν τι μόνον ὑπὸ τοῦ θυμοειδοῦς κρατοῦντος, φιλονεικίαι καὶ φιλοτιμίαι.

19. μέν is probably not taken up either by ἀλλὰ μὴν . . . γε, 20 or by δέ, 22: it seems here as in 1270 a 34 to stand by itself, the course of the sentence being broken at ἀλλὰ μήν.

20. ἄλλος ἔστω λόγος, 3. 14–17.

ἀλλὰ μὴν . . . γε, 'but certainly': cp. 3. 4. 1276 b 18, 1277 a 25, and see Ast, Lex. Platon. 1. 103.

21. μὴ καθάπερ νῦν. Göttl. 'intellige κατὰ τὸ γένος.' Cp. on this subject c. 11. 1272 b 38–41. Aristotle appears to have agreed with Lysander, if the object of the latter was not, as some thought (7 (5). 1. 1301 b 19 sq.), the abolition of the kingship, but the opening of it to the best men irrespectively of descent. Lysander's scheme was, according to Ephorus (ap. Plutarch. Lysand. c. 30), ὡς χρὴ τῶν Εὐρυπωντιδῶν καὶ Ἀγιαδῶν τὴν βασιλείαν ἀφελομένους εἰς μέσον θεῖναι καὶ ποιεῖσθαι τὴν αἵρεσιν ἐκ τῶν ἀρίστων—a sentence continued as follows in the version of the same story given in [Plutarch,] Apophth. Lac. 229 E sqq. (Lysand. 14), ἵνα μὴ τῶν ἀφ' Ἡρακλέους, ἀλλ' οἷος Ἡρακλῆς τῇ ἀρετῇ κρινομένων τὸ γέρας ᾖ, ᾗ κἀκεῖνος εἰς θεῶν τιμὰς ἀνήχθη. Cp. also Plutarch, Comp. Lysandri et Sullae c. 2. Aristotle does not approve of the restriction of the kingship to the Heraclids, nor of the mode in which the kings were selected from their number. The merits of a father or a family should not help the son; his claims should be decided according to the life led by him personally (cp. for *βίον* Eth. Nic. 10. 9. 1179 a 18 sq., and for *κρίνεσθαι* Pol. 8 (6). 7. 1321 a 30). Aristotle's language reminds us of the views expressed in the composition of Lysander, the substance of which appears to be given in the passage from the Apophthegmata Laconica quoted above.

22. ὅτι δὲ ὁ νομοθέτης κ.τ.λ. The connexion perhaps is—'it is impossible to make sure of educating men taken simply on grounds of seniority from a given family (1272 b 40) into models of manhood, and this the lawgiver himself seems virtually to admit.' *Ποιεῖν* 23, sc. *τοὺς βασιλέας*.

24. συμπρεσβευτάς, i.e. with the kings or one of them. Two ephors usually accompanied the king on campaigns, and it is to their presence, according to Schömann (Gr. Alterth. 1. 250), that Aristotle here refers. If so, however, the use of the word *συμπρεσβευτάς* seems strange. It is more likely that Aristotle refers to occasions on which the kings were sent on embassies. The lawgiver is here viewed as the author of these administrative traditions.

25. σωτηρίαν ἐνόμιζον τῇ πόλει κ.τ.λ. Contrast c. 2. 1261 a 30, *διόπερ τὸ ἴσον τὸ ἀντιπεπονθὸς σώζει τὰς πόλεις*, and Rhet. 1. 4. 1360 a 19, *ἐν γὰρ τοῖς νόμοις ἐστὶν ἡ σωτηρία τῆς πόλεως*.

26. οὐ καλῶς δ' οὐδὲ κ.τ.λ. The defect in the arrangements respecting the syssitia here noticed does not seem to have occurred to Plato: cp. Laws 842 B.

28. ἀπὸ κοινοῦ, 'at the public expense': see the references in Liddell and Scott s.v. In c. 10. 1272 a 20 we have *ἐκ κοινοῦ τρέφεσθαι*: in 6 (4). 6. 1293 a 19, *τρέφεσθαι ἀπὸ τῆς πόλεως*. For the Cretan system, cp. c. 10. 1272 a 12 sqq. For *τὴν σύνοδον* ('meeting' or 'gathering'), Bonitz (Ind. 731 b 25) compares 4 (7). 12. 1331 b 10: 8 (6). 4. 1319 a 32. Compare also Plato, Laws 640 A, and Theaet. 173 D.

30. καί intensifies *σφόδρα* ('though some citizens are extremely poor' etc.).

32. βούλεται μὲν γὰρ κ.τ.λ. 'For he intends' etc. Cp. c. 6. 1265 b 40 sq. The rich are said (Plutarch, Lyc. c. 11) to have been violent in their opposition to the institution of syssitia.

33. κατασκεύασμα, 'device' perhaps rather than 'institution' (Lamb. 'inventum'). Compare the use of the word in 8 (6). 4. 1319 b 19–30.

γίνεται. See note on 1264 a 14.

35. ὅρος δὲ κ.τ.λ., 'and this is the traditional standard by which participation in the advantages of the constitution is regulated in the Lacedaemonian State.' Cp. c. 10. 1272 a 15, εἰ δὲ μή, μετέχειν νόμος κωλύει τῆς πολιτείας, καθάπερ εἴρηται καὶ πρότερον, and Plato, Rep. 551 A–B, a passage which throws light on the meaning of ὅρος τῆς πολιτείας here. In 8 (6). 2. 1317 b 11 the phrase seems to bear a different meaning, 'the criterion of a democratic constitution.'

38. καὶ ἕτεροί τινες. 'Critiae tyranni Λακεδαιμονίων πολιτείαν vel similes libros respici probabile est,' Bon. Ind. 822 a 37 sq.

39. στάσεως, as in Lysander's case, 7 (5). 1. 1301 b 19 sq.: 7 (5). 7. 1306 b 33.

ἐπὶ γὰρ τοῖς βασιλεῦσιν. Bonitz (Ind. 268 b 36) compares Rhet. 2. 6. 1384 a 9, ἐπὶ τούτοις, 'praeterea,' apparently making the meaning 'for in addition to the kings,' but perhaps something more than this is meant—'as a check upon the kings' (cp. 1271 a 23 sq.: 6 (4). 15. 1299 b 36, οἱ πρόβουλοι καθεστᾶσιν ἐπὶ τοῖς βουλευταῖς).

40. οὖσι στρατηγοῖς ἀϊδίοις. Cp. 3. 15. 1285 b 38. These words are probably added to show how it is that the Admiralship can fairly be called an additional Kingship. It is because the Kingship is nothing more than a perpetual Generalship. It should be noted that an ἀΐδιος ἀρχή is apparently distinguished from one held for life in Polyb. 6. 45. 5.

1271 b. **1. Πλάτων ἐν τοῖς νόμοις,** 'p. 625 C–638 B: cf. p. 660 sqq.: p. 666 E: p. 688 A sq.: p. 705 D' Sus.[1].

3. χρησίμη. 'Feminini forma et χρήσιμος et (fortasse paullo rarius) χρησίμη exhibetur' (Bon. Ind. 854 b 19).

4. ἀπώλλυντο δὲ ἄρξαντες. Cp. 4 (7). 14. 1334 a 6, αἱ γὰρ πλεῖσται τῶν τοιούτων πόλεων πολεμοῦσαι μὲν σώζονται, κατακτησάμεναι δὲ τὴν ἀρχὴν ἀπόλλυνται. For ἄρξαντες in the sense of 'having acquired empire,' cp. σχολάσαντες, 1270 a 4, and κοινωνήσαντες, c. 5. 1263 b 28, and see Schömann's note on ἐφορεύσας δέ τις ἀνὴρ δυνατός in his edition of Plutarch's Agis and Cleomenes, p. 106. As to the fact, see Plutarch, Agis 5. 1. The ruin of the Lacedaemonian State is also traced to ὀλιγανθρωπία in 1270 a 33, but the deeper cause of it is now for the first time dwelt upon. A fuller culture, moral and intellectual, would have taught the Spartans to resist the temptations of their newly acquired wealth and power: cp. 4 (7). 15. 1334 a 22–34. Ephorus had said much the same thing of the Thebans in a striking passage of his history (Fr. 67: Müller, Fr. Hist. Gr. 1. 254): compare also Plutarch's remarks on the character of Marius (Marius c. 2).

6. κυριωτέραν, 'more sovereign, more ἀρχιτεκτονική,' as in Eth. Nic. 1. 1. 1094 a 26.

τούτου δὲ κ.τ.λ. The fault now noticed is hinted by Plato, Laws

661 D–662 B. Isocrates had said much the same thing (Panath. §§ 187–8, 228). Aristotle virtually repeats the charge in 4 (7). 14. 1333 b 9: cp. Eth. Eud. 7. 15. 1248 b 37 sqq. He finds much the same fault with Carthage in c. 11. 1273 a 37 sqq.

7. τἀγαθὰ τὰ περιμάχητα are goods for which the many strive (cp. Rhet. 1. 6. 1363 a 8 sqq.), such as wealth, honours, bodily pleasures, Eth. Nic. 9. 8. 1168 b 16 sqq.

9. καλῶς. Sus.[2] (Note 346b) compares 4 (7). 1. 1323 a 40.

ὅτι μέντοι ταῦτα κ.τ.λ. Cp. 4 (7). 15. 1334 a 40–b 3.

10. φαύλως δὲ ἔχει κ.τ.λ. In this passage the words of Archidamus (Thuc. 1. 80. 4)—*οὔτε ἐν κοινῷ ἔχομεν (χρήματα) οὔτε ἑτοίμως ἐκ τῶν ἰδίων φέρομεν*—seem to be present to the mind of Aristotle. Polybius (6. 49. 8 sqq.) draws a contrast between the Lacedaemonian and Roman States in this respect.

11. οὔτε . . τε. 'Not only is there nothing in the public treasury, but they also are slow to pay extraordinary contributions.' For *οὔτε* followed by *τε*, cp. c. 10. 1272 b 19 sqq.

ἐν τῷ κοινῷ, 'in the public treasury.' See Liddell and Scott s. v. for this sense of the word; they refer among other passages to Thuc. 6. 8. 2, *καὶ περὶ τῶν χρημάτων ὡς εἴη ἑτοῖμα ἔν τε τοῖς ἱεροῖς πολλὰ καὶ ἐν τοῖς κοινοῖς.*

12. ἀναγκαζομένοις, 'though they are compelled': cp. c. 5. 1264 a 32 and 7 (5). 9. 1309 b 12.

13. διὰ γὰρ κ.τ.λ. Here most of the territory is said to belong to the citizens. In Plutarch's life of Lycurgus (c. 8), on the contrary, we are told that Lycurgus made 9000 lots for the Spartans and 30,000 for the Perioeci, nor is there anything to show that the Spartan lots were larger than the Perioecic. In the division made by Agis (Plutarch, Agis c. 8)—4500 Spartan lots against 15,000 for Perioecic hoplites—much the same proportion obtains. It is very possible (cp. 7 (5). 7. 1307 a 34 sq.) that the portion of Laconia belonging to the citizens increased as time went on, and that the aim of Agis was to restore what he conceived to have been the proportion at the outset. We see that the *εἰσφοραί* of the State fell to a large extent, if not wholly, on land: as to Athens, see Boeckh, Publ. Econ. of Athens E. T., p. 506.

16. τὴν μὲν γὰρ κ.τ.λ. Aristotle here describes the result of the lawgiver's arrangements.

17. φιλοχρημάτους, for the lawgiver has not brought the extravagant habits of the women, who nevertheless rule their husbands, under the control of the State, and he has taught his citizens to prefer wealth to virtue (1271 b 7 sqq.).

18. τ**αῦτα γὰρ κ.τ.λ.** The translation probably is, 'for these are the main points for censure,' not 'for these are the main censures which one may pass upon it': cp. Demosth. in Lept. c. 148, *οὐ τοῦτ' ἐπιτιμῶ*. It is true that *ἐπιτιμᾶν* is used in 1271 a 38 with a dative of the thing found fault with, and that Aristotle does not seem to use *ἐπιτιμᾶν* with an accusative in this sense anywhere else; still we have *τῶν ἐπιτιμηθέντων ἂν* in c. 11. 1273 a 2 and *αἱ ἐπιτιμώμεναι τῶν κακιῶν* in Eth. Nic. 3. 7. 1114 a 30.

C. 10. **20.** The similarity of the Cretan institutions to those of the Lacedaemonian State must have been early recognized, for Herodotus found the belief prevailing among the Lacedaemonians that Lycurgus had derived his institutions from Crete (Hdt. 1. 65). Plato in the Republic (544 C) classes the Cretan and Lacedaemonian constitutions together as timocracies and makes the same description serve for both (547 A sqq.). And so again in the Laws the chief interlocutor draws little or no distinction between the constitutions under which his Cretan and Lacedaemonian comrades live; he applies the same criticisms to both (631 B sqq., 634, 635 sqq., 780 E sqq.). He finds in the one constitution no less than in the other a mixture of monarchy, or authoritative government, with democracy, or the principle of freedom; both are constitutions in the truest sense of the word, inasmuch as they are framed with a view to the common good, whereas in many States part of the citizens are slaves to the rest. It is as hard to decide with regard to the constitution of Cnosus as it is with regard to the Lacedaemonian constitution, whether it is a democracy, oligarchy, aristocracy, or kingship (712 E). Not only Plato, but Xenophon, Ephorus, and Callisthenes are said by Polybius (6. 45 sq.) to have treated the Cretan and Lacedaemonian constitutions as the same, and we see from Strabo, p. 481 sq., that Ephorus did in fact trace many resemblances between them, though he mentioned certain customs as peculiar to Crete (Strab. p. 483) and also spoke of the Lacedaemonians as having 'perfected' the Cretan institutions, which implies that they had altered them to a certain extent. He describes how Cretan freedom was guaranteed by the unanimity and valour which were the fruits of the constitution, in language which contrasts strangely with Aristotle's remark, *σώζεται διὰ τὸν τόπον*, and with his reference to intervals of civil discord during which the Cretan States were at the mercy of any one who chose to assail them. Ephorus probably wrote, as Plato certainly did, before the raid of Phalaecus (345 B.C.) had revealed the weakness of the Cretan laws, whereas Aristotle wrote after it. It is perhaps for this reason that Aristotle is far more alive than Plato or Ephorus to the differences between the Cretan and the Lacedaemonian constitution. So far indeed as deviations from the best constitution are concerned, he agrees that the same criticisms are applicable to both (c. 11. 1273 a 2 sq.), but while in the chapters on the Lacedaemonian and Carthaginian constitutions he inquires how far the lawgiver has succeeded in his design of constructing an *ἀριστοκρατία*, he seems to think it hardly worth while to raise this question as to the Cretan constitution; the doubt is rather whether it is a legally ordered constitution at all. Still there seem to have been points in which the Cretan laws were superior to the Lacedaemonian. The freedom of the Cretan States from troubles with their serfs appears indeed to have been no more than a happy accident. But the Cretan syssitia were better organized than the Lacedaemonian, for the citizens were not expected to contribute a quota to them, and poverty cost no man his rights under the constitution. No fear can have been felt in Crete of a paucity of citizens, for while in the Lacedaemonian State rewards were given to the father of more than two sons, the Cretan lawgiver discouraged large families. The Cretan women, again, though Plato speaks of them in the Laws (780 E sqq.) as equally *ἀνομοθέτητοι* with the Spartan, seem to have been less indulged, for dowries were limited in amount to half a son's share (see above on 1270 a 21), and, at Gortyna at any rate, certain important portions of the inheritance were reserved for sons and could not pass to daughters (see below on 1272 a 17). If in the Lacedaemonian State the caprice of testators was, as Aristotle implies, among the causes which led to the concentration of the land in a few hands, Gortyna would seem to have had nothing to fear on this score, for there is no indication in the fragment which we possess of its laws that wills were known there (Bücheler und Zitelmann, Das Recht von Gortyn, p. 134). The inheritor of an heiress, again, unlike his Spartan compeer, had no right to give her in marriage to any one he pleased: if he were unwilling to marry her, the right to her hand passed to the next in succession (Bücheler und Zitelmann, p. 151 sq.). How far Crete had its reward in a comparatively even distribution of landed property, we are hardly in a position to say; the language of Polybius (6. 46. 1) points the other way, at any rate as to his own time. A further fact may be noted to the credit of the Cretan States, that though, unlike the Lacedaemonian, they had no ambitious dreams of empire, they nevertheless maintained and enforced a laborious system of gymnastic training.

On the other hand, the constitutional organization of the Cretan States was very defective. The government in each of them was in the hands of ten Cosmi and of a Boulê composed of persons who had held the office of Cosmus. We see that this office was not held for life, but whether it was an annual office in the time of Aristotle, as it seems to have been in that of Polybius (6. 46. 4), is uncertain. Aristotle's use of the word μεταξύ in 1272 b 5 appears to imply that it was held for some definite term or other, though Zitelmann points out (Bücheler und Zitelmann, p. 54) that the expression '*if* he quits office,' and not '*when* he quits office,' is used of a Cosmus in the law of Gortyna (col. 1. 52). The Cosmi had large powers, for they were not only the rulers of the State, but also its generals in war. It would perhaps be hardly safe to infer from αἱροῦνται, 1272 a 34, that they were elected by the whole citizen-body, but we are distinctly told that only the members of certain *gentes* were eligible; the people, however, acquiesced in their exclusion from the office, because it brought those who held it no illicit gains; nevertheless the monopoly of supreme authority by a few families, which was all the more marked as the powers of the popular assembly were small, cost the Cretan States dear, for it led to the occasional displacement of the Cosmi by violent means. The worst point in the working of Cretan institutions, however, was the insubordination of the most powerful men. They occasionally carried their turbulence to the length of declaring an abeyance of the office of Cosmus, the result being a temporary dissolution of the body politic. The δυνατοί here referred to would probably belong to the families whose members were alone eligible to this office. It is evident that whatever the effect of the syssitia may have been in equalizing rich and poor, the people in Crete readily rallied round δυνατοί, just as in youth they formed ἀγέλαι under the leadership of a δυνατός (Ephor. ap. Strab. p. 483). In an island so rich in legend as Crete the great families would be likely to be strong.

Ἡ δὲ Κρητικὴ πολιτεία. This must mean the constitution which prevailed in the Cretan cities, for Crete was not gathered into one State. 'The forms of government established in the Dorian colonies in Crete' (and, it would seem, in the Cretan cities generally) 'so closely resembled each other, that we find one only described as common to all' (Thirlwall, Hist. of Greece 1. 284).

According to Ephorus, Lyctus Gortyna and some petty towns had remained truer to the primitive institutions of Crete than Cnosus (Ephor. ap. Strab. p. 481). How much Aristotle has drawn in this chapter from Ephorus will best be seen, if a few extracts from Strabo's summary of Ephorus' account of the Cretan constitution are appended (Strab. pp. 481–2)—*λέγεσθαι δ' ὑπό τινων ὡς Λακωνικὰ εἴη τὰ πολλὰ τῶν νομιζομένων Κρητικῶν, τὸ δ' ἀληθὲς εὑρῆσθαι μὲν ὑπ' ἐκείνων, ἠκριβωκέναι δὲ τοὺς Σπαρτιάτας . . . καὶ δὴ καὶ τὰ Λυττίων νόμιμα ποιεῖσθαι μαρτύρια τοὺς τὰ Λακωνικὰ πρεσβύτερα ἀποφαίνοντας· ἀποίκους γὰρ ὄντας φυλάττειν τὰ τῆς μητροπόλεως ἔθη, ἐπεὶ ἄλλως γε εὔηθες εἶναι τὸ τοὺς βέλτιον συνεστῶτας καὶ πολιτευομένους τῶν χειρόνων ζηλωτὰς ἀποφαίνειν· οὐκ εὖ δὲ ταῦτα λέγεσθαι . . . πολλὰς γοῦν τῶν ἀποικίδων μὴ φυλάττειν τὰ πάτρια, πολλὰς δὲ καὶ τῶν μὴ ἀποικίδων ἐν Κρήτῃ τὰ αὐτὰ ἔχειν τοῖς ἀποίκοις ἔθη* (cp. 1271 b 28 sq., where Aristotle adopts Ephorus' view that the colonists of Lyctus found the characteristic Cretan institutions already existing there on their arrival). Besides (Ephorus continues) Althaemenes the founder of the settlement lived five generations before Lycurgus: *τῶν δ' ἀρχείων τὰ μὲν καὶ τὰς διοικήσεις ἔχειν τὰς αὐτὰς καὶ τὰς ἐπωνυμίας, ὥσπερ καὶ τὴν τῶν γερόντων ἀρχὴν . . . τοὺς ἐφόρους δὲ τὰ αὐτὰ τοῖς ἐν Κρήτῃ κόσμοις διοικοῦντας ἑτέρως ὠνομάσθαι· τὰ δὲ συσσίτια ἀνδρεῖα παρὰ μὲν τοῖς Κρησὶν καὶ νῦν ἔτι καλεῖσθαι* (cp. Dosiadas ap. Athen. Deipn. 143 b), *παρὰ δὲ τοῖς Σπαρτιάταις μὴ διαμεῖναι καλούμενα ὁμοίως πρότερον· παρ' Ἀλκμᾶνι γοῦν οὕτω κεῖσθαι "φοίναις δὲ καὶ ἐν θιάσοισιν ἀνδρείων παρὰ δαιτυμόνεσσι πρέπει παιᾶνα κατάρχειν."* Then follows, in the form in which it was current among the Cretans, the story of Lycurgus' visit to Crete after giving up his guardianship of the child Charilaus; this is told at greater length than Aristotle tells it in 1271 b 24 sqq., but to the same effect, except that Aristotle does not allow (cp. 6 (4). 11. 1296 a 20) that Lycurgus ever was king, while the next allegation of these Cretan informants of Ephorus—the statement that Thaletas was the instructor of Lycurgus—is rejected in c. 12. 1274 a 29 sqq. on grounds of chronology, and Aristotle is silent in the Politics as to Lycurgus having, like Minos, asked for guidance in his legislation from a god, though in the Polities (Aristot. Fragm. 492. 1558 a 30 sqq.) he would seem to have followed Ephorus and his Cretan authorities in this matter. Cp. also Strab. p. 476, *ἱστόρηται δ' ὁ Μίνως νομοθέτης γενέσθαι σπουδαῖος θαλαττοκρατῆσαί τε πρῶτος*, where Ephorus is perhaps again referred to, for he is quoted a few lines lower. The germ of some of the statements in 1271 b 32 sqq. may, in fact, be detected in some lines of the poem which passes under the name of Scymnus Chius—lines which evidently reproduce passages of Ephorus: see Ephor. Fragm. 61 (Müller, Fr. Hist. Gr. 1. 249):—

> Πρώτους δὲ Κρῆτάς φασι τῆς Ἑλληνικῆς
> ἄρξαι θαλάττης, ὥς τε νησιωτίδας
> πόλεις κατασχεῖν, ἅς τε καὶ συνοικίσαι (cp. 1271 b 38)
> αὐτῶν Ἔφορος εἴρηκεν, εἶναι φησί τε
> ἐπώνυμον τὴν νῆσον ἀπὸ Κρητός τινος,
> τοῦ δὴ γενομένου βασιλέως αὐτόχθονος·
> πλοῦν ἡμέρας ἀπέχειν δὲ τῆς Λακωνικῆς (cp. 1271 b 35).

The statements of Diodorus 5. 78. 3–4 seem to be based on the same passage of Ephorus. I have not observed that any commentator has pointed out its resemblance to the passage 1271 b 35 sqq.

πάρεγγυς. Ephorus, according to Polybius (6. 45: cp. 6. 46. 9 sq.), treated the Lacedaemonian and Cretan constitutions as identical. Polybius says the same thing less emphatically of Xenophon, Callisthenes, and Plato.

21. μικρὰ μὲν οὐ χεῖρον, e.g. the syssitia.

ἧττον γλαφυρῶς, 'with less neatness of finish,' explained by ἧττον διήρθρωται, 24. It is an exception to the general rule, when Charondas is found, c. 12. 1274 b 7, to be τῇ ἀκριβείᾳ τῶν νόμων γλαφυρώτερος καὶ τῶν νῦν νομοθετῶν.

22. λέγεται, by Herodotus (1. 65), who says that according to the Lacedaemonians themselves Lycurgus derived his laws from Crete (contrast Plato, Laws 624 A), whereas others ascribed them to the counsels of the Pythia; and by Ephorus, as we have seen, who appears to have blended the two accounts and to have traced the institutions to Crete, though he adds that Lycurgus promulgated them as proceeding from the Delphian Apollo (Strabo, pp. 481–2). Xenophon (Rep. Lac. c. 8. 5) and Plato (Laws 624 A: 632 D: 634 A: contrast Minos 318 C sq.) say nothing of the derivation from Crete (Trieber, Forschungen p. 73 sq.). Isocrates boldly alleges that Lycurgus borrowed from Thesean Athens (Panath. §§ 152–3), but this is only 'his way.' On καὶ . . . δέ, 'and also,' see Liddell and Scott δέ iii, and cp. Pol. 3. 16. 1287 a 7.

24. ἧττον διήρθρωται, 'less elaborated,' 'less fully worked out in detail': cp. Oecon. 1. 3. 1343 b 16. The word is sometimes used of the change of an embryo into a fully articulated animal—e.g. in Hist. An. 7. 3. 583 b 23: so διαρθροῦν in Probl. 3. 31. 875 b 22 is replaced by διακριβοῦν, 24 (ἠκριβωκέναι δὲ τοὺς Σπαρτιάτας is the expression used by Ephorus, ap. Strab. p. 481): cp. de Gen. An.

1. 17. 721 b 34, συγκεχυμένον καὶ οὐ διηρθρωμένον τὸ γράμμα, and Eth. Nic. 1. 7. 1098 a 22, δόξειε δ' ἂν παντὸς εἶναι προαγαγεῖν καὶ διαρθρῶσαι τὰ καλῶς ἔχοντα τῇ περιγραφῇ, καὶ ὁ χρόνος τῶν τοιούτων εὑρετὴς ἢ συνεργὸς ἀγαθὸς εἶναι, which confirms what is here said as to the difference between that which is earlier in date and that which is later.

25. **τὴν ἐπιτροπείαν.** Cp. 6 (4). 11. 1296 a 20, οὐ γὰρ ἦν βασιλεύς. However, the guardianship after the birth of Charilaus was admitted by some who, like Ephorus (Strabo p. 482), held that Lycurgus was king till Charilaus was born.

Χαρίλλου. See critical note.

26. **καταλιπών.** Cp. Andoc. c. Alcib. c. 17, κατέλιπε τὸ ἔργον.

27. **διὰ τὴν συγγένειαν,** i. e. the relationship of Lyctus, a Laconian colony in Crete, to its mother-city. The same expression is used in 1. 2. 1252 b 21 sq., and probably of the same relation. Strabo (p. 476) found Λύκτος the name of the city in Homer, but he writes it himself Λύττος (cp. νυττί=νυκτί in the Law of Gortyna, col. 2. 14), and this is the form used on coins and in inscriptions (Bursian, Geogr. von Griechenland, 2. 569. 3). On its remarkable situation commanding the one zig-zag track which leads from its fertile plain to the mountain-pastures, see Bursian ibid. p. 570. Λύττος is 'Cretan for ὑψηλός' (Liddell and Scott, s. v.).

30. **διὸ καὶ νῦν κ.τ.λ.** Cp. 4 (7). 10. 1329 b 16, διὸ καὶ νῦν ἔτι τῶν ἀπ' ἐκείνου τινὲς χρῶνται τοῖς συσσιτίοις καὶ τῶν νόμων ἐνίοις, and see vol. i. Appendix E (p. 575, note 2). For τὸν αὐτὸν τρόπον, cp. 3. 3. 1276 a 13, εἴπερ οὖν καὶ δημοκρατοῦνταί τινες κατὰ τὸν τρόπον τοῦτον.

31. **ὡς κατασκευάσαντος,** 'their view being that' etc.

32. **δοκεῖ δ' ἡ νῆσος κ.τ.λ.** What follows down to Κάμικον (40) is evidently taken from Ephorus: this is clear from the lines of Scymnus Chius quoted above. The passage may be an interpolation, but it is more probable that it was placed where it stands by the hand of Aristotle himself, who has already drawn largely in this chapter from Ephorus, and may well have added it in order to show that there was nothing improbable in the view that the Lacedaemonians owed their famous laws to Crete. Crete, he in effect says, though now so out of the world, is well adapted by nature for supremacy over the Greek race, for it commands the Aegean sea, round which the Greek race is planted. This the Lacedaemonian king Agis III saw, when in B.C. 333 in preparation for an attack on the power of Macedon he despatched his brother Agesilaus to secure Crete.

καί before πρὸς τὴν ἀρχήν is translated by Sus. 'also,' not 'both,' and he is probably right. For πεφυκέναι πρός, cp. Rhet. 1. 5. 1361 b 10 sq.

34. πάσῃ . . . τῇ θαλάσσῃ, 'the sea as a whole' (see above on 1. 4. 1253 b 33). What sea, however, is referred to? Evidently ἡ Ἑλληνικὴ θάλασσα, if we compare the lines of Scymnus Chius quoted above on 1271 b 20, with which σχεδὸν τῶν Ἑλλήνων κ.τ.λ., 34, agrees, and ἡ Ἑλληνικὴ θάλασσα would seem to be the Aegean ('the sea by the Greeks familiarly called their own,' Thirlwall, Hist. of Greece, 1. 2), not the Mediterranean: cp. Thuc. 1. 4, and Plutarch, Eumenes c. 19, ὅπως μηδεὶς αὐτῶν εἰς Μακεδονίαν ἄπεισι μηδὲ ὄψεται τὴν Ἑλληνικὴν θάλατταν. The explanation ἀπέχει γὰρ κ.τ.λ., 35, seems to suggest a reference to the Aegean. We find, in fact, that Eudoxus placed Crete in the Aegean (Strabo p. 474), a view to which Strabo objects. For the connexion of empire in Greece with the sea, cp. Thuc. 1. 15. Ephorus (Fr. 67: Müller, Fr. Hist. Gr. 1. 254) praised Boeotia for being τριθάλαττος and pronounced it well-adapted for hegemony. So in Pol. 4 (7). 6. 1327 b 4 an adequate fleet is considered essential for hegemony over other States.

ἐπίκειται, 'lies close to,' perhaps with some notion of commanding or dominating: cp. Polyb. 1. 42. 6, and 5. 44. 4, 5, ἐπίκειται δὲ καὶ κρατεῖ τῶν καλουμένων Κασπίων πυλῶν.

35. ἀπέχει γὰρ κ.τ.λ. 'From the isle of Cythera, which is parted by a narrow channel from Laconia, the snowy summits of the Cretan Ida are clearly visible, and from them the eye can probably reach the Rhodian Atabyrus and the mountains of Asia Minor' (Thirlwall, Hist. of Greece, 1. 2). Cp. Diod. 5. 59. 2, Διὸς ἱερὸν τοῦ προσαγορευομένου Ἀταβυρίου . . . κείμενον ἐπί τινος ὑψηλῆς ἄκρας, ἀφ' ἧς ἔστιν ἀφορᾶν τὴν Κρήτην. This temple was in Rhodes.

39. τῇ Σικελίᾳ, also an island.

40. ἀνάλογον, here an adverb: see on this word Liddell and Scott, and Bon. Ind. 48 a 51 sqq. The Cretan institutions are said to be 'analogous' to the Lacedaemonian, whereas in c. 11. 1272 b 33 sqq. some of the Carthaginian institutions are said to be 'analogous,' and others 'similar' (παραπλήσια) to the Lacedaemonian. Things may be 'analogous' without being 'alike' (Hist. An. 2. 1. 497 b 33: de Part. An. 1. 4. 644 a 16 sqq.: see Bon. Ind. 48 a 46), but here a certain amount of likeness is no doubt implied; still 'analogous' is probably a less strong word than 'similar.'

ἡ Κρητικὴ τάξις. Not only τῆς πολιτείας ἡ τάξις, 1272 a 4, but the whole body of Cretan institutions (see above on 1269 a 9).

41. γεωργοῦσί τε γὰρ κ.τ.λ. On the importance of this severance between the military and cultivating classes, which was common to the Lacedaemonian and Cretan States and also to Egypt, see 4 (7). 10. 1329 a 40 sqq. Here as there the syssitia are mentioned in immediate connexion with it, perhaps as an institution tending to mark off soldiers from cultivators (cp. Hdt. 1. 65, where syssitia are included under *τὰ ἐς πόλεμον ἔχοντα*). Compare Strabo, p. 542, *εἴρηται δὲ καὶ τοῦτο, ὅτι πρῶτοι τὴν Ἡράκλειαν κτίσαντες Μιλήσιοι τοὺς Μαριανδυνοὺς εἱλωτεύειν ἠνάγκασαν τοὺς προκατέχοντας τὸν τόπον, ὥστε καὶ πιπράσκεσθαι ὑπ' αὐτῶν, μὴ εἰς τὴν ὑπερορίαν δέ (συμβῆναι γὰρ ἐπὶ τούτοις), καθάπερ Κρησὶ μὲν ἐθήτευεν ἡ Μνῴα καλουμένη σύνοδος, Θετταλοῖς δὲ οἱ Πενέσται.*

4. ἔτι δὲ τῆς πολιτείας ἡ τάξις (sc. *ἔχει ἀνάλογον*). See note on 1264 b 31. 1272 a.

οἱ μὲν γὰρ ἔφοροι κ.τ.λ. Trieber (Forschungen, p. 90 n.) justly remarks that Aristotle seems to be in conflict with himself, when he derives the ephorship from Crete as if it had been introduced by Lycurgus, while nevertheless he ascribes its institution to Theopompus (7 (5). 11. 1313 a 25 sq.), unless indeed he supposes that Theopompus also borrowed from Crete. The functions of the cosmi do not seem to have been quite the same as those of the ephors, for they commanded the troops on a campaign (1272 a 9), which the ephors did not.

8. ἴσοι, 'correspond to': cp. *ἀνάλογον*, 1271 b 40. Cp. Soph. O. T. 845, 1498, and see Prof. Jebb's notes. Cp. also Lysias Or. 19. 36.

βασιλεία δὲ κ.τ.λ. Aristotle goes on to mention other similarities between the Lacedaemonian and Cretan constitutions. Kingship once existed in Crete, as it still does in the Lacedaemonian State, and the popular assembly in Crete is like the Lacedaemonian. Thirlwall (Hist. of Greece, 1. 285) thinks that Aristotle probably 'has the age of Minos in his view,' but, as he points out, Herodotus mentions (4. 154) a King of Axus in Crete as grandfather of the founder of Cyrene according to the Cyrenean tradition. We are perhaps in the region of fable when we read in Diodorus (5. 59. 1) the moving history of 'Althaemenes, son of Catreus, king of the Cretans,' and still more when we mount up to the autochthonous King Cres mentioned in the lines of Scymnus Chius. For *πρότερον μέν* answered by *εἶτα*, see Bon. Ind. s.v. *εἶτα*.

11. κυρία δ' οὐδενὸς κ.τ.λ. With the passage before us should be compared Aristot. Fragm. 493. 1558 b 9 (Plut. Lycurg. c. 6)—for what Plutarch here says may well be based on the *Λακεδαιμονίων*

Πολιτεία of Aristotle, whom he mentions by name shortly before—τοῦ δὲ πλήθους ἀθροισθέντος εἰπεῖν μὲν οὐδενὶ γνώμην τῶν ἄλλων ἐφεῖτο, τὴν δ' ὑπὸ τῶν γερόντων καὶ τῶν βασιλέων προτεθεῖσαν ἐπικρῖναι κύριος ἦν ὁ δῆμος, and also Pol. 2. 11. 1273 a 9, ἃ δ' ἂν εἰσφέρωσιν οὗτοι (i. e. the Carthaginian Suffetes and senators), οὐ διακοῦσαι μόνον ἀποδιδόασι τῷ δήμῳ τὰ δόξαντα τοῖς ἄρχουσιν, ἀλλὰ κύριοι κρίνειν εἰσὶ καὶ τῷ βουλομένῳ τοῖς εἰσφερομένοις ἀντειπεῖν ἔξεστιν, ὅπερ ἐν ταῖς ἑτέραις πολιτείαις οὐκ ἔστιν (i. e. in the Lacedaemonian and Cretan constitutions). It is not quite clear whether ὅπερ—ἔστιν refers to both κύριοι—εἰσί and τῷ βουλομένῳ—ἔξεστιν, or only to the latter clause. We have, however, a definite intimation in the passage before us that the only power possessed by the assembly in Crete was that of confirming the resolutions of the senators and cosmi (cp. Polyb. 22. 15. 1 [21. 32. 1, Hultsch], referred to by Liddell and Scott s. v. συνεπιψηφίζω—δόξαντος δὲ τῷ συνεδρίῳ καὶ τοῦ δήμου συνεπιψηφίσαντος, ἐκυρώθη τὰ κατὰ τὰς διαλύσεις). It might probably withhold that confirmation, and most authorities think that, if it did so, the resolution laid before it remained without legal force, but Gilbert (Gr. Staatsalt. 2. 221) thinks otherwise, and there is much to be said for his view, if we take ὅπερ—ἔστιν to refer to κύριοι κρίνειν εἰσί as well as to τῷ βουλομένῳ—ἔξεστιν. In any case the fact that it was not open to any member of the assembly who pleased to speak against the proposals of the senate and cosmi—whether any one at all was empowered to do so, we are not distinctly told, though we gather that any member who pleased might speak in support of them—must have tended to make a refusal to confirm an event of rare occurrence. Still the rights of the members of the assembly in Crete were in this matter of speaking the same as those possessed by the members of the Lacedaemonian assembly, and that the Lacedaemonian assembly possessed real authority we see from such passages as Thuc. 1. 87: Xen. Hell. 2. 2. 19: Plutarch, Ages. c. 6. The various ways of limiting the powers of the popular assembly are described in 6 (4). 14. 1298 b 26 sqq. One of them is ἢ ταὐτὰ ψηφίζεσθαι τὸν δῆμον ἢ μηδὲν ἐναντίον τοῖς εἰσφερομένοις, a plan not very unlike the Cretan. In some States no such thing as a popular assembly existed (3. 1. 1275 b 7). The Speaker of the English House of Commons of 1593 in answer to his request for liberty of speech, was told that it is granted, 'but not to speak every one what he listeth or what cometh into his brain to utter; their privilege was Ay or No' (Acland and Ransome, Political History of England, p. 82).

12. μὲν οὖν here, as in c. 6. 1265 a 10 and c. 11. 1273 a 2, introduces a transition from description to criticism: we have been told that the syssitia and cosmi in Crete correspond to the Lacedaemonian syssitia and ephors, but now we learn that while the organization of the Cretan syssitia is better than that of the Lacedaemonian, the Board of Cosmi is a less satisfactory institution even than the ephorate. The sentence introduced by μὲν οὖν is repeated in 26, and then the answering δέ comes in 28.

15. **νόμος**, 'a law': see above on 1270 b 3.

16. **πρότερον**, c. 9. 1271 a 26–37.

κοινοτέρως, sc. τὰ τῶν συσσιτίων ἔχει: 'the syssitia are placed on a more public footing': cp. c. 9. 1271 a 28, ἔδει γὰρ ἀπὸ κοινοῦ μᾶλλον εἶναι τὴν σύνοδον, καθάπερ ἐν Κρήτῃ, and below 1272 a 20, ὥστ' ἐκ κοινοῦ τρέφεσθαι πάντας. Ephorus had already mentioned that the Cretan syssitia were maintained at the public expense (ap. Strab. p. 480)—τοὺς δὲ τελείους ἐν τοῖς συσσιτίοις ἃ καλοῦσιν ἀνδρεῖα συσσιτεῖν, ὅπως τῶν ἴσων μετάσχοιεν τοῖς εὐπόροις οἱ πενέστεροι δημοσίᾳ τρεφόμενοι (cp. Pol. 2. 5. 1263 b 40 sq.)—but whether he also stated that this was otherwise in the Lacedaemonian State, we do not know. In Crete we see that the provision for the syssitia was put on a level with that for the worship of the gods and the public liturgies.

17. 'For from the whole of the agricultural produce and live stock raised on the public land and the tributes rendered by the serfs one part is assigned for the service of the gods and the discharge of the public liturgies, and the other for the syssitia.' For the order of τῶν γινομένων καρπῶν τε καὶ βοσκημάτων ἐκ τῶν δημοσίων, cp. de Part. An. 4. 10. 690 a 23, τὸ ἐκλεῖπον ὀστῶδες ἐκ τοῦ ποδός: 4. 1. 676 b 15, διὰ τὰς εἰρημένας αἰτίας πρότερον. For τὰς κοινὰς λειτουργίας, cp. Rhet. ad Alex. 3. 1424 a 23, τοῖς δὲ πλουτοῦσιν εἰς τὰς κοινὰς λειτουργίας ἑκουσίαν ἅπασαν φιλοτιμίαν ἐμποιήσωσιν. It would seem that the liturgies, elsewhere borne by rich men, were undertaken in Crete by the State. Compare Aristotle's own arrangement as to the public land (4 (7). 10. 1330 a 9 sqq.), which is not very dissimilar from the Cretan, though no provision is made for the liturgies, many of which he would be glad to abolish (8 (6). 5. 1320 b 3 sq.). The scheme for the division of the produce adopted in Plato's Laws 847 E is said to 'approach near to that sanctioned by the Cretan law,' but it is not easy to combine it with that described here. It is enough to say, with Thirlwall (Hist. of Greece, 1. 288), of Dosiadas' account (ap. Athen. Deipn. p. 143) of the syssitia at Lyctus, that the system which prevailed at Lyctus seems to have been different from that which Aristotle here describes as obtaining generally in Crete. The public land was evidently in part arable, in part pasture. Bücheler und Zitelmann (Das Recht von Gortyn, p. 138 sqq.) infer from some provisions of the succession-law of Gortyna (col. 4. 31 sqq.), which reserve for the sons, where there are sons and daughters, the succession to houses in Gortyna itself and to cattle and sheep, no mention being made of land, that the citizens of Gortyna grazed their cattle and sheep on the public pastures, which consequently must have lain, in part at all events, near the city. If this was so, the *βοσκήματα* here referred to would probably be private property. It is not quite clear from Aristotle's language, whether the produce from the public lands and the *φόροι* of the serfs were used for these purposes exclusively, no balance being left for others. The term *φόροι* applied to the contributions of the serfs indicates subjection, and probably conquest. These *φόροι* would seem to have been due to the State: a rent would perhaps be payable to the owner of the land in addition.

20. ὥστ' ἐκ κοινοῦ κ.τ.λ. If we understand this to mean that women and girls took part in the Cretan syssitia, it conflicts with Plato, Laws 780 E, as Oncken points out (Staatslehre des Aristoteles, 2. 386 sq.), and also with c. 12. 1274 b 11, not to dwell on the name *ἀνδρεῖα*. Probably all that is meant is that the share of produce given to each householder was sufficient to provide not only for the needs of himself and his sons at the public tables, but also for his wife and daughters at home. See Sus.[2], Note 366.

22. πρὸς δὲ τὴν ὀλιγοσιτίαν κ.τ.λ. 'And for securing scantiness of fare, in the view that it is beneficial, the lawgiver has devised many contrivances.' The transition from syssitia to *ὀλιγοσιτία*, and next to preventives of *πολυτεκνία*, is, as we shall see, easy. *'Ωφέλιμον* includes considerations both of health and morality. The aim of the Lacedaemonian lawgiver in studying the same thing is explained in Xen. Rep. Lac. 2. 5–6, Plutarch, Lycurg. c. 10, and [Plutarch,] Inst. Lac. c. 13. Ephorus confirms Aristotle's statement as to Crete (Strab. p. 480, *σωφρόνως καὶ λιτῶς ζῶσιν ἅπασιν*). Epimenides the Cretan is, in fact, said (Plato, Laws 677 E) to have achieved by his 'device' (*μηχάνημα*) what Hesiod divined before him: the reference no doubt is to the lines (Op. et Dies, 40)—

Νήπιοι, οὐδὲ ἴσασιν ὅσῳ πλέον ἥμισυ παντός,
οὐδ' ὅσον ἐν μαλάχῃ τε καὶ ἀσφοδέλῳ μέγ' ὄνειαρ.

The *μηχάνημα* referred to by Plato may possibly be the famous *ἄλιμος*, 'of which a small quantity satisfied both hunger and thirst': see Herodor. Fr. 19 (Müller, Fr. Hist. Gr. 2. 33) and Hermipp. Callim. Fr. 18 (Müller, Fr. Hist. Gr. 3. 40), together with Stallbaum's note on Laws 677 E, and also the note of Mr. Purves (Selections from Plato, p. 376), to whose references may be added Plutarch de Facie in Orbe Lunae c. 25. 940 C, ᾐνίξατο μὲν Ἡσίοδος, εἰπὼν

Οὐδ' ὅσον ἐν μαλάχῃ τε καὶ ἀσφοδέλῳ μέγ' ὄνειαρ,

ἔργῳ δ' ἐμφανῆ παρέσχεν Ἐπιμενίδης, διδάξας ὅτι μικρῷ παντάπασιν ἡ φύσις ὑπεκκαύματι ζωπυρεῖ καὶ συνέχει τὸ ζῷον, ἂν ὅσον ἐλαίας μέγεθος λάβῃ, μηδεμιᾶς ἔτι τροφῆς δεόμενον. It is possible that Aristotle here includes the invention of Epimenides among the expedients which he ascribes to the Cretan lawgiver. At any rate, Crete seems to have given birth to, or derived from Egypt (Diod. 1. 82. 2), an idea which came to be widely diffused in Greece. The object of the original lawgiver probably was to make hardy soldiers of his Cretans (cp. Xen. Cyrop. 8. 1. 43, where we are told that Cyrus, in the case of those whom he destined for slavery, ἐπεμέλετο ὅπως μήτε ἄσιτοι μήτε ἄποτοί ποτε ἔσοιντο ἐλευθερίων ἕνεκα μελετημάτων): it is hardly likely that he shared the mystical and ascetic tendency of Epimenides, still less that he found the virtues in a spare diet which Xenophon and others attributed to it. To them scanty food meant scanty περιττώματα, and scanty περιττώματα meant freedom from disease: thus the Persians of the Cyropaedia owed it, we are told, to the scantiness of their food that they rarely needed to spit or to blow their noses (Cyrop. 1. 2. 16: 8. 8. 8–9): cp. Plutarch de Sanitate Tuenda c. 14, μάλιστα δὲ τροφαῖς κεχρημένους ἐμβριθέσι καὶ κρεώδεσιν ἢ ποικίλαις, ὀλιγοσιτεῖν, καὶ μηδὲν ὑπολιπεῖν περιττώματος πλῆθος ἐν τῷ σώματι: so too Dicaearchus ap. Porphyr. de Abstinentia 4. 2 (ed. Nauck, p. 158. 14 sqq.: Müller, Fr. Hist. Gr. 2. 233–4), and Porphyry in the account of the Essenes which he gives on Josephus' authority (de Abstin. 4. 13, p. 174. 21 sqq. ed. Nauck: Bernays, Theophrastos' Schrift über Frömmigkeit, p. 155). Compare also [Aristot.] Probl. 1. 46. 865 a 1, ἢ ὅτι τοῦ νοσεῖν αἴτιον περιττώματος πλῆθος, τοῦτο δὲ γίνεται ἡνίκα τροφῆς ὑπερβολὴ ἢ πόνων ἔνδεια: Theopomp. Fr. 57 (Müller, Fr. Hist. Gr. 1. 286). Aristotle himself holds that luxurious living accelerates puberty (Phys. 5. 6. 230 b 1, αὐξήσεις αἱ τῶν ταχὺ διὰ τρυφὴν ἡβώντων). Thus the transition from ὀλιγοσιτία to checks on πολυτεκνία is easy. Aristotle's ὅρος, however, is not γλίσχρως, but σωφρόνως καὶ ἐλευθερίως . . . ζῆν (c. 6. 1265 a 29 sqq.: 4 (7). 5. 1326 b 30 sqq.); he is for avoiding either extreme.

23. καὶ πρὸς κ.τ.λ. Cp. Ephor. ap. Strab. p. 482, γαμεῖν μὲν ἅμα πάντες ἀναγκάζονται παρ' αὐτοῖς οἱ κατὰ τὸν αὐτὸν χρόνον ἐκ τῆς τῶν παίδων ἀγέλης ἐκκριθέντες, οὐκ εὐθὺς δ' ἄγονται παρ' ἑαυτοὺς τὰς γαμηθείσας παῖδας, ἀλλ' ἐπὰν ἤδη διοικεῖν ἱκαναὶ ὦσι τὰ περὶ τοὺς οἴκους, and see Gilbert, Gr. Staatsalt. 2. 223 sq., who refers to Heraclid. Pont. De

Rebuspubl. 3. 3 *sub fin.* (Müller, Fr. Hist. Gr. 2. 211). Aristotle approves the end (cp. 4 (7). 16. 1335 a 36–b 2), but not the means used in Crete, for though the discussion on this point is postponed, his judgment is not doubtful. Contrast the law of the Lacedaemonian State which encouraged πολυτεκνία (c. 9. 1270 b 1 sqq.).

24. ποιήσας, cp. ἐποίησε, c. 12. 1274 b 7. For ποιεῖν in the sense of 'constituere, sancire legibus,' see Sturz, Lex. Xenoph. s. v., P 29.

26. In place of δέ Sus.[23] following Lambinus reads δή, but compare 7 (5). 10. 1311 a 8, ὅτι δ' ἡ τυραννὶς ἔχει κακὰ καὶ τὰ τῆς δημοκρατίας καὶ τὰ τῆς ὀλιγαρχίας, φανερόν.

28. δέ answers to μὲν οὖν, 12.

29. γίνονται, 'are elected': cp. γινομένων, 36, and c. 9. 1270 b 8.

30. συμφέρει πρὸς τὴν πολιτείαν, 'is of advantage in relation to the constitution' (explained by βούλεται μένειν τὴν πολιτείαν, 33): cp. c. 6. 1265 b 25, συμφέρει πρὸς οἰκονομίαν, and see Bon. Ind. 719 a 35 sqq.

35. περὶ ὧν κ.τ.λ. The third of these criticisms, that relating to 'rule exercised without the check of law,' reminds us of Aristotle's remark as to the Lacedaemonian Ephors (c. 9. 1270 b 28 sqq.), that they 'judge without the check of law,' while his first and second criticisms repeat those which he has passed on the Lacedaemonian Senators (c. 9. 1270 b 38 sqq.), but to refer ὧν both to the Cosmi and to the Senators makes the sentence read awkwardly, and it is more likely that Aristotle is here speaking of the Senators only, though he has not said of the Lacedaemonian Senators that they 'rule without the check of law.' For this expression, which is not quite the same as 'judge without the check of law,' cp. 3. 15. 1286 a 12. Demosthenes (in Lept. c. 107) speaks of the Lacedaemonian Senator as δεσπότης τῶν πολλῶν. We see that while the magistracy of the Cosmi is more defective than the Ephorate, the Cretan Senate may be characterized in the same way as the Lacedaemonian. For γινομένων 36, cp. 7 (5). 8. 1308 a 5, τοὺς ἐν ταῖς ἀρχαῖς γινομένους.

40. 'De οὐδέν τι v. Jacobs. ad Achill. Tat. p. 728' (Göttl.). See critical note. For the happy results which follow when office is not a source of gain, see 7 (5). 8. 1308 b 31 sqq., and Isocr. Panath. § 145, who speaks of τὰ λήμματα τὰ εἰθισμένα δίδοσθαι ταῖς ἀρχαῖς.

41. ὥσπερ. Cp. c. 9. 1269 b 38.

πόρρω γε κ.τ.λ. Aristotle probably regarded Persia or the Greek States of the mainland of Europe and Asia as the most likely sources of corruption (cp. Hdt. 5. 51): the Greek islands were usually poor (Isocr. Paneg. § 132: cp. also Xen. Hell. 6. 1. 12, *οἶσθα δὲ δήπου ὅτι καὶ βασιλεὺς ὁ Περσῶν οὐ νήσους ἀλλ' ἤπειρον καρπούμενος πλουσιώτατος ἀνθρώπων ἐστίν*). In cities like Athens corrupting agencies might no doubt be found within the State: cp. Aristot. Fragm. 371. 1540 a 17 sq. (Harpocr. s. v. *δεκάζων*), *Ἀριστοτέλης δ' ἐν Ἀθηναίων πολιτείᾳ Ἄνυτόν φησι καταδεῖξαι τὸ δεκάζειν τὰ δικαστήρια.* Has Aristotle the passage before us (cp. also 1272 b 17) in his mind, when he says in 7 (5). 8. 1308 a 24, *σώζονται δ' αἱ πολιτεῖαι οὐ μόνον διὰ τὸ πόρρω εἶναι τῶν διαφθειρόντων, ἀλλ' ἐνίοτε καὶ διὰ τὸ ἐγγύς?* If so, he uses *διαφθείρειν* in a different sense from that in which he uses it in 1272 b 1.

1. τῆς ἁμαρτίας ταύτης, i.e. the restriction of the offices of Cosmus and Senator to certain families, notwithstanding the largeness of their powers. 1272 b.

2. οὐ πολιτικὴ ἀλλὰ δυναστευτική. Cp. 10, and 4 (7). 2. 1324 b 26, *πῶς γὰρ ἂν εἴη τοῦτο πολιτικὸν ἢ νομοθετικόν, ὅ γε μηδὲ νόμιμόν ἐστιν; οὐ νόμιμον δὲ τὸ μὴ μόνον δικαίως ἀλλὰ καὶ ἀδίκως ἄρχειν, κρατεῖν δ' ἔστι καὶ μὴ δικαίως.* The remedy employed involves a resort to arbitrary measures on the part of a handful of powerful men quite out of character with a constitution governed by law: hence it is *δυναστευτική*, for a *δυναστεία* is the tyranny of a handful, as the *τυραννίς* is the tyranny of one man and the extreme democracy the tyranny of the Many (6 (4). 14. 1298 a 31 sq.), and tyranny is least of all a constitution (6 (4). 8. 1293 b 29). See below on 10.

4. αὐτῶν, 'their colleagues themselves,' whom one would least expect to do such a thing.

ἔξεστι δὲ κ.τ.λ. It would seem that not only might individual cosmi resign before the expiration of their term of office, but that the cosmi might resign in a body, thus leaving the State without cosmi. Apart from this, however, Aristotle objects to the magistrate resigning in the midst of his term, for, as he says in c. 9. 1271 a 11, *δεῖ καὶ βουλόμενον καὶ μὴ βουλόμενον ἄρχειν τὸν ἄξιον τῆς ἀρχῆς.* Possibly, however, resignation before the close of the official term was not usually allowed in Greece. It seems to have been allowed at Rome (Mommsen, Römisches Staatsrecht 1. 508 sqq.: Dict. of Greek and Roman Antiquities, art. Magistratus, p. 724 a).

6. Congreve, followed by Welldon, would read *δέ* in place of *δή*, but perhaps *δή* is defensible (it is the reading of all the MSS. and the Vet. Int.). 'As the present method leads to violence and other inconveniences, it is therefore better to regulate the matter by law.'

7. οὐ γὰρ ἀσφαλὴς ὁ κανών. Cp. 3. 15. 1286 a 17 sq.: Eth. Nic. 5. 10. 1134 a 35: Hyperid. Or. Fun. col. 9. 23 sqq. (p. 63 Blass). Aristotle may possibly here have in his mind a familiar line from the Peirithous of Euripides (Fr. 600 Nauck), which seems also to be present to his memory in 3. 16. 1287 b 6 sq.:

Τρόπος ἐστὶ χρηστὸς ἀσφαλέστερος νόμου.

8. τὸ τῆς ἀκοσμίας κ.τ.λ., 'the way the great men have of declaring an abeyance of the magistracy of the Cosmi': cp. 7 (5). 7. 1307 b 18, δυναστείαν τῶν ἐπιχειρησάντων νεωτερίζειν. Ἀκοσμία is formed on the model of ἀναρχία, 'the abeyance of the archonship,' Xen. Hell. 2. 3. 1. I have retained in the text the reading of Π^2, but not without much hesitation. Π^1 read πάντων δὲ φαυλότατον τὸ τῆς ἀκοσμίας, ἣν καθιστᾶσι πολλάκις ὅταν μὴ δίκας βούλωνται δοῦναι τῶν δυναστῶν. This is unintelligible without Coray's slight emendation of οἳ ἂν for ὅταν, but with this it is certainly smoother Greek, though perhaps not more Aristotelian, than the reading of Π^2. But all the MSS. and also the Vet. Int. have ὅταν. As to the reading of Π^1 τῶν δυναστῶν, perhaps we rather expect to hear of δυνατοί than δυνάσται, notwithstanding δυναστευτική, 3. The Cretan constitution is not pronounced to be a δυναστεία μᾶλλον till 10, and even then is probably regarded rather as a virtual, than as an actual, δυναστεία. The mention of δυνάσται no doubt makes the inference that the constitution is a δυναστεία easy: perhaps indeed it makes it too easy. For if Aristotle had already spoken of δυνάσται, he would hardly need to draw the inference that the Cretan constitution approaches a δυναστεία, as he does in 1272 b 9 sq. We find a reference to δυνατοί in Crete in the account of Ephorus ap. Strab. p. 483, τὰς δ' ἀγέλας συνάγουσιν οἱ ἐπιφανέστατοι τῶν παίδων καὶ δυνατώτατοι. Cretan methods remind us of the 'liberum veto' of Poland. They far transcend the turbulence of medieval Genoa (Machiavelli, History of Florence, p. 211 E. T. Bohn).

10. οὐ πολιτεία, because a constitution is not compatible with these moments of surrender to the will of powerful individuals: cp. 6 (4). 4. 1292 a 32, ὅπου γὰρ μὴ νόμοι ἄρχουσιν, οὐκ ἔστι πολιτεία. Intentionally or not, Aristotle negatives here the remark of the Athenian interlocutor of the Laws (712 E) to Cleinias the Cretan and Megillus the Lacedaemonian—ὄντως γάρ, ὦ ἄριστοι, πολιτειῶν μετέχετε· ἃς δὲ ὠνομάκαμεν νῦν, οὐκ εἰσὶ πολιτεῖαι. A δυναστεία is thus described in Pol. 6 (4). 5. 1292 b 5—τέταρτον δ' [εἶδος ὀλιγαρχίας], ὅταν ὑπάρχῃ τό τε νῦν λεχθὲν (i. e. ὅταν παῖς ἀντὶ πατρὸς εἰσίῃ), καὶ ἄρχῃ μὴ ὁ νόμος ἀλλ' οἱ ἄρχοντες· καὶ ἔστιν ἀντίστροφος αὕτη ἐν ταῖς ὀλιγαρχίαις ὥσπερ ἡ τυραννὶς ἐν ταῖς μοναρχίαις καὶ περὶ ἧς τελευταίας εἴπαμεν δημοκρατίας ἐν ταῖς δημο-

κρατίαις· καὶ καλοῦσι δὴ τὴν τοιαύτην ὀλιγαρχίαν δυναστείαν: cp. 6 (4). 6. 1293 a 30, *ὅταν δὲ ἤδη πολὺ ὑπερτείνωσι ταῖς οὐσίαις καὶ ταῖς πολυφιλίαις, ἐγγὺς ἡ τοιαύτη δυναστεία μοναρχίας ἐστίν, καὶ κύριοι γίνονται οἱ ἄνθρωποι ἀλλ' οὐχ ὁ νόμος.* Aristotle holds that the Cretan constitution is rather a *δυναστεία* than a constitution regulated by law, because, though in its ordinary course the magistrates are appointed by election, and the popular assembly possesses certain rights of a definite, though narrow, kind, and so far the constitution does not resemble a *δυναστεία*, it is subject to intervals of license, in which the will of a few powerful individuals overmasters all law.

11. εἰώθασι δὲ κ.τ.λ. We see from the passages quoted in the preceding note that Aristotle regards a *δυναστεία* as 'near to monarchy,' and now we are told that the leading men form followings for themselves by breaking up the demos and their friends into factions, and so set up a monarchy (cp. 6 (4). 12. 1297 a 8, *τῶν τὰς ἀριστοκρατικὰς βουλομένων ποιεῖν πολιτείας*), just as Peisistratus did according to Herodotus (Hdt. 1. 59, *ὃς στασιαζόντων τῶν παράλων καὶ τῶν ἐκ τοῦ πεδίου Ἀθηναίων . . . καταφρονήσας τὴν τυραννίδα, ἤγειρε τρίτην στάσιν*). As to *διαλαμβάνοντες* ('dividing into parties'), cp. 8 (6). 5. 1320 b 8, *διαλαμβάνοντας τοὺς ἀπόρους*, and 6 (4). 11. 1296 a 10, *ἐν δὲ ταῖς μικραῖς ῥᾴδιόν τε διαλαβεῖν εἰς δύο πάντας κ.τ.λ.* With this picture of Cretan feuds compare Polyb. 4. 53. 5, *ἐγγενομένης δὲ φιλοτιμίας ἐκ τῶν τυχόντων, ὅπερ ἔθος ἐστὶ Κρησίν, ἐστασίασαν πρὸς τοὺς ἄλλους.*

13. τὸ τοιοῦτον, 'the state of things just described.' For the thought here expressed, cp. c. 11. 1272 b 30–33, where the absence of *στάσις* and of any *τύραννος* is said to be *σημεῖον πολιτείας συντεταγμένης*, and Thuc. 1. 18. 1, *ἡ γὰρ Λακεδαίμων . . . ἐπὶ πλεῖστον ὧν ἴσμεν χρόνον στασιάσασα, ὅμως ἐκ παλαιοτάτου καὶ ηὐνομήθη καὶ ἀεὶ ἀτυράννευτος ἦν.*

15. ἔστι δ' ἐπικίνδυνος κ.τ.λ. 'A State in this condition' (subject to intervals of non-existence) 'is in peril, as' (or 'if') 'those who wish to attack it are also able to do so.' Stahr, however, translates, 'läuft derselbe (Staat) Gefahr, jedem der ihn angreifen will und kann zur Beute zu werden,' but in the absence of other instances of this use of *ἐπικίνδυνος* with a genitive it is hardly safe to interpret the passage thus.

17. εἴρηται, 1272 a 41.

σώζεται, sc. *ἡ πόλις*, for Aristotle seems to forget that he is speaking not of one State, but of the many States of Crete.

ξενηλασίας plural, as usual. 'Distance has produced the effect of a law expelling foreigners.' Hoeck (Kreta 3. 442 sqq.) illustrates the isolation of Crete, but also points out (p. 450 sqq.) that there are many indications that foreigners were not excluded from the island. He refers to Plato, Laws 848 A among other passages.

18. **καί** may perhaps here mean 'for instance,' as occasionally elsewhere (e.g. in 1. 12. 1259 b 8).

μένει τοῖς Κρησίν. 'The perioeci stand firm in the Cretan States' (not, I think, 'are faithful to the Cretans,' as some translate, though the dative *τοῖς Κρησίν* probably implies some advantage to the Cretans from their attitude). Cp. 1272 a 26, *ὅτι δὲ τὰ περὶ τὰ συσσίτια βέλτιον τέτακται τοῖς Κρησὶν ἢ τοῖς Λάκωσι, φανερόν*, and 1270 a 37, *τοῖς Σπαρτιάταις*, and for *μένει*, 8 (6). 5. 1319 b 35, *μίαν γὰρ ἢ δύο ἢ τρεῖς ἡμέρας οὐ χαλεπὸν μεῖναι πολιτευομένους ὁπωσοῦν.*

19. **ἀφίστανται.** Cp. Plato, Laws 777 B, *χαλεπὸν δὴ τὸ κτῆμα· ἔργῳ γὰρ πολλάκις ἐπιδέδεικται περὶ τὰς Μεσσηνίων συχνὰς εἰωθυίας ἀποστάσεις γίγνεσθαι.*

οὔτε γὰρ κ.τ.λ. apparently gives the reason why the Cretan perioeci do not revolt like the Helots; but Aristotle does not explain how external dominion leads to the revolt of serfs. Does he hint that it was the foreign empire of the Lacedaemonians that led to the liberation of Messenia by Thebes? Perhaps he only means that external dominion involves foreign war, which he has stated in c. 9. 1269 b 5 to be one main reason for serf-revolts. 'Not only,' we are told, 'do they not possess any external dominion, but' (*οὔτε—τε*) 'it is only lately that a foreign war' (*πόλεμος ξενικός*—cp. *ξενηλασίας*, 17—not, probably, 'a mercenary war,' for its being waged by mercenaries is not to the point) 'has passed over to the island' (cp. Choerilus ap. Rhet. 3. 14. 1415 a 17, *ὅπως Ἀσίας ἀπὸ γαίης ἦλθεν ἐς Εὐρώπην πόλεμος μέγας*). Wars between one Cretan city and another, he has already said, did not lead to revolts of the serfs (c. 9. 1269 a 40 sqq.): indeed it would seem from the language of this passage—*περὶ δὲ τοὺς Κρῆτας οὐδέν πω τοιοῦτον συμβέβηκεν*—that even the 'foreign war' here referred to did not, though it manifested the weakness of their institutions. Whether Aristotle refers here to the operations of Phalaecus and his mercenaries in the island (345 B.C.), or to its subjugation by Agesilaus, brother of the Lacedaemonian king Agis III, in 333 B.C., is uncertain, but perhaps it is more probable that Phalaecus is referred to, for Aristotle is evidently speaking of the first intrusion of a foreign war into Crete. Though Phalaecus was ultimately foiled and slain before Cydonia, he had previously taken Lyctus.

C. 11. **25.** **περιττῶς**, 'in a vein above the common.' See note on 1265 a 11.

μάλιστα δ' ἔνια κ.τ.λ., 'but so far as the Carthaginian constitution can be said to resemble any other, it comes nearest in some points at least to the Laconian.' Cp. σύνεγγύς πως, 27.

26. αὗται γὰρ αἱ πολιτεῖαι τρεῖς. For the order, which is quite regular, see note on 1269 a 23. The Cretan constitution is now brought in, which had already been said to be the model on which the Lacedaemonian was framed.

29. The older editors place a full stop after Καρχηδονίων (as do Bernays and Susemihl), whereas Bekker places only a comma there, thus making αὐτοῖς, 30, refer to all three States. There is something to be said in favour of Bekker's view, but on the whole I am inclined to think that Bern. and Sus. are right. If we place a full stop or colon after Καρχηδονίων, καὶ πολλά 29 will take up πολλά 25.

30. σημεῖον δὲ κ.τ.λ. 'And it is an indication of a constitution carefully framed with a definite aim that, possessing though it does its well-known popular element, Carthage remains faithful to the arrangements of its constitution.' In most States the laws are not συντεταγμένοι, but χύδην κείμενοι, 4 (7). 2. 1324 b 5–9. The meaning of the word comes out clearly in 4 (7). 14. 1333 b 7 sq.: 8 (6). 1. 1317 a 6: Metaph. Λ. 10. 1075 a 18 sq. Schneider, followed by Bernays and others, would insert εὖ before συντεταγμένης, but this is probably unnecessary: cp. Democrit. Fragm. 45, τοῖσι δ τρόπος ἐστὶ εὔτακτος, τουτέοισι καὶ βίος ξυντέτακται. Τεταγμένη πολιτεία is a term used by Plato (Rep. 619 C)—in a different sense, however, for it seems to be used in that passage of a constitution favourable to the formation of habits of virtuous action. With ἔχουσαν (which Π² Vet. Int. have, though it is omitted in Mˢ P¹), I supply τὴν πόλιν, which, as has been already noticed in the note on 1266 b 1, is often omitted by Aristotle. Τὸν δῆμον, as in c. 12. 1274 a 2, τὸν δὲ δῆμον καταστῆσαι, and 7 (5). 3. 1303 a 30, τὸ ἄγος: it was well-known that the citizen-body at Carthage comprised a mass of poor (cp. 7 (5). 12. 1316 b 5, where Carthage is even described as δημοκρατουμένη, if the reading is right, and Plutarch, Praecepta Reipubl. Gerend. c. 3, where the character of the Carthaginian demos is sketched and contrasted with the character of the Athenian in a striking passage probably based on some earlier authority). For δῆμος in the sense of 'a popular element,' cp. c. 12. 1274 a 2: c. 6. 1265 b 39. For ἡ τάξις τῆς πολιτείας, cp. c. 10. 1272 a 4. The quiescence of the demos, it appears later (1273 b 21), is due to a fortunate accident rather than to the skill of the lawgiver.

32. **στάσιν.** The design of Hanno, however, is mentioned in 7 (5). 7. 1307 a 5.

καί, 'at all' (Riddell, Apology of Plato, p. 168).

τύραννον. Yet in 7 (5). 12. 1316 a 34 a tyranny is said to have changed into an ἀριστοκρατία at Carthage, if the reading is right. Perhaps Aristotle intends to confine his assertion to the duration of the ἀριστοκρατία, and does not reckon what preceded it. It is, we note, in this same twelfth chapter of the book on Revolutions (B. 7)—a chapter somewhat loosely hung on to the book and not impossibly later in date—that Carthage is referred to as δημοκρατουμένη (1316 b 5).

33. **ἔχει δὲ κ.τ.λ.** Some remarks on the Carthaginian constitution will be found in Appendix B. The word ἑταιρία is used in so many different senses that it is hardly possible to determine the exact nature of these συσσίτια τῶν ἑταιριῶν at Carthage. Its most usual meaning is 'a political club or association,' but Aristotle would hardly compare gatherings of this nature with the Lacedaemonian Phiditia. Ἑταιρία is used by Dosiadas in his description of the syssitia of Lyctus in much the same sense apparently as συσσίτιον (cp. Athen. Deipn. p. 143, διῄρηνται δ' οἱ πολῖται πάντες καθ' ἑταιρίας, καλοῦσι δὲ ταύτας ἀνδρεῖα· τήν τ' ἐπιμέλειαν ἔχει τοῦ συσσιτίου γυνή), so that τὰ συσσίτια τῶν ἑταιριῶν may here only mean 'the common meals of the messes.' One would suppose from the comparison of them with the Phiditia, that they must have comprised the whole citizen-body, and that they must have been designed, like them, to promote efficiency in war.

36. **ἐκ τῶν τυχόντων**, cp. ἐξ ἁπάντων, c. 9. 1270 b 26.

38. **καὶ βέλτιον δὲ κ.τ.λ.**, 'and it is also better that the kings (at Carthage) neither belong to one and the same family, nor that again an ordinary one; and that if the family from which they are taken is of marked excellence, they are appointed from it by election rather than by seniority.' I have adopted the reading of Π^2, κατὰ τὸ αὐτὸ εἶναι γένος (κατ' αὐτὸ pr. P^1, καυτωτὸ pr. M^s, καταυτὸ corr. M^s, 'per se' Vet. Int.), but Susemihl's reading, καθ' αὑτὸ εἶναι γένος ('do not form a family apart'), has many claims to attention. The κατ' αὐτὸ of P^1 and καταυτὸ of M^s, however, may easily have originated in a miswriting of κατὰ ταὐτὸ, the second τα being omitted, as often happens (cp. 6 (4). 15. 1299 b 27, where κατὰ ταύτας τὰς διαφοράς, which is probably the right reading, has undergone similar changes); and there is some roughness in the expression τοὺς βασιλεῖς καθ' αὑτὸ εἶναι γένος. Besides, no MS. gives καθ' αὑτό. There is also some awkward-

ness in the sequence of μηδὲ (or μήτε, Sus.) τοῦτο τὸ τυχόν, if we read καθ' αὑτό, for we shall have to translate—'it is better that the kings do not form a family apart, nor this an ordinary one': we seem to need 'do not belong to' instead of 'do not form,' but it is not easy to get this meaning from the words μήτε καθ' αὑτὸ εἶναι γένος. And how can it be said that the kings form a whole family? On the other hand, it must be admitted that the use of κατά in κατὰ τὸ αὐτὸ εἶναι γένος is not a common one. Κατά with the acc., however, occasionally bears much the same meaning as ἐν: thus κατὰ τὴν αὐτὴν ἡλικίαν, de Gen. An. 1. 19. 727 a 5, is replaced by ἐν τῇ αὐτῇ ἡλικίᾳ, de Gen. An. 1. 20. 728 b 24. (The use of the phrase εἶναι κατά is slightly different in 3. 4. 1276 b 33, where ἀγαθόν should perhaps be supplied.) Aristotle objects to a single family monopolizing two posts of such importance as the Lacedaemonian kingships: cp. 7 (5). 7. 1306 b 22 sqq. and 7. (5). 6. 1305 b 2 sqq. Arrangements of this kind often led to στάσις, especially when the favoured family was not one of conspicuous merit, and Aristotle does not seem to think that the Heracleidae of the Lacedaemonian State were so: hence the design of Lysander (7 (5). 7. 1306 b 31 sq.). We have in this passage μήτε followed by μηδέ and τε, much as we have μήτε—μηδὲ—μήτε in Plato, Gorg. 500 B, μήτε αὐτὸς οἴου δεῖν πρὸς ἐμὲ παίζειν, μηδ' ὅ τι ἂν τύχῃς παρὰ τὰ δοκοῦντα ἀποκρίνου, μήτ' αὖ τὰ παρ' ἐμοῦ οὕτως ἀποδέχου ὡς παίζοντος. On μήτε—μηδέ, see Jelf, Gr. Gr. § 775. 2. d and Obs. 5 (where this passage from the Gorgias is quoted), and Ast, Lex. Plat. s. vv. μηδέ, οὐδέ. Μηδέ following μήτε 'gives its clause an adversative or emphatic force,' 'neither—nor yet' (Jelf, ibid.). No change, therefore, is called for in μηδέ. As to the view here expressed by Aristotle, cp. Cic. de Rep. 2. 12. 24, quo quidem tempore novus ille populus (the Roman) vidit tamen id quod fugit Lacedaemonium Lycurgum, qui regem non deligendum duxit, si modo hoc in Lycurgi potestate potuit esse, sed habendum, qualiscunque is foret, qui modo esset Herculis stirpe generatus. Nostri illi etiam tum agrestes viderunt virtutem et sapientiam regalem, non progeniem, quaeri oportere. Herodotus (5. 39, 42) evidently bears no goodwill to the rule of succession by which Cleomenes was preferred to Dorieus.

41. εὐτελεῖς, 'insignificant in character': Bonitz (Ind. s. v.) compares Rhet. 2. 15. 1390 b 24, εἰσὶν οἱ πολλοὶ (τῶν εὐγενῶν) εὐτελεῖς.

2. τὰ μὲν οὖν κ.τ.λ. Aristotle here passes with μὲν οὖν from fact 1273 a.
to criticism, as in c. 6. 1265 a 10 and c. 10. 1272 a 12, but he

continues to make the Carthaginian constitution the subject of his remarks, so that it hardly seems necessary to add (*e conj.*) τοῖς Καρχηδονίοις either (with Thurot, Études p. 32) after μᾶλλον, 6, or (with Sus.) after πολιτείας, 5. The Carthaginian and Cretan States, no less than the Lacedaemonian, are open to the charge of making military success and predominance their aim and thinking τὰ ἀγαθὰ τὰ περιμάχητα better than virtue. The same thing is said in 4 (7). 14. 1333 b 5 sqq. of the lawgivers of all the best-constituted Hellenic States. Cp. also below, 1273 a 37 sq. Τῶν ἐπιτιμηθέντων ἄν must here mean 'of the points open to censure' (not 'of the censures one might pass'): cp. Eth. Nic. 3. 7. 1114 a 30, αἱ ἐπιτιμώμεναι τῶν κακιῶν. See note on 1271 b 18. Here the παρεκβάσεις referred to are παρεκβάσεις τῆς ἀρίστης πολιτείας (cp. c. 9. 1269 a 31), as in 6 (4). 3. 1290 a 24 sqq., not παρεκβάσεις τῶν ὀρθῶν πολιτειῶν as in 3. 7.

4. **τῶν δέ**, sc. ἐπιτιμηθέντων ἄν. The framers of 'aristocratic' constitutions are said in 6 (4). 12. 1297 a 7 sqq. often to give the rich too much power.

πρὸς τὴν ὑπόθεσιν κ.τ.λ., 'in relation to its aim of being an Aristocracy or Polity.' For καί = 'or,' see Bon. Ind. 357 b 20 sq. It is possible, however, that καὶ τῆς πολιτείας is added (cp. 1. 9. 1257 b 9, τὴν χρηματιστικὴν καὶ τὴν καπηλικήν) to explain the sense in which the word ἀριστοκρατία is used, for it might mean 'the best constitution' (6 (4). 7. 1293 b 1).

5. **δῆμον** = δημοκρατίαν, as (e.g.) in 6 (4). 3. 1290 a 16.

6. **μᾶλλον**, 'rather than in the opposite direction' (cp. c. 7. 1266 a 36 and c. 9. 1270 b 33).

τοῦ μὲν γὰρ κ.τ.λ. A deviation in a democratic direction is here noticed. Μέν (= 'while') is answered, I think, by δ' in ἃ δ' ἂν εἰσφέρωσιν. For the parenthesis εἰ δὲ μὴ κ.τ.λ., cp. c. 10. 1272 a 15.

8. If πάντες is read (which P[2] omits) after ὁμογνωμονῶσι, two explanations are possible: either πάντες means 'both authorities,' as it frequently does in the style of Aristotle (Bon. Ind. 571 b 50 sqq.), or absolute unanimity not only of the Suffetes but of the senators was required. The latter is improbable: Sus.[2] (Note 387) refers to Liv. 21. 3 sq.: 21. 9. 3–11. 2: 23. 12 sqq. to disprove it. Aristotle most likely means by 'are unanimous' 'are unanimous as to bringing or not bringing a given question before the popular assembly.' Καὶ τούτων, 9, will then mean 'over matters as to the reference of which to the popular assembly the kings and senators are not unanimous, as well as over those which they agree to refer to it.' If, on the other hand, 'are unanimous' means 'are agreed

on a measure,' then καὶ τούτων will mean 'over the measure which is the subject of that difference of opinion, as well as over matters voluntarily referred to the assembly in cases of unanimity.' In either case the power possessed by the assembly was a very real and substantial one, though it would seem that it had not, like most popular assemblies in Greece (6 (4). 14), an absolute claim to have certain specified matters, such as questions of war, peace, alliance, and the like, referred to it. If the kings and the senate agreed not to refer a question to the assembly, they could effectually prevent this question coming before it Susemihl (Note 387) remarks that the Second Punic War was decided on by Suffetes and Senate alone, notwithstanding that the assembly had by that time (Polyb. 6. 51. 6) gained the chief voice in deliberation.

9. **ἃ . . . ἂν εἰσφέρωσιν οὗτοι**, 'as to any matters brought by them before the assembly' (cp. εἰσφοράν, 8 (6). 8. 1322 b 14). See note on 1264 b 39.

οὐ διακοῦσαι μόνον κ.τ.λ. Cp. Eth. Nic. 3. 5. 1113 a 7, δῆλον δὲ τοῦτο καὶ ἐκ τῶν ἀρχαίων πολιτειῶν, ἃς Ὅμηρος ἐμιμεῖτο· οἱ γὰρ βασιλεῖς ἃ προέλοιντο ἀνήγγελλον τῷ δήμῳ.

10. **ἀποδιδόασι.** See note on 1265 a 6. Ἀποδιδόναι often means 'dare id quod convenit vel par est' (Ast, Lex. Platon. s. v.), as for instance in Plat. Polit. 295 A, ἀκριβῶς ἑνὶ ἑκάστῳ τὸ προσῆκον ἀποδιδόναι.

11. **κρίνειν**, 'to come to a decision of their own.' The word used in Plut. Lycurg. c. 6 (Aristot. Fragm. 493. 1558 b 9 sqq.) to describe the powers of the Lacedaemonian assembly is ἐπικρῖναι—τοῦ δὲ πλήθους ἀθροισθέντος εἰπεῖν μὲν οὐδενὶ γνώμην τῶν ἄλλων ἐφεῖτο, τὴν δ' ὑπὸ τῶν γερόντων καὶ τῶν βασιλέων προτεθεῖσαν ἐπικρῖναι κύριος ἦν ὁ δῆμος. For the meaning of ἐπικρῖναι, cp. Plato, Laws 768 A, ἐὰν δὲ μὴ δύνησθον κοινωνῆσαι τῆς ὁμολογίας αὐτοί, τὴν βουλὴν ἐπικρίνειν αὐτῶν τὴν αἵρεσιν ἑκατέρου, and for that of κρίνειν, Aristot. Eth. Nic. 3. 5. 1113 a 11, ἐκ τοῦ βουλεύσασθαι κρίναντες. See note on 1272 a 11.

12. **ὅπερ.** See note on 1272 a 11.

ἐν ταῖς ἑτέραις πολιτείαις, i. e. the Lacedaemonian and Cretan.

13. **τὰς πενταρχίας.** As δεκαρχίαι = 'decemviratus' (cp. Xen. Hell. 3. 4. 2), so πενταρχίαι = 'quinqueviratus' (Kluge, Aristoteles de politia Carthaginiensium, p. 121–2). Nothing is known about these bodies of five magistrates. On self-election as an oligarchical feature, cp. 6 (4). 5. 1292 b 1 sqq.: it is so only if eligibility is confined to a few.

16. **πλείονα ἄρχειν χρόνον τῶν ἄλλων.** So ὀλιγοχρόνιοι ἀρχαί are a sign of democracy (8 (6). 2. 1317 b 24). Τῶν ἄλλων is translated

by Bern. 'als die Mitglieder anderer Behörden,' and by Mr. Welldon 'than any other board of officers,' but Sus. translates 'than all other magistrates,' and, I incline to think, rightly.

ἐξεληλυθότες, 'after exit from office.' Kluge compares εἰς τὰς ἀρχὰς βαδίζειν, 2. 7. 1266 b 24: cp. also εἰς τὰς ἀρχὰς παριέναι, 7 (5). 3. 1303 a 17.

17. τὸ δὲ ἀμίσθους καὶ μὴ κληρωτάς, sc. εἶναι. Here Aristotle notices one or two points which might seem to be deviations in an oligarchical direction, but are not. The payment of magistrates is democratic (8 (6). 2. 1317 b 35–38), but the non-payment of them is compatible with aristocracy as well as with oligarchy. The same may be said of appointment by election, not by lot (cp. 6 (4). 9. 1294 b 7–13, 32–33, etc.). No deviation from the aristocratic ὑπόθεσις of the constitution is involved in these arrangements.

19. καὶ τὸ τὰς δίκας κ.τ.λ. The Carthaginian and Lacedaemonian States had this feature of judicial procedure in common, that in them all suits came before magistrates of the State for adjudication, not before the citizen-body (3. 1. 1275 b 8 sqq.). In the latter State, however, each magistracy had its own exclusive field of judicial competence, so that a very small number of persons possessed the right of dealing with this or that offence—of inflicting, for instance, the punishment of death or exile (6 (4). 9. 1294 b 33, where this is noted as an oligarchical feature of the constitution)—whereas at Carthage this was not so: all magistracies were competent to try any suit—whether severally or in combination, we do not learn. We are left to guess why this arrangement is more suitable to an aristocracy than the other, just as in 4 (7). 11. 1330 b 20 we are not told why a plurality of 'strong places' in a city is suitable to an aristocracy; but the reason may perhaps be that under the Carthaginian system less is left to the decision of a very few, for it must be remembered that an ἀριστοκρατία takes account of ἐλευθερία (or δῆμος) as well as of wealth and virtue (6 (4). 7. 1293 b 14 sq.: 6 (4). 8. 1294 a 19–25). Or possibly the Carthaginian system may be regarded as more suitable to an aristocracy, because it assumes and implies a greater diffusion of virtue among the holders of magistracies than the other.

21. For **παρεκβαίνειν** followed by a genitive, see Bon. Ind. 568 a 27 sqq.

22. διάνοιαν here = δόξαν, Bon. Ind. 186 b 4 sqq.

23. συνδοκεῖ, i. e. approves itself not only to the Carthaginian constitution but also to the mass of men. Cp. Plato, Laws 763 D, δεῖ δὴ καὶ τούτους δυνατούς τε εἶναι καὶ σχολάζοντας τῶν κοινῶν ἐπιμελεῖσθαι, and see the criticisms which Aristotle passes on the Laws in c. 6. 1266 a 12 sqq.

25. καλῶς probably qualifies both *ἄρχειν* and *σχολάζειν*: cp. 4 (7). 5. 1326 b 30, *πλήθει δὲ καὶ μεγέθει τοσαύτην ὥστε δύνασθαι τοὺς οἰκοῦντας ζῆν σχολάζοντας ἐλευθερίως ἅμα καὶ σωφρόνως*. *Καλῶς σχολάζειν* is a condition of *καλῶς ἄρχειν*.

28. καί, 'among others,' 'for example': cp. 4 (7). 12. 1331 a 31, *οἷαν καὶ περὶ Θετταλίαν ὀνομάζουσιν*: 4 (7). 1. 1323 b 26: 1. 12. 1259 b 8.

29. εἰς δύο ταῦτα βλέποντες. In 35 (cp. c. 12. 1274 b 21) we have *βλέπειν* used with *πρός*: for *βλέπειν* with *εἰς*, see Bon. Ind. 138 a 51 sqq.

30. τὰς μεγίστας. *Ἀρχάς* is omitted, though it is some time since even *ἄρχοντες* were referred to (24); but no one will be at a loss to supply the missing word, so it drops out.

31. ἁμάρτημα νομοθέτου, 'a lawgiver's error': cp. 3. 4. 1277 a 20, *ὡς οὖσάν τινα ἄρχοντος παιδείαν*. Lawgivers are regarded as responsible, if what ought to be attended to at the outset (*ἐξ ἀρχῆς*, cp. c. 9. 1269 b 39) is not attended to. Here Aristotle traces back the practice of the Carthaginians in paying regard to wealth as well as excellence, when they elect magistrates, to an omission on the part of the lawgiver or founder of the State (cp. c. 9. 1270 a 18, *τοῦτο δὲ καὶ διὰ τῶν νόμων τέτακται φαύλως*), who ought to have done what Aristotle himself does in constructing his best State (4 (7). 9. 1329 a 17 sqq.), and secured *εὐπορία* to the best men of the State. Cp. Isocr. Busir. § 18, *ἔτι δὲ τὸ μηδένα (τῶν μαχίμων) τῶν ἀναγκαίων ἀποροῦντα τῶν κοινῶν προσταγμάτων ἀμελεῖν*.

35. εἰ δὲ κ.τ.λ., i.e. but if it is right to look to wealth as well as to virtue in electing to offices, it is not right or necessary to go to the extreme of making the greatest offices in the State purchaseable; yet there is a law at Carthage to this effect. For the fact, cp. Polyb. 6. 56. 4, *παρὰ μὲν Καρχηδονίοις δῶρα φανερῶς διδόντες λαμβάνουσι τὰς ἀρχάς*. Plato perhaps was thinking of Carthage, when he speaks (Rep. 544 D) of *ὠνηταὶ βασιλεῖαι*.

χάριν σχολῆς. '*Χάριν* plerumque ipsi nomini postponitur; aliquoties antepositum legitur,' Bon. Ind. 846 a 42.

37. ἔντιμον γὰρ κ.τ.λ. The phrase *ἔντιμον ποιεῖν* recurs in 3. 15. 1286 b 14, *ἐπεὶ δὲ χείρους γιγνόμενοι ἐχρηματίζοντο ἀπὸ τῶν κοινῶν, ἐντεῦθέν ποθεν εὔλογον γενέσθαι τὰς ὀλιγαρχίας· ἔντιμον γὰρ ἐποίησαν τὸν πλοῦτον*. Cp. also Plato, Rep. 550 E sqq. referred to by Giph., and 554 B.

38. τὴν πόλιν ὅλην. Compare the use of this phrase in c. 5. 1264 b 16 sqq., in 3. 13. 1283 b 40, where it seems to be explained by τῶν πολιτῶν 41, and in 2. 9. 1269 b 19, where it includes not only the citizens, but also the women of the citizen class.

39. ὅτι δ' ἂν κ.τ.λ. Susemihl reads γάρ, though all the MSS. as well as Vet. Int. have δέ. Δέ seems to be quite in place here, for the sentence which it introduces does not appear to be added in proof of that which precedes (ἔντιμον γὰρ—φιλοχρήματον), in which no reference is made to τὸ κύριον. Aristotle's meaning probably is—'the law makes wealth to be esteemed more than virtue, and renders the whole city fond of money, and those who purchase these high offices will come to prize above all other things the wealth by which they are won, yet what the possessors of supreme authority prize most will be most prized by the other citizens also.' We read already in Xen. Cyrop. 8. 8. 5, ὁποῖοί τινες γὰρ ἂν οἱ προστάται ὦσι, τοιοῦτοι καὶ οἱ ὑπ' αὐτοὺς ὡς ἐπὶ τὸ πολὺ γίγνονται, and the same thing is said by Isocrates (ad Nicocl. § 31, τὸ τῆς πόλεως ὅλης ἦθος ὁμοιοῦται τοῖς ἄρχουσιν: cp. Areopag. § 22: Nicocl. § 37). Cp. also Plato, Laws 711 B sqq.

41. τούτοις = τῇ τούτων, just as in the passage quoted in the last note from Isocr. ad Nicocl. τοῖς ἄρχουσιν = τῷ τῶν ἀρχόντων (see Jelf, Gr. Gr. § 781 d. Obs. 2). Τούτοις refers to τὸ κύριον: for the plural, cp. 1273 a 11, κύριοι, which refers to τῷ δήμῳ, 10. We are reminded of Plato, Laws 711 C, καὶ πῶς οἰόμεθα ταχὺ ξυνακολουθήσειν τοὺς ἄλλους πολίτας τῷ τὴν τοιαύτην πειθὼ καὶ ἅμα βίαν εἰληφότι;

1273 b. **1. οὐχ οἷόν τε βεβαίως ἀριστοκρατεῖσθαι τὴν πολιτείαν.** So Π^1: οὐχ οἷόν τ' εἶναι βεβαίως ἀριστοκρατικὴν πολιτείαν, Π^2. With ἀριστοκρατεῖσθαι we expect πόλιν rather than πολιτείαν, but it may possibly be right to supply τὴν τῶν Λακεδαιμονίων (πολιτείαν) with δημοκρατεῖσθαι in 2. 6. 1265 b 35–38 (see note on this passage). Perhaps on the whole it is probable that the reading of Π^1 is the original reading, and that of Π^2 the result of an attempt on the part of some one or other (possibly Aristotle himself, though that is not very likely) to soften the harshness of ἀριστοκρατεῖσθαι. As to the thought, we must bear the passage before us in mind when we are told in 6 (4). 7. 1293 b 14 sqq., that an ἀριστοκρατία will pay regard to πλοῦτος, ἀρετή, and δῆμος. It will not be durable, if it does not honour virtue most. Compare the passages referred to above on 37, and also 7 (5). 12. 1316 b 5 sqq. Aristotle seems to have thought it likely that the Carthaginian ἀριστοκρατία would ultimately pass into an oligarchy.

ἐθίζεσθαι δ' εὔλογον κ.τ.λ. This is a further objection. Not only does this law lead the citizens to count wealth more precious than virtue, and thus tend to imperil the aristocratic character of the constitution, but the purchasers of these great offices will probably learn by degrees to seek to replace the money spent in their purchase by dishonest gains.

3. εἰ πένης μὲν ὢν . . . κερδαίνειν. And this is the view implied by the law making these offices purchaseable (cp. 1273 a 24 sq.). After *φαυλότερους δ' ὢν* we should supply, with Bernays, 'like those purchasers of office.' The argument is an *argumentum ad hominem* addressed to the lawgiver or the supporters of this law.

5. διὸ κ.τ.λ. This amounts to saying—'therefore the *ἐπιεικεῖς* should be put in a position to rule': *εὐπορία* should be secured to them. And then, in the next sentence, Aristotle goes on—'but even if the lawgiver neglected to secure a sufficiency of means to the best men both in and out of office, still it is better that he should provide for their leisure when in office.' As to *τούτους*, 5, see note on 1260 b 35 and Bon. Ind. 546 a 47. For *προεῖτο*, Liddell and Scott (s. v.) compare 7 (5). 7. 1307 b 4: see also Bon. Ind. 638 b 54 sqq.

9. ὅπερ κ.τ.λ. M. Yriarte says of the Venetian system of government (Vie d'un Patricien de Venise, p. 95)—'il permet le cumul de plusieurs fonctions, et le permet à un tel point qu'il n'est pas rare de voir un Sénateur occuper en même temps jusqu'à cinq ou six postes très-importants dans l'État.' See also Dr. Arnold, History of Rome 2. 550, note 6. We learn from Pol. 7 (5). 10. 1310 b 22, that some of the earlier tyrannies owed their origin to the practice adopted by certain oligarchies of entrusting the most important magistracies to a single holder.

11. προστάττειν. Cp. 6 (4). 15. 1299 b 7 sq.

12. ὅπου μὴ μικρὰ πόλις. Cp. 6 (4). 15. 1299 a 34 sqq. and 8 (6). 8. 1321 b 8 sqq.

πολιτικώτερον here seems to be taken by Bonitz (Ind. 614 a 30–39, b 10–24) in a similar sense to that which it bears in 6 (4). 9. 1294 a 41, *κοινὸν δὲ καὶ μέσον τούτων ἀμφότερα ταῦτα, διὸ καὶ πολιτικόν, μέμικται γὰρ ἐξ ἀμφοῖν*: i.e. in a sense contrasted with *δημοκρατικόν, ὀλιγαρχικόν* etc., 'aptum ad moderatum quoddam imperium populare.' But must it not be used here in some sense in which *καὶ κάλλιον—θᾶττον* can serve as a justification of it? Its meaning is probably 'more statesmanlike,' 'more agreeable to political science,' as in 4 (7). 2. 1324 b 26 (cp. *ἔργον τοῦ πολιτικοῦ*, 24) and 4 (7). 14. 1333 b 35. Cp. also Demosth. de Falsa Legatione § 114 Shilleto (p. 373), *καίτοι τῶν σκήψεων τούτων οὐδεμία ἐστὶ πολιτικὴ οὐδὲ δικαία*, where Shilleto translates 'one which you would take from a statesman.'

13. κοινότερόν τε γὰρ κ.τ.λ. 'For it is fairer to all, as we said' (the reference probably is to 2. 2. 1261 b 1 sqq.), 'and work of one and the same kind, whatever it is (ἕκαστον), is done better and more quickly.' Cp. Plato, Rep. 370 C, ἐκ δὴ τούτων πλείω τε ἕκαστα γίγνεται καὶ κάλλιον καὶ ῥᾷον, ὅταν εἷς ἓν κατὰ φύσιν καὶ ἐν καιρῷ σχολὴν τῶν ἄλλων ἄγων πράττῃ, and Aristot. Pol. 1. 2. 1252 b 3 sqq. For κοινότερον, cp. Rhet. ad Alex. 9. 1430 a 1, καὶ ἡμεῖς δέ, ἂν ἴσως καὶ κοινῶς πρὸς αὐτοὺς προσφερώμεθα, πολὺν χρόνον τὴν συμμαχίαν φυλάξομεν, where κοινῶς is conjoined with ἴσως (see Liddell and Scott s. v. ἴσος, ii. 3) and opposed to πλεονεκτικῶς, 1429 b 38. Ἕκαστον τῶν αὐτῶν seems = ἓν ἔργον, 1273 b 9, e. g. τὸ σκυτοτομεῖν as distinguished from a combination of αὐλεῖν καὶ σκυτοτομεῖν: cp. Isocr. Busir. § 16, ἅπαντας δὲ τοὺς ἀριθμοὺς περιλαβὼν ἐξ ὧν ἄριστ' ἄν τις τὰ κοινὰ διοικήσειεν, ἀεὶ τοῖς αὐτοῖς τὰς αὐτὰς πράξεις μεταχειρίζεσθαι προσέταξεν, εἰδὼς τοὺς μὲν μεταβαλλομένους τὰς ἐργασίας οὐδὲ πρὸς ἓν τῶν ἔργων ἀκριβῶς ἔχοντας, τοὺς δ' ἐπὶ ταῖς αὐταῖς πράξεσι συνεχῶς διαμένοντας εἰς ὑπερβολὴν ἕκαστον ἀποτελοῦντας, and Nicocl. § 18, οἱ δ' ἀεὶ τοῖς αὐτοῖς ἐπιστατοῦντες κ.τ.λ. Yet there is much to be said for Bernays' conjecture of τῶν ἔργων in place of τῶν αὐτῶν. Has Cicero this passage in his memory when he writes to Atticus (13. 10. 2)—Ad Dolabellam, ut scribis, ita puto faciendum, κοινότερα quaedam et πολιτικώτερα? We perhaps find an echo of it in Plutarch, Reip. Gerend. Praecepta c. 15. 812 D, οὐ γὰρ μόνον τῆς δυνάμεως εἰς πολλοὺς διανέμεσθαι δοκούσης, ἧττον ἐνοχλεῖ τὸν φθόνον τὸ μέγεθος, ἀλλὰ καὶ τὰ τῶν χρειῶν ἐπιτελεῖται μᾶλλον.

15. τοῦτο, i. e. the advantage of a diffusion of ἀρχή. It is not quite certain whether ἐπὶ τῶν πολεμικῶν καὶ τῶν ναυτικῶν means 'in military and naval affairs' or 'in affairs of war and in maritime affairs.' I rather incline to the former view. In fleets and armies almost every one may be said both to rule and to be ruled, for each has a superior at the same time as he commands inferiors. There were in the Lacedaemonian army even enomotarchs, i. e. leaders of 30 or 40 men, and very possibly commanders on even a smaller scale. Lord Napier of Magdala remarks (*Times*, July 25, 1885), that 'the command even of a small body of soldiers involves . . . the exercise both of subordinate discipline and of discipline in command.' In civic life a share of ruling and being ruled is secured in a different way—by alternation (2. 2. 1261 b 1 sqq.)—but the result is the same.

17. διὰ πάντων διελήλυθε. This phrase recurs in 6 (4). 14. 1298 a 17 and 6 (4). 15. 1300 a 26, where however it is used of office, not of ruling and being ruled.

18. ὀλιγαρχικῆς, and hence exposed to much danger of being upset (7 (5). 12. 1315 b 11 : 7 (5). 1. 1302 a 4 sqq.: compare the transition in c. 6. 1266 a 11 sqq. from ὀλιγαρχικόν, 12, to ἐπικίνδυνον, 27). As oligarchies rest on wealth, the remedy employed at Carthage (that of enrichment) was an excellent one, for it brought fresh blood into the ruling class, or at all events made the people less hostile. See on this subject 8 (6). 5. 1320 a 35–b 16, τεχναστέον οὖν ὅπως ἂν εὐπορία γένοιτο χρόνιος κ.τ.λ. Ischomachus (Xen. Oecon. 14. 4 sqq.) contrasts the laws of Draco and Solon, which punish those who do wrong, with the 'royal laws' (i. e. those of kings, or perhaps those of the king of Persia—see Holden, Oeconomicus, p. 217), which enrich those who do right, and says that in his management of his slaves he employs both methods, and that further, when he finds slaves anxious to be commended by him, τούτοις ὥσπερ ἐλευθέροις ἤδη χρῶμαι, οὐ μόνον πλουτίζων ἀλλὰ καὶ τιμῶν ὡς καλούς τε κἀγαθούς. See also Xen. Cyrop. 8. 2. 22.

ἐκφεύγουσι, sc. τὸν κίνδυνον (Coray). Bernays, ingeniously enough, would insert (*e conj.*) στάσιν after ἄριστα, but it is doubtful whether anything has dropped out. Aristotle often omits a word where it will be readily supplied. See note on 1266 b 1, and cp. 5 (8). 5. 1340 b 17, where πρὸς τὴν ψυχὴν is left to be supplied by the reader. We find ἐκφεύγειν, however, used absolutely now and then, and διαφεύγειν is frequently thus used (e. g. in Hdt. 1. 10).

19. τῷ πλουτεῖν. So all MSS. Τῷ πλουτίζειν (Schn.) would certainly be much simpler, but perhaps τῷ πλουτεῖν (which Bernays leaves unaltered) is defensible. Πλουτεῖν means 'to become rich' as well as 'to be rich,' cp. 8 (6). 4. 1318 b 20, and Menand. Κόλαξ, Fr. 6 (Meineke, Fr. Com. Gr. 4. 154), οὐδεὶς ἐπλούτησεν ταχέως δίκαιος ὤν: thus τῷ πλουτεῖν may here be translated 'by becoming rich,' 'by enrichment.' Members of the demos became rich and contented through being despatched to the cities dependent on Carthage in some capacity the exact nature of which is uncertain (as officials, if we follow Susemihl—as colonists, if we follow Grote, History of Greece 10. 545): cp. 8 (6). 5. 1320 b 4, τοιοῦτον δέ τινα τρόπον Καρχηδόνιοι πολιτευόμενοι φίλον κέκτηνται τὸν δῆμον· ἀεὶ γάρ τινας ἐκπέμποντες τοῦ δήμου πρὸς τὰς περιοικίδας ποιοῦσιν εὐπόρους. See Sus.[2], Note 398, who explains the 'cities' here mentioned to be cities of the agricultural section of the indigenous Libyans subject to Carthage, as distinguished on the one hand from Phoenician cities ruled by her and on the other from pastoral Libyan tribes.

ἐπὶ τὰς πόλεις. In 1320 b 4 sqq. (quoted in the last note) ἐκπέμπειν is used with πρός. Ἐπί perhaps implies that they were sent out to rule the cities: cp. Xen. Hell. 3. 4. 20, τούτων Ξενοκλέα μὲν καὶ ἄλλον ἔταξεν ἐπὶ τοὺς ἱππέας κ.τ.λ. Ἐκπέμπειν is used of sending out officials in c. 9. 1271 a 24, but it is also commonly used of colonists (see Liddell and Scott s. v.). For τὰς πόλεις, 'the cities dependent on Carthage,' compare the use of ἀπὸ τῶν πόλεων in Xen. Hell. 3. 4. 20 and of ἐν ταῖς πόλεσιν in [Xen.] Rep. Ath. 1. 14.

21. ἀλλὰ κ.τ.λ. Cp. 6 (4). 9. 1294 b 36 and 4 (7). 13. 1332 a 28 sq.

τουτί. Aristotle would seem, if we may judge from the Index Aristotelicus, to use οὑτοσί but rarely. For the contrast between τύχης ἔργον and διὰ τὸν νομοθέτην, cp. 4 (7). 13. 1332 a 29 sqq., and for διὰ τὸν νομοθέτην, see above on 1270 b 19.

23. φάρμακον . . . τῆς ἡσυχίας. Compare the use of ἄκος in 7 (5). 5. 1305 a 32 sq.

25. Κρητικῆς. For the omission of the article, see Bon. Ind. 109 b 44 sqq. and Vahlen, Beitr. zu d. Poet. 4. 409.

δικαίως surprises us, but still the Cretan constitution had its merits.

C. 12. **27. Τῶν δὲ κ.τ.λ.** Looking to the programme of the Second Book which we find in its opening chapter, we might well expect it to close with the review of the Carthaginian constitution. We are there prepared for a review of the constitutions subsisting in reputedly well-governed States and of schemes of constitution put forth by individuals and generally well thought of; but now Aristotle speaks as if he had promised a review of οἱ ἀποφηνάμενοι περὶ πολιτείας, divides them into two classes, those who had not taken an active part in politics and those who had, and calls to mind that he has not yet spoken of anyone except Lycurgus belonging to the latter class. He will now, we gather, enter on a review, not of existing constitutions or of schemes of constitution, but of lawgivers who had played a part in politics. It is no doubt true that, as Aristotle ranks Solon among the best lawgivers in 6 (4). 11. 1296 a 18 sqq., we look for a criticism of the Solonian constitution from him, and that this constitution, having passed away and given place to another, is not in strictness included in either of the two classes of constitution marked out for treatment in the first chapter of the Second Book. Still there is some awkwardness about this addition to the programme, and the purpose of the book—the indication of what is good and useful in the constitutions reviewed and the revelation of their general inadequacy (2. 1. 1260 b 32–35)—seems to be but little served by the inquiries of this concluding chapter. The more valuable portion of it —that relating to Solon—rather corrects current mistakes as to the nature of his legislation than criticises it, and the remainder is little more than a collection of jottings. The notice of Solon's legislation, though possibly incomplete, seems to be Aristotelian, but it may have been tacked on by some later hand to the notice of the Carthaginian constitution, and the authenticity of the rest of the chapter in its present shape is very questionable. See note on 1274 a 22.

35. Σόλωνα δ' ἔνιοι κ.τ.λ. This approval is mentioned because good repute confers a claim to notice (c. 1. 1260 b 32). Plato had already said in Rep. 599 E, *σὲ δέ τίς αἰτιᾶται πόλις νομοθέτην ἀγαθὸν γεγονέναι καὶ σφᾶς ὠφεληκέναι; Χαρώνδαν μὲν γὰρ Ἰταλία καὶ Σικελία, καὶ ἡμεῖς Σόλωνα.* Aristotle himself ranks Solon among the 'best lawgivers' (see above on 27). It is not clear whether Isocrates is referred to among these *ἔνιοι*, though he was an eulogist of Solon and of the *πάτριος δημοκρατία* (cp. Areopag. §§ 16–17, 26–27, 37: de Antid. § 232). They regarded Solon as the destroyer of an extreme oligarchy, on the ruins of which he constructed the *πάτριος δημοκρατία*, a wisely mixed constitution: they took him to have founded the Areopagus, to have introduced the system of filling magistracies by election, and to have created the popular dicastery, thus as it were equipping the State with a complete set of new institutions. 'Most writers,' says Plutarch (Solon c. 19), 'made Solon the author of the Areopagus': Plutarch himself, however, doubts the fact for the reason he there mentions. To this view of Solon's work Aristotle objects; he says that Solon would seem to have found the council of the Areopagus and the system of filling the magistracies by election already established, and that he was only so far responsible in relation to those matters that he left them as he found them, whereas he did institute the popular element in the constitution by founding the popular dicasteries. He appeals in support of his contention to the opinion of a second set of critics, who made Solon responsible for the existing extreme democracy. They complained that so far from being the author of a mixed constitution, he overpowered the oligarchical element of the constitution by the democratic, inasmuch as he gave supreme power to the popular dicastery. Armed with this judicial authority, the people became masters of the State; one statesman after another had to play into their hands, and so the extreme democracy gradually came into being. Aristotle, however, holds that these inquirers ascribed to Solon's institution of popular dicasteries consequences which would not have resulted from it, if it had not been for accidental circumstances. Solon was far from intending to found an extreme democracy; he gave, in fact, only a modicum of power to the people—enough to content them and no more—and reserved office for the better-to-do classes. On the other hand, he was not the contriver of an elaborate mixed constitution, but rather the founder of the beginnings of popular liberty; still less was he the undoer of the power of the Few. He left office in their hands, and gave the people only just enough power to make the holders of office govern well (8 (6). 4. 1318 b 27–1319 a 6). That Aristotle approved of Solon's legislation is evident from 6 (4). 11. 1296 a 18 sq.: 8 (6). 4. 1318 b 27 sqq.: 3. 11. 1281 b 21–1282 a 41.

39. **μίξαντα καλῶς τὴν πολιτείαν κ.τ.λ.** These critics appear to have thought that a good mixed constitution should include oligarchical, aristocratical, and popular elements: compare the view referred to in c. 6. 1265 b 33 sqq. Aristotle may perhaps have regarded the Areopagus as an oligarchical rather than an aristocratic institution (7 (5). 4. 1304 a 20: cp. 6 (4). 3. 1290 a 27), but he would hardly agree that election to office, unless it is *κατ' ἀρετήν*, is an aristocratic feature (cp. 6 (4). 9. 1294 b 7 sqq.), or think that the mere admissibility of all citizens to serve on the dicasteries, without the accompaniment of pay to the poor for serving, is a large step in the democratic direction.

41. Here, as it seems to me, Aristotle's statement of his own opinion begins.

1274 a. **2.** **τὸν δὲ δῆμον καταστῆσαι κ.τ.λ.**, 'set up the demos' (gave a place in the constitution to the demos) 'by enacting that all the citizens should be admitted to sit on the dicasteries.' Aristotle uses the same words—*καταλῦσαι, καταστῆσαι*—as had been used by the critics to whom he refers, in order to bring out clearly the difference of his own view. Solon is here so far connected with the dicasteries that he is said to have provided that membership of them should be open to all citizens.

5. **ὥσπερ τυράννῳ τῷ δήμῳ χαριζόμενοι.** An indication of the *τελευταία δημοκρατία*: cp. 6 (4). 4. 1292 a 11, *μόναρχος γὰρ ὁ δῆμος γίνεται κ.τ.λ.*: 7 (5). 11. 1313 b 38: 8 (6). 5. 1320 a 4 sq.

6. **τὴν νῦν δημοκρατίαν.** Cp. 10, where this expression is repeated. It is implied that the Athenian democracy was in the writer's time a democracy of an advanced kind—perhaps a *τελευταία δημοκρατία*. The passage is noticeable, because Aristotle commonly avoids mentioning Athens in connexion with his censures of extreme democracy. Some have doubted its genuineness because of its unwonted outspokenness.

8. **Ἐφιάλτης . . . καὶ Περικλῆς**, cp. Plutarch, Praecepta Reip.

Gerend. c. 15. 812 D, ὡς Περικλῆς Μενίππῳ μὲν ἐχρῆτο πρὸς τὰς στρατηγίας, δι' Ἐφιάλτου δὲ τὴν ἐξ Ἀρείου πάγου βουλὴν ἐταπείνωσε, διὰ δὲ Χαρίνου τὸ κατὰ Μεγαρέων ἐκύρωσε ψήφισμα, Λάμπωνα δὲ Θουρίων οἰκιστὴν ἐξέπεμψεν.

10. αὔξων. Cp. 8 (6). 4. 1319 b 21, οἷς Κλεισθένης Ἀθήνησιν ἐχρήσατο βουλόμενος αὐξῆσαι τὴν δημοκρατίαν.

12. ἀπὸ συμπτώματος. Cp. 7 (5). 6. 1306 b 6.

τῆς ναυαρχίας, a rare word, apparently, in the sense in which it is here used.

13. ἐν τοῖς Μηδικοῖς. Cp. 7 (5). 4. 1304 a 20, οἷον ἡ ἐν Ἀρείῳ πάγῳ βουλὴ εὐδοκιμήσασα ἐν τοῖς Μηδικοῖς ἔδοξε συντονωτέραν ποιῆσαι τὴν πολιτείαν, καὶ πάλιν ὁ ναυτικὸς ὄχλος γενόμενος αἴτιος τῆς περὶ Σαλαμῖνα νίκης καὶ διὰ ταύτης τῆς ἡγεμονίας διὰ τὴν κατὰ θάλατταν δύναμιν τὴν δημοκρατίαν ἰσχυροτέραν ἐποίησεν: Isocr. de Antid. § 316 sq.: Plato, Laws 707, and also 708 E, ἔμελλον λέγειν, ὡς οὐδείς ποτε ἀνθρώπων οὐδὲν νομοθετεῖ, τύχαι δὲ καὶ ξυμφοραὶ παντοῖαι πίπτουσαι παντοίως νομοθετοῦσι τὰ πάντα ἡμῖν· ἢ γὰρ πόλεμός τις βιασάμενος ἀνέτρεψε πολιτείας καὶ μετέβαλε νόμους κ.τ.λ.

14. δημαγωγοὺς φαύλους. Probably those alluded to by Isocrates, de Antidosi §§ 316–7, a passage which Aristotle evidently has in his mind here. Aristotle had a good opinion of the antagonist of Pericles, Thucydides son of Melesias (Plutarch, Nicias c. 2), but would hardly have applied this expression to Pericles, even for the sake of contradicting Isocrates, who calls him δημαγωγὸς ἀγαθός (de Antid. § 234).

15. ἐπεὶ Σόλων γε κ.τ.λ. Cp. Solon, Fragm. 5 (Bergk), and Pol. 3. 11. 1281 b 32 sqq. It would seem, however, from 8 (6). 4. 1318 b 21 sqq., that Solon might have given the people less; and Plato in the Laws, though he allows the people some share in judicial and deliberative functions, reserves the review of the conduct of magistrates in office for his great college of the priests of Apollo.

16. ἀποδιδόναι. See note on 1273 a 10, ἀποδιδόασι τῷ δήμῳ.

17. μηδὲ γὰρ τούτου κ.τ.λ. Cp. Plato, Laws 767 E–768 B, and Pol. 8 (6). 5. 1320 a 14 sqq.

18. ἀρχάς, here as in 6 (4). 14. 1298 a 1–3 (contrast 3. 1. 1275 a 23–29) distinguished from τὸ δικάζον. Cp. 3. 4. 1277 b 1, διὸ παρ' ἐνίοις οὐ μετεῖχον οἱ δημιουργοὶ τὸ παλαιὸν ἀρχῶν, πρὶν δῆμον γενέσθαι τὸν ἔσχατον, where Athens may be among the States referred to, for, as Schömann says (Gr. Alterth. 1. 342), 'it is clear that as the three upper classes of the Solonian Constitution were framed in relation to the amount of their landed property, all those who owned no land must have been placed in the fourth, even when well endowed with other kinds of property.' The Archonship was probably confined to the first class (Plut. Aristid. c. 1).

19. ἐκ τῶν πεντακοσιομεδίμνων κ.τ.λ. Diels (Über die Berliner Fragmente der *'Αθηναίων Πολιτεία* des Aristoteles, p. 33. 3) regards 1274 a 19–21 as an interpolation, and if with Susemihl we regard all that follows *νομοθέται δέ*, 22, as spurious, there is something to be said for rejecting *ἐκ τῶν πεντακοσιομεδίμνων—μετῆν*, 21, also. These words, however, seem to be added to justify and enforce *τῶν γνωρίμων καὶ τῶν εὐπόρων*, and to show that Solon not only confined office to well-to-do men, but did so by the requirement of a property qualification (cp. 8 (6). 4. 1318 b 30, *ἄρχειν δὲ τὰς μεγίστας αἱρετοὺς καὶ ἀπὸ τιμημάτων . . . ἢ καὶ ἀπὸ τιμημάτων μὲν μηδεμίαν, ἀλλὰ τοὺς δυναμένους*).

20. τρίτου τέλους probably means 'third in mention' (cp. c. 6. 1264 b 33: c. 11. 1272 b 28), not necessarily 'third in point of dignity.' Susemihl brackets (though doubtfully) these two words as spurious, but *τέλους* seems to be needed for *τὸ τέταρτον*, 21.

21. οἷς κ.τ.λ. The fact was mentioned by Aristotle in the *'Αθηναίων Πολιτεία* also (Aristot. Fragm. 350. 1537 a 20 sqq.).

22. νομοθέται δὲ ἐγένοντο κ.τ.λ. The review of Solon's legislation seems, as has been said, hardly to be complete. Be that, however, as it may, we expect it to be followed by a review of lawgivers who legislated for their own States or for others after taking an active part in politics (*πολιτευθέντες αὐτοί*, 1273 b 31), whether they were the authors of laws only or of constitutions as well as laws, for it is doubtful whether Susemihl is right in thinking that the authors of laws only are dismissed in 1273 b 32 from consideration. And we do find that in what follows lawgivers who legislated for other States than their own (Charondas, Philolaus, Androdamas) are specially noted. Nothing, however, is said as to the lawgivers now enumerated having taken an active part in politics, and we are even more at a loss in this part of the chapter than in that relating to Solon to see how the scanty notices given of their legislation serve the main purpose of the book, which is set forth in c. 1. 1260 b 32–36. Of Zaleucus all that we are told is that he legislated for the Epizephyrian Locrians, and it would even seem (see next note) that Aristotle elsewhere gave an account of him which would at all events exclude the idea of his having legislated *after* taking an active part in politics, for according to the *Πολιτεῖαι* he was a shepherd and a slave when he became a lawgiver. About Charondas we learn a little more, and perhaps there is a reason for the insertion of the story about Philolaus and

Diocles, though it seems out of keeping in the Politics. From this point onward the object of the writer appears to be to note anything special and peculiar to each lawgiver. This aim had not, to say the least, been equally prominent in previous chapters, though we find, it is true, some traces of it in c. 7. 1266 a 33–36, 39 and c. 8. 1267 b 29. The passage 1274 b 9–15 is especially open to suspicion. A recurrence to Phaleas and Plato seems quite out of place, especially now that we are concerned with lawgivers, and with lawgivers who had taken an active part in politics, of whom Plato was not one. The statement (1274 b 9 sq.) that Plato was the first to propose a community of property conflicts with c. 7. 1266 a 34 sq. It is true that there is much that is characteristic of Aristotle in the style of the passage which begins at 1274 a 22 and extends to the end of the chapter. The quiet correction of Ephorus (1274 a 25 sqq.), and of the too patriotic Locrian legend which traced back the beginnings of the legislative art to the Locrian Onomacritus, is also quite in Aristotle's vein.

On the whole, the guess is perhaps permissible that Aristotle may have left only the fragment about Solon and a few rough data for insertion after the notice of the Carthaginian constitution, and that some member of the school, not very long after his death, completed them as he best could. Zeller, it should be noticed, holds that the chapter has suffered from interpolation (Gr. Ph. 2. 2. 676).

Ζάλευκός τε κ.τ.λ. Of the lawgivers noticed in the remaining portion of the chapter, some seem to have been authors of constitutions as well as laws, others of laws only. We cannot be certain that the 'ill-compounded *ἀριστοκρατία*' at the Epizephyrian Locri which Aristotle criticises in 7 (5). 7. 1307 a 38 sq. was regarded by him as the work of Zaleucus, but Plutarch speaks of Zaleucus as the author of a constitution (Numa c. 4). Charondas, however, appears to be referred to in 6 (4). 12. 1297 a 7 sqq. as the founder of an *ἀριστοκρατία*, or at all events of a constitution of some kind: cp. 6 (4). 11. 1296 a 21: 6 (4). 13. 1297 a 21 sqq. Draco and Pittacus, on the contrary, are stated to be authors of laws only in 1274 b 15, 18. It is hardly likely that Cicero refers to this passage in Ep. ad Att. 6. 1. 18: Quis Zaleucum leges Locris scripsisse non dixit? Num igitur iacet Theophrastus, si id a Timaeo reprehensum est? Cp. Cic. de Leg. 2. 6. 15, where Timaeus is said to have denied that Zaleucus ever existed. There were perhaps some who ascribed the Politics to Theophrastus, but Cicero can hardly have been among them, for, as has been pointed out elsewhere, he says in the De Finibus (5. 4. 11) that both Aristotle and Theophrastus had written 'de optimo statu rei publicae,' so that at all events the two books of the Politics which relate to this subject cannot have been attributed by him to Theophrastus. It has apparently escaped notice, that while Zaleucus is here classed among those who had become lawgivers after taking an active part in politics (πολιτευθέντες αὐτοί, 1273 b 31), he is said by the Scholiast on Pindar on the authority of Aristotle to have been a shepherd and a slave when he was called on to legislate (Aristot. Fragm. 505. 1561 a 5 sqq.). Perhaps, however, the words πολιτευθέντες αὐτοί need not be interpreted as implying that the participation in political life preceded the legislation; the intention may be only to contrast lawgivers who took an active part in politics at some time in their life with those who διετέλεσαν ἰδιωτεύοντες τὸν βίον (1273 b 28).

24. ταῖς Χαλκιδικαῖς. Some would omit ταῖς, but cp. 1. 11. 1258 b 19, τῶν ἄλλων ζῴων τῶν πλωτῶν ἢ πτηνῶν, ἀφ' ὅσων ἔστι τυγχάνειν βοηθείας, where τῶν ἄλλων ζῴων undergoes a similar series of limitations.

25. πειρῶνται δὲ κ.τ.λ. 'And some attempt even to put facts together, their view being that' etc. Welldon, following Congreve, translates συνάγειν 'to make out a catena of legislators,' and so also Bernays, 'eine ununterbrochene Reihenfolge von Gesetzgebern nachzuweisen,' but the correctness of this rendering seems doubtful. For the construction, cp. 6 (4). 9. 1294 b 20. Who were these τινες? Trieber (Forschungen, pp. 67, 72, 101) and Sus.[2] (Note 418) say Ephorus; and it is true that Ephorus (ap. Strab. 10. p. 482), on the authority of 'the Cretans,' brings Lycurgus into communication with Thales—μελοποιῷ ἀνδρὶ καὶ νομοθετικῷ—from whom he is said to learn in particular the way in which Rhadamanthus, and afterwards Minos, fathered their laws on Zeus. But we nowhere learn that Ephorus connected Thales with Onomacritus; and as to Zaleucus, Ephorus would seem from Strabo 6. p. 260 to have regarded his laws as a compilation ἔκ τε τῶν Κρητικῶν νομίμων καὶ Λακωνικῶν καὶ ἐκ τῶν Ἀρεοπαγιτικῶν. This hardly looks as if he made Zaleucus and Lycurgus disciples of Thales, and therefore contemporaries or nearly so. Ephorus, it is true, was an enthusiast for things Cretan, and may well have pointed to Crete as the birthplace of the legislative art among others—indeed, those who traced the beginnings of Greek civilization to Crete were probably very much in the right (see E. Curtius, History of Greece

E. T. 1. 73)—but one would rather suspect a Locrian origin for a tradition which made a Locrian the first skilled legislator, and placed Zaleucus and Lycurgus on a level, thus virtually denying the debt of the former to the latter. We know that the Italian Locri claimed to have been the first State to use written laws, those which Zaleucus had given it (Scymnus Chius, 314 sqq.). If again the Locrian Onomacritus mentioned here is the same man as the well-known Athenian oracle-monger of Peisistratid times, the anachronism is very great—too great, probably, for Ephorus to have committed. We should also expect Ephorus, with his strong interest in Crete, to look back to Rhadamanthus or Minos as the earliest able lawgiver.

26. γυμνασθῆναι δ' αὐτὸν κ.τ.λ., 'and that he trained himself by practice in Crete, though a Locrian and sojourning there in the exercise of the prophetic art.' For *γυμνασθῆναι*, cp. Isocr. de Antid. § 187, where it is coupled with *ἐντριβεὶς γενέσθαι*.

28. Θάλητα. Thales the Cretan, in contradistinction to whom Thales the Milesian is thus designated in 1. 11. 1259 a 6. On Thales the Cretan, the other and probably later form of whose name is Thaletas, see Dict. of Greek and Roman Biography, and Sus.[2], Note 419. In associating Thales with Lycurgus, Ephorus and the authorities here criticised gave currency to a long-enduring and widespread error, which survives not only in Plutarch, Lycurgus c. 4, but also in Sextus Empiricus adv. Math. 2. 21, and Diog. Laert. 1. 38. We probably learn the true date of Thales the Cretan from the De Musica attributed to Plutarch (c. 10), where he is said on the authority of Glaucus (a Rhegian, contemporary with Democritus) to have lived after Archilochus. The contradiction given in the text on chronological grounds to the ingenious combination of these *τινες* may perhaps apply to the whole of it. Lawgivers do not fall so easily into an order of filiation: Lycurgus was not the pupil of Thales, nor Thales the contemporary of Onomacritus, nor Zaleucus the contemporary of Lycurgus, nor Charondas the pupil of Zaleucus.

30. ἀλλὰ ταῦτα κ.τ.λ. For the transition, cp. 1. 5. 1254 a 33, *ἀλλὰ ταῦτα μὲν ἴσως ἐξωτερικωτέρας ἐστὶ σκέψεως, τὸ δὲ ζῷον πρῶτον συνέστηκεν ἐκ ψυχῆς καὶ σώματος*, where Aristotle turns from a question lying somewhat off his path to the inquiry which he is pursuing. So here the meaning seems to be—'but all this rests on an error of chronology, and to return to our subject, Philolaus the Corinthian also legislated for a city not his own, Thebes.' It seems doubtful whether, as some have thought, the *τινες* of 25 are found fault with here for omitting Philolaus in their enumeration. Ἐγένετο δὲ καὶ Φιλόλαος is repeated in 1274 b 18, ἐγένετο δὲ καὶ Πιττακός, and 23, ἐγένετο δὲ καὶ Ἀνδροδάμας.

τῷ χρόνῳ. So Π, Vet. Int., Bekk.: Ar. 'sed qui ista dicunt, tempora non supputant,' on the strength of which rendering Schneider, Coray, and Susemihl read τῶν χρόνων. Τοῖς χρόνοις seems to be read by Bonitz (Ind. 856 a 20), who groups this passage with 6 (4). 6. 1293 a 1 and 4 (7). 10. 1329 b 24, and the plural is certainly far more usual in this sense. As to λέγουσιν . . . λέγοντες, the repetition, though harsh, may perhaps be explained by such phrases as ἐποίησεν οὐ καλόν, ὀρθῶς ποιήσας, c. 9. 1270 a 20.

32. ἦν δὲ κ.τ.λ. The purpose of this narrative seems to be partly to show how remarkable the career of Philolaus was, but still more to explain how a Corinthian came to live at Thebes: we were informed a few lines back how it was that a Locrian came to sojourn in Crete. The striking feature of the story to the mind of a Greek would be that a member of the ruling family of Corinth should have been willing to give up country and home, honours and power, and to accompany Diocles into a life-long exile. A tale like this was not out of place at the head of the legislative traditions of Thebes: cp. Plutarch, Pelopid. c. 19, ὅλως δὲ τῆς περὶ τοὺς ἐραστὰς συνηθείας οὐχ, ὥσπερ οἱ ποιηταὶ λέγουσι, Θηβαίοις τὸ Λαΐου πάθος ἀρχὴν παρέσχεν, ἀλλ' οἱ νομοθέται τὸ φύσει θυμοειδὲς αὐτῶν καὶ ἄκρατον ἀνιέναι καὶ ἀνυγραίνειν εὐθὺς ἐκ παίδων βουλόμενοι πολὺν μὲν ἀνεμίξαντο καὶ σπουδῇ καὶ παιδιᾷ πάσῃ τὸν αὐλὸν εἰς τιμὴν καὶ προεδρίαν ἄγοντες, λαμπρὸν δὲ τὸν ἔρωτα ταῖς παλαίστραις ἐνεθρέψαντο συγκεραννύντες τὰ ἤθη τῶν νέων. Plutarch's reference to the untempered strength of the spirited element in the Theban nature suggests that the Thebans may be present to Aristotle's mind when he says (4 (7). 7. 1327 b 34), τὰ μὲν γὰρ (τῶν Ἑλλήνων ἔθνη) ἔχει τὴν φύσιν μονόκωλον.

36. καὶ νῦν ἔτι κ.τ.λ. Aristotle seems also to have mentioned (perhaps in his Ἐρωτικός) a tomb of Iolaus, probably at Thebes, at which lovers exchanged pledges of fidelity (Plutarch, Pelopid. c. 18: Aristot. Fragm. 92. 1492 a 39).

37. πρὸς δὲ τὴν τῶν Κορινθίων χώραν, 'in the direction of the Corinthian territory.' The tombs were mounds, but the distance would be not far from 40 miles, as the crow flies. So Althaemenes, after exiling himself from Crete lest he should fulfil prophecy and kill his father, built the temple of the Atabyrian Zeus on a high peak in the island of Rhodes, from which his native land could be descried on the horizon (Diod. 5. 59. 2). As to the position of the tomb of Diocles, compare the last stanza of Wordsworth's Laodamia:

even the elm-trees planted on the grave of Protesilaus could not bear the sight of Ilium (Anth. Pal. 7. 141).

40. διὰ τὴν ἀπέχθειαν τοῦ πάθους. Vict. 'propter odium illius affectus' (cp. *διαμισήσας τὸν ἔρωτα*, 34).

ὅπως . . . ἔσται after *τάξασθαι*. Weber (Die Absichtssätze bei Aristot., p. 36) compares Soph. El. 33. 183 b 3 sq.

ἄποπτος here 'visible,' not, as in Soph. Aj. 15, 'invisible.'

3. παιδοποιίας, not *τεκνοποιίας*. *Τεκνοποιία*, 'the begetting of off- 1274 b. spring,' is common to man with the lower animals; not so *παιδοποιία*, which means 'the begetting of children': we often find *παιδοποιία* conjoined with *γάμοι* (e.g. in Plato, Rep. 423 E, 459 A, Symp. 192 B: Plutarch, Solon c. 6). But C. F. Hermann (Gr. Ant. 1. 180. 10) may possibly be right in translating the word here 'adoption,' for in Plutarch, Quaest. Platon. 1. 3. 1000 D we find *παιδοποιεῖσθαι* used in the sense of 'adopt' (*ὥσπερ ὁ μὴ τεκὼν παιδοποιεῖται τὸν ἄριστον*, where however Wyttenbach would read *παῖδα ποιεῖται*, comparing Paus. 7. 1. 3). On the other hand, it should be remembered that the laws referred to might be called *θετικοί* without relating solely to adoption. No other instance of the occurrence of *παιδοποιία* in Aristotle's writings is given in the Index Aristotelicus, though *τεκνοποιία*, which is never used by Plato or by the Attic Orators, is of frequent occurrence in them.

The antecedent of **οὓς** seems to be in the gen. after *νομοθέτης*: it is, however, as often happens, caught into the relative clause.

4. θετικούς, 'relating to adoption.' See Büchsenschütz, Besitz und Erwerb, p. 32, and C. F. Hermann, Gr. Ant. 3. § 65. 2, who points out that Philolaus, if he was the first to permit adoption at Thebes, in effect introduced testation. This would be the case even if the form of adoption introduced by him was, like that prescribed by the law of Gortyna (Bücheler und Zitelmann, p. 161), *adoptio inter vivos*. The aim of Philolaus in permitting adoption was very different from that which Isaeus ascribes to the Attic lawgiver—*ὁ γὰρ νομοθέτης, ὦ ἄνδρες, διὰ τοῦτο τὸν νόμον ἔθηκεν οὕτως, ὁρῶν μόνην ταύτην καταφυγὴν οὖσαν τῆς ἐρημίας καὶ παραψυχὴν τοῦ βίου τοῖς ἄπαισι τῶν ἀνθρώπων, τὸ ἐξεῖναι ποιήσασθαι ὅν τινα ἂν βούλωνται* (2. 13).

ἰδίως. His aim he shared with Pheidon, who was, like himself, a Corinthian (c. 6. 1265 b 12 sqq.), and perhaps earlier than Philolaus, but the means used were peculiar to the latter. From this point onwards we note an effort to point out anything special and peculiar to each lawgiver. Some attention had been paid to this before (c. 7. 1266 a 33–36, 39: c. 8. 1267 b 29), but now the thing is done systematically. Probably the view is that enactments peculiar to a lawgiver are those which are most likely to deserve attention. To produce something ἴδιον was held to be the surest sign of capacity and training: cp. Plutarch adv. Colot. c. 26. 1121 E, τοῦ δ' Ἀρκεσιλάου τὸν Ἐπίκουρον οὐ μετρίως ἔοικεν ἡ δόξα παραλυπεῖν . . . μηδὲν γὰρ αὐτὸν ἴδιον λέγοντα, φησίν, ὑπόληψιν ἐμποιεῖν καὶ δόξαν ἀνθρώποις ἀγραμμάτοις, ἅτε δὴ πολυγράμματος αὐτὸς ὢν καὶ μεμουσωμένος: Aristot. Metaph. A. 1. 981 b 13 sqq.: Metaph. A. 4. 984 b 31: see also de Soph. El. 33. 183 b 20 sqq. Ephorus and others are said by Polybius (6. 45. 3) to have pointed out certain things as ἴδια τῆς Λακεδαιμονίων πολιτείας. Inquiries respecting εὑρήματα and their authors were popular in Greece (Pol. 5 (8). 6. 1341 b 2 sqq.: Aeschyl. Prom. Vinct. 476 sqq.: Plato, Phaedrus 274 C, Rep. 600 A), and they were especially popular in Aristotle's day: Ephorus paid much attention to the subject in his History (Müller, Fr. Hist. Gr. vol. 1. p. lxi), and is also said to have written a separate work on εὑρήματα, as did two successive heads of the Peripatetic School, Theophrastus and Strato (Diog. Laert. 5. 47, 60): Hermippus also in his book on Lawgivers concerned himself with εὑρέσεις (Athen. Deipn. 154 d). Isocrates, in arguing (Paneg. § 10) that honour should be paid rather to the best practitioners of an art than to its originators, implies that the prevailing tendency was in the latter direction. It is not surprising, then, that the authors of anything ἴδιον in legislation should be noted here; still the aim of the Second Book is not history but criticism, and of criticism there is hardly anything in this concluding chapter.

6. **ψευδομαρτύρων.** See critical note.

7. **πρῶτος γὰρ κ.τ.λ.** 'For he was the first to introduce the denunciation for false witness.' See Mr. Sandys' note on Demosth. Or. 2 adv. Steph. c. 7 (p. 115 of his edition), and, on the general significance of the innovation, which gave unsuccessful litigants an opportunity of re-opening questions decided against them, C. F. Hermann, Gr. Ant. 3. § 72 (in Thalheim's edition, Rechtsalterth. § 17. p. 119 sq.), who refers to [Demosth.] contra Evurg. c. 1. These suits had evidently become in Aristotle's time a great social nuisance: cp. c. 5. 1263 b 20 sq. Ἐποίησε is here used of a legislator, as e.g. in c. 9. 1270 a 20.

8. **γλαφυρώτερος**, 'more finished': see note on 1271 b 21.

9. **[Φαλέου . . . ἄχρηστον.]** As to this passage, see note on 1274 a 22. In c. 7. 1266 a 34 we read οὐδεὶς γὰρ οὔτε τὴν περὶ τὰ τέκνα κοινότητα καὶ τὰς γυναῖκας ἄλλος κεκαινοτόμηκεν (except Plato) οὔτε περὶ τὰ συσσίτια τῶν γυναικῶν: here, on the contrary, the suggestion of a community of property is said to be also peculiar to him. The

two passages seem inconsistent, and probably the earlier statement is the truer. Most of the suggestions with which Plato is here credited are trivial enough, and it may well be doubted whether this paragraph is anything more than a marginal annotation from the pen of some reader of the treatise, which has crept into the text. Its style, however, resembles that of Aristotle, and its date may well be very early. Φαλέου seems to be the correct reading, not Φιλολάου, though Φιλολάου has the weight of MS. authority in its favour, for a re-equalization, or at any rate an equalization, of οὐσίαι (the word οὐσίαι is used also in 1266 a 37 and 1267 b 5, though, as Aristotle points out in 1267 b 9, his project extended only to land) has been ascribed to Phaleas (c. 7. 1266 b 1 sq.), whereas nothing of the kind has been attributed to Philolaus.

ἀνομάλωσις. Here all the MSS. read ἀνωμάλωσις (Vet. Int. 'irregularitas')—i. e. 'partitio inaequalis,' which is evidently not the sense intended. 'Ανομάλωσις ('aequalitatis restitutio': see Bon. Ind. s. v.) is probably the true reading: the word does not, however, occur elsewhere in Aristotle: still we have ἀνωμαλίσθαι (from ἀνομαλίζειν) in Rhet. 3. 11. 1412 a 16, and some would read ἀνομαλισθησομένην for ἂν ὁμαλισθησομένην in Pol. 2. 6. 1265 a 40.

11. ὁ . . . συμποσιαρχεῖν. Cp. Plato, Laws 671 D–672 A. For the construction ὁ νόμος, τὸ κ.τ.λ., cp. c. 8. 1268 b 4, ὁ περὶ τῆς κρίσεως νόμος, τὸ κρίνειν ἀξιοῦν διαιροῦντα κ.τ.λ., and below 19–20.

12. καὶ τὴν . . . ἄχρηστον. Sus. compares Plato, Laws 794 D–795 D. Τὴν . . . ἄσκησιν is governed by περί, 11: see the passages collected by Bonitz (Ind. 630 a 39 sqq.), and cp. also Pol. 7 (5). 10. 1311 b 37, and de Gen. An. 3. 1. 749 b 24, where PZ omit διά. Κατὰ τὴν μελέτην (13), 'by practice': cp. κατὰ φύσιν, κατὰ τύχην. Plato's view was that the difference between the right hand and the left has arisen διὰ τὰ ἔθη, οὐκ ὀρθῶς χρωμένων, there being by nature none whatever (Laws 794 E). Aristotle, on the contrary, held that this difference existed by nature (Eth. Nic. 5. 10. 1134 b 33 sqq.: de Caelo 2. 2. 284 b 6 sqq.: Hist. An. 2. 1. 497 b 31), though men might make themselves ambidextrous by practice: cp. Magn. Mor. 1. 34. 1194 b 32, τὰ φύσει ὄντα μεταλαμβάνουσι μεταβολῆς· λέγω δ' οἷον εἰ τῇ ἀριστερᾷ μελετῷμεν πάντες ἀεὶ βάλλειν, γινοίμεθ' ἂν ἀμφιδέξιοι· ἀλλὰ φύσει γε ἀριστερά ἐστι κ.τ.λ. He would probably, however, be opposed to attempts to counteract nature by habituation (4 (7). 17. 1337 a 1: 4 (7). 14. 1332 b 35 sqq.).

14. ὡς δέον κ.τ.λ. Cp. Plato, Laws 795 C, ὅτι τὸν διττὰ δεῖ κεκτημένον οἷς ἀμύνοιτό τ' ἂν καὶ ἐπιτιθεῖτο ἄλλοις, μηδὲν ἀργὸν τούτων μηδὲ ἀνεπιστήμον ἐᾶν εἶναι κατὰ δύναμιν.

τοῖν χεροῖν. 'In Attic the dual of *ὁ, ἡ, τό* has commonly but one gender *τώ, τοῖν*' (Liddell and Scott s. v.). See Jelf, Gr. Gr. § 388. 3 b, and cp. Plato, Protag. 314 D: Theaetet. 155 E.

17. καί, 'at all': see Riddell, Apology of Plato, p. 168.

ἡ χαλεπότης. Cp. Rhet. 2. 23. 1400 b 21. See C. F. Hermann, Gr. Ant. 3. § 73. 10 (in Thalheim's edition, Rechtsalt. § 18. p. 122. 5).

18. A transition is made from Draco to Pittacus, because Pittacus also was the author of laws only: the two lawgivers, however, had more than this in common, for Pittacus' law about drunkards was, like those of Draco, famous for its severity ([Plutarch,] Sept. Sap. Conv. 13, *τὸν σὸν ἐκεῖνον τὸν χαλεπὸν νόμον*).

20. τι πταίσωσι. See critical note.

21. οὐ πρὸς τὴν κ.τ.λ. Literally, 'he paid regard not to the greater consideration which it might be pleaded is due to men who offend when drunk, but' etc. *Ὅτι* is used, and not *ἥν*, because the writer does not wish to affirm that this greater consideration is due. The question with regard to which neutrality is here maintained, a neutrality perhaps slightly benevolent to the drunkard, is solved without hesitation in Eth. Nic. 3. 2. 1110 b 24 sqq., where the drunken offender is said not to act *δι' ἄγνοιαν*, much less involuntarily (in which case alone *συγγνώμη* is called for, Eth. Nic. 3. 1. 1109 b 31 sq.), but only *ἀγνοῶν*: thus Pittacus was quite right, *ἡ γὰρ ἀρχὴ ἐν αὐτῷ· κύριος γὰρ τοῦ μὴ μεθυσθῆναι, τοῦτο δ' αἴτιον τῆς ἀγνοίας* (Eth. Nic. 3. 7. 1113 b 30 sqq.). Lesbos, we remember, was a wine-producing island, and Pittacus was engaged in restoring order to Mytilene. According to the English law, if intoxication amounts to stupidity, it reduces the crime (Ruling of an English Judge, *Times,* Feb. 4, 1881). It should be noted that Pittacus was credited with the exclamation *Συγγνώμη τιμωρίας κρείσσων*, on liberating his opponent Alcaeus (Diog. Laert. 1. 76).

24. οὗ, sc. *νόμος*, latent in *νομοθέτης*.

26. τὰ μὲν οὖν κ.τ.λ. Constitutions which 'took effect' (*κυρίας*) seem to be here distinguished from schemes which remained mere schemes. *Κυρίας*, however, would more naturally mean 'actually in force,' and this winding-up would be more in place at the close of the notice of the Carthaginian constitution, than at the end of a chapter on *νομοθέται*, for it makes no reference to *νομοθέται*. We note also that *μὲν οὖν* is not taken up by *δέ* at the commencement of the next book, which begins *τῷ περὶ πολιτείας ἐπισκοποῦντι* without any connecting particle, as does the Sixth Book likewise. This is hardly reassuring as to the state of the text, though it is impossible to say what precisely has happened to it.

APPENDIX A.

The Relation of the teaching of the Nicomachean Ethics to that of the Politics.

It is proposed to examine in the present Appendix, so far as limits of space will allow, the relation in which the Politics stands to the Nicomachean Ethics, and also to ask how far its teaching agrees with that of the latter treatise—how far the two works can be said to form well-planned parts of a coherent whole.

In dealing with these questions, it will be necessary for us to take the Nicomachean Ethics as it stands, without pausing to inquire whether parts of it are due to other hands than Aristotle's, or whether intrusive or interpolated matter is present in the work, or again whether its component parts were designed at the time of composition to form part of the whole which they at present constitute. To enter on these and other vexed questions with regard to the state of the text of this work would carry us too far.

That the Nicomachean Ethics should have a sequel was necessary for more reasons than one. As we have already seen, Aristotle himself mentions one of these reasons at the beginning of the last chapter of the treatise. Moral Philosophy is to him a practical science with a practical aim: *οὐκ ἔστιν ἐν τοῖς πρακτοῖς τέλος τὸ θεωρῆσαι ἕκαστα καὶ γνῶναι, ἀλλὰ μᾶλλον τὸ πράττειν αὐτά* (Eth. Nic. 10. 10. 1179 a 35)—*οὐ γὰρ ἵν' εἰδῶμεν τί ἐστιν ἡ ἀρετὴ σκεπτόμεθα, ἀλλ' ἵν' ἀγαθοὶ γενώμεθα, ἐπεὶ οὐδὲν ἂν ἦν ὄφελος αὐτῆς* (Eth. Nic. 2. 2. 1103 b 27): the study of Morals thus involves a study of the means by which men are made good. It involves therefore a study of the State. To stop short at the close of the Nicomachean Ethics would be to leave the science of moral action incomplete, to balk its aim and rob it of its effectiveness.

But then again it is in the State that happiness assumes its noblest form (Eth. Nic. 1. 1. 1094 b 7 sqq.). We must study it in the State if we wish to see it at its best. Nor is this all. Aristotle would probably say that we have not fully explored the nature of the σπουδαῖος till we have explored the State of which he is a part. We do not fully understand what the σπουδαῖος is until we have viewed him as a part of a whole—as a husband, father, citizen, soldier, and ruler.

Plato had treated of Ethics and Politics in one and the same dialogue. He had not only traced a parallel between the State and the soul of the individual, but had laid stress on the mutual reaction of individual and State. As is the individual, so is the State; as is the State, so is the individual. The individual, he seemed to say, could no more be understood apart from the State than a limb apart from the body to which it belongs. Ethics and Politics, according to this view, gain by being treated together; the individual must not be severed from the State which makes him what he is, nor the State from the individual who gives it its character. The Republic of Plato gains in concreteness by its adoption of this method. We study the good man and his opposites, as we see them in actual life, in a 'setting' of institutions. We view them in connexion with the little world of which they form a part. We recognize not only what the σπουδαῖος is, but what makes him what he is, and see the medium in which he lives and moves. The relation between the individual and the State has never been more vigorously portrayed than in the Republic. The unsound State, we see, is fatal even to sound philosophy. The four virtues of the Republic are public virtues, all of them relative to the Whole of which they are the pillars; they presuppose the State and the State presupposes them.

Aristotle's plan, on the contrary, is to part the study of εὐδαιμονία and the virtues of which it is the outcome from the study of the State and its various forms. He thus severs what Plato had joined together. Plato's plan of dealing with Ethics and Politics in one work had, in fact, its disadvantages. Pent within so narrow a space, neither could really thrive. It brought out, indeed, more effectively than any other method could have done the pressing need of a return to justice and of a reform of the State, and this was precisely what Plato sought to do; but a full scientific treatment of the two subjects was hardly possible without a double inquiry. In dealing with them separately Aristotle took a great step in advance. In the interest of science, he concerns himself in the Nicomachean Ethics primarily with the individual viewed as the subject of εὐδαιμονία and as exercising the various moral and intellectual virtues. He asks what constitutes virtuous action and happiness, and dwells only incidentally on the forces external to the individual which bring them into being, and the field in which they are realized. His aim is for the time to view virtue as an internal fact, a psychological diathesis, rather than as the life-breath of society or its product—to approach it rather from the side of Psychology than from that of Politics. But he too, in his turn, as he passes from virtues like Temperance or Liberality to virtues like Justice and Moral Prudence, and then to Friendship, is led further and further into the domain of Politics. If we are not yet asked to analyse the State, we are taught to study the work of Justice in the State. If the objects in the foreground are still virtues, we look through them into a background of Politics, and thus the study of Ethics leads Aristotle on to the study of Politics. If, unlike Plato, he treats of Ethics in one work and Politics in another, he is far from intending to break the link which binds the two subjects together, or to stop short in his inquiries at the close of the Nicomachean Ethics.

It was necessary then that this treatise should have a sequel, but how far is the Politics an appropriate sequel to it and in accord with it?

It is easy to see that the two treatises have much in common. Not only do both of them presuppose the great central principles of the Aristotelian philosophy, but a broad similarity of method and treatment is traceable throughout them. We find evidence in both of a desire to gather up all that is sound in the work of previous inquirers and in the beliefs of ordinary men, to do justice to all aspects of truth, and to frame a creed in which all the jarring schools would find their best results embodied. Half-truths were to vanish before the whole truth, as the stars disappear before the light of day. Aristotle sought to mediate between contending doctrines, and to sum up the best traditions of the Greek race and the net result of Greek inquiry in a broad-based and broad-minded system[1]. This could only be done by steering a midway course. Truth no less than moral virtue lay in a mean; the conception of the mean is of the very essence of Aristotle's philosophy. We

[1] *Τὸ διορίζειν* was precisely that of which the Many are incapable (Eth. Nic. 10. 1. 1172 b 3) and of which the philosopher should be capable. *Ἴσως οὖν τοὺς τοιούτους δεῖ τῶν λόγων διαιρεῖν καὶ διορίζειν ἐφ᾽ ὅσον ἑκάτεροι καὶ πῇ ἀληθεύουσιν* (Eth. Nic. 9. 8. 1168 b 12). *Ληπτέος δὴ τρόπος ὅστις ἡμῖν ἅμα τά τε δοκοῦντα περὶ τούτων μάλιστα ἀποδώσει καὶ τὰς ἀπορίας λύσει καὶ τὰς ἐναντιώσεις. τοῦτο δ᾽ ἔσται, ἐὰν εὐλόγως φαίνηται τὰ ἐναντία δοκοῦντα· μάλιστα γὰρ ὁμολογούμενος ὁ τοιοῦτος ἔσται λόγος τοῖς φαινομένοις. συμβαίνει δὲ μένειν τὰς ἐναντιώσεις, ἐὰν ἔστι μὲν ὡς ἀληθὲς ᾖ τὸ λεγόμενον, ἔστι δ᾽ ὡς οὔ* (Eth. Eud. 7. 2. 1235 b 13 sqq.).

hear less of the mean in the Politics than in the Nicomachean Ethics, but the idea is very present there also[1]. The same breadth of view appears in Aristotle's readiness to recognize higher and lower forms of things. Just as in the Nicomachean Ethics the recognition of higher forms of virtue, or justice, or pleasure, or friendship does not preclude the recognition of lower forms also, so in the Politics, side by side with the true citizen and the best constitution, the citizen of the deviation-forms and the deviation-forms themselves receive recognition. Aristotle declines to say, as Cicero in effect said[2], that the lower forms of State are not States at all. Many a problem is solved in both treatises by the use of this method. It enables Aristotle to do justice both to the higher and to the lower forms of things without sinning either against truth or against the ordinary use of language[3], and authorizes a careful study both of the more and of the less perfect. The Nicomachean Ethics and the Politics would have been far less comprehensive in treatment than they are, if Aristotle had followed a different course in this respect. So again, the two works agree in aiming both at speculative truth and practical utility[4]. Another common feature is an unwillingness to rest content with generalities. Broad general descriptions of things are wanting, Aristotle feels, in clearness; they seem to say much, but really say little. We learn but little when we are told that virtue is *τὸ εὖ ἔχειν τὴν ψυχὴν* (Pol. 1. 13. 1260 a 25 sq.). Plato and the contemporary Academy dealt too much in these generalities. Aristotle insists on *τὸ διορίζειν* (e.g. in Pol. 2. 5. 1264 a 14, 37, and 2. 6. 1265 a 28 sqq., b 18 sqq.), and his definition of virtue is full and particular. This effort to be clear and detailed is traceable in both treatises. In both Aristotle learns the nature of the Whole (e.g. *εὐδαιμονία, οἰκία, πόλις*) by beginning with the part and working up from it to the Whole.

But these broad similarities do not carry us very far, and if we are to judge to what extent the two works are in accord, we must recall some of the more important passages in the Nicomachean

[1] See for instance Pol. 6 (4). 11. 1295 a 35 sqq.: 6 (4). 9. 1294 a 41: 2. 6. 1265 a 32 sqq. (cp. 4 (7). 5. 1326 b 30–39): 4 (7). 7. 1327 b 29 sqq.

[2] See vol. i. p. 216 note, and above p. xiv.

[3] Cp. Eth. Nic. 8. 5. 1157 a 25, *ἐπεὶ γὰρ οἱ ἄνθρωποι λέγουσι φίλους καὶ τοὺς διὰ τὸ χρήσιμον . . . καὶ τοὺς δι' ἡδονὴν ἀλλήλους στέργοντας . . . ἴσως λέγειν μὲν δεῖ καὶ ἡμᾶς φίλους τοὺς τοιούτους, εἴδη δὲ τῆς φιλίας πλείω, καὶ πρώτως μὲν καὶ κυρίως τὴν τῶν ἀγαθῶν ᾗ ἀγαθοί, τὰς δὲ λοιπὰς καθ' ὁμοιότητα.*

[4] See Eth. Nic. 2. 2. 1103 b 26 sqq., 10. 10. 1179 a 35 sqq., and above on 1. 3. 1253 b 14 as to the Politics.

Ethics in which light is thrown on the State, its functions and organization.

The reader of the Nicomachean Ethics, as he passes on from book to book, finds the relation of virtue to the State and of Ethics to Politics coming ever more prominently before him. Virtue, he learns, is the offspring of law, and law is an incident of the State. Virtue varies with the constitution, and reaches its full height only in the best constitution. Some virtues, again, belong exclusively or especially to the ruler. In these and other ways we are constantly being reminded of the importance of the State.

The earliest pages of the treatise bring the πολιτικὴ ἐπιστήμη before us, the Science which is at once the Science of the State and the Science of Life. Its end is nothing less than the end of human life; it is supreme over the State as over the individual, 'determining what sciences are to exist in the State, and what each man is to learn, and how far'—'legislating what is to be done and not done.' (Not a word, we note, is said here about those lower problems of πολιτική, of which we hear so much in the first chapter of the Sixth Book of the Politics.) We are told further, that the happiness of a State or nation is a nobler and more divine thing than the happiness of an individual; later (Eth. Nic. 1. 5. 1097 b 8 sqq.: cp. 9. 9. 1169 b 16 sqq.), we learn that man is by nature a political animal, and that his needs are not fully satisfied unless the needs of the persons who live in society with him—his parents, wife, children, and fellow-citizens—are also satisfied. In all this the Nicomachean Ethics anticipates the teaching of the Politics, that man is more fully a political animal than any of the gregarious animals (Pol. 1. 2. 1253 a 7 sqq.), that the training which produces a πολιτικός is the same as that which produces a σπουδαῖος, so that the πολιτικός cannot be far other than the σπουδαῖος (Pol. 3. 18), and that the πολιτικός must know both the end of human life and the best means of attaining it (Pol. 4 (7). 13. 1331 b 26 sqq.).

Later on in the first book of the Nicomachean Ethics (c. 13. 1102 a 18 sqq.), we are told that broad psychological data, such as the division of the soul into a rational and an irrational part, have an interest and importance for the true πολιτικός, and we soon learn why: the appetitive section of the irrational part of the soul needs to be brought under the control of right reason (λόγος), so that moral virtue may be developed, but this can only be accomplished through habituation, and habituation to virtue is the business of the lawgiver, or in other words, of the State. The true statesman—the lawgivers of the Lacedaemonian and Cretan

States, for instance—is generally held to concern himself with the development of virtue (Eth. Nic. 1. 13. 1102 a 7 sqq.); every lawgiver aims at making his citizens virtuous, and the only difference between lawgivers is that some do this well and others not; it is in this that a good constitution differs from a bad one (Eth. Nic. 2. 1. 1103 b 2 sqq.). In fact, as those are held to be bravest whose States honour the brave and disgrace the coward (Eth. Nic. 3. 11. 1116 a 18 sqq.), the virtue of the individual appears to depend on the distribution of reward and punishment, pleasure and pain, by the State. Often as in this treatise the ordinary πολιτικοί are weighed in the balance and found wanting, νομοθέται are always treated with respect: νομοθετική, we are told in a later book (Eth. Nic. 6. 8. 1141 b 24 sqq.), is the architectonic form of φρόνησις περὶ πόλιν: the makers of ψηφίσματα are mere χειροτέχναι.

Aristotle's psychology and ethics reveal to him, in fact, the necessity of a power capable of disciplining the lower nature by habituation, and he ascribes a power of this kind to the lawgiver. Not all lawgivers were wise enough to begin their training of the citizen in childhood, or to supervise education and the habits of adult life (Eth. Nic. 10. 10. 1180 a 24 sqq.), but all sought more or less wisely and well to make their citizens virtuous by a skilful use of pain and pleasure, or, in other words, by habituation. The account of Universal Justice in the Fifth Book confirms all this, for what the laws prescribe (or 'normally constituted laws,' at all events) is there said to be universally just (c. 3. 1129 b 14 sqq.); and if (c. 5. 1130 b 26 sqq.) a question is raised, whether πολιτική has to do with the training which makes a good man as distinguished from a good citizen, this is perhaps nothing more than an anticipation of the teaching of the Politics, that πολιτική is concerned with other forms of State than the best, in which alone the virtue of the citizen is identical with that of the good man.

Already then we discern the ethical necessity of the lawgiver and the State, but the study of Particular Justice brings the State more vividly before us. Aristotle's account of it incidentally corrects Plato's account of Justice in the Republic, according to which a just man is he who does the work for which he is fit (τὰ αὑτοῦ πράττει). Justice, in Aristotle's view, has rather to do with external goods—honour, wealth, and the like—than with work. He is just who gives these to those to whom they are due, not he who does the work for which he is fit. Justice is a question of external goods, not of functions. But the main purpose of the

Fifth Book probably is to show that Justice, like all other moral virtues, has to do with a mean—that it is ἀνάλογον and ὡς ὁ λόγος [1] (the word for reason and proportion in Greek being the same), and that it has more kinds than one [2]. True justice does not, as Plato thought (Laws 757 A–D), always take account of virtue in the award it makes. The justice of the lawgiver and ruler does so, but not that of the judge.

We see in Aristotle's account of Justice an effort to be more definite than Plato had been, and to keep closer to facts. We learn that Justice differs with the social function. The justice of the ruler is not as the justice of the judge. Far more than any other moral virtue, justice presupposes the κοινωνία of the State, for it especially appertains to the lawgiver, the ruler, the judge, and the citizen, if it also appears in the ἀλλακτικὴ κοινωνία [3], which need not, of course, be between fellow-citizens. Its highest type apparently implies rule. It is to be found rather in the relations of the State than in those of the household—ἐπὶ κοινωνῶν βίου πρὸς τὸ εἶναι αὐτάρκειαν, ἐλευθέρων καὶ ἴσων ἢ κατ' ἀναλογίαν ἢ κατ' ἀριθμόν (Eth. Nic. 5. 10. 1134 a 26)—between those between whom law subsists (30) [4], or can subsist (Eth. Nic. 8. 13. 1161 b 6 sq.). But then there are two kinds even of τὸ πολιτικὸν δίκαιον, one natural, the other conventional, and we gather that the true standard of that which is naturally just among men is to be found in the best constitution (μία μόνον πανταχοῦ κατὰ φύσιν ἡ ἀρίστη, Eth. Nic. 5. 10. 1135 a 5).

[1] Cp. Eth. Nic. 3. 10. 1115 b 17, ὁ μὲν οὖν ἃ δεῖ καὶ οὗ ἕνεκα ὑπομένων καὶ φοβούμενος καὶ ὡς δεῖ καὶ ὅτε, ὁμοίως δὲ καὶ θαρρῶν, ἀνδρεῖος· κατ' ἀξίαν γὰρ καὶ ὡς ἂν ὁ λόγος πάσχει καὶ πράττει ὁ ἀνδρεῖος.

[2] 'In my opinion,' says Mr. Jackson (Fifth Book of the Nic. Ethics, p. 87), 'c. 5 [of Eth. Nic. 5] should be read in close connection with cc. 2–4, the passage as a whole being an attempt at once to connect and to distinguish three kinds of particular justice. In order to connect these three kinds of particular justice, the author regards them each as ἀνάλογόν τι: in order to distinguish them, he represents each by a special and appropriate kind of ἀναλογία.'

[3] In the account of the ἀλλακτικὴ κοινωνία (Eth. Nic. 5. 8) and the part that money plays in making it possible, a social value is assigned to money different from that which it is implied to possess in the First Book of the Politics, though there too money is said to be the στοιχεῖον καὶ πέρας τῆς ἀλλαγῆς, just as here it is said to be the μέσον, or standard, by which the value of the commodities exchanged is measured and determined (cp. Eth. Nic. 9. 1. 1164 a 1 sq.).

[4] This would appear to exclude the παμβασιλεία: cp. Pol. 3. 13. 1284 a 11 sqq. It of course implies that the relation of man to the lower animals is in strictness one with which justice has nothing to do: they have, in Aristotle's view, no rights against man and cannot be wronged (ἀδικεῖσθαι) by him: they are merely ὄργανα for his use, not κοινωνοί: they are not even, like the slave, human ὄργανα and therefore capable of being the objects of friendship (cp. Eth. Nic. 8. 13. 1161 a 32 sqq.). See as to this view Porphyry de Abstinentia, 1. 4–6. It justified the slaughter of animals, the rightfulness of which had been questioned by some.

Already we have been told (5. 6. 1131 a 26 sqq.) that different constitutions distribute what they have to distribute on different principles, and now we are made aware that justice varies with the constitution, and attains its true form only in the best constitution. This quite agrees with the teaching of the Politics (cp. Pol. 7 (5). 9. 1309 a 37, εἰ γὰρ μὴ ταὐτὸν τὸ δίκαιον κατὰ πάσας τὰς πολιτείας, ἀνάγκη καὶ τῆς δικαιοσύνης εἶναι διαφοράς).

Aristotle's ethical treatise is pervaded by the half-mathematical conceptions of the mean and the proportional, and we nowhere learn more clearly than in its Fifth Book how important is the part played by 'proportion' (τὸ κατ' ἀναλογίαν ἴσον) in holding the State together (Eth. Nic. 5. 8. 1132 b 33, τῷ ἀντιποιεῖν ἀνάλογον συμμένει ἡ πόλις: cp. Pol. 2. 2. 1261 a 30, τὸ ἴσον τὸ ἀντιπεπονθὸς σώζει τὰς πόλεις, ὥσπερ ἐν τοῖς ἠθικοῖς εἴρηται πρότερον).

The books on Friendship possess an especial interest for the student of the Politics, both on account of the importance of Friendship to the State (Eth. Nic. 8. 1. 1155 a 22 sqq.: Pol. 2. 4. 1262 b 7 sqq.) and because they study Friendship not only in its highest form—the friendship of the good—but also as a concomitant of every kind of κοινωνία. The less temporary and the more comprehensive are the aims with which a κοινωνία is formed, the stronger is the link which binds one member of it to another, and the fuller the friendship. The link which binds together a band of merchants making a voyage for gain is a far less close one than that which binds together the members of a State, for the latter have joined together not for the sake of that which is advantageous for the moment, but to win that which will benefit their life as a whole (Eth. Nic. 8. 11. 1160 a 21). We learn in these books how all κοινωνίαι should be constituted, if friendship is to prevail within them. We learn the true form both of the parental relation and of the manifold relations of kinship which spring from it; we study the relation of husband and wife, the relation of master and slave, and then again the political relations on which the family relations seem to be modelled—those which prevail between ruler and ruled in a Kingship, an Aristocracy, and a Timocracy, or again those prevailing in a Tyranny, an Oligarchy, and a Democracy. The study of all these κοινωνίαι, and especially of the six constitutions, makes it clear that justice is a condition of friendship in κοινωνίαι. The members of a κοινωνία must render honour and advantage (ὠφέλεια) to each other κατ' ἀξίαν, if friendship is to prevail in it. The father must benefit the child, and the child must honour the father. The king must rule for the advantage of his subjects and they must render him honour. It is because in Tyranny, Oligarchy, and Democracy the rulers rule, not for the advantage of the ruled, but for their own advantage, thus monopolising both honour and advantage—it is because, in fact, they rule unjustly—that there is so little friendship in States thus governed. Honour belongs justly to rulers, benefit to those ruled, but the rulers in a deviation-form grasp both at honour and gain[1].

Thus the books on Friendship enforce anew the importance of Justice: we learn more clearly than before how essential Justice is to *κοινωνίαι*: we see that not only the lawgiver, the ruler, the judge, and the trader need to be just, but that all members of *κοινωνίαι* need to be so—even children and slaves—and that precisely in so far as they are so, will Friendship be present in the *κοινωνία*. This holds good both of equal and unequal *κοινωνίαι* (Eth. Nic. 8. 15. 1162 b 2 sq.): *τὸ ἰσάζειν* is necessary in both. It is best, indeed, that in friendship 'the same thing should be rendered on both sides' (Eth. Nic. 8. 5. 1156 b 33 sqq.)—that the friendship should rest, not on the return of an equivalent amount of different things, but on an identical return: in the relations of the State, however, and in many of those of the household this is not possible; hence here a return must be made *κατ' ἀξίαν*.

Political society rests on *τὸ ἀνάλογον*, on *τὸ κατ' ἀξίαν*: this is the far-reaching principle laid down in these books of the Nicomachean Ethics. It is an infraction of the principles of political society, when the ruler draws to himself the whole advantage: rule to be justifiable must be *πρὸς τὸ κοινῇ συμφέρον*. The just is that which is for the common advantage. Aristotle's ethical treatise thus contains the germ and something more of his Politics. The former treatise gives us at all events one of the main laws which govern *κοινωνίαι*: the latter works it out in its application to the State.

And yet there are points in which the teaching of these books of the Nicomachean Ethics is not quite borne out by that of the Politics. Take, for instance, the account they give of the deviation-forms of constitution. These are implied in the Eighth Book of the Nicomachean Ethics to arise from the deterioration of the rulers of the normal constitutions. The rulers of an oligarchy are 'few and bad' (Eth. Nic. 8. 12. 1160 b 12 sqq.). The Politics appears to be more ready to recognize that even the deviation-forms are founded on *δίκαιόν τι*. The book on Revolutions,

[1] Cp. Pol. 8 (6). 7. 1321 a 40 sq.

indeed, goes so far as to say that it is not safe to base a constitution wholly on ἡ κατ' ἀξίαν ἰσότης (7 (5). 1. 1302 a 2 sq.)[1]: the most durable constitutions are those which are partly based on this kind of equality, partly on arithmetical equality. We learn in the Sixth Book of the Politics that the deviation-forms are not mere gratuitous embodiments of injustice: we are taught, on the contrary, to trace the law of their appearance; the social conditions of a community, we find, have much to do with its government. A deviation-form of some kind is often the only possible constitution. Aristotle had also learnt by the time at which the Sixth Book of the Politics was written, that there are better and worse shades of each deviation-form. So again, the scheme of constitutional change given in Eth. Nic. 8. 12, according to which Kingship passes into Tyranny, and Aristocracy into Oligarchy, and Timocracy into Democracy, is quite different from any of those given in the Politics (cp. Pol. 3. 15. 1286 b 8 sqq.: 6 (4). 13. 1297 b 16 sqq.). In the former of these passages Kingship is made to change into Polity, in the latter first into Oligarchy, and then into Polity. In the Politics (7 (5). 7. 1307 a 20–25: 7 (5). 12. 1316 a 17 sqq.) Aristotle is far from thinking that constitutions change most often into the forms most akin to them. His view of the just or normal constitution in the Politics seems also to be different. Justice, we are there told, requires that all elements which contribute to the being and well-being of a State—not only virtue, but also wealth and free birth—should receive due recognition (Pol. 3. 13. 1283 a 26 sqq.). Constitutions which rest on a bare superiority in one such element only, even if that element be virtue, are unjust. Superiority in virtue must be transcendent if it is to confer an exclusive title to rule.

We are further surprised to find Aristotle speaking in Eth. Nic. 8. 14. 1161 b 13 sqq. of πολιτικαὶ φιλίαι as resting on compact (οἷον γὰρ καθ' ὁμολογίαν τινὰ φαίνονται εἶναι), when we remember the decided way in which at the outset of the Politics he de-

[1] The view that the constitution should rest partly on ἀριθμητικὴ ἰσότης, partly on ἡ κατ' ἀξίαν ἰσότης is, it should be noticed, derived from Plato's Laws 757 D, ἀναγκαῖόν γε μὴν καὶ τούτοις παρωνυμίοισί ('his quae iusta quidem vocantur, nec tamen revera iusta sunt,' Stallbaum) ποτε προσχρήσασθαι πόλιν ἅπασαν, εἰ μέλλει στάσεων ἑαυτῇ μὴ προσκοινωνήσειν κατά τι μέρος . . . διὸ τῷ τοῦ κλήρου ἴσῳ ἀνάγκῃ προσχρήσασθαι δυσκολίας τῶν πολλῶν ἕνεκα . . . οὕτω δὴ χρηστέον ἀναγκαίως μὲν τοῖν ἰσοτήτοιν ἀμφοῖν, ὡς δ' ὅτι μάλιστα ἐπ' ὀλιγίστοις τῇ ἑτέρᾳ, τῇ τῆς τύχης δεομένῃ. Plutarch (Solon, c. 14) even carries the idea back to Solon—λέγεται δὲ καὶ φωνή τις αὐτοῦ περιφερομένη πρότερον εἰπόντος ὡς τὸ ἴσον πόλεμον οὐ ποιεῖ καὶ τοῖς κτηματικοῖς ἀρέσκειν καὶ τοῖς ἀκτήμοσι, τῶν μὲν ἀξίᾳ καὶ ἀρετῇ, τῶν δὲ μέτρῳ καὶ ἀριθμῷ τὸ ἴσον ἕξειν προσδοκώντων.

clares the State to be based on nature. The relation of kinship, again, seems in this book of the Nicomachean Ethics to count for more in comparison with the political relation, than in the Politics, and man is said to be by nature συνδυαστικὸν μᾶλλον ἢ πολιτικόν (Eth. Nic. 8. 14. 1162 a 17). On the other hand, when we read that πολιτικὴ φιλία thrives best between good men (Eth. Nic. 9. 6. 1167 b 4 sqq.: cp. 9. 8. 1169 a 8 sqq.), we recognize an anticipation of the teaching of the Politics, that the best State is the State whose citizens are ἁπλῶς σπουδαῖοι. The same book also prepares us for the limitation of the number of the citizens in the best State (Eth. Nic. 9. 10. 1170 b 29 sqq.: cp. Pol. 4 (7). 4).

The whole tenour of the Nicomachean Ethics points to the conclusion that virtue not only presupposes a life in relation to others, but life in a State, and further a good State, or even the best State. Nay more, one kind of Justice presupposes the exercise of rule, for it appears only in the ruler. That φρόνησις is peculiar to the ruler, Aristotle asserts in the Politics (3. 4. 1277 b 25)[1], but not, it would seem, in the Nicomachean Ethics.

So largely indeed does the latter treatise admit virtue to be modified by the constitution and by the social function discharged, that we might almost expect it, seeing that it has a practical aim in view, to deal with the variations of duty under different constitutions and in different social positions. But this it does not do. Its moral teaching seems to apply indifferently to all constitutions, for all that we hear to the contrary. And then again, if the State is represented in the Nicomachean Ethics as essential to virtue, it seems to be essential rather to moral than to intellectual virtue. We do not learn whether the State does as much for the highest element of man's nature, the speculative intelligence, as it does for the appetitive nature and for moral virtue. At all events, we are not told what it is that the State does for σοφία, though we know that it 'rules for its sake' (ἐπιτάττει σοφίας ἕνεκα, Eth. Nic. 6. 13. 1145 a 9)[2].

The last book of the treatise, which finds τελεία εὐδαιμονία in the contemplative life and exalts this life above the political life, should have traced the dependence of the highest of man's energies on the excellence of the State. So far however is it from doing this, and completing the indications given us earlier in the work of the intimate relation between virtue and the State, that it closes with a

[1] Following Plato (Rep. 433 C) and Xenophon (Cyrop. 1. 6. 22).

[2] We learn from the Republic of Plato how much a defective State could do to corrupt philosophy.

chapter (c. 10), which, though it points to the State as the most effective agency in the production of virtue, seems half to hint that its place may to a certain extent be filled by heads of families trained in legislative science. We are conscious, as has been observed elsewhere, of some change of tone, when we pass to the commencement of the Politics. We there learn that man is by nature a part of a Whole; he is a part of the State, born to rule and be ruled with a view to the highest and most complete life. The Politics asserts emphatically and in unmistakable terms the truth which the abstract method of the Nicomachean Ethics had kept somewhat in the background, though even there facts constantly force it on our notice—the truth that the life of the State is marked out for man by nature. Even the virtue of the wife and the child, we are here told, is relative to the constitution (Pol. 1. 13. 1260 b 8 sqq.); much more is this true of the virtue of the citizen. The citizen varies with the constitution, but the citizen of the best constitution, and therefore the σπουδαῖος, is he who is able and purposed to rule and be ruled with a view to a life in accordance with virtue (Pol. 3. 13. 1284 a 1 sq.). We might well infer that the life of ruling and being ruled, or in other words the political life, is the highest life open to man. It is not till we reach the Fourth Book of the Politics, that the lesson of the last book of the Nicomachean Ethics is again impressed on us—the lesson that the supreme end of man is not work (ἀσχολία) but leisure (σχολή)—not the political life, not even the life of the ruler in the best State, but rather the life of leisure and contemplation. The highest employment of man, we are again told, is the employment of leisure; his highest and most godlike moments are moments of speculation, not of political activity. True, the right use of leisure presupposes the active virtues (Pol. 4 (7). 15. 1334 a 16 sqq.); still the ruler rules for the sake of speculative virtue (σοφία), not over her. But the Politics couples this doctrine with the emphatic assertion that man is a part of the State. Many of the virtues enumerated in the Nicomachean Ethics drop out of sight in the Politics, but some features in the character of the σπουδαῖος acquire a fresh prominence. We see him in a 'setting' of institutions, as we know him in actual life; we see him as a member of a πόλις, and therefore as one who is 'his brother's keeper'[1], and who cares for the virtue of all his equals and dependents in the community to which he belongs. We see him in connexion with the social positions which he fills—a husband, a father, a master, a proprietor, a citizen, and

[1] Pol. 3. 9. 1280 b 1 sqq.

a ruler. Virtue is depicted diffusive of itself and radiating its influence through household and State. We learn to know happiness better, when it is embodied for us in an entire State of happy men.

Thus the Politics completes the Nicomachean Ethics. The latter treatise is, in fact, presupposed by the former. It would not have been possible to discover the best constitution, if the nature of the most desirable life, or in other words of εὐδαιμονία, had not been ascertained previously (Pol. 4 (7). 1. 1323 a 14 sq.: 4 (7). 13. 1332 a 7 sqq.).

But then again, the last three books of the Politics teach us a lesson of which we have heard but little in the Nicomachean Ethics. If the State is at its best when it is realizing εὐδαιμονία, Political Science falls short of completeness unless it can deal with cases in which the production of σπουδαῖοι and εὐδαίμονες is out of the question. The highest mission of Political Science is not its only mission; it needs to understand the deviation-forms and to know how to constitute them, as much as it needs to understand the best State. Political Science has its technical side; it is not a mere handmaid to Ethics. Thus if the Nicomachean Ethics sought in some measure to view the moral agent apart from the State, one portion of the Politics studies the State apart in some degree from ethical aims. In Aristotle's hands, Ethics and Politics show to this extent an inclination to draw away from each other.

Not all the Politics, we see, is a strictly necessary sequel to the Nicomachean Ethics. When Aristotle announces his intention to study all constitutions—which he does as early as the close of his ethical treatise—he goes beyond the limits of the task which the interests of Moral Philosophy obliged him to undertake. He in effect implies that his purpose is to deal with Political Science not simply as a sequel to Ethics, but as a science deserving of study even apart from ethical considerations. Plato had studied the inferior constitutions in the Republic, only to show how fatal they are to justice and happiness; Aristotle will study them because it is the business of the πολιτικός to know how to construct even these lower forms of the State.

Aristotle, in fact, worked out to its results the parallel between πολιτική on the one hand, and γυμναστική and ἰατρική on the other, which he inherited from the Gorgias of Plato (464 B sqq.) and from Socrates. These are arts, while πολιτική is a practical science; yet on the whole a resemblance exists between them[1], though it is

[1] Cp. Pol. 6 (4). 1. 1288 b 10 sqq.: 3. 6. 1278 b 37 sqq.: Eth. Nic. 10. 10. 1180 b 7 sqq.

not complete at all points[1]. Πολιτική, no less than δυνάμεις like Rhetoric and Dialectic[2], resembles the arts in dealing with cases in which an imperfect success is alone attainable as readily as with others; 'it is quite possible to treat scientifically patients who can never enjoy health' (Rhet. 1. 1. 1355 b 13). Just as it is the business of Medicine to treat any one who may be proposed for treatment (τὸν προτεθέντα, Eth. Nic. 10. 10. 1180 b 26[3]), so it is the business of πολιτική to study how any given constitution is to be brought into being, and how, having been brought into being, it is to be kept in being as long as possible, even if the constitution thus demanded at its hands falls short of that to which the circumstances of the particular State enable it to attain (μήτε τὴν ἐνδεχομένην ἐκ τῶν ὑπαρχόντων ἀλλά τινα φαυλοτέραν, Pol. 6 (4). 1. 1288 b 28 sqq.).

Thus the political branch of πολιτική seems, as it were, to waver between two levels; it is, on the one hand, a practical science closely akin to Ethics, if indeed it does not deal with a nobler subject-matter; it is, on the other, an art or productive science like Medicine, ready to construct on demand any constitutional form which may be asked of it, whatever its merits or demerits, in such a way as to be as durable as possible; indeed, stooping even lower than Medicine, for while Medicine seeks in all cases to restore some degree of health, Political Science is not in every case to require States to adopt a good constitution.

Why, we ask, does not the Nicomachean Ethics also make it its business to deal with τὸν προτεθέντα and to do as much as possible for the virtue and happiness of the ill-circumstanced individual, just as the Politics does its best for the ill-circumstanced State?[4] We do, in fact, find lower as well as higher virtues described in the Nicomachean Ethics—continence as well as temperance; the lower kinds of friendship as well as the higher; justice as well as equity and friendship; prudence as well as speculative virtue—but why does not the treatise go on to trace out a life for the less favourably constituted individual, as the Politics traces a fitting organization for the less favourably circumstanced State? The answer is that

[1] Pol. 2. 8. 1269 a 19 sqq.: 3. 16. 1287 a 32 sqq.

[2] Rhet. 1. 4. 1359 b 12 sq.: 1. 1. 1355 b 10 sqq.: Top. 1. 3. 101 b 5 sqq.

[3] Cp. Eth. Nic. 1. 11. 1101 a 3, καθάπερ καὶ στρατηγὸν ἀγαθὸν τῷ παρόντι στρατοπέδῳ χρῆσθαι πολεμικώτατα καὶ σκυτοτόμον ἐκ τῶν δοθέντων σκυτῶν κάλλιστον ὑπόδημα ποιεῖν, τὸν αὐτὸν δὲ τρόπον καὶ τοὺς ἄλλους τεχνίτας ἅπαντας.

[4] See on this subject the remarks of Teichmüller, Einheit des Aristotel. Eudämonie, pp. 103–108, though perhaps there is more difference between the Nicomachean Ethics and the Politics in this matter than Teichmüller here allows.

in strictness it has to do only with the virtues and the virtuous action which culminate in εὐδαιμονία: it seeks to draw out the contents of εὐδαιμονία: thus its aim is essentially ideal, and any attempt to do for the less well-endowed individual what the Politics does for the less favoured State would have conflicted with its plan. The question, however, remains, why the work was constructed on this plan—why Aristotle's treatment of Ethics is more ideal than his treatment of Politics. Perhaps the steps which Plato had already taken in the direction of sketching lower and more easily attainable forms of the State (Laws 739 E) may have suggested to Aristotle a broader and more practical treatment of Politics.

But if the Politics is something more than a sequel to the Nicomachean Ethics, the teaching of the latter treatise seems also to be less adjusted to that of the former than we might have expected. We learn in the Politics to regard man as a part of a greater Whole, the State, and we expect to find this fact kept in view by Aristotle in his ethical treatise. Virtue, we anticipate, will be the sum of the qualities which tend to the maintenance and excellence of the Whole, and the first question discussed in the work will be the question what these qualities are. The course followed, however, is quite different. Aristotle's ethical ideal is deduced partly from psychological facts, or alleged psychological facts, such as the natural supremacy of a certain part of the soul over other parts, partly from opinion, and especially opinion evidenced in action, or the opinion of wise and good men; in no way from the nature of the State or the conditions of its successful working. On the contrary, the State seems rather to be adjusted to the σπουδαῖος than the σπουδαῖος to the State; we are nowhere taught by Aristotle to deduce the nature of virtue from the nature of the State. If this had been otherwise, the ethical ideal of Aristotle might have been somewhat different from what it is. The virtues which tend to make men valuable members of a Whole would probably have assumed a more conspicuous place in it. The highest virtue would have been discovered not by asking what is the virtue of the most divine part of the soul, but by asking what virtue tends most to the harmony and excellence of the State. We do, in fact, find that in the Politics the highest virtue, that virtue whose exercise is more the end of human life than the exercise of any other—speculative virtue—is placed in a new light, as being (together with temperance, prudence, and justice) preservative of the State in those times of peace and leisure which are fatal to the exclusively military

State (4 (7). 15. 1334 a 22 sqq.). But we hear nothing about this in the Nicomachean Ethics. There, on the whole, the principle that man is by nature a part of the State seems to find less application than might have been expected[1]. Virtue is described rather as the supremacy of that part of the soul which is rightfully supreme, than as the adaptation of the individual to the maintenance of the highest type of society. Ethical Science dominates Political Science, not Political Science Ethical. The supreme end of the State is contemplative activity, precisely the activity in the exercise of which the individual is most independent of his fellows.

But then again, as we have seen, Political Science claims freedom for itself. The Politics studies the πόλις and the various πολιτεῖαι more independently of Ethics than we might have expected. If Aristotle's only object had been to complete the Nicomachean Ethics, the Politics would have been a very different work from what it is. It would have been more ideal and less technical.

We see then that the two treatises are to a certain extent correlated, but that they are not perfectly adjusted to each other.

One remark may be added. There is no sign that Aristotle deduced from the Politics the lesson which it would seem clearly to imply, as to man's chance of attaining full virtue and happiness. The further we advance in the Politics, the more clearly we see how dependent the moral virtue of the individual is on the constitution—that is, on the ethical creed adopted by the State as a whole—and also how much the constitution depends on causes not altogether subject to man's control. The result is—as the reader of the Politics can hardly fail to see, whether Aristotle himself saw it or not—that virtue can rarely be attainable in its purity, for only the citizen of the best constitution is ἁπλῶς σπουδαῖος, and that if virtue is rarely attainable, still more must this be the case with happiness, for happiness presupposes not only pure and complete virtue, but also a certain measure of external and bodily goods. We hardly saw this, while we were

[1] Some virtues which are implied in the Politics to be essential to the successful working of the State appear to escape notice in the Nicomachean Ethics: e.g. that which is exercised in caring that others shall be virtuous (Pol. 3. 9. 1280 b 1 sqq.: 1. 13. 1259 b 18 sqq.)—unless indeed, as is probably the case, φρόνησις is the virtue whose existence is here implied. But then, how imperfect is the sketch of φρόνησις or πολιτική in the Nicomachean Ethics, if this important feature of its action is not dwelt on there.

absorbed in the Nicomachean Ethics with the analysis of the nature of happiness: it is when we turn to the question how happiness is produced, that we learn how little it can really be said to be *πολύκοινον*, as it is said to be in Eth. Nic. 1. 10. 1099 b 18—how little we are able without the aid of Nature and Fortune to bring the best State into being[1], or in other words, to realize the indispensable condition of full virtue and happiness. The ideal picture of *εὐδαιμονία* in the Nicomachean Ethics turns out to be little else than a glorious vision. We see the goal of human life, but the road to it seems to be well-nigh blocked.

APPENDIX B.

On the Carthaginian Constitution[2].

THE Carthaginian State was not a declining State when Aristotle wrote, like the Lacedaemonian and Cretan States, but was perhaps in its prime or approaching it. Carthage was a seaport, unlike Sparta and most of the Cretan cities, and a very populous seaport, for even in the days of its decline it is said to have had seven hundred thousand inhabitants[3]; the number of its citizens, therefore, was probably also very great—great enough, one would have thought, to remove Carthage from the category of well-governed States, if in these the citizen-body was never allowed to pass moderate limits (4 (7). 4. 1326 a 27 sq.). We know not who had written on the Carthaginian constitution before Aristotle—he himself may have already sketched it in his Polities—but it evidently enjoyed a high reputation. Aristotle remarks that the fact of its stability, notwithstanding that a demos existed at Carthage, proved it to be a well-designed constitution, and that under it Carthage had been free from serious civil trouble, and also from tyrants. It is clear that whatever Aristotle may say as to the political weaknesses of Asiatic

[1] Cp. Pol. 6 (4). 11. 1295 a 25 sqq.

[2] See on this subject Susemihl's notes (Sus.[2], Notes 376–398), which have been of much use to me.

[3] It is thus that Grote (History of Greece, 10. 542) interprets the words of Strabo, p. 833, *πόλεις μὲν εἶχον τριακοσίας ἐν τῇ Λιβύῃ, ἀνθρώπων δ' ἐν τῇ πόλει μυριάδας ἑβδομήκοντα*. Mommsen, however, takes Strabo to refer, not to the inhabitants, but to the citizens of Carthage, 'whether dwelling in the city or its neighbourhood, or resident in its subject-territory or in other lands' (History of Rome, E. T. 2. 24 n.).

races (4 (7). 7), the Carthaginians deserve the credit, often ascribed too exclusively to Greece and Rome, of being among the earliest pioneers of free institutions.

We do not hear that, like the Lacedaemonian State, Carthage forbade its citizens to practise agriculture, trade, and the handicrafts, but it seems to have sought to encourage a military spirit in them (4 (7). 2. 1324 b 12 sqq.), and though we are not told that anything corresponding to the Lacedaemonian and Cretan systems of gymnastic training existed at Carthage, we hear of the existence of syssitia, and these may well have been there also, no less than at Sparta and in Crete, designed with a view to war.

It is, however, on the political constitution that Aristotle mainly dwells. His chapter on the Lacedaemonian constitution throws much light on the social organization of the Lacedaemonian State, but this cannot be said of his chapter on the Carthaginian constitution. We learn far less from him, indeed, than we could wish even as to the political constitution, for he is mainly preoccupied with the question, how far the Carthaginian constitution fulfilled its aim of being an *ἀριστοκρατία*, and not an oligarchy or a democracy. His remarks on this question throw some light on the arrangements of the constitution, but only enough to make us wish for more.

He had mentioned at the outset of the chapter that the Carthaginian constitution was similar in some respects to the Lacedaemonian, and he is thus led to enumerate, though in the briefest and baldest way, first those Carthaginian institutions which were similar (*παραπλήσια*, 33), and next those which were analogous (*ἀνάλογον*, 37), to Lacedaemonian institutions. The former epithet is applied to the Carthaginian syssitia and to the Council of the Hundred and Four, which are respectively compared with the Phiditia and the Ephors, while the Carthaginian kings and senate are described as analogous to their Lacedaemonian correlatives. The Carthaginian constitution, though an *ἀριστοκρατία* (6 (4). 7. 1293 b 14 sqq.), is held by Aristotle to deviate from the true model of an *ἀριστοκρατία* both in an oligarchical and in a democratic direction. It sometimes conceded too much to the people and sometimes too much to the rich. A strict *ἀριστοκρατία* would not have given as much power to the popular assembly as the Carthaginian constitution gave it[1]—would not have given it full power to arrive at decisions of its own or have allowed any one who pleased to speak against the pro-

[1] See Sus.[2], Note 388, who points out how limited were the powers of the people even in a democracy of the more moderate type.

posals of the magistrates. On the other hand, poor men of high merit had a career open to them in the Lacedaemonian State which was not open to them at Carthage. Carthage, indeed, not only tended to exclude poor men from high office, but confined two at least of its highest magistracies to wealthy men, actually making them purchaseable. The Carthaginian practice of allowing several offices to be held by one man also had an oligarchical tendency, inasmuch as it diminished the number of office-holders. Many even of the wealthy would find that office came to them but rarely. Thus, if we can understand how the Carthage of Aristotle's day could be described, not quite baselessly, as δημοκρατουμένη (7 (5). 12. 1316 b 5), we can still better understand the language which Isocrates puts into the mouth of Nicocles with regard to it—ἔτι δὲ Καρχηδονίους καὶ Λακεδαιμονίους τοὺς ἄριστα τῶν Ἑλλήνων πολιτευομένους οἴκοι μὲν ὀλιγαρχουμένους, παρὰ δὲ τὸν πόλεμον βασιλευομένους (Nicocl. § 24). Carthage, he holds, was oligarchically ruled at home, but ruled by kings in the field. Aristotle, on the contrary, would say that the Carthaginian constitution was an aristocracy, though it deviated from the true standard partly in the direction of democracy and still more in that of oligarchy. It was an aristocracy because it did homage to virtue as well as to wealth and popular power (6 (4). 7. 1293 b 14 sqq.), but it was so much mastered by a worship of wealth that Aristotle doubted whether it was a durable aristocracy, and would seem to have anticipated that it would ultimately become an oligarchy (1273 a 41 sq.). If it is allowable slightly to alter a phrase of Mr. Lowell's, the Carthaginian aristocracy was 'an aristocracy with oligarchical instincts.'

When we pass from the broad outline of the constitution to details, we find ourselves much at a loss, but it would seem that till the fifth century before Christ, when the Council of the Hundred and Four was instituted, the Kings (i.e. the Suffetes or Judges) and the Senate were supreme at Carthage, and that even after that event they probably retained to a large extent the immediate administration of affairs, for we are told that nothing came before the popular assembly except matters referred to it by them, or matters as to the reference of which to the popular assembly the kings and senate were not agreed (1273 a 6 sqq.). It would appear, therefore, that in practice either the kings or the senate could compel the reference of a question to the popular assembly. It does not seem that there were any determinate subjects with which the popular assembly had the exclusive right of dealing, and no doubt the kings and the senate would commonly deal with administrative questions themselves. For all we hear to the contrary, they may have had the right to legislate also.

The Kings, or Suffetes, who were probably two in number, and who are compared by Livy to the Roman Consuls (30. 7. 5, suffetes, quod velut consulare imperium apud eos erat), cannot have held office for life, as Cicero appears to imply that they did (De Rep. 2. 23. 42–43), for Aristotle tells us (1273 a 15 sqq.) that the members of the Pentarchies held office for a longer term than any other magistrates, and they did not hold office for life. The kingship was probably an annual office, but those who held it may have been indefinitely re-eligible. We gather from Aristotle's language (1272 b 38 sqq.) that the kings were not taken, like the Lacedaemonian, from a single family, and that they were elected from families of merit, and were men of mark themselves, though they needed also to be wealthy men, but we know not by whom they were elected; Aristotle speaks, indeed, of the kingship as a purchaseable office (cp. Plato, Rep. 544 D). Isocrates, in the passage of the Nicocles which has already been quoted (§ 24), appears to regard the kings as the generals of the State, but Aristotle distinguishes the offices of King and General (1273 a 36 sq.). These two offices, however, may often have been combined. They are described by Aristotle in 1273 a 30, 36 as the greatest in the State, but in 1273 a 15 he refers in similar terms to 'the Hundred.' We have seen that in comparing the Carthaginian kingship with the Lacedaemonian he uses the epithet 'analogous,' not 'similar,' and it is clear that these two forms of kingship differed in many respects; the Carthaginian kingship was elective and purchaseable, was not held for life, and was not always combined with the Generalship.

We learn little from Aristotle as to the Senate. We have already seen that it probably shared with the Kings or Suffetes the ordinary administration of the State, and that he speaks of it as 'analogous' to the Lacedaemonian. It must have been a far more numerous body than the Lacedaemonian Senate, for the inner council by which it was to a large extent guided itself numbered thirty members (Liv. 30. 16. 3: oratores ad pacem petendam mittunt triginta seniorum principes; id erat sanctius apud illos consilium, maximaque ad ipsum senatum regendum vis), and the Carthaginian Senators cannot, like the Lacedaemonian, have held office for life, at any rate in the time of Aristotle, for Aristotle implies that no magistracies at Carthage were held for life (1273 a 15 sqq.). Valerius Maximus (Facta et Dicta Memorabilia, 9. 5. 4) remarks on the arrogance of the Carthaginian Senate in using a bath of their own, distinct from that used by the plebs, and the contrast of Roman and Carthaginian custom in this matter is not without significance. See on the subject of the Carthaginian Senate Sus.[2], Note 382.

The Council of the Hundred and Four is described by Aristotle as 'similar' to the Lacedaemonian Ephorate. He probably means that its function in the State was similar, and that, like the Ephorate (c. 9. 1271 a 6), it exercised a control over the other magistracies, and especially over the kings. He mentions a body called 'the Hundred' as the greatest magistracy of the State (1273 a 14 sq.), and the question arises whether he means by 'the Hundred' the Hundred and Four. It is not absolutely certain that he does, for the use of the word αἱροῦνται (1272 b 36) in reference to the election of the Hundred and Four might be taken to suggest (if we supply οἱ Καρχηδόνιοι, as in 1273 a 29) that they were elected by the citizens generally, whereas we are told that the Hundred were elected by certain Boards of Five called Pentarchies; it is also true that, if we identify the Hundred with the Hundred and Four, we shall have to suppose that the Pentarchies, which Aristotle criticises as defectively constituted (1273 a 13 sqq.), nevertheless elected the Hundred and Four well and fairly, for Aristotle says that the Hundred and Four were chosen on grounds of merit (1272 b 36). Still it is difficult to believe that a Council answering, as the Hundred and Four did, to the Lacedaemonian Ephorate, which, as Susemihl points out (Note 379), is itself called ἡ μεγίστη ἀρχή in 2. 9. 1270 b 18 sq., can have been second to any other magistracy at Carthage; it seems, therefore, on the whole, likely that it is to be identified with the Hundred, ἡ μεγίστη ἀρχή. If, however, we identify the Hundred and the Hundred and Four, the resemblance which Aristotle traces between the Hundred and Four and the Ephorate cannot have extended to the mode in which the members of these two magistracies were appointed, for the Ephors were not elected by Pentarchies. Nor can the Hundred and Four have resembled the Ephorate in being recruited from the people and in forming a bulwark of popular power, for it was a principle at Carthage to prefer rich men to poor men in elections to office. Aristotle himself implies that the Hundred and Four were far superior to the Ephors in character, position, and capacity (1272 b 35 sq.). The resemblance between the two magistracies must probably have lain, as has been said, in similarity of function. The Hundred and Four, like the Ephors, seem to have controlled the Kings and the Generals, and perhaps also the Senate.

This great council has commonly been identified with the magistracy, the original creation of which in the fifth century before Christ is thus described by Justin (19. 2. 5–6)—dein, cum familia tanta imperatorum (the descendants of Mago) gravis liberae civitati esset omniaque ipsi agerent simul et iudicarent, centum ex numero senatorum iudices deliguntur, qui reversis a bello ducibus rationem rerum gestarum exigerent, ut hoc metu ita in bello imperia cogitarent, ut domi iudicia legesque respicerent. Aristotle says nothing about the Hundred and Four being senators, and Justin speaks of the 'centum iudices' as reviewing the conduct of the generals after their return from the field, not as controlling the kings and senate, but they may have added to their functions as time went on, and we have already seen that the kings were often the generals of the State. It is a further question whether Livy alludes to the Hundred and Four, or even to the 'centum iudices' of Justin, in the well-known passage (33. 46) in which he depicts the 'impotens regnum' of the 'ordo iudicum' at Carthage in the time of Hannibal. 'Iudicum ordo Carthagine ea tempestate dominabatur, eo maxime quod idem perpetui iudices erant. Res fama vitaque omnium in illorum potestate erat. Qui unum eius ordinis offendisset, omnes adversos habebat, nec accusator apud infensos iudices deerat.' The term 'ordo iudicum' would seem to be a wider one than 'centum iudices,' and may perhaps include the whole 'order' of judges at Carthage, not merely a single court, however important. And then again, if 'the property, the good fame, and the life of every one lay in the power' of the 'centum iudices,' their jurisdiction must have at this time extended far beyond its original limits, for their functions were confined at the outset, as we have seen, to the control of the Generals. The 'ordo iudicum' of Livy, again, is recruited by the accession to it of quaestors, and probably other magistrates, at the expiration of their term of office (Liv. 33. 46. 4); we hear nothing of this in relation to the Hundred and Four, or indeed the 'centum iudices.' And if Livy means by saying 'idem perpetui iudices erant,' that the members of the 'ordo iudicum' held office for life, this certainly was not true of the Hundred and Four in Aristotle's time. It is evident, indeed, from the expression 'ea tempestate,' that Livy is describing a state of things which had not always existed. He is speaking of a time a century and a quarter after that of Aristotle.

We have seen that Isocrates puts in the mouth of Nicocles an interesting remark on the dual character of the Lacedaemonian and Carthaginian constitutions. They were, he says, oligarchies at home and kingships in the field. It was probably with a view to diminish this duality and to bring the Kingship and the Generalship under the control of the oligarchy, that the Council of the Hundred and Four was instituted. The Lacedaemonian Ephorate was intended to serve a similar purpose, but a democratic character was skilfully imparted to it which was wanting in the Hundred and Four, and the services of the Lacedaemonian demos were thus enlisted in the task of checking and controlling the Kings.

In the Lacedaemonian and Cretan constitutions, and indeed in the earlier constitutions of Greece generally (7 (5). 5. 1305 a 15 sqq.: 7 (5). 10. 1310 b 21 sqq.), not a few great magistracies found a place. This is true of the Carthaginian constitution also, though the great magistracies tenable for life, which form so conspicuous a feature of the Lacedaemonian and Cretan constitutions, seem to have been wanting in it. The democratic spirit (8 (6). 2. 1317 b 24 sqq.), though stronger at Carthage than in the Lacedaemonian and Cretan States, had not yet begun in Aristotle's day to abolish or cripple the great magistracies. When in the fifth century before Christ the House of Mago had threatened to become too powerful for the safety of the State (Mommsen, History of Rome, E. T. 2. 16), its ascendency was checked by the creation of a new great magistracy, not by the abolition of the Kingship and Generalship, the offices through which it asserted its influence, or by the aggrandisement of the popular assembly. The Carthaginian constitution, after this great change had been made in it, came to belong to the class of constitutions in which the magistracies are ranged, as it were, in two tiers, one or more magistracies being charged with the control of the rest. At Carthage this controlling authority was lodged with the Hundred and Four, just as in the Lacedaemonian State it was lodged with the Ephors, in early Athens with the Council of the Areopagus, and in the State described in Plato's Laws with the Nomophylakes, the priests of Apollo, and the Nocturnal Council.

In reading Aristotle's remarks on the Carthaginian constitution, we must not forget that he criticises it from a point of view from which it was probably seldom regarded by its framers. Their desire was for a constitution which, while it favoured the acquisition and preservation of empire by the State, would also guard its liberties—a constitution under which the virtues and the ascendency of great leaders like those of the House of Mago might be made as useful to the community and as little perilous to it as possible; Aristotle, on the other hand, is mainly interested in the inquiry, how far does the Carthaginian constitution give supremacy to virtue and place power in the hands of virtuous men?

APPENDIX C.

THE following are the variations of MS. Phillipps 891 (z) from the text of the first two books of the *Vetus Versio* of the Politics printed by Susemihl in his edition of 1872. Some unimportant variations of spelling are omitted.

BOOK I.

Sus. p. **1**. 2. om. *et* pr. z; it is added in the darker ink used in the marginal glosses: 4. om. *quidem* (with a b g n t): 6. om. *et* pr. z (it is added in darker ink): 8. om. *et* before *regale*. **2**. 2. om. *puta* (with a): 3. patremfamiliae] *patrem familias*: yconomum] *yconomicum*: 5. aut] *et* (with almost all MSS.). **3**. 4. hiis] *his*, and so mostly: 5. itaque] *utique* (with a): combinari] *combinare*: 9. quod quidem] *quicquid*: 11. haec] *hoc* (with a m t). **4**. 2. *servum* pr. z altered to *servus* in lighter ink: 4. om. *paupere* (with a): om. *utique*: om. *optime*: 6. femina] the first two letters are over an erasure: 8. om. *ipsorum*. **5**. 1. domum] *dominum*: praeeminenter] *praeeminentem*: 2. om. *que*: 4. *karondas*: *omosiphios*: 5. *epymenides*: *otres*: *omokapnos*: 7. *et* is added before *vicinia*. **6**. 1. om. *et* before *primum*: 3. viciniae] *vicine* pr. z: 5. *dispersim*: 6. om. *hii*: 10. consequens] *q̄ns*. **7**. 4. om. *et* before *finis*: 8. *qui* is added after *fortunam* (*quia* in a) and followed by *at* in place of *aut*; *qui* is expunged and *at* corrected in a different ink from that of the MS. **8**. 4. *et* is added after *homo* (as in a). **9**. 1. om. *est*: 2. *hominibus* after *proprium est* (as in a): 5. om. *natura*: 9. autem] *enim*: definita] *diffinita*, and so elsewhere. **10**. 1. *est* is added after *manifestum* (as in a): 4. persesufficientiam] *sufficientiam*: 6. the first half of *communitatem* is over an erasure and in darker ink: 10. *nascitur autem homo habens arma*: 12. *ad* is added after *venerea et*. **11**. 1. *diki*: 2. *diki*: 9. *servis* pr. z?: om. *et* before *maritus*: 11. om. *sunt*: 12. *teknofactiva*. **12**. 3. om. *his autem* pr. z, but the words are added above the line (with a caret) in an ink very similar to that of the MS.: 5. *trimatistica*: despota] *despotia*: 7. *ut* is added before *utique*: 9. *despotica* is expunged by dots placed beneath (the ink of these dots is perhaps different from that of the MS.): politia] *pollitica*. **13.** 4. *manifestum quod* is added after *est*: 5. om. *est*. **14.** 1. om. *quidem*: *proratius* (with a): 7. *subinducere*: 9. *citarizarent*: *architetoribus*. **15.** 1. *igitur* is added after *quidem*: 4. om. *autem* after *adhuc*: differt] *differunt*: 6. om. *hanc* (so a g n): 8. *autem* after *possessa* (so a b t): quae] *quod*: 9. om. *quidem*. **16.** 4. *autem* is added after *iste* in pr. z, but expunged in a different ink from that of the MS.: *est* after *homo* (so a): 6. *natura* after *talis* (with a): 8. *post* after *considerandum*: om. *haec*. **17.** 2. *adiscere*: 4. *seggregata*: 5. om. *et* after *multae*: 10. om. *sive* after *commune*: 13. *armonie*. **18.** 5. in corruptis] *incorruptis*: om. *et* after *quod* (so a Alb.): 8. om. *utique*: 9. dicimus] *diximus* (with a c m Alb.): 12. *autem* written twice (the second *autem* expunged, but in a darker ink than that of the MS.). **19.** 3. aequo] *quo* pr. z, but *e* is added above the line (with a caret) in the ink of the MS.: aut e] *aut*, but this word is written over an erasure and in darker ink than that of the MS.: 9 om. *omnibus*: 12. *est* after *opus* (with a). **20.** 7. corpori] *corporibus*: om. *a* before *domesticis*: 9. quae liberorum et servorum] *quae servorum et quae liberorum*: 11. om. *et* (with a). **21.** 1. fuerint] *sunt* (with a): 5. *facile* is in the margin, but in the same hand and ink as the MS.: 7. quod] the original reading in z was not *quod*, but something different (probably *qui*), which has been altered into *quod* in darker ink: 11. *superata* pr. z, altered into *superati* by erasure. **22.** 1. rhetora scribunt] *rectorici scribunt* pr. z, but these words have been expunged by dots placed beneath them, and *rhetora scribit* has been written in the margin in a different ink: 4. *illo* pr. z, altered into *alio* in a different ink: sapientum] *sapientium*: 6. *et* is added before *violentiam*: 8. violentia] *violentiam* (with a o y): 9. *benivolentia*: 10. sepositis] *positis*. **23.** 1. *est* is added: 5. om. *aliquis*: 8. equidem] *et quidem*: 9. hos] *hoc*: 10. necesse enim esse aliquos dicere] *necesse enim est dicere aliquos esse*. **24.** 2. om. *et*: autem] *quidem*: 3. om. *et*: Eleloga] *egloga* (*elegia* in the margin in darker ink): om. *enim*: 4. progenetricibus] the four or five letters which precede *-bus* are over an erasure: addicere] *addere*: 6. om. *et* before *nobiles* (with a): ignobiles] *innobiles*: 9. *quidem* after *hoc* (with a). **25.** 1. om. *natura* (with pr. a): 2. om. *quod* (with a): 4. nata] *nati*: *principatu* after the second *principari* (so a): 7. veluti] *velut*. **26.** 3. hic quidem] *haec quidem*: hic autem] *haec autem*: 9. quidem qui] *quidam* (with a): *Siracusis*: 11. plus] *plura*. **27**. 3. om. *omnes*: 4. quae est] *quae et*: 6. *magnum* after *habens* (with a): 7. haec] *hoc*. **28**. 3. om. *utique*: 8. *et* is added before *ex* (as in a): 10. om. *quidem*: 12. utrum autem] *utrum autem enim*, but *enim* is expunged by dots placed beneath it (by whom, is uncertain) and *utrum autem* (except the first *u*) is written over an erasure in darker ink than that of the MS. **29**. 3. multae] *multa* pr. z; *s* is added above the line in a different ink: 4. agricultiva] *agricultura* (with a t): 5. universaliter] *utiliter*: 7. om. *et* before *animalium* (with a): 9. enim] *et enim* (so a): quidem] *quod*: 10. *que* is added in a different ink above *utro*: 11. *esse* is added after *quidem*. **30**. 8. *necessarium* after *fuerit* (with a b t): 9. *m* of *viventem* is over an erasure. **31**. 1. *tot* before, not after, *fere*: 2. quicunque] *quaecunque*: sponte natam] *spontaneam* (with a): 3. per commutationem] *percontationem* pr. z?, but the word has been touched up with darker ink and made hardly legible, so that it is not easy to say what the original reading was (*i. commutationem* is written above in similar ink to the MS.): 7. *simul* after *furativam*: 10. *videtur* after *natura* (with a): 11. perfectionem] *perfectam*: 13. *coe* of *coepariunt* is over an erasure (as in a). **32**. 1. om. *utique* (with a): om. *sibi ipsi*: 3. generatis] *genitis*: om. *in se ipsis*: 7. om. *cibi*: 8. ipsis] *eis*: 10. *ipsa* after *omnia*. **33**. 2. om. *et*: 3. *possessivae* after *naturam* (with a): 4. quorum] *quarum*: 5. *communione* (with b c): 6. videntur] *universaliter* was first written, then expunged, and *videntur* added in the margin probably by the writer of the MS. **34**. 1. om. *ponitur* after *viris* pr. z (it is added above in darker ink): 2. organum] *organorum*: nullius] *ullius*: 7. vocare] *vocari*: om. *quam*: 8. *terminus* after *esse* (with a t Alb.): 12. *fit* after *magis* (with a): 13. autem] *enim*. **35**. 2. om. *rei*: 6. *factum* after *est* (with a): 10. qua] *quare*. **36**. 1. *est* after *opus* (with a): 9. nulla] *ulla*: 11. *magis* is joined to the preceding sentence in z, and not to *peregrino*. **37**. 1. *enim* after *facile*: 6. *pondere et magnitudine* (so a): 7. *absolvant*: 9. *species* after *pecuniativae*. **38**. 2. *rursum deliramentum esse* after *videtur* (so a): 4. om. *nullo dignum*: 6. *sit* is added after *inconveniens* (as in a): *perit*: 7. om. *propter* (with pr. a): 8. om. *factis*: 9. *alterum* after *aliquid* (as in a): 11. full stop after *yconomica*, the next word *Campsoria* beginning with a capital letter: 12. per] *propter*. **39**. 3. in infinitum] *infinitorum*: 5. *-um* of *illum* is over an erasure: om. *in* before *infinitum* (with a c m Alb.): 10. necessarium] *necessariarum*: 11. video] *vide'* (= *videmus*), but the *e* is followed by an erasure, and I do not feel absolutely certain that the symbol for *-mus* is in the ink of the MS.; still it resembles other symbols in the MS. of the same import: 13. variat] *variatur*. **40**. 1. *uterque*, I think, pr. z, but it has been altered into *utrique* in ink somewhat darker than that of the MS.: after *est* is added *geca*, but this is expunged by dots placed beneath: *et* is added after *usus*: 8. *et* is added before *ipsius*: 9. quoniam] *quia*: om. *et* (with a): 10. in possessione] *impossibile*: *et* is added before *omnis*: 12. om. *non*. **41**. 1. factivam] *factiva* (with b c): om. *si* pr. z (it is added in a darker ink): possint] *possunt* (with a c m Alb.): 2. *hoc* is added before *acquirere* (as in a): 6. om. *hoc*. **42**. 4. naturam] *natura* (with c Alb.): 6. yconomo] so pr. z, but *ic* is inserted (with a caret) before the final *o* in the ink of the MS.: 7. autem] *etiam*: 10. om. *aut* pr. z (with a); it is added in a lighter ink. **43**. 1. subservientis] *ut servientis*: 3. exhibere] *exibere*: omni] *omnium* (with a and pr. b): 9. om. *est*: *habentur*, but the *e* is over an erasure and in darker ink: obolostatica] *ob olostatica*: 10. sit] *fit*: 11. om. *usura*; *i. usura*, however, is written above the line in darker ink. **44**. 1. se ipsum] *se ipsam*: 2. parta] *partu*: *fiunt* is added after *ipsa*, but expunged by dots placed beneath, apparently in the same ink as the MS.: 3. om. *maxime*: 12. qualibus] *quibus*: 14. nudae] the second and third letters are over an erasure and are touched with darker ink. **45**. 1. convenit] *9tin*ᵗ (*contingit?*): 2. *igitur pecuniativae* is added in the margin in the same handwriting and ink as the MS.: 4. *nacleria* pr. z: *fortigia*: 7. mistarnia] *ministrativa*: 12. terra] *altera*: 14. *ex terra* before *species*: unoquoque] *unaquaque*. **46**. 1. horum] *harum*: 5. *banausike*: 7. after *minimum* is written *reoperatur* but expunged by dots placed beneath, and *requiritur* is written above in the same hand and apparently the same ink: 8. *Karitide Paris*: *Limnio*: 13. om. *et*. **47**. 2. contingit] *contigit*: 3. ipsi] *ipsis*: 5. *olivarum* after *ubertatem*: 6. hieme] *yeme*: 7. *kio*: *pro* before *omnibus modico* (with a): 8. adiciente] *addiciente*. **48**. 1. *Tales*: after *quidem h* crossed through: 2. *fecisse* before *ostensionem* (so a): 4. *praeparare* is added in the margin in the hand and ink of the MS. in substitution for a word which is expunged by dots placed beneath it: 6. venalium] *venalem*: 10. *assumpsit* pr. z, altered in the ink of the MS. to *supersumpsit*: *Dionisius*: 11. absportare] *asportare*: 12. *Siracusis*. **49**. 3. *in* is added before *domibus*: 6. yconomicae] *yconomie*: 11. *natura* after *femella*. **50**. 2. ex aequali enim vult esse] *exaequari enim vult*: 3. at tamen] *attamen*: 4. quaerit] *quaerunt*: 11. *horum* after *omnium*: 12. regem quidem differre] *quidem differre regem*. **51**. 1. iuvenem] *iuvenius*: 5. horum] *eorum*: 6. om. *quidem*: 7. om. *utique*: 8. *aliis* is added before *hiis*: 9. om. *et* before *fortitudo*: 11. different] *differunt*. **52.** 1. *uxore* is written above *muliere* and *filio* above *puero* in the hand and ink of the MS.: sunt] *sint*: 2. *esse* before *temperatam* (with a): intemperatus] *in* is added above *temperatus* (with a caret) in the hand and ink of the MS.: 4. *et* is crossed through before *natura*: 6. *kalokatia*: 14. *est* is added after *necesse*. **53.** 1. om. *esse*: *differentiae* is over an erasure: 2. exemplificatur] *exemplificabitur* (with a): 6. et in aliis. quare natura quae plura principantia et subiecta] *et in aliis quae natura sunt, puta principantia et subiecta*, but the words *quae natura sunt puta* are written in the hand and ink of the MS. over an erasure: 9. *quidem* after *servus* runs into the margin: 11. the first *habet* is added above the line with a caret, but in the hand and ink of the MS. **54.** 4. immittit] *immittitur*: 5. et] *est*: 9. *hoc* is over an erasure: 11. aut] *est*, but over an erasure: 12. *dicunt* is added above the line (with a caret) in the hand and ink of the MS. **55.** 1. dixit] *dicit* (with a): 11. aut differt] *differt autem*: 12. hic] *hoc* (so a). **56.** 4. *esse* after *oportet*: 9. isto] *hoc* (so Alb.): 10. *autem* om. pr. z, but it is added above the line with a caret, I think in the hand and ink of the MS.: 11. homilia] *omelia*: quod] *quidem*: 12. quod quidem bene] *bene quidem*. **57.** 6. *esse* is added before *studiosas* (as in a m Alb.): 7. politiae] *policiae*: 8. de hiis quidem] *quidem de his*: 9. om. *dicendum*: om. *finem*: 11. politia] *policia*.

BOOK II.

58. 2. qui] *quae*: 4. *legibus* after *dicuntur* (so a): 7. *sophyzare*: 8. *propter* after *non*: has] *eas* (with a): 10. om. *est* (with a m). **59.** 1. civitas] *civilitas*: 3. om. *quidem* pr. z (it is added in lighter ink, but in the hand of the MS.): 4. *sotii*: 10. sic] *sit*: 12. caussam] *caussa*. **60.** 5. omnem] *omnium* (with a): 11. *esset* before *quis* (with Alb.): *operari* before *hoc* (with a): 13. om. *et* (with a m). **61.** 4. differet] *differret*: 6. *Archades*: *et* is added before *ex*: 8. om. *et* pr. z (it is added with a caret in lighter ink but in the hand of the MS.): 11. *alium* before *aliquem*. **62.** 1. eidem] *idem hiidem*: 3. *semper* after 4. *principari* (so a): 7. in parte] *imperate*. **63.** 6. om. *quidem*: 10. om. *magis*: 11. *est* before *optimum* (with a): scilicet] *sed*. **64.** 4. dicet] *dicit*: 7. om. *ut* pr. z, but something which may possibly stand for it is added above the line (with a caret) in a similar ink to that of the MS.: 8. om. *autem*: 9. om. *ut*. **65.** 2. omnes] *omnis*: 4. ad haec] *adhuc*: 7. quam quantum] *quamquam tamen*: 8. neglegunt] *negliguntur* (with a b t Alb.): 11.

est before *similiter*: 12. *autem* is added after *adhuc*, but struck out. **66.** 1. quotuscunque contingit] *et quotcunque contingat*: 3. aut] *autem*: quorumcunque] *quotcunque*: 6. sic] so pr. z, but it has been altered into *sit* in a different ink: 7. om. *millium* after *decem*: 11. aut] *autem*: ad haec] *adhuc*: contribulem] *contribuelem* with a dot under the first *e*. **67.** 1. *proprium* after *nepotem* (with a): 3. secundum] *sed*: 5. *quidam* before *accidere*: 7. *libia*: 8. sunt autem quaedam etiam femellae etiam] *sunt etiam quaedam et femellae*: 11. *Farsalo.* **68.** 4. *et* is added before *ad.* **69.** 8. ordinare] *ordinari* (with a): 10. *in* is added before *civitatibus.* **70.** 4. *unum fieri ambos* (with a): 5. om. *quidem*: 8. om. *modicum*: 11. fili] *filii*: 12. om. *ut.* **71.** 1. *dilligere*: *dillectum*: 3. transferre] *transferri*: 7. om. *in* (so a). **72.** 3. om. *modo*: 6. quis] *aliquis* (with a): 8. om. *omnes.* **73.** 1. communes] *omnes*: 3. sibi] *sic*: 5. *in operibus et in fruitionibus* is altered in the margin by the writer of the MS. to *in fruitionibus et operibus*: 13. ad ministrationes] *administrationes.* **74.** 1. *ancilares*: 3. superornatum] *semper ornatum*: 4. *differret* altered into *differet.* **75.** 3. velut] *velud*: 4. qui] *quidem*: *est* is added before *dicere* (as in a t Alb.): 11. *est* after *hoc* (as in a Alb.): 12. *esse autem phylauton.* **76.** 1. *amare oportet* (omitting *se ipsum* with a): 5. om. *in* (with a): haec itaque accidunt] *hoc utique accusat* (not, I think, *accidat*): 6. ad haec] *adhuc*: 7. manifeste] *maxime vel manifeste*: 12. *philantropos.* **77.** 1. *et* is added before *cum*: 4. testimoniorum] *testium* (with a): 5. adulationes] *allocutiones vel adulationes*: 6. possidentes] *possi* pr. z at the end of a line (*tes* is added above the line in darker ink): 11. communicantes] *incommunicantes*: 12. *esse* after *omnino* (with b c m). **78.** 4. prope] *proprie* (with a): 5. *simphoniam*: 6. *rithmon*: 8. futurum] *futuram*: 12. in] *et.* **79.** 5. *utique* after *fiet* (with a b m t Alb.): 7. civitatem] *civilitatem*: 8. *tribum* pr. z ?, altered into *tribubus* in darker ink: 10. *facere* before *Lacedaemonii* (with a). **80.** 2. no stop after *est*, a full stop after *prius*: 3. *oportet* after *possessiones* (with a): unumquemque] *unumquodque*: 5. *communia* after *omnia* (with a): different] possibly *differunt*, but a worm-hole in the parchment makes the reading uncertain: 6. illis] *aliis* (with Alb.): 7. nisi] *si nihil* (with a): 8. om. *tale*: 10. om. *et.* **81.** 4. om. *et disceptationes*: 5. existent] *existunt* (with a): hiis] *hi*: 6. legalibus] *legibus* (with a c): 7. municipia] *municipium*: 10. om. *esse.* **82.** 2. om. *autem*: 3. municipum] *municipium*: 5. communes possessiones] *omnes*: 8. eadem] *eodem.* **83.** 3. semper] *super*: 4. miscere] *misceri*: 6. auferens] *aufferens*: om. *felicem*: 7. felicitare] *felicita-*

tem was first written; it is changed into *felicitare* in the hand and ink of the MS. **84.** 5. politia] *polithia.* **85.** 7. om. *oportere* (with a): 9. om. *de.* **86.** 3. communiorem facere] *facere communionem* (with a): *circumducit* after *iterum*: 4. alteram] *aliam* (with a): mulierum] the original reading is uncertain, but, whatever it was, it has been made into *mulierum* in darker ink: 9. quinque] *quimque* pr. z? **87.** 2. *alia* before *aliqua* (with a). **88.** 3. acceptat] *aceptat*: 5. om. *et* before *multitudinem* (with t Alb.): 9. universale] *naturale*: 11. utrumque] *utrum.* **89.** 5. sinere] *si vere*: *puerorum* after *procreationem* (with a): 10. quidem] *equidem*: sunt] *sint* (with a c m): 12. iugarios] so z, but in the margin *aliter deiectos.* **90.** 3. *plures numero quidam*: 6. sinere] *si vere*: 8. *Fudon* altered into *Fydon* in darker ink: om. *quidem.* **91.** 3. omnem] *omnium*: sinit] *scivit*: 10. politiam] *polityam*: ex utentibus] *existentibus.* **92.** 1. igitur] *enim*: constituit] *constituerit*: 3. politiam] *politeyam*: 6. politiam] *politeiam*, and so mostly: 7. *aiunt* is added after *enim*, but is expunged by dots placed beneath in the ink of the MS.: 9. regnum] *regum*: 10. *plebeiorum* after *principatum* (with a): 11. ephoros] *eternos.* **93.** 2. *dictum est* after *hiis*: 3. aut] *haud* pr. z, changed into *aut* apparently in the same ink as the MS.: 7. oligarchiam] *oligarkica*: 9. electis] *ellectos*, but *ellectis* may have been first written: 12. tentare] *temptare.* **94.** 2. consili] *concilii* pr. z, but *s* is added above the line (with a caret) before *c* in the darker ink used for some of the glosses. **95.** 3. honorabilitatibus] *honorabilibus* (with a): 7. politia] *policia*: 9. institui] *instituti*: 10. mediocres] *mediocris.* **96.** 2. habent] *habet*: 3. omnes] *summis*: 7. incohant] *inchoant*: 8. quod] *quidem*: 9. aiunt] *autem*: 10. *felleas*, and so elsewhere. **97.** 1. *celerime*: 3. an erasure between *leges* and *scribens*: 5. minimae] *miniuem* (with a cross in faint ink above it): 6. om. *et* (with a m): 9. magnitudinem] *multitudinem*: 12. om. *quidem* (with a). **98.** 4. *leges* after *prohibent*: 9. autem vel] *aut*: 10. vivat] *vivatur*: 11. vivat] *vivatur*: *est* is expunged after *non.* **99.** 2. eruditis] *eruditi*: 3. haec] *hoc*?: 4. om. *existere* (with a). **100.** 2. putat] *putant* (with a): 3. esurire] *exurire* (with a): 4. habeant] *habent* (with b): 6. sine] *sive*: 9. possint] *possunt* (with b c t Alb.): *utique* before *non*: 11. maxima] *maxime.* **101.** 1. magni] *magis*: 8. sufficientem] *sufficienter.* **102.** 3. prolem] *pro levi*: *bellum inferre* before *propter habundanciam* (with a): 4. om. *ut*: 5. *cuboilus*: *autofradati*: *artaneam*: 8. *atraneam*: 12. *utique* after *gratiosi.* **103.** 1. existentes] *existente* pr. z (with pr. a), *s* being added above the line in a different ink: 6. *replectionem* or *replettionem.* **104.** 6. *dnofantus*: 9. dixit] *dixerit* (with a): om. *bene* after *non* (with a): the first letter of *Ipodamus* is not filled in: 10. *eurifontis milisios*: 13. *curiosus* (with a b). **105.** 1. et] *etiam* (with c): 3. *aliquid* after *de policia*: 9. deputata facient] *reputata faciant*: 10. vivent] *vivant*: 12. disceptationes] *disceptati omnes?*: 13. iniuriam] *iniuriarum* altered in the ink of the MS. to *iniuriam*. **106.** 3. constituit] *construxit*: 4. non per sententiae collationem] *non propter senum collationem*: 6. condemnetur] *condempnet*: 9. haec vel haec] *hoc vel hoc?* **107.** 5. om. *igitur*: 6. *Ipodami*: ordinationis] *oportet dignationis*: haec] *hee* (with b c): 10. servi] *secundum*. **108.** 5. oportet] *oportebit*: 7. quid] *quidem* (with c): 9. om. *in*: 12. om. *propriam* before *colent*. **109.** 4. propria] *propriam*: 8. non] *nunc*: 9. sument] *summent*: 11. om. *lex*. **110.** 3. collocuntur] *colloquentur*: 4. *ut* is added in the margin at the end of the line in a lighter ink, but apparently in the same hand as the MS.: 8. mnas] *minas*, and so elsewhere: 10. partientur] *patientur* (with b): 11. *condempnabunt*, as elsewhere: *erit* before *modus*: 12. sententiarum] *summarum*: om. *nullus* (with pr. a). **111.** 1. abiudicans] *adiudicans*: 3. aliquod] *aliquid*: 5. *aspectus*: *calumpnias*: 7. om. *et*: 11. politiae] *pollitice*: 12. *autem* is added after *memoriam*. **112.** 2. videbitur] *videtur* (with a): 3. *medicinalī*, but the stroke above the final *i* may have been added at a later time or by a later hand: 5. etiam] *et*: 8. *barbaticas*: 9. ab invicem] *adinvicem* (with a Alb.): 11. *komi* (with a): si multitudo] *similitudo* (with pr. a b): 12. homicidium] *homicidam*. **113.** 1. *homicidii*: 4. *et* after *dicitur* (with a): 6. ad haec] *adhuc*: 7. diligenter] *diligentius* (with a): 13. *facile* is added in the margin in the hand and ink of the MS. **114.** 1. enim] *erit* pr. z, but it is expunged and *enim* substituted in perhaps a slightly different ink: mutaverit] *mulctaverit*: 2. *asuescens*: 3. *simile* after *movere*: 4. haec] *hoc?*: 6. om. *ex*: om. *leges*: 11. temporum] *ipsorum*. **115.** 1. *quidem* is added (with a caret) above the line in the hand and ink of the MS.: 5. scholam] *scolam*: 6. *Tessallorum*: 7. *Tessallis*: 8. *perversant* (with a). **116.** 2. *archades*: 3. om. *a*: *et* is added before *adhuc* (as in a): 4. *achaycis*: om. *et* before *perebiis*: 5. operosum] *operose* (with a): 9. optimum] *oportunum*: 10. mulieres] *multitudines* pr. z, but this is expunged in darker ink, and *mulieres* written above, also in darker ink. **117.** 7. *et* is added before *ad*. **118.** 2. *matrem* pr. z, *martem* substituted in the hand and ink of the MS.: 7. autem] *enim* (with b t): 9. om. *nocivae* (with pr. a): haec] *hoc*: *lakosensum*: 13. *lakosensibus*. **119.** 2. om. *et* before *messenios*: 4. om. *habet*: 5. om. *autem*: conatum] *cognatum* pr. z, *conatum* written above in darker ink: 6. ut] *ubi*: 7. peccati] *peccata*: 9. et] *aut*: 10. *et* is added above the line (with a caret) in the hand and ink of the MS. **120.** 1. post ea enim] *postea vero* (with a): 5. om. *quidem*. **121.** 2. derelinquet] *derelinquat* (with b c t Alb.): 8. sub prioribus] *superioribus*: 10. om. *et* before *decem* (with Alb.): *attamen*. **122.** 4. enim] *autem*: eum] *cum*: *tres* after *filios*: 5. *afruron*: 6. quod] *quia* (with a c): 9. *ut et*: 10. principum] *praecipuum*: 11. penuriam] *pecuniam* (with pr. m and pr. a). **123.** 1. autem] *quidem*: 3. aequityrannum] *sequi tirannum*: 4. laedatur politia] *politeia politeiam ledant*: 8. evenerit] *venit*. **124.** 1. *kaikagati*, but the first *i* is not in the ink of the MS.: 8. *dicta* pr. z, but it is crossed through and *dieta* written above in the hand and ink of the MS.: 13. *epieikesi* was probably the original reading, for there is an erasure after the final letter of *epieikes*. **125.** 1. *andragarchiam* (so a): *forsitam*: 4. om. *ut et* (with a): 5. diffidat] *discredat*: 6. velle videri dativi et inutiliter tribuentes] *velle videri dativi et lucrativi tribuentes*: 8. correctione] *coruptione* probably pr. z, altered into *coreptione*: 10. donum] *domum* z, *donum* in lighter ink in the margin: 11. correctiones] *coruptiones* pr. z, altered in darker ink into *coreptiones*. **126.** 1. *dignificabantur*: 4. amatores] the last letter but one has been written over and is indistinct: 5. usus] *usu* (with pr. a): 6. om. *existens*: 8. honoris] *honorum*. **127.** 1. iudicari regum] *iudicare regnum*: autem] *aut*: 2. kaloskagathos] *kaluskatus* pr. z, but *ga* is inserted with a caret before *t* and the last *u* is altered into *a*, perhaps in a different ink from the MS.: 4. emittebant] *emittebat*: 8. Creta] *cata* pr. z; *creta* is written above in the hand and ink of the marginal glosses: 11. voluntatis] *voluntati*: om. *quidem*. **128.** 3. ista] *ita* (with a): 5. eam] *eum* altered into *eam*: *navigii*: quidam] *quidem*: 8. om. *constituit*: 10. increpuit] *increpavit* (with a). **129.** 6. communes] *omnes*: 7. coactis] *coacti*: 8. que] *quae*: 10. fecit] the second letter has been written over, and what it originally was is uncertain; *e* is written above it, apparently in the ink of the MS.: 12. in tantum] *iterum*. **130.** 3. modica] *modicam*: 6. iunioribus] *in moribus*: *likurgum* (with a): 7. *karuli* (with a): 8. om. *est*: 13. *minus* (*mi* pr. a): *et* is added before *insula*. **131.** 3. om. *quidem*: 4. *triopisci*: 5. *quidem* before *has*: 6. *scicilie*: 9. servi] *servis*: 11. *filicia*. **132.** 2. *eandem* after *habent* (with t): 3. om. *quidem*: 5. *boulin*: autem] *quidem*: om. *quidem*: 6. kosmoi] *kosmois*: 8. consententiandi] *consenciendi*: 10. in Lacedaemonia] *Illacedemonia*: 12. lex] *hoc* or *haec*: om. *et*: 13. in Creta] *Incata* with a dot under the first *a* to expunge it and what is probably an *e* written above. **133.** 1. *et* is added before *ex* (as in a): ferunt] *fuerunt*: 3. haec] *huius*: *et* is added after *ut* (as in a b c t Alb.): 4. omnes] *homines*: *et* is added before *ad*: 5. disiugationem] *disiungationem* (with a Alb.): 9. sunt] *sint*: *in* is added after *quam*: manifestum] *infra*: kosmos] *komos*: 11. ephororum] *fororum*: ephororum] *efororum*. **134.** 2. enim] *est*: 3. *datus* is added after *omnibus*, and *esse participans populus maximi principatus vult* omitted: 4. hic] *hii*: 5. e] *ex*: 6. after *kosmi* follows *de* at the beginning of the next line but projecting into the margin, and between *de* and *quibus* is inserted *esse participans populus maximi praesidi*: 8. ipsis] *temporis*: 9. autognomonas] *antogmonas*. **135.** 4. intermedie] *intermedium* (with a): kosmois] *kosmis* (with a): 6. *omnia* is added after *quam*: 7. id] *ad*: 8. sententias] *sententia* (with a): 10. assumentes] *consumentes* (with a). **136.** 1. *at* pr. z, altered into *aut* not (I think) in the ink of the MS.: 6. *et quod* pr. z, altered to *et quidam*, perhaps in the ink of the MS.: 12. *calcedonii*. **137.** 3. sunt] *sibi*: 5. *se* is added in the margin in the hand and ink of the MS.: 7. dici] *dicit*: 9. societatum] *civitatum*: philitiois] *filicios* (with a): 10. ephoris] *ephorus*. **138.** 1. om. *autem*: 2. *gerusiam*] *gerusia* (with a): 3. autem] *esse*: 4. quid] *quod*: differens] *differrens*: 6. *et* is added before *multum* (as in a): 8. om. *utique*: 10. demum] *demoticum*. **139.** 3. quaecunque] *quodcunque*: *et* is added after *intulerint*: 4. audire] *audite*: solum] *solis*: 5. volenti] *nollenti*: 6. dominas existentes] *dominans existens*: 9. *qui* is added after *hos* (as in a). **140.** 1. aliis] *his*: 7. igitur] *enim*: om. *autem*: 8. quidam] *quidem*: 13. *hoc* after *videre*. **141.** 2. *-spicere*: 4. regnum] *regum*: 6. quodcunque autem] *quicunque enim*: om. *esse*. **142.** 3. praeferret] *praefert* (with a): legislator] *legum lator*: *sed et*: 4. om. *utique*: 5. *aceptatur*, and so elsewhere: 7. *legum latorem*: 8. ubi] *ibi* (with a): 9. participare principatibus] *percipe principantibus*: 11. *velotius*. **143.** 2. *efugiunt*: inditando] *in ditando*: 3. emittentes] *eminentes*: 6. abscesserit] *abscenserit*: 7. est] *esse*. **144.** 1. perseverarunt] *perseveraverunt*: 2. singulari] *singuli* pr. z, corrected in a different ink: 4. om. *fuerunt*: 5. politice] *politeye*: quidem] *enim quidem*: 6. *licurgus*: 9. *legum latorem*: 10. *intemperatum* pr. z, altered to *intemperatam*: 12. quod quidem] *quod quod*, but a dot beside the first *quod* is perhaps intended to expunge it. **145.** 1. scilicet] *sed*: 2. om. *et*: 3. quod] *quidem*: 4. fecerit] *fecit*: 5. tyranno] *titano*: 8. *peridoes* pr. z, but *pericles ?* is written in the margin in the same hand: 9. populi] *populum*. **146.** 1. epieikeis] *epieikis*: 4. erit] *esset*: 6. *medicinis* altered into *medignis*: 8. *legum latores*: *Zalentus*: Locris] *loc'*: 9. *karondas catameus*: 11. *legum lationem*: 12. Locrus] *locris*.

147. 1. om. *fuisse*: 2. *thelecam*: *thelece*: om. *et Zaleucum* (with a): *Zalenti* (with a b m): 4. *tempori*] *temporais* pr. z, but the *a* has been partly erased: Philolaus] *Filolaus*, but the *F* is written in dark ink over some letter now undecipherable: 5. *Filolaus*: 6. *Diobleis* pr. z, but this is expunged by dots placed beneath, and *Dioclis* is added in the margin, apparently in the same hand: *olimpiasem* pr. z, altered into *olimpiadem*: 7. *anchiones*: abiit] *ab his*: 8. finiverunt] *finierunt*: 9. *conspectibilia*, and so elsewhere: 11. *et* is added before *fabulantur*: om. *enim*. **148.** 4. *legum lator*: ipsis fuit] *fit ipsis*: 5. leges] *legis*: 8. vindictae] *in dōce?* (*in doctae?*, but *vindictae* is right, cp. 1320 a 12): 9. *legum latoribus*: 10. *filolia* (with a): 11. om. *et substantiae* (with a). **149.** 1. *coa* is added after *lex*, but is expunged by dots placed beneath which seem to be in the ink of the MS.: 2. *semposiarchizare* (with a): 3. hac] *hanc*: 4. *utile* pr. z?, for the stroke over the *e*, which makes it *utilem*, is in darker ink: hac autem inutile] *hanc autem inutilem*: 5. existenti] the original reading, which is now undecipherable, has been altered into *existentes*: posuit] *possidere* (with a): 6. om. *est* (with a): 7. *pitachus*: 8. politiae] *polithis*: 9. damni] *damnum*: 11. *conferrens*. **150.** 1. *reginus*: *calcidibus*: om. *qui*: in Thracia] *intracia*: 3. dicere aliquis] *ducere eis* (with a): 7. sint] *sunt*.

ADDITIONS AND CORRECTIONS.

P. xii, line 17. An epic fragment of Rhianus (Meineke, Analecta Alexandrina, p. 199: Prof. Mahaffy, Greek Life and Thought from the Age of Alexander to the Roman Conquest, Appendix C) reminds us here and there of Pol. 6 (4). 11. 1295 b 6 sqq., but we cannot be sure that Rhianus was acquainted with this passage.

P. xxxiii, line 11, *for* γεγονότες *read* γενόμενοι

P. 26, last line but one, *dele* the commas

P. 31, line 22, *read* τοῖς μὲν

P. 87, last line, *read* in

P. 93, heading, *for* 15 *read* 7

P. 95, heading, *read* 1273 b 15—1274 b 20.

P. 120, line 1, *for* 3 a *read* 32

P. 151, line 9, *for* of one *read* alone

P. 169, line 4, *read* ἀλλήλους

P. 185, line 17, *dele* bracket after 649

P. 194, line 14, *for* 8. c. *read* c. 8.

P. 200, end of note on κτήματα, *add* The shepherds of a hamlet near Elympos in the island of Carpathus 'call their mules κτήματα or possessions . . . This use of the word κτήματα is, I take it, of distinctly classical origin' (Mr. J. T. Bent, *Journal of Hellenic Studies*, vol. 6, p. 241).

P. 212, line 1, *read* βασιλείας

P. 213, line 13, *read* [ἀγαθῶν].

P. 221, line 29, *for* ἄρα *read* ἆρα

P. 245, line 2, *add* Compare the use of λέγω δέ in Oecon. 1. 6. 1345 a 26 sqq.

P. 262, line 4, *after* οἰκεῖν *add* Compare Oecon. 2. 1352 b 1 sqq.

P. 294, line 1, *after* labour *add* (cp. Oecon. 2. 1350 b 30 sqq.)

P. 294, line 30, *read* ἐργολαβία

P. 309, last line but eleven, *for* of a not very dissimilar custom to that mentioned by Aristotle *read* of the employment of witnesses of this kind

P. 316, note on 1269 a 35, *add* Cp. also Magn. Mor. 1. 35. 1198 b 14 sqq.

P. 322, last line but six, *read* ἐπαύσατο

P. 323, note on προωδοπεποιημένους, *add* See also Veitch, Greek Verbs Irregular and Defective, s. v. 'Οδοιπορέω.

P. 334, line 25, *after* ἀριστοκρατίας *add* and Aristot. Pol. 7 (5). 3. 1303 a 5.

P. 376, line 2. Plutarch here speaks only of the Eponymous Archonship, but C. F. Hermann (Gr. Ant. 1. § 109), Schömann (Gr. Alterth. 1. 343), and Gilbert (Gr. Staatsalt. 1. 134) hold that the restriction applied to all the Archonships.

P. 386, lines 24–27. I believe that this remark was suggested by a remark in Mr. J. Cook Wilson's unpublished Essay for the Conington Prize, which I read with much interest some years ago.

www.ingramcontent.com/pod-product-compliance
Lightning Source LLC
Chambersburg PA
CBHW031347290326
41932CB00044B/356
9783743376755